EU EXTERNAL RELATI

The first edition of this seminal textbook made a significant impact on the teaching of EU external relations law. This new edition retains the hallmarks of that success, while providing a fully revised and updated account of this burgeoning field. It offers a dual perspective, looking at questions from both the EU constitutional law perspective (the principles underpinning EU external action, the EU's powers, and the role of the Court of Justice of the EU); and the international law perspective (the effect of international law in the EU legal order and the position of the EU in international organisations such as the WTO). A number of key substantive policy areas are explored, including trade, security and defence, police and judicial cooperation, the environment, human rights, and development cooperation. Taking a 'text, cases and materials' approach, it allows students to gain a thorough understanding of milestones in the evolution of EU law in this area, their judicial interpretation and scholarly appraisal. Linking these pieces together through the authors' commentary and analysis ensures that students are given the necessary guidance to properly position and digest these materials. Lastly, each chapter concludes with a section entitled 'The Big Picture of EU External Relations Law', which weaves together the diverse and complex materials into a coherent whole and stimulates critical discussion of the topics covered.

EU External Relations Law

Text, Cases and Materials

Second Edition

Edited by
Ramses A Wessel
and
Joris Larik

• HART •
OXFORD • LONDON • NEW YORK • NEW DELHI • SYDNEY

HART PUBLISHING

Bloomsbury Publishing Plc

Kemp House, Chawley Park, Cumnor Hill, Oxford, OX2 9PH, UK

1385 Broadway, New York, NY 10018, USA

HART PUBLISHING, the Hart/Stag logo, BLOOMSBURY and the Diana logo are trademarks of Bloomsbury Publishing Plc

First published in Great Britain 2020

A catalogue record for this book is available from the British Library.

Library of Congress Cataloging-in-Publication data

Names: Wessel, Ramses A, editor. | Larik, Joris, editor.

Title: EU external relations law : text, cases and materials / edited by Ramses A. Wessel and Joris Larik.

Description: Second edition. | Oxford, UK ; New York, NY : Hart Publishing, Bloomsbury Publishing Plc, 2020. | Includes bibliographical references and index.

Identifiers: LCCN 2020001990 (print) | LCCN 2020001991 (ebook) | ISBN 9781509926763 (pb) | ISBN 9781509926749 (ePDF) | ISBN 9781509926756 (EPub)

Subjects: LCSH: European Union countries—Foreign relations—Law and legislation. | International cooperation—European Union countries. | International and municipal law—European Union countries. | LCGFT: Casebooks (Law)

Classification: LCC KJE5105 .V3575 2020 (print) | LCC KJE5105 (ebook) | DDC 341.242/2—dc23

LC record available at https://lccn.loc.gov/2020001990

LC ebook record available at https://lccn.loc.gov/2020001991

ISBN: PB: 978-1-50992-676-3
ePDF: 978-1-50992-674-9
ePub: 978-1-50992-675-6

Typeset by Compuscript Ltd, Shannon
Printed and bound in Great Britain by CPI Group (UK) Ltd, Croydon CR0 4YY

FSC www.fsc.org MIX Paper from responsible sources FSC® C013604

Preface

'Any meaningful study of the constitutional order of the EU
must include the external relations of the Union.
In fact, EU external relations law offers one of the best ways of understanding
the essential features of the Union legal order in general.'

Judge Allan Rosas[1]

The patchwork of EU external policies and instruments is the result of more than 60 years of European integration. The present book conceptualises EU external relations law as a body of rules matured as a discipline against an historical and present-day political backdrop: on the one hand, the project of European integration and, on the other, the reality of international politics which requires a coherent and effective European response.

Indeed, EU external relation law has developed into a sub-discipline of its own, with its own conferences, journals, and academic community. Yet, it has become equally clear that all EU internal policies have an external dimension. While the popular and perhaps exciting image of EU External Relations Law is indeed its global perspective and its focus on grand challenges, the day-to-day implementation of EU external action can prove more mundane. EU External Relations Law is largely about who can do what and when and on which legal basis. Yes, it is about how the EU deals with China, the United States, Africa or Latin America, how it operates in the United Nations or the World Trade Organization, and about the EU's contribution to sustainable development, human rights protection, peace and security issues or managing refugee crises. At the same time, to a large extent, the legal questions relate to the division of powers ('competences') between the Union and its Member States and between the different EU institutions. While the case law is often characterised by technical complexities, we should never forget the institutional battles and constitutional questions that loom behind them.

The present book aims to provide an in-depth analysis of the field of EU External Relations Law by discussing relevant actors, principles, instruments, and competences as well as also by zooming in on the key policy areas. The book's purpose is to allow students, scholars, and practitioners to understand the central concepts and salient developments in this field and explain these by pointing to the pertinent Treaty provisions, legislation, case law, and institutional practice.

Whereas the first edition of this book was written by two authors, the current version is based on contributions by various experts. The main reason for this is the increasing complexity of the field and, consequently, the wish to use specialists in the

[1] A Rosas, 'Mixity Past, Present and Future: Some Observations' in M Chamon and I Govaere (eds) *EU External Relations Post-Lisbon: The Law and Practice of Facultative Mixity* (Leiden, Brill/Nijhoff, forthcoming 2020).

various sub-fields of EU External Relations Law. This second edition also benefited from the many constructive comments we received over the years from both colleagues and students, which we have taken into account as far as possible.

Our 'text, cases, and materials' approach has remained the same: we analyse legal provisions and case law by partly reproducing these. This implies that readers do not need additional sources to follow the line of argumentation and that the most relevant provisions are used as part of the analysis. In addition, shorter or more lengthy quotes from relevant key scholarly publications or policy documents are introduced to clarify certain specific issues. Within these excerpts some original references have been left out to save space, so for full quotations it is advised to go back to the original sources.

The development of this edition has also benefitted from two research clinics at Leiden University College The Hague, in the framework of which a group of dedicated students helped with editing and proofing the various chapters. We are very grateful to Tess Baker, Louise Bekkers, Hannah Koole, Angela Pandita Gunavardana, Rebecca Poort, Michael Scullion-Mindorff, Sterre van Campen, and Femke van der Eijk for their hard work and valuable contributions.

Last but not least, as editors we are indebted to Bart Van Vooren, who first came up with the idea for this textbook and together with Ramses Wessel wrote the first edition. We are happy that we were able to convince Bart – who has taken to contributing to the development of the EU's legal order first-hand as a practitioner – to contribute to the final chapter of this book, so he is still part of the team. Moreover, throughout the book, the reader will find many sentences that originate from his thinking.

We hope that you will enjoy this new, updated version.

Ramses A Wessel and Joris Larik

Contents

Abbreviations

AA	Association Agreement
ACP	African, Caribbean, Pacific
AETR	European Road Transport Agreement
AFSJ	Area of Freedom, Security and Justice
AG	Advocate General
ARIO	Articles on the Responsibility of International Organizations
ASEAN	Association of South-East Asian Nations
ATAA	Air Transport Association of America
BIT	Bilateral Investment Treaty
CAC	Codex Alimentarius Commission
CAP	Common Agricultural Policy
CBD	Convention on Biological Diversity
CBP	Bureau of Customs and Border Protection
CCP	Common Commercial Policy
CCT	Common Customs Tariff
CEECs	Central and Eastern European Countries
CEPOL	European Police College
CETA	Comprehensive Economic and Trade Agreement
CFSP	Common Foreign and Security Policy
CITES	Convention on International Trade in Endangered Species
CIVCOM	Committee for Civilian Aspects of Crisis Management
CJEU	Court of Justice of the European Union
CMPD	Crisis Management and Planning Directorate
COM	Communication
COREPER	Committee of Permanent Representatives
COREU	Correspondance Européenne
COTIF	Convention concerning International Carriage by Rail

CPCC	Civilian Planning and Conduct Capability
CSDP	Common Security and Defence Policy
CTC	Counter-terrorism Coordinator
DCFTA	Deep and Comprehensive Free Trade Agreement
DG	Directorate General
DSB	Dispute Settlement Body
DSU	Understanding on Rules and Procedures Governing the Settlement of Disputes
EA	Europe Agreement
EASO	European Asylum Support Office
EBA	Everything But Arms
EC	European Community
ECHR	European Convention on Human Rights
ECJ	European Court of Justice
ECLI	European Case Law Identifier
ECOSOC	UN Economic and Social Council
ECOWAS	Economic Community of West African States
ECR	European Court Reports
ECSC	European Coal and Steel Community
EDA	European Defence Agency
EDC	European Defence Community
EDF	European Development Fund
Ed(s)	Editor(s)
EEA	European Economic Area
EEAS	European External Action Service
EEC	European Economic Community
EFTA	European Free Trade Association
EIB	European Investment Bank
EIDHR	European Instrument for Democracy and Human Rights
EMU	Economic and Monetary Union
ENP	European Neighbourhood Policy

ENPI	European Neighbourhood and Partnership Instrument
EP	European Parliament
EPC	European Political Cooperation
ERTA	European Road Transport Agreement
EU	European Union
EUCO	European Council
EUMC	European Union Military Committee
EUMM	European Union Monitoring Mission
EUMS	European Union Military Staff
EUPM	European Union Police Mission
EURATOM	Atomic Energy Community Treaty
Eurojust	European Union Judicial Cooperation Unit
Europol	European Police Office
EUTM	European Union Training Mission
FAC	Foreign Affairs Council
FAO	Food and Agricultural Organization
FDI	Foreign Direct Investment
FIAMM	Fabbrica Italiana Accumulatori Motocarri Montecchio
FLEGT	Forest Law Enforcement, Governance and Trade
FREMP	Fundamental Rights, Citizens Rights and Free Movement of Persons
FRONTEX	European Agency for the Management of Operational Cooperation at the External Borders of the Member States of the European Union
FTA	Free Trade Agreement
FYROM	Former Yugoslav Republic of Macedonia
G-8/20	Group of 8/20
GATS	General Agreement on Trade in Services
GATT	General Agreement on Tariffs and Trade
GC	General Court
GMO	genetically modified organism
GNP	Gross National Product

GSP	Generalised System of Preferences
HR	High Representative
IATA	International Air Transport Association
ICAO	International Civil Aviation Organization
IGC	Inter-Governmental Conference
IHL	International Humanitarian Law
ILC	International Law Commission
ILO	International Labour Organization
IMF	International Monetary Fund
IMO	International Maritime Organization
IO	International Organization
EU ISS	EU Institute for Security Studies
JAIEX	External JHA Issues
JCCM	judicial cooperation in criminal matters
JHA	Justice and Home Affairs
MARPOL	Marine Pollution (eg, the International Convention for the Prevention of Pollution from Ships)
MDGs	Millennium Development Goals
MEA	Multilateral Environmental Agreement
MFF	Multi-annual Financial Framework
MFN	most-favoured nation
MLA	Mutual Legal Assistance
MoU	Memorandum of Understanding
MOX	Mixed Oxide Fuel
MS	Member States
NAFO	Northwest Atlantic Fisheries Organization
NATO	North Atlantic Treaty Organization
NPT	Non-Proliferation Treaty
OCTs	overseas countries and territories
OECD	Organization for Economic Cooperation and Development
OIV	International Organization for Vine and Wine

OJ	Official Journal (of the European Union)
OSCE	Organization for Security and Cooperation in Europe
PCA	Partnership and Cooperation Agreement
PCD	Policy Coherence for Development
PESCO	Permanent Structured Cooperation
PFOS	Perfluorooctoane Sulfonate
PHARE	Pologne, Hongrie – Assistance à la Réstructuration des Economies
PNR	Passenger Name Records
PSC	Political and Security Committee
QMV	Qualified Majority Voting
REIO	Regional Economic Integration Organization
RELEX	External Relations
REV	Revision
RGA	Remote Gambling Association
SAA	Stabilisation and Association Agreement
SAP	Stability and Association Process
SDGs	Sustainable Development Goals
SEA	Single European Act
SMEs	Small and Medium Sized Enterprises
SOFAs	Status of Forces Agreements
SOMAs	Status of Missions Agreements
SP	Stability Pact
SPS	Agreement on the Application of Sanitary and Phytosanitary Measures
SWIFT	Society for Worldwide Interbank Financial Telecommunication
TAIEX	Technical Assistance and Information Exchange Office
TBR	Trade Barriers Regulation
TCA	Trade and Cooperation agreement
TEC	Treaty Establishing the European Community
TEU	Treaty on European Union
TFEU	Treaty on the Functioning of the European Union

TREN	Transport and Energy
TRIPS	Agreement on Trade-related Aspects of Intellectual Property Rights
TTIP	Transatlantic Trade and Investment Partnership
UMED	Union for the Mediterranean
UN	United Nations
UNCLOS	United Nations Convention on the Law of the Sea
UNCTAD	United Nations Conference on Trade and Development
UNESCO	UN Educational, Scientific and Cultural Organization
UNGA	United Nations General Assembly
UNHCR	UN High Commissioner for Refugees
UNODC	United Nations Office on Drugs and Crime
UNSC	United Nations Security Council
UNSCR	United Nations Security Council Resolution
USTR	United States Trade Representative
VCLT	Vienna Convention on the Law of Treaties
VP	Vice President
VPA	Voluntary Partnership Agreement
WB	World Bank
WCO	World Customs Organization
WEU	Western European Union
WHO	World Health Organization
WIPO	World Intellectual Property Organization
WTO	World Trade Organization

Table of Cases

Court of Justice and the General Court: Judgments

Numerical

Alphabetical

Court of Justice: Rulings

Court of Justice: Opinions

Opinions of the Advocates General

National Courts

Germany

United Kingdom

WTO Disputes

Table of Instruments and Legislation

1

The European Union as a Global Legal Actor

Central Issues

- This chapter introduces the legal dimension of the EU as an international actor. We define this notion as an entity which interacts with third countries and international organisations (and even its own Member States) in ways which are legally and politically distinguishable from its constitutive Member States. In the global context, this entity thus has a stand-alone identity composed of values, interests, and policies which it seeks to define and promote internationally as its own.
- This chapter shows the importance of legal rules in organising EU international action and indicates that EU external relations law consists of an internal and an external dimension. In its internal dimension it consists of the set of rules which govern the constitutional and institutional legal organisation of this legal entity in pursuit of its interests in the world. The external dimension comprises the rules governing the relationship of the European Union with the international legal order in which it is active.
- In order to study EU external relations law in all its complexity, this Chapter provides an overview of the architecture of EU external relations. It outlines the existence of the European Union as an international organisation with legal personality, which exists legally distinctly from its Member States. It also shows that the European Union is based on the Treaty on European Union and the Treaty on the Functioning of the European Union, which each contain crucial legal principles constituting the body of EU external relations law.
- Finally, in order to carry out its external *action*, the European Union needs *actors* to make the decisions and represent the EU at the global stage. These include the EU institutions, but also other key players in the law of EU external relations.

I. The Nature of the European Union as an International Actor

A. An International Organisation or Something Else?

A textbook on EU external relations law is founded on the premise that the European Union can have legal relations with third states (non-Member States) and other international organisations. Hence, it is an international actor with a distinct legal existence akin to the EU Member States or international organisations such as the United Nations. What does it mean to say that the European Union is an international actor?

With the 1957 Rome Treaty having founded the European Economic Community, this new international organisation was explicitly given competence to conduct international trade relations through its Common Commercial Policy and to conclude international agreements through which it could associate itself with third countries. As European integration progressed, the EEC, later the European Community and now the European Union, acquired powers in other areas such as foreign and security policy, environmental policy, energy policy, and so on. Scholars have been struggling with the nature of the European Union as it is clearly different from other international organisations and has features that come close to a (federal) state. Often, the easy way out is to state that the Union is a *sui generis* international actor which cannot be defined by using any pre-existing terminology.

In this textbook we are primarily concerned with the rules and principles which govern the legal existence and functioning of this international actor. Consequently, we define the EU as an international actor in abstract terms as *an entity which interacts with third countries and international organisations (and even its own Member States), in ways which are legally and politically distinguishable from its constitutive Member States. In the global context, this entity thus has a stand-alone identity composed of values, interests, and policies which it seeks to define and promote internationally as its own.*[1]

The term 'entity' may nevertheless not be too helpful to explain the nature of this 'beast' and the question emerges as to whether we can see the EU as an international organisation. To lawyers, being an international actor usually means being an international *legal* actor. This means that, although the European Union is not a state – which has been confirmed by the Court of Justice in its Opinion 2/13[2] – it is subject to the rules of international law when it wishes to take action on the global stage. International law, however, is still quite traditional. Created as 'inter-state' law, it continues to struggle with the presence of non-state actors in the international order. Yet, international

[1] This definition is inspired by Cremona's description of the different roles of the EU in the world. See M Cremona, 'The Union as a Global Actor: Roles, Models and Identity' (2004) 42 *Common Market Law Review* 553.

[2] Opinion 2/13 *(ECHR II)*, ECLI:EU:C:2014:2454.

organisations have obviously found their place as international legal actors while other fora, networks and actors are also increasingly recognised as legally relevant. It is a truism that the European Union is not a regular international organisation. From the outset, Member States have been prepared to transfer important sovereign powers and pool them at the level of the Community and later the Union. The current EU Treaties again herald a new phase in which the Union's international actorness in the global legal order will be further developed. This is exactly why it is important to classify the European Union under international law.

C Eckes and RA Wessel, 'The European Union: An International Perspective' in T Tridimas and R Schütze (eds) *Oxford Principles of European Union Law – Volume 1: The European Union Legal Order* (Oxford, Oxford University Press, 2018) 74–102, 81

Most international rules apply to states, some (also) to international organisations and a limited set also to other internationally active entities (such as liberation movements or multinationals). Few would argue that the EU is a state; many would say that it is an international entity sui generis. International law, however, only works when it is applied across the board for certain categories of international actors. Its rationale is to offer clarity and set the conditions for a smooth cooperation between different subjects. At the same time, it is of course possible to create special rules for special entities. The clauses on Regional Economic Integration Organisations (REIOs) in some multilateral agreements are a good example.

The European Treaties are still silent on the international legal status of the Union. They do not give an answer to the classic question of whether the EU is an international organisation or something else. This may be the reason that also textbooks are still uncertain about the legal nature of the Union and seem to have a preference for more political notions. In their leading textbook, Chalmers et al. refer to the EU as 'amongst other things, a legal system established to deal with a series of contemporary problems and realise a set of goals that individual states felt unable to manage alone.'[3] And, the 'nature of the Union's international presence' is related to its international legal personality only, whereas the nature of the entity as such is left open.[4]

In its famous ruling on the Lisbon Treaty, the German Federal Constitutional Court held that the Union was 'designed as an association of sovereign states (*Staatenverbund*) to which sovereign powers are transferred'. Yet, the further description by the Court

[3] D Chalmers, G Davies and G Monti, *European Union Law*, 2nd edn (Cambridge, Cambridge University Press, 2010) 3.

[4] Ibid, 632.

comes close to generally accepted definitions of international organisations: 'The concept of *Verbund* covers a close long-term association of states which remain sovereign, an association which exercises public authority on the basis of a treaty, whose fundamental order, however, is subject to the disposal of the Member States alone and in which the peoples of their Member States (ie the citizens of the states) remain the subjects of democratic legitimisation.'[5]

Could the EU be qualified as an international organisation? When it looks like a banana and smells like a banana, it may very well be a banana.[6] Indeed, many would agree with Curtin and Dekker 'that the legal system of the European Union is most accurately analysed in terms of the institutional legal concept of an international organization'.[7] But even this quote reveals how difficult it seems to simply argue that the European Union *is* an international organisation – albeit a very special one 'of its own kind'.[8] Throughout their handbook on the law of international organisations, Schermers and Blokker take the EU along as an international organisation, while noting, of course, the 'stronger constraints on domestic policies of the member states' and its 'more far-reaching objectives'.[9] The EU is indeed 'considered special not because of its identity problems but because of the high degree of "constitutional" development, supranational components and the rule of law features within this organization making it look almost like a federation of states …', as argued by Bengoetxea in one of the few publications focussing on this question.[10]

As an international organisation, the European Union is subject to international law in its relations with third states and other international organisations. While international law can also be part of the EU's internal set of rules (see Chapter 5), this chapter's focus is on the external dimension. There we would need to start from the presumption that the EU is bound by the international agreements to which it is a party as well as to customary international law. Yet, third states experience that the EU remains special. It may be an international organisation, but the fact that it is exclusively competent to act in certain areas – at the expense of its own Member States – is unprecedented. The same holds true for the rule that EU Member States, in the end,

[5] *Bundesverfassungsgericht*, Judgment of the Second Senate of 30 June 2009, 2 BvE 2/08, ECLI:DE:BVerfG:2009:es20090630.2bve000208, para 229. See also A Steinbach, 'The Lisbon Judgment of the German Federal Constitutional Court – New Guidance on the Limits of European Integration' (2010) 11 *German Law Journal* 367.

[6] As we will see in Chapter 7, the choice for 'banana' as a metaphor in a textbook on EU external relations law is less random than it seems.

[7] DM Curtin and IF Dekker, 'The European Union from Maastricht to Lisbon: Institutional and Legal Unity out of the Shadow' in P Craig and G De Búrca (eds) *The Evolution of EU Law* (Oxford, Oxford University Press, 2011) 163.

[8] Compare the qualification as 'eine internationale Organisation eigener Art' by W Schroeder, 'Die Europäische Union als Völkerrechtssubjekt' (2012) Beiheft 2 *Europarecht* 9, 18. More generally, the status of the EU as an 'international organization' seems to be accepted implicitly by many authors, see P Eeckhout, *EU External Relations Law*, 2nd edn (Oxford, Oxford University Press, 2011), who does not address the external legal nature of the EU, but merely refers to the fact that '[t]he EU is also a member of a number of *other* international organizations …' (at 3, emphasis added).

[9] HG Schermers and NM Blokker, *International Institutional Law: Unity in Diversity*, 6th edn (Leiden, Martinus Nijhoff, 2018) 33.

[10] J Bengoetxea, 'The EU as (More Than) an International Organization' in J Klabbers and Å Wallendahl (eds) *Research Handbook on the Law of International Organizations* (Cheltenham, Edward Elgar Publishing, 2011) 449. The author argues that it is above all the 'transitional' status of the EU (from international organisation to federation) which justifies its 'specialness' (at 450).

should give priority to EU law in cases of a conflict with international law. Indeed, as underlined by case law, the loyalty towards the Union (*Unionstreue* in German) is believed to take precedence over international law obligations (see Chapter 5). While for EU Member States (and most EU lawyers) these may be logical consequences of a dynamic division of competences, third states (and most public international lawyers) would remind us of the rule of *pacta tertiis nec nocent nec prosunt*; third states are not, in principle, bound by the EU Treaties as to them these are agreements between others.[11] From a legal perspective, they should not be bothered with a complex division of competences that was part of a deal between the EU and its Member States. Yet, these days, one may expect a certain knowledge of the division of competences on the side of third states, not least because it would be useful to know which actors on the European side are the most appropriate interlocutors.

S Sheth, 'Angela Merkel Reportedly Had to Explain the "Fundamentals" of EU Trade to Trump 11 times', *Business Insider*, 22 April 2017

President Trump did not understand that the US cannot negotiate a trade deal with Germany alone and must deal with the European Union as a bloc, a senior German official told The Times of London.

'Ten times Trump asked (German chancellor Angela Merkel) if he could negotiate a trade deal with Germany. Every time she replied, "You can't do a trade deal with Germany, only the EU,"' the official said.

They continued: 'On the eleventh refusal, Trump finally got the message, "Oh, we'll do a deal with Europe then."'

Merkel reportedly told her cabinet members that Trump had 'very basic misunderstandings' on the 'fundamentals' of the EU and trade.

B. The EU and its Member States in the International Legal Order

The above discussion points to the core difficulty of EU external relations: who represents the 'European interest' on the international scene – the EU or its Member States? How do these actions relate to each other – are they coherent, mutually supportive or perhaps contradictory? The following excerpt serves as a good illustration of the diverse policy areas encompassed by the EU as an international actor. In this Communication, the European Commission provides a succinct summary of the diverse challenges facing the EU in the twenty-first century. Subsequently, it indicates the wide range of policies and instruments the EU has developed in the past six decades

[11] This rule is laid down in Art 34 of the Vienna Convention on the Law of Treaties, adopted in Vienna on 22 May 1969 (hereinafter: VCLT): 'A treaty does not create either obligations or rights for a third State without its consent.'

in response, and how they could be improved.[12] Notice how the excerpt makes the distinction between 'Europe' and 'EU'. The latter is a reference to the international organisation of which the Commission is an institution, the former is a reference to the EU and its Member States acting together across a vast range of subjects in a challenging global environment.

Communication from the Commission, *Europe in the World – Some Practical Proposals for Greater Coherence, Effectiveness and Visibility*, Brussels, 8 June 2006, COM(2006) 278 final, 2

Since the end of the Cold War, the world has changed very fast. Europe faces strong economic competition and new threats to its security. While Europe's mature economies have many strengths, they also suffer from sluggish growth and ageing populations. The economic balance of power has shifted. Countries such as China and India are growing fast and there is increasing competition for access to raw materials, energy resources and markets. Terrorism, the proliferation of weapons of mass destruction, regional conflicts, failed states and organised crime remain as pressing as ever.

Europe has the potential to rise to these challenges and to share in the new opportunities created by emerging markets and globalisation. It has an open society that can absorb people, ideas and new technologies. Successive enlargements over the last three-and-a-half decades have demonstrated the EU's ability to promote stability and prosperity and the success of this model of regional integration. With a combined population of 470m and a quarter of the world's income, the EU now accounts for over a fifth of world trade. We provide more than half of development and humanitarian assistance worldwide. European countries make a central contribution to all the important global institutions. The EU model of co-operation and integration is a pole of attraction for countries in our neighbourhood and beyond.

Over the last fifty years the EU has developed a series of external policy instruments, political, economic, commercial and financial, which help us to protect and promote our interests and our values. More recently these instruments have been diversified in areas where member states felt they needed to work in common, and a High Representative for Common Foreign and Security Policy was appointed, to enhance the scope and effectiveness of the EU's external action. Military instruments have been created to reinforce civil instruments of crisis management.

Increasingly the EU's internal policies – for example the environment, energy, competition policy, agriculture and fisheries, transport, the fight against

[12] The quoted Communication followed in the wake of the Dutch and French referenda rejecting the Draft Constitutional Treaty. Through this document, the Commission sought to stimulate pragmatic advances in EU external relations without the need for changes to EU primary law.

terrorism and illegal migration, dealing with global pandemics – impact on international relationships and play a vital part in the EU's external influence. Conversely, many of Europe's internal policy goals depend on the effective use of external policies.

This paper seeks to ... make pragmatic proposals to enable the Union to define a strong sense of collective purpose in our external action and to ensure that this is backed by the necessary policy instruments.

The first two paragraphs are a highly dense summary of the vast range of policies pursued by the EU as an international actor. To explicitly name but three of them: First, it starts out by referring to access to raw materials and markets in a global competitive environment, which is generally within the purview of the EU's Common Commercial Policy (Article 207 TFEU; see Chapter 7). Second, the Communication further mentions the challenge of terrorism and the proliferation of weapons of mass destruction, which falls within the scope of the EU's Common Foreign and Security Policy (Article 24 TEU; see Chapter 9), but certainly also within the scope of Member States' own foreign policies. Third and finally, the excerpt refers to the fact that 'we' provide more than half of global development and humanitarian aid, by which the document refers to funds dispersed by the Union and its Member States within their respective development policies (Article 208 TFEU; see Chapter 8). In sum, the excerpt illustrates that the European Union 'as an international actor' is an umbrella term for a set of external policies, instruments and actors across a vast range of substantive domains. It also illustrates the ambiguity as to who is acting: the European Union alone, the EU Member States, or both simultaneously.

Yet, from a legal perspective, it makes sense to continue to distinguish between the European Union as an international organisation of which states can be members, and the (Member) States themselves. In that sense, the EU is clearly something more than merely a collection of several states. It has a distinct legal status, both in relation to its own members as well as towards third states. The European Union as an international actor then refers to the entity which has express legal personality and capacity to act in the international legal order.

Article 47 TEU

The Union shall have legal personality.

Despite this autonomous legal standing, like any other international organisation, the EU is based on the principle of conferred powers (eg it can only act where its Member States have given it the competence to do so). But, importantly, the Member

States may no longer be allowed to act once competences have been transferred and have been placed 'exclusively' in the hands of the Union. As a consequence, depending on the legal existence, scope and nature of the EU's external powers (a synonym for competence, see Chapter 3), the Member States have, to a greater or lesser degree, a prominent role in the formation and execution of international action in the relevant area. Conversely, the role of the European Union (as the legal person) and its supranational institutions will then shift depending on the policy area at issue. This is why it possesses significant legal competences and political clout which is distinct from that of its Member States. However, its Member States remain equally significant on the international scene and the core of EU external relations law is based on finding out who is competent to act externally: the EU, its Member States or both together. Perhaps ironically, this has turned EU *external* relations law largely into a story about *internal* competence battles; either between the EU and its Member States or between the different EU institutions.

II. EU External Relations in the Treaties

A. A Tale of Two Treaties

The European Union is a single legal person, but it is not based on a single constitutive document. In the following sections we explain the legal structure of the Treaty on European Union and the Treaty on the Functioning of the European Union – with specific emphasis on how external relations are organised in EU primary law.[13]

The European Union and its competences are based on the Treaty on European Union (TEU) and the Treaty on the Functioning of the European Union (TFEU). These are not in a relationship of hierarchy but have the same legal value; together they constitute 'the Treaties' on which the Union is founded (Article 1 TEU and Article 1 TFEU). The Treaties are supplemented by the Charter of Fundamental Rights ('the Charter') and the Treaty establishing the Atomic Energy Community Treaty ('Euratom'). The latter still exists as a separate legal instrument which has not been merged with the TEU and TFEU. Though it shares the EU's institutions, Euratom exists as a distinct legal personality from the European Union. In this book, the focus is on the Union as based on the TEU and TFEU; we only discuss Euratom and the Charter in an ancillary fashion.

The Treaties are the result of numerous modifications over the years. These changes are usually implemented based on separate modification treaties that contain changes that take effect after their entry into force. The 2007 Treaty of Lisbon (entry into force in 2009) was the latest modification treaty and the modifications it contained led to

[13] In referring to the Treaties, this book will use the following acronyms: For the pre-Lisbon, post-Nice situation this text refers to 'TEC' for the EC Treaty and 'EU' for the EU Treaty. For the post-Lisbon situation, the text uses 'TFEU' for Treaty on the Functioning of the European Union and 'TEU' for the Treaty on European Union.

the new and current consolidated versions of the TEU and the TFEU. References are always to these consolidated treaties and not to the modification treaties (eg, a reference to 'Article 50 of the Lisbon Treaty' does not make any sense; the actual Lisbon Treaty only contains seven articles[14]).

The TEU with its 55 articles is the shorter of the two EU Treaties and is considered the framework treaty. It sets out the most fundamental legal properties of the European Union: the aims and objectives for which it was set up, which of its organs has what role in making decisions binding the legal person, essential principles of conduct within the organisation, how to leave or become a member of the Union and how its constitutional rules can be changed. In the TEU, the key provisions of EU external relations are those stating the core legal principles governing all EU action, including its international relations; the values and objectives of the EU in conducting its international relations; the EU institutions' roles in pursuing EU foreign policy; and the relationship between the TEU and the TFEU. For historical reasons (examined in Chapter 9), the TEU also contains the rules and procedures governing the EU's common foreign and security policy, the only substantive EU competence to be found in the TEU. Similarly, for reasons pertaining to the drafting of the Treaty of Lisbon, following the failed Constitutional Treaty, the TEU contains an article on the European Neighbourhood Policy, examined in Chapter 13.

The Treaty on the Functioning of the European Union, in comparison, as is clear from its name and with its 358 articles, 'fleshes out' the functioning of this international organisation. In which areas can the EU institutions adopt measures in pursuit of the external objectives set out in the TEU? Which procedures should its institutions adhere to? Which (legally binding) instruments can they use? Furthermore, the TFEU contains crucial provisions governing the relationship between the EU and international law both as regards itself, its own international agreements and the legal position of the Member States and their international commitments. Finally, relevant to both the TEU and the TFEU are the legally binding protocols attached to the TFEU, and the political declarations, which serve to interpret or contextualise some of the provisions in the TEU and TFEU.

B. Values and Objectives

The objectives of EU external relations deserve an in-depth look for two reasons. First, they govern the inner workings of the entire EU machinery: the principles of conferral, cooperation and institutional balance (see Chapter 2) exist in light of them. Second, they shape the EU's relationship to the legal and political global reality in which it exists. Articles 3(5) and 21 TEU mention the key external objectives of the Union.

[14] Treaty of Lisbon amending the Treaty on European Union and the Treaty establishing the European Community, 13 December 2007 [2007] OJ C 306/1.

Article 3(5) TEU

In its relations with the wider world, the Union shall uphold and promote its values and interests and contribute to the protection of its citizens. It shall contribute to peace, security, the sustainable development of the Earth, solidarity and mutual respect among peoples, free and fair trade, eradication of poverty and the protection of human rights, in particular the rights of the child, as well as to the strict observance and the development of international law, including respect for the principles of the United Nations Charter.

Article 21 TEU

1. The Union's action on the international scene shall be guided by the principles which have inspired its own creation, development and enlargement, and which it seeks to advance in the wider world: democracy, the rule of law, the universality and indivisibility of human rights and fundamental freedoms, respect for human dignity, the principles of equality and solidarity, and respect for the principles of the United Nations Charter and international law.

   The Union shall seek to develop relations and build partnerships with third countries, and international, regional or global organisations which share the principles referred to in the first subparagraph. It shall promote multilateral solutions to common problems, in particular in the framework of the United Nations.
2. The Union shall define and pursue common policies and actions, and shall work for a high degree of cooperation in all fields of international relations, in order to:
   (a) safeguard its values, fundamental interests, security, independence and integrity;
   (b) consolidate and support democracy, the rule of law, human rights and the principles of international law;
   (c) preserve peace, prevent conflicts and strengthen international security, in accordance with the purposes and principles of the United Nations Charter, with the principles of the Helsinki Final Act and with the aims of the Charter of Paris, including those relating to external borders;
   (d) foster the sustainable economic, social and environmental development of developing countries, with the primary aim of eradicating poverty;

(e) encourage the integration of all countries into the world economy, including through the progressive abolition of restrictions on international trade;
(f) help develop international measures to preserve and improve the quality of the environment and the sustainable management of global natural resources, in order to ensure sustainable development;
(g) assist populations, countries and regions confronting natural or man-made disasters; and
(h) promote an international system based on stronger multilateral cooperation and good global governance.

3. The Union shall respect the principles and pursue the objectives set out in paragraphs 1 and 2 in the development and implementation of the different areas of the Union's external action covered by this Title and by Part Five of the Treaty on the Functioning of the European Union, and of the external aspects of its other policies.

The Union shall ensure consistency between the different areas of its external action and between these and its other policies. The Council and the Commission, assisted by the High Representative of the Union for Foreign Affairs and Security Policy, shall ensure that consistency and shall cooperate to that effect.

Articles 3(5) and 21 TEU give a double response to the question as to what kind of international actor the EU is and how it relates to the international order. On the one hand, there is the substantive answer. As explained in the extract below, these provisions in the TEU impose substantive requirements on EU international relations by stating that there are certain fundamental objectives which shall guide its internal and external policies. On the other hand, these provisions also impose a strong methodological imperative upon EU international action: it must pursue its action through a multilateral approach based on the rule of law. It is then also clear that the scope of objectives which EU action in the world must pursue is extraordinarily broad. Aside from perhaps issuing a declaration of war, there is very little that does not fall within the purview of these objectives. In order to legally and conclusively establish what the EU can do in international relations, Chapter 3 will examine the existence, nature and scope of EU external competence, in light of these objectives. Chapter 5 will examine the relationship between the EU and international law. On the basis of Articles 3(5) and 21 TEU and, as a creation of international law, we may assume that the Union legal order should be open, supportive and receptive to international legal norms. This is partially true but must be qualified in many respects.

J Larik, 'Entrenching Global Governance: The EU's Constitutional Objectives Caught Between a Sanguine World View and a Daunting Reality' in B Van Vooren, S Blockmans and J Wouters (eds) *The Legal Dimension of Global Governance, What Role for the EU?* (Oxford, Oxford University Press, 2013) 10–12

The Lisbon Treaty has both expanded and streamlined the Union's global objectives. The EU Treaties include now a set of general objectives of the Union, including their external dimension (Art. 3(5) TEU), an article containing general principles and goals of EU external action (Art. 21 TEU), and in some cases objectives specific to certain external policies (Arts. 206, 207, 208, 214 TFEU) …

While being careful to refer also to the pursuit of 'interests' (Arts. 3(5) TEU and 21(2)(a) TEU), thus keeping the door open for the pursuit of 'possession goals', the Treaties contain a wealth of substantive objectives that squarely fall into the category of milieu goals. These include contributions to 'peace, security, the sustainable development of the Earth, solidarity and mutual respect among peoples, free and fair trade, eradication of poverty and the protection of human rights, in particular the rights of the child' (Arts. 3(5) TEU and 21 TEU). The Treaties also make clear that this is largely an extrapolation of the Union's internal values to the outside world (Art. 21(1) TEU). Nevertheless, these goals are not all autonomously defined by the Union, but are indeed open to input from external sources by drawing on internationally-defined concepts such as sustainable development, universal human rights or internationally agreed goals for development cooperation (Art. 208(2) TFEU).

In addition, we find a strong emphasis on law-based goals. The various references to human rights (Arts. 3(5); 21(1), first subpara; 21(2)(b) TEU), as *rights*, can also be seen as a matter of law. More straightforwardly, the Treaties oblige the Union to contribute 'to the strict observance and the development of international law' (Art. 3(5) TEU) and to spread and consolidate the rule of law in the world at large (Arts. 3(5) and 21(2)(b) TEU). They furthermore identify the United Nations as the forum of choice to 'promote multilateral solutions to common problems' (Art. 21(1), second subpara TEU and 220(1) TFEU), which suggests abiding by and utilising the procedures and means provided under its Charter. Indeed, according to the Treaties 'stronger multilateral cooperation and good global governance' (Art. 21(2)(h) TEU) go hand in hand …

In sum, we see that the EU Treaties codify a range of global objectives both in terms of substance but also specifically harnessing law … Together, these elements coincide with the idea of the Union as a 'transformative power', changing not only fundamentally the relations among its members but also of the world around it …

C. Protocols and Declarations

Attached to the TEU and TFEU are no fewer than 37 legally binding Protocols, as well as 65 political Declarations. Many of these are of indirect relevance to EU external relations,[15] but of direct interest are the following Protocols: Protocol No 2 on the application of the principles of subsidiarity and proportionality; Protocol No 7 on the privileges and immunities of the European Union; Protocol No 8 relating to accession to the European Convention on Human Rights; Protocols 19, 21, 22 and 23 as regards the external dimension of the area of freedom, security and justice; and Protocol 25 on the exercise of shared competence. The most pertinent Declarations are 13 and 14 on the common foreign and security policy; Declaration 15 concerning establishment of the European External Action Service; Declaration 18 on the delimitation of competences; Declaration 24 on legal personality of the Union; Declaration 36 on the negotiation and conclusion of international agreements by Member States relating to the AFSJ; Declaration 37 concerning the solidarity obligation in Article 222 TFEU; and finally, Declaration 41 stating for which objectives of Article 3 TEU Article 352 TFEU can be used. We discuss these in more depth in the relevant chapters.

Protocols form an integral part of the Treaty structure on which the Union is based. They are as such equal to the TEU and the TFEU. Declarations are not legally binding, though have an important interpretative effect in relation to the TEU or TFEU provisions to which they refer.

III. Introducing the Key Players

A. The European External Action Service and the High Representative

In dealing with the institutions, textbooks usually follow the order presented in Article 13 TEU which lists the EU institutions starting from the European Council. Given the external relations angle of this book, we focus first on the European External Action Service (EEAS) and the role of the High Representative of the Union for Foreign Affairs and Security Policy (HR) as envisaged by the post-Lisbon EU Treaties. This will be followed by an analysis of the role of the traditional institutions (European Council, Council, Commission, European Parliament and Court of Justice) in EU external relations. The reason is that the EEAS and the HR both play a pivotal role in EU external relations, to which can subsequently be referred when analysing the actual EU institutions.

[15] Though some can be of direct relevance, they are not further discussed in this book, such as Protocol 31 concerning petroleum imports into the EU from the Netherlands Antilles and Protocol 34 on special arrangements for Greenland. See further D Kochenov (ed) *EU Law of the Overseas: Outermost Regions, Associated Overseas Countries and Territories, Territories Sui Generis* (The Hague, Wolters Kluwer, 2011).

Article 27 TEU

1. The High Representative of the Union for Foreign Affairs and Security Policy, who shall chair the Foreign Affairs Council, shall contribute through his proposals to the development of the common foreign and security policy and shall ensure implementation of the decisions adopted by the European Council and the Council.
2. The High Representative shall represent the Union for matters relating to the common foreign and security policy. He shall conduct political dialogue with third parties on the Union's behalf and shall express the Union's position in international organisations and at international conferences.
3. In fulfilling his mandate, the High Representative shall be assisted by a European External Action Service. This service shall work in cooperation with the diplomatic services of the Member States and shall comprise officials from relevant departments of the General Secretariat of the Council and of the Commission as well as staff seconded from national diplomatic services of the Member States. The organisation and functioning of the European External Action Service shall be established by a decision of the Council. The Council shall act on a proposal from the High Representative after consulting the European Parliament and after obtaining the consent of the Commission.

The EEAS, mentioned only in Article 27(3) TEU, was formally established by a Council Decision in 2010 and was officially launched in January 2011.

Council Decision 2010/427/EU of 26 July 2010 establishing the organisation and functioning of the European External Action Service [2010] OJ L201/30

...

Article 1

Nature and scope

1. This Decision establishes the organisation and functioning of the European External Action Service ('EEAS').
2. The EEAS, which has its headquarters in Brussels, shall be a functionally autonomous body of the European Union, separate from the General Secretariat of the Council and from the Commission with the legal capacity necessary to perform its tasks and attain its objectives.
3. The EEAS shall be placed under the authority of the High Representative of the Union for Foreign Affairs and Security Policy ('High Representative').

4. The EEAS shall be made up of a central administration and of the Union Delegations to third countries and to international organisations.

Article 2

Tasks

1. The EEAS shall support the High Representative in fulfilling his/her mandates as outlined, notably, in Articles 18 and 27 TEU:
   — in fulfilling his/her mandate to conduct the Common Foreign and Security Policy ('CFSP') of the European Union, including the Common Security and Defence Policy ('CSDP'), to contribute by his/her proposals to the development of that policy, which he/she shall carry out as mandated by the Council and to ensure the consistency of the Union's external action,
   — in his/her capacity as President of the Foreign Affairs Council, without prejudice to the normal tasks of the General Secretariat of the Council,
   — in his/her capacity as Vice-President of the Commission for fulfilling within the Commission the responsibilities incumbent on it in external relations, and in coordinating other aspects of the Union's external action, without prejudice to the normal tasks of the services of the Commission.
2. The EEAS shall assist the President of the European Council, the President of the Commission, and the Commission in the exercise of their respective functions in the area of external relations.

…

The way the position of the Union as an autonomous international actor developed could only partially be said to be by purposive design. By most standards, it is a piecemeal construction of political and legal developments pushed forward by geopolitical and socio-economic *stimuli*. As will be further elaborated in Chapter 9, the early years of European Political Cooperation coincided with the process leading up to the Helsinki Final Act, as well as events in the Middle East. The birth of CFSP in the Maastricht Treaty is intimately connected to the collapse of the Soviet Union and the Gulf War. The subsequent failure to formulate a common response to the conflicts in the former Yugoslavia gave impetus to CFSP reforms in the Amsterdam Treaty. This dynamic has continued in the twenty-first century. For example, the first ever European Security Strategy was drawn up after deep disagreement among EU Member States over the 2003 Iraq War. Each of these geopolitical realities prompted EU-internal change to the legal and political machinery making up 'European Union' external action. The EEAS is, then, a continuation of that process: a new institutional structure set up against a decades-old struggle of the Union seeking to project a strong, coherent voice on the international scene; counterbalanced by the Member States' wish to retain control over various aspects of international relations. The EEAS was created to overcome this fragmentation. The idea is to bring together policy preparation and implementation on external relations into one new body, under the auspices of the High Representative for Foreign Affairs and Security Policy, who is also vice-President of the Commission and Chairperson of the Foreign Affairs Council (Article 18 TEU). This is referred to as 'triple-hatting', and together with an EU external action service is hoped to support attaining consistency in EU external relations (Article 21(3) TEU).

In terms of policy fields covered by the new EEAS, the current structure is a typical EU-type compromise. It is *not* an EU institution, which significantly constrains its power to legally influence EU external decision-making. Furthermore, the EU external action service has no say whatsoever in the Common Commercial Policy ('the mother of all EU external policies', see Chapter 7), where the Commission remains very firmly in the driver's seat. Development policy is opaquer, where both the EEAS and the Commission have been given a role in the policy-making process (see Chapter 8).

Council Decision 2010/427/EU of 26 July 2010 establishing the organisation and functioning of the European External Action Service [2010] OJ L201/30

Preamble

...

(2) In accordance with the second subparagraph of Article 21(3) TEU, the Union will ensure consistency between the different areas of its external action and between those areas and its other policies. The Council and the Commission, assisted by the High Representative, will ensure that consistency and will cooperate to that effect ...

The preamble of the Council Decision reaffirms that coherence remains the final objective of setting up the EEAS and does this by copying and pasting the text of Article 21(3)(2) TEU. Article 2 of the EEAS Decision then describes the two tasks of the EEAS attaining that objective: first, Article 2(1) states that it 'shall support' the High Representative in fulfilling his mandates as outlined in Articles 18 and 27 TFEU. Three indents follow that statement, one for each of the HR's hats. The first requires the EEAS to support the High Representative while carrying out CFSP and ensuring the consistency of the Union's external action. The second and third indents require the EEAS to support her in her mandate as President of the Foreign Affairs Council and as Vice President of the Commission, respectively. All of this is in function of a coherent EU international policy, though each time qualified by stating that 'this is without prejudice to the normal tasks' of the General Secretariat of the Council and the 'normal tasks' of the Commission services respectively. Article 2(2) adds that the EEAS also function to assist the President of the European Council, the President of the Commission, as well as the Commission itself, 'in the exercise of their respective functions in the area of external relations'.

Article 1(2) of the EEAS Decision (see above) provides: 'The EEAS, which has its headquarters in Brussels, *shall be a functionally autonomous body* of the European Union, *separate* from the General Secretariat of the Council and from the Commission with the *legal capacity necessary* to perform its tasks and attain its objectives' (emphasis added). Deep disagreement existed throughout the negotiation process on the EEAS' position in the EU institutional set-up. On the one hand, there was Member State agreement that 'the EEAS should be a service of a *sui generis* nature separate from the Commission and the Council Secretariat'.[16] On the other hand, the European Parliament's opinion was that it should be connected to the Commission. The final result laid down in Article 1(2) of the Decision reveals that Parliament has lost out in the final compromise.

In Article 1 of the EEAS Decision we found that the EEAS is 'functionally autonomous' and 'separate' from the Council Secretariat and Commission. Given the negotiation history to the EEAS, these notions should be interpreted as meaning that in supporting the High Representative, the EU diplomatic service does not take instructions from either the Council or the Commission ('equidistance'). Its instructions come from the *office of* the High Representative,[17] who is accountable to the EU institutions proper – notably also the Parliament. The EEAS is certainly part of a 'command structure' which runs vertically via the High Representative, then through to the Council and up to the European Council, with a strand of accountability connecting it to Parliament. However, the EEAS is horizontally not an institutional participant in the EU's institutional balance nor part of an institution itself.

M Gatti, *European External Action Service: Promoting Coherence through Autonomy and Coordination* (Leiden, Brill/Nijhoff, 2016) 1

The EEAS is one of the most significant innovations introduced by the Lisbon Treaty and constitutes the first case of a non-national 'foreign ministry'.

Given the idea behind the establishment of the EEAS, does setting up such a complex new body do anything to resolve decades-old tensions of EU external relations? No inter-institutional reconfiguration is perfect, and the EEAS is clearly a compromise between the many different interests involved.

[16] October 2009 Presidency Report, DOC 14930/09, 6.

[17] Heads of the EU delegations can also receive instructions from the Commission 'in areas where they exercise powers conferred upon it by the Treaties'. Otherwise, the Delegations only receive instructions from the High Representative (Art 5(3) EEAS Decision).

Council Decision 2010/427/EU of 26 July 2010 establishing the organisation and functioning of the European External Action Service [2010] OJ L201/30

…

Article 3

Cooperation

1. The EEAS shall support, and work in cooperation with, the diplomatic services of the Member States, as well as with the General Secretariat of the Council and the services of the Commission, in order to ensure consistency between the different areas of the Union's external action and between those areas and its other policies.
2. The EEAS and the services of the Commission shall consult each other on all matters relating to the external action of the Union in the exercise of their respective functions, except on matters covered by the CSDP. The EEAS shall take part in the preparatory work and procedures relating to acts to be prepared by the Commission in this area.

   This paragraph shall be implemented in accordance with Chapter 1 of Title V of the TEU, and with Article 205 TFEU.
3. The EEAS may enter into service-level arrangements with relevant services of the General Secretariat of the Council, the Commission, or other offices or interinstitutional bodies of the Union.
4. The EEAS shall extend appropriate support and cooperation to the other institutions and bodies of the Union, in particular to the European Parliament. The EEAS may also benefit from the support and cooperation of those institutions and bodies, including agencies, as appropriate. The EEAS internal auditor will cooperate with the internal auditor of the Commission to ensure a consistent audit policy, with particular reference to the Commission's responsibility for operational expenditure. In addition, the EEAS shall cooperate with the European Anti-Fraud Office ('OLAF') in accordance with Regulation (EC) No 1073/1999. It shall, in particular, adopt without delay the decision required by that Regulation on the terms and conditions for internal investigations. As provided in that Regulation, both Member States, in accordance with national provisions, and the institutions shall give the necessary support to enable OLAF's agents to fulfil their tasks.

Article 3 of the 2010 EEAS Decision on the duty of cooperation is exemplary of the carefully crafted new institutional balance in EU external relations: links have been established with national diplomatic services, though practice will show whether that is a reciprocal cooperative relationship. The legal obligations of cooperation are the strongest between the Commission and the EEAS, while relations with the Council and its 'normal tasks' are less clear. Accountability of the EEAS to Parliament is extensive but will have to be given form and substance in practice. In many areas the new diplomatic service has merged elements that used to function separately, while past tendencies of delimitation remain. Undoubtedly, the EEAS has also created new schisms, and new 'institutional interests'. While the EEAS's role as an interlocutor provides good ground to work towards a single EU voice, the legal and institutional innovations are far from perfect and will require further legal and practical elaboration in the near future.

A key role is indeed played by the High Representative. After Javier Solana as the first HR, Catherine Ashton was the first person appointed in the new system both as High Representative and as Vice President of the Commission at the end of 2009. She was succeeded by Federica Mogherini in 2014 and by Josep Borrell in 2019. This combination of the functions of HR and Vice-President of the Commission is, without doubt, one of the key innovations of the Lisbon Treaty. Since the entry into force of that Treaty the High Representative for the Common Foreign and Security Policy has been renamed *High Representative of the Union for Foreign Affairs and Security Policy*. The name change reflects the fact that it has become clear that the HR indeed represents the Union and not the (collective) Member States. The HR's powers are clearly laid down in the EU Treaty and form part of the institutional framework. Although the term 'Foreign Minister', which was used in the Constitutional Treaty, has been abandoned, the new provisions make clear that the HR will indeed be the prime representative of the Union in international affairs. Even the President of the European Council (note: not the European *Union*) exercises that position's external competences 'without prejudice to the powers of the High Representative of the Union for Foreign Affairs and Security Policy' (Article 15(6)(d) TEU).

The HR is appointed by the European Council (with the agreement of the President of the Commission) by qualified majority voting (QMV). This again underlines the HR's role as a person who can act on behalf of the Union and who is perhaps competent to act even in the absence of a full consensus among the Member States.

Article 18(2) TEU

The High Representative shall conduct the Union's common foreign and security policy. He shall contribute by his proposals to the development of that policy, which he shall carry out as mandated by the Council. The same shall apply to the common security and defence policy.

In addition, the HR's de facto membership of the European Council is codified in Article 15 TEU (although strictly speaking it is stated that the HR only 'takes part in the work' of the European Council). The HR is further to assist the Council and the Commission in ensuring consistency between the different areas of the Union's external action (Article 21 TEU) and, together with the Council, ensures compliance by the Member States with their CFSP obligations (Article 24(3) TEU). All in all, the position of HR has been upgraded to allow for stronger and more independent development and implementation of the Union's foreign, security and defence policy, which – potentially – allows for a more coherent and more effective role for the EU in the world.

B. The European Council

Article 22(1) TEU

On the basis of the principles and objectives set out in Article 21, the European Council shall identify the strategic interests and objectives of the Union.

The European Council is one of the EU institutions and adopts its own 'Decisions'. However, most often, this institution carries out this task through the adoption of 'Conclusions' at the end of its meetings. These can be considered an 'instrument' of EU external relations, though they are not listed in Article 288 TFEU alongside the legal instruments. They are thus not considered to be legally binding instruments as the European Council does not 'exercise legislative functions' (Article 15(1) TEU). Yet, what is certain is that they are 'politically important' for EU external relations because the European Council is the top EU institution tasked with setting out the future policy direction of EU external action. Procedurally, it is clear that we cannot neatly capture EU external policymaking through the ordinary legislative procedure for internal instruments, or the Article 218 TFEU procedure for international agreements (see Chapter 4). Conclusions of the European Council may trigger action at all levels of governance within the EU as an international actor: both within the Member States themselves and within and between the EU institutions. It may lead the Commission to propose a new Regulation (eg, autonomous internal legally binding instrument) or lead to the proposition by the Commission and/or EEAS of the negotiation of an international agreement (eg, conventional external legally binding instrument). However, it may also lead to non-legal but important foreign policy activity: for example, the opening of a political dialogue with an important strategic partner (eg, the USA or Russia), the adoption of a political démarche rejecting a certain international state of affairs (eg, Iran's pursuit of nuclear weapons). Thus, different 'actors' will be implementing the strategic vision set out by the European Council in accordance with Article 22 TEU. In order to implement European Council Conclusions adopted in carrying out Article 22 TEU, the High Representative, the European External Action Service or the President of the European Council may all have an important function.

Article 15(6) TEU

The President of the European Council shall, at his level and in that capacity, ensure the external representation of the Union on issues concerning its common foreign and security policy, without prejudice to the powers of the High Representative of the Union for Foreign Affairs and Security Policy.

The President of the European Council is thus one of the Union's external representatives. Article 15(6) TEU explicitly refers to the fact that the President ensures the representation *at his level*. The President would therefore be the contact person for heads of state of third countries, whereas the High Representative would generally act at the level of ministers.

C. The Council

Article 16(6) TEU

The Council shall meet in different configurations, the list of which shall be adopted in accordance with Article 236 of the Treaty on the Functioning of the European Union.

The General Affairs Council shall ensure consistency in the work of the different Council configurations. It shall prepare and ensure the follow-up to meetings of the European Council, in liaison with the President of the European Council and the Commission.

The Foreign Affairs Council shall elaborate the Union's external action on the basis of strategic guidelines laid down by the European Council and ensure that the Union's action is consistent.

In general, the Council of the European Union, which meets at the level of ministers in the Member States' governments, exercises legislative and budgetary functions and carries out policy making and coordinating functions, jointly with the European Parliament (Article 16(1) TEU). This is not different in the area of external relations. Like the European Council, the Council also adopts 'Conclusions' which will reflect what has been discussed and decided during each meeting. Again, these are not legally binding instruments of the Union, but they are crucial in driving forward the decision-making process that underpins EU external action. As will be illustrated in Chapter 13 on 'The EU and its Neighbours', the European Neighbourhood Policy was originally crafted entirely on the basis of a succession of non-legally binding policy documents, with the Council firmly directing the heading of EU policy in this domain.

Article 16(6) TEU points to the 'Foreign Affairs Council' (FAC) as the key configuration in the area of external action. In this configuration, the Council is generally composed of the Ministers for Foreign Affairs, but it is up to the Member States to decide to send either their Minister for Foreign Affairs or, for instance, a Minister or Deputy Minister for European Affairs. The Council deals with the whole of the EU's external action, including Common Foreign and Security Policy, Common Security and Defence Policy, foreign trade and development cooperation, which occasionally calls for other ministers (Development or Trade) to join in. Defence Ministers traditionally participate in Foreign Affairs Council meetings twice a year, in addition to their informal meetings (also twice a year). In contrast to other Council configurations – which are presided by the six-monthly Presidency held by the Member States representatives in the Council on the basis of equal rotation (Articles 16(9) TEU and 236 TFEU) – the FAC is chaired by the High Representative. Given the busy schedule of the High Representative, (s)he may, where necessary, ask to be replaced by the member of the FAC holding the rotating Presidency (Article 2(5) of the Council's Rules of Procedure).

As indicated above, however, external relations not only relate to CFSP, but also include other external policies and can be a considered a dimension of most other EU policies. This implies that other Council configurations have an external dimension and it would be mistaken to only take account of the FAC Council's work in analysing EU external relations. Thus, negotiations on EU enlargement are dealt with by the General Affairs Council and issues concerning borders and visas may be on the agenda of the Justice and Home Affairs Council (see Chapter 12). The same holds true for the other configurations (Economic and Financial Affairs; Transport, Telecommunications and Energy; Agriculture and Fisheries; Environment; Education, Youth, Culture and Sport; Employment, Social Policy, Health and Consumer Affairs; and Competitiveness).

The role of the Committee of Permanent Representatives (COREPER) is similar in external relations issues as in other policy areas. There are two COREPER configurations, named COREPER I and COREPER II. COREPER I consists of EU Member State representatives at ambassadorial level and deals with political, commercial, economic or institutional matters. COREPER II consists of representatives at deputy ambassadorial level, dealing with what are considered 'technical matters'.

D. The Commission

In terms of decision-making, the area of external relations does not differ from internal policies in the sense that, generally, the Commission is in the lead and should initiate new decisions and legislation. With the introduction of the EEAS, the dedicated external relations Directorate General was removed from the Commission. Yet, given the external dimension of most policy areas (energy, environment, financial system etc), the Commission has remained a key player. Apart from its general role in negotiations with third states and other international organisations, some external relations domains were not transferred to the EEAS, but maintained in the Commission, including Trade, Energy or Humanitarian Aid.

Article 17(1) TEU

With the exception of the common foreign and security policy, and other cases provided for in the Treaties, it shall ensure the Union's external representation.

Apart from the general role of the Commission in the decision-making process, this provision allows the Commission to represent the Union externally. This is only the case with respect to non-CFSP issues and 'other cases provided for in the Treaties'. A clear example of such an 'other' case is formed by Article 218 TFEU. This provision addresses the specific cases of negotiation of international agreements and expression of the EU's position in international bodies in certain circumstances (see Chapter 4). It clearly indicates the many roles of different institutions: it is for the Council to authorise the opening of negotiations, to adopt negotiation directives and to authorise the signing of agreements and conclude them (with the consent or consultation of the European Parliament). Yet, the negotiations themselves are conducted by the Commission and in certain cases by the High Representative. Subsequently, the Council exercises a certain control over the negotiations by addressing directives to the negotiator and designating a special committee which is to be consulted during the negotiations. Moreover, the European Parliament should be immediately and fully informed at all stages (see further Chapter 4).

Most importantly, however, the Commission's competences are defined by the principle of conferral, which may limit the Commission's powers in international conferences and international organisations. Thus, the Commission represents the Union in the areas of exclusive Union competence listed in Article 3 TFEU (customs union, competition, monetary policy for Member States whose currency is the euro, the conservation of marine biological resources under the fisheries policy, the common commercial policy); whereas in the areas of shared competence of the Union with the Member States listed in Article 4 TFEU, both the Commission and the Member States have powers of representation in respect of their respective competences (see also Chapters 3 and 4 on mixed agreements).

E. The European Parliament

Despite its formally modest role in the area of external relations, the European Parliament has maximised the use of its powers and has proven itself to be a very active player. After the entry into force of the Lisbon Treaty this was supported by a number of innovations:

- For basically all a wide range of international agreements, Parliament is required to give consent before the agreement can be concluded by the Council (Article 218(6)(a) TFEU).
- The TFEU foresees a Multiannual Financial Framework for at least a period of five years (Article 312 TFEU), which is adopted by the Council but following consent

of the EP. The latter now has a say, as the Council, on expenses related to the EU external relations, in particular concerning CFSP.

- A specific section of the EU budget (Section X) relates to the EEAS, which implies that the EP has to agree with this part of the budget. It also has competence to decide on the discharge of the EEAS, which provides a degree of political control on how the EEAS is organised. The EP Committee on budgetary control is particularly concerned with verifying how the EU budget is spent on external relations, in particular regarding CFSP.
- 'The President, the High Representative of the Union for Foreign Affairs and Security Policy and the other members of the Commission shall be subject as a body to a vote of consent by the European Parliament' (Article 17(7) TEU).

In general, the European Parliament is regularly consulted by the High Representative on the main aspects and basic choices of CFSP and is informed of how those policies evolve (Article 36 TEU) (Chapter 9). Throughout this book, there are many examples whereby the Parliament has proactively sought to defend and even expand its influence on EU external policymaking. For example, in Chapter 7 on the Common Commercial Policy, we illustrate that the Parliament does not hesitate to remind the Commission that its consent will be required for the Union to conclude trade agreements. In other policy fields the Parliament has shown that it will, in fact, utilise its veto power if its views are not taken into account. This, together with its budgetary powers, render the Parliament a force to be reckoned with in EU external decision making. Beyond these formal aspects, the European Parliament has Committees such as the AFET (foreign affairs) or DEVE (development) committees, which are proactive in commissioning studies, adopting non-binding Resolutions, organising hearings, carrying out fact-finding missions and so on, to place a parliamentary stamp on EU external relations. In its view, this provides an important element of democratic input to EU external action.

F. The Court of Justice

Since, in particular in the early years, references to external relations in the Treaties were minimal, the role of the Court in this area simply cannot be overstated. Large parts of what we now consider to be part and parcel of the external relations legal doctrine find their basis in CJEU case law. Throughout this book we will come across many key examples: the doctrine of implied powers, the exclusive nature of the Common Commercial Policy, the scope of development policy, the effects of international law (United Nations, WTO, law of the sea, etc) on the EU legal order and many other crucial elements of EU external relations law, are all based on judge-made law – parts of which were later codified in the Treaties.

The Court's jurisdiction with respect to CFSP is limited. Its main tasks include monitoring compliance with the dividing line between CFSP and non-CFSP matters laid down in Article 40 TEU and reviewing the legality of the external restrictive measures laid down in Article 275(2) TFEU (Article 24(1) TEU). Yet, as Chapter 9 will reveal, the Court does also have jurisdiction in relation to general EU rules and principles even when these emerge in a CFSP context.

A core task of the Court has been (and still is) to decide on the delimitation of external competences between the Union and its Member States. With the further intensification of the European integration process, more and more internal competences ended up in the hands of the European institutions. This, in turn, also led to an incremental transfer of external powers from the Member States to the Union. After all, once competences have become 'exclusive' internally, there is not much left for Member States to decide on externally (see also Chapter 3).

G. The Member States

While we will further elaborate on the issue of competences (exclusive, shared, etc) in Chapter 3 it is clear that, despite their membership of the European Union, the Member States have not ceased to be international actors in their own capacity. In fact, all Member States would argue that statehood – rather than EU membership – is still their primary identity. The principle of conferral means that the European Union is only competent to act once a competence exists (see further Chapter 2). In principle, this implies that where the Union is not competent to act or where it shares its competences with the Member States, the latter can engage in legal relations with third states and other international organisations. As we will see throughout this book, it is this tension in particular (between being a state and being a *Member* State) which lies behind many of the rules in EU external relations law. The irony seems to be that Member States are generally happy with the benefits of European integration, in particular the internal market, but are not always equally happy with the consequences this entails in terms of losing (external) powers.

IV. The Broader Picture of EU External Relations Law

This chapter has provided a roadmap explaining the reasons why EU external relations law is such a complex field and subsequently pointing to the essential features of the EU's architecture and the key institutional actors in this area. The starting point is the peculiar nature of the Union itself; neither state nor classic international organisation, it is a unique species of international (integration) organisation with a legal existence distinct from that of its Member States and with a standalone identity – and legal personality – composed of values, interests and policies which it promotes internationally as its own. EU external relations law, then, is the body of law that governs the actions of the European Union in the world both internally and externally. In its internal dimension, it consists of the set of rules which governs the constitutional and institutional legal organisation of this legal entity in pursuit of its interests in the world. In its external dimension, it includes the rules which govern its relationship and interaction with other entities of the international (legal) order.

What renders this field particularly complex is the fact that the functioning, interpretation, and application of the rules it comprises is shaped by its specific *telos* as well as the context of progressing integration. The purpose of EU external relations law is to organise the European Union and its Member States to exert their influence on the world stage in a coherent and effective fashion. This *telos* is then deeply intertwined with the project of European integration and debates how far this process should continue. The consequence is then that law, even constitutional law, plays a far more significant role in international relations of the Union than is common at the national level. First, a large body of legal rules is required to ensure that this *sui generis* entity is a sufficient coagulant to ensure effective external action. Secondly, this internal law-based integration experience is then also translated into substantive external relations. Indeed, EU Treaty objectives also point to the Union as seeking to contribute 'to the strict observance and the development of international law' and to spread and consolidate the rule of law in the world at large.

Taking a step back and looking at the broader picture of the material presented in this first chapter, we can now ask the following tantalising question raised by Bruno de Witte: Is there too much constitutional law in the European Union's foreign relations?

B de Witte, 'Too Much Constitutional Law in the European Union's Foreign Relations?' in M Cremona and B de Witte (eds) *EU Foreign Relations Law: Constitutional Fundamentals* (Oxford, Hart Publishing, 2008) 5–15

The argument that there is 'too much constitutional law' in the EU is mainly based on the overabundance of primary law norms, which unduly constrains the normal democratic process. It is made worse by two other elements, namely the structural complexity of EU constitutional law which leads to a lack of 'legibility' for citizens, and the rigidity of the EU's rules of change ...

EU primary law tends to deal with many [issues of EU external relations] in a much more detailed way than national constitutions. In purely quantitative terms, a greater proportion of articles of the founding Treaties deal, entirely or in part, with foreign relations. This overabundant written text is complemented by an unusually abundant case law which has designed a fine pattern of rules on such foreign relations matters as the implied powers doctrine, the distinction between exclusive and shared competences, the duty of sincere cooperation in the context of mixed agreements, and the conditions under which international agreements have direct effect in the EC legal order ...

[T]here are too many 'un-fundamentals' in the foreign relations constitution of the EU. The formal constitutional law of the EU, which consists of the primary law of the Treaties as interpreted by the Court of Justice and supplemented by general principles, contains many norms that are not constitutional in their substance. They do not serve the useful purpose of constitutional rules, namely to limit and steer the activity of the institutions, but are merely obstructive ... [T]he drafters of the Treaties have not sufficiently reflected on the need for constitutional parsimony.

V. Sources and Further Reading

Bengoetxea, J, 'The EU as (More Than) an International Organization' in J Klabbers and Å Wallendahl (eds) *Research Handbook on the Law of International Organizations* (Cheltenham, Edward Elgar Publishing, 2011) 448–65.

Bretherton, C and J Vogler, *The European Union as a Global Actor* (Abingdon, Routledge, 2006).

Cannizzaro, E, P Palchetti and RA Wessel (eds) *International Law as Law of the European Union* (Leiden, Martinus Brill Nijhoff, 2011).

Cremona, M, 'The Draft Constitutional Treaty: External Relations and External Action' (2003) 40 *Common Market Law Review* 1347.

Cremona, M, 'The Union as a Global Actor: Roles, Models and Identity' (2004) 42 *Common Market Law Review* 553.

Curtin, DM and IF Dekker, 'The European Union from Maastricht to Lisbon: Institutional and Legal Unity out of the Shadow' in P Craig and G De Búrca (eds) *The Evolution of EU Law* (Oxford, Oxford University Press, 2011) 155–85.

De Baere, G, *Constitutional Principles of EU External Relations* (Oxford, Oxford University Press, 2008).

De Burca, G, 'EU International Relations: The Governance Mode of Foreign Policy' in B Van Vooren, S Blockmans and J Wouters (eds) *The Legal Dimension of Global Governance: What Role For the EU?* (Oxford, Oxford University Press, 2012) 39–58.

de Witte, B, 'Too Much Constitutional Law in the European Union's Foreign Relations?' in M Cremona and B de Witte (eds) *EU Foreign Relations Law: Constitutional Fundamentals* (Oxford, Hart Publishing, 2008) 3–15.

Eckes, C, *EU Powers Under External Pressure: How the EU's External Actions Alter its Internal Structures* (Oxford, Oxford University Press, 2019).

Eeckhout, P, *EU External Relations Law*, 2nd edn (Oxford, Oxford University Press, 2011).

Eeckhout, P and M Lopez-Escudero (eds) *The European Union's External Action in Times of Crisis* (Oxford, Hart Publishing, 2016).

Gosalbo Bono, R, 'The Organization of the External Relations of the European Union in the Treaty of Lisbon' in P Koutrakos (ed) *The European Union's External Relations A Year after Lisbon,* CLEER Working Papers 2011/3, 13–38.

Govaere, I, E Lannon, P Van Elsuwege, S Adam (eds) *The European Union in the World: Essays in Honour of Marc Maresceau* (Leiden, Brill/Nijhoff, 2013).

Hillion, C, 'Tous pour un, un pour tous! Coherence in the External Relations of the European Union' in M Cremona (ed) *Developments in EU External Relations Law* (Oxford, Oxford University Press, 2008) 10–36.

Kaddous, C, 'Role and Position of the High Representative of the Union for Foreign Affairs and Security Policy under the Lisbon Treaty' in S Griller and J Ziller (eds) *The Lisbon Treaty: Constitutionalism without a Constitutional Treaty?* (Vienna, Springer, 2008) 205–21.

Kochenov, D (ed) *EU Law of the Overseas: Outermost Regions, Associated Overseas Countries and Territories, Territories Sui Generis* (The Hague, Wolters Kluwer, 2011).

Koutrakos, P, *EU International Relations Law*, 2nd edn (Oxford, Hart, 2015).

Kuijper, PJ, J Wouters, F Hoffmeister, G De Baere and T Ramopoulos, *The Law of EU External Relations: Cases, Materials, and Commentary on the EU as an International Legal Actor*, 2nd edn (Oxford, Oxford University Press, 2015).

Larik, J, 'Entrenching Global Governance: The EU's Constitutional Objectives caught Between A Sanguine World View and a Daunting Reality' in B Van Vooren, S Blockmans and J Wouters (eds) *The Legal Dimension of Global Governance, What Role for the EU?* (Oxford, Oxford University Press, 2013) 7–22.

Manners, I, 'Normative Power Europe: A Contradiction in Terms?' (2002) 40 *Journal of Common Market Studies* 235.

Neframi, E and M Gatti (eds) *Constitutional Issues of EU External Relations Law* (Baden-Baden, Nomos, 2018).

Paasivirta, E, 'The EU's External Representation after Lisbon: New Rules, A New Era?' in P Koutrakos (ed) *The European Union's External Relations A Year after Lisbon,* CLEER Working Papers 2011/3, 39–47.

Schroeder, W, 'Die Europäische Union als Völkerrechtssubject' (2012) Beiheft 2 *Europarecht* 9.

Steinbach, A, 'The Lisbon Judgment of the German Federal Constitutional Court – New Guidance on the Limits of European Integration' (2010) 11 *German Law Journal* 367.

Thym, D, 'Parliamentary Involvement in European International Relations' in M Cremona and B de Witte (eds) *EU Foreign Relations Law: Constitutional Fundamentals* (Oxford, Hart Publishing, 2008) 201–32.

Van Vooren, B, 'A Legal institutional Perspective on the European External Action Service' (2011) 48 *Common Market Law Review* 475.

Van Vooren, B, S Blockmans and J Wouters (eds) *The EU's Role in Global Governance: The Legal Dimension* (Oxford, Oxford University Press, 2013).

Wessel, RA, 'The International Legal Status of the European Union' (1997) 2 *European Foreign Affairs Review* 10.

2

Principles of EU External Action

Central Issues

- Principles of EU law in the external relations context have been employed by the Court of Justice of the European Union (CJEU) and have helped structure the space in which Member States and EU institutions exercise exclusive and shared external competences as well as Common Foreign and Security Policy (CFSP) competences. One can distinguish between relational principles that, inter alia, help to address power struggles between EU institutions and Member States (eg, principles of conferral, sincere cooperation and institutional balance) and systemic principles, which have been employed to further define the nature and 'actorness' of the EU as a global actor in its own rights (eg, coherence, autonomy and effectiveness).
- The CJEU has applied established principles (such as fundamental rights) as legality benchmarks for EU measures adopted in the context of external action on the one hand, and as a basis for recognising remedies for individuals affected by operational action, even if taken in the context of CFSP, on the other. Yet, the Court has been reluctant to employ the tool of judge-made EU principles to develop new substantive law in its case law in the field of external relations, leaving it to the other EU institutions and their international counterparts to establish such law on the international stage.
- Since the Treaty of Lisbon, the Treaty on European Union (TEU) makes additional reference to principles, requiring that EU external action is guided and shaped by EU (substantive) principles that have played an important role in the creation and development of the EU's internal legal order, including democracy, the rule of law, human rights and equality (Article 21(1) TEU; see also, with regard to any EU action, eg, Articles 9 TEU and 8 TFEU on the principle of equality). At the same time, the Treaties require the EU to ensure consistency in its external action (Article 21(3) TEU, Article 7 TFEU).

I. The Role and Development of EU Principles

The Court of Justice of the European Union (CJEU) has recognised 'general principles' of EU law in its case law since the beginning of European integration.[1] General principles have been acknowledged as judge-made EU law that sits below the Treaties and above secondary EU law in the hierarchy of EU norms.[2] They include fundamental rights, but also other principles, such as direct effect, supremacy, proportionality, sincere cooperation and state liability.

In the context of the EU internal legal order, the CJEU would rely on objectives, such as the establishment and functioning of the internal market, to justify Member State constraints on the basis of its principles. In light of EU objectives, the CJEU established principles and recognised Member State obligations related to the ranking of conflicting norms (eg, supremacy of EU law),[3] the need for collaboration between institutions and Member States (eg, sincere cooperation,[4] institutional balance[5]) or the need for the protection of individuals as participants in the EU legal order (eg, fundamental rights,[6] direct effect,[7] legal certainty and legitimate expectations[8]).

In short, the CJEU has employed general principles as tools for further integration and constitutionalisation of the EU's legal order, shaping rules regarding the exercise of power by the EU and its Member States, recognising the role of individuals as right holders and enforcers of EU law and establishing a catalogue of fundamental and citizenship rights. While some principles have (later) been codified in the Treaties or related instruments (eg, principle of proportionality,[9] fundamental rights[10]), others have remained unwritten but important parts of EU law (eg, the principles of direct

[1] T Tridimas, *The General Principles of EU Law*, 2nd edn (Oxford, Oxford University Press, 2006); K Ziegler, P Neuvonen, V Moreno-Lax (eds) *Research Handbook on General Principles of EU Law* (Cheltenham, Edward Elgar, 2020).

[2] P Craig and G De Búrca, *EU Law: Text, Cases and Materials*, 6th edn (Oxford, Oxford University Press, 2015) 111.

[3] Case 6/64 *Costa v Enel*, ECLI:EU:C:1964:66.

[4] Cases C-36/97 and 37/97 *Hilmar Kellinghusen*, ECLI:EU:C:2006:101, para 30.

[5] Case C-70/88 *Parliament v Council*, ECLI:EU:C:1992:325, paras 21 et seq.

[6] Case 4/73 *Nold v Commission*, ECLI:EU:C:1974:51, 502 et seq.

[7] Case 26/62 *Van Gend en Loos*, ECLI:EU:C:1963:1.

[8] Case 120/86 *Mulder v Minister van Landbouw en Visserij*, ECLI:EU:C:1988:213, para 27.

[9] Art 5(4) TEU states:

> 'Under the principle of proportionality, the content and form of Union action shall not exceed what is necessary to achieve the objectives of the Treaties.
>
> The institutions of the Union shall apply the principle of proportionality as laid down in the Protocol on the application of the principles of subsidiarity and proportionality.'
>
> See also Protocol (No 2) on the application of the principles of subsidiarity and proportionality [2008] OJ C 115/206.

[10] Art 6(1), (3) TEU; Charter of Fundamental Rights of the European Union.

effect, supremacy, legal certainty). The application and enforcement of principles have helped to ensure the effectiveness of EU law, the uniformity of its application and the overall functioning of the EU legal order. They have served as benchmark for the lawfulness of EU[11] and Member State measures and as interpretation aid when dealing with EU Treaty and secondary law provisions.[12]

As this chapter shows, many EU principles developed within the context of the EU internal legal order are, in an equal or at least similar way, applicable to the field of external action.[13] At the same time, there are several characteristics of the legal framework for EU external action that are worth highlighting, as they pose additional challenges for the CJEU in the development of EU principles. First, the notion of 'principles' features more prominently in the Treaty provisions on external action, raising questions of how they relate to previously existing (unwritten) principles and their application and interpretation. Secondly, the Lisbon Treaty introduced a catalogue of specific external action objectives that complements the pool of EU objectives related to the internal legal order, which the CJEU has relied on when developing EU principles. Thirdly, the CJEU has been reluctant to interfere with policy choices of the EU's political institutions, which has made the development of new substantive EU principles concerning the EU's external identity or agenda less likely.

A. Principles Guiding EU External Action

The EU Treaties have made explicit the Member States' commitment that certain core EU principles should guide the EU's external action and be 'advance[d] in the wider world' (eg, democracy, the rule of law, human rights, equality). However, the pertinent Treaty provisions have not specified what the legal implications of such commitment should be regarding the named principles' particular scope, implications for EU institutions, Member States, non-EU actors and individuals, or to what extent they might be enforceable before the EU courts, compared to (unwritten) EU principles previously recognised and employed by the CJEU.[14]

[11] See for a classification of general principles as 'additional limits on EU institutional activity' and reference to case law on fundamental and procedural rights T Horsley, *The Court of Justice of the European Union as an Institutional Actor – Judicial Lawmaking and its Limits* (Cambridge, Cambridge University Press, 2018) 69.

[12] Craig and De Búrca (n 2) 111 et seq. For instance, the CJEU asked national courts to set aside national law conflicting with the EU principle of non-discrimination to ensure its effectiveness, even where the implementation period for the relevant directive had not yet expired, see Case C-144/04 *Mangold v Helm*, ECLI:EU:C:2005:709, paras 75 et seq.

[13] For a comprehensive study of how EU external actions, including the interpretation of principles, have affected EU law and practice see C Eckes, *EU Powers Under External Pressure: How the EU's External Actions Alter its Internal Structures* (Oxford, Oxford University Press, 2019).

[14] With regard to the implications of fundamental rights obligations and the rule of law for the EU external action see section IV below.

Article 21(1) TEU

The Union's action on the international scene *shall be guided by the principles* which have inspired its own creation, development and enlargement, and which it seeks to advance in the wider world: democracy, the rule of law, the universality and indivisibility of human rights and fundamental freedoms, respect for human dignity, the principles of equality and solidarity, and respect for the principles of the United Nations Charter and international law. [emphasis added]

Article 21(1) TEU does not clarify what the consequences would be of EU external action taking different listed principles into account. The provision does not provide detail on how different principles relate to each other nor how potential conflicts between them can be resolved. The Treaty is also silent with regard to reconciling potential clashes between the commitment to EU principles and the EU and its Member States' commitment to international law, including the rights and obligations conferred by it. It still needs to be seen to what extent the EU institutions, including the CJEU, will be in a position to clarify the reach of such core principles and their implications for the EU as a global actor.

Since the entry into force of the Lisbon Treaty, also in the field of the Common Foreign and Security Policy (CFSP) '[t]he Union's action on the international scene … shall be guided by the principles, shall pursue the objectives of, and be conducted in accordance with, the general provisions laid down in Chapter 1'.[15] Moreover, '[w]ithin the framework of the principles and objectives of its external action, the Union shall conduct, define and implement a common foreign and security policy, based on the development of mutual political solidarity among Member States, the identification of questions of general interest and the achievement of an ever-increasing degree of convergence of Member States' actions'.[16] In spite of the CJEU's limited jurisdiction in the field of CFSP, which reflects states' traditional interest in protecting a high degree of EU and Member States' political discretion by placing it outside the remit of the Court, the Court has begun to apply EU principles in its CFSP case law (see Chapter 9).

B. Developing Principles in Light of Objectives

As we have seen in the previous chapter, the Treaty of Lisbon introduced a catalogue of specific EU external action objectives (Articles 3(5), 21(2) TEU) that is different in nature from the EU's internal objectives, which have been relied on in the development

[15] Art 23 TEU. Chapter 1 includes Art 3(5) TEU, which will be discussed in the following section.
[16] Art 24(2) TEU.

of EU principles. Whereas internal objectives focused primarily on specific goals, such as the introduction and functioning of the internal market or the creation of an area of security and justice, external objectives are more open-ended and concern the EU's contribution and identity as a rules-based global actor.[17] The EU's external action objectives are 'orientational and general rather than functional',[18] and do not prescribe concrete end-goals to be achieved in foreign affairs. Such lack of finality of EU external objectives arguably makes it more difficult for the CJEU to crystallise the content and reach of EU principles.[19] At the same time, the wording of the relevant Treaty provisions makes clear that Member States have committed to establishing the EU as a strong and rules-based global actor, even if its empowerment has been limited by Member States' explicit retention of powers and the jurisdiction of the CJEU on most matters of CFSP remains limited (see Chapter 9).

According to Articles 3(5) and 21(2) TEU – presented in the previous chapter – the objectives that the EU pursues on the international scene are linked to international law principles, objectives and mechanisms.[20] Such openness and commitment to the international legal order poses additional challenges to the CJEU's capacity to develop and employ EU principles in the context of external action, as objectives that could possibly legitimise Member State constraints (when exercising their own external powers), or shape the scope of individuals' legal position when affected by EU external action, are not exclusively defined by the EU internal order (for which the CJEU holds jurisdiction). Moreover, the extent to which EU external objectives can be achieved does not just depend on the EU institutions and Member States and how the CJEU interprets the meaning of principles and related obligations. Instead, EU external action is shaped by the international law obligations of the EU and its Member States, as well as (sometimes unpredictable) interests or preferences of non-EU actors and possibly the international community as a whole.[21]

[17] For a comprehensive study of the codification of EU foreign policy objectives as a growing part of European constitutional law see J Larik, *Foreign Policy Objectives in European Constitutional Law* (Oxford, Oxford University Press, 2016).

[18] M Cremona, 'Structural Principles and their Role in EU External Relations Law' in M Cremona (ed), *Structural Principles in EU External Relations Law* (Oxford, Hart Publishing, 2018) 29, see also 3 et seq; see on the lack of end-goals also M Cremona, 'A Reticent Court? Policy Objectives and the Court of Justice' in M Cremona and A Thies (eds) *The European Court of Justice and External Relations Law: Constitutional Challenges* (Oxford, Hart Publishing, 2014) 19; and A Thies, 'General Principles in the Development of EU External Relations Law' in Cremona and Thies (eds) *The European Court of Justice and External Relations Law: Constitutional Challenges* 161.

[19] One exception is arguably Art 6(2) TEU, according to which the EU 'shall accede to the European Convention for the Protection of Human Rights and Fundamental Freedoms', even if not very successful (and possibly evidence of the challenges of finality elements in EU external action objectives), given the CJEU's Opinion on the incompatibility of the Draft Accession Agreement with the EU Treaties, Opinion 2/13 (*ECHR II*), ECLI:EU:C:2014:2454.

[20] Eg Art 21(1) TEU refers to 'respect for the principles of the United Nations Charter and international law' as one of the guiding principles; Art 21(2) TEU codifies the EU's commitment to multilateralism, linking it to EU and international objectives.

[21] Thies, A, 'General Principles in the Development of EU External Relations Law' in M Cremona and A Thies (eds) *The European Court of Justice and External Relations Law: Constitutional Challenges* (Oxford, Hart Publishing, 2014) 140; for a discussion of how the international dimension/context has affected the scope of protection of general principles, see 148 et seq.

C. Principles and Policy Choices

With regard to the EU internal legal order, Treaty objectives and Member States' commitment to an overall direction of further integration have legitimised the recognition and judicial development of EU substantive law principles.[22] Yet, the CJEU has been reluctant in its judicial activity to interfere with policy choices made by other EU institutions in the field of external relations.

M Cremona, 'A Reticent Court? Policy Objectives and the Court of Justice' in M Cremona and A Thies (eds) *The European Court of Justice and External Relations Law: Constitutional Challenges* (Oxford, Hart Publishing, 2014) 15

'[T]he Court appears to be reticent (non-interventionist), if not deferential as regards the policy choices of the political institutions in external relations. It tends to take those choices at face value (basing itself on statements in legal instruments and policy documents); it does not question them, nor seek to define or shape them. More than this, it emphasises the need for the political institutions to retain their policy discretion, their room for manoeuvre. This is in contrast to its interventionist – if not activist – stance in relation to the definition of the scope of EU external competence and its implications for Member States, and its 'gatekeeper' – if not defensive – role in relation to the status of international law within the EU legal system …'

The judicial self-restraint with regard to policy choices and the EU's external agenda makes the development of substantive EU external relations law in form of judge-made principles less likely. This observation, however, does not affect the CJEU's willingness to apply existing substantive EU principles, such as fundamental rights, when assessing the lawfulness of EU measures adopted in the context of external action.

II. The Significance of Structural Principles

In spite of some uncertainty created by Treaty reference to external relations specific principles and objectives, as discussed in the previous paragraphs, the Court's employment of EU law principles has played an important role in complementing EU

[22] Eg the principle of equality, see LS Rossi and F Casolari (eds) *The Principle of Equality in EU Law* (Berlin, Springer, 2017); fundamental rights, including the principle of *ne bis in idem* in criminal matters, see B Van Bockel, *The Ne Bis in Idem Principle in EU Law* (The Hague, Kluwer, 2010).

objectives and values in the development of EU external relations law.[23] Most importantly, EU principles have helped to structure the system, functioning and exercise of EU external competences both within the EU institutions and in international fora. The application of EU principles has further shaped the EU's 'actorness', addressing challenges related to the co-existence of the EU and its Member States as distinct global actors.

M Cremona, 'Structural Principles and their Role in EU External Relations Law' in M Cremona (ed) *Structural Principles in EU External Relations Law* (Oxford, Hart Publishing, 2018) 11

'Whereas in its internal policies, the Union is generally instructed to construct something (an internal market, an area of freedom, security and justice, a system of undistorted competition), in its external policy, the Union is called upon to construct itself, to build its actorness and agency. As a result, the law (and the Court) does not interfere with the institutions' choice of specific policy objectives or with the use of external competences for varied purposes. When, on the other hand, we turn to the issues which define the institutional structure of EU external policy-making, we see law being used, through structural principles, to construct the Union as an autonomous international actor.'

The CJEU has engaged with the implications of what Cremona has called 'relational principles' when assessing the legal relations between Member States, Member States and the EU institutions, between EU institutions, and between the EU and individuals, third states and international organisations.[24] In that context, the CJEU has also applied principles – in particular, fundamental rights but also the rule of law more generally – as benchmark for the lawfulness of EU external action when challenged by individuals. Moreover, the CJEU has employed what Cremona has categorised as 'systemic principles', which have helped to build 'the EU's identity as a *coherent*, *effective* and *autonomous* actor in the world'.[25]

III. Structuring the Space and Protecting the EU's 'Actorness'

The following section introduces case law and scholarship on selected relational principles, taking account of how their content and reach have been affected by the systemic

[23] Cremona (2018) (n 18) 5 et seq.
[24] See Cremona (2018) (n 18).
[25] Ibid.

principle of effectiveness to strengthen the EU's 'actorness' on the international stage (on the basis of EU law). Subsequently, the chapter addresses the systemic principle of autonomy, which has increasingly been applied by the CJEU and become the subject of extensive academic debate. The final section turns to the CJEU's employment of (established) EU principles for the protection of individuals in the context of EU external action. The analysis thereby focuses on the way the CJEU has addressed the implications of the EU's increased global involvement for the legal position of affected individuals. It thereby highlights the recognition of fundamental rights as important legality benchmark for EU external action and the significance of the principle of the rule of law for the recognition of individuals' rights and remedies in that context, also with regard to the CJEU's own jurisdiction in the area of the EU's Common Foreign and Security Policy.

As mentioned above, the CJEU has been reluctant (so far) to develop substantive EU principles. Yet, external relations law – like any other area of EU law – has required the CJEU to address the *delimitation* of EU and Member State competences as well as the *exercise* of these competences on the global stage; principles have helped to structure the system, its functioning and exercise of EU external competences.[26] The following paragraphs introduce the principles of *conferral*, *sincere cooperation* and *institutional balance* with a particular focus on how they operate in the context of EU external relations law. The discussion includes some systemic principles to the extent they have shaped, complemented or interacted with the assessed relational principles in the context of external action.

A. The Principle of Conferral

The principle of conferral is concerned with the competence that Member States have given to the EU, and the competence that Member States have retained themselves.

Article 5 TEU

1. The limits of Union competences are governed by the principle of conferral. The use of Union competences is governed by the principles of subsidiarity and proportionality.
2. Under the principle of conferral, the Union shall act only within the limits of the competences conferred upon it by the Member States in the Treaties to attain the objectives set out therein. Competences not conferred upon the Union in the Treaties remain with the Member States. ...

The Lisbon Treaty brought some clarity to the nature and reach of EU competences by categorising competences as exclusive, shared and complementary and listing them

[26] Ibid at 3–29.

in a catalogue of competences for each of them.[27] The Treaty on European Union also states that those powers not conferred to the EU remain with the Member States (see Chapter 3). The EU Treaties continue to refer to some specific external competences of the EU, most importantly in the areas of trade (see Chapter 7), development cooperation and humanitarian aid (see Chapter 8). Yet, most EU competences are not specific to EU external relations but cover both internal and external matters in principle.

With the Lisbon Treaty, Member States conferred also comprehensive competence in the field of the Common Foreign and Security Policy to the EU, even if making its exercise 'subject to specific rules and procedures' (Article 24 (1) TEU), and thus arguably protecting Member States' say in an area that has long been distinct from more 'communitarised' areas (see Chapter 9).

In addition to express (external) competences, the EU holds implied external competences, to which the principle of conferral is also applicable.[28]

I Govaere, 'To Give or to Grab: The Principle of Full, Crippled and Split Conferral of Powers Post-Lisbon' in M Cremona (ed), *Structural Principles in EU External Relations Law* (Oxford, Hart Publishing, 2018) 72

'The importance of the principle of conferral to determine the structure, functioning and exercise of European Union (EU) law can hardly be over-estimated. From a sequential perspective, the principle of conferral is necessarily the very first of all the structural principles to be applied …

The principle of conferral is first and foremost the core principle that determines the delimitation of competence between the Member States and the EU.[29] At the same time it impacts directly on the relations between the EU and/or its Member States with third countries and other international organisations as it underpins the limitations that may be placed on the legal personality of the Union.[30]

The application of the principle of conferral also determines whether or not a subject matter comes within the ambit of the autonomous EU legal order, which is characterised by the exclusive jurisdiction of the CJEU [Article 19 TEU in conjunction with Art 344 TFEU], primacy and direct effect …'

[27] Arts 2 et seq TFEU.

[28] M Cremona, 'The Principle of Conferral and Express and Implied External Competences' in E Neframi and M Gatti (eds) *Constitutional Issues of EU External Relations Law* (Baden-Baden, Nomos, 2018) 30.

[29] Cremona points to the following two dimensions for allocation of competence: the relationship between the EU-Member States and the relationship between internal and external powers, see M Cremona, 'EU External Relations: Unity and Conferral of Powers' in L Azoulai (ed), *The Questions of Competence in the European Union* (Oxford, Oxford University Press, 2014) 65.

[30] Art 47 TEU reads: 'The Union shall have legal personality'.

In addition to the vertical delimitation of competence between the EU and its Member States, the principle of conferral is also concerned with the horizontal division of EU competences between different EU institutions. According to Article 13(2) TEU: '[e]ach institution shall act within the limits of the powers conferred on it in the Treaties, and in conformity with the procedures, conditions and objectives set out in them. The institutions shall practice mutual sincere cooperation'.

The CJEU has regularly been asked to decide on both vertical and horizontal division of competence in cases involving the EU and its Member States and/or different EU institutions. Cases have often concerned the choice of correct legal basis, which has implications for the level of involvement of different EU institutions, representing a variety of interests and stakeholders. The Court has recognised the 'constitutional significance' of choosing the appropriate legal basis, linking it to the principle of conferral.[31]

Opinion 2/00 (*Cartagena Protocol*), ECLI:EU:C:2001:664, para 5

The *choice of the appropriate legal basis has constitutional significance*. Since the Community has *conferred powers only*, it must tie the Protocol to a Treaty provision which empowers it to approve such a measure. To proceed on an incorrect legal basis is therefore liable to invalidate the act concluding the agreement and so vitiate the Community's consent to be bound by the agreement it has signed. That is so in particular where the Treaty does not confer on the Community sufficient competence to ratify the agreement in its entirety, a situation which entails examining the allocation as between the Community and the Member States of the powers to conclude the agreement that is envisaged with non-member countries, or where the appropriate legal basis for the measure concluding the agreement lays down a legislative procedure different from that which has in fact been followed by the Community institutions. [emphasis added]

The CJEU has reiterated the need to match the correct choice of substantive legal basis and applicable procedural rules in the context of international treaty-making, which has determined the level of involvement of the European Parliament also in the context of CFSP (see Chapter 9).

[31] Opinion 2/00 (*Cartagena Protocol*), ECLI:EU:C:2001:664, para 5; Opinion 1/08 (*Amendments to EU Schedules of Commitments under GATS*), ECLI:EU:C:2009:739, para 110, and eg Case C-263/14 Parliament *v* Council (*Tanzania*), ECLI:EU:C:2016:435, para 42, and Case C-600/14 *Germany v Council (COTIF)*, ECLI:EU:C:2017:935, para 80.

B. The Principle of Sincere Cooperation and Effectiveness Considerations

While the principle of conferral determines whether, or the extent to which the EU and/or its Member States hold competence to take (external) action altogether, there are other structural EU principles that determine the way in which EU and Member State competence is to be exercised. The CJEU has played an important role in further defining how conferred/retained competence must be exercised through its interpretation and application of EU principles.[32]

The CJEU has applied EU principles and, in particular, the principle of sincere cooperation, to organise the EU and its Member States' individual and joined external action in accordance with the EU Treaty framework. In most cases, the CJEU had been asked to define the scope of Member States' constraints and obligations in the interest of empowering the EU as a global actor as well as the unity of EU representation.

E Neframi, 'The Duty of Loyalty: Rethinking its Scope through its Application in the Field of EU External Relations' (2010) 47 *Common Market Law Review* 323, 359

'The duty of loyalty is a general principle inherent in membership of the EU. [Its] transcription in Article 4(3) TEU and its specification through the duty of loyal cooperation allows the CJEU to determine its scope and impact and to restrict the Member States' autonomy through the recognition of duties contributing to the constitutionalization of the European Union. The duties stemming from Article 4(3) TEU may cover effectiveness in the context of implementation of common rules, or other aspects in the interest of the Union, such as the respect for the *effet utile* of EU law, the contribution to the effective exercise of Union competence, or the fulfilment of the requirement of unity with a view to asserting the identity of the EU on the international scene. The effectiveness of EU law can thus be considered as the tangible facet of the duty of loyalty, specified through obligations of loyal cooperation incumbent on the national authorities, including the national courts. The duty of loyalty is thus the legal basis for both procedural duties and substantive principles, while the specific obligations stemming from it interfere and converge in the pursuit of the interest of the Union.

In the field of external relations, the duty of loyalty may constrain the exercise of the member states' competence, both at legislative and implementation levels, following principles developed internally and by means of a procedural or substantive duty of cooperation. Such a constraint has a particular meaning

[32] According to Art 19(1) TEU, the CJEU 'shall ensure that in the interpretation and application of the Treaties the law is observed'.

in the external relations field, as the duty of loyalty impacts on the EU relations with non-member countries and on the international status of the Member States, while the parallel to the internal field confirms the general character of the duty. Giving rise to a best-endeavours obligation, without excluding an obligation of result – namely when common rules are at stake –, the constraints of loyalty are reconciled with the autonomy of Member States, the latter being of particular importance when Member States act as subjects of international law.'

Article 4(3) TEU refers to the principle of sincere cooperation and recognises that both the Member States and the EU need to 'assist each other carrying out tasks which flow from the Treaties'.

Article 4(3) TEU

'Pursuant to the principle of sincere cooperation, the Union and the Member States shall, in full mutual respect, assist each other in carrying out tasks which flow from the Treaties.

The Member States shall take any appropriate measure, general or particular, to ensure fulfilment of the obligations arising out of the Treaties or resulting from the acts of the institutions of the Union.

The Member States shall facilitate the achievement of the Union's tasks and refrain from any measure which could jeopardise the attainment of the Union's objectives.'

The obligations arising from Article 4(3) TEU are manifold and have been subject to academic debate with regard to both the internal and external sphere of the EU legal order. According to the provision's actual wording, Member States, first, need to make sure that they fulfil 'the obligations arising out of the Treaties or resulting from the acts of the institutions of the Union'. In addition to confirming the international principle '*pacta sunt servanda*', Article 4(3) subparagraph 2 TEU also refers to EU institutional acts that trigger Member State obligations. In other words, this subparagraph obliges Member States to comply with the Treaties as well as EU acts that have been (lawfully) adopted by the institutions, either in form of EU secondary legislation or other. Second, Member State obligations arise under Article 4(3) subparagraph 3 TEU, which require them to 'facilitate the achievement of the Union's tasks' one the one hand, and to 'refrain from any measure which could jeopardise the attainment of the Union's objectives' on the other. This second category of obligations goes beyond protecting the effectiveness of Treaties, legislation and other adopted institutional acts. It asks Member State to support the EU in doing its work and not to act in any way that could hinder attaining the EU's objectives.[33]

In the context of EU external relations law, the principle of sincere cooperation has often been applied by the CJEU in connection with effectiveness considerations to establish Member State obligations limiting the exercise of their own external powers, even if the Court has not always explicitly linked obligations to the wording of [what is now] Article 4(3) TEU. Some of such obligations are quite obvious, as they affirm the need for Member States to comply with their *legal obligations* under existing EU law. For instance, Member States need to exercise their (retained) external powers 'in a manner consistent with [EU] law'[34] and are required to 'take all appropriate steps to eliminate the incompatibilities [with the Treaties]' that result from international treaty obligations that came into existence prior to their EU membership.[35] What is at the core of such obligations is the necessity to make space for EU law and its implementation, even if that implies a reduced capacity of Member States to take part in international law-making.

Moreover, Member States 'cannot, outside the framework of the [EU] institutions, assume obligations which might affect [EU] rules [promulgated to attain Treaty objectives] or alter their scope'.[36] This dimension of the principle of sincere cooperation is closely linked to principles of conferral and pre-emption, because existing EU law constrains significantly the Member States' capacity to act at all. As will be discussed further in Chapter 3, the Lisbon Treaty has codified the principles of implied powers and exclusivity in two Treaty provisions, which enable the EU to conclude international agreements (Article 216 TFEU, which does not require exclusivity of EU competence to start with) and affirms exclusive EU competence where the conclusion of such agreement 'is provided for in a legislative act of the Union or is necessary to enable the Union to exercise its internal competence, or in so far as its conclusion may affect common rules or alter their scope' (Article 3(2) TEU).

The CJEU has also protected the uniform application of EU law (stemming from an international agreement concluded by the EU and its Member States) by limiting Member States' capacity to participate in international dispute settlement, focusing in its reasoning on the Court's own exclusive jurisdiction for matters of EU law

[33] See, for a discussion of the meaning of 'institutional acts' and 'objectives' under Art 4(3) TEU, A Thies, 'Shared Competence and the EU Member States' Obligation to Refrain from Unilateral External Action: PFOS and Beyond' in J Díez-Hochleitner et al (eds) *Recent Trends in the Case Law of the Court of Justice of the EU (2008–2011)* (Madrid, La Ley – Grupo Wolters Kluwer, 2012).

[34] Case C-124/95 *Centro-Com*, ECLI:EU:C:1997:8, para 25, with reference to Joined Cases 6/69 and 11/69 *Commission v France*, ECLI:EU:C:1969:68, para 17; Case 57/86 *Greece v Commission*, ECLI:EU:C:1988:284, para 9; Case 127/87 *Commission v Greece*, ECLI:EU:C:1988:331, para 7; and Case C-221/89 *Factortame*, ECLI:EU:C:1991:320, para 14. All these cases concerned the Member States' obligation to comply with Treaty obligations.

[35] Art 351(2) TFEU; see for cases on the scope of that obligation Case C-205/06 *Commission v Austria (BITs)*, ECLI:EU:C:2009:118, para 45; Case C-249/06 *Commission v Sweden (BITs)*, ECLI:EU:C:2009:119, para 46; for further discussion of 'effectiveness considerations' in those cases see A Thies, 'The Search for Effectiveness and the Need for Loyalty in EU External Action' in Cremona (2018) (n 18) 273 et seq.

[36] Case 22/70 *Commission v Council (ERTA)*, ECLI:EU:C:1971:32, para 22.

(now Article 344 TFEU) and related loyalty obligations.[37] In *Mox Plant*, the CJEU emphasised that submitting a dispute under the UN Convention on the Law of the Sea (UNCLOS) – which had been concluded by the EU and its Member States in form of a mixed agreement – involved 'the risk that a judicial forum other than the Court will rule on the scope of obligations imposed on the Member States pursuant to Community law'.[38] In a next step, the CJEU referred explicitly to the 'obligation of close cooperation' that would be applicable in such circumstances and established the Member State's obligation to inform and consult the EU Commission prior to initiating international arbitration.[39]

In addition to requiring Member States to allow EU *law* to be uniformly applied and effective, the CJEU has recognised Member State constraints to enable the EU to speak with one voice and to thereby strengthen its *functionality* as a global actor in its own right, even in the absence of existing or evolving EU law that delineates the Member States' remaining scope for manoeuvre.[40] Such cases have, again, concerned the stage of international treaty-/law-making at the international level as well as the stage of implementation of international agreements, covering areas of both exclusive and shared EU competence. In areas of EU exclusive competence, the Member States were reminded of their role as 'trustees of the common interest'.[41] The Member States' obligation to act on behalf of the EU in areas of exclusive competence in international fora that preclude the EU's own membership was established in Opinion 2/91 *(ILO Convention No. 170)*.[42] They have been required to act on behalf of the EU[43] or refrain from external action to enable the EU to exercise its competence fully and efficiently on the international stage.

In areas of EU *shared* competence, the Court has identified Member State obligations based on the principle of sincere cooperation, applying it in combination with considerations of effectiveness, coherence and unity. This line of case law has been more controversial, as it arguably affected Member States' capacity to exercise their (retained) competence altogether, rather than simply shaping the way Member States exercise such competence. Some authors have emphasised that Member State obligations in areas of shared competence are/should be limited to 'best effort' or 'conduct' obligations and, if no common ground can be found, Member States can act alone.[44]

[37] Case C-459/03 *Commission v Ireland (Mox Plant)*, ECLI:EU:C:2006:345, paras 177 et seq. In Opinion 2/13 (*ECHR II*), ECLI:EU:C:2014:2454, para 201 et seq, the CJEU confirmed its exclusive jurisdiction for disputes between Member States and between the EU and Member States, which required an 'express exclusion of the ECtHR's jurisdiction' in the accession agreement to be compatible with Art 344 TFEU.

[38] Case C-459/03 *Commission v Ireland (Mox Plant)*, ECLI:EU:C:2006:345, para 177.

[39] Ibid, para 179.

[40] Thies (n 35) 288–89.

[41] Case 804/79 *Commission v United Kingdom*, ECLI:EU:C:1981:93, para 30.

[42] Opinion 2/91 (*ILO Convention No. 170*), ECLI:EU:C:1993:106, para 5.

[43] See, for analysis of relevant case law until 2011, M Cremona, 'Member States as Trustees of the Union Interest: Participating in International Agreements on Behalf of the European Union' in A Arnull et al (eds) *A Constitutional Order of States? Essays in EU Law in Honour of Alan Dashwood* (Oxford, Hart Publishing, 2011) 435.

[44] For a recent discussion of 'the concrete procedural and substantive implications of the duty of sincere cooperation in order to identify the rooms of manoeuvre for individual Member States' see P Van Elsuwege, 'The Duty of Sincere Cooperation and its Implications for Autonomous Member State Action in the Field of External Relations' in M Varju (ed), *Between Compliance and Particularism: Member State Interests and European Union Law* (Berlin, Springer, 2018) 283–98.

Yet, the CJEU – having identified EU institutional measures that acted as trigger – affirmed a variety of Member State obligations, reaching from the obligation to cooperate, bring their position in line with the EU's position, or even to refrain from unilateral action altogether on the basis of Article 4 (3) TEU.

A Thies, 'The Search for Effectiveness and the Need for Loyalty in EU External Action' in M Cremona (ed), *Structural Principles in EU External Relations Law* (Oxford, Hart Publishing, 2018) 275–276

'[T]here have been other cases in which the CJEU has acknowledged Member State obligations, where the Court's reasoning has focused more on the EU's capacity to speak with one voice and act effectively as global actor than merely on the effective enforcement of EU law. In those cases, the Court has identified negative and positive Member State obligations that correlate with joined representation and/or an increased scope for manoeuvre of the EU institutions in the interest of the EU's effectiveness on the international stage. As a consequence, the capacity of the EU to act (effectively) on the international stage in itself gained significance. It is argued here that the Court has started to protect the EU's external functionality as global actor through a combined application of the principles of effectiveness and sincere cooperation as laid down in Article 4(3) TEU. In that context, the Court has referred to concepts of coherence, consistency and unity to fill the gap of substantive EU law that could determine Member State external action. It has been on the basis of those concepts that the Court has provided the basis and rationale for Member State obligations that go beyond the mere enforcement of EU law in the interest of the EU' s effectiveness as global actor in international fora.

... It should be emphasised ..., however, that the EU's capacity to act internationally itself or through the Member States, which has been protected by the Court in that context, continues to be firmly rooted in the internal EU legal order in that it had been legitimised by lawfully adopted EU law or other institutional acts. In that respect the reach of the principles of effectiveness and sincere cooperation is (again) comparable to the way they interact within the EU internal legal order.'

For instance, where a Council decision had authorised the Commission to negotiate an international agreement, the CJEU recognised such decision as the 'point of departure' of concerted action and held that from that point on, [EU law] would require 'if not a duty of abstention on the part of the Member States, at the very least a duty of close cooperation between the latter and the Community institutions in order to facilitate the achievement of the Community tasks and to ensure the coherence and consistency of the action and its international representation'.[45] Without distinguishing between the different subparagraphs of Article 4(3)TEU, the CJEU identified an institutional act – namely the EU decision under [what is now] Article 218(2)TEU – that triggered Member State obligations under the principle of sincere cooperation.

According to the CJEU's interpretation of the principle of sincere cooperation, Member States are not only prevented from contributing to the making of international treaties and international dispute settlement that could affect EU common rules, but also their capacity to submit unilateral positions within international fora is constrained, even in areas of shared competence, and even where the EU was not itself a member of the international forum.

In the *Commission v Hellenic Republic (IMO)* case, the CJEU concluded that Member States were prohibited to take unilateral action in the International Maritime Organisation, because it would undermine the EU Regulation, according to which 'Member States and the Commission shall cooperate, through coordination meetings and/or any other appropriate means, in order to define, as appropriate, a common position or approach in the competent international fora'.[46]

Case C-45/07 *Commission v Hellenic Republic (IMO)*, ECLI:EU:C:2009:81, para 30

Similarly, the Hellenic Republic's argument that an obligation to abstain from active participation in the IMO will not ensure that the Community interest is protected, since the Community is not a member of that international organisation, cannot be accepted. The mere fact that the Community is not a member of an international organisation in no way authorises a Member State, acting individually in the context of its participation in an international organisation, to assume obligations likely to affect Community rules promulgated for the attainment of the objectives of the Treaty.

In the landmark case *Commission v Sweden (PFOS)*, the CJEU recognised an EU 'strategy' regarding its further contribution to internal and international law-making on particular chemical substances as sufficient to trigger the Member State's obligation to refrain from unilateral action in the international forum.

[45] Case C-433/03 *Commission v Germany (Inland Waterway)*, ECLI:EU:C:2005:462, para 66; C-266/03 *Commission v Luxembourg (Inland Waterway)*, ECLI:EU:C:2005:341, para 60; reiterated in Case C-246/07 *Commission v Sweden (PFOS)*, ECLI:EU:C:2010:203, para 75.

[46] Regulation (EC) No 725/2004 of the European Parliament and of the Council of 31 March 2004 on enhancing ship and port facility security [2004] OJ L 129/6, Art 10(4).

Case C-246/07 *Commission v Sweden (PFOS)*, ECLI:EU:C:2010:203

73 Where it is apparent that the subject-matter of an agreement or convention falls partly within the competence of the Community and partly within that of its Member States, it is essential to ensure close cooperation between the Member States and the Community institutions, both in the process of negotiation and conclusion and in the fulfilment of the commitments entered into. That obligation to cooperate flows from the requirement of unity in the international representation of the Community (Ruling 1/78 [1978] ECR 2151, paragraphs 34 to 36 (by analogy with the EAEC Treaty); Opinion 2/91 [1993] ECR I-1061, paragraph 36; Opinion 1/94 [1994] ECR I-5267, paragraph 108; and Case C-25/94 *Commission* v *Council* [1996] ECR I-1469, paragraph 48).

74 The Court has held that Member States are subject to special duties of action and abstention in a situation in which the Commission has submitted to the Council proposals which, although they have not been adopted by the Council, represent the point of departure for concerted Community action (Case 804/79 *Commission* v *United Kingdom* [1981] ECR I-1045, paragraph 28; *Commission* v *Luxembourg*, paragraph 59; and *Commission* v *Germany*, paragraph 65).

75 Likewise, the Court has held that the adoption of a decision authorising the Commission to negotiate a multilateral agreement on behalf of the Community marks the start of a concerted Community action at international level and requires for that purpose, if not a duty of abstention on the part of the Member States, at the very least a duty of close cooperation between the latter and the Community institutions in order to facilitate the achievement of the Community tasks and to ensure the coherence and consistency of the action and its international representation (*Commission* v *Luxembourg*, paragraph 60, and *Commission* v *Germany*, paragraph 66).

...

102 ... The Union could be bound by an amendment to an Annex to the Stockholm Convention ....

103 As was pointed out in paragraph 74 of this judgment, the Court has held that Member States are subject to special duties of action and abstention in a situation in which the Commission has submitted to the Council proposals which, although they have not been adopted by the Council, represent the point of departure for concerted Community action (*Commission* v *Germany*, paragraph 65). That is especially true in a situation such as that in the present case which is characterised, as established in paragraph 91 of this judgment, by a unilateral proposal which dissociates the Member State in question from a concerted common strategy within the Council and was submitted within an institutional and procedural framework such as that of the Stockholm Convention.

104 Such a situation is likely to compromise the principle of unity in the international representation of the Union and its Member States and weaken their negotiating power with regard to the other parties to the Convention concerned.

105 Consequently, the Commission's first complaint, alleging breach of Article 10 EC, is well founded.

As the excerpt above shows, the CJEU based its reasoning to establish Member State obligations on two grounds. In addition to including a 'strategy' in the list of institutional acts that can trigger obligations under Article 4(3) TEU,[47] the CJEU also referred to the potential implications Sweden's action and a subsequent amendment to the international legal instrument would have on the EU's own law as member of the international convention in question.[48] The Court thereby followed its established case law on the need for Member States to refrain from international action where this could affect common rules or alter their scope. Yet, the Court's approach in this case has led to criticism, because of its far-reaching consequences for the exercise of retained Member State competence.

A Thies, 'Shared Competence and the EU Member States' Obligation to Refrain from Unilateral External Action: *PFOS* and Beyond' in J Díez-Hochleitner et al (eds) *Recent Trends in the Case Law of the Court of Justice of the EU (2008–2011)* (Madrid, La Ley–Grupo Wolters Kluwer, 2012) 703–28

'Scholars have welcomed the existence and enforcement of loyalty obligations as an alternative to exclusivity and instrumental for further European integration. ... In particular, in the context of shared competence and the implementation of mixed agreements, loyalty obligations have been considered a helpful tool for the smooth running or functioning of the EU legal order/decision-making, as both the EU institutions and the Member States remain involved in the process. However, the CJEU's recognition of a potential Member State obligation to completely refrain from unilateral action in *PFOS* in areas of shared competence has been received less enthusiastically. The Court has been criticised for establishing a Member States' 'duty to remain silent', which could lead to a stalemate in EU external action altogether and thus even negatively affect the attainment of external objectives. Furthermore, the strict obligation to abstain from unilateral action in such a scenario was considered to 'involve the risk of blurring the essential distinction between exclusive and shared Union competence' where it

[47] Case C-246/07 *Commission v Sweden (PFOS)*, ECLI:EU:C:2010:203, para 103.
[48] Ibid, para 102.

went beyond the procedural obligation to inform and consult on the basis of a 'common strategy' the requirement for which were 'not very high'.

It is claimed here that in principle a set of loyalty obligations is indeed a useful tool both to improve the EU internal decision-making preceding external action and to increase the coherence of EU and Member States 'external action on the international plane. What is problematic, however, is that the CJEU has so far decided on Member States' loyalty obligations in a line of case-law, which has left open the duties' precise constitutional justification and limits in the light of Member States' retained sovereignty.

It is unfortunate that the Court missed the opportunity in *PFOS* (a) to clearly differentiate those Member State constraints regarding the *exercise* of shared competence from the *termination* of Member State competence due to EU external competence becoming exclusive under the principle of pre-emption, and (b) to further conceptualise the constitutional basis, trigger and scope of loyalty obligations in the interest of legal certainty, functionality and sustainability of the EU's external action framework, in particular with regard to policy areas for which the EU and the Member States continue to share external competence in principle.

…

What makes it difficult to reach legal certainty with regard to loyalty and cooperation duties is that they are a particularly dynamic kind of Treaty obligations. Not only are they applicable in principle to any kind of policy area or Member State activity, but also their coming into existence as well as their scope remain open to change and evolve alongside further integration of the Union.[49] They are triggered and shaped not only by Treaty amendments, the adoption of secondary law and case law of the CJEU, but also by EU policy making, such as the formulation of EU objectives and strategies for particular policy areas. This does, however, not alleviate the need for precise judicial reasoning with regard to those scenarios, in which Member States' sovereignty to exercise retained external competence is substantially affected.'

In sum, the principle of sincere cooperation has been employed to protect EU law (and its uniform interpretation) as well as the EU's functionality as a global actor more broadly. The question whether Member States had retained no competence or shared their competence with the EU seems to have been increasingly less important for the CJEU when identifying Member State obligations.

[49] With regard to [now] Article 4(3) TEU to be understood as 'dynamisch-evolutiv', see also W Kahl, 'Commentary on "Art. 10 EGV"' in C Callies and M Ruffert (eds) *EUV/EGV Kommentar*, 3rd edn (Munich, CH Beck, 2007) 431.

C. The Principle of Institutional Balance

The principle of institutional balance has been recognised in EU law for a long time.[50]

Case 70/88 *European Parliament v Council of the European Communities (Chernobyl)*, ECLI:EU:C:1990:217

21 [t]he Treaties set up a system for distributing powers among the different Community institutions, assigning to each institution its own role in the institutional structure of the Community and the accomplishment of the tasks entrusted to the Community.

22 Observance of the institutional balance means that each of the institutions must exercise its powers with due regard for the powers of the other institutions. It also requires that it should be possible to penalize any breach of that rule which may occur.

While the Lisbon Treaty aimed to bring more clarity to the division of (external) competences and allocation of tasks, the CJEU has been busy with inter-institutional litigation concerning, inter alia, the negotiation, conclusion and implementation of international treaties. Those cases have given the CJEU the opportunity to apply and develop the principle of institutional balance in the context of EU external action and triggered scholarly analysis.

S Platon, 'The Principle of institutional Balance: Rise, Eclipse and Revival of a General Principle of EU Constitutional Law' in K Ziegler, P Neuvonen, V Moreno-Lax (eds) *Research Handbook on General Principles of EU Law* (Cheltenham, Edward Elgar Publishing, forthcoming 2020)

[B]efore 2014, the principle of institutional balance was mostly limited to internal affairs of the European Union. This is clearly no longer the case. The Court does not hesitate to use the principle of institutional balance as a regulatory principle as regards the action of the various EU institutions when involved in the external action of the European Union.

[50] In 1958, the Court of Justice referred to 'the balance of powers which is characteristic of the institutional structure of the Community', see Case 9/56 *Meroni v High Authority of the European Coal and Steel Community*, ECLI:EU:C:1958:7, 152.

In this context, the Court has mostly used the institutional balance to guarantee the European Commission, which usually represents the European Union in international matters, a certain degree of autonomy.

On the one hand, the principle of institutional balance seems to give the Commission some leeway in its relations with the Council. For example, in the 2015 case *Council v Commission*, the Court stated that the principle of institutional balance does not prevent the Commission from submitting a written statement to the International Tribunal for the Law of the Sea on behalf of the European Union, without prior approval of the content of that statement by the Council of the European Union.[51] On the other hand, the Court sometimes utilises the principle of institutional balance to protect the Commission from the Council. For example, in the *Commission v Council* case 2015, the Court found that the principle of institutional balance forbids the Council and the special committee designated by the Council in accordance with Article 218(4) TFEU from imposing detailed negotiating positions on the negotiator, usually the Commission. By doing so, the Council would go beyond its power to address negotiation directives and would, in fact, interfere with the negotiation itself, therefore trespassing the attributions of the negotiator.[52] It is noteworthy that, according to the Court, the principle of institutional balance also sometimes prohibits the Council to remain 'below' its own powers, for example by adopting mere 'conclusions' when the treaties provide that the Council must adopt a decision.[53]

There are, however, limits to the level of discretion that the Commission enjoys when representing the European Union in its international relations. In the *Council v Commission* case 2016,[54] the Court found that Art. 13(2) TEU and the principle of institutional balance forbid the Commission to sign even a non-binding international agreement without the Council's prior approval. ...

The Court also considers that institutional balance implies that the Parliament and the Council shall enjoy the same powers in relation to a given field, both internally and externally. This is the reason why Article 218(6) TFEU establishes a symmetry between the procedure for adopting EU measures internally and the procedure for adopting international agreements.[55] More recently, the General Court used the principle of institutional balance to the 'Stop TTIP' European citizens' initiative (ECI) in the Efler case. On 15 July 2014, the applicants submitted a request for registration of an ECI proposal stating that the European Commission should recommend that the Council cancel the

[51] Case C-73/14 *Council v Commission*, ECLI:EU:C:2015:663.
[52] Case C-425/13 *Commission v Council*, ECLI:EU:C:2015:483.
[53] Case C-687/15 *Commission v Council*, ECLI:EU:C:2017:803, paras 42–7.
[54] Case C-660/13 *Council v Commission*, ECLI:EU:C:2016:616.
[55] Case C-658/11 *Parliament v Council (Mauritius)*, ECLI:EU:C:2014:2025, para 56.

negotiating mandate for the Transatlantic Trade and Investment Partnership with the United States of America and not conclude the Comprehensive Economic and Trade Agreement with Canada. The Commission refused to register the ECI proposal, which led the applicants to challenge this decision. The Commission notably argued that this ECI proposal would lead to an inadmissible interference in an ongoing legislative procedure. The General Court replied to this argument saying that such a possibility does not infringe the principle of institutional balance in so far as it is for the Commission to decide whether or not it will accept the ECI by presenting its legal and political conclusions on the ECI, the action it intends to take, if any, and its reasons for taking or not taking that action.[56]

The CJEU has employed the principle of institutional balance in the context of the EU's international treaty-making and the preparation of EU positions to be submitted to international fora. In spite of institutional disagreement regarding the interpretation of procedural rules (eg, Article 218 TFEU) following the Lisbon Treaty reforms, the CJEU has arguably taken a balanced approach and managed to accommodate all EU institutions in a way that reflects the principle of democracy and the EU's particular system of checks and balances.

P Koutrakos, 'Institutional Balance and the Duty of Cooperation in Treaty-making under EU Law' (2019) 68 *International and Comparative Law Quarterly* 1, 22–23

The [recent] case-law … is not tilted towards a specific institution. Overall, the Court's approach to the principle of institutional balance is rather balanced. Whilst the Commission has the power to represent the EU in international judicial proceedings and to withdraw a proposal, it may not sign even non-binding international agreements. The Council's power to impose rigorous reporting duties on the Commission may not extend to impinging on the latter's right to negotiate international treaties. Put differently, both the powers of the Commission to negotiate international agreements and of the Council to sign them is affirmed. As for the Parliament, the absence of a formal role in CFSP treaty-making may not lead to depriving the institution from its right to be informed promptly and at all stages of the treaty-making procedure. In fact, it is the Parliament that emerges as the clear winner in the institutional stakes, a conclusion that is hardly surprising given the significant enhancement of its position under the Lisbon Treaty. The case-law, furthermore, conveys a broader

[56] Case T-754/14 *Efler v Commission*, ECLI:EU:T:2017:323, para 45.

message: the procedures laid down in primary law have teeth, their scope is construed broadly, and, as the *Hybrid Decisions* judgment suggests, they may not be marginalized by the legal ingenuity of the Union's institutions and the Member States.

The volume, however, and intensity of inter-institutional disputes examined in this article are striking. For all its ambition to rationalize the Union's institutional structure and streamline decision-making, the Lisbon Treaty has not provided greater clarity as to the allocation of tasks to different institutions, neither has it reduced the institutions' appetite for legal disputes about turf wars. This development may be understood in the light of the broader scope of Article 218 TFEU which, therefore, provides more scope for inter-institutional argument. It may also be due to the ambiguity of the relevant primary rules and the central role of open-ended principles that govern the Union's external action. Finally, the Union's inherently idiosyncratic constitutional set up is also relevant: the position, for instance, of CFSP in the EU's legal order provides ample scope for inter-institutional disputes, especially given the merging of the objectives of the Union's external action in Article 21 TEU.

D. The Systemic Principle of Autonomy

The autonomy of the EU legal order relates to the EU's unique constitutional framework and exists with regard to both the law of the Member States and international law.[57] It dates back to the early *Van Gend & Loos* and *Costa v ENEL* case law, in which the Court stressed that the Community was to be seen as a new legal order. In the context of EU external relations law, the CJEU has referred to the autonomy of the EU legal order, in particular when dealing with the implications of international law for the EU legal order and institutional structure (see also Chapter 5). In addition to the effects of international law invoked in litigation before the CJEU, the CJEU has relied on autonomy considerations to protect its own (exclusive) jurisdiction. It has denied the compatibility of international agreements that provided international dispute settlement mechanisms with the EU Treaties where it saw a threat to the CJEU's final say on the interpretation of EU law.[58] For instance, in *Opinion 2/13*, the Court noted a number of problematic aspects in the accession agreement through which the EU wished to accede to the European Convention on Human Rights.[59]

[57] Opinion 1/17 (*CETA*), ECLI:EU:C:2019:341, para 110.

[58] Opinion 1/09 (*Agreement creating a Unified Patent Litigation System*), ECLI:EU:C:2011:123, paras 78, 89; Opinion 2/13 (*ECHR II*), ECLI:EU:C:2014:2454, paras 170 et seq, 200. See for an analysis of the Court's approach until 2013 B De Witte, 'A Selfish Court? The European Court of Justice and the Design of International Dispute Settlement beyond the European Union' in Cremona and Thies (n 18) 41.

[59] See for analysis and reference to academic debate P Eeckhout, 'Opinion 2/13 on EU Accession to the ECHR and Judicial Dialogue: Autonomy or Autarky?' (2015) 38 *Fordham International Law Journal* 1.

The Court considered the accession agreement incompatible with the EU Treaties, mainly in light of its own prerogative to decide on the validity and the interpretation of EU law, including the division of competences between the EU and its Member States (see further Chapters 5 and 10).

J Odermatt, 'The Principle of Autonomy: An Adolescent Disease of EU External Relations Law?' in M Cremona (ed) *Structural Principles in EU External Relations Law* (Oxford, Hart Publishing, 2018) 291–316

The EU has become a global actor in its own right and, especially since the Lisbon Treaty, it has espoused the principles of multilateralism and international cooperation. At the same time, its recent case-law has stressed the autonomy of the EU legal order, in a way that emphasises the Court as the gatekeeper able to decide the conditions under which international law can take effect within the EU. The way in which the Court has sought to preserve this autonomy has meant that it has appeared rather hostile to international law and towards international dispute settlement mechanisms. This approach to autonomy can in turn undermine another goal, the EU's ability to become a strong and effective global actor. The EU is a part of, and seeks to participate in, the international legal order, but at the same time seeks to preserve its autonomy vis-à-vis that legal order: 'On the one hand, the EU's autonomy is a product of international law; on the other, it must distance itself from the international legal order to cement and strengthen its autonomy.' Cannizzarro, Palchetti and Wessel point out this apparent contradiction: 'The ambiguity lies in its claim to be an open society, which aims to play an increasingly active role in the global legal order, while simultaneously presenting itself as an isolated monad, safeguarding the autonomy of its domestic system of values.'

In the context of the Opinion on the compatibility of the Comprehensive Economic and Trade Agreement between Canada, of the one part, and the European Union and its Member States, of the other part (CETA) with the EU Treaties, Advocate General Bot suggested that 'the Court should interpret the principle of the autonomy of EU law not only in such a way as to maintain the specific characteristics of EU law but also to ensure the European Union's involvement in the development of international law and of a rules-based international legal order'.[60] The CJEU considered CETA's investment dispute mechanism compatible with the EU Treaties; however, the CJEU highlighted the need for the investment court to respect the autonomy of the EU legal order in its future decision-making.[61] The latter requirement comes close to the Court's reasoning

[60] Opinion 1/17 (*CETA*), Opinion of AG Bot, ECLI:EU:C:2019:72, para 174.

[61] Opinion 1/17 (*CETA*), ECLI:EU:C:2019:341, paras 106–161. See for further discussion C Eckes, P Eeckhout and A Thies (eds) 'Reflection Essays on Opinion 1/17' (2020) *Europe and the World: A Law Review* (Special Issue) (forthcoming).

in Opinion 2/13, which blocked the conclusion of the ECHR accession agreement. Yet, in relation to CETA, the Court referred to the autonomy of the EU legal order as imposing a (legal) constraint on the future investment court, rather than preventing the EU's participation in the agreement altogether as was the case with the ECHR.

E. Ensuring Coherence and Consistency

Given the fact that most internal EU policies have an external dimension, the Treaties are quite clear about the need for coherence and consistency in EU external relations. In the previous chapter we pointed to Article 21 TEU, which combines the various external objectives of the Union and at the same time establishes a legal connection between all these objectives. Indeed, Article 21(3) TEU imposes a binding obligation of coherence in EU external relations, illustrating that coherence is not merely an academic notion but a tangible legal principle of EU primary law. This provision can be considered the *lex generalis* coherence obligation in EU external relations. There are, then, a number of *lex specialis* provisions in the TEU and TFEU imposing derived obligations in specific instances of vertical, horizontal, institutional etc coherence. For example, in Chapter 8 we shall see that, for instance, EU development policy cannot function without a strong emphasis on coherence in all its facets. Thus, what paragraph 21(3) TEU does is connect the list of policy objectives in 21(2) to each other, and to the functioning of pertinent legal principles, by imposing a legally binding obligation of coherence between all EU internal and external policies which must pursue them. Specifically, through the case law of the Court of Justice the obligation of loyalty has become directly connected to the objective of 'ensur[ing] the coherence and consistency of the action and its [the Union's] international representation'.[62]

The third paragraph of Article 21 specifically obliges the Commission, Council and High Representative to put coherence into effect, but the TEU contains four other provisions which pertain to coherence in its material and institutional dimensions. We name them at this juncture to point to the importance of coherence in EU external relations but shall return to them throughout this book.

- Article 13(1) TEU imposes coherence as one of the over-arching purposes for the activities of the EU institutions: 'The Union shall have an institutional framework which shall aim to promote its values, advance its objectives, serve its interests, those of its citizens and those of the Member States, and ensure the consistency, effectiveness and continuity of its policies and actions.' The explicit reference to the Member States can be read as meaning that it concerns not merely coherence between policies and action of the Union itself (horizontal), but also between that of the Union and its Member States (vertical).
- Article 16(6) TEU imposes on the General Affairs Council an obligation of substantive policy coherence between the work of the different Councils and a specific

[62] Case C-266/03 *Commission v Luxembourg (Inland Waterway)*, ECLI:EU:C:2005:341, para 60, and Case C-476/98 *Commission v Germany (Open Skies)*, ECLI:EU:C:2002:631, para 66.

obligation for the Foreign Affairs Council since it 'shall elaborate the Union's external action on the basis of strategic guidelines laid down by the European Council and ensure that the Union's action is consistent'.

- Article 18(4) TEU imposes a specific coherence obligation on the EU High Representative (HR) with a strong institutional dimension, as it relates to the connection between the work of the HR and that of the Commission: 'The High Representative shall be one of the Vice-Presidents of the Commission. He shall ensure the consistency of the Union's external action. He shall be responsible within the Commission for responsibilities incumbent on it in external relations and for coordinating other aspects of the Union's external action ….'
- Article 26(2) TEU contains an obligation of substantive policy coherence specifically for the EU's Common Foreign and Security Policy: 'The Council and the High Representative of the Union for Foreign Affairs and Security Policy shall ensure the unity, consistency and effectiveness of action by the Union.'

In the Treaty on the Functioning of the European Union, we find coherence obligations that do not relate to the institutions as such but are predominantly substantive in the nature of their requirement.

- Article 7 TFEU is found in Title II of that Treaty, under the heading 'provisions having general application' and states that: 'The Union shall ensure consistency between its policies and activities, taking all of its objectives into account and in accordance with the principle of conferral of powers.' Because this article is of general application and not specific to EU external relations, it must be read as requiring substantive, positive coherence between EU internal policies and EU external policies.
- Part Five of the Treaty on the Functioning of the European Union concerns 'external action by the Union'. Article 205 TFEU is the first and general provision of that Title and reads that 'the Union's action on the international scene, pursuant to this Part, shall be guided by the principles, pursue the objectives and be conducted in accordance with the general provisions laid down in Chapter 1 of Title V of the Treaty on European Union'. This Article is a cross-reference to Articles 21 and 22 TEU and has a triple consequence: First, any of the external competences listed in Part Five of the TFEU (common commercial policy, development policy, and so on) must be conducted in line with the coherence obligation of Article 21(3) TEU. Second, any of these competences must all pursue the objectives listed in Article 21(2) TEU. Third, where Article 22(1) TEU states that 'the European Council shall identify the strategic interests and objectives of the Union', Article 205 TFEU is yet another confirmation that this EU institution is given the principal role in ensuring over-arching coherence across all EU external policies.

In three competence-specific articles we also find obligations to maintain coherence. In Article 208(1) TFEU concerning development policy there is an obligation that it pursue 'the principles and objectives of the Union's external action' (eg, an obligation of horizontal coherence with Articles 3(5) TEU and 21(2) TEU), and a vertical obligation of coherence stating that 'the Union's development cooperation policy and that of the Member States complement and reinforce each other'. In Article 212 TFEU concerning economic, financial and technical cooperation with third countries we find similar obligations: one of horizontal coherence but this time with EU development policy and one of vertical coherence with Member States' respective policies. Finally, Article 214 TFEU concerning humanitarian aid, is formulated in similar terms: a general reference to the EU's principles and objectives in external relations and the need for EU measures and those of Member States to 'complement and reinforce each other'. This is thus a reciprocal obligation of substantive, positive, policy coherence.

C Hillion, '*Tous pour un, un pour tous!* Coherence in the External Relations of the European Union' in M Cremona (ed) *Developments in EU External Relations Law* (Oxford, Oxford University Press, 2008) 35 [The text was slightly adapted towards post-Lisbon language]

'[C]onsistency', understood as absence of legal contradiction, is an essential element of coherence. Such consistency is ensured notably through the observance of EU rules on distribution of powers, and thanks to mechanisms to handle conflicts between acts adopted by each actor of the EU system of external relations. In the Member States–EU interface, the principles of the attribution of powers and primacy of EU law play a key role in ensuring consistency ... Importantly, consistency between the actions of the Member States ... is guaranteed by the Council and thus by the Member States themselves, given the limited supranational nature of the CFSP ...

[C]oherence in EU external relations not only depends on the absence of legal contradiction between the different instruments of EU external action. It also stems from the *degree of cooperation* between the different actors in the system, particularly between the Member States, on the one hand, and the Union's institutions on the other; as well as cooperation between the institutions themselves when acting in the different EU procedural frameworks. In its respective field of power, each actor is bound by a multifarious principle of cooperation. In essence, this entails procedural obligations, whose purpose is to ensure that each actor's competence is exercised with the ultimate purpose of contributing to the general Union's objective of asserting its identity on the international scene. Rather than aiming at policing the boundaries between the different areas of competences, the duty of cooperation aims at moderating the implications of such division. It has a more positive undertone, suggesting that the Union's external action is not a zero-sum game.

Across all these articles, Article 21(3) TEU is the most prominent as it renders coherence into a general and legally binding obligation of EU external relations applicable to all external *and* internal policies of the European Union. Notably, since the Lisbon Treaty, these obligations fall within the jurisdiction of the Court of Justice. This is not insignificant: the Lisbon Treaty has set up a carefully crafted legal regime governing

EU external action, whereby vertically and horizontally operating legal principles interact towards a common purpose. In subsequent chapters, we point to the crucial importance of the Court in shaping the EU as an international actor, and this legal obligation of coherence only strengthens this role.

IV. EU Principles and the Protection of Individuals: Rights and Remedies

The Court has reiterated the necessity for all EU measures – whether taken in the internal or external sphere of the EU legal order – to comply with fundamental right obligations under EU general principles and the Charter. Moreover, recent case law has shed further light on the reach of the rule of law and the recognition of remedies for individuals affected by EU (administrative) conduct in the context of external action.[63]

Advocate General Bot reiterated in his Opinion in Opinion 1/17 the need for any exercise of EU competence, including the conclusion of international (trade) agreements to respect fundamental rights.

Opinion 1/17 (*CETA*), Opinion of AG Bot, ECLI:EU:C:2019:72, para 195

In relation to this issue, it is necessary to clarify that it follows from the second sentence of Article 207(1) TFEU, read in conjunction with Article 21 TEU, that the European Union must, when exercising the competences conferred on it by the EU and FEU Treaties, including those relating to the common commercial policy, respect fundamental rights, of which the principle of equal treatment forms part. The European Union is a union based on the rule of law in which all acts of its institutions are subject to review of their compatibility with, in particular, the Treaties, general principles of law and fundamental rights. This also includes the European Union's external action. I note, in this regard, that, in accordance with settled case-law, international agreements concluded by the European Union 'are, from the date of their entry into force, an integral part of the EU legal order … The provisions of such agreements must therefore be entirely compatible with the Treaties and with the constitutional principles

[63] For further discussion of the principles of the rule of law, legitimacy and accountability as part of the constitutional foundations of the EU see T Konstadinides, 'The Rule of Law as the Constitutional Foundation of the General Principles of EU Law' in K Ziegler, P Neuvonen, V Moreno-Lax (eds) *Research Handbook on General Principles of EU Law* (Cheltenham, Edward Elgar, forthcoming 2020). See also I Vianello, 'The Rule of Law as a Relational Principle Structuring the Union's Action Towards its External Partners' in Cremona (n 18).

stemming therefrom'.[64] This, of course, includes the Charter, pursuant to Article 51 thereof, which has 'the same legal value as the Treaties' in accordance with Article 6(1) TEU. Even prior to the formal entry into force of the Charter, the Court had already established the principle that the conduct of the European Union's external relations must be consistent with the fundamental rights of the European Union.

EU principles, including fundamental rights, are also applicable in the area of the EU's Common Foreign and Security Policy. The CJEU has recognised the need to focus on the implications of EU measures on natural and legal persons and their fundamental rights protection, rather than the political sphere in which they have been adopted. In the famous *Kadi* cases, the CJEU clarified that EU legislation needs to comply with EU fundamental rights in form of general principles also when jointly implementing international obligations of the EU Member States. Instead of assessing the international (law) trigger and foreign policy dimension of the pertinent EU legislation, the Court focused on the need for any kind of EU measure, including those of a legislative nature, to comply with EU fundamental rights in order to be lawful.[65] While the Court's jurisdiction in matters of CFSP remains limited in principle, it has affirmed its jurisdiction in the cases *H* and *Rosneft* to protect individuals on the basis of EU principles (see Chapters 5 and 9).

V. The Broader Picture of EU External Relations Law

The recognition, development and employment of general principles have helped to achieve the creation of the internal market and legal integration *within* the EU legal order, in that they have strengthened EU law effectiveness, addressed the co-existence and responsibilities of the EU and its Member States and established the protection of individuals through rights and remedies. EU principles have also played an important role in the development of EU *external* relations law: they guide and frame the EU and its Member States' external action, as well as their interaction, in procedural and substantive terms and help 'building the EU's identity as a *coherent*, *effective* and *autonomous* actor in the world'.[66] Moreover, EU principles have been employed for the protection of individuals affected by EU/Member State conduct in the context of

[64] See, inter alia, Case C-266/16 *Western Sahara Campaign UK*, ECLI:EU:C:2018:118, para 46 and the case law cited there.
[65] See also Joined Cases C-584/10 P, C-593/10 P and C-595/10 P *Commission and Others v Kadi*, ECLI:EU:C:2013:518, para 97.
[66] Cremona (2018) (n 18) 27.

external action. The latter is true even in the context of CFSP for which the jurisdiction of the CJEU is explicitly limited.

Several aspects make the study of EU principles in the context of EU external relations law particularly challenging and interesting. Traditionally, EU principles have either been established by the CJEU, often without any explicit basis in the EU Treaties (eg, supremacy, direct effect, fundamental rights), or their content and reach have at least been subject to extensive judicial development or clarification (eg, conferral, proportionality, sincere cooperation). In the context of external relations law, the Lisbon Treaty has introduced more explicit Treaty reference to EU core (constitutional) principles as guiding EU external action, while also committing to international principles and structures when taking external action. It remains to be seen how these two commitments will be reflected in the CJEU's case law in the longer term. So far, the CJEU has exercised judicial self-restraint and refrained from interfering with EU policy choices for external action, respecting other EU institutions' scope for manoeuvre on the international stage. At the same time, the CJEU has been willing to further develop principles concerning the EU's internal/constitutional order for external action and the EU's empowerment as global actor, which has affected Member States' capacity (under EU law) to exercise their sovereignty on the international stage. While the jurisdiction of the CJEU is explicitly limited in the field of CFSP, which arguably prevents full constitutionalisation through judicial activity, the CJEU has confirmed the applicability of principles for the protection of individuals.

Overall, the employment of EU principles has contributed to the further constitutionalisation of the EU legal order, including its external dimension. What remains challenging, however, is the extent to which EU principles, both in procedural and substantive terms, can actually be accommodated by the international (legal) order which frames EU external action 'from the outside'. At the same time, the fact that international law and international institutions pose limits on the practicalities or actual reach of EU principles does not put into question their relevance for the EU internal allocation of powers, rules on collaboration, coherence or accountability, and the EU's value-based approach to external action.

VI. Sources and Further Reading

Chamon, M, 'The Institutional Balance, An Ill-fated Principle of EU Law?' (2015) 21 *European Public Law* 371.

Cremona, M, 'Defending the Community Interest: The Duties of Cooperation and Compliance' in M Cremona and B de Witte (eds) *EU Foreign Relations Law: Constitutional Fundamentals* (Oxford, Hart Publishing, 2008) 125–70.

Cremona, M, 'Member States as Trustees of the Union Interest: Participating in International Agreements on Behalf of the European Union' in A Arnull, C Barnard, M Dougan and E Spaventa (eds) *A Constitutional Order of States? Essays in EU law in Honour of Alan Dashwood* (Oxford, Hart Publishing, 2011) 435–57.

Cremona, M, 'Case Comment on C-246/07, *Commission* v *Sweden (PFOS)*' (2011) 48 *Common Market Law Review* 1639.
Cremona, M, 'EU Treaty-Making after the Lisbon Treaty – A Test Case for Mutual Sincere Cooperation?' in J Czuczai and F Naert (eds) *The EU as a Global Actor – Bridging Legal Theory and Practice, Liber Amicorum in Honour of Ricardo Gosalbo Bono* (Leiden, Brill/Nijhoff, 2017) 424–39.
Cremona, M, '"Effective Judicial Review Is of the Essence of the Rule of Law": Challenging Common Foreign and Security Policy Measures Before the Court of Justice' (2017) 2 *European Papers* 671–97.
Cremona, M, 'Structural Principles and their Role in EU External Relations Law' in M Cremona (ed) *Structural Principles in EU External Relations Law* (Oxford, Hart Publishing, 2018) 3–29.
Cremona, M (ed), *Structural Principles in EU External Relations Law* (Oxford, Hart Publishing, 2018).
Dashwood, A, 'The Limits of European Community Powers' (1996) 21 *European Law Review* 113.
Dashwood, A, 'EU Acts and Member State Acts in the Negotiation, Conclusion, and Implementation of International Agreements' in M Cremona and C Kilpatrick (eds) *EU Legal Acts: Challenges and Transformations* (Oxford, Oxford University Press, 2018) 189–249.
Govaere, I, 'To Give or to Grab: The Principle of Full, Crippled and Split Conferral of Powers Post-Lisbon' in M Cremona (ed) *Structural Principles in EU External Relations Law* (Oxford, Hart Publishing, 2018) 71–91.
Hillion, C, 'Mixity and Coherence in EU External Relations: The Significance of the Duty of Cooperation' in C Hillion and P Koutrakos (eds) *Mixed Agreements Revisited – The EU and its Member States in the World* (Oxford, Hart Publishing, 2010) 87–115.
Hillion, C, 'Conferral, Cooperation and Balance in the Institutional Framework' in M Cremona (ed) *Structural Principles* (Oxford, Hart Publishing, 2018) 117–74.
Jacqué, J-P, 'The Principle of Institutional Balance' (2004) 41 *Common Market Law Review* 383.
Klamert, M, *The Principle of Loyalty in EU Law* (Oxford, Oxford University Press, 2014).
Koutrakos, P, 'Judicial Review in the EU's Common Foreign and Security Policy' (2018) 67 *International and Comparative Law Quarterly* 1.
Koutrakos, P, 'Institutional Balance and the Duty of Cooperation in Treaty-making under EU Law' (2019) 68 *International and Comparative Law Quarterly* 1.
Kube, V, *EU Human Rights, International Investment Law and Participation – Operationalizing the EU Foreign Policy Objective to Global Human Rights Protection* (Berlin, Springer, 2019).
Larik, J, *Foreign Policy Objectives in European Constitutional Law* (Oxford, Oxford University Press, 2016).
Larik, J and A Delgado Casteleiro, 'The Duty to Remain Silent: Limitless Loyalty in EU External Relations' (2011) 36 *European Law Review* 524.
Neframi, E, 'The Duty of Loyalty: Rethinking its Scope through its Application in the Field of EU External Relations' (2010) 47 *Common Market Law Review* 323.
Platon, S, 'The Principle of Institutional Balance: Rise, Eclipse and Revival of a General Principle of EU Constitutional Law' in K Ziegler, P Neuvonen, V Moreno-Lax (eds) *Research Handbook on General Principles of EU Law* (Cheltenham, Edward Elgar Publishing, forthcoming 2020).
Poli, S, 'The Common Foreign Security Policy after Rosneft: Still Imperfect but Gradually Subject to the Rule of Law' (2017) 54 *Common Market Law Review* 1799.
Rosas, A, 'Mixed Union – Mixed Agreements' in M Koskenniemi (ed) *International Law Aspects of the European Union* (The Hague, Kluwer Law International, 1998) 125–48.
Thies, A, 'Shared Competence and the EU Member States' Obligation to Refrain from Unilateral External Action: *PFOS* and Beyond' in J Díez-Hochleitner, C Martínez Capdevila, I Blázquez Navarro, J Frutos Miranda (eds) *Recent Trends in the Case Law of the Court of Justice of the EU (2008–2011)* (Madrid, La Ley–Grupo Wolters Kluwer, 2012) 703–28.
Thies, A, 'General Principles in the Development of EU External Relations Law' in M Cremona and A Thies (eds) *The European Court of Justice and External Relations Law: Constitutional Challenges* (Oxford, Hart Publishing, 2014) 139–63.

Thies, A, 'The Search for Effectiveness and the Need for Loyalty in EU External Action' in M Cremona (ed) *Structural Principles in EU External Relations Law* (Oxford, Hart Publishing, 2018) 263–90.

Van Elsuwege, P, 'Securing the Institutional Balance in the Procedure for Concluding International Agreements: European Parliament v Council (Pirate Transfer Agreement with Mauritius)' (2015) 52 *Common Market Law Review* 1379.

Van Elsuwege, P, 'Upholding the Rule of Law in the Common Foreign and Security Policy: *H* v *Council*' (2017) 54 *Common Market Law Review* 841.

Van Elsuwege, P, 'Judicial Review of the EU's Common Foreign and Security Policy: Lessons from the Rosneft case', *Verfassungsblog.de*, 6 April 2017. Available at: https://verfassungsblog.de/judicial-review-of-the-eus-common-foreign-and-security-policy-lessons-from-the-rosneft-case/.

Van Elsuwege, P, 'The Duty of Sincere Cooperation and its Implications for Autonomous Member State Action in the Field of External Relations' in M Varju (ed) *Between Compliance and Particularism: Member State Interests and European Union Law* (New York, Springer, 2018) 283–98.

Van Vooren, B, *EU External Relations Law and the European Neighbourhood Policy: A Paradigm for Coherence* (Abingdon, Routledge, 2012).

Wessel, RA, 'The Inside Looking Out: Consistency and Delimitation in EU External Relations' (2000) 37 *Common Market Law Review* 1135.

3

EU External Competence

Central Issues

- As indicated in the previous chapters, the European Union possesses legal personality and capacity to act as a legal subject in international relations. However, the EU cannot undertake whatever international action it wishes. Its treaty-making capacity is governed by the principle of conferral laid down in Article 5 TEU, which states that the Union shall act within the powers conferred on it by the Member States.
- In this chapter, we examine the conditions under which the Union acts externally. The general conditions to conclude international agreements are laid down in Article 216(1) TFEU. First, this is the case when the Treaty expressly confers such external competence on the Union. Secondly, such competence may also be implied when, according to the *ERTA* principle, the EU has adopted internal rules based on expressly conferred internal powers; or when, exceptionally, action of the Union is required to attain EU Treaty objectives and the Union is installed with a legal basis to act.
- Competences and legal bases determine the role the EU can play as a global actor but also decisively influence the interinstitutional relationship and the relations between the EU and its Member States. Consequently, political battles and arguments colour the legal provisions and arguments. From the outset, the CJEU has played a decisive role as final arbiter between the institutional actors and Member States in establishing the specific competences of the Union. While the integrationist agenda is visible in the first rulings establishing the *ERTA* doctrine, the judges

* Credit is due to Bruno De Witte, Rebecca Poort, Simona Popan, Jonah Thompson, and Yannick Weber for their valuable comments. The usual disclaimer applies.

have been more careful in subsequent meticulous rulings on competences. These rulings have contributed to the careful balancing of interests but also added to the complex web of competences and conditions for their use. These complexities have not diminished since the Lisbon codification.

I. Current State of Affairs in EU External Competences

A. Treaty-making Power of the European Union

As we will see, international agreements are the tools 'par excellence' for the Union to engage in external relations. In contrast to states, which possess an inherent treaty-making capacity (Article 6 VCLT), international organisations such as the European Union are endowed with treaty-making capacity only when this is conferred upon them. This capacity or power is based on their constituent rules and the necessity to perform their functions and to fulfil their purposes.[1] One of these constituent rules limiting this capacity is the general principle of conferral in the TEU which 'must be observed with respect to both the internal and international action of the European Union'[2] (see also Chapter 2).

The EU's treaty-making capacity is now addressed in EU primary law by Article 216 TFEU but was already reflected early on, in *Costa v Enel* (1963)[3] and *ERTA* (1971).[4]

Article 216(1) TFEU

The Union may conclude an agreement with one or more third countries or international organisations where the Treaties so provide or where the conclusion of an agreement is necessary in order to achieve, within the framework of the Union's policies, one of the objectives referred to in the Treaties, or is provided for in a legally binding Union act or is likely to affect common rules or alter their scope.

[1] Vienna Convention on the Law of Treaties (adopted 23 May 1969, entered into force 27 January 1980), 1155 UNTS 331, Art 6. See also A Peters, 'Treaty Making Power' in *Max Planck Encyclopaedia of Public International Law* (Oxford, Oxford University Press, 2009) paras 35–48; HG Schermers and NM Blokker, *International Institutional Law*, 6th edn (Leiden, Brill/Nijhoff, 2018) para 209.

[2] Case C-600/14 *Germany v Council* (*COTIF*), ECLI:EU:C:2017:935, para 44, citing Opinion 2/94 (*Accession of the Community to the ECHR*), ECLI:EU:C:1996:140, para 24.

[3] Case 6/64 *Costa v ENEL*, ECLI:EU:C:1964:66, para 3: 'By creating a Community of unlimited duration, having its own institutions, its own legal capacity and capacity of representation on the international plane'; Case 22/70 *Commission v Council* (*ERTA*), ECLI:EU:C:1971:32, para 15: 'To determine in a particular case the Community's authority to enter into international agreements, regard must be had to the whole scheme of the Treaty and no less than to its substantive provisions.'

[4] Case 22/70 *Commission v Council* (*ERTA*), ECLI:EU:C:1971:32. The case is also known in English under its French abbreviation: AETR.

Article 216(1) TFEU does not only codify the so-called *ERTA* doctrine but captures the essence of dozens of CJEU cases spanning more than half a century. This body of case law addresses two aspects, namely: (1) the *existence* and (2) the *nature* and *scope* of external competences. As will be further developed below, *existence* refers to the question of whether the EU is competent at all; *nature* deals with the question of whether the Union can act on its own; and *scope* asks the question of what is and is not covered by a certain legal basis. The first aspect is incorporated in Article 216(1) TFEU, which addresses the general conditions under which the EU has the mandate to conclude international agreements (the existence of an external competence). The nature and scope of external competences is addressed in Article 3(2) TFEU by explaining when such power becomes exclusive for the Union.

Article 3 TFEU

2. The Union shall also have exclusive competence for the conclusion of an international agreement when its conclusion is provided for in a legislative act of the Union or is necessary to enable the Union to exercise its internal competence, or in so far as its conclusion may affect common rules or alter their scope.

B. The Competence Catalogue and the *ERTA* Codification

The clarification and codification of competences were one of the major aims of the failed Draft Constitutional Treaty and the subsequent Lisbon Treaty. The EU intended to 'clarify, simplify and adjust the division of competence between the Union and the Member States'.[5] To this end, Articles 216 TFEU and 3 TFEU are complemented by a competence catalogue listing the categories of EU competences (mainly exclusive or shared) in Articles 2 to 6 TFEU, ranging from *exclusive* competences (only the Union may act or empower the Member States), to *shared* competences (the Union and the Member States may act together under specific conditions), to supporting, coordinating or supplementing competences. This codification was not only an important step in the consolidation of power under EU law but also held important implications for EU external relations law. Its management and implementation were burdened by a growing amount of detailed CJEU cases on (external) competences. CJEU judgments on external competences were often submerged in case-specific technicalities, with judges meticulously comparing international agreement norms with secondary EU law rules. CJEU judges provided specific examples for exclusive competences but the general conditions of treaty-making power and exclusive competences remained more obscure.[6]

[5] See the Laeken Declaration on the Future of the European Union, Annexes to the Presidency Conclusions – Laeken, European Council meeting in Laeken, 14–15 December 2001, SN 300/1/01 REV 1, 21.

[6] Claes and De Witte speak of 'pointillist case law' in M Claes and B De Witte 'Competences: Codification and Contestation' in A Łazowski and S Blockmans (eds) *Research Handbook on EU Institutional Law*

The codification of the treaty-making power and competences combined three aims: the strengthening of the EU as a global actor by reinforcing and creating more coherence and visibility of EU external action; the prevention at the same time of a further competence creep by clarifying the competence division between the EU and its Member States;[7] and finally, the codification of important case law, especially the *ERTA* doctrine. However, judging by the number of cases brought before the Court post-Lisbon on the issue of competences, the codification failed to serve the purposes outlined above.[8]

This recurring constitutional conflict on competences can be primarily explained by the unfortunate and incomplete wording of Articles 216(1) and 3(2) TFEU with unnecessary and misleading overlaps.[9] Articles 216(1) TFEU and 3(2) TFEU codify in two sentences fundamental elements of the case law on (external) competences, dating back from dozens of cases between the *ERTA* case (1971) until the *Open Skies* judgments (2002). It is, however, also a judge-made failure. These judgments on external competences by different generations of judges argue against the backdrop of the evolution of external relations. More dynamic rulings in the 1970s interchanged with a more cautious approach in the 1990s.[10] Decisively, the CJEU judges only took the opportunity with the *Lugano Convention* Opinion in 2006 to restate its intricate case law in a more structured and complete way.[11] Nevertheless, it takes the Court five pages in the *Lugano Convention* Opinion to unravel the conditions of existence and especially exclusivity of competences.[12] Consequently, any codification would probably fail to grasp the full dimension of the Court's assessment of the politically sensitive issue of EU (exclusive) competences. This is why it is important to always return to the case law.

(Cheltenham, Edward Elgar Publishing, 2016) 66. See also, PJ Kuijper, 'Fifty Years of EC/EU External Relations: Continuity and the Dialogue Between Judges and Member States as Constitutional Legislators' (2007) 31 *Fordham International Law Review* 1571, 1588; Pescatore describes 'microscopic arguments' in P Pescatore, 'Opinion 1/94 on Conclusion of The WTO Agreement: Is There an Escape From a Programmed Disaster?' (1999) *Common Market Law Review* 387, 395.

[7] See on this: A von Bogdandy and J Bast, 'The Vertical Order of Competences' in A von Bogdandy and J Bast (eds) *Principles of European Constitutional Law*, 2nd edn (Oxford, Hart Publishing, 2011) 276.

[8] All of the cases decided in post-Lisbon since 2013 are grand chamber rulings: Case C-414/11 *Daiichi Sankyo v DEMO*, ECLI:EU:C:2013:520; Case C-137/12 *Commission v Council* (*Services*), ECLI:EU:C:2013:675; Case C-114/12 *Commission v Council* (*Broadcasters*), ECLI:EU:C:2014:2151; Opinion 1/13 (*Hague Convention*), ECLI:EU:C:2014:2303; Case C-66/13 *Green Network v Autorità per l'energia elettrica e il gas*, ECLI:EU:C:2014:2399; Opinion 3/15 (*Marrakesh Treaty*), ECLI:EU:C:2016:657; Opinion 2/15 (*Singapore*), ECLI:EU:C:2017:376; Case C-600/14 *Germany v Council* (*COTIF*), ECLI:EU:C:2017:935. See also in this regard F Castillo de la Torre, 'The Court of Justice and External Competences after Lisbon: Some Reflections on the Latest Case Law' in P Eeckhout and M López-Escudero (eds) *The European Union's External Action in Times of Crisis* (Oxford, Hart Publishing, 2016).

[9] Criticised by M Cremona, 'Defining Competence in EU External Relations: Lessons From the Treaty Reform Process' in A Dashwood and M Maresceau (eds) *Law and Practice of EU External Relations: Salient Features of a Changing Landscape* (Cambridge, Cambridge University Press, 2008) 59–63; Claes and De Witte, (n 6); B De Witte, 'Too Much Constitutional Law in the European Union's Foreign Relations?' in M Cremona and B De Witte (eds) *EU Foreign Relations Law* (Oxford, Hart Publishing, 2008) 11.

[10] See, for example, P Mengozzi, 'The EC External Competencies: From ERTA Case to the Opinion in the Lugano Convention' in L Azoulai and M P Maduro (eds) *The Past and Future of EU Law: The Classics of EU Law Revised on the 50th Anniversary of the Rome Treaty* (Oxford, Hart Publishing, 2010) 127.

[11] This clarification came after the finalisation of the Draft Constitutional Treaty in May 2003. Opinion 1/03 (*Lugano Convention*), ECLI:EU:C:2006:81. See also on this point, P Eeckhout, *EU External Relations Law*, 2nd edn (Oxford, Oxford University Press, 2011) 113.

[12] Opinion 1/03 (*Lugano Convention*), ECLI:EU:C:2006:81, paras 114–33.

Opinion 1/03 (*Lugano Convention*), ECLI:EU:C:2006:81

Competence of the Community to conclude international agreements

114 The competence of the Community to conclude international agreements may arise not only from an express conferment by the Treaty but may equally flow implicitly from other provisions of the Treaty and from measures adopted, within the framework of those provisions, by the Community institutions (see ERTA, paragraph 16).

115 *That competence of the Community may be exclusive or shared with the Member States.* [emphasis added]

This important distinction between the existence and nature of external competences, emphasised in *Lugano*, was less prominent in the early case law. The first cases on external competences not only confirmed an external competence but also concluded that this resulted in an EU exclusive competence.[13] This (misleading) interconnection between existence and exclusivity of external competences is already visible in the *ERTA* case. The *ERTA* (or *AETR* according to its French abbreviation) judgment addressed the power of the Member States to participate in an international agreement on European Road Transport (*ERTA*). In this area, the EU has and had no express competence to conclude international agreements. Instead, the policy provisions on transport in Articles 95 and 100 TFEU only cover the right of Union institutions to enact *internal* legislation in the field of transport. This, however, did not hinder the judges in arguing the following:

Case C-22/70 *Commission v Council* (*ERTA*), ECLI:EU:C:1971:32

15 To determine in a particular case the Community's authority to enter into international agreements, regard must be had to *the whole scheme of the Treaty no less than its substantive provisions.*

16 Such authority arises not only from an express conferment by the Treaty – as in the case with Articles 113 and 114 for tariff and trade agreements and with Article 238 for association agreements – *but may equally flow from other provisions of the Treaty and from measures adopted*, within the framework of those provisions, by the Community institutions. [emphasis added]

[13] Case 22/70 *Commission v Council* (*ERTA*); ECLI:EU:C:1971:32, paras 27–29, 31; Joined Cases 3/76, 4/76 and 6/76 *Kramer and others*; ECLI:EU:C:1976:114, para 40; Opinion 1/75 *(Re Understanding on a Local Costs Standard)*, ECLI:EU:C:1975:145; Opinion 1/76 (*European laying-up fund*), ECLI:EU:C:1977:63.

In the *ERTA* case, the CJEU also defined for the first time one condition of exclusive competences of the Union (now codified in Article 3(2) TEU).

> 17 In particular, each time the Community, with the view to implementing a common policy envisaged by the Treaty, adopts provisions laying down common rules, whatever form these may take, *the Member States no longer have the right, acting individually or even collectively, to undertake obligations with third countries which affect those rules.*
>
> 21 Under Article 5, the Member States are required on the one hand to take all appropriate measures to ensure fulfilment of the obligations arising out of the Treaty or resulting from action taken by the institutions and, on the other hand, *to abstain from any measure which might jeopardise the attainment of the objectives of the Treaty.*
>
> 22 If these provisions are read in conjunction, it follows that to the extent to which Community rules are promulgated for the attainment of the objectives of the Treaty, *the Member States cannot, outside the framework of the Community institutions, assume obligations which might affect those rules or alter their scope.* [emphasis added]

The so-called 'parallelism' between internal and external competences consolidated and broadened the external powers of the European Communities in the 1970s. At the time of the *ERTA* ruling (and as emphasised in that ruling in para 16), the Community had an express mandate to conclude international agreements in only two cases: the Common Commercial Policy and the Association Policy. The *ERTA* doctrine extended the Union's treaty-making power to any field of internal policy and legislation, potentially leading, depending on the individual circumstances, to an exclusive competence.

> **JHH Weiler, 'The Transformation of Europe' (1991) 100 *Yale Law Journal* 2405, 2416**
>
> The significance of this ruling goes beyond the issue of treaty-making power. With this decision, subsequently replicated in different contexts, the European Court added another rung to its constitutional ladder: powers would be implied in favour of the Community where they are necessary to serve legitimate ends pursued by it. Beyond its enormous practical ramifications, the critical point was the willingness of the Court to sidestep the presumptive rule of interpretation typical in international law, that treaties must be interpreted in a manner that minimises encroachment on state sovereignty. The Court favoured a teleological, purposive rule drawn from the book of constitutional interpretation.

The judge-rapporteur in the *ERTA* case, Pierre Pescatore, explained this *constitutional interpretation* with the special nature of the supranational legal order. He differentiated the restrictive principle of explicitly attributed powers applying to international organisations such as the United Nations[14] from principles developed for the supranational entity in the form of sincere cooperation to be respected by the Member States and influenced by the principle of *effet utile* to attain the common objectives effectively in practice.[15] The 'sincere cooperation principle' (see Chapter 2), in particular, features prominently in the *ERTA* judgment, obliging Member States to take all measures or abstain from action for the attainment of the Treaty objectives (the *ERTA* judgment refers to the former Article 5 EEC Treaty in paragraphs 21 and 22, mentioned above (now Article 4(3) TEU)).

Applying a parallelism between internal and external competences was a bold act of judicial engineering. This synchronised the Community external action with the other two supranational Treaties Euratom and ECSC.[16] The *ERTA* judgment took inspiration from the more open-ended norm in the ECSC Treaty. The former Article 6 ECSC Treaty stipulated that the Community could act if required to 'perform its functions and attain its objectives'.[17] The first judgments on external competences (*ERTA* case, Opinion 1/76 and *Kramer* judgment)[18] demonstrated that external policies were and are a vehicle to achieve internal policies. An effective common transport and fishery policy of the initially six Member States in the 1970s could only be shaped if third countries were included in legal regimes and thus required the conclusion of international agreements with these third countries.[19] So could the Rhine navigation between some of the EU Member States only be effectively regulated by an international agreement, including the third state Switzerland as a Rhine riparian country.[20] This logic of an implied connectivity between internal and external action also springs from the wording of the common transport norm in Article 91(1)(a) TFEU. The EU has a legislative mandate to achieve a common transport policy by laying down rules 'applicable to international transport to or from the territory of a Member State or passing across the territory of one or more Member States'. From this wording the Court concluded that the power to enter into international agreements to bring these common rules into effect is 'necessarily vested' in the EU.[21]

[14] See, Schermers and Blokker (n 1) at para 209.

[15] P Pescatore, *The Law of Integration* (Leiden, Sijthoff International Publishing, 1974) 37–44.

[16] I MacLeod, ID Henry and S Hyett, *The External Relations of the European Communities* (Oxford, Clarendon Press, 1996) 48.

[17] See P Pescatore, 'External Relations in the Case Law of the CJEU' (1979) 16 *Common Market Law Review* 615, 618 who admits that the justification for ERTA derives from Paul Reuter and his writing on the ECSC Treaty in P Reuter, *La Communauté Européenne du charbon et de l'acier* (Paris, LGDJ, 1953) 116–40.

[18] Joined Cases 3/76, 4/76 and 6/76 *Kramer and others*, ECLI:EU:C:1976:114.

[19] See also JHH Weiler, 'The Transformation of Europe' in JHH Weiler (ed) *The Constitution of Europe* (Cambridge, Cambridge University Press, 1999) 22.

[20] The Rhine navigation is managed by one of the oldest regional international organisations, the Central Commission for the Navigation of the Rhine. See Schermers and Blokker (n 1) para 631.

[21] Case 22/70 *Commission v Council (ERTA)*, ECLI:EU:C:1971:32, para 28.

The Union is enabled by this case law and its codification in Article 216(1) TFEU to conclude international agreements which are 'necessary' to achieve Treaty objectives. As we have seen in the previous chapter, this built-in flexibility is limited by the more static principle of conferral in Article 5(2) TEU.

Article 5 TEU

1. The limits of Union competences are governed by the principle of conferral. The use of Union competences is governed by the principles of subsidiarity and proportionality.
2. Under the principle of conferral, the Union shall act *only within the limits of the competences conferred upon it by the Member States in the Treaties to attain the objectives set out therein.* Competences not conferred upon the Union in the Treaties remain with the Member States [emphasis added].

The *ERTA* doctrine and its follow-up case law, especially the restatement of the principles in the *Lugano Convention* Opinion, still play a role in the interpretation of the current norms. Hence, the relevance of pre-Lisbon case law in the post-Lisbon judgments is decisively explained by the deficiencies of the codification and the Court's structuring exercise in the *Lugano* Opinion, occurring *after* the codification. At the same time, this judicial exercise undermines the value of the codification[22] and the CJEU reaffirms itself in its decisive role as the final arbiter on competences.[23] In the first judgments post-Lisbon, the judges explain in great detail the conditions and circumstances of the exercise and nature of external competences in light of *ERTA* and the subsequent case law.[24] This 'integrated' approach is displayed in Opinion 1/13 (*Hague Convention*) which refers to the *Lugano* Opinion (Opinion 1/03) and *ERTA* case, as if no codification had taken place.

[22] See critically on this fine pattern of rules, De Witte, 'Too Much Constitutional Law in The European Union's Foreign Relations?' (n 9).

[23] Case C-114/12 *Commission v Council (Broadcasters)*, ECLI:EU:C:2014:2151, paras 67–68; Opinion 1/13 (*Hague Convention*), ECLI:EU:C:2014:2303, paras 71–72.

[24] Case C-114/12 *Commission v Council (Broadcasters)*, ECLI:EU:C:2014:2151, paras 66–67 and subsequently, Case C-66/13 *Green Network v Autorità per l'energia elettrica e il gas*, ECLI:EU:C:2014:2399; Opinion 1/13 (*Hague Convention*), ECLI:EU:C:2014:2303; Opinion 3/15 (*Marrakesh Treaty*), ECLI:EU:C:2016:657; Opinion 2/15 (*Singapore*), ECLI:EU:C:2017:376; Case C-600/14 *Germany v Council* (*COTIF*), ECLI:EU:C:2017:935. See generally, C Timmermans, 'The Competence Divide of the Lisbon Treaty Six Years After' in S Garben and I Govaere (eds) *The Division of Competences between the EU and the Member States: Reflections on the Past, the Present and the Future* (Oxford, Hart Publishing, 2017) 19.

Opinion 1/13 (*Hague Convention*), ECLI:EU:C:2014:23

The existence of EU competence

67 The competence of the EU to conclude international agreements may arise not only from an express conferment by the Treaties but may equally flow implicitly from other provisions of the Treaties and from measures adopted, within the framework of those provisions, by the EU institutions. In particular, whenever EU law creates for those institutions powers within its internal system for the purpose of attaining a specific objective, the EU has authority to undertake international commitments necessary for the attainment of that objective even in the absence of an express provision to that effect (*Opinion 1/03, ECLI:EU:C:2006:81, paragraph 114 and the case-law cited*). The last-mentioned possibility is also referred to in Article 216(1) TFEU.

The nature of the competence

69 The FEU Treaty specifies, in particular in Article 3(2), the circumstances in which the EU has exclusive external competence.

71 … *(see, to that effect, judgments in Commission v Council ('ERTA'), 22/70, ECLI:EU:C:1971:32, paragraph 30; Commission v Denmark, C-467/98, ECLI:EU:C:2002:625, paragraph 82; and Commission v Council, C-114/12, ECLI:EU:C:2014:2151, paragraphs 66 to 68).* [emphasis added]

In addition to the critical reception the codification of the rules on existence and nature of a competence received by scholars,[25] the literature perceives the competence catalogue as an unfinished job and a mismatch between the typology and the concrete legal basis found in the respective Chapters of the TFEU.[26] The competence catalogue categorises competences into exclusive, shared and supporting or complementary.

Article 2 TFEU

1. When the Treaties confer on the Union exclusive competence in a specific area, only the Union may legislate and adopt legally binding acts, the Member States being able to do so themselves only if so empowered by the Union or for the implementation of acts of the Union.

[25] M Cremona, 'The Draft Constitutional Treaty: External Relations and External Action' (2003) 40 *Common Market Law Review* 1347; P Craig, *The Lisbon Treaty* (Oxford, Oxford University Press, 2010) 166–67; D Thym, 'Foreign Affairs' in A von Bogdandy and J Bast (eds) *Principles of European Constitutional Law*, 2nd edn (Oxford, Hart Publishing, 2011) 318.

[26] Claes and De Witte (n 6) 56–60.

2. When the Treaties confer on the Union a competence shared with the Member States in a specific area, the Union and the Member States may legislate and adopt legally binding acts in that area. The Member States shall exercise their competence to the extent that the Union has not exercised its competence. The Member States shall exercise their competence again to the extent that the Union has decided to cease exercising its competence.
3. The Member States shall coordinate their economic and employment policies within arrangements as determined by this Treaty, which the Union shall have competence to provide.
4. The Union shall have competence, in accordance with the provisions of the Treaty on European Union, to define and implement a common foreign and security policy, including the progressive framing of a common defence policy.
5. In certain areas and under the conditions laid down in the Treaties, the Union shall have competence to carry out actions to support, coordinate or supplement the actions of the Member States, without thereby superseding their competence in these areas.

   Legally binding acts of the Union adopted on the basis of the provisions in the Treaties relating to these areas shall not entail harmonisation of Member States' laws or regulations.
6. The scope of and arrangements for exercising the Union's competences shall be determined by the provisions of the Treaties relating to each area.

Exclusive Union competences prevent the Member States from acting internally and externally. A shared competence might pre-empt Member States action (Article 2(2) TFEU). And supporting competences are competences in which the EU only complements the Member States action without replacing it (Article 6 TFEU). Supporting competences such as human health protection or education and training exclude the harmonisation of Member States rules, as their policy chapters explain.[27] However, a further subcategory exists within shared competences for the parallel competences development and research. These competences do not fall under the pre-emption norm in Article 2(2) TFEU. In these policy areas, shared competences cannot become exclusive by exercise of the EU competence, thus allowing Member States to engage in parallel actions. In addition, the CFSP competence is briefly mentioned in the competence catalogue but it is a hybrid competence which falls outside the categories listed above. Although it is clearly presented as a Union competence in both Articles 2(4) TFEU and Article 24(1) TEU, it is generally assumed that Member States are not

[27] See for example, Art 167(3) TFEU.

pre-empted from acting once the Union has done so. The CFSP competence can thus be compared with the parallel competences of development and humanitarian aid (see more extensively Chapter 9).

A closer look at the competence catalogue and its categories reveal that the clear-cut categorisation is challenged by the underlying complexity that competences are to be linked to the respective policy field and the legal bases found in the policy chapters of the TFEU (and exceptionally in the TEU). For instance, Article 3(2) TFEU and the case law stipulate exclusivity by nature where the Union adopts common rules and harmonises a certain field of EU acquis. However, minimum harmonisation allows for stricter rules of Member States in the policy field of the internal market or environmental law (in the category of shared competences). Consequently, in this case, the EU might legislate internally but Member State rule-making is not pre-empted, consequently preventing exclusivity and resulting in the form of concurrent or parallel competence.[28] On the other hand, a discrepancy between internal and external exclusivity might exist. Internally, a non-exclusive competence might nevertheless lead to an exclusive competence externally if the conclusion of an international agreement is foreseen in a legislative act or is necessary to enable the Union to exercise its internal competence.

Article 3 TFEU

1. The Union shall have exclusive competence in the following areas:
   (a) customs union;
   (b) the establishing of the competition rules necessary for the functioning of the internal market;
   (c) monetary policy for the Member States whose currency is the euro;
   (d) the conservation of marine biological resources under the common fisheries policy;
   (e) common commercial policy.

Only one of the a priori exclusive competences listed in Article 3(1) TFEU coincides with the policy fields presented by the TFEU, namely the common commercial policy (Article 207 TFEU). The other areas concern a limited field within a broader policy chapter of the Treaty, such as the conservation of marine biological resources under the common fisheries policy, which forms part of the common agricultural policy.[29]

[28] See also, R Schütze, 'Classifying EU Competences: German Constitutional Lessons?' in S Garben and I Govaere (eds) *The Division of Competences between the EU and the Member States* (Oxford, Hart Publishing, 2017) 33. See also the pre-Lisbon case law, Opinion 2/91 (*ILO Convention No. 170*), ECLI:EU:C:1993:106, the Court held that the European Union did not have exclusive competence because both the provisions of EU law and those of the international convention in question laid down minimum requirements.

[29] This was established in Joined Cases 3/76, 4/76 and 6/76 *Kramer and others*, ECLI:EU:C:1976:114.

In addition, while the competence in regard to the Euro currency is exclusive, the specific provisions addressing treaty-making in Article 219 TFEU and external representation in Article 138 TFEU establish doubts about a priori unified external representation.[30] Protocol No. 25 annexed to the Lisbon Treaty on the exercise of shared competences clarifies that if the Union has taken action in a certain area, 'the scope of this exercise of competence only covers those elements governed by the Union act in question and therefore does not cover the whole area'.[31]

Finally, the list of shared competences (Article 4(2) TFEU) are the 'principal areas' and constitute a non-exhaustive list.[32] This is emphasised by such missing competences as the Association and Neighbourhood Policy (Articles 217 TFEU and 8 TEU) and the flexibility clause under Article 352 TFEU.[33] Some competences escape clear categorisation. The field of the Union's social policy falls into shared competences for the aspects defined in this Treaty (Article 4(1)(b) TFEU) but provide the EU only with a role of coordination for the Member States' social policies (Article 5(3) TFEU).[34]

II. The Existence of an External Competence

Article 216(1) TFEU carves out four situations under which the Union is assigned treaty-making powers to conclude international agreements. These external competences can basically be divided into an express and implicit (internal) EU power to act externally. For instance, Article 207(1) TFEU refers to the conclusion of bilateral trade agreements with third countries ('the conclusion of tariff and trade agreement'). This constitutes an express power to act as it is clearly laid down in the Treaty. The Union, however, is also endowed with the power to conclude an agreement on air transport or competition law with a third country or an international organisation. This external competence is not expressly spelled-out in the Treaty, but international agreements in that area can be based on the internal legal base (Article 95 TFEU for transport or Article 103 TFEU on competition law) – the so-called implicit or internal competence.

Article 216 TFEU addresses the express competence with the words 'where the Treaty so provides'. The implicit competence is covered by 'where the conclusion of an agreement is necessary in order to achieve, within the framework of the Union's policies, one of the objectives referred to in the Treaties'. The third and fourth alternatives

[30] A Rosas, 'Exclusive, Shared and National Competence in the Context of EU External Relations: Do Such Distinctions Matter?' in I Govaere, E Lannon, P van Elsuwege and S Adam (eds) *The European Union in the World* (Leiden, Brill/Nijhoff, 2013) 21.

[31] Protocol No 25 on the exercise of shared competences [2008] OJ C 115/*307*.

[32] Opinion 2/15 (*Singapore*), Opinion of AG Sharpston, ECLI:EU:C:2016:992, para 59; R Gosalbo-Bono and F Naert, 'The Reluctant (Lisbon) Treaty and its implementation in the practice of the Council' in P Eeckhout and M Lopez-Escudero (eds) *The European Union's External Action in Times of Crisis* (Oxford, Hart Publishing, 2016) 20.

[33] C Timmermans, 'CJEU Doctrines on Competences' in L Azoulai (ed) *The Question of Competence in the European Union* (Oxford, Oxford University Press, 2014) 161. See also, Declaration No 41 on Article 352 TFEU [2012] OJ C326/352.

[34] Timmermans, ibid, 162; Claes and De Witte (n 6) 56–57.

in Article 216(1) TFEU cover situations where the EU is provided with treaty-making competence 'by a legally binding Union act' or 'is likely to affect common rules or alter their scope'. However, the interpretation of these two latter alternatives is burdened by the overlap between Article 216 TFEU and Article 3(2) TFEU and the difficult task of disentangling the conditions of exercise and scope of competences in the case law. The following parts (A to D) will address the four different alternatives laid down in Article 216(1) TFEU and explain them in greater detail.

A. Express External Powers Based on Primary Law

Express powers (also referred to as explicit powers) in the Treaties are legal norms which refer to the treaty-making power of the Union in the policy chapters of the TEU and the TFEU; these powers can be exclusive or shared. Hence, Article 216 TFEU (on the conclusion of international agreements) does not determine whether the EU competence is exclusive, this can be only be judged by Article 3(1) or (2) TFEU. Examples of such express (exclusive and shared) competences are trade (Article 207 TFEU), association policy (Article 217 TFEU) or development policy (Article 209(2) TFEU).[35] These norms have in common that they state explicitly that the EU can conclude international agreements with third countries and international organisations.

Furthermore, some internal policy areas with an external dimension include an express legal base to conclude international agreements. According to Article 79(3) TFEU, the Union may conclude readmission agreements with third countries. However, international agreements can also be concluded based on Article 186 (research, technological development and space); or Article 191(4) TFEU (environment). In other policy fields, namely education and training (Article 165(3)), culture (Article 167(3) TFEU), or public health (Article 168(3) TFEU) the norms merely state that 'the Union and the Member States shall foster cooperation with third countries and the competent international organisations'.[36] Subsequently, this leads to the question of whether these provisions also can be considered an express competence to conclude international agreements in those areas. This can be confirmed but, at the same time, the EU's scope of action is limited by the wording and the nature of these competences as supporting and coordinating powers in accordance with Article 6 TFEU.[37]

Furthermore, legal dispute arises whether Article 220 TFEU – on the cooperation with international organisations – contains a mandate for the European Commission and the High Representative to agree on legally binding international agreements on organisational matters with international organisations. This issue will be further dealt with in Chapter 6.

[35] Further norms are Art 37 TEU (CFSP); Arts 212(3), 214(4) TFEU.

[36] In the case of Art 171(3) TFEU on trans-European networks, the norm stipulates that the Union may decide to cooperate with third countries to promote projects of mutual interest.

[37] See also Macleod, Henry and Hyett (n 16) 47. See to the contrary, A Dashwood, M Dougan et al, *Wyatt and Dashwood's European Union law*, 6th edn (Oxford, Hart Publishing, 2011) 919.

Lastly, Article 219 TFEU needs to be singled out. This provision covers the conclusion of monetary agreements with third countries.[38] Similar to the predecessor norm Article 218 TFEU before Lisbon, it combines procedure and competence norm in one single provision. The provision explains which agreements can be concluded (formal agreements on an exchange-rate system for the euro in relation to the currencies of third states and agreements concerning monetary and exchange regime matters) and it outlines the procedure monetary agreements must follow.

B. Implied External Power Necessary to Attain Treaty Objectives

Implied external powers and their conditions result in most of the debates surrounding competences and persistent misunderstandings prevail. The subtleties and ramifications of the pre-Lisbon case law are insufficiently captured by the wording in Article 216 TFEU ('where the conclusion of an agreement is necessary in order to achieve, within the framework of the Union's policies, one of the objectives referred to in the Treaties'). The wording finds its origin in the reasoning applied in the *Open Skies* judgments.[39] The *Open Skies* judgments stressed that implied powers could derive from an internal Treaty norm upon which secondary rules have been adopted or where these internal rules are only adopted on the occasion of the conclusion and implementation of an international agreement.[40] These two forms of implied powers were for the first time circumscribed in *ERTA* but also played a decisive role in the *Kramer* judgment and Opinion 1/76 (*European Laying-up Fund*). These rulings concerned the internal policies of common transport and common fisheries, both of which address the organisation of common policies among Member States with no reference to an explicit mandate for the Union to conclude international agreements.[41] In the *ERTA* and *Kramer* cases, EU internal common rules were already adopted. In *Kramer*, to have effective and equitable rules on the conservation of fishing resources, it required to cover vessels of EU and non-EU members and thus necessitating external competence.[42] This *effet utile* reading of secondary law ('the very duties and powers', *Kramer* judgment, paragraph 33) was further unpacked in Opinion 1/76 (*European Laying-up Fund*). In this case, however, no internal measures were yet adopted, but external action was nevertheless considered necessary for the attainment of a specific Treaty objective.[43] The Draft

[38] Such agreements have been concluded with the micro-states Monaco, Andorra, San Marino and Vatican City. See for instance, Art 3 of Council Decision (EC) 2009/904 of 26 November 2009 on the position to be taken by the European Community regarding the renegotiations of the Monetary Agreement with the Republic of San Marino [2009] OJ L322/12; Monetary Agreement between the European Union and the Republic of San Marino [2012] OJ C121/5.

[39] Case C-469/98 *Commission v Finland* (*Open Skies*), ECLI:EU:C:2002:627, para 57: 'thus, the competence to bind the Community in relation to non-member countries may arise by implication from the Treaty provisions establishing internal competence, provided that participation of the Community in the international agreement is necessary for attaining one of the Community's objectives'.

[40] For instance, Case C-469/98 *Commission v Finland* (*Open Skies*), ECLI:EU:C:2002:627, para 57.

[41] Though Art 91(1)(a) TFEU refers in its objectives to common rules applicable to international transport.

[42] Joined Cases 3/76, 4/76 and 6/76 *Kramer and others*, ECLI:EU:C:1976:114, para 30/33.

[43] Opinion 1/76 (*European layer-up funds for inland waterway vessels*), ECLI:EU:C:1977:63, para 3.

agreement on a European Laying-up fund produced a unique situation. This draft agreement aimed to improve the inland waterway freight market within the Dutch and German waterways of Rhine and Moselle, foreseeing a compensation system in case of periods of excess capacity. Crucially, such regimes had under international law traditionally involved Switzerland and covered Swiss vessels.[44] Therefore this objective of establishing autonomous common rules in the internal sphere could only be established by integrating the third country of Switzerland by concluding a multilateral international agreement.

Opinion 1/76 (*European Laying-Up Fund*), ECLI:EU:C:1977:63, para 4

This is particularly so in all cases in which internal power has already been used to adopt measures which come within the attainment of common policies. It is, however, not limited to that eventuality. Although the internal Community measures are only adopted when the international agreement is concluded and made enforceable, as is envisaged in the present case by the proposal for a regulation to be submitted by the Commission *the power to bind the Community vis-à-vis third countries nevertheless flows by implication from the provisions of the Treaty creating the internal power and in so far as the participation of the Community in the international agreement is, as here, necessary for the attainment of one of the objectives of the Community*. [emphasis added]

Article 216(1) TFEU refers to objectives in the Treaties and does not mention the purpose of attaining a specific Treaty objective.[45] It is not clear how the condition of Article 216 TFEU 'necessary in order to achieve one of the objectives referred to in the Treaties' relates to or differentiates from the Article 3(2) TFEU condition 'necessary to enable the Union to exercise its internal competence'. In addition, it can be questioned whether a lighter test regarding the necessity of action is applied if the international agreement is based on the internal primary norm and EU internal rules have already been adopted. Hence, the necessity test appears to be stricter if the secondary law measures have not yet been adopted and the international agreement can only be based on an internal power (such as, eg, the common agricultural policy and its internal legal basis in Article 43 TFEU).[46] In Opinion 2/92 (*OECD*), the Court explained that this relates to a situation where the conclusion of an international agreement is necessary to achieve Treaty objectives which cannot be attained by the adoption of secondary rules.[47]

[44] Switzerland has been involved in the international organisation Central Commission for Navigation on the Rhine since 1920.

[45] Macleod, Henry and Hyett (n 16) 51.

[46] Another comparable example is competition policy and the legal basis in Art 103 TFEU.

[47] Opinion 2/92 (*OECD*), ECLI:EU:C:1994:116, para 32.

This incomplete incorporation of case law has led to two misconceptions. One is the argument that Article 216 TFEU broadens the power to act within the purpose of achieving objectives mentioned under Article 3 TEU and Article 21 TEU. These latter provisions, however, differ in nature to Article 216 TFEU as they refer generally to the objectives of the EU and of EU external action, not all of which are reflected in a specific policy norm and concrete legal bases.[48] Therefore this observation lacks both practical relevance and support in the post-Lisbon case law. The above-mentioned Opinion 1/13 (*Hague Convention*) stresses that a competence exists 'whenever EU law creates for those institutions *powers* within its internal system for the purpose of attaining a specific objective'. The objectives found in Article 3 and 21 TEU do not create such institutional *powers* and consequently cannot extend external action beyond powers granted to the Union by, for instance, primary or secondary legal bases.

The second misconception is that an implied power always results in an exclusive power.[49] This confusion stems not only from the overlaps in the wording of Articles 216 TFEU and 3(2) TFEU but also from the above highlighted judgments of the Court where an implied power in those specific cases did indeed lead to an exclusive power.[50] In later pre-Lisbon case law both aspects were even merged in the Court's argumentation.[51] Post-Lisbon, the Court took the opportunity in the grand chamber *COTIF* ruling (and before in Opinion 2/15 (*Singapore*)), to clarify the relation between internal and external competences in underlining that the existence of an external European Union competence is not dependent on the prior Union exercise of its internal legislative competences.[52]

Case C-600/14 *Germany v Council (COTIF)*, ECLI:EU:C:2017:935

49 It follows from the very wording of that provision [Article 216], in which no distinction is made according to whether the European Union's external competence is exclusive or shared, that the Union possesses such a competence in four situations. ... *the scenario in which the conclusion of an agreement is liable to affect common rules or to alter their scope, a scenario where the Union competence is, under Article 3(2) TFEU, exclusive, constitutes only one of those situations.*

[48] Craig (n 25) 399; M Cremona, 'EU External Relations: Unity and Conferral of Powers' in L Azoulai (ed) *The Question of Competence in the European Union* (Oxford, Oxford University Press, 2014) 73–74.

[49] See, in this regard, Schermers and Blokker (n 1) para 1754.

[50] See, Joined Cases 3/76, 4/76 and 6/76 *Kramer and others*, ECLI:EU:C:1976:114, paras 44/45; Case 22/70 *Commission v Council* (*ERTA*), ECLI:EU:C:1971:32, para 22.

[51] See Opinion 2/92 (*OECD*), ECLI:EU:C:1994:116, para 32; Opinion 1/94 (*WTO*), ECLI:EU:C:1994:384, para 85; Case C-469/98 *Commission v Finland* (*Open Skies*), ECLI:EU:C:2002:627, para 77; and especially, Opinion 1/03 (*Lugano Convention*), ECLI:EU:C:2006:81, para 115.

[52] Case C-600/14 *Germany v Council* (*COTIF*), ECLI:EU:C:2017:935, para 67; Opinion 2/15 (*Singapore*), ECLI:EU:C:2017:376, para 243.

67 The fact *that the existence of an external European Union competence is not, in any event, dependent on the prior exercise, by the Union, of its internal legislative competence* in the area concerned is also apparent from paragraph 243 of Opinion 2/15 (*Free Trade Agreement with Singapore*) of 16 May 2017 (EU:C:2017:376) … [emphasis added]

C. Provided for in a Legally Binding Act

The third option, covered by Article 216(1) TFEU, is that a legally binding act assigns a treaty-making power to the European Union. This alternative was already mentioned in the *ERTA* judgment, namely that EU secondary law grants the Union institutions the power to enter into negotiations with third countries.[53] It is decisively illustrated in Opinion 1/94 (*WTO*) with the example that 'the Community has included in its internal legislative acts provisions relating to the treatment of nationals of non-member countries or expressly conferred on its institutions powers to negotiate with non-member countries'.[54] Notably, in Opinion 1/94 this is explained by the judges in such a way as to indicate an exclusive competence. Such judicial analysis has resulted in the wrong assumption, as highlighted above, either that the existence of a competence and its exclusivity are one and the same or that only an exclusive competence provides for the power to make an international agreement.[55] This is clearly rebutted by, again, the *COTIF* case.

Case C-600/14 *Germany v Council* (*COTIF*), ECLI:EU:C:2017:935, para 50

Moreover, it is clear from a comparison of the respective wording of Article 216(1) TFEU and Article 3(2) TFEU *that the situations in which the Union has an external competence*, in accordance with the former provision, *are not limited to the various scenarios set out in the latter provision, where the Union has exclusive external competence*. [emphasis added]

It is remarkable that the wording of the Article 216 TFEU condition of a 'legally binding act' is similar but not identical to Article 3(2) TFEU which states 'when its conclusion is provided in a legislative act of the Union'. This difference might be

[53] Case 22/70 *Commission v Council* (*ERTA*), ECLI:EU:C:1971:32, para 29.

[54] Opinion 1/94 (*WTO*), ECLI:EU:C:1994:384, para 95; Case C-467/98 *Commission v Denmark* (*Open Skies*), ECLI:EU:C:2002:625, para 85.

[55] On this point see, Castillo de la Torre, 'The Court of Justice and External Competences after Lisbon' (n 8) 140.

explained by the fact that the Chapter in which Article 216 TFEU appears combines the treaty-making functions under the TEU and TFEU. This becomes clear when considering the treaty-making procedure in Article 218 TFEU. In effect, this broader wording within Article 216 TFEU could also cover a CFSP decision, a legally binding act that is not adopted based on the legislative procedure. As such, a CFSP legal act can also provide for powers to conclude international agreements (see Chapter 9).

Legal acts which empower the Union to act can be legislative acts, legal acts under Articles 290 and 291 TFEU and Article 25 TEU or international agreements (adopted through a Council Decision).[56] The latter is especially highlighted by other examples of specific – delegated – treaty-making competences where the Commission was mandated to conclude financial, technical and cooperation agreements with international organisations and third countries. The mandate then primarily flows from secondary law, but it might also be derived from international agreements and, exceptionally, primary rules.[57]

D. Likely to Affect Common Rules or Alter their Scope

The last situation, namely that common rules are affected, has been covered by the case law only in relation to the exclusivity of the competence. A parallel can once again be drawn with Article 3(2) TFEU, which almost exactly repeats Article 216 TFEU in one of its conditions for exclusivity ('in so far as its conclusion may affect common rules or alter their scope').

It holds no separate importance in relation to the other alternatives mandating the conclusion of international agreements. If common rules are adopted in certain fields of Union law internally, the second condition establishing implied powers, discussed in section IIIB, is also fulfilled.

E. The Function of the Flexibility Clause, Article 352 TFEU

Pre-Lisbon, the flexibility clause has been considered as a potential legal basis for action to conclude an international agreement; 'in absence of express or implied power for this purpose'.[58] It was used, before the relevant specific legal bases had been introduced into the Treaties, for financial instruments and bilateral agreements concerning

[56] See, for example, for the conclusion framework and subsidiary agreements Art 8 of Council Regulation (EU) No 231/2014 of 11 March 2014 establishing an Instrument for Pre-accession Assistance [2014] OJ L77/11 (IPA II Regulation), which is further specified in Art 5 of the IPA II Commission Implementing Regulation [2014] OJ L 132/32. Another example is an international agreement such as Art 141 of the Association Agreement with Moldova and Art 5 of the annexed Protocol I which set out the terms and conditions of an international agreement regarding the participation of Moldova in particular EU programmes.

[57] Art 8 of Council Regulation (EU) No 231/2014 of 11 March 2014 establishing an Instrument for Pre-accession Assistance [2014] OJ L77/11 (IPA II Regulation); and Arts 58, 60(5) and 184(2)(b) and 58 of Regulation (EU) No 966/2012 [2012] OJ L298/1 (Euratom Regulation).

[58] Opinion 2/94 (*ECHR*), ECLI:EU:C:1996:140, para 28.

third country aid and development policy.[59] The Court acknowledged a gap-filling function under very strict conditions[60] but denied that an *exclusive* power could be derived from it.[61] The role of this norm has further diminished and its limits are now clearly reflected in Article 352 TFEU:[62]

> **Article 352 TFEU**
>
> 1. If action by the Union should prove necessary, within the framework of the policies defined in the Treaties, to attain one of the objectives set out in the Treaties, and the Treaties have not provided the necessary powers, the Council, acting unanimously on a proposal from the Commission and after obtaining the consent of the European Parliament, shall adopt the appropriate measures. Where the measures in question are adopted by the Council in accordance with a special legislative procedure, it shall also act unanimously on a proposal from the Commission and after obtaining the consent of the European Parliament.
> 3. *Measures based on this Article shall not entail harmonisation of Member States' laws or regulations in cases where the Treaties exclude such harmonisation.*
> 4. This Article cannot serve as a basis for attaining objectives pertaining to the common foreign and security policy and any acts adopted pursuant to this Article shall respect the limits set out in Article 40, second paragraph, of the Treaty on European Union. [emphasis added]

III. The Nature and Scope of EU External Competences: The Question of Exclusivity

As highlighted above, the discussion of the *existence* of a competence is continuously and unfortunately intertwined with the question on *exclusivity*. This leads to the question of how to differentiate Article 3(2) from Article 216(1) TFEU in light of their overlaps. The areas in which either case law or Treaty drafters agreed on a priori exclusivity are listed under Article 3(1) TFEU. These areas address internal as well as external policy fields and only the Union can legislate and conclude international agreements.

[59] For instance, pre-accession financial support PHARE for CEEC countries was based on this norm. See Council Regulation (EEC) No 3906/89 of 18 December 1989 on economic aid to the Republic of Hungary and the Polish People's Republic [1989] OJ L375/11.

[60] Opinion 2/94 (*ECHR*), ECLI:EU:C:1996:140, paras 28–30.

[61] Opinion 2/94 (*OECD*), ECLI:EU:C:1994:116, para 36.

[62] See also Declaration No 41 on Article 352 TFEU [2012] OJ C326/352.

Thus, the customs union (Article 3(1)(a) and Articles 31 and 32 TFEU) and monetary policy for the Member States whose currency is the euro (Article 3(1)(c) TFEU) are exclusive based on primary law. Article 3(1)(b) TFEU only covers competition policy in so far as it is necessary for the functioning of the internal market. The EU's exclusively competence is limited to the establishment of rules in line with Articles 101 and 102 TFEU and does not concern the application which falls under Member States' responsibilities.[63] Originally, the first draft version of the Constitutional Treaty also included internal market as an exclusive competence. However, Member States finally insisted it is a shared competence (now listed in Article 4(a) TFEU).[64] The conservation of marine biological resources under the common fisheries policy and common commercial policy have been confirmed by case law as exclusive competences and have only later been codified as such.[65]

Exclusivity does not entail that the Member States are fully excluded from acting. The Union can empower the Member States to act in an area of exclusive competence (Article 2(1) TFEU). This situation, for instance, occurred when the Member States negotiated the multilateral Arms Trade Treaty (ATT) under the UN regime.[66] While the EU contributed actively to the negotiations, it could not ratify the ATT, though parts of the subject fell under the exclusive CCP. Council Decision 2013/269/CFSP stipulated in Article 1 that 'with respect to those matters falling under the exclusive competence of the Union, Member States are hereby authorised to sign the Arms Trade Treaty in the interests of the Union'.[67]

Article 3(2) TFEU establishes three abstract conditions under which an area can become exclusive, (a) when the conclusion of international agreement is provided for in a legislative act of the Union, (b) it is necessary to enable the Union to exercise its internal competence or (c) in so far as the conclusion of the EU international agreement may affect common rules or alter their scope.

Comparing Article 3(2) TFEU with the *Lugano Convention* Opinion, it becomes clear that this wording cannot capture the evolution of exclusive competences since *ERTA* and has several flaws. It may appear from the wording of Article 3(2) TFEU that an assessment only takes place between the EU envisaged international agreement and adopted EU legislation. However, case law reveals that a decisive part of the assessment concerns whether the Member States' (potential) action interferes with EU law. The starting point of the Court's argumentation was always that the Member States are prevented from acting externally when they could obstruct EU common

[63] See, with reference to the decentralisation through Council Regulation 1/2003, Craig (n 25) 160. Van Cleynenbruegel speaks of *de facto* shared power, sharing powers within exclusive competences in P van Cleynenbruegel, 'Rethinking EU Antitrust Law Enforcement' (2016) 12 *Croatian Yearbook of European Law & Policy* 49, 54.

[64] On the reasons see, Craig (n 25) 160.

[65] Joined Cases 3/76, 4/76 and 6/76 *Kramer and others*, ECLI:EU:C:1976:114, paras 44–45; Opinion 1/75 *(Re Understanding on a Local Costs Standard)*, ECLI:EU:C:1975:145 1363.

[66] For other examples, A Rosas, 'The Status in EU Law of International Agreements Concluded by EU Member States' (2011) 34 *Fordham International Law Journal* 1304, 1307.

[67] Council Decision (CFSP) 2013/269 authorising Member States to sign, in the interests of the European Union, the Arms Trade Treaty [2013] OJ L155/9.

policies and the unity of the internal market.[68] Moreover, the risk that Member States could affect the uniform application of Union law or interfere with the nature of the existing Union provisions has proven to be relevant. Finally, the pre-Lisbon case law alternates between general conditions of exclusivity (incompatibility with the unity of the common market, complete or almost complete harmonisation of a particular issue) and concrete examples (legislative measures containing clauses relating to the treatment of third-country nationals). Some, but not all, examples have been codified in Treaty law. This will be now analysed in greater detail.

A. Provided for in a Legislative Act

The condition 'provided in a legislative act' was for the first time taken up in Opinion 1/94 on the accession of the Community to the WTO. Whenever the Union has included 'in its internal legislative acts provisions relating to the treatment of nationals of non-member countries or expressly conferred on its institutions powers to negotiate with non-member countries, it acquires exclusive external competence in the spheres covered by those acts'.[69] The codification in Articles 216 and 3(2) TFEU give the misleading impression that this has been split up and that Article 216 TFEU covers part of it (provided in a legally binding act) and Article 3(2) TFEU the other part of this *WTO* Opinion. It has been argued by scholars that this codification must be interpreted more narrowly as the Union cannot assign itself more competences than awarded by the Treaties. Equally, the EU cannot obtain exclusive competences in an area of shared or complementary competences by simply adopting legislative acts.[70]

B. Necessary to Enable to Exercise its Internal Competence

As explained above, this condition is decisively connected to exclusivity in the past case law. However, the *necessity* test has no self-standing role for the question of exclusivity in relations to the other alternative covered in point III.C. In all the cases pre-Lisbon, the *necessity* to exclude the individual action of the Member States was related to the situation that it either concerned the common policy or the unity of the internal market. Hence, the area was largely covered by EU rules or completely harmonised.[71]

In Opinion 1/94 on the WTO agreements *an inextricable link* between an internal and external aspect was required in case no internal legislation had been adopted

[68] See for instance, Case 22/70 *Commission v Council* (*ERTA*), ECLI:EU:C:1971:32, paras 16–19; Opinion 2/92 (*OECD*), ECLI:EU:C:1994:116, para 31; Opinion 1/03 (*Lugano Convention*), ECLI:EU:C:2006:81, paras 121–22.

[69] Opinion 1/94 (*WTO*), ECLI:EU:C:1994:384, para 95.

[70] G De Baere, 'External Action' in C Barnard and S Peers (eds) *European Union Law*, 2nd edn (Oxford, Oxford University Press, 2017); M Klamert, *The Principle of Loyalty in EU Law* (Oxford, Oxford University Press, 2017) 153.

[71] Case C-469/98 *Commission v Finland* (*Open Skies*), ECLI:EU:C:2002:627, paras 81–82.

before the conclusion of an international agreement.[72] In that Opinion, such an *inextricable link* between external and internal rules was not found concerning the rules on freedom of establishment and the treatment of nationals of non-Member States,[73] nor was it found for the common air aviation rules in the *Open Skies* judgments.[74] In addition, in the ruling of the *Lugano Convention* Opinion, *necessity* only played a role in as far as it was argued that any agreement by the Member States under these conditions would *necessarily* affect the Union rules.[75] Post-Lisbon this criteria have been so far not been analysed and a lot speaks for the argument that it holds no separate role next to other conditions in Article 3(2) TFEU.

C. Affecting Common Rules or Altering their Scope

In all the cases post-Lisbon addressing exclusive competences, the Court has analysed this condition. This is explained by the fact that it abbreviates the extensive conditions established in the evolving case law pre-Lisbon in an insufficient way. The Court established early on in its case law that the adoption of common rules prevents Member States from acting collectively or individually. Exclusivity is, however, also established if the EU adopts within a certain policy or parts of it, particular rules which result in harmonisation.[76] The question of whether common rules only equate internal secondary EU rules or also could refer to EU international agreements or primary law has been settled by the *Singapore* Opinion.

Opinion 2/15 (*Singapore*), ECLI:EU:C:2017:376

234 Regard would not be had to the reasoning inherent in the rule as to exclusive internal competence contained in the judgment of 31 March 1971, *Commission* v *Council* (22/70, ECLI:EU:C:1971:32), a judgment confirmed by the Court's subsequent case-law (see, *inter alia*, judgment of 5 November 2002, *Commission* v *Denmark*, C-467/98, ECLI:EU:C:2002:625, paragraphs 77 to 80), *if the scope of that rule, currently laid down in the final limb of Article 3(2) TFEU, were extended to a situation which, as in the present instance, concerns not rules of secondary law laid down by the European Union in the exercise of an internal competence that has been conferred upon it by the Treaties, but a rule of primary EU law adopted by the framers of those Treaties.*

[72] Opinion 1/94 (*WTO*), ECLI:EU:C:1994:384, para 85.
[73] Opinion 1/94 (*WTO*), ECLI:EU:C:1994:384.
[74] Case C-469/98 *Commission v Finland* (*Open Skies*), ECLI:EU:C:2002:627, paras 58–59.
[75] Opinion 1/03 (*Lugano Convention*), ECLI:EU:C:2006:81, para 122.
[76] Ibid, paras 116–18, with reference to Opinion 2/91 (*ILO Convention No. 170*), ECLI:EU:C:1993:106.

235 Secondly, in the light of the primacy of the EU and FEU Treaties over acts adopted on their basis, those acts, including agreements concluded by the European Union with third States, derive their legitimacy from those Treaties and cannot, on the other hand, have an impact on the meaning or scope of the Treaties' provisions. *Those agreements accordingly cannot 'affect' rules of primary EU law or 'alter their scope', within the meaning of Article 3 (2) TFEU.* [emphasis added]

The different perspectives, above already highlighted and reflected in the pre-Lisbon case law in assessing exclusivity, are not sufficiently reflected in Article 3(2) TFEU. This Treaty provision states that exclusivity is triggered by the conclusion of *an international agreement affecting EU common rules or altering their scope.* Article 3(2) is thus limited to the conclusion of international agreements *by the EU.* However, the starting point for exclusivity since *ERTA* is that the *Member States* affect with their action and international commitments the EU common regime and rules;[77] a criterion that does not return in Article 3(2), but that has been underlined in the case law:

Opinion 1/13 (*Hague Convention*), ECLI:EU:C:2014:23

71 The question as to whether that condition is met must be examined in the light of the Court's case-law according to which *there is a risk that common EU rules may be adversely affected by international commitments undertaken by the Member States, or that the scope of those rules may be altered, which is such as to justify an exclusive external competence of the EU, where those commitments fall within the scope of those rules.*

72 A finding that there is such a risk does not presuppose that the areas covered by the international commitments and those covered by the EU rules coincide fully (see Opinion 1/03, ECLI:EU:C:2006:81, paragraph 126, and judgment in *Commission v Council*, ECLI:EU:C:2014:2151, paragraph 69).

73 In particular, the scope of EU rules may be affected or altered by international commitments where such commitments are concerned *with an area which is already covered to a large extent by such rules* (see, to that effect, Opinion 2/91, ECLI:EU:C:1993:106, paragraphs 25 and 26).

[77] Case 22/70 *Commission v Council* (*ERTA*), ECLI:EU:C:1971:32, para 31; Case C-469/98 *Commission v Finland* (*Open Skies*), ECLI:EU:C:2002:627, para 77.

> 74 That said, since the EU has only conferred powers, *any competence, especially where it is exclusive, must have its basis in conclusions drawn from a comprehensive and detailed analysis of the relationship between the envisaged international agreement and the EU law in force.* That analysis must take into account the areas covered by the EU rules and by the provisions of the agreement envisaged, their foreseeable future development and the nature and content of those rules and those provisions, in order to determine whether the agreement is capable of undermining the uniform and consistent application of the EU rules and the proper functioning of the system which they establish (see Opinion 1/03, ECLI:EU:C:2006:81, paragraphs 126, 128 and 133, and judgment in *Commission v Council*, ECLI:EU:C:2014:2151, paragraph 74). [emphasis added]

In addition, Article 3(2) TFEU takes effect not only at the conclusion of an agreement, but also before at negotiation and later in the implementation phase.[78]

> **Joined Cases C-626/15 and C-659/16 *Antarctique*, ECLI:EU:C:2018:925**
>
> 112 In the light of that objective, Article 3(2) TFEU must therefore be interpreted, in order to preserve its practical effect, as meaning that, although its wording refers solely to the conclusion of an international agreement, *it also applies, at an earlier stage, when such an agreement is being negotiated and, at a later stage, when a body established by the agreement is called upon to adopt measures implementing it.*
>
> 114 Furthermore, such a risk of common EU rules being affected may be found to exist where the international commitments at issue, without necessarily conflicting with those rules, may have an effect on their meaning, scope and effectiveness. [emphasis added]

Thus, the condition 'may affect common rules or alter their scope' is assessed by determining whether the risk exists that EU common rules are adversely affected or altered by Member States' international commitments. A broad risk assessment thus takes place. International commitments by the Member States and EU rules do not have to overlap fully and a coverage to a large extent is sufficient.[79]

These considerations – reflected already in the *ERTA* findings – are all left unmentioned by Article 3(2) TFEU. Instead it abbreviates the conditions in Article 3(2) which

[78] Joined Cases C-626/15 and C-659/16 *Antarctique*, ECLI:EU:C:2018:925.
[79] Opinion 3/15 (*Marrakesh Treaty*), ECLI:EU:C:2016:657, paras 105–7.

are found in 'longhand' form in paragraph 74 of Opinion 1/13 (with reference to the *Lugano* Opinion, see above),[80] 'since the EU has only conferred powers', a comprehensive and detailed analysis is conducted comparing *the EU's envisaged international agreement and the EU law in force and the latter's foreseeable future development*.[81]

In sum, in establishing exclusivity, the following two aspects find consideration:

- A risk assessment of whether common rules are affected by the Member States' international commitments or whether the risk exists that EU rules are altered by those Member States commitments. The risk assessment is broad; considering future developments and the effect on EU rules, their meaning, scope and effectiveness, is sufficient, no conflict needs to be established.
- To determine this risk and define the scope of analysis, a comparison needs to be drawn between the EU's envisaged international agreement field of application and existing or foreseeable EU secondary rules. This analysis compares the areas covered by the current or foreseeable EU rules with the provisions of the agreement envisaged. It is sufficient if an area of the international agreement is largely covered by EU rules and the nature and content of the international commitment effects EU rules.

This comprehensive risk assessment for current and future EU rules, which are capable of undermining EU rules and the proper functioning of the system, necessitates an elaborate and technical review. It also invites the Court's assessment back in to illustrate the conditions through examples, as demonstrated since the beginning. In Opinion 2/15 (*Singapore*) the Court specified the limiting factor that common rules are only secondary rules, as highlighted above.[82] In the same ruling, the Court also confirmed a more diffuse exception. Provisions that are extremely limited in scope do not have to be considered when assessing the competence divide between EU and Member States.[83] In other words: an exclusive competence to conclude an international agreement is not per se affected by the inclusion in that agreement of a minor non-exclusive element. This 'limited scope' argument is inspired by previous case law.[84] In the *WTO* Opinion 1/94, the Commission argued that secondary provisions could be affected in the area of intellectual property rights but the Court countered with the explanation that they were limited in their scope of application under EU law.[85] In the *Singapore* Opinion this argument was for the first time applied not against a Union competence, but in its favour. The Court held that institutional norms are of ancillary nature in regard to the substantive norms.[86] This assessment only changes if it concerns institutional norms which include dispute settlement provisions removing disputes from Member States' courts.[87] The limited scope argument is introduced by the Court as settled case law in

[80] Opinion 1/03 (*Lugano Convention*), ECLI:EU:C:2006:81, para 133.

[81] Opinion 1/13 *(Hague Convention)*, ECLI:EU:C:2014:23; and Case C-114/12 *Commission v Council* (*Broadcasters*), ECLI:EU:C:2014:2151, para 74.

[82] Opinion 2/15 (*Singapore*), ECLI:EU:C:2017:376.

[83] Ibid, paras 216–17.

[84] Opinion 1/94 (*WTO*), ECLI:EU:C:1994:384; Opinion 1/08 (*GATS*), ECLI:EU:C:2009:739.

[85] Opinion 1/94, ECLI:EU:C:1994:384, para 67.

[86] Opinion 2/15 (*Singapore*), ECLI:EU:C:2017:376, para 276.

[87] Ibid, para 292.

the *Singapore* Opinion. However, when a norm is of limited scope, it must be assessed in the framework of the choice of a legal basis and not in relations to competences. This criterion, instead, introduces an element of unpredictability for future conflicts (see further Chapter 4 on mixed agreements).

Another unresolved interpretation question is the relationship between Article 3(2) and Article 2(2) TFEU – the relationship between pre-emption and exclusivity.[88]

Article 2(2) TFEU

When the Treaties confer on the Union a competence shared with the Member States in a specific area, the Union and the Member States may legislate and adopt legally binding acts in that area. The Member States shall exercise their competence to the extent that the Union has not exercised its competence. The Member States shall exercise their competence again to the extent that the Union has decided to cease exercising its competence.

C Timmermans, 'ECJ Doctrines on competences' in L Azoulai (ed) *The Question of Competence in the European Union* (Oxford, Oxford University Press, 2014) 159 and 163

As far as EU law is concerned, it seems to me that the concept of pre-emption may be useful to distinguish with regard to shared competences between two, entirely different approaches:

1. The exercise of Union competence is considered to block the exercise of national competence. Member States may not at all act unilaterally anymore in the field in which, and to the extent to which, the Union has exercised its competence. Whether or not the national measure can be considered in conflict with Union rules, is completely irrelevant. Each national measure, whatever its contents, will be invalid. This approach establishes a rule of competence; it solves a conflict of competences, not of norms. Here the notion of pre-emption seems useful.
2. In the second approach national competences as such remain unaffected. Member States may continue to exercise their competence in spite of the exercise of Union competences, provided that they respect Union rules. We have to do here with a rule, not of competence, per se, but of conflict. I do not think that applying to this approach the concept of pre-emption has

[88] M Cremona, 'EU External Competence – Rationales for Exclusivity' in S Garben and I Govaere, *The Division of Competences between the EU and its Member States* (Oxford, Hart Publishing, 2017).

any added value. Where a conflict of norms arises, applying the principle of primacy of Union law will be sufficient to solve it.

... I might draw attention to the relationship between Articles 2(2) (blocking effect in case of exercise of shared competences) and 3(2) TFEU. According to the latter provision, external competences become exclusive in three particular situations, well-known from the case law, related to the exercise of internal competences amongst which the *ERTA* situation. So, no blocking effect but exclusivity. This raises the question of whether Article 2(2) TFEU is at all applicable to the exercise of non-exclusive external competences. There should be no doubt about that. But then it is interesting to note that only the exercise of internal competences may make an external competence exclusive, not the exercise of the external competence itself. The latter may only entail the blocking effect of Article 2(2) TFEU, which, as already mentioned, is not the same as exclusivity.

This distinction between the two norms can be demonstrated with the EU competence in Article 79(3) TFEU to conclude readmission agreements with third countries. This competence is shared under the area of freedom, security and justice, but at the same time pre-empts Member States from acting, without resulting necessarily in an exclusive competence.

M Cremona, 'EU External Competence' in S Garben and I Govaere (eds) *The Division of Competences between the EU and the Member States*, (Oxford, Hart Publishing, 2017) 150

Exclusivity thus carries different connotations in the case of express and implied external powers. In the case of powers expressly granted for the purpose of external action (in particular CCP, the common foreign and security policy, development co-operation and association agreements), the breadth and open-ended nature of these powers mean that competence carries with it the power to shape external policy, to define the scope of EU international action. In most cases this is not a power which excludes the Member States, but when it does (in the case of the CCP) its boundaries will of course be contested.

Where implied external powers are linked to internal policy fields, they need to demonstrate either the AETR *(aka ERTA)* or the *effet utile rationale*, as now expressed in Article 216(1) TFEU, and will tend to be sectoral in nature, tied to the Treaty-based objectives of those specific policies. In such cases exclusivity is internally oriented; it is aligned to the need to preserve the integrity and functioning of the internal acquis.

IV. The Choice of a Legal Basis and the Scope of Specific Policies

The competence categories (Articles 3 to 6 TFEU) do not include specific legal bases; concrete legal bases are primarily found in the policy chapters of the Treaties. Also, Article 21 TEU cannot create competences in external action but merely contains a list of objectives guiding the Union's external action. The extent of the EU's competences in external action thus depends on the areas covered in the policies chapters. Article 216 TFEU offers a general competence for the EU to conclude international agreements, but a concrete and substantive legal basis is still required in line with the principle of conferral (Article 5 TEU). Competences and legal basis disputes are closely linked.[89] The competence question addresses the scope of a competence or policy while the legal basis addresses the existence of legal basis and competence.

As we have seen, in Opinion 2/15 (*Singapore*), a correlation appears between the scope of a policy legal basis and the nature of the competence in such a way that no provisions have to be taken into account which are extremely limited in scope – so in being ancillary. However, the choice of legal basis impacts the nature of the competence: exclusive or shared.[90] This also explains the tendency of the Council to add legal bases to an international agreement to secure that parts of international agreements fall into a shared competence, often with the intention of creating a mixed agreement (see further Chapter 4).

A. The Criteria for the Choice of a Legal Basis

Under the principle of conferral, the adoption of an international agreement or a legislative/legal act requires a concrete legal basis or several legal bases. A legal basis is found in the policy norms of the Treaty (TFEU or exceptionally the TEU).[91] Furthermore, legal bases can be further specified in EU secondary law and international agreements as delegated legislation/treaty-making (see further on this Chapter 4). A concrete legal basis refers to the procedure under which the legislating institutions act. In the case of the conclusion of international agreements, the detailed procedure is found in Article 218(6) TFEU (see Chapters 4 and 5).

[89] Opinion 1/08 (*GATS*), ECLI:EU:C:2009:739, para 111.

[90] In Opinion 2/00 (*Cartagena*), ECLI:EU:C:2001:664, para 41, the Court stressed that 'the practical difficulties associated with the implementation of mixed agreements … cannot be accepted as relevant when selecting the legal basis for a Community measure'.

[91] For instance, Art 45(2) TEU for the establishment of the European Defence Agency.

Case C-263/14 *Parliament v Council* (*Tanzania*), ECLI:EU:C:2016:435, para 42

The choice of the appropriate legal basis of a European Union act has constitutional significance, since to proceed on an incorrect legal basis is liable to invalidate such an act, particularly where the appropriate legal basis lays down a procedure for adopting acts that is different from that which has in fact been followed.

The Court has developed two criteria for determining the correct legal basis when a legislative act is enacted: namely (1) that it is necessary to identify the main aim and content of the measure at hand; and (2) and that exceptionally two or more legal bases can be combined if several objectives of a legislative act are inseparably linked, no hierarchy between the norms exist and they are compatible in their respective legislative procedure.[92] For international agreements, the Court has added in the *Tanzania* case that also the context of the agreement must be considered.[93]

Case C-244/17 *Commission v Council* (*Kazakhstan*), ECLI:EU:C:2018:662

36 According to settled case-law, the choice of the legal basis for an EU measure must rest on objective factors amenable to judicial review, which include the aim and content of that measure.

37 If examination of an EU measure reveals that it pursues two purposes or that it comprises two components and if one of these is identifiable as the main or predominant purpose or component, whereas the other is merely incidental, the measure must be founded on a single legal basis, namely that required by the main or predominant purpose or component. Exceptionally, if it is established, on the other hand, that the measure simultaneously pursues a number of objectives, or has several components, which are inextricably linked without one being incidental to the other, so that various provisions of the Treaty are applicable, the measure must be founded on the various corresponding legal bases.

[92] A Dashwood, 'EU and Member State Acts in the Negotiation, Conclusion, and Implementation of International Agreements' in M Cremona and C Kilpatrick (eds) *EU Legal Acts* (Oxford, Oxford University Press, 2018) 210–11.

[93] Case C-263/14 *Parliament v Council (Tanzania)*, ECLI:EU:C:2016:435, paras 48–50.

(i) Identifying the Centre of Gravity: An Objective Test Amenable to Legal Review?

The legal basis follows the predominate aim and purpose of a measure at hand – the centre of gravity. According to case law, the centre of gravity test implies that if one policy is predominant and the other incidental, the choice will be made for the predominant norm.[94]

Literature has defined this as an absorption theory: '… the dominant objective 'absorbs' the possible other substantive legal bases which are pursuing objectives of a subsidiary or ancillary nature'.[95] The choice of predominant objective 'does not follow from its author's conviction alone, but must rest on objective factors which are amenable to judicial review'.[96]

This centre of gravity test helps to identify the just and correct legal basis, but the EU legislator can steer this choice by emphasising certain aims in the preamble of a legislative instrument.

P Koutrakos, 'Legal Basis and Delimitation of Competence' in M Cremona and B De Witte (eds) *EU Foreign Relations Law* (Oxford, Hart Publishing, 2008) 184

A degree of uncertainty is inevitable in the process underpinning the choice of a legal basis. In a legal order where the institutional balance is ill-defined and, at times, incrementally redefined, the choice of legal basis is, in any case, a potentially politicised matter.

These uncertainties become even more visible in recent more complex and elaborate international agreements. While the EU cooperates with third countries in sectoral agreements (on fisheries, air transport or energy) with a specific aim and limited purposes, association agreements or development and trade agreements – so-called horizontal agreements – are multi-aimed and include cooperation in several policies and objectives ranging from political to trade cooperation.[97] In these agreements, several legal bases can be considered by the treaty-making institutions.

(ii) Several Legal Bases

Exceptionally two or more legal bases for a legislative act or an international agreement can be chosen if the legal procedures applied are compatible. This compatibility

[94] Case C-338/01 *Commission v Council*, ECLI:EU:C:2004:253, paras 54–55.

[95] P Van Elsuwege, 'The Potential for Inter-institutional Conflicts before the Court of Justice: Impact of the Lisbon Treaty' 117 in M Cremona and A Thies (eds) *The European Court of Justice and External Relations Law* (Oxford, Hart Publishing, 2014) with reference to M Maresceau, *Bilateral Agreements Concluded by the European Community, Collected Courses of the Hague Academy of International Law* (Leiden, Brill/Nijhoff, 2004) 156–58.

[96] Opinion 2/00 (*Cartagena*), ECLI:EU:C:2001:664, paras 22–23.

[97] F Naert, 'Use of CFSP Legal Basis for EU International Agreements' in J Czuczai and F Naert (eds) *The EU as a Global Actor Bridging Legal Theory and Practice* (Leiden, Brill/Nijhoff, 2017) 409.

is assessed on the basis of the respective legal bases in Treaty norms and the procedures indicated in Article 218(6) and (8) TFEU.[98] These norms determine the voting procedure in the Council (unanimous or qualified majority voting) and the participation of the European Parliament for a legislative act or an international agreement. It is, however, not clear whether both procedural conditions must be in line with each other or one incompatibility (such as the voting in the Council) can be reconciled when more than one legal basis is chosen.

Before the Lisbon reform, it was undisputed that it was incompatible to combine procedures deriving from the different EU 'pillars'. This was prohibited by reference to Article 47 TEU (pre-Lisbon) and the supranational 'Community' pillar took precedence over the more intergovernmental pillars. For this not only the *ECOWAS* case bears witness but also the CJEU's *Kadi* judgment, with its emphasis on integrated but separated legal orders.[99] However, on the question of when the procedures are incompatible in other situations, the Court has not always been consistent.[100] While the CJEU held in one case, pre-Lisbon, that Treaty Articles providing unanimity and a qualified majority vote in the Council could not be applied conjointly,[101] a later judgment accepted this 'inconsistency' as long as the Council would act unanimously.[102]

In the *Smart Sanctions* case, a grand chamber ruling, the Court for the first time addressed the question of procedures under CFSP and TFEU legal bases under the current TFEU and TEU for a unilateral act and concluded on their incompatibility.[103] This judgment left open whether differences in the Council's decision-making procedures (so unanimous voting and qualified majority voting) can be reconciled, but confirms that differences in both procedural aspects – the legislation-making and, especially, the involvement of the European Parliament – cannot be overcome or reconciled.

In contrast, for international agreements, Article 218(6) TFEU reveals one treaty-making procedure only. Except when agreements are exclusively related to CFSP, the participatory right of the European Parliament is determined by paragraph 6(a) and (b) and manifests itself – as a rule – in a consent right of the European Parliament (see Chapter 9). The voting in the Council follows Article 218(8) TFEU where, as a rule, the Council votes by qualified majority voting – with a few exceptions such as when

[98] Case C-130/10 *Parliament v Council (Smart Sanctions)*, ECLI:EU:C:2012:472; Joined Cases C-164/97 and C-165/97 *Parliament v Council*, ECLI:EU:C:1999:99, para 14.

[99] Joined Cases C-402/05P and C-415/05P *Kadi and Al Barakaat International Foundation v Council and Commission*, ECLI:EU:C:2008:461.

[100] See also, K St Clair Bradley, 'Powers and Procedures in the EU Constitution' in G de Búrca and P Craig (eds) *The Evolution of EU Law*, 2nd edn (Oxford, Oxford University Press, 2011) 92–93.

[101] Case C-338/01 *Commission v Council*, ECLI:EU:C:2004:253, para 58. Though in the judgment the Court seemed to rely more on a more specific norm argument which gets preference over the other (former Art 95 [now Art 114 TFEU] states 'save where otherwise provided in the Treaty' than on this argument mentioned above (para 60). However, in Case C-178/03 *Commission v European Parliament and Council*, ECLI:EU:C:2006:4, it seemed again of relevance, as already before in Case C-300/89 *Commission v Council (Titanium Dioxide)*, ECLI:EU:C:1991:244, para 19. Case C-300/89 *Commission v Council*, ECLI:EU:C:1991:244.

[102] Case C-166/07 *European Parliament v Council*, ECLI:EU:C:2009:499, para 69; Case C-178/03 *Commission v European Parliament and Council*, ECLI:EU:C:2006:4.

[103] Case C-130/10 *Parliament v Council (Smart Sanctions)*, ECLI:EU:C:2012:472.

concluding association agreements. Different voting procedures for this single procedure can become an issue when the international agreement relies on two legal bases with one requiring unanimous voting and the other qualified majority voting.

B. The Centre of Gravity Test and the Scope of Policies

To determine whether a policy is dominant, the Court will look at the aim and content of the piece of legislation or international agreement at stake.[104] For determining the predominant aim and purpose, the preamble forms a decisive factor in a legislative act.[105] However, the choice of the correct legal basis encounters two problems. One problem is that this choice is not necessarily a neutral one as it defines the role of the institutions and the Member States, as explained above. In addition, the scope of the individual policies and their relation have an influence. A possible hierarchy between norms could help to establish the best suited legal basis. However, no hierarchy between the policies in EU external relations can be identified. Article 21(2) TEU lists principles and objectives of EU external relations and these objectives are streamlined with each other in specific policies.

Especially the exclusive competence of trade is investigated regarding its scope. In *Daiichi Sankyo*, the Court argued 'a European Union act falls within the common commercial policy if it relates specifically to international trade in that it is essentially intended to promote, facilitate or govern trade and has direct and immediate effects on trade'.[106] Also other objectives, such as sustainable development, can be covered by trade if the provisions in the international agreement are not intended 'to regulate the levels of social and environmental protection in the Parties' respective territory'.[107] In the development policy, characterised as a parallel competence, the Court turns the test around by focusing on the content of the non-development norms. However, development, endowed with broad objectives[108] or a broad 'notion'[109] incorporates other objectives and can absorb them as long as these other policies and their norms in the international agreement do not contain 'distinct objectives that neither are secondary nor indirect to the objectives of development cooperation'[110] (see Chapter 8).

In the case of international agreements, the centre of gravity remains an issue but multiple CFSP and TFEU legal bases could be reconciled in their procedure. Article 218 TFEU serves as single treaty-making procedure and paragraphs 6 and 8

[104] See for instance Case C-300/89 *Commission v Council* (*Titanium Dioxide*), ECLI:EU:C:1991:244, para 10.

[105] P Leino, 'The Institutional Politics of Objective Choice: Competence as a Framework for Argumentation' in S Garben and I Govaere (eds) *The Division of Competences between the EU and the Member States: Reflections on the Past, the Present and the Future* (Oxford, Hart Publishing, 2017) 227.

[106] Case C-414/11 *Daiichi Sankyo v DEMO*, ECLI:EU:C:2013:520, para 51.

[107] Opinion 2/15 (*Singapore*), ECLI:EU:C:2017:376, paras 147 and 166.

[108] Case C-268/94 *Portugal v Council*, ECLI:EU:C:1996:461, para 7.

[109] Case C-377/12 *Commission v Council* (*Philippines*), ECLI:EU:C:2014:1903, para 43. The Advocate General Mengozzi defined it as multi-faceted, see, Case C-377/12 *Commission v Council* (*Philippines*), Opinion of AG Mengozzi ECLI:EU:C:2014:29, para 40.

[110] Case C-377/12 *Commission v Council* (*Philippines*), ECLI:EU:C:2014:1903.

determine the voting procedure. Article 37 TEU confirms that the EU can conclude a CFSP international agreement and the procedure is solely determined by Article 218 TFEU. However, if the agreement is exclusively CFSP, Article 218(6) does not apply. The participation of the EP through consultation or consent is then excluded and limited to an information right (Article 218(10) TFEU) (see Chapter 9).

In practice, several TFEU-based horizontal agreements (association agreements and framework partnership and cooperation agreements) include CFSP provisions but not all of these agreements have a CFSP legal base. This is the case, for example, for the Association Agreement with Kosovo, which covers political dialogue (Articles 11–15). The agreement is based on Articles 31, 37 TEU and Article 217 TFEU.[111] In this case, the association agreement requires unanimously voting according to Article 218(8)(2). Hence, the primarily non-CFSP agreement has the same voting requirement in the Council and the participation of the EP remains the same despite including a CFSP legal base. This situation, however, changes decisively when the legal basis is found in the trade and/or development policy. For these legal bases, the Council decides by qualified majority voting. All new and comprehensive FTAs[112] are linked to a separate partnership and cooperation agreement. The Framework Agreement on Comprehensive Partnership and Cooperation between the EU (and its Member States) and Vietnam also addresses in Articles 8 to 10 political provisions covering the prohibition of the proliferation of weapons of mass destruction, small and light arms and combatting terrorism.[113] The Council decision on the signing of the agreement, however, does not refer to Articles 31 and 37 TEU as legal bases.[114]

With regard to the choice of a legal basis, the Council demonstrates a flexibility (or inconsistency) which is more a political than a legal choice. For instance, the Council has exceptionally based its adopting measure on two legal bases with different voting requirements. The accession of the EU to the Treaty of Amity and Cooperation in Southeast Asia refers to Articles 37 and 31(1) TEU as well as Articles 209 and 212 in conjunction with Articles 218(6) and 218(8)(2) TFEU.[115] This indicated that the Council held the position that the differences in the voting could be reconciled by

[111] Council Decision (EU) 2015/1988 of 22 October 2015 on the signing, on behalf of the Union, of the Stabilisation and Association Agreement between the European Union and the European Atomic Energy Community, of the one part, and Kosovo, of the other part [2015] OJ L290/4.

[112] In reaction to the *Singapore* Opinion, the new approach of the Council is that a separate Investments Agreement (IPA) will be negotiated next to an FTA. Draft Council Conclusions on the negotiation and conclusion of EU trade agreements, Brussels, 8 May 2018, 8622/18.

[113] Framework Agreement on Comprehensive Partnership and Cooperation between the European Union and its Member States, of the one part, and the Socialist Republic of Vietnam, of the other part [2016] OJ L329/8.

[114] Instead the following legal bases apply: 'Articles 79(3), 91, 100, 207 and 209 in conjunction with Article 218(5)', Council Decision (EU) 2012/279 of 14 May 2012 on the signing, on behalf of the Union, of the Framework Agreement on Comprehensive Partnership and Cooperation between the European Union and its Member States, of the one part, and the Socialist Republic of Vietnam, of the other part [2012] OJ L137/1.

[115] Council Decision (CFSP) 2012/308 of 26 April 2012 on the accession of the European Union to the Treaty of Amity and Cooperation in Southeast Asia [2012] OJ L154/1. At the stage of the signature and conclusion, the CFSP legal base was dropped. See on this and another example, Agreement continuing the International Science and Technology Centre [2017] OJ L37/3; Naert (n 97) 403–8.

voting unanimously.[116] In addition, the Council is open to the addition of legal bases for procedural purposes and in addressing Member States' concerns about competences.[117] These practices have been attacked by the Commission for contaminating supranational procedures and derailing the centre of gravity test by compromising legal certainty – similar to the illegal practice of hybrid acts in case of mixed agreements.[118] In the case of the Association Agreement with Ukraine, the authorisation to sign of the agreement was based on three Council decisions.[119] The first found its legal basis in Articles 31(1), and 37 TEU for the CFSP aspects,[120] the second is founded on Article 217 TFEU but excludes rights under Article 17 of the Association Agreement with Ukraine which covers equal treatment of workers.[121] This provision was adopted by a separate third Council decision finding its legal basis in Article 79 (2)(b).[122] The inclusion of a separate Council decision based on the legal base from Title V of Part Three of the TFEU (Area of Freedom, Security and Justice) was thought to be necessary because these legal bases trigger the application of Protocol 21 to the benefit of Ireland and UK and Protocol 22 to the benefit of Denmark.[123] These Protocols explain the opt-out of these countries and allow them to decide for themselves whether

[116] See, however, the Cooperation agreement with Afghanistan where Art 37 is mentioned in the Council Decision (next to Arts 207 and 209 TFEU) but only forms a procedural and not a substantial legal base): Council Decision (EU) 2017/434 of 13 February 2017 on the signing, on behalf of the Union, and provisional application of the Cooperation Agreement on Partnership and Development between the European Union and its Member States, of the one part, and the Islamic Republic of Afghanistan, of the other part [2017] OJ L67/1.

[117] On this motivation and dropping CFSP legal bases and leaving it for the Member States to exercise it as part of their national competences in the framework of a mixed agreement, Gosalbo-Bono and Naert (n 32) 28–29.

[118] Case C-28/12 *Commission v Council* (*Hybrid Act*), ECLI:EU:C:2015:282, concerning Decision (EU) 2011/708 of the Council and of the Representatives of the Governments of the Member States of the European Union [2011] OJ L283/1 adopted in one hybrid supranational and intergovernmental act an international agreement for EU and Member States (signing and provisional application of the agreement), which stated expressly that the Council and the representative of the governments of the EU Member states adopted this decision in a meeting within the Council. This consequently changed the voting rules for this decision from qualified majority voting foreseen in Art 218 TFEU to intergovernmental unanimity.

[119] This number is excluding the separate Council decision approving the conclusion of Euratom based on Art 101 Euratom: Council Decision (EU) 2014/670 of 23 June 2014 approving the conclusion, by the European Commission, on behalf of the European Atomic Energy Community, of the Association Agreement between the European Union and the European Atomic Energy Community and their Member States, of the one part, and Ukraine, of the other part [2014] OJ L278/8 (Council Decision Approving The Conclusion Of Euratom).

[120] Council Decision (EU) 2014/295 of 17 March 2014 on the signing, on behalf of the European Union, and provisional application of the Association Agreement between the European Union and the European Atomic Energy Community and their Member States, of the one part, and Ukraine, of the other part [2014] OJ L161/1.

[121] Council Decision (EU) 2014/668 of 23 June 2014 on the signing, on behalf of the European Union, and provisional application of the Association Agreement between the European Union and the European Atomic Energy Community and their Member States, of the one part, and Ukraine, of the other part [2014] OJ L 278/1.

[122] Council Decision (EU) 2014/669 of 23 June 2014 on the signing, on behalf of the European Union, of the Association Agreement between the European Union and the European Atomic Energy Community and their Member States, of the one part, and Ukraine, of the other part, as regards the provisions relating to the treatment of third-country nationals legally employed as workers in the territory of the other party [2014] OJ L 278/6.

[123] For other examples of an inconsistent practice see, Gosalbo-Bono and Naert, 'The Reluctant (Lisbon) Treaty and its implementation in the practice of the Council' (n 32) 52.

they wish to be bound by this provision of the agreement.[124] However, this practice is only justifiable for sectoral readmission agreements but, in this case, contradicts the principle that the procedure has to follow the legal base and not the other way around.

In addition to the Council's tendency to add legal bases for political and pragmatic reasons, the question arises of how the centre of gravity test can apply when policies are inherently multi-aimed as in these so-called horizontal trade or association agreements. All EU external relations policies can pursue multiple aims as highlighted by the chapeau clauses in Article 21 TEU and Article 205 TFEU. As far as this practice has reached the Court of Justice (PCAs with *Philippines* and *Kazakhstan* cases) it confirms a strict centre of gravity test and the absorption of other policies and potential other legal bases under certain conditions.

In the *Philippines* case, the Council added separate legal bases for migration, environment and transport next to development and trade for the Partnership and Cooperation Agreement with the Philippines. The Commission disputed these additions and argued that this was covered by development policy and its legal and political instruments. In such, the Commission specifically relied on the pre-Lisbon case *Portugal v Council* (Case C-268/94) on the qualification as a development agreement with India.

Case C-268/94 *Portugal v Council*, ECLI:EU:C:1996:461

7 In order to qualify as a development cooperation agreement for the purposes of Article 130y of the Treaty, an agreement must pursue the objectives referred to in Article 130u. Article 130u(1) in particular makes it clear that those are broad objectives in the sense that it must be possible for the measures required for their pursuit to concern a variety of specific matters.

39 It must therefore be held that the fact that a development cooperation agreement contains clauses concerning various specific matters cannot alter the characterization of the agreement, *which must be determined having regard to its essential object and not in terms of individual clauses, provided that those clauses do not impose such extensive obligations concerning the specific matters referred to that those obligations in fact constitute objectives distinct from those of development cooperation.* [emphasis added]

Analysing the objective and content of each of the provisions in the fields of energy, tourism, culture, drug abuse control and protection of intellectual property, the Court concluded that the provisions were not distinct from those of development cooperation. In the *Philippines* case, the Court added that, for a development and trade

[124] See a comparable situation with the social security and Switzerland, EEA and Turkey Agreement and the UK's initiated annulment proceeding, for instance: Case C-431/11 *United Kingdom of Great Britain and Northern Ireland v Council*, ECLI:EU:C:2013:589; see also on this, Dashwood, 'EU and Member State Acts in the Negotiation, Conclusion, and Implementation of International Agreements' (n 92) 217.

agreement, the centre of gravity is assessed by reviewing the provisions in the agreement and assessing whether these provisions include specific obligation changing the character of the development agreement.

Case C-377/12 *Commission v Council (Philippines)*, ECLI:EU:C:2014:1903

35 In this instance, it must be determined whether, among the provisions of the Framework Agreement, those relating to the readmission of nationals of the contracting parties, to transport and to the environment also fall within development cooperation policy or whether they go beyond the framework of that policy and therefore require the contested decision to be founded on additional legal bases.

48 In light of all those considerations, it is necessary, for the purposes of the determination specified in paragraph 35 of the present judgment, to examine whether the provisions of the Framework Agreement relating to readmission of nationals of the contracting parties, to transport and to the environment also contribute to the pursuit of the objectives of development cooperation and, if so, whether those provisions do not nevertheless contain obligations so extensive that they constitute distinct objectives that are neither secondary nor indirect in relation to the objectives of development cooperation.

The Court could not deny that the provision of readmission of nationals of the contracting parties, Article 26(3) of the Framework Agreement, contained specific obligations. However, they were not considered extensive enough to 'constitute objectives distinct from those of development cooperation that are neither secondary nor indirect in relation to the latter objectives'.[125] This finding was based on the argument that the readmission of nationals still necessitates the separate conclusion of an international readmission agreement.

The *Philippines* case enabled the multifaceted development policy to absorb other policies with the limitation that they may not cover separate and extensive legal obligations that constitute distinct objectives separate from development policy. Accordingly, individual provisions will be investigated for their legal content. Norms must prove that they create direct and distinct obligations to justify a separate legal basis. However, if the definition of a policy is based on its context found in policy documents and its inherent objectives of the international agreement, other 'multifaceted' policies next to development policy can be identified.

Especially association policy has a broad notion and Association Agreements comprehensively cover cooperation throughout all EU policies. Consequently, similar

[125] Case C-377/12 *Commission v Council (Philippines)*, ECLI:EU:C:2014:1903, para 59.

conclusions should be drawn and Article 217 TFEU can absorb other legal bases in line with the *Philippines* case. However, do these findings also extend to the CFSP norms found in Association Agreements or partnership and cooperation agreements or is the distinct nature of CFSP norms (Article 40 TEU) to be honoured by including a CFSP legal base?

The addition of a CFSP legal basis was tested with the Enhanced Partnership and Cooperation Agreement with Kazakhstan, the signing and provisional application found its legal basis in Articles 37 and 31(1) TEU and Articles 91, 100(2) and 207 and 209 TFEU (see also Chapter 9).[126] Whereas the Commission did not challenge these legal bases, it did attack the Council decision on the position to be adopted on behalf of the EU in the Cooperation Council established under the Partnership Agreement based on Article 218(9) TFEU to which Article 31(1) TEU was added and the unanimous voting procedure in the Council applied. The Court concluded that in this specific case, the substantive legal basis must be assessed to determine the voting procedure for paragraph 9.[127]

The *Kazakhstan* ruling confirms the centre of gravity for multi-aim or horizontal agreements. These agreements do not require other legal bases of different sectoral policies for quantitative and qualitative reasons. Quantitative because the majority of the provisions fall into one main horizontal policy and qualitative because the other provisions, such as CFSP-related provisions, are not concrete enough in their obligation nor distinct enough to justify a separate CFSP legal base. This ruling is, however, not unproblematic because CFSP-related provisions cannot *qua* nature determine in detail concrete obligations. Secondly, the Court did not address how to do justice to Article 40 TEU and to respect the specific nature of CFSP. The Council could possibly either not execute the CFSP competence or decide to 'outsource' the CFSP cooperation into sectoral CFSP agreements and separate from the Partnership and Cooperation Agreements or Association Agreements. The practice of including CFSP legal bases in horizontal agreements could, however, exceptionally prevail if the agreement has two components and a strong CFSP aim (see further Chapter 9).[128]

[126] Council Decision (EU) 2016/123 of 26 October 2015 on the signing, on behalf of the European Union, and provisional application of the Enhanced Partnership and Cooperation Agreement between the European Union and its Member States, of the one part, and the Republic of Kazakhstan, of the other part [2016] OJ L 29/1. See also for the same legal bases, Council Decision (EU) 2018/1552 of 28 September 2018 on the position to be taken, on behalf of the European Union, within the Cooperation Council established by the Partnership and Cooperation Agreement between the European Communities and their Member States, of the one part, and the Republic of Azerbaijan, of the other part, with regard to the adoption of the EU-Azerbaijan Partnership Priorities [2018] OJ L260/20.

[127] And in difference to the Case C-81/13 *United Kingdom of Great Britain and Northern Ireland v Council of the European Union*, ECLI:EU:C:2014:2449 where the decision falling within the field covered in Art 48 TFEU and adopted in the context of an association agreement was intended not to supplement or amend the institutional framework of that agreement.

[128] Examples of this practice are the so-called Strategic Partnership Agreements, as for instance, the one with Japan, where the political and security element is an important component. Legal bases were Arts 37 TEU and 212 TFEU, Council Decision (EU) 2018/1197 of 26 June 2018 on the signing on behalf of the European Union, and provisional application of the Strategic Partnership Agreement between the European Union and its Member States, of the one part, and Japan, of the other part [2018] OJ L216/1.

M Cremona, 'The Principle of Conferral and Express and Implied External Competences' in E Neframi and M Gatti (eds) *Constitutional Issues of EU External Relations Law* (Baden-Baden, Nomos, 2018) 33–34

The prevailing impression is that ... external competence is still highly fragmented. Certainly, there are many different potential legal bases in the Treaties, express and implied, and disagreements about the appropriate legal basis for international action have not diminished. But if we examine the reality of practice over the last few years we can identify a different trend, towards a consolidation of EU external action ...

Two factors have certainly contributed to this trend. The first is the distinct preference on the part of the Court for choosing a single legal basis for a Union act, whether an autonomous measure or the decision concluding an international agreement ... The second factor is the wide scope of the EU's express external competences, and in particular to certain central external policy fields: the Common Foreign and Security Policy (CFSP), the Common Commercial Policy (CCP), development cooperation policy and Association Agreements.

V. The Broader Picture of EU External Relations Law

The relationship between EU and Member States competences is an intricate issue touching upon fundamental issues of the EU's external action. It also one of the most disputed fields between the EU and its Member States. EU competences and the choice of a legal basis, at first sight, appear to be based on extensive legal rules and principles developed over many years but at the same time cannot be detached from political struggles and choices of EU external actors and Member States. The 'complex mosaic of the external competences of the Union and its Member States'[129] has evolved over many years of jurisdiction and proceeds despite the attempt of its codification. At the same time, competence conflicts and the principles surrounding them have remained surprisingly 'frozen in time'. The *ERTA* case law from 1971 and its TFEU codification still dominate the academic and judicial discussion. The Advocate General in the *ERTA* case at the time argued in favour of a more restrictive approach to EU external competences. He denied (and contrary to the evolutionary verdict of the judges) a parallelism between internal and external competences with the arguments that it would contribute to legal ambiguity and might hamper the development of Union law.[130] And indeed, the so-called *ERTA* effect can contribute to the Member States'

[129] Joined Cases C-626/15 and C-659/16 *Antarctique*, Opinion of AG Kokott ECLI:EU:C:2018:362, para 6.
[130] Case 22/70 *Commission v Council* (*ERTA*), Opinion of AG Dutheillet de Lamothe, ECLI:EU:C:1971:23, paras 291–92.

unwillingness to legislate internally[131] and legal ambiguity has accompanied the evolution of implied external competences. The debate did not come to a standstill with the introduction of Article 3(2) TFEU and, in contrast, has gained pace. The lack of a proper distinction between the existence of an external power and its possible exclusivity, and the inapt codification (in light of the intricate case law rulings) have contributed to an avalanche of grand chamber rulings by the CJEU since Lisbon. Especially, the scope of policy of external policies and the combination of exclusive competences in form of trade and common fisheries policies with shared competences such as environment or CFSP resulted in legal conflicts.

The divisions between Council and Member States, and Commission and European Parliament run deep because competences, as much as the choice of the legal basis, influence the standing of the EU as a global actor but at the same time limit the room of international action for the individual Member States or specific institutions. The Court ends up in an ambivalent situation of becoming the final arbiter in political conflicts and reaffirming its meticulous pre-Lisbon case law as decisive for the codification and interpretation post-Lisbon. Consequently, the Treaty can only be understood under the backdrop of the complex case law of the CJEU and will remain a focus to understand the competences divide and legal bases. The undergrowth of procedural rules and principles created through external relations case law require sincere cooperation and an interinstitutional agreement between all external actors.

VI. Sources and Further Reading

Castillo de la Torre, F, 'The Court of Justice and External Competences after Lisbon: Some Reflections on the Latest Case Law' in P Eeckhout and M López-Escudero (eds) *The European Union's External Action in Times of Crisis* (Oxford, Hart Publishing, 2016) 129–86.

Claes, M and B De Witte, 'Competences: Codification and Contestation' in S Blockmans and A Lazowski (eds) *Research Handbook on EU institutional Law* (Cheltenham, Edgar Elgar Publishing, 2016) 46–87.

Cremona, M, 'Who Can Make Treaties? The European Union' in DB Hollis (ed) *The Oxford Guide to Treaties* (Oxford, Oxford University Press, 2012) 93–124.

Cremona, M, 'EU External Competence – Rationales for Exclusivity' in S Garben and I Govaere (eds) *The Division of Competences between the EU and its Member States* (Oxford, Hart Publishing, 2017) 133–50.

Cremona, M, 'External Competences and the Principle of Conferral' in R Schütze and T Tridimas (eds) *Oxford Principles of EU Law* (Oxford, Oxford University Press, 2018) 1110–40.

Cremona, M, 'The Principle of Conferral and Express and Implied External Competences' in E Neframi and M Gatti (eds) *Constitutional Issues of EU External Relations Law* (Baden-Baden, Nomos, 2018) 29–62.

[131] See also on this, PJ Kuijper 'Of "Mixity" and "Double-hatting", EU External Relations Law Explained', Inaugural Lecture (Amsterdam, Vossiuspers UvA, 2008) 8.

De Baere, G, 'EU External Action' in C Barnard and S Peers (eds) *European Union Law*, 2nd edn (Oxford, Oxford University Press) 710–60.

Gosalbo-Bono, R and F Naert, 'The Reluctant (Lisbon) Treaty and its Implementation in the Practice of the Council' in P Eeckhout and M López-Escudero (eds) *The European Union's External Action in Times of Crisis* (Oxford, Hart Publishing, 2018) 13–84.

Koutrakos, P, *EU International Relations Law*, 2nd edn (Oxford, Hart Publishing, 2015).

Kuijper, PJ, 'An Introduction to the Union External Action, Its Scope, Its Institutions and Its Instruments' in PJ Kuijper et al (eds) *The Law of the European Union*, 5th edn (Alphen aan den Rijn, Kluwer law International, 2018) 1231–62.

Kuijper, PJ, J Wouters, F Hoffmeister, G De Baere and T Ramopoulos, *The Law of EU External Relations: Cases, Materials, and Commentary on the EU as an International Legal Actor*, 2nd edn (Oxford, Oxford University Press, 2016).

Naert, F, 'The Use of the CFSP Legal Basis for EU International Agreements in Combination with Other Legal Bases' in J Czuczai and F Naert (eds) *The EU as a Global Actor Bridging Legal Theory and Practice*, liber amicorum *in Honour of Ricardo Gosalbo Bono* (Leiden, Brill/Nijhoff, 2017) 394–423.

Timmermans, C, 'CJEU Doctrine on Competences' in L Azoulai (ed) *The Question of Competence in the European Union* (Oxford, Oxford University Press, 2014) 155–67.

4

Instruments of EU External Action

Central Issues

- The European Union makes use of a variety of instruments in the conduct of its external relations. This chapter gives insight into the Union's 'toolbox' of instruments, distinguishing between 'hard law' and 'soft law' as well as between internal and international instruments.
- International agreements are the EU's legal external relations tools *par excellence*. They form the key instrument to allow the Union to interact with others in the global legal order and to establish legal relationships with third states and international organisations. If the EU lacked the competence to conclude international agreements, its external relations would be the object of study of mainly political scientists and international relations experts and not so much of lawyers. The main part of this chapter will therefore be devoted to the EU as an international treaty-maker.

I. A Typology of Instruments of EU External Action

In the typology of instruments used to carry out the EU's external action, we distinguish between instruments that are adopted within the EU legal order (internal) and those that are adopted by the Union in the international legal order (international). These may be instruments adopted by the EU alone (autonomous) or as a result of agreement between the Union and one or several other parties (conventional). These instruments can then be legally binding (hard law) or binding in other ways (soft law).

Within the Union, the legally binding, autonomous instruments are those stated in Article 288 TFEU: regulations, directives and decisions. The other instruments, sometimes referred to as 'non-legally binding' autonomous instruments, are recommendations and opinions listed in that article, but in practice there are many more 'soft law' instruments through which the EU acts on the international scene. In their international dimension, the legally binding, conventional instruments are the international agreements concluded by the Union; and in accordance with general international public law, the EU can also adopt unilaterally positions by which it will be legally bound. On the soft law side, the EU also regularly adopts conventional instruments such as Joint Declarations, or Memoranda of Understanding, or expresses its opinion through démarches which are diplomatic and political in nature. Despite the frequent reference to these instruments as 'non-legally binding', we treat these instruments as forming part of the EU legal order given that they may produce (interpretative) legal effects or may be committing the EU and/or its Member States in other ways.

A typology such as this one is of an ideal type. In practice, the line between internal and external, autonomous or conventional, soft or hard law, can be difficult to draw. In the day-to-day process of EU external relations policymaking, these three dimensions will intertwine into a complex mix of law and politics to reach desirable external policy outcomes. It is then crucial to keep in mind that in EU external relations *law*, politics matters to a great extent. When an instrument has been adopted as soft law and is therefore non-legally binding on the parties, and may have limited legal enforcement possibilities, that does not mean that it is not important. For example: the EU's 2016 Global Strategy on Foreign and Security Policy (see also Chapter 9) is an autonomous instrument of the Union that cannot be categorised within Article 288 TFEU, yet it is an influential conceptual rallying point in external policymaking. Since each external policy area possesses its own dynamic as to which of these instruments will be used more often and in which form, we refer the reader to the policy-specific chapters in this book.

II. Internal Instruments

A. Hard Law in EU External Relations

Article 288 TFEU

To exercise the Union's competences, the institutions shall adopt regulations, directives, decisions, recommendations and opinions.

A regulation shall have general application. It shall be binding in its entirety and directly applicable in all Member States.

A directive shall be binding, as to the result to be achieved, upon each Member State to which it is addressed, but shall leave to the national authorities the choice of form and methods.

A decision shall be binding in its entirety. A decision which specifies those to whom it is addressed shall be binding only on them.

Recommendations and opinions shall have no binding force.

All instruments the Union uses for legislating internal policy matters can and are being used in the context of EU external relations. A good knowledge of EU legislative and non-legislative instruments and the procedures through which they are adopted (Article 289 TFEU etc) is therefore imperative and for that we refer to relevant literature.[1]

The first three instruments named in Article 288 TFEU are legally binding, and will only enjoy that status if they are duly adopted in accordance with the procedure set out in the relevant competence-conferring article. For example, Article 194 TFEU (on energy) requires that the ordinary legislative procedure be used to adopt instruments in this domain (Article 289 TFEU) and only exceptionally the special legislative procedure. Regulations, Directives and Decisions all have their role to play in EU external relations.

Regulations can be relevant for external relations in at least two ways: they may regulate specifically a matter purely of external relevance or, where they organise an internal policy aspect, they may also have a degree of external relevance. Examples of the first aspect include the Trade Barriers Regulation and the many regulations adopted in relation to anti-dumping and countervailing duties as part of the EU's trade policy (see Chapter 7), the Financing Regulations of EU development cooperation (see Chapter 8) or Regulations organizing EU-Member State cooperation in certain areas.[2] These are examples which legally organise an aspect purely of EU external relations and, by their nature, have general application, are binding in their entirety and are directly applicable in all Member States.

Directives are focused on the result to be achieved, giving Member States a choice of form and method. It is uncommon that a Directive organises a purely external policy aspect, but where they regulate some aspect of the internal market, they very often acquire an international dimension.

Decisions mentioned in Article 288 TFEU may equally be relevant in external relations. Within the EU legal order, most Decisions are addressed to Member States, with fewer addressed to private parties and mostly in the area of competition law. Among others, decisions may also be found in anti-dumping and anti-subsidy proceedings (Chapter 7).

In the area of the Common Foreign and Security Policy (CFSP), the EU may also adopt Decisions, for instance imposing restrictive measures (sanctions) against other countries as well as legal and natural persons according to Article 215 TFEU (see Chapter 9).

These three legally binding instruments need to be adopted in accordance with the procedures set out in the relevant competence-conferring provision. Most often, this will be the ordinary legislative procedure as set out in Article 289 TFEU.

B. Soft Law in EU External Relations

Article 288 TFEU states that recommendations and opinions shall have no binding force. Beyond these two non-binding instruments mentioned in the Treaties, there are

[1] See D Chalmers, G Davies and G Monti, *European Union Law*, 4th edn (Cambridge, Cambridge University Press, 2019) ch 3 on 'Law-making'.

[2] See, for example, Regulation 847/2004/EC of the European Parliament and of the Council of 29 April 2004 on the negotiation and implementation of air service agreements between member states and third countries [2004] OJ L157/7.

many other measures which are generically referred to as 'soft law'. These are defined as 'rules of conduct that are laid down in instruments which have not been attributed legally binding force as such, but nevertheless may have certain (indirect) legal effects, and that are aimed at and may produce practical effects'.[3] In EU external relations, soft law occupies a prominent position. A non-exhaustive summary of soft law instruments includes: European Council Conclusions, Council Conclusions, Commission Communications, Joint Communications, Green Papers, White Papers, Non-Papers, Joint Papers, Joint Letters, Resolutions, Strategies, Statements, Arrangements, Working Arrangements, Inter-institutional Arrangements, Declarations, Resolutions, Action Plans, Reports, Interim Reports, Progress Reports, Programmes, and Memoranda.

One thing that soft law instruments all have in common is that they do not possess the legal effect of a Regulation or Directive because they have not been adopted through procedures laid down in the Treaties. However, they often will produce practical effects by setting in motion, or being part of, the external policy-making or legislative process. In that sense, soft law instruments will have to be 'adopted' by the relevant EU body within the scope of the role accorded to it by the Treaties. Soft law may not be utilised to avoid the principles of conferred powers (Article 5 TEU) or institutional balance (Article 13 TEU) and the absence of legal binding force does not allow an EU body to act as it pleases. In *France v Commission*, France sought an annulment of the Decision by which the Commission had adopted non-legally binding 'Guidelines on Regulatory Cooperation and Transparency' between the Commission and the US Trade Representative (USTR). France argued that the prerogatives of the Council had been infringed under what is now Article 218 TFEU, insofar as it constituted a binding agreement which the Council should adopt. The Commission stated that the institutional balance could not be affected since the guidelines were to be applied on a voluntary basis and lacked legal binding force.[4]

Case C-233/02 *France* v *Commission*, ECLI:EU:C:2004:173

38 By its first plea, the French Government merely submits that the Guidelines should have been concluded by the Council rather than by the Commission, in accordance with Article 300 EC [now in amended form Article 218 TFEU], since they constitute a legally binding agreement.

39 On the other hand, the French Government in no way claims that a measure exhibiting the characteristics of the Guidelines must, even if it has no binding force, come under the sole competence of the Council. There is therefore no need for the Court to extend the subject-matter of the action of which it is seized.

40 Nevertheless, this judgment cannot be construed as upholding the Commission's argument that the fact that a measure such as the Guidelines is

[3] The definition of soft law which we entertain is that of L Senden, *Soft Law in European Community Law* (Portland, Oregon, Hart Publishing, 2004) 112.

[4] Case C-233/02 *France v Commission*, ECLI:EU:C:2004:173, para 33.

> not binding is sufficient to confer on that institution the competence to adopt it. Determining the conditions under which such a measure may be adopted requires that the division of powers and the institutional balance established by the Treaty in the field of the common commercial policy be duly taken into account, since in this case the measure seeks to reduce the risk of conflict related to the existence of technical barriers to trade in goods.
>
> 41 Moreover, both the Transatlantic Economic Partnership and the Action Plan were approved by the Council, as is made clear in the memorandum of 9 April 2002 sent by the Commission to the committee set up pursuant to Article 133(3) EC [now in its amended form Article 207(3) TFEU] and the committee was regularly informed of the progress of the negotiations relating to the drafting of the Guidelines by the Commission's services.
>
> 42 In the light of that clarification, the intention of the parties must in principle be the decisive criterion for the purpose of determining whether the Guidelines are binding, as the Commission rightly contends.
>
> 43 In the present case, that intention is clearly expressed, ... in the text of the Guidelines itself, paragraph 7 of which specifies that the purpose of the document is to establish guidelines which regulators of the United States Federal Government and the services of the Commission 'intend to apply on a voluntary basis'. In those circumstances, and without its being necessary to consider the specific importance which the use of the terms 'should' or 'will' rather than 'shall' could assume in an international agreement concluded by the Community, it need only be stated that on the basis of that information, the parties had no intention of entering into legally binding commitments when they concluded the Guidelines.
>
> 44 As pointed out by the Commission, without contradiction by the French Government, the history of the negotiations confirms that the intention of the parties not to enter into binding commitments was expressly reiterated throughout the negotiations on the Guidelines.
>
> 45 It follows that the Guidelines do not constitute a binding agreement and therefore do not fall within the scope of Article 300 EC.

The Court ruled that even if a given instrument is non-binding, that this does not give an institution the power to adopt it. The application of the principles of conferral (Article 5 TEU) and institutional balance (Article 13 TEU) continue to apply and must be respected (see Chapter 2). While this case concerned an international soft legal instrument, the principle evidently applies across all kinds of soft law utilised by the European Union, internal or international. In paragraph 41, the Court then confirmed that the prerogatives of the Council had been duly respected by the Commission through approval of the overall Action Plan with the USA (another soft law instrument), and by regularly informing the working party responsible for Common Commercial Policy.

Many actors in EU external relations adopt a wide range of soft law instruments. In the following paragraphs we highlight 'Conclusions' adopted by the European Council and Council and 'Communications' adopted by the Commission and possibly the High Representative. Of all soft law instruments, these form the bread and butter of EU external policy making.

In the General Provisions on EU external action (Title V TEU), Article 22(1) TEU states that the European Council 'shall identify the strategic interests and objectives of the Union'. The European Council is one of the EU institutions and is legally empowered to adopt 'Decisions' to carry out its task. However, most often this institution executes its mandate to steer the Union through the adoption of 'Conclusions' at the end of its meetings. These are (meticulously) negotiated outcomes of meetings by the Heads of State and government and are crucial soft-law instruments because the Treaty endows the European Council with setting out the future direction of EU external action. Conclusions of the European Council will therefore trigger action at all levels of governance within the Union: within the Member States themselves, and within and between the EU institutions. European Council Conclusions may call on the Member States to refrain from certain action, may prompt the Council to flesh out a new policy direction, may approve the accession of a new Member State, or may decide the EU's position towards important international events. Thus, different actors will be implementing the strategic vision set out by the European Council in accordance with Article 22 TEU.

A constant interaction and cross-referencing takes place through the progressive adoption of Conclusions by the European Council and the Council. In all policy areas of EU (external) action, a steady stream of Conclusions is adopted to follow up ongoing policy matters and push them in the desirable direction. The substance of these Conclusions will be prepared in the preparatory bodies of the Council (see Chapter 1), notably COREPER and the Working Groups. These bodies will receive much of their input not only from Member State representatives, but also from the Commission and the European External Action Service.

Communications are most often adopted by the Commission, sometimes jointly with the High Representative if it falls within the scope of his/her competence. The extract below explains the role of the Commission in formulating the European Neighbourhood Policy (see also Chapter 13) and analyses the importance of soft legal Communications in doing so.

B Van Vooren, 'A Case Study of "Soft Law" in EU External Relations: The European Neighbourhood Policy' (2009) 34 *European Law Review* 696, 704–06

The first ENP Communication was published in March 2003, entitled, 'Wider Europe –Neighbourhood: A New Framework for Relations with our Eastern and Southern Neighbours' ... In subsequent years, Commission Communications have at regular (yearly) intervals evaluated and redirected the course of this policy, and it is no exaggeration to state that these milestone Communications have formed the backbone of this policy ... The role of the Wider Europe Communication includes a definite steering function. Recall that steering instruments independently indicate the direction of future policy and the principles on which such action is based. The Wider Europe Communication is evidently not independent in that it exists in a policy vacuum, and is undoubtedly interrelated with [relevant European Council Conclusions, Council Conclusions,] the financing instruments of that time and the existing bilateral agreements with third countries. Nevertheless, as the title of the instrument indicates, it seeks to lay down '[a] new framework for relations with the Eastern and Southern Neighbours' and can be considered steering both in terms of its substantive and methodological proposals. In terms of substance, this Communication famously stated that the neighbours should be offered the prospect of participation in the four freedoms and their 'stake in the internal market' .... Subsequent Council Conclusions also did nothing to refute that position: the Council Conclusions of March 18, 2003 welcomed this Communication, and the ensuing debate focused on issues which were more contentious: the need to differentiate between third countries and the fact that the ENP is separate from the question of EU membership. The Communication is thus a steering instrument since it adds a distinct direction to a policy which is a priority for the Union as a whole [as decided at the level of the Council and European Council].

Soft law is also increasingly used as an alternative to the formal international agreements that we will address in the next section.

III. International Agreements

A. The Legal Nature of International Agreements

International agreements remain the key legal tool to regulate the EU's external relations. Perhaps surprisingly, they are not defined by the Treaties. Article 216 TFEU merely provides the following:

Article 216(1) TFEU

The Union may conclude an agreement with one or more third countries or international organisations where the Treaties so provide or where the conclusion of an agreement is necessary in order to achieve, within the framework of the Union's policies, one of the objectives referred to in the Treaties, or is provided for in a legally binding Union act or is likely to affect common rules or alter their scope.

Notwithstanding the absence of a definition (or perhaps exactly because of this) it is obvious that the term should be read in its international context and thus the international law definitions apply. The 1969 Vienna Convention on the Law of Treaties (Article 2(1)(a)) does not define international agreements but provides a definition of the concept of a 'treaty'.

Vienna Convention on the Law of Treaties, Article 2(1)(a)

'Treaty' means an international agreement concluded between States in written form and governed by international law, whether embodied in a single instrument or in two or more instruments and whatever its particular designation.

As we will see, the international agreements concluded by the EU can be said to follow this description and are therefore 'treaties' in the sense of the Vienna Convention. The same may hold true for international contractual obligations that have not been given the heading of 'international agreement', but bear labels such as 'Convention'. Agreements may also be concluded in the form of an exchange of letters. As long as parties agree that they have entered into a legal commitment, the EU Treaty procedures apply. This has been confirmed by the Court of Justice when it described an international agreement as any undertaking entered into by entities subject to international law which has binding force, whatever its formal designation.[5] The fact that the 1969 Vienna Convention refers to states only is solved by the 1986 Vienna Convention on the Law of Treaties between States and International Organizations and between International Organizations (not yet in force), which contains a similar definition in Article 2(1)(a), taking into account the fact that international organisations may also conclude treaties. Although the concluding procedure is 'governed by EU law' (as the conclusion of treaties between states is usually regulated by domestic foreign relations law), there is no doubt that the final agreement between the EU and a third state or international organisation is an instrument of international law.

The use of the term 'international agreement' rather than 'treaty' therefore has no specific legal meaning, but at least prevents confusion; in EU law, the term '(the) Treaties' is usually reserved for the TEU and the TFEU as well as for the accession Treaties – in other words, for EU primary law.

[5] See Opinion 1/75 *(Re Understanding on a Local Cost Standard)*, ECLI:EU:C:1975:145. See also Case C-327/91 *France* v *Commission*, ECLI:EU:C:1994:305, para 27.

The internal binding nature of concluded international agreements is confirmed by Article 216(2) TFEU.

Article 216(2) TFEU

Agreements concluded by the Union are binding upon the institutions of the Union and on its Member States.

The first part of this sentence follows from the international law concept of *pacta sunt servanda*, codified in the Vienna Convention on the Law of Treaties (Article 26), which states: 'Every treaty in force is binding upon the parties to it and must be performed by them in good faith.' This also implies that the second part of Article 216(2) is, in fact, not a reflection of that principle, as the Member States are not (necessarily) parties to agreements concluded by the Union. Member States are therefore bound by EU international agreements on the basis of EU law, rather than international, law. In many cases, the implementation of these agreements calls for Member State action. In a way, international agreements are similar to secondary legislation enacted by the EU and, as an 'integral part' of the EU legal order, they cannot be ignored by the Member States. Yet, as will be explained in Chapter 5, this does not automatically lead to supremacy and direct effect of all agreements concluded by the EU.

B. The EU as a Treaty-Maker

Article 216(1) TFEU provides for a competence of the EU in various circumstances, which were discussed in Chapter 3. In addition, the current Treaties list a number of areas in which the EU has an express competence to conclude international agreements, such as for the readmission of illegal immigrants (Article 79(3) TFEU); environmental policy (Article 191(4) TFEU); common commercial policy (Article 207 TFEU); development cooperation (Article 209(2) TFEU; association agreements (Article 217 TFEU); the monetary union (Article 219(1) and (3) TFEU); and common foreign, security and defence policy (Article 37 TEU).

The EU is a party to well over 1,200 international agreements. As the graph below shows, it has become an increasingly active treaty-maker during the first half-century of its existence, with its activity slowing down in the last couple of years.[6]

[6] See the Treaties Office Database of the European External Action Service. Available at: http://ec.europa.eu/world/agreements/default.home.do.

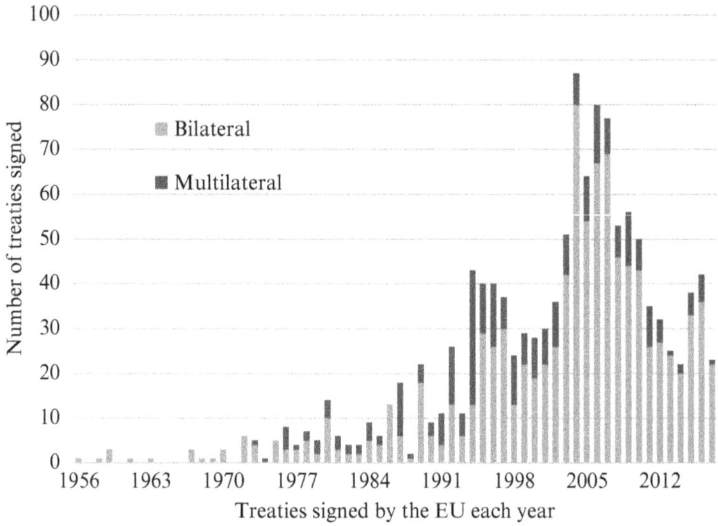

Graph: The EU as an international treaty maker: Bilateral and multilateral agreements signed by the EU in the course of its history (1956–2017).
Source: Joris Larik, Louise Bekkers and Tess Baker, based on data from the Treaties Office Database of the European External Action Service. Available at: http://ec.europa.eu/world/agreements/default.home.do.

With its increasing internal competences, the scope of the Unions' legal dealings with third states was extended to almost all areas covered by the Treaties. The EU's Treaties Office Database lists international agreements in the areas of Agriculture, Coal and Steel, Commercial Policy, Competition, Consumers, Culture, Customs, Development, Economic and Monetary Affairs, Education, Training, Youth, Energy, Enlargement, Enterprise, Environment, External Relations, Fisheries, Food Safety, Foreign and Security Policy, Fraud, Information Society, Internal Market, Justice, freedom and security, Public Health, Research and Innovation, Taxation, Trade, and Transport.

C. Concluding International Agreements

The Vienna Convention on the Law of Treaties uses the term 'conclusion' for the entire treaty-making process, which encompasses, inter alia, the phases of negotiation, initialling and signing. By contrast, the EU Treaties clearly differentiate between the different phases. While the procedures in principle apply to all EU policy areas, we will note that special rules apply for international agreements concluded in the area of CFSP (see also Chapter 9).

(i) Negotiating an International Agreement

According to Article 218 TFEU, which lists the entire procedure, the process is very much in the hands of the Council. In practice the Commission is also a central actor in both the preparation and the negotiations themselves.

Article 218(2) TFEU

The Council shall authorise the opening of negotiations, adopt negotiating directives, authorise the signing of agreements and conclude them.

Yet, it starts with a recommendation to the Council from the Commission or the High Representative, as noted in the subsequent paragraph:

Article 218(3) TFEU

The Commission, or the High Representative of the Union for Foreign Affairs and Security Policy where the agreement envisaged relates exclusively or principally to the common foreign and security policy, shall submit recommendations to the Council, which shall adopt a decision authorising the opening of negotiations and, depending on the subject of the agreement envisaged, nominating the Union negotiator or the head of the Union's negotiating team.

Thus, apart from the situation where an agreement 'relates exclusively or principally' to CFSP – in which case the High Representative is in charge of making recommendations – the Commission shall submit recommendations to the Council. History has shown that the question of whether an agreement 'relates exclusively or principally' to CFSP (including CSDP) may be difficult to answer (Chapters 3 and 9). Based on an (unpublished) recommendation by either the Commission or the High Representative, the Council adopts a decision which, in turn, forms the basis for the negotiations. Depending on the subject matter of the agreement this is done by qualified majority voting or unanimity. The context of paragraph 3 suggests that the Commission will be appointed as the negotiator, unless it is a CFSP agreement, in which case it will be the High Representative. This would also be in line with the general role of the Commission in the Union's external representation (Article 17(1) TEU). In a hybrid agreement, which covers both CFSP and other matters, both the Commission and the High Representative may be part of the negotiating team.

The negotiator acts within the framework of special directives issued by the Council.

Article 218(4) TFEU

The Council may address directives to the negotiator and designate a special committee in consultation with which the negotiations must be conducted.

The special committees are usually composed of national governmental experts, through which the Council will be able to control the process.

For the common commercial policy, such a special committee is specifically designated, in addition to several other rules applying to treaty-making in this area (see also Chapter 7). Article 218(1) TFEU refers to 'specific provisions laid down in Article 207 [TFEU]', which reads:

Article 207(3) TFEU

The Commission shall make recommendations to the Council, which shall authorise it to open the necessary negotiations. The Council and the Commission shall be responsible for ensuring that the agreements negotiated are compatible with internal Union policies and rules.

The Commission shall conduct these negotiations in consultation with a special committee appointed by the Council to assist the Commission in this task and within the framework of such directives as the Council may issue to it. The Commission shall report regularly to the special committee and to the European Parliament on the progress of negotiations.

This provision ensures that the Commission is the only negotiator in the CCP. At the same time, it is to report to the European Parliament. While the latter institution is not mentioned explicitly in the regular negotiating procedure, based on Article 218(10) TFEU the 'European Parliament shall be immediately and fully informed at all stages of the procedure'. Whenever consent of the Parliament is required, it can obviously use this as an instrument to claim to be heard during the earlier stages. In any case, the EP's involvement seems to be better guaranteed since the conclusion of the 2010 inter-institutional agreement, on the basis of which the Commission agreed to involve Parliament during the various stages of the process.[7] The role of the European Parliament in the procedure to conclude international agreements in the area of CFSP was further addressed by the Court in cases such as *Mauritius* and *Tanzania* (see below and Chapter 9).

Article 218(5) TFEU

5. The Council, on a proposal by the negotiator, shall adopt a decision authorising the signing of the agreement and, if necessary, its provisional application before entry into force.

[7] Framework Agreement on Relations between the European Parliament and the European Commission [2010] OJ L 304/47.

In general, negotiations end with the 'signing' of the text. As the excerpt below shows, a specific Decision to sign must first be taken at EU-level. Unless the agreement enters into force upon signature, it must still go through the domestic legal processes before it can be ratified and enter into force.

Council Decision 2012/471/EU of 13 December 2011 on the signing, on behalf of the Union, of the Agreement between the United States of America and the European Union on the use and transfer of Passenger Name Records to the United States Department of Homeland Security [2012] OJ L 215/1

THE COUNCIL OF THE EUROPEAN UNION,

Having regard to the Treaty on the Functioning of the European Union, and in particular Articles 82(1)(d) and 87(2)(a), in conjunction with Article 218(5) thereof,

Having regard to the proposal from the European Commission,

...

HAS ADOPTED THIS DECISION:

Article 1

The signing of the Agreement between the United States of America and the European Union on the use and transfer of Passenger Name Records to the United States Department of Homeland Security is hereby authorised on behalf of the Union, subject to the conclusion of the said Agreement.

Article 2

The President of the Council is authorised to designate the person(s) empowered to sign the Agreement on behalf of the Union.

...

Article 4

This Decision shall enter into force on the day of its adoption.

Done at Brussels, 13 December 2011.

For the Council

The President

Article 218(5) TFEU also refers to the possibility of provisional application (compare Article 25 Vienna Convention), which allows the parties to provisionally apply the treaty provision, pending the entry into force of the agreement. Considering the long period of time that is usually needed for the ratification of mixed agreements (see below), this is a useful transitional arrangement.

(ii) Concluding an International Agreement

The actual conclusion of an international agreement takes place on the basis of another Decision by the Council:

Article 218(6) TFEU

6. The Council, on a proposal by the negotiator, shall adopt a decision concluding the agreement …

Such concluding decisions are comparable to other decisions taken by the Council and lists the considerations leading to the decision, the legal basis as well as further procedural points.

Council Decision 2012/472/EU of 26 April 2012 on the conclusion of the Agreement between the United States of America and the European Union on the use and transfer of passenger name records to the United States Department of Homeland Security [2012] OJ L 215/4

THE COUNCIL OF THE EUROPEAN UNION,

Having regard to the Treaty on the Functioning of the European Union, and in particular Article 82(1)(d) and Article 87(2)(a), in conjunction with Article 218(6)(a) thereof,

Having regard to the proposal from the European Commission,

Having regard to the consent of the European Parliament

…

HAS ADOPTED THIS DECISION:

Article 1

The Agreement between the United States of America and the European Union on the use and transfer of passenger name records to the United States Department of Homeland Security is hereby approved on behalf of the Union.

The text of the Agreement is attached to this Decision.

Article 2

The President of the Council shall designate the person(s) empowered to proceed, on behalf of the Union, to the exchange of the notifications provided for in Article 27 of the Agreement, in order to express the consent of the Union to be bound by the Agreement.

Article 3

This Decision shall enter into force on the day following that of its publication in the Official Journal of the European Union.

Done at Luxembourg, 26 April 2012.

For the Council

The President

Although in practice sometimes signature and conclusion are combined in one Decision, the EU procedure follows the logic presented in the Vienna Conventions on the Law of Treaties. Even before a formal entry into force, signing the agreement already has legal consequences. As Article 18 of the Vienna Convention notes, 'a State is obliged to refrain from acts which would defeat the object and purpose of a treaty' that it has signed.

While the Council Decision is the *internal* instrument needed for conclusion of the agreement, *externally*, the EU's expression of its consent to be bound and to become a party to the agreement is usually done by notifying the other parties or the depositary by way of an instrument of ratification (a letter in which the ratification is expressed).

Article 218(8) TFEU provides the voting rules applicable within the Council when taking the abovementioned decisions.

Article 218(8) TFEU

The Council shall act by a qualified majority throughout the procedure.

However, it shall act unanimously when the agreement covers a field for which unanimity is required for the adoption of a Union act as well as for association agreements and the agreements referred to in Article 212 [TFEU] with the States which are candidates for accession. The Council shall also act unanimously for the agreement on accession of the Union to the European Convention for the Protection of Human Rights and Fundamental Freedoms; the decision concluding this agreement shall enter into force after it has been approved by the Member States in accordance with their respective constitutional requirements.

Hence, QMV is the rule, but unanimity shall be used in certain specific cases as well as in relation to subject matters that would internally also require unanimity. Examples include CFSP/CSDP matters (Article 24(1)(2) TEU) or indirect taxation (Article 113 TFEU). In addition, Article 207(4) TFEU refers to the need for unanimity in relation to certain 'sensitive' trade agreements.

The above-mentioned decision to conclude the Agreement with the United States refers to the 'consent of the European Parliament'. Indeed, taking into account the fact that, once concluded, international agreements form an integral part of the Union's legal order and that their content may directly affect EU citizens and companies, it should not come as a surprise that the European Parliament enjoys a prominent role in the regular legislative procedure as well as in the adoption of international agreements. Article 218(6) TFEU calls for the consent of the European Parliament in the following cases:

Article 218(6)(a) TFEU

…

(i) association agreements;
(ii) agreement on Union accession to the European Convention for the Protection of Human Rights and Fundamental Freedoms;
(iii) agreements establishing a specific institutional framework by organising cooperation procedures;
(iv) agreements with important budgetary implications for the Union;
(v) agreements covering fields to which either the ordinary legislative procedure applies, or the special legislative procedure where consent by the European Parliament is required.

The European Parliament and the Council may, in an urgent situation, agree upon a time limit for consent.

In other cases, the European Parliament shall just be 'consulted' and shall deliver its opinion within a time limit which the Council may set depending on the urgency of the matter. In the absence of an opinion within that time limit, the Council may act. The only exception is for cases 'where agreements relate exclusively to the common foreign and security policy'. However, based on the general rule in Article 218(10) TFEU, the 'European Parliament shall be immediately and fully informed at all stages of the procedure'. As the CJEU clarified in a case relating to the transfer of suspected pirates to Mauritius, 'the information requirement laid down in Article 218(10) TFEU applies to any procedure for concluding an international agreement, including agreements relating exclusively to the CFSP'.[8] In the words of the Court, failing to keep the EP properly informed would inhibit its ability to exercise democratic scrutiny of EU external action and can lead to the invalidity of Council Decisions.

[8] Case C-658/11 *Parliament and Commission v Council (Mauritius)*, ECLI:EU:C:2014:2025, para 85.

Case C-658/11 *Parliament v Council (Mauritius)*, ECLI:EU:C:2014:2025

79 ... the information requirement arising under Article 218(10) TFEU is prescribed in order to ensure that the Parliament is in a position to exercise democratic scrutiny of the European Union's external action and, more specifically, to verify that its powers are respected precisely in consequence of the choice of legal basis for a decision concluding an agreement.

80 Lastly, as regards the consequences of infringement of Article 218(10) TFEU in terms of the validity of the contested decision, it should be noted that the procedural rule laid down in that provision constitutes an essential procedural requirement within the meaning of the second paragraph of Article 263 TFEU and its infringement leads to the nullity of the measure thereby vitiated.

81 That rule is an expression of the democratic principles on which the European Union is founded. In particular, the Court has already stated that the Parliament's involvement in the decision-making process is the reflection, at EU level, of the fundamental democratic principle that the people should participate in the exercise of power through the intermediary of a representative assembly ...

(iii) Terminating or Suspending an International Agreement

Article 218 TFEU not only provides for the creation of new international agreements, but also contains rules regarding their 'suspension':

Article 218(9) TFEU

The Council, on a proposal from the Commission or the High Representative of the Union for Foreign Affairs and Security Policy, shall adopt a decision suspending application of an agreement and establishing the positions to be adopted on the Union's behalf in a body set up by an agreement, when that body is called upon to adopt acts having legal effects, with the exception of acts supplementing or amending the institutional framework of the agreement.

This is an internal rule only. Any suspension of an international agreement should be in accordance with the international law of treaties. This may also be the reason why suspension clauses are included in agreements with third states. Reasons for the EU to suspend an agreement may relate to violations of 'essential elements' such as human rights protection and the rule of law (see also Chapter 10).

Partnership and Cooperation Agreement between the European Union and its Member States, of the one part, and the Republic of Iraq, of the other part [2012] OJ L 204/20

Article 2: *Basis*

Respect for democratic principles and human rights, as laid down in the Universal Declaration of Human Rights and other relevant international human rights instruments, as well as for the principle of the rule of law, underpins the internal and international policies of both Parties and constitutes an essential element of this Agreement.

...

Article 12: *Non-execution of agreement*

...

2. If one of the Parties considers that the other Party has failed to fulfill an obligation under this Agreement it may take appropriate measures. Before doing so, it must supply the Cooperation Council within 30 days with all the relevant information required for a thorough examination of the situation with a view to seeking a solution acceptable to the Parties. ...

3. By way of derogation from paragraph 2, any Party may immediately take appropriate measures in accordance with international law in case of:

...

(b) violation by the other Party of the essential elements of this Agreement referred to in Articles 2 and 5. ...

The termination of international agreements by the EU should be in line with the international law of treaties, in particular the procedure provided for within the agreement in question. Article 218(9) TFEU does not explicitly address the issue of which procedure is to be followed within the EU, though it would seem reasonable to assume that the same procedure should be followed as for the suspension of an agreement and due regard should be had for parliamentary involvement in the case of politically significant agreements.

(iv) Soft Legal International Agreements

Apart from the international agreements concluded on the basis of Article 218 TFEU, the Union may enter into international soft law commitments such as codes of conduct, declarations, or joint statements. Despite their intended 'non-binding' nature, such international soft legal agreements cannot be ignored in the EU legal order.

They may form the interpretative context for legal agreements and may even commit the Union through the development of customary law or as unilateral declarations. They are usually described as 'political commitments', rather than legal commitments. However, this may be misleading: soft and hard law instruments may both be politically important. Nevertheless, in international instruments, the EU often underlines their non-legal binding nature by reference to their 'political nature only'.

A key example of a political commitment is a memorandum of understanding (MoU). MoUs reflect a political agreement between the Union and one or more third states or international organisations, with the express intention not to become bound in a legal sense. A legal basis is not always necessary to establish a competence for the institutions to enact such commitments. Notably, Article 17(1) TEU calls upon the Commission 'to ensure the Union's external representation', while Article 18(2) TEU states that the 'High Representative shall conduct the Union's common foreign and security policy'. This leaves ample room for these actors to choose the means through which to do so. In practice, the conclusion of political commitments does not differ much from the conclusion of international agreements: the Commission – or in the case of MoUs in the area of CFSP, the High Representative – will negotiate and sign the agreement, whereas the actual conclusion is in the hands of the Council.

Memorandum of Understanding Between the African Union and the European Union on Peace, Security and Governance, 23 May 2018

The African Union (hereinafter referred to as 'AU') and the European Union (hereinafter referred to as 'EU')

jointly referred to as 'Participants' to this Memorandum of Understanding (hereinafter referred to as the 'MoU');

Share the following understanding:

1. PRINCIPLES

EU and AU security interests are closely intertwined and this calls for a strategic approach between the AU and the EU. Through the Joint Africa-EU Strategy (JAES), the Africa-EU Peace and Security Partnership was defined as one of its strategic priority areas. This was more recently reaffirmed during the AU-EU Summit in Abidjan in 2017, where the Participants recognised the need to strengthen the relationship and agreed to put their partnership on peace and security on a more solid and structured basis. The Participants intend to steadily expand their longstanding cooperation ...

3. AREAS OF COOPERATION

(i) In order to facilitate the attainment of the objectives listed under point 2 above, the Participants endeavour to cooperate in relevant areas for the promotion of good governance and maintenance of peace, security and stability in the AU and the EU, including by:

a. Deepening their strategic coordination and enhancing joint action, where appropriate, during all phases of the conflict cycle: tackling root causes, prevention, early warning, early response, crisis management, conflict resolution, resilience, Security Sector Reform, stabilisation, mediation and fight against impunity;

...

p. Jointly cooperate on climate-related security threats across peace and security policy areas, to strengthen the capacity to address the risks of instability, insecurity and conflict arising from the interaction of climate change and social, economic, demographic and political factors. ...

6. NON-BINDING CHARACTER

This MoU is not intended to create rights or impose any legal obligations under domestic or international law in respect of either Participant.

7. FINAL PROVISIONS

The collaboration based on this MoU is to start on the date of signature.

Either Participant may end the collaboration based on this MoU by giving three (3) months' advance notice to the other Participant.

Signed in Brussels on the 23rd of May 2018.

For the African Union Commission	For the European Union
Chairperson of the African Union Commission	High Representative of the Union for Foreign Affairs and Security Policy/ Vice-President of the Commission

We may further also distinguish administrative and exploratory arrangements. The former are non-binding arrangements that are functional to the cooperation between the administration of the Union and the administration of third countries or international organisations. They may be considered executive agreements which are necessary to allow (mainly) the Commission and the High Representative to fulfil the administrative and operational parts of their mandate. Examples include the Trust Funds and Co-Financing Framework Agreement between the Commission and the World Bank or the Administrative Agreement concluded between the Central Commission for the Navigation of the Rhine and the European Commission on a systematic exchange of information and regular meetings to coordinate activities. Exploratory arrangements are the outcome of the talks that precede the negotiation of an international agreement. They are thus part of the negotiation process and are negotiated by the Commission or the High Representative.

In general, the reason for soft arrangements is that the EU and third states may wish to settle their relations but wish to avoid being taken to Court in case of non-compliance. The downside is that these arrangements run the risk of by-passing some valuable procedural rules. In the scarce case law on informal arrangements concluded by the EU, however, the Court had no difficulty in deciding positively on admissibility and, in fact, underlined the value of EU law principles, both in a procedural and a substantive sense. The claim that an arrangement is not meant to 'create legal rights or obligations under international law' does not always imply that it falls completely outside EU law.[9]

RA Wessel, 'Normative Transformations in EU External Relations: The Phenomenon of "Soft" International Agreements' (2020) 43 *West European Politics* (forthcoming)

Where the concept of 'legalization' has been addressed in political science literature in particular, the choice for 'softer' arrangements rather than international agreements seems to form an example of what can perhaps be termed 'de-legalisation'. Possible consequences of this shift have also been prescribed and include the risk that these instruments are not subject to appropriate safeguards, that parliamentary influence (by the European Parliament as well as by national parliaments) is by-passed and that transparency is affected. …

Soft law instruments in EU external relations may bear various labels, including Joint Communications, Joint Letters, Strategies, Arrangements, Progress Reports, Programmes or Memoranda of Understanding. Recent examples include the EU-Turkey 'Statement' on refugees or the EU-Libya 'Memorandum of Understanding' concerning the observation of the 2017 presidential and representatives' elections, the 2016 'Decision' of the European Council to clarify the objective and purpose of the EU-Ukraine Association Agreement, or the 'Joint Way Forward' on migration issues between Afghanistan and the EU of 2016.

… [S]everal reasons are mentioned in the literature that account for the use of soft arrangements in EU external relations, such as 'the need to increase the efficiency of external action, to allow greater smoothness in negotiation and conclusion of the instrument, or to enhance the margin of discretion of the signatories in the fulfilment of commitments. In addition, non-binding agreements may be more suitable to the political sensitivity of the subject of the agreement or to its changing nature …'[10]

[9] See for instance Case C-660/13 *Council v Commission* (*Swiss MoU*), ECLI:EU:C:2016:616.

[10] P García Andrade, 'The Distribution of Powers Between EU Institutions for Conducting External Affairs through Non-Binding Instruments' (2016) 1 *European Papers* 115, 116.

In general, however, this comes at a price as the legislator is by-passed in favour of the executive. The use of the many forms of soft law in EU external relations runs the risk of creating a parallel universe, inside the EU legal order, with the potential of violating basic EU principles. Hence, while both the procedures to conclude international agreements and the Court's abundant case law on these procedures are meant to guarantee consistency within the Union's legal order and a well-balanced role of the institutions, arrangements not following the procedural rules of Article 218 TFEU may seriously disturb this system of checks and balances and possibilities for legal review.

IV. Types of International Agreements

A. Mixed Agreements

International agreements may be concluded in all areas of Union activity (see Chapter 4). The reason is that whenever the Union exercises more competences internally, there is simply no possibility that external relations will be left solely in the hands of the Member States. Only in few instances are competences fully and exclusively in the hands of the European Union. This is the source of the notion of 'mixity': in its external relations the Union will have to combine ('mix') its competences with those that are still in the hands of the Member States so as to cover the full spectrum of the external action at stake. In the case of international agreements, this often implies that both the Union and its Member States need to become a party to the agreement. Depending on the kinds of competences at hand, mixity can be either compulsory of 'facultative' (optional).

Allan Rosas, 'Mixity Past, Present and Future: Some Observations' in M Chamon and I Govaere (eds), *EU External Relations Post-Lisbon: The Law and Practice of Facultative Mixity* (Leiden, Brill/Nijhoff, forthcoming 2020)

A … distinction may be made between *obligatory* and *facultative* mixity, the former arising in the case of coexistent competence (the existence of an exclusive national competence makes a Union-only agreement legally impossible) and the latter arising in the case of a concurrent competence. It goes without saying that mixity is facultative also in the case of a parallel competence (but in the areas of development cooperation and humanitarian aid it is common that the Union and the Member States act separately although in parallel). The following typology emerges:

I. Parallel competence -> facultative mixity
II. Shared competence
   A. Coexistent competence -> obligatory mixity
   B. Concurrent competence -> facultative mixity

The distinction between obligatory and facultative mixity is thus relevant for any general attempt to avoid mixity altogether and opt for Union-only agreements. ...

While some dicta contained in Opinion 2/15 relating to a trade agreement with Singapore[11] could have been interpreted as suggesting that mixity in such a case is not facultative but obligatory, the subsequent judgment in *Germany v Council* confirmed that a shared competence (supposing that it is of a 'concurrent' nature) may be fully exercised by the Council, implying the conclusion of a Union-only agreement.[12]

(i) Negotiation and Conclusion of Mixed Agreements

As indicated above, the notion of mixity follows from the fact that, in many cases, both the EU and the Member States are competent to engage in external action or that international agreements cover a variety of areas, all of which are subject to different divisions of competence. Only in a few cases would the EU be exclusively competent to conclude an agreement, which implies that, in many cases, the Member States will also have to become a party. While, for political reasons, this allows Member States to remain present and visible on the international stage, the need to have a mixed agreement obviously complicates, as well as prolongs, the process of concluding international agreements. Mixed agreements can be both bilateral (between the EU/MS and a third state or international organisation) and multilateral (between the EU/MS and several other states and/or organisations).

While for the EU the general procedure in Article 218 TFEU continues to apply, several issues render the conclusion of mixed agreements special. At all stages of the process, account will have to be taken of the possibly different positions of the EU and its Member States. It is essential for the EU and its Member States to speak with one voice during the negotiations, to prevent a third party from abusing a possible difference of opinion. The European Union (read: European Commission) therefore

[11] Opinion 2/15 (*Singapore*), ECLI:EU:C:2017:376, eg para 244.
[12] Case C-600/14 *Germany v Council (COTIF)*, ECLI:EU:C:2017:935.

has a strong preference to act as the sole negotiator on behalf of the Member States. However, this depends on the sensitivity of the topic. In any case, it is important to agree on a common position, but as negotiations, by definition, require some flexibility on both sides, negotiators would need some freedom to change their position.

The complexity is strengthened by the fact that it is virtually impossible to clearly distinguish between the areas falling under (exclusive) EU competence and areas in which the Member States still have a (perhaps large) role to play. Many agreements are a clear mix of issues, which calls for both the EU and the Member States to accept a certain lack of clarity. A strict division of competences would call for separate roles for the EU and the Member States during the process, but this could seriously harm the negotiating position and would make it very unattractive for third states to enter into negotiations on a mixed agreement. Indeed, for third states, it is often far from clear where the competence lies; they would rather deal with one combined counterpart.

A way to clarify the division of competences is through 'declarations of competence', which lay down the respective competences of the EU and its Member States in the different fields addressed by the agreement. However, in practice, this often encounters some difficulties.

A Delgado Casteleiro, 'EU Declarations of Competence to Multilateral Agreements: A Useful Reference Base?' (2012) 17 *European Foreign Affairs Review* 491, 509

In theory, declarations of competence are supposed to give legal certainty to non-EU parties to mixed agreements with regard to where responsibilities reside. By externalizing the internal division of competence, the declarations of competence give an a priori solution to the questions of implementation and compliance with mixed agreements. They also provide legal certainty to third parties that neither the EU nor its Member States will try to avoid their responsibility in case of a breach by hiding behind the other. …

Although in theory, declarations could provide an easy solution to the different responsibility scenarios which were identified in the introduction, a closer look suggests otherwise. First, the internal division of competence is anything but simple. Competences do not only change over time, but also vary depending on the stage of the life-cycle of the agreement (eg, negotiation, conclusion or implementation). Second, it appears that declarations create more problems than they solve. In terms of content, they are vague and fail really to clarify when the EU is responsible under each specific mixed agreement. … Moreover, they need to be constantly updated so as to keep up with the evolution of the EU's powers, but they are not. Consequently, after close examination, it is clear that declarations of competence do not answer the question of EU competence to implement mixed agreements but instead create more uncertainty.

The problem with these declarations is that the division of competences is dynamic: what can be a reasonable description for the division at the time of the conclusion of an agreement may very well change over the years. From an internal point of view, the exact delimitation of competences is not required, as confirmed by the Court in Ruling 1/78.[13] Nevertheless, third states may demand it, so they know who to address in cases of conflicts on the interpretation or implementation.

Because they become full parties to them, Member States also need to sign and conclude mixed agreements. This implies that a ratification procedure is necessary in each Member State. Although swift ratification is possible even in very complex cases (as the case of the WTO agreement showed), the fact that each Member State can delay the process because of complex parliamentary or federal reasons usually creates a time-consuming exercise. The latter is illustrated by the negotiations on the Comprehensive Economic and Trade Agreement between the EU and Canada, the signature of which was delayed due to the Belgian region of Wallonia withholding its consent in late 2016. While in certain cases provisional application may be possible as a stopgap (see above), in practice, the Council will await ratification by all Member States before concluding the agreement on behalf of the EU. In case the process takes too much time, the Council can propose an interim agreement, to which the Member States are not a party, but which will at least allow the Union and the third party to proceed in an area controlled by the EU.

Once they become parties, Member States are bound to the agreement. Considering the rule that 'Agreements concluded by the Union are binding upon the institutions of the Union and on its Member States' (Article 216(2) TFEU) and the fact that mixed agreements are also to be considered an 'integral part of EU law',[14] the question may arise as to why we have mixed agreements at all. The answer lies in the fact that the Union is simply not competent to exclusively claim all areas of Union law; the Treaties foresee a division of competences which is also to be reflected in external relations. Nonetheless, in both cases, the Member States are bound by the agreements. The difference is that in agreements concluded by the EU they are bound by EU law as they do not have a direct legal relationship with the third party. By contrast, in mixed agreements, Member States are bound by international treaty law; at the same time, they will have to abide by the relevant rule of EU law (eg, in relation to the duty of sincere cooperation; see below).

In some cases, not all Member States become party to a mixed agreement ('partial mixity', or 'incomplete mixity'). When we follow the above rules, this would imply that those Member States that have not themselves become a party are not bound under international law, but they are still bound under EU law according to Article 216(2) TFEU.

[13] Ruling 1/78 *Re Convention on the Physical Protection of Nuclear Materials, Facilities and Transports*, ECLI:EU:C:1978:202.

[14] Case C-431/05 *Merck Genéricos-Produtos Farmacêuticos v Merck*, ECLI:EU:C:2007:496.

(ii) Mixed Agreements and the Duty of Sincere Cooperation

As was shown in Chapter 2, the 'duty of sincere cooperation' as laid down in Article 4(3) TEU is an important principle in EU external relations law. Here, we revisit this duty specifically in the context of mixed agreements.

C Hillion, 'Mixity and Coherence in EU External Relations: The Significance of the Duty of Cooperation' in C Hillion and P Koutrakos (eds), *Mixed Agreements Revisited: The EU and its Member States in the World* (Oxford, Hart Publishing, 2010) 114

It has been argued that the duty of [sincere] cooperation plays an increasingly significant role in the law of mixed agreements. Its greater significance stems from its progressive legalisation and the elaboration of its normative content by the Court. While it has mostly entailed an obligation of conduct, the normative strength of which may vary depending on the specific form of mixity of the agreement at hand, the duty of cooperation may also involve, albeit exceptionally, an obligation of result. Hence, Member States and EU judicial authorities may be called upon to ensure uniformity in the application of provisions of the agreement, where those have a procedural nature and are capable of applying at national and Union levels. The Court has also articulated enforceable procedural obligations (eg of consultation and information) that bind Member States and EU institutions, including where they exercise their powers. Such procedural obligations, which are still being elaborated, entail that while exercising their recognised powers, Member States and institutions should be aware and respectful of each other's undertakings, if not responsible for facilitating each other's tasks ultimately to promote the common good. The Court thus fosters an attitude of mutual support, rather than an instinctive territoriality reflex in the EU–Member States interactions. That apparent increasing jurisprudential emphasis on cooperation as a contribution to consistency and coherence in the organisation of the EU external relations counterbalances the traditional competence-distribution case law. It may signal lesser judicial apprehension, and perhaps more acceptance of the plurality that characterises the EU posture on the international stage.

Ruling 1/78 is generally seen as the starting point of the case law on the duty of sincere cooperation. This judgment was delivered in the framework of the European Atomic Energy Community (EAEC) and contained an interpretation of Article 192 EURATOM, which is phrased in similar terms as in Article 4(3) TEU.

Several subsequent cases revolve around the situations related to (collective) Member State action which negatively affected independent external action by the

Union, especially in mixed agreements. The CJEU stressed the importance of sincere cooperation in Opinion 1/94 regarding the WTO, where both the EU and the Member States are represented.

Opinion 1/94 *(WTO)*, ECLI:EU:C:1994:384, para 108

... where it is apparent that the subject-matter of an agreement or convention falls in part within the competence of the Community and in part within that of the Member States, it is essential to ensure close cooperation between the Member States and the Community institutions, both in the process of negotiation and conclusion and in the fulfilment of the commitments entered into. That obligation to cooperate flows from the requirement of unity in the international representation of the Community ....

Another prominent case in this context is *PFOS*, which was discussed in Chapter 2.[15] The case concerned unliteral action by a Member State in the framework of the Stockholm Convention on Persistent Organic Pollutants – also a mixed agreement. While mixity is the logical – although, as we have seen, not automatic – consequence of the existence of a shared competence, cases such as *PFOS* underline that Member States cannot act entirely on their own and must take into account existing or planned Union action.

The developments in relation to 'mixity' will have consequences for the relationship between international and EU law as Member States' powers to act internationally may be further restrained on the basis not only of ongoing but also future EU action. One may regard this as the inevitable result of the (external) coming of age of the EU.

(iii) The Question of International Responsibility

It would seem logical that the EU itself would be responsible for violations of international (treaty) law (see Chapter 5). In relation to mixed agreements, however, the question of responsibility is even more complex. Under international treaty law, third parties have a right to address both the EU and its Member States in cases of (perceived) violations. When a declaration of competence (see above) has been drafted, this may guide third parties to the most appropriate addressee but, in other cases, a general joint responsibility is to be assumed.[16] At the same time, international dispute settlement mechanisms such as those at the WTO have come to accept the prominent role of the EU as more than just a collective 'veil' draped over the Member States.

[15] Case C-246/07 *Commission v Sweden (PFOS)*, ECLI:EU:C:2010:203.
[16] See Case C-53/96 *Hermès International*, ECLI:EU:C:1998:292.

PJ Kuijper, 'International Responsibility for EU Mixed Agreements' in C Hillion and P Koutrakos (eds), *Mixed Agreements Revisited: The EU and its Member States in the World* (Oxford, Hart Publishing, 2010) 226

What the cases tell us is that international tribunals, notably WTO Panels, are close to accepting the special character of the executive federalism of the European Union, and to not assuming that Member State acts in the framework of such federalism require attribution of these acts to the Member States instead of to the Union. The cases also show that tribunals are, without much ado, also ready to accept that certain matters within a mixed agreement, such as customs in the WTO Agreement, fall within exclusive Union competence and should be treated as such, in spite of assertions by other WTO Members that EU Member States as WTO Members are equally fully responsible for the performance of these obligations.

B. Association Agreements

Article 217 TFEU

The Union may conclude with one or more third countries or international organisations agreements establishing an association involving reciprocal rights and obligations, common action and special procedure.

Although the notion of 'association' is not defined by the Treaties (apart from the fact that it would involve 'reciprocal rights and obligations, common action and special procedure'), practice has revealed that association agreements are indeed a special type of agreement, used to establish far-reaching relationships with third countries. Association agreements are characterised by a number of specific features:

- The legal basis for their conclusion is Article 217 TFEU.
- There is an intention to establish close economic and political cooperation.
- Joint bodies for the management of the cooperation are created, which are competent to take decisions that bind the contracting parties.
- Most Favoured Nation treatment is included.
- A privileged relationship between the European Union and its partner is established (in the words of the Court: 'a special, privileged link').[17]
- A clause on the respect of human rights and democratic principles is systematically included and constitutes an essential element of the agreement (see above).

[17] Case 12/86 *Demirel v Stadt Schwabusch Gmünd*, ECLI:EU:C:1987:400, para 9.

Association agreements (albeit not always under that name) currently exist, among others, with countries in the EU's neighbourhood (see also Chapter 13), including Turkey (entered into force in 1964), Iceland, Norway, and Liechtenstein (1994), the Palestinian Authority (1997 on an interim basis), Tunisia (1998), Israel (2000), Morocco (2000), Jordan (2002), North Macedonia (2004), Algeria (2005), Albania (2009), Montenegro (2010), Serbia (2013), Bosnia and Herzegovina (2015), and Ukraine (2017). Moreover, association agreements also exist with countries farther away from the EU, such as the African, Caribbean and Pacific (ACP) group of states (2003) and Chile (2005).

The different associations have led to a complex web of relations between the Union, its Member States and several third countries. This has led to varying degrees of integration with the EU short of becoming a Member State.

A Łazowski, 'Enhanced Multilateralism and Enhanced Bilateralism: Integration Without Membership in the European Union' (2008) 45 *Common Market Law Review* 1433, 1437–38

The origins of enhanced multilateralism go back to the 1980s when EFTA countries and EEC Member States embarked on negotiations on the European Economic Space. The outcome of those was the emergence of the European Economic Area in 1994. As already argued, thus far it is the most advanced model of integration without membership in the European Union. In substantive terms it covers almost the entire internal market *acquis* as supplemented by numerous flanking policies (ie environmental protection). The sophisticated institutional arrangement serves as a guarantor of the homogeneity of the legal space. One has to admit that so far is has been very successful in this respect.

The first years of the XXIst century have seen further deepening of the relations between the EU/EC and the EEA-EFTA countries. It merits attention that this process has been arranged alongside the EEA; nevertheless is full of integration flavours. The prime example is the extension of the Schengen framework to Norway and Iceland (as well as the envisaged extension to Liechtenstein). ...

Association agreements were often used as a first step towards accession and, indeed, many of the current Members first enjoyed an association status. In other cases, they are the follow-ups to so-called cooperation agreements, which may be concluded on the basis of Article 212 TFEU.

C. Accession to International Organisations

As will be discussed in Chapter 6, the Union may become a member of other international organisations once its competence can be established and the other organisation is (as per its own founding document as well as politically) willing to welcome the EU as a member, despite it not being a state. Membership of international organisations typically implies joining the constituent treaty of the organization, which may include the need to become party to an accession treaty.

In relation to the question as to whether an agreement 'establishing a European laying-up fund for inland waterway vessels' is compatible with the provisions of the EU Treaties, the Court argued the following:

Opinion 1/76 *(Draft Agreement establishing a European laying-up fund for inland waterway vessels)*, ECLI:EU:C:1977:63, para 5

[T]he Community is ... not only entitled to enter into contractual relations with a third country in this connexion but also has the power, while observing the provisions of the Treaty, to cooperate with that country in setting up an appropriate organism such as the public international institution which it is proposed to establish under the name of the 'European laying-up fund for inland waterway vessels'.

The Treaties do not provide for a specific procedure for agreements to establish or join international organisations, which implies that the general rules of Article 218 TFEU apply.

D. (The Future of) International Agreements Concluded by the Member States Only

(i) Member States' Treaty-Making Capacity

Obviously, the competence of the EU to conclude international agreements did not deprive the Member States of their individual competence to conclude treaties. Over the years, however, the expansion of the competences of the EU and of its external activities called for a careful assessment of the extent to which the agreements concluded by the Member States would be in conflict with EU law.

As far as international agreements concluded prior to the establishment of the European Economic Community or prior to a country's accession to the EU are concerned, the matter is regulated by Article 351 TFEU:

Article 351 TFEU

The rights and obligations arising from agreements concluded before 1 January 1958 or, for acceding States, before the date of their accession, between one or more Member States on the one hand, and one or more third countries on the other, shall not be affected by the provisions of the Treaties.

To the extent that such agreements are not compatible with the Treaties, the Member State or States concerned shall take all appropriate steps to eliminate the incompatibilities established. Member States shall, where necessary, assist each other to this end and shall, where appropriate, adopt a common attitude.

In applying the agreements referred to in the first paragraph, Member States shall take into account the fact that the advantages accorded under the Treaties by each Member State form an integral part of the establishment of the Union and are thereby inseparably linked with the creation of common institutions, the conferring of powers upon them and the granting of the same advantages by all the other Member States.

In other words: these agreements shall not be affected, but any incompatibility with EU law should be removed. This again reveals an uneasy relationship between international treaty law and the primacy of EU law. After all, in case of conflicts between provisions in an international agreement and EU law, Member States may be obliged to give priority to EU law based on the general rules on primacy but, whenever these arguments are not accepted by a third party (which is not bound on the basis of the *pacta tertiis nec nocent nec prosunt* rule, see above), they have every right to ask for a correct implementation of the agreement.

From the EU side, the pressure on Member States to at least find interpretations which would allow for EU law to work properly may be difficult. In its case law, the Court held that international agreements 'may in no circumstances permit any challenge to the principles that form part of the very foundations of the [EU] legal order'.[18] As the Court noted in the *Burgoa* case, Article 351 TFEU is about protecting the rights of the third countries (rather than the Member States) and the duties of the Member States (rather than their rights) under both EU and international law.

Case C-812/79 *Attorney General* v *Juan C Burgoa*, ECLI:EU:C:1980:231

8 … the purpose of [Article 351 TFEU] is to lay down, in accordance with the principles of international law, that the application of the Treaty does not affect the duty of the Member State concerned to respect the rights of non-member countries under a prior agreement and to perform its obligations thereunder.

[18] Joined Cases C-402/05 P and C-415/05 P *Kadi and Al Barakaat International Foundation v Council and Commission,* ECLI:EU:C:2008:461, para 304.

> 9 Although the first paragraph of [Article 351 TFEU] makes mention only of the obligations of the Member States, it would not achieve its purpose if it did not imply a duty on the part of the institutions of the Community not to impede the performance of the obligations of Member States which stem from a prior agreement. However, that duty of the Community institutions is directed only to permitting the Member State concerned to perform its obligations under the prior agreement and does not bind the Community as regards the non-member country in question.

Considering the extensive legal relations Member States maintain with third states, the potential for conflict is real. Several options have been developed in practice to prevent conflicts with EU law. Firstly, for new agreements the best solution seems to be to prevent Member States from negotiating and concluding agreements in areas which fall under EU competence. In the case of an exclusive competence it is clear that the Member States are simply no longer allowed to conclude the agreement. In a shared or parallel competence the case law indicates that they would be strongly recommended to cooperate with the EU institutions, in particular the Commission, to prevent conflict with (planned) EU activities. In *Kramer*, the Court held that Member States are 'not to enter into any commitment within the framework of these [fisheries] conventions which could hinder the Community in carrying out the tasks entrusted to it'.[19]

Secondly, regarding agreements which have already been concluded by the Member States, the principle of primacy implies that such agreements are seen as a form of national legislation. In contrast to agreements concluded by the EU, they do not rank above secondary EU law. This means that they will simply have to be implemented in accordance with EU law and that Member States have an obligation to renegotiate possible conflicting provisions with the respective third parties. If such agreements have been concluded by Member States after their membership of the EU started, the special protection enshrined in Article 351 TFEU does not apply.

EU membership and the evolution of EU law has serious consequences for a large number of existing international agreements. This is exemplified by the so-called *BITs* (Bilateral Investment Treaties) cases.[20] The EU's increasing powers in the field of foreign investment not only serve as an example of new international activity, but also has repercussions for BITs between the Member States and third countries. The outcome of the *BITs* cases is that all (over 1,000) of these BITs have to be renegotiated to prevent incompatibilities with EU law. The long-term objective of the EU is to replace Member State BITs with EU Investment Agreements.[21] In the meantime,

[19] Joined Cases C-3/76, C-4/76 & C-6/76 *Kramer*, ECLI:EU:C:1976:114, para 44.

[20] Case C-205/06 *Commission v Austria*, ECLI:EU:C:2009:118; Case C-249/06 *Commission v Sweden*, ECLI:EU:C:2009:119; Case C-118/07 *Commission v Finland*, ECLI:EU:C:2009:715.

[21] A Dimopoulos, 'The BITs Cases and their Practical and Doctrinal Implications' in J Díez-Hochleitner et al (eds), *Recent Trends in the Case Law of the Court of Justice of the European Union (2008–2011)* (Madrid, La Ley, 2012) 737–58.

an authorisation system should combine the validity of the BITs that were concluded based on international treaty law with the primacy of EU law.[22]

Where, traditionally, Member States are not a priori pre-empted from rule-making in an area of shared competence, the *BITs* cases reveal a number of Member States obligations (even when the EU itself has not legislated) caused by the 'hypothetical incompatibility' of existing international agreements with EU law.[23] The Court argued that even a perceived – but not yet materialised – conflict between the international agreements and EU law (in this case relating to the free movement of capital) brings Article 351 TFEU into play. The incompatibilities could jeopardise the future exercise of EU competences. In that sense, the judgments indeed continue the trend of 'decoupling the international law obligations from the EU law obligations and subsequently subordinating the former from the latter'.[24]

As in earlier case law, in the *BITs* cases, the Court does not simply deny the relevance of international law, but claims that it cannot be used in this case. Indeed, the fact that the EU has powers 'on a matter which is identical to or connected with that covered by an earlier agreement concluded between a Member State and a third country, reveals the incompatibility with that agreement where, first the agreement does not contain a provision allowing the member State concerned to exercise its rights and to fulfil its obligations as a member of the [EU] and, second, there is also no international law mechanism which makes that possible'.[25] By arguing that international law itself does not offer solutions, the Court has no choice but to preserve the autonomy of EU law by limiting Member States' traditional treaty-making competences under international law.

Another area where agreements between the Member States and third countries were kept in place but put under EU supervision due to progressing EU legislation is civil aviation.[26] This concerns approximately 2,000 so-called 'Open Skies' agreements that require amendment.[27]

(ii) Member States' Agreements in Areas of Exclusive Competence

A somewhat ironic situation occurs in areas where the EU enjoys an exclusive competence but lacks the possibility to use it. For several reasons, Member States may participate in international agreements falling (at least partly) within exclusive Union competence. The case law of the CJEU illustrates this possibly complex situation.

[22] Regulation 1219/2012 of the European Parliament and of the Council of 12 December 2012 establishing transitional arrangements for bilateral investment agreements between Member States and third countries [2012] OJ L351/40.

[23] N Lavranos, 'Case Note, Cases C-205/06 and C-249/06' (2009) 103 *American Journal of International Law* 716, 717.

[24] Ibid, 720.

[25] Case C-205/06 *Commission v Austria*, ECLI:EU:C:2009:118, para 37.

[26] Regulation (EC) 847/2004 on the negotiation and implementation of air service agreements between Member States and third countries [2004] OJ L 157/7.

[27] See from the relevant litigation at the CJEU, eg, C-467/98 *Commission v Denmark (Open Skies)*, ECLI:EU:C:2007:244; C-476/98 *Commission v Germany (Open Skies)*, ECLI:EU:C:2002:63.

The *Intertanko* case was about a request for a preliminary ruling on the compatibility between a Directive on ship-source pollution and the International Convention for the Prevention of Pollution from Ships (also known as Marpol 73/78). The CJEU ruled that the Convention, to which the EU is not a party, fell outside its jurisdiction as there was no transfer of powers: 'It is true that all the Member States are parties to Marpol 73/78. Nevertheless, in the absence of a full transfer of the powers previously exercised by the Member States to the Community, the latter cannot, simply because all those states are parties to Marpol 73/78, be bound by the rules set out therein, which it has not itself approved.'[28] The content of such agreements can become part of EU law through secondary legislation. Through 'good faith' and the duty of sincere cooperation, conventions such as Marpol get an interpretative function within EU law. These situations illustrate the need for the Union to occasionally accept a role by the Member States in areas of exclusive competence.

M Cremona, 'Member States Agreements as Union Law' in E Cannizzaro, P Palcheti and RA Wessel (eds), *International Law as Law of the European Union* (Leiden, Martinus Nijhoff, 2011) 291–93

While not common, the participation of the Member States in international agreements falling within exclusive Union competence is not as unusual as we might imagine, and it gives rise to a number of interesting legal questions as to the status of the agreement, if any, in Union law and the Member States' obligations under Union law arising as a consequence. Such a situation may occur for several reasons:

1. It is decided that it is in the Union interest, for political or other reasons, that the Member States rather than the Union should participate in an agreement ...

2. In some cases, an individual Member State may be given authorisation to enter into an agreement that falls within exclusive Union competence. Here a distinction needs to be made between those cases where the Member State acts *on behalf of* the Union and those where it acts on its own account, albeit under Union authorisation. In the first case, the Member State acts in the Union interest, and the position will be similar to the previous scenario. In the second case, the authorization is given on the ground that it is not contrary to the Union interest for the Member State to conclude the agreement ...

3. It may be the case that only States, and not regional economic integration organisations (REIOs) such as the EC or EU, are entitled to participate in the agreement. This is the case for agreements concluded under the aegis of many UN agencies such as the ILO and the IMO ...

[28] Case C-308/06 *Intertanko*, ECLI:EU:C:2008:312, para 49.

(iii) Member States' inter se *Agreements*

Apart from pre-existing agreements with third states, agreements among the Member States (so-called agreements *inter se*) potentially challenge the principles and foundation of the EU legal order. After all, they run the risk of allowing Member States to bypass EU law. These agreements are not covered by Article 351 TFEU. It is clear that Member States cannot freely choose whenever the subject is covered by EU law, which implies that agreements *inter se* should be limited to topics that are not covered by the EU Treaties.

Consequently, the CJEU ruled in *Achmea* that certain BITs *between* Member States have become incompatible with EU law, especially since the arbitral panels they establish may be interpreting EU law, which is the exclusive prerogative of the CJEU.[29] As to the way forward, the Member States issued a declaration in January 2019, which underscored some of the underlying foundational principles of EU law at play and illustrates the wide-ranging impact of EU law on their treaty relations.

Declaration of the Representatives of the Governments of the Member States of 15 January 2019 on the legal consequences of the *Achmea* judgment and on investment protection in the European Union

…

Union law takes precedence over bilateral investment treaties concluded between Member States. As a consequence, all investor-State arbitration clauses contained in bilateral investment treaties concluded between Member States are contrary to Union law and are thus inapplicable. They do not produce effects including as regards provisions that provide for extended protection of investments made prior to termination for a further period of time (so called 'sunset' or 'grandfathering' clauses). An arbitral tribunal established on the basis of investor-State arbitration clauses lacks jurisdiction, due to a lack of a valid offer to arbitrate by the Member State party to the underlying bilateral investment Treaty …

This declaration is without prejudice to the division of competences between the Member States and the Union.

Taking into account the foregoing, Member States declare that they will undertake the following actions without undue delay:

1. By the present declaration, Member States inform investment arbitration tribunals about the legal consequences of the *Achmea* judgment, as set out in this declaration, in all pending intra-EU investment arbitration proceedings

[29] Case C-284/16 *Achmea*, ECLI:EU:C:2018:158.

brought either under bilateral investment treaties concluded between Member States or under the Energy Charter Treaty ...

5. In light of the *Achmea* judgment, Member States will terminate all bilateral investment treaties concluded between them by means of a plurilateral treaty or, where that is mutually recognised as more expedient, bilaterally ...

8. Member States will make best efforts to deposit their instruments of ratification, approval or acceptance of that plurilateral treaty or of any bilateral treaty terminating bilateral investment treaties between Member States no later than 6 December 2019. They will inform each other and the Secretary General of the Council of the European Union in due time of any obstacle they encounter, and of measures they envisage in order to overcome that obstacle ...

V. The Broader Picture of EU External Relations Law

As this chapter has shown, firstly, we must keep in mind that all instruments used by the EU to regulate or legislate internal policy matters can have external ramifications. Moreover, they can and are also being used directly as tools of EU external action. In addition to 'hard' legal instruments, the toolbox also contains a range of 'soft' instruments such as actions plans and démarches.

When engaging with external partners, international agreements are essential for the EU to be able to play its role as a global actor. In the current Treaties, the conclusion of international agreements is laid down in detailed terms. Over the years, the EU has made full and dynamic use of its treaty-making competences so that '[t]oday few parts of the world remain unconnected to the EU by some form of bilateral or regional trade-related agreement'.[30]

This global treaty-making activity notwithstanding, the need for mixity remains apparent and reveals that the EU's powers are far from exclusive in most areas. Member States have not ceased to conclude treaties themselves; in fact they have expanded their activity.[31] Mixity reflects the tension between the EU's own (sometimes exclusive) competences and the wish of Member States to stay connected once elements in the agreements fall under their competences. For third states, the division of competences remains a complex element in international negotiations, in particular since this division is not fixed but may change based on treaty modifications or new case law.

While tariffs and trade formed the subject of many early agreements, the EU has clearly expanded the scope of its external legal relations to its other policy areas.

[30] M Mendez, *The Legal Effects of EU Agreements: Maximalist Treaty Enforcement and Judicial Avoidance Techniques* (Oxford, Oxford University Press, 2013) xvii.

[31] Ibid, xv. Mendez points to the fact that since the 1990s France, for instance, has been negotiating roughly 200 bilateral treaties a year which is equivalent to 2.5 times the annual number of treaties negotiated during the 1950s.

Subsequent chapters will reveal the EU entering into international agreements following developments in the internal market or other areas such as freedom, security and justice, development cooperation, the Common Security and Defence Policy or, indeed, when it comes to joining and leaving the EU.

VI. Sources and Further Reading

Chalmers, D, G Davies, and G Monti, *European Union Law*, 4th edn (Cambridge, Cambridge University Press, 2019).

Chamon, M and I Govaere (eds) *EU External Relations Post-Lisbon: The Law and Practice of Facultative Mixity* (Leiden, Brill/Nijhoff, 2020).

Cremona, M, 'Member States Agreements as Union Law' in E Cannizzaro, P Palchetti and RA Wessel (eds) *International Law as Law of the European Union* (Leiden, Brill/Nijhoff Publishers, 2011) 291–324.

Czuczai, J, 'Mixity in Practice: Some Problems and Their (Real or Possible) Solution' in C Hillion and P Koutrakos (eds) *Mixed Agreements Revisited – The EU and its Member States in the World* (Oxford, Hart Publishing, 2010) 231–48.

Delgado Casteleiro, A, 'EU Declarations of Competence to Multilateral Agreements: A Useful Reference Base?' (2012) 17 *European Foreign Affairs Review* 491.

Dimopoulos, A, 'The BITs Cases and their Practical and Doctrinal Implications' in J Díez-Hochleitner et al (eds) *Recent Trends in the Case Law of the Court of Justice of the European Union (2008–2011)* (Madrid, La Ley, 2012) 737–58.

Gatti, M and P Manzini, 'External Representation of The European Union in the Conclusion of International Agreements' (2012) 49 *Common Market Law Review* 1703.

Heliskoski, J, 'The Procedural Law of International Agreements: A Thematic Journey through Article 218 TFEU' (2020) 57 *Common Market Law Review*, 79.

Hillion, C, 'Mixity and Coherence in EU External Relations: The Significance of the Duty of Cooperation' in C Hillion and P Koutrakos (eds) *Mixed Agreements Revisited – The EU and its Member States in the World* (Oxford, Hart Publishing, 2010) 87–115.

Hoffmeister, F, 'Curse or Blessing? Mixed Agreements in the Recent Practice of the European Union and its Member States' in C Hillion and P Koutrakos (eds) *Mixed Agreements Revisited – The EU and its Member States in the World* (Oxford, Hart Publishing, 2010) 249–68.

Klabbers, J, *Treaty Conflict and the European Union* (Cambridge, Cambridge University Press, 2009).

Kuijper, PJ, 'International Responsibility for EU Mixed Agreements' in C Hillion and P Koutrakos (eds) *Mixed Agreements Revisited – The EU and its Member States in the World* (Oxford, Hart Publishing, 2010) 208–27.

Lavranos, N, 'Case Note, Cases C-205/06 and C-249/06' (2009) 103 *American Journal of International Law* 716.

Łazowski, A, 'Enhanced Multilateralism and Enhanced Bilateralism: Integration Without Membership in the European Union' (2008) 45 *Common Market Law Review* 1433.

Maresceau, M, 'A Typology of Mixed Bilateral Agreements' in C Hillion and P Koutrakos (eds) *Mixed Agreements Revisited – The EU and its Member States in the World* (Oxford, Hart Publishing, 2010) 11–29.

Mendez, M, *The Legal Effects of EU Agreements: Maximalist Treaty Enforcement and Judicial Avoidance Techniques* (Oxford, Oxford University Press, 2013).

Senden, L, *Soft Law in European Community Law* (Portland, Oregon, Hart Publishing, 2004).

Van Vooren, B, 'A Case Study of "Soft Law" in EU External Relations: The European Neighbourhood Policy' (2009) 34 *European Law Review* 696.

5

The EU and International Law

Central Issues

- The European Union is usually considered a special or *sui generis* organisation (see Chapter 1). This special status would not only flow from the relationship with its Member States (which indeed differentiates it from other international organisations) but also from its position towards international law. The Court of Justice tends to underline this special position by referring to the 'autonomous' legal order that was created in which the relationship between the Member States is no longer primarily regulated by international law, but by EU law. In many ways, the states are first and foremost *Member* States.
- Yet, without international law, the EU would not exist. It is based on treaties concluded within the framework of international treaty law. At the same time, third states are in principle not bound by the EU Treaties since to them it is an agreement between others (known as the principle of *pacta tertiis nec nocent nec prosunt*).[1] This implies that in its external legal relations the EU will have to act under international law and will also have to respect its basic rules. Within the EU legal order, however, this may lead to conflicting norms and over the years the Court has had quite a task in finding solutions for these conflicts.
- This leads to several questions that will be addressed in this chapter: What is the hierarchical position of international law within the EU legal order? What are the effects of international law in the EU legal order? How did the CJEU solve conflicts between EU law and international law?

[1] This rule is laid down in Article 34 of the Vienna Convention on the Law of Treaties, adopted in Vienna, 22 of May 1969 (hereinafter: VCLT): 'A treaty does not create either obligations or rights for a third State without its consent'.

- Despite their EU membership, the Member States did not cease to be states. They continue to conclude international agreements; not only with third states, but also between themselves (*inter se*). The dynamic shift of external competences (see Chapter 3) frequently results in Member States facing diverging EU and international law obligations, which raises specific questions.

I. The Relationship between EU Law and International Law

A. An Autonomous EU Legal Order …?

(i) … or International Law as an Integral Part of the EU Legal Order?

The European Union's status in the international legal system is related to its international legal personality (Article 47 TEU), which – as we have seen in Chapter 1 – implies that it exists as a legal entity in the international system. At the same time, the relationship between EU law and international law has always been complicated. While over the years the EU's global actorness pointed to the increasing need to study parts of EU law in close relation to international law, the two academic fields have rather drifted further apart.

RA Wessel, 'Studying International and European Law: Confronting Perspectives and Combining Interests', in S Garben and I Govaere (eds) *The Interface between International and EU Law* (Oxford, Hart Publishing, 2019) 73–97, 96

Noticing a deepening of the divide between international and EU law scholarship and the reflection of this in our educational programmes, the question [is] whether we could indicate issues in one discipline of which it makes sense to be included in analyses of the other. While there are certainly exceptions, it is quite strange that in EU law programmes hardly any attention is paid to treaty law, trade law, statehood, the law of international responsibility, international organisations law or (these days) diplomatic law. Similarly, why do courses on the law of international organisations mostly continue to exclude the EU and the institutional developments in that organisation? And, why do we hardly see a comparison to EU enforcement mechanisms, negotiations and decision-making, institutional solutions, democratic experiments or variations of legal acts in general courses on international law?

A striking tension underlies the many judicial cases on the effects of international law in the EU legal order: the EU's struggle to find solutions between autonomy and dependence.[2] To make certain key principles of EU law (including primacy and direct effect) work, the EU needs to stress its autonomy vis-à-vis international law. At the same time, as an international actor, there is a need for the EU to live up to the rules that make up the international legal order and that are binding on it. We have analysed the principle of autonomy in Chapter 2.

Both the CJEU and the General Court felt obliged to stress the EU's autonomous legal order in the *Kadi* cases on the question of whether the EU would be bound by UN Security Council resolutions: 'the institutions ... had no *autonomous* discretion [in relation to UNSC resolutions]'[3] and 'the validity of any Community measure ... must be considered to be the expression ... of a constitutional guarantee stemming from the EC Treaty as an *autonomous* legal system'.[4] The notion of 'autonomy' was a central element in the discussion between the CJEU and the General Court in the *Kadi* saga when the latter argued: 'the Court of Justice thus seems to have regarded the constitutional framework created by the EC Treaty as a wholly *autonomous* legal order, not subject to the higher rules of international law ...'[5]

'A wholly autonomous legal order, not subject to the higher rules of international law.' Phrases like these meant to indicate that the EU as such is not automatically bound by international law. They seem to suggest the dualism that many Member States are familiar with: international law can only be part of a domestic legal order once it has been transposed or incorporated into that legal order. Yet, the legal order of the Union is widely identified as 'monist' in its relation to public international law: international law that binds the Union is believed to be valid within the Union's legal order. One observer even noted the Union's 'good international citizenship'.[6]

This 'good citizenship' was questioned when, after *Kadi*, the question of autonomy returned in Opinion 2/13 on the accession of the EU to the European Convention of Human Rights (see also Chapter 10). One of the main arguments of the Court to advise against the text of the accession agreement was related to the autonomy of the Union and, in particular, to the possibility of an international court – the European Court of Human Rights – to influence questions of validity and interpretation of EU law and to adjudicate in areas that were left out of the CJEU's own jurisdiction, in particular CFSP (see Chapter 9).

B De Witte, 'The Relative Autonomy of the European Union's Fundamental Rights Regime' (2019) 88 *Nordic Journal of International Law* 1, 4

The use of the autonomy doctrine in Opinion 2/13 is very different from its use in the *Kadi* case. In the latter case, as we saw, the EU's own human rights

[2] RA Wessel and S Blockmans (eds) *Between Autonomy and Dependence: The EU Legal Order Under the Influence of International Organisations* (TMC Asser Press/Springer, 2013) 297–312.

[3] Case T-315/01 *Kadi v Council and Commission*, ECLI:EU:T:2005:332, para 214 (emphasis added).

[4] Joined Cases C-402/05 P & C-415/05 *P Kadi and Al Barakaat International Foundation v Council*, ECLI:EU:C:2008:461, para 316 (emphasis added).

[5] T-85/09 *Kadi v Commission*, ECLI:EU:T:2010:418, para 119 (emphasis added).

[6] T Dunne, 'Good Citizen Europe' (2008) 84 *International Affairs* 13.

guarantees were shielded with the help of the concept of autonomy, from external threats stemming from an international law source. Whereas, in Opinion 2/13, the concept of autonomy was not displayed in order to give better protection to human rights, but in order to allow for human rights protection in the Court's own way without being hindered by an outside actor such as the European Court of Human Rights. The CJEU effectively vetoed accession of the European Union to Europe's leading international human rights instrument so as to preserve its own manoeuvrability in deciding the appropriate level and procedures of human rights protection in the EU legal order.

The principle of autonomy is, to a large extent, related to the Court's exclusive jurisdiction to decide on the validity of EU law and on its interpretation and thus affects the possibilities for the Union to participate in international dispute settlement.[7] As is well known, from the outset, the novel and special nature of the European Union (then European Economic Community) was stressed by the Court. In *Van Gend & Loos*, the Court argued 'that the Community constitutes *a new legal order of international law* for the benefit of which the states have limited their sovereign rights'.[8] In *Costa v ENEL*, the Court further stressed the 'special' nature of the EU: 'By contrast with *ordinary* international treaties, the EEC Treaty has created its own legal system.'[9] The phrase 'a new legal order *of international law*' is not without importance, despite the fact that, in later case law, the phrase was limited to 'a new legal order'.

In the early case law, the need to distinguish EU law from international law was above all triggered by the existence and development of the two notions that are so characteristic for EU law (and generally absent in international law): primacy and direct effect. Although over time the EU adopted a more relaxed attitude towards international law (see below), in more recent cases the Court frequently used the term 'autonomy' to indicate the need for the Union to live up to its own rules (and perhaps to preserve its own prerogatives). Thus, the 'preservation of the autonomy of the Community legal order' formed a crucial element in Opinion 1/00 on the possible establishment of a European Common Aviation Area.[10] Similar references could already be found in Opinion 1/76 (on the possible establishment of a European laying-up fund for inland waterway vessels) and Opinion 1/91 (on the creation of the European Economic Area). The safeguarding of the EU's judicial system was at stake when in *Mox Plant* (Case C-459/03) the Court held that '... an international agreement cannot affect ... the autonomy of the Community legal system ...'[11]

[7] See M Cremona, A Thies and RA Wessel (eds) *The European Union and International Dispute Settlement* (Oxford, Hart Publishing, 2017).

[8] Case C-26/62 *Van Gend en Loos v Nederlandse Administratie der Belastingen*, ECLI:EU:C:1963:1 (emphasis added).

[9] Case C-6/64 *Costa v ENEL*, ECLI:EU:C:1964:66 (emphasis added).

[10] Opinion 1/00 (*Common Aviation Area*), ECLI:EU:C:2002:231, para 12.

[11] Case C-459/03 *Commission of the European Communities v Ireland*, ECLI:EU:C:2006:345, para 123.

T Molnár, 'Revisiting the External Dimension of the Autonomy of EU Law: Is There Anything New Under the Sun?' (2016) 57 *Hungarian Journal of Legal Studies* 178, 179

The Opinion 2/13 of the Court of Justice of the European Union (CJEU), delivered on 18 December 2014, reignited interest in the content and meaning of the autonomy of EU law, even though this well-settled doctrine, elaborated by the CJEU case law, had been around for a long time. After this Opinion, a new wave of scholarly writings has focused on the ramifications of the autonomy of EU law, contributing to the renaissance of the concept, but principally in connection with the Union's accession to the European Convention on Human Rights (ECHR) … Autonomy, despite being in the background for the majority of its more than fifty years' existence, is an undisputed fundamental and structural principle of the EU legal order and is believed to be part of 'the very foundations of the Union legal order'.

In essence, the concept of autonomy oversteps the traditional divide between international law and domestic law by giving birth to a new category of law, a 'new legal order', which is meant to be the EU legal system. In order for a normative system be autonomous, it must not be subject to external legal norms. In the EU context, this has been stipulated by the CJEU 'the very nature of EU law … requires that relations between Member States be governed by EU law to the exclusion … of any other law.'

Autonomy, however, does not mean that international treaties that are binding on the Union are not to be considered a part of EU law. Their binding nature was already indicated by the Court in the 1970s.

Article 216(2) TFEU

Agreements concluded by the Union are binding upon the institutions of the Union and on its Member States.

Case 181/73 *Haegeman v Belgian State*, ECLI:EU:C:1974:41

3 The Athens Agreement was concluded by the Council under Articles 228 and 238 of the Treaty as appears from the terms of the Decision dated 25 September 1961.

4 This Agreement is therefore, in so far as concerns the Community, an Act of one of the institutions of the Community within the meaning of subparagraph (b) of the first paragraph of Article 177.

> 5 The provisions of the Agreement, from the coming into force thereof, form an integral part of Community law.
>
> 6 Within the framework of this law, the Court accordingly has jurisdiction to give preliminary rulings concerning the interpretation of this Agreement.

International agreements concluded by the European Union thus form 'an integral part' of Union law. As we will see below, this status of international law is not restricted to international agreements (including mixed agreements[12]), but also holds true for customary law[13] and secondary international law created in the framework of international agreements, such as Association Council decisions.[14]

Accepting that international law forms part of the EU legal order raises the question of where to place it in the EU's hierarchy of norms. The Court frequently dealt with this question and concluded that international law ranks between primary and secondary law.[15] This leads to the following hierarchy:

1. The EU Treaties.
2. International law binding upon the EU.
3. Secondary EU law.

Obviously, this hierarchy may work quite well internally, but it raises problems in relation to obligations both the Member States and the EU may have *vis-à-vis* third states and international organisations. In *Kadi*, the CJEU was challenged to reconcile UN Security Council obligations with the protection of fundamental rights as part of the general principles of law to be ensured by the Court. In this case, the Court held that the obligations imposed by an international agreement (in this case the UN Charter) could not have the effect of prejudicing the constitutional principles of the EU Treaty. Thus, it confirmed the hierarchy scheme presented above.

(ii) The Kadi *Case: Hierarchy Settled?*

On 3 September 2008, the CJEU delivered its first judgment in the so-called *Kadi* case. This judgment is often seen as a deviation from the traditional monist approach of the European Union towards international law and hence on the way we look at hierarchy in the international legal order. With regard to the question of whether or

[12] In Case C-239/03 *Commission v France (Étang de Berre)*, para 25, the Court held that mixed agreements have the same status in the EU legal order as EU-only agreements.

[13] Case C-162/96 *Racke GmbH & Co v Hauptzollamt Mainz* ECLI:EU:C:1998:293, para 45; Case T-115/94 *Opel Austria GmbH v Council*, ECLI:EU:T:1997:3; as well as Case C-84/95 *Bosphorus Hava Yollari Turizm ve Ticaret AS v Minister for Transport, Energy and Communications and Others*, ECLI:EU:C:1996:312.

[14] See for instance: Case C-192/89 *Sevince v Staatssecretaris van Justitie* ECLI:EU:C:1990:322.

[15] See for instance: Case C-179/97 *Spain v Commission*, ECLI:EU:C:1999:109; Case C-162/96 *Racke GmbH & Co v Hauptzollamt Mainz*, ECLI:EU:C:1998:293, para 45.

not UN Security Council Resolutions should enjoy immunity from jurisdiction as to their lawfulness in the Union's legal order, the General Court held the following in its 2005 decision:[16]

Case T-315/01 *Kadi v Council and Commission*, ECLI:EU:T:2005:332

215 Any review of the internal lawfulness of the contested regulation, especially having regard to the provisions or general principles of Community law relating to the protection of fundamental rights, would therefore imply that the Court is to consider, indirectly, the lawfulness of those resolutions ...

225 It must therefore be considered that the resolutions of the Security Council at issue fall, in principle, outside the ambit of the Court's judicial review and that the Court has no authority to call in question, even indirectly, their lawfulness in the light of Community law. On the contrary, the Court is bound, so far as possible, to interpret and apply that law in a manner compatible with the obligations of the Member States under the Charter of the United Nations.

In this case the acts of the European Union[17] were to be seen as a direct implementation of Security Council Resolution 1267 (1999).[18] Mr Kadi was one of the persons on the UN list of individuals and entities associated with Usama bin Laden or the Al-Qaeda network and hence appeared on the sanctions list of the European Union. Apart from a check against *jus cogens* (see further below), the General Court saw no way to assess the listing by the EU of Mr Kadi as that, it its view, would indirectly question the legality of the underlying decision by the UN Security Council. The

[16] See also Case T-306/01 *Yusuf and Al Barakaat International Foundation v Council and Commission*, ECLI:EU:T:2005:331.

[17] Respectively EU Common Position 2002/402/CFSP concerning restrictive measures against Usama bin Laden, members of the Al-Qaeda organization and the Taliban and other individuals, groups, undertakings and entities associated with them [2002] OJ L139/4; and Regulation 881/2002/EC imposing certain specific restrictive measurements directed against certain persons and entities associated with Usama bin Laden, the Al-Qaeda network and the Taliban [2002] OJ L139/9.

[18] Security Council Resolution 1267 (1999) provides that all the States must, in particular, 'freeze funds and other financial resources, including funds derived or generated from property owned or controlled directly or indirectly by the Taliban, or by any undertaking owned or controlled by the Taliban, as designated by the Committee established by paragraph 6 below, and ensure that neither they nor any other funds or financial resources so designated are made available, by their nationals or by any persons within their territory, to or for the benefit of the Taliban or any undertaking owned or controlled, directly or indirectly, by the Taliban, except as may be authorised by the Committee on a case-by-case basis on the grounds of humanitarian need' (para 4b).

subsequent appeals case has become essential to understand the relationship between EU law and international law. The Court of Justice argued as follows:

Joined Cases C-402/05 P & C-415/05 *P Kadi and Al Barakaat International Foundation v Council*, ECLI:EU:C:2008:461

283 In addition, according to settled case law, fundamental rights form an integral part of the general principles of law whose observance the Court ensures. For that purpose, the Court draws inspiration from the constitutional traditions common to the Member States and from the guidelines supplied by international instruments for the protection of human rights on which the Member States have collaborated or to which they are signatories. In that regard, the ECHR has special significance (see, *inter alia*, Case C-305/05 Ordre des barreaux francophones et germanophone and Others, paragraph 29 and case-law cited).

284 It is also clear from the case-law that respect for human rights is a condition of the lawfulness of Community acts (Opinion 2/94, paragraph 34) and that measures incompatible with respect for human rights are not acceptable in the Community (Case C-112/00 Schmidberger, paragraph 73).

285 It follows from all those considerations that the obligations imposed by an international agreement cannot have the effect of prejudicing the constitutional principles of the EC Treaty, which include the principle that all Community acts must respect fundamental rights, that respect constituting a condition of their lawfulness which it is for the Court to review in the framework of the complete system of legal remedies established by the Treaty.

286 In this regard it must be emphasised that, in circumstances such as those of these cases, the review of lawfulness thus to be ensured by the Community judicature applies to the Community act intended to give effect to the international agreement at issue, and not to the latter as such.

326 … the Community judicature must … ensure the review, in principle the full review, of the lawfulness of all Community acts in the light of the fundamental rights forming an integral part of the general principles of Community law, including review of Community measures which, like the contested regulation, are designed to give effect to the resolutions adopted by the Security Council under Chapter VII of the Charter of the United Nations …

To arrive at this conclusion without having to challenge the validity of norms flowing from UN Security Council resolutions, the Court pointed to the fact that the UN Charter leaves the members 'the free choice among the various possible models for transposition of those resolutions into their domestic legal order'.[19] This would allow for judicial review of the 'internal lawfulness' of the EU and EC acts, keeping in mind that fundamental rights form an integral part of the general principles of law, the observance of which is to be ensured by the Court.

Although the Court's focus is on the *implementation* of the Security Council resolutions by the Union and the Community, rather than on the validity of the international norms as such, the consequence of this exercise could very well be that any implementation of a Security Council resolution could entail the violation of fundamental EU rights. In this concrete case the Court annulled the contested acts, while their legal effects were maintained basically until Mr Kadi was taken off the UN sanctions list in October 2012, including by imposing slightly adapted new measures and through appeals. The primacy of the EU Treaties over international law was confirmed, while avoiding an overt conflict in practice.

J Larik, 'The Kadi Saga as a Tale of "Strict Observance" of International Law: Obligations Under the UN Charter, Targeted Sanctions and Judicial Review in the European Union' (2014) 61 *Netherlands International Law Review* 23, 39–40

The clamour on the autonomy of the Union legal order and the majesty of human rights aside, in reality, the EU and its Member States successfully cloaked themselves in a seamless coat of compliance with their international obligations, covering the entire period from October 2001 until Mr Kadi's delisting. While vocally upholding human rights as constitutional principles of the EU legal order, also against attacks from the UNSC bolstered by the supremacy of the UN Charter, what the institutions of the EU achieved in fact was living up, all this time, to the objective of strictly observing international law as stipulated in Article 3(5) TEU … For Mr Kadi, certainly, his repeated victories in court retain a Pyrrhic character. He had to wait almost twelve years before his judicial successes became effective.

Rather than taking the formal hierarchical relationship between UN law and EU law as the basis for establishing the immunity from jurisdiction of Security Council resolutions (as was done by the General Court in 2005, whose judgment was overturned by the CJEU), the Court chose to look at this hierarchy in more substantive terms. Security Council resolutions remain 'untouchable', but the acts by which the EU implements the resolutions are not and are subject to the fundamental rights and principles that form the basis of the Union legal order. This certainly offered the Court a smart way out of the dilemma, but in the virtual absence of judicial remedies at the UN level, the consequence can (and perhaps should) be that the EU may not be able to fully implement Security

[19] Joined Cases C-402/05 P and C-415/05 *P Kadi and Al Barakaat International Foundation v Council*, ECLI:EU:C:2008:461, para 298.

Council resolutions that are in conflict with fundamental human rights obligations flowing not only from the EU legal order and the European Convention for the Protection of Human Rights and Fundamental Freedoms, but also from the UN Charter itself.

B. A Monist or Dualist Relationship?

The terms 'monism' and 'dualism' are generally used to characterise the relationship between domestic legal orders and international law. Although in their extreme form both notions cannot be found in practice, a monist system regards international law as being part of the national legal order, whereas in a dualist system international rules need to be 'transposed' to national law before being able to be recognised as valid law. Although labelling the relationship between international and European law in terms of 'monism' may be helpful to indicate that international law forms part of the EU legal order from the moment an international norm is (lawfully) concluded, it has been pointed out that it may also raise questions.

First of all, the complexity of the Union's legal order is related to the role of the Member States in this order. When the fact that international agreements are an 'integral part' of Union law is linked to the notion of primacy, the effects of international agreements reach the internal law of (both monist and dualist) Member States and hence would lead to their supremacy over this national law. This has led one observer to point to European law as a 'door opener' for international law, '[i]n that event, the traditional approaches of the Member States for explaining the relationship between municipal law and public international law do not matter anymore'.[20] At the same time the status as an 'integral part' of Union law does not settle the hierarchical position of international law in relation to other (secondary) sources of Union law.

Secondly, 'monism' and 'dualism' are often used to describe the relationship between legal orders in far too general terms. Claims based on 'monism' often confuse the 'validity' of norms with their 'direct applicability', 'direct effect', or even their 'primacy'. At least at a theoretical level, it may still be helpful to differentiate between the different notions. 'Monism' and 'dualism' would relate formally only to the status of international norms within the European or domestic legal orders. In that sense, 'monism/dualism' relates to the 'validity' (or existence) of international norms in those orders. In monist systems, international norms enjoy automatic validity, whereas in dualist systems, they need to be transferred into domestic law to become a 'valid' part of that legal order.

Thirdly, this validity does not imply a direct effect, in the sense that all international norms (as part of the EU legal order) may be invoked to challenge existing, conflicting Union law. The classic example is formed by WTO law, in which area the Court generally denied direct effect as a possibility of individuals to refer to WTO law, both before national courts and the court of the European Union (see Chapter 7 on the Common Commercial Policy).

[20] FC Mayer, 'European Law as a Door Opener for Public International Law?' in JMM Thouvenin and C Tomuschat (eds) *Droit International et Diversité des Cultures Juridiques – International Law and Diversity of Legal Cultures* (Paris, Pédone, 2008) 253.

II. The Effects of International Law within the EU Legal Order

A. Internal Effects of International Law and External Effects of EU Law

Thus far we have established that international law may be binding on the EU. The current section looks at the consequences of this assertion, in particular within the EU legal order. In other words, we look at the internal effects of international law. As an introduction to this theme we consider a 2011 judgment in which the Court not only summarised some of the relevant issues, but also addressed the question of whether non-EU states can be bound by EU legislation.

The case concerned the applicability of rules of written and customary international law in relation to a directive to include aviation activities in the scheme for greenhouse gas emission allowance trading within the Union.[21] This directive not only affects EU Member States, but every aircraft operator when their flight schedule departs or arrives in the territory of one of the Member States and, more specifically, at an airport situated there. Obviously, third states are not too eager to pay for greenhouse gas emission for miles they do not fly in EU airspace. The Air Transport Association of America (ATAA) and others brought judicial review proceedings asking the referring court to quash the measures implementing the directive in the United Kingdom.[22] In support of their action, they pleaded that that directive was unlawful in light of international treaty law and customary international law. In this ruling, the Court succinctly summarised the main principles related to the effect of international law in the EU legal order, to which we will return below.

Case C-366/10 *Air Transport Association of America and Others*, ECLI:EU:C:2011:864

[On the criteria to assess the effects of international agreements]

52 First, the European Union must be bound by those rules (see Joined Cases 21/72 to 24/72 *International Fruit Company*, paragraph 7, and *Intertanko*, paragraph 44).

53 Second, the Court can examine the validity of an act of European Union law in the light of an international treaty only where the nature and the broad logic of the latter do not preclude this (see Joined Cases C-120/06 P and C-121/06 P *FIAMM and Others v Council and Commission*, paragraph 110).

[21] Directive 2008/101/EC to include aviation activities in the scheme for greenhouse gas emission allowance trading within the Community [2009] OJ L8/3.

[22] Case C-366/10 *Air Transport Association of America and Others*, ECLI:EU:C:2011:864.

54 Finally, where the nature and the broad logic of the treaty in question permit the validity of the act of European Union law to be reviewed in the light of the provisions of that treaty, it is also necessary that the provisions of that treaty which are relied upon for the purpose of examining the validity of the act of European Union law appear, as regards their content, to be unconditional and sufficiently precise (see IATA and ELFAA, paragraph 39, and *Intertanko and Others*, paragraph 45) …

[On the question of whether the EU is bound to an international agreement to which it is not a party: the Chicago Convention]

63 Indeed, in order for the European Union to be capable of being bound, it must have assumed, and thus had transferred to it, all the powers previously exercised by the Member States that fall within the convention in question (see, to this effect, *Intertanko and Others*, paragraph 49, and *Bogiatzi*, paragraph 33). Therefore, the fact that one or more acts of European Union law may have the object or effect of incorporating into European Union law certain provisions that are set out in an international agreement which the European Union has not itself approved is not sufficient for it to be incumbent upon the Court to review the legality of the act or acts of European Union law in the light of that agreement (see, to this effect, *Intertanko and Others*, paragraph 50) …

69 Nevertheless, whilst it is true that the European Union has in addition acquired certain exclusive powers to agree with third States commitments falling within the field of application of the European Union legislation on international air transport and, consequently, of the Chicago Convention (see, to this effect, Case C-476/98 *Commission v Germany*, paragraph 124), that does not mean that it has exclusive competence in the entire field of international civil aviation as covered by that convention. …

71 Consequently, it must be concluded that, since the powers previously exercised by the Member States in the field of application of the Chicago Convention have not to date been assumed in their entirety by the European Union, the latter is not bound by that convention.

72 It follows that in the context of the present reference for a preliminary ruling the Court cannot examine the validity of Directive 2008/101 in the light of the Chicago Convention as such.

[On the question of whether the EU is bound to an international agreement to which it is a party: the Kyoto Protocol]

73 It is apparent from Decisions 94/69 and 2002/358 that the European Union has approved the Kyoto Protocol. Consequently, its provisions form an integral part of the legal order of the European Union as from its entry into force (see Case 181/73 Haegeman, paragraph 5). …

76 It is thus clear that, even though the Kyoto Protocol imposes quantified greenhouse gas reduction commitments with regard to the commitment period corresponding to the years 2008 to 2012, the parties to the protocol may comply with their obligations in the manner and at the speed upon which they agree.

77 In particular, Article 2(2) of the Kyoto Protocol, mentioned by the referring court, provides that the parties thereto are to pursue limitation or reduction of emissions of certain greenhouse gases from aviation bunker fuels, working through the ICAO. Thus, that provision, as regards its content, cannot in any event be considered to be unconditional and sufficiently precise so as to confer on individuals the right to rely on it in legal proceedings in order to contest the validity of Directive 2008/101 …

[On the question of whether the EU is bound to an international agreement to which it is a party: the Open Skies Agreement]

79 The Open Skies Agreement has been approved on behalf of the European Union by Decisions 2007/339 and 2010/465. Consequently, its provisions form an integral part of the legal order of the European Union as from its entry into force (see Haegeman, paragraph 5). …

84 Since the Open Skies Agreement establishes certain rules designed to apply directly and immediately to airlines and thereby to confer upon them rights and freedoms which are capable of being relied upon against the parties to that agreement, and the nature and the broad logic of the agreement do not so preclude, the conclusion can be drawn that the Court may assess the validity of an act of European Union law, such as Directive 2008/101, in the light of the provisions of the agreement …

[On the question of whether the EU is bound by customary international law]

101 Under Article 3(5) TEU, the European Union is to contribute to the strict observance and the development of international law. Consequently, when it adopts an act, it is bound to observe international law in its entirety, including customary international law, which is binding upon the institutions of the European Union (see, to this effect, Case C-86/90 Poulsen and Diva Navigation [1992] ECR I-6019, paragraphs 9 and 10, and Case C-162/96 Racke [1998] ECR I-3655, paragraphs 45 and 46).

102 Thus, it should be examined first whether the principles to which the referring court makes reference are recognised as forming part of customary international law. If they are, it should, secondly, then be determined whether and to what extent they may be relied upon by individuals to call into question the validity of an act of the European Union, such as Directive 2008/101, in a situation such as that in the main proceedings …

108 In the main proceedings, those principles of customary international law are relied upon, in essence, in order for the Court to determine whether the European Union had competence, in the light thereof, to adopt Directive 2008/101 in that it extends the application of Directive 2003/87 to aircraft operators of third States whose flights which arrive at and depart from an aerodrome situated in the territory of a Member State of the European Union are carried out in part over the high seas and over the third States' territory.

109 Therefore, even though the principles at issue appear only to have the effect of creating obligations between States, it is nevertheless possible, in circumstances such as those of the case which has been brought before the referring court, in which Directive 2008/101 is liable to create obligations under European Union law as regards the claimants in the main proceedings, that the latter may rely on those principles and that the Court may thus examine the validity of Directive 2008/101 in the light of such principles.

110 However, since a principle of customary international law does not have the same degree of precision as a provision of an international agreement, judicial review must necessarily be limited to the question whether, in adopting the act in question, the institutions of the European Union made manifest errors of assessment concerning the conditions for applying those principles (see, to this effect, Racke, paragraph 52) …

[On the question of whether the EU is competent to adopt rules binding on third parties in the light of international law]

123 The European Union must respect international law in the exercise of its powers, and therefore Directive 2008/101 must be interpreted, and its scope delimited, in the light of the relevant rules of the international law of the sea and international law of the air (see, to this effect, Poulsen and Diva Navigation, paragraph 9).

124 On the other hand, European Union legislation may be applied to an aircraft operator when its aircraft is in the territory of one of the Member States and, more specifically, on an aerodrome situated in such territory, since, in such a case, that aircraft is subject to the unlimited jurisdiction of that Member State and the European Union (see, by analogy, Poulsen and Diva Navigation, paragraph 28) …

127 It is only if the operator of such an aircraft has chosen to operate a commercial air route arriving at or departing from an aerodrome situated in the territory of a Member State that the operator, because its aircraft is in the territory of that Member State, will be subject to the allowance trading scheme …

130 It follows that the European Union had competence, in the light of the principles of customary international law capable of being relied upon in the context of the main proceedings, to adopt Directive 2008/101, in so far as the latter extends the allowance trading scheme laid down by Directive 2003/87 to all flights which arrive at or depart from an aerodrome situated in the territory of a Member State.

First, the Court confirmed that the EU is, in principle, bound by international law. This has indeed been standard case law ever since the *International Fruit Company* case in 1972.[23] Secondly, the Court can examine the validity of an act of European Union law in the light of an international treaty only where the nature and the broad logic of the latter do not preclude this.[24] Finally, where the nature and the broad logic of the treaty in question permit the validity of the act of European Union law to be reviewed in the light of the provisions of that treaty, it is also necessary that the provisions of that treaty which are relied upon for the purpose of examining the validity of the act of European Union law appear, as regards their content, to be unconditional and sufficiently precise.[25]

Yet, the question is, of course, different when the European Union is not a party to a particular international agreement. In that case, for the Union to be capable of being bound, it must have assumed, and thus had transferred to it, the powers previously exercised by the Member States that fall within the international agreement in question. In this case, the question related to the Chicago Convention and the Court held that regarding this particular agreement the powers previously exercised by the Member States had not been assumed in their entirety by the European Union, the latter is thus not bound by it. In other words: the European Union was not bound because it was not itself a party to the agreement and it had not replaced the Member States. This led to the conclusion that the provisions of the Chicago Convention cannot be said to form part of the EU legal order.

But what if the EU *is* a party to an international agreement? In *ATAA*, the Court answered this question as follows. This case involved the Kyoto Protocol, an international agreement on CO_2 emissions. Since the EU is a party to it, the provisions of the Kyoto Protocol form an integral part of the legal order of the European Union as from its entry into force.[26] And, since the agreement 'establishes certain rules designed to apply directly and immediately to airlines and thereby to confer upon them rights and freedoms which are capable of being relied upon against the parties to that agreement, and the nature and the broad logic of the agreement do not so preclude, the conclusion can be drawn that the Court may assess the validity of an act of European Union law … in the light of the provisions of the agreement' (para 84).

Hence, in order to know whether international agreements can play a role within the EU (primarily to set aside internal EU legislation) the EU will have to be bound by the agreement and the agreement must be directly applicable to individuals or companies. We will come back to this in the next sub-section, but at this point it is important to underline that international law is not only seen as an integral part of the Union's legal order (the *validity* question), but that it can also be relied upon by legal actors within that legal order for the purpose of challenging internal EU legislation (the *applicability* and *primacy* issues).

[23] Joined Cases C-21/72 – 24/72 *International Fruit Company and Others v Produktschap voor Groenten en Fruit*, ECLI:EU:C:1972:115.

[24] See also Joined Cases C-120/06 & C-121/06 *FIAMM and Others v Council and Commission*, ECLI:EU:C:2008:476, para 110.

[25] Case C-344/04 *R, ex parte IATA v Department for Transport*, ECLI:EU:C:2006:10, para 39; and Case C-308/06 *Intertanko and Others*, ECLI:EU:C:2008:312, para 45.

[26] See also Case 181/73 *Haegemann v Belgian State*, ECLI:EU:C:1974:41, para 5.

The main question the American airline companies were interested in, however, was whether they could be subjected to rules based on treaties (the EU Treaties) to which neither they nor their home country were a party. The Court held that EU legislation applies in the territory of the EU Member States and may thus be applied to an aircraft operator when its aircraft is in the territory of one of the Member States and, more specifically, on an airport situated in such a territory. In such a case, that aircraft is subject to the unlimited jurisdiction of that Member State and the European Union. It follows that the Union has competence to apply its *internal* rules to *external* parties once they enter 'EU territory' and, since the emission rules in the Kyoto Protocol concern complete flights, the directive could be applied to all flights which arrive or depart from an airport situated in the territory of a Member State, even when, for the most part, they would not fly over EU territory. International law is thus not only applicable in the EU, international actors may also be subject to EU law, including for activities that partly take place outside the EU. This is a consequence of the fact that external actors will have to abide by EU rules whenever they wish to be active in the EU, including the internal market. This is known as the 'extraterritorial' effect of EU law.

E Fahey, *The Global Reach of EU Law* (Abingdon, Routledge 2016) 1

The global reach and effect of EU law, or simply put for now, the 'spread' of EU law, is increasingly the subject of legal scholarship, which considers a broad range of its manifestations to other legal order or systems, organisations or third countries, as an empirical phenomenon. For example, the so-called 'Brussels effect' is the subject of recent scholarship, assessing the perceived 'spillover' effect of EU regulatory standards on US rules in the realm of, *inter alia*, genetically modified foods, data privacy standards and chemical safety rules. Equally, recent accounts consider the extent to which EU legal rules are actually transplanted in the US – for example, the transposition of EU environmental standards in California, Boston and Maine. Included in these theorisations is the view that the size and scale of the EU, as a market and as a polity, has generated what is understood here as a 'rule transfer'. It has entailed that the EU has adopted rules and standards that other policies and markets have in turn adopted, compelled to do so or acting out of sheer necessity.

A final point in this section on the status of international agreements in the EU legal order concerns the application of international law by the Court to assess the validity of international agreements; or, to be more precise, to review the validity of the EU act approving the international agreement. In *Front Polisario*, the Court was faced with the question of the validity of an international agreement with Morocco on trade in agricultural and fishery products due to its application to the disputed territory of Western

Sahara.[27] In this case the Court had to rely on rules of international (treaty) law to establish whether or not the agreement violated these rules. In the end, it concluded that this was not the case as the agreement did not extend to the Western Sahara. The way in which the Court, somewhat selectively, applied international law in this case, has been criticised in the literature.

E Kassoti, 'The *Council v Front Polisario* Case: The Court of Justice's Selective Reliance on International Rules on Treaty Interpretation (Second Part)' (2017) 2 *European Papers* 23, 40

... the Court's artificial and selective reliance on international law in *Front Polisario* adds a new dimension to the ever-burgeoning debate on the relationship between international and EU law. In the past, the Court has arguably shown a great deal of judicial recalcitrance towards international law and a tendency to guard its own identity and the autonomy of the EU legal order through its reluctance to engage with international law. However, the *Front Polisario* judgment manifests a different and more worrisome judicial strategy. While seemingly anchoring its findings in international law, the Court, in essence, showed here a great degree of willingness to stretch international rules on treaty interpretation to a breaking point in order to avoid addressing the political disinterest that the EU has demonstrated in relation to the situation in *Western Sahara*.

Front Polisario was followed up by a similar case one year later. In *Western Sahara*,[28] the Court again had to assess the validity of an international agreement (the EU–Morocco Fisheries Partnership Agreement (FPA) and its 2013 Protocol) and the EU implementing acts. Again, the question concerned the application of the agreement to the territory of and products originating in Western Sahara. For the first time, the Court was confronted with a request for a preliminary reference concerning the validity of international agreements concluded by the EU. In line with other case law (eg *Rosneft*[29]), the Court stressed the importance of the 'complete system' of judicial review that flows from Article 19 TEU. In *Western Sahara*, the Court again extensively applied international law, also to determine the EU's own obligations. By accepting Morocco's sovereignty over the Western Saharan waters, the EU would, inter alia,

[27] Case C-104/16 P *Council of the European Union v Front Polisario*, ECLI:EU:C:2016:973.

[28] Case C-266/16 Request for a preliminary ruling under Article 267 TFEU from the High Court of Justice (England & Wales), Queen's Bench Division (Administrative Court) (United Kingdom), made by decision of 27 April 2016, received at the Court on 13 May 2016, in the proceedings The Queen, on the application of: *Western Sahara Campaign UK v Commissioners for Her Majesty's Revenue and Customs, Secretary of State for Environment, Food and Rural Affairs*, ECLI:EU:C:2018:118.

[29] Case C-72/15 *PJSC Rosneft Oil Company, formerly OJSC Rosneft Oil Company v Her Majesty's Treasury, Secretary of State for Business, Innovation and Skills, The Financial Conduct Authority*, ECLI:EU:C:2017:236 (see also Chapter 9).

accept Morocco's breach of the right to self-determination of Western Sahara (and thus, the EU might also be found responsible for that breach by way of complicity).[30] As in *Front Polisario*, a way out was found in arguing that 'Moroccan fishing zones' did not include Western Sahara territory; hence, the agreements did not – in the eyes of the Court – apply to any illegally occupied territory.

The remaining part of this chapter will zoom in more closely on the effects of written and unwritten international law in the EU legal order.

III. Direct Applicability of International Agreements

As far as international agreements are concerned, we have seen that the *Haegeman* doctrine – international law forms an integral part of EU law – implies what is now laid down in Article 216(2) TFEU, which reads that 'agreements concluded by the Union are binding upon the institutions of the Union and on its Member States'. This means that there is no specific need to transpose international agreements to Union law or to the domestic law of the Member States (for instance by means of a special Regulation).

A. Direct Effect of International Agreements

'Direct effect' relates to the question of whether these norms can be invoked by individuals before a domestic or EU court (see also above). As we have seen, the basic rule is that this is the case for provisions international agreements to which the Union is a party. In *Bresciani*,[31] the Court of Justice established that the EU's association agreements could be used in national courts to challenge national law. In addition, in the seminal case of *Kupferberg*,[32] the CJEU confirmed the direct effect of an 'ordinary' bilateral trade agreement. Indeed, all international agreements concluded by the EU can have direct effect if the conditions are fulfilled.

Case 104/81 *Hauptzollamt Mainz v Kupferberg*, ECLI:EU:C:1982:362

9 In the first place the Bundesfinanzhof wishes to know whether the German importer may rely on the said Article 21 before the German Court in the proceedings which it has brought against the decision of the tax authorities ...

[30] Again, the Court seems to have been selective in using international law arguments. See E Kassoti, 'The ECJ and the Art of Treaty Interpretation: Western Sahara Campaign UK' (2019) 56 *Common Market Law Review* 209.

[31] Case 87/75 *Conceria Daniele Bresciani v Amministrazione delle finanze dello Stato*, ECLI:EU:C:1976:18.

[32] Case 104/81 *Hauptzollamt Mainz v Kupferberg & Cie.*, ECLI:EU:C:1982:362.

13 In ensuring respect for commitments arising from an agreement concluded by the Community institutions the Member States fulfil an obligation not only in relation to the non-member country concerned but also and above all in relation to the Community which has assumed responsibility for the due performance of the agreement. That is why the provisions of such an agreement, as the Court has already stated in its judgment of 30 April 1974 in Case 181/73 *Haegeman* form an integral part of the Community legal system.

14 It follows from the Community nature of such provisions that their effect in the Community may not be allowed to vary according to whether their application is in practice the responsibility of the Community institutions or of the Member States and, in the latter case, according to the effects in the internal legal order of each Member State which the law of that state assigns to international agreements concluded by it. Therefore it is for the Court, within the framework of its jurisdiction in interpreting the provisions of agreements, to ensure their uniform application throughout the Community …

17 It is true that the effects within the Community of provisions of an agreement concluded by the Community with a non-member country may not be determined without taking account of the international origin of the provisions in question. In conformity with the principles of public international law Community institutions which have power to negotiate and conclude an agreement with a non-member country are free to agree with that country what effect the provisions of the agreement are to have in the internal legal order of the contracting parties. Only if that question has not been settled by the agreement does it fall for decision by the courts having jurisdiction in the matter, and in particular by the court of justice within the framework of its jurisdiction under the treaty, in the same manner as any question of interpretation relating to the application of the agreement in the Community.

18 According to the general rules of international law there must be bona fide performance of every agreement. Although each contracting party is responsible for executing fully the commitments which it has undertaken it is nevertheless free to determine the legal means appropriate for attaining that end in its legal system unless the agreement, interpreted in the light of its subject-matter and purpose, itself specifies those means. Subject to that reservation the fact that the courts of one of the parties consider that certain of the stipulations in the agreement are of direct application whereas the courts of the other party do not recognize such direct application is not in itself such as to constitute a lack of reciprocity in the implementation of the agreement …

22 It follows from all the foregoing considerations that neither the nature nor the structure of the agreement concluded with Portugal may prevent a trader from relying on the provisions of the said agreement before a court in the Community.

> 23 Nevertheless the question whether such a stipulation is unconditional and sufficiently precise to have direct effect must be considered in the context of the agreement of which it forms part. In order to reply to the question on the direct effect of the first paragraph of article 21 of the agreement between the Community and Portugal it is necessary to analyse the provision in the light of both the object and purpose of the agreement and of its context.

In *Sevince*, the Court also found that decisions adopted by an Association Council and created by an association agreement were capable of having direct effect, provided they fulfil the same criteria that determine whether an international agreement has direct effect.[33] Similarly, it was confirmed that third-country nationals could rely on the provisions of agreements concluded with the European Union. Thus, the Russian football player Igor Simutenkov, at the time employed by the Spanish club Deportivo Tenerife, could invoke relevant provisions of the Partnership and Cooperation Agreement (PCA) with Russia.[34] Article 23(1) of that PCA provided the following: 'Subject to the laws, conditions and procedures applicable in each Member State, the Community and its Member States shall ensure that the treatment accorded to Russian nationals, legally employed in the territory of a Member State shall be free from any discrimination based on nationality, as regards working conditions, remuneration or dismissal, as compared to its own nationals.' In examining this provision, the Court of Justice found that it laid down 'in clear, precise and unconditional terms, a prohibition precluding any Member State from discriminating on grounds of nationality, against Russian workers vis-à-vis their own nationals'.[35] This judgment further affirmed that even Partnership and Cooperation agreements which do not establish the 'special relationship' that Association Agreements do (217 TFEU), can produce direct effect.

B. Limits to the Direct Effect

Ten years after *Haegeman*, the Court proved to be more restrictive in applying its doctrine. In *Kupferberg* (see above) the Court not only confirmed the possible direct effect of international agreements but, at the same time, argued that 'the effects within the Community of provisions of an agreement concluded by the Community with a non-member country may not be determined without taking account of the

[33] Case C-192/89 *Sevince v Staatssecretaris van Justitie*, ECLI:EU:C:1990:322.

[34] Agreement on partnership and cooperation establishing a partnership between the European Communities and their Member States, of one part, and the Russian Federation, of the other part, signed in Corfu on 24 June 1994 and approved on behalf of the Communities by Decision 97/800/ECSC, EC, Euratom: Council and Commission Decision of 30 October 1997 [1997] OJ L327/1).

[35] Case C-265/03 *Igor Simutenkov v Ministerio de Educación y Cultura, Real Federación Española de Fútbol*, ECLI:EU:C:2005:213.

international origin of the provisions in question'. This idea was elaborated in further case law, starting with *Demirel.*

Case 12/86 *Demirel v Stadt Schwäbisch Gmünd*, ECLI:EU:C:1987:400, para 14

A provision in an Agreement concluded by the Community with non-member countries must be regarded as being directly applicable when, regard being had to its wording and the purpose and nature of the Agreement itself, the provision contains a clear and precise obligation which is not subject, in its implementation or effects, to the adoption of any subsequent measure.

Indeed, this implies that the original monistic starting point (international law as an integral part of EU law) does not automatically entail direct effect of all provisions in international agreements concluded by the Union. Reasons for the Court to limit the domestic effects of international agreements vary. A classic argument is *reciprocity*: third states also limit the direct effect of the same agreement. This argument was leading in for instance *Kupferberg* and returned in *Van Parys*.[36]

Case C-377/02 *Van Parys v BIRB*, ECLI:EU:C:2005:121, para 53

To accept that the Community Courts have the direct responsibility for ensuring that Community law complies with the WTO rules would deprive the Community's legislative or executive bodies of the discretion which the equivalent bodies of the Community's commercial partners enjoy. It is not in dispute that some of the contracting parties, which are amongst the most important commercial partners of the Community, have concluded from the subject-matter and purpose of the WTO agreements that they are not among the rules applicable by their courts when reviewing the legality of their rules of domestic law. Such lack of reciprocity, if admitted, would risk introducing an anomaly in the application of the WTO rules.

More generally, the Court held that 'having regard to their nature and structure, the WTO agreements are not in principle among the rules in the light of which the Court is to review the legality of measures adopted by the Community institutions'.[37] The nature of WTO law thus prevents the Court from giving effect to these norms within

[36] Later confirmed in Joined Cases C-120/06 & C-121/06 *FIAMM and Others v Council and Commission*, ECLI:EU:C: 2008:476.

[37] Case C-377/02 *Van Parys v BIRB*, ECLI:EU:C:2005:121, para 39; but established case law ever since Case 21/72– 24/72 *International Fruit Company*.

the EU legal order. This may be referred to as a dualist exception in a mostly monist system, but is it really? There is perhaps no doubt that the norms of WTO agreements are valid within the EU legal order; the problem lies more in the possibilities to *apply* them in case of a conflict (see further Chapter 7).

While WTO law had long been the odd one out, the Court seems to have extended the idea in relation to the United Nations Convention on the Law of the Sea (UNCLOS). Here, however, it was not so much reciprocity that triggered the Court to be careful with the domestic application of an international agreement, but rather the *effects on individual rights*.

Case C-308/06 *Intertanko and Others*, ECLI:EU:C:2008:312

64 In those circumstances, it must be found that UNCLOS does not establish rules intended to apply directly and immediately to individuals and to confer upon them rights or freedoms capable of being relied upon against States, irrespective of the attitude of the ship's flag State.

65 It follows that the nature and the broad logic of UNCLOS prevent the Court from being able to assess the validity of a Community measure in the light of that Convention.

Earlier, in *Simutenkov*, the Court had established that 'when an agreement established cooperation between the parties, some of the provisions of that agreement may … directly govern the legal position of individuals'.[38] Now, in *Intertanko*, the absence of individual rights and obligations, together with 'the nature and broad logic of UNCLOS' prevented the Court from being able to assess the validity of a Community measure in the light of that Convention. It seems that the absence of direct effect causes the problem; the Court does not deny the legal status of the Convention within the EU legal order. The question may rightfully be posed whether the criterion of the governance of 'the legal position of individuals' – which seems to be relevant for the acceptance of direct effect[39] – would not virtually rule out the legal effects of most international law within the EU legal order and hence *de facto* limit the much applauded international law friendly attitude of the Union.[40]

Another argument used by the Court to limit the internal effects of international agreements relates to the possible existence of a dispute settlement mechanism in the agreement. However, the argument is not used in a consistent manner. It played a role

[38] Case C-265/03 *Simutenkov*, ECLI:EU:C: 2005:213.

[39] See more extensively and eloquently E Cannizzaro, 'The Neo-Monism of the European Legal Order' in E Cannizzaro, P Palchetti and RA Wessel (eds) *International Law as Law of the European Union* (Martinus Nijhoff Publishers, 2011) 35–58.

[40] Ibid.

in several classic cases[41] (see further Chapter 7) before in *Portugal v Council* the Court held the following:

Case C-149/96 *Portugal v Council*, ECLI:EU:C:1999:574, para 40

To require [domestic] courts to refrain from applying rules of domestic law which are inconsistent with the WTO agreements would have the consequence of depriving the legislative or executive organs of the contracting parties of the possibility afforded by Article 22 of [the WTO Understanding on Rules and Procedures Governing the Settlement of Disputes] of reaching a negotiated settlement, even on a temporary basis.

The idea was that the existence of a dispute settlement system in the WTO agreement was the proper forum for the Member States to settle conflicts related to the agreement.[42] Again, however, one could argue that this does not affect the status of international agreements in the EU legal order. Yet, these exceptions seriously limit the effects of international law in concrete situations. In the words of AG Poiares Maduro:

Joined Cases C-120/06 & C-121/06 *FIAMM and Others v Council and Commission*, Opinion of AG Poiares Maduro, ECLI:EU:C:2008:98, para 37

… the fact that WTO law cannot be relied upon before a court does not mean that it does not form part of the Community legal system. From this point of view, the formulation used by the Court in *Portugal v Council* is undoubtedly unfortunate. It nurtures a belief that an international agreement does not form part of the body of Community legality, whereas it is merely a question of the provision's enforceability, of the jurisdiction of the courts to take cognisance of it.

International law does not regulate its own status in the domestic legal orders of states or the legal orders of international organisations. Nevertheless, one may argue that the international principle of *pacta sunt servanda* may call for internal measures to facilitate the state or international organisation to live up to its international obligations. Whether this is done by accepting the international norms as valid norms in the domestic legal order or by transferring international norms into domestic law (or even by accepting a conflict between national and international obligations) is up to the state or international organisation.

[41] Including Case C-469/93 *Chiquita*, ECLI:EU:C:1995:435; Case 270/80 *Polydor*, ECLI:EU:C:1982:43; and Case 21/72–24/72 *International Fruit Company*, ECLI:EU:C:1972:115.

[42] See also Case C-27/00 *R v Secretary of State for the Environment, Transport and the Regions, ex parte Omega Air Limited*, ECLI:EU:C:2002:161.

C. International Customary Law and EU Law

So far, we have mainly focused on the status and effect of international agreements binding upon the EU. Yet, generally the CJEU does take unwritten international law into account. In *Kadi*, the General Court even checked the acts of the UN Security Council against *jus cogens* (as the type of customary international law from which no deviation is allowed); without, by the way, concluding that norms of *jus cogens* were violated. The Treaties are silent on the status of customary international law in the EU legal order, but in general terms, Article 3(5) TEU hints at the idea that the EU considers itself bound by international law in general. This was confirmed by the Court in the ATAA judgment discussed at the outset of this section.

Article 3(5) TEU

In its relations with the wider world, the Union … shall contribute to … the strict observance and development of international law including respect for the principles of the United Nations Charter.

The last part is repeated in the General Provisions on the Union's External Action in the TEU, where Article 21(1) refers to 'respect for the principles of the United Nations Charter and international law'. As we will see, over the years, the Court accepted the fact that the Union is bound by international law 'in its entirety, including customary international law, which is binding upon the institution of the European Union' – to quote AG Kokott.[43] The idea that the respect for international law relates to both written and unwritten law had already been underlined by the Court in *Poulsen*, in which references were made to the customary law rules in the law of the sea.[44] This extends the scope of international law binding on the EU, including the substance of treaties to which the EU is not a party, to the extent that they reflect customary international law. Clear examples are the 1969 and 1986 Vienna Conventions on the Law of Treaties, which are largely considered to reflect international custom.

Yet, the hierarchical position of customary international law (see Section II above) is less clear. In the landmark case of *Racke*, the Court for the first time shed some light on the effects of customary international law in the EU legal order and the possibilities for individuals to invoke it to challenge an EU Regulation. This case was about the rule of *rebus sic stantibus* (a fundamental change in circumstances as a legitimate reason to suspend an international agreement) which is laid down in Article 62 of the Vienna Convention on the Law of Treaties. As the European Community was not a party to that Convention, the Court had to rely on the customary nature of that rule.

[43] Case C-398/13 P *Inuit Tapiriit Kanatami v Commission*, Opinion of AG Kokott, ECLI:EU:C:2015:190, para 86.

[44] Case C-286/90 *Anklagemindigheden v Poulsen and Diva Navigation*, ECLI:EU:C:1992:453, para 10.

Case C-162/96 *Racke GmbH & Co v Hauptzollamt Mainz*, ECLI:EU:C:1998:293

41 As far as the Community is concerned, an agreement concluded by the Council with a non-member country in accordance with the provisions of the EC Treaty is an act of a Community institution, and the provisions of such an agreement form an integral part of Community law (see *Demirel*, paragraph 7).

42 If, therefore, the disputed regulation had to be declared invalid, the trade concessions granted by the Cooperation Agreement would remain applicable in Community law until the Community brought that Agreement to an end in accordance with the relevant rules of international law.

43 It follows that a declaration of the invalidity of the disputed regulation by reason of its being contrary to rules of customary international law would allow individuals to rely directly on the rights to preferential treatment granted to them by the Cooperation Agreement.

44 For its part, the Commission doubts whether, in the absence of an express clause in the EC Treaty, the international law rules referred to in the order for reference may be regarded as forming part of the Community legal order. Thus, in order to challenge the validity of a regulation, an individual might rely on grounds based on the relationship between him and the Community, but does not, the Commission argues, have the right to rely on grounds deriving from the legal relationship between the Community and a non-member country, which fall within the scope of international law.

45 It should be noted in that respect that, as is demonstrated by the Court's judgment in Case C-286/90 Poulsen and Diva Navigation, paragraph 9, the European Community must respect international law in the exercise of its powers. It is therefore required to comply with the rules of customary international law when adopting a regulation suspending the trade concessions granted by, or by virtue of, an agreement which it has concluded with a non-member country.

46 It follows that the rules of customary international law concerning the termination and the suspension of treaty relations by reason of a fundamental change of circumstances are binding upon the Community institutions and form part of the Community legal order.

Although in this particular case the Court held that there was no manifest violation of the law of treaties, it did not hesitate to state that 'it is required to comply with the rules of customary international law'. In fact, the last sentence of paragraph 46 strongly resembles the legal status of international agreements laid down in current Article 216(2) TFEU. As one observer holds, '[b]ased on these observations, one can proceed on the assumption that it is unlikely that the EU system should adopt a very different approach in its relationship with international agreements and custom'.[45] A similar reasoning can be found in *Opel Austria*.

Case T-115/94 *Opel Austria v Council*, ECLI:EU:T:1997:3

84 The Council does not take issue with the applicant's statement that Article 18 of the First Vienna Convention and Article 18 of the Second Vienna Convention codify rules of customary international law which are binding on the Community ...

90 The Court holds in this connection, first, that the principle of good faith is a rule of customary international law whose existence is recognized by the International Court of Justice (see the judgment of 25 May 1926, German interests in *Polish Upper Silesia*, CPJI, Series A, No 7, pp 30 and 39) and is therefore binding on the Community.

Obviously, the obligation to respect international customary law holds in particular with regard to relations with third states (compare also Article 3(5) TEU referred to above). Unless we are dealing with *jus cogens* norms, the EU – in both primary and secondary law – may deviate from international law to regulate the relationship with and between its Member States.[46]

More recent case law on the one hand confirms the idea expressed in *Racke* that 'the rules of customary international law ... form part of the Union legal order', but at the same time it is not completely consistent. The statements in Articles 3(5) and 21 TEU indicating that the Union shall contribute to the strict observance and development of international law lead to the presumption that in its relations with other international actors the EU is bound by international law, be it written or unwritten. The question, however, is how this can be squared with the statement in *Kadi* that, in the end, priority should be granted to the constitutional principles of the EU itself. One answer is that at the time of *Kadi*, Articles 3 and 21 TEU did not yet exist. A post-Lisbon *Kadi* may have had to use a slightly different reasoning but the outcome may have been the same: the duty to respect international law today amounts to a constitutional principle of the EU.[47] Obviously, the Court would still have a task to balance this constitutional principle against other constitutional principles, including the protection of fundamental rights, which are considered to 'form part of the very foundations of the Community legal order'.[48]

[45] A Gianelli, 'Customary International Law in the European Union' in E Cannizzaro, P Palchetti and RA Wessel (eds) *International Law as Law of the European Union* (Leiden, Martinus Nijhoff, 2011) 99.

[46] Ibid.

[47] Ibid, 105.

[48] Joined Cases C-402/05 P and C-415/05 P *Kadi and Al Barakaat*, ECLI:EU:C:2008:461, para 304.

D. The Doctrine of Consistent Interpretation

The above analyses reveal the possibility of a direct effect of international law in the EU legal order. At the same time, the case law of the Court introduced another possibility: *indirect* effect of international law. This mode of application is usually referred to as the doctrine of consistent interpretation.

Case C-61/94 *Commission v Germany*, ECLI:EU:C:1996:313, para 52

When the wording of secondary Community legislation is open to more than one interpretation, preference should be given as far as possible to the interpretation which renders the provision consistent with the Treaty. Likewise, an implementing regulation must, if possible, be given an interpretation consistent with the basic regulation (see Case C-90/92 *Dr Tretter v Hauptzollamt Stuttgart-Ost*, paragraph 11). Similarly, the primacy of international agreements concluded by the Community over provisions of secondary Community legislation means that such provisions must, so far as is possible, be interpreted in a manner that is consistent with those agreements.

Given the notion that agreements concluded by the EU form an integral part of the EU legal order, the principle of consistent interpretation did not appear out of the blue.[49] It is an elegant way of solving (potential) conflicts between EU law and international obligations when international agreements lack direct effect (as is the case with the WTO agreements and, as we have seen, UNCLOS). The duty to interpret secondary EU law in conformity with binding international law stems from the superior hierarchical status of international law within the EU legal order as discussed above. The WTO agreements, in particular, have been a source of inspiration in this respect. The principle of consistent interpretation has been said to be relevant for the Anti-Dumping Agreement, the Anti-Subsidy Agreements and for the Agreement on Trade-Related Aspects of Intellectual Property Rights (TRIPs).[50] In the *Werner* and *Leifer* judgments the Court argued that Article XI GATT was relevant for the interpretation of a Community Regulation establishing common rules for exports (Cases C-70/94 and C-83/94).

While these cases were about the lack of direct effect of the 1947 GATT and thus concerned the need to assess the indirect effect of provisions of an international

[49] In fact, a more implicit reference could already be found in Case 92/71 *Interfood GmbH v Hauptzollamt Hamburg-Ericus* ECLI:EU:C:1972:30, para 6: 'Since agreements regarding the Common Custom Tariff were reached between the Community and its partners in GATT the principles underlying those agreements *may be of assistance* in interpreting the rules of classification applicable to it' (emphasis added).

[50] Cases C-61/94 *Commission v Germany*, ECLI:EU:C:1996:313, para 52; C-286/02 *Bellio F.lli Srl v Prefettura di Treviso* ECLI:EU:C:2004:212, para 33; and C-49/02 *Heidelberger Bauchemie GmbH*, ECLI:EU:C:2004:384, para 20.

agreement, in *Poulsen* the Court confirmed that this also holds true for customary international law.

Case C-286/90 *Poulsen and Diva Navigation*, ECLI:EU:C:1992:453, para 9

As a preliminary point, it must be observed, first, that the European Community must respect international law in the exercise of its powers and that, consequently, Article 6 [of Regulation 3094/86 on certain technical measures for the conservation of fishery resources] must be interpreted, and its scope limited, in the light of the relevant rules of the international law of the sea.

It is important to note that the principle of consistent interpretation not only applies in relation to the international agreements themselves but also to decisions flowing from those agreements. In general terms this was made clear by the Court in *Sevince* (Case C-192/89): 'in order to be recognized as having direct effect, the provisions of a decision of the council of association must satisfy the same conditions as those applicable to the provisions of the Agreements itself'.[51] EU law should be interpreted in the light of the provisions in international decisions that are binding upon the EU. The main area of concern is WTO decisions. Interpretation and application of WTO law is regularly influenced by the reports of WTO panels and of the Appellate Body. However, so far, the Court has been hesitant to interpret EU secondary legislation in the light of WTO dispute decisions.[52] Yet, in general, decisions by international organisations have an impact on the EU legal order and may be of interpretative assistance.[53]

The duty of consistent interpretation may also be applicable in the domestic legal order of the Member States in the case of an agreement to which the Member States are a party. In *Commune de Mesquer*,[54] the Court pointed to the possible necessity for Member States to interpret EU law in the light of international obligations to allow EU law to function well. Similarly, in *Intertanko* (see above) it became clear that there is a role for the Court to prevent a clash between Member States' international agreements and EU obligations by way of a consistent interpretation. The rationale behind the doctrine of consistent interpretation therefore seems the need to assure the principle of respect for international law.

Finally, it is important to note that the conclusion of the above analysis cannot be used the other way around: that provisions in international agreements should always be interpreted in exactly the same manner as under EU law. Even if the provisions are

[51] See also Case 30/88 *Greece v Commission*, ECLI:EU:C:1989:422.

[52] See, for instance, Case C-351/04 *Ikea Wholesale v Commissioners of Customs & Excise*, ECLI:EU:C:2007:547.

[53] RA Wessel and S Blockmans, 'The Legal Status and Influence of Decisions of International Organizations and other Bodies in the European Union' in P Eeckhout and M Lopez-Escudero (eds) *The European Union's External Action in Times of Crisis* (Oxford, Hart Publishing, 2016).

[54] Case C-188/07 *Commune de Mesquer v Total France SA, Total International Ltd*, ECLI:EU:C:2008:359.

identical (which may be the case in, for instance, trade agreements which have as their main goal to extend certain internal market rules to external parties), there remains a difference between international law and EU law. A classic case in this regard is *Polydor*,[55] in which the question was raised whether the internal market interpretation of the exhaustion of intellectual property rights could also be applied to trade with Portugal (which was not yet an EU member at the time) on the basis of the free trade agreement with that country, which contained identical provisions. The Court noted the differences between Community law and international law and concluded that different interpretations were justified. A similar conclusion was drawn in *Kupferberg*, referred to above.

Case 270/80 *Polydor v Harlequin Record Shop*, ECLI:EU:C:1982:43

14 The provisions of the agreement on the elimination of restrictions on trade between the Community and Portugal are expressed in terms which in several respects are similar to those of the EEC Treaty on the abolition of restrictions on intra-Community trade. Harlequin and Simons pointed out in particular the similarity between the terms of Articles 14(2) and 23 of the agreement on the one hand and those of Articles 30 and 36 of the EEC Treaty on the other.

15 However, such similarity of terms is not a sufficient reason for transposing to the provisions of the agreement the above-mentioned case-law, which determines in the context of the Community the relationship between the protection of industrial and commercial property rights and the rules on the free movement of goods.

16 The scope of that case law must indeed be determined in the light of the Community's objectives and activities as defined by articles 2 and 3 of the EEC Treaty. As the Court has had occasion to emphasize in various contexts, the Treaty, by establishing a common market and progressively approximating the economic policies of the Member States, seeks to unite national markets into a single market having the characteristics of a domestic market.

IV. International Responsibility

In Chapter 1 we addressed the international legal personality of the European Union. We argued that, as an international legal person, the EU occupies a separate position in the international legal order. This position as an international actor

[55] Case 270/80 *Polydor*, ECLI:EU:C:1982:43.

implies that in its relations with third states and other international organisations the EU must adhere to the norms that make up that international legal order. This leads to the question of whether and to what extent the EU may be held responsible by its international partners where there is a violation of international law. This question may occur in relation to all international obligations of the Union, but is particularly salient in the context of the EU's Common Foreign, Security and Defence Policy (see Chapter 9).

From an international law perspective it is difficult not to regard the European Union as an international organisation and hence within the scope of the Articles on the International Responsibility of International Organizations (ARIO) as adopted by the International Law Commission (ILC) of the UN in August 2011 and endorsed by the UN General Assembly in December 2011.[56] While these Articles are not to be seen as a formal agreement between states on the issue of the international responsibility of international organisations, they are regarded the most authoritative source of interpretation at the moment. At the same time, the Union is not a regular international organisation and the general rules on the responsibility of international organisations sit uneasily with, in particular, the complex (and indeed unique) division of competences between the Union and its Member States.

The present section does not do justice to the many complex questions related to the EU's possible responsibility under international law. Yet, is has at least become widely accepted that the EU as such may bear international responsibility for an internationally wrongful act. It indeed seems to fit the definition of an international organisation used in the ARIO, Article 2(a): '"international organization" means an organisation established by a treaty or other instrument governed by international law and possessing its own international legal personality' and which 'may include as members, in addition to States, other entities.'

On the basis of Article 1, the ARIO 'apply to the international responsibility of an international organisation for an internationally wrongful act' as well as 'to the international responsibility of a State for an internationally wrongful act in connection with the conduct of an international organisation'. The latter paragraph is meant to, inter alia, incorporate those cases of State responsibility for internationally wrongful acts by an international organisation where a State is a member of that organisation, such as the Member States of the Union.[57]

The ARIO suggest in Article 3 that, as a point of departure, the EU is responsible for its own internationally wrongful acts. Article 4 lists the conditions for an internationally wrongful act by an international organisation that entails the international responsibility of that organisation.

[56] International Law Commission (ILC), 'Draft Arts. on the responsibility of international organisations, with commentaries 2011', Adopted by the ILC at its sixty-third session, in 2011, and submitted to the General Assembly as part of the Commission's report covering the work of that session (A/66/10) (2011) *Yearbook of the International Law Commission*, vol II, Part Two, 5, see in particular Pt 6 where the Commentary refers to Art 57 of the Arts. on responsibility of States for internationally wrongful acts.

[57] See, in particular, Pt 6 of the ARIO Commentaries where the Commentary refers to Art 57 of the Arts on responsibility of States for internationally wrongful acts.

Article 3 ARIO

Every internationally wrongful act of an international organization entails the international responsibility of that organization.

Article 4 ARIO

There is an internationally wrongful act of an international organization when conduct consisting of an action or omission: (a) Is attributable to the international organization under international law; and (b) constitutes a breach of an international obligation of that organization.

The next question is: What conduct can be attributed to the Union? Article 6(1) ARIO indicates that conduct by organs and agents can establish the international responsibility of the Union. According to Article 6(2) ARIO, the 'rules of the organisation' shall be applied when determining these 'organs and agents'. In view of the Union rules on 'internal' responsibility, there are good reasons to interpret this term as 'institutions, bodies, offices and agencies and their servants' as used is in the TFEU.[58]

Yet, the EU is not a normal international organisation and the division of external competences is both complex and dynamic (see Chapters 1 and 4). One of the key questions, therefore, is how to divide the responsibility between the EU and its Member States, for instance in the case of mixed agreements. Would a joint responsibility between the EU and its Member States be possible?

A Delgado Casteleiro, *The International Responsibility of the European Union: From Competence to Normative Control* (Cambridge, Cambridge University Press, 2016) 5

The debate within the CJEU focuses, perhaps in excess, on how the division of competences might a priori affect the international responsibility of the EU. However, it does not further articulate how the exercise of that competence plays out in relation to the attribution of responsibility. By focusing only on the division of competences, the CJEU disregards how the constitutional architecture of the EU determines the relationship between the EU and its Member States.

[58] Cf F Hoffmeister, 'Litigating Against the European Union and its Member States' (2010) 21 *European Journal of International Law* 723, 740, who refers to Arts 340(2) and 263 TFEU as well as to Art 51(1) of the EU Charter of Fundamental Rights. Article 10(2) confirms that also 'the breach of any international obligation that may arise for an international organisation towards its members under the rules of the organisation' is included in the ARIO.

> ... The EU seems to be favouring joint responsibility as the default rule in the European Convention on Human Rights (ECHR) ... Conversely, in relation to the responsibility stemming from International investor-State arbitration, joint responsibility is not the general rule.

In general, as also argued by the above study, the EU's 'normative control' over the actions by its Member States in a particular setting plays an essential role. The division of competences does not always reveal the ways in which Member States are actually following EU rules in their international activities. Or, indeed, when they even merely act as agents of a Union that may have a competence it is unable to exercise in an international (state-centred) setting (see Chapter 6 on the role of the EU in international organisations).

Irrespective of the notion that the EU itself can be responsible under international law for internationally wrongful acts, it is worth keeping in mind that it is quite difficult to actually enforce the rules. The immunity of international organisations makes proceedings before (domestic or international) courts extremely difficult and the same may apply to the EU.[59] At the same time, the International Court of Justice may only rule in conflicts between states. This means that the role of the ARIO in establishing an international responsibility of the Union may be limited to an argumentative function.

F Hoffmeister, 'Litigating Against the European Union and its Member States' (2010) 21 *European Journal of International Law* 723, 745

> When one compares the results of the analysis of international case law and of the special rules of the European Union, there is considerable overlap. Both international case law and European Union rules attach significance to the actor but are also aware of the situation that a Member State may not act on his own behalf, but merely as an agent of the Union. International practice also takes account of the fact that the Union is exclusively competent or has exercised its shared competence in a certain policy field, with the consequence that the Union is considered to have the power to bring an end to the alleged breach, provided that it has assumed an international obligation in the field. That leads inevitably to the rules of the European Union on external competences and their differentiation between exclusive, shared, and parallel competences. Such rules are hence of primordial importance for both the third state or applicant in question and the Union and its Member States alike.

[59] RA Wessel, 'Immunities of the European Union' (2014) 10 *International Organizations Law Review* 395.

In view of this remarkable overlap, it is suggested that one should always examine and evaluate three criteria in order to determine whether action can be attributed to the Union or its Member States under international law:

(a) Who is the factual actor of the alleged breach?
(b) Who has the legal power to bring an end to the alleged breach?
(c) Who bears the international obligation invoked concerning the alleged breach? …

Certainly, the exact application of the three criteria may be subject to debate and controversy. But codifying and progressively developing international law is a tremendous task in any event. Having finished its first reading on responsibility of international organizations, the ILC has so far decided not to propose a special rule for the attribution of Member States' conduct to the European Union in particular circumstances. But it opened the door to accepting such a rule as *lex specialis* under Draft Article 63 Provided that it can be firmly rooted in international law, including the rules of the organization applicable between the international organization and its members.

V. The Broader Picture of EU External Relations Law

As this chapter has shown, while the EU and its legal order have traditionally been portrayed as 'friendly' towards international law, this 'friendship' has evolved over time and has not been without its difficulties. There are many connections but also tensions that exist between EU and international law. The tensions were already inherent in the original idea of creating an entity that would have a certain autonomous relation vis-à-vis international law, and the need for that entity to live up to the international rules in order to be able to interact with others on the global stage. Over the years, the Court of Justice has had an important role in balancing interests in the relationship between EU and international law and taking account of the sensitive links between law and policy/politics in EU external relations law.

The Court of Justice's case law in *Kadi* serves as a prime example of that tension. The CJEU found itself in a difficult position, attempting to square some of the foundations of EU law with the obligations flowing from UN law. But, also in the WTO cases, it became clear that legal analysis was interspersed with political considerations. While the EU Treaties contain a general commitment to respect and develop international law, its application in practice is complex. Hence, the Court's role in this area cannot be underestimated. The Court made clear that there is a certain hierarchy and that international law, in most cases, has an internal effect in the EU legal order and that it can even set aside the application of EU rules. At the same time, we have seen some of the external effects that EU law can produce and which create their own tensions with outside actors and existing international legal frameworks.

This chapter also highlighted the interconnectedness between the internal division of competences and external responsibilities. The complex combination of roles of the EU and its Member States make it difficult to apply, for instance, the general rules on the international responsibility of international organisations to the European Union.

VI. Sources and Further Reading

Cannizzaro, E, P Palchetti, and RA Wessel (eds) *International Law as Law of the European Union* (Leiden, Brill/Nijhoff, 2011).

Contartese, C, 'The Autonomy of the EU Legal Order in the CJEU's External Relations Case-Law: From the "Essential" to the "Specific Characteristics" of the Union and Back Again' (2017) 54 *Common Market Law Review* 1627.

De Búrca, G, 'The European Court of Justice and the International Legal Order After *Kadi*' (2010) 51 *Harvard International Law Journal* 1.

Delgado, A, *The International Responsibility of the European Union: From Competence to Normative Control* (Cambridge, Cambridge University Press, 2016).

Fahey, E, *The Global Reach of EU Law* (Abingdon, Routledge, 2016).

Garben, S and I Govaere (eds) *The Interface between International and EU Law* (Oxford, Hart Publishing, 2019).

Griller, S, 'International Law, Human Rights and the European Community's Autonomous Legal Order: Notes on the European Court of Justice Decision in *Kadi*' (2008) 4 *European Constitutional Law Review* 528.

Hoffmeister, F, 'Litigating Against the European Union and its Member States – Who Responds under the ILC's Draft Articles on International Responsibility of International Organizations?' (2010) 21 *European Journal of International Law* 723.

Klabbers, J, 'International Law in Community Law: The Law and Politics of Direct Effect' (2001) 21 *Yearbook of European Law* 263.

Klabbers, J, *Treaty Conflict and the European Union* (Cambridge, Cambridge University Press, 2009).

Kuijper, PJ, 'Customary International Law, Decisions of International Organisations and other Techniques for Ensuring Respect for International Legal Rules in European Community Law' in J Wouters, A Nollkaemper and E de Wet (eds) *The Europeanisation of International Law: The Status of International Law in the EU and its Member States* (The Hague, TMC Asser Press, 2008) 87–106.

Larik, J, 'The Kadi Saga as a Tale of "Strict Observance" of International Law: Obligations Under the UN Charter, Targeted Sanctions and Judicial Review in the European Union' (2014) 61 *Netherlands International Law Review* 23.

Mayer, FC, 'European Law as a Door Opener for Public International Law?' in JM Thouvenin and C Tomuschat (eds) *Droit International et Diversité des Cultures Juridiques – International Law and Diversity of Legal Cultures* (Paris, Pédone, 2008) 241–55.

Moreno-Lax, V and Gragl, P (eds) 'EU Law and Public International Law: Co-Implication, Embeddedness and Interdependency', Special section in (2016) 35 *Yearbook of European Law*.

Van Rossem, JW, 'Interaction between EU Law and International Law in the Light of *Intertanko* and *Kadi*: The Dilemma of Norms Binding the Member States but not the Community' (2009) 40 *Netherlands Yearbook of International Law* 183.

Wessel, RA, and Blockmans, S (eds) *Between Autonomy and Dependence: The EU Legal Order Under the Influence of International Organisations* (The Hague, TMC Asser Press/Springer, 2013).

Wessel, RA, 'Studying International and European Law: Confronting Perspectives and Combining Interests' in S Garben and I Govaere (eds) *The Interface between International and EU Law* (Oxford, Hart Publishing, 2019) 73–97.

Wouters, J, 'The Tormented Relationship between International Law and EU Law' in PHF Bekker, R Dolzer, and M Waibel (eds) *Making Transnational Law Work in the Global Economy: Essays in Honour of Detlev Vagts* (Cambridge, Cambridge University Press, 2010) 98–221.

Wouters, J and D Van Eeckhoute, 'Giving Effect to Customary International Law through European Community Law' in JN Prinssen and A Schrauwen (eds) *Direct Effect* (Groningen, European Law Publishing, 2004) 183–234.

Wouters, J, A Nollkaemper and E de Wet (eds) *The Europeanisation of International Law: The Status of International Law in the EU and its Member States* (The Hague, TMC Asser Press, 2008).

Ziegler, KS, 'The Relationship between EU Law and International Law' in D Patterson and A Södersten (eds) *A Companion to European Union Law and International Law* (Chichester, Wiley, 2016) 42–61.

6

The EU and International Institutions

Central Issues

- This chapter looks at how the EU Treaties, secondary legislation and case law regulate the position of the EU in international institutions. This includes both formal international organisations and less formal regimes. As highlighted by the position of the EU in the WTO, the division of competences between the EU and its Member States is an important part of this legal framework.
- The Treaties list several general and specific competences related to the participation of the EU in international institutions, which are described and analysed in this chapter.
- The European Union participates in many international organisations and other international fora, but the position of the EU in these bodies varies.
- The chapter focuses on two examples: The EU's presence in the World Trade Organization and the United Nations.

I. Introduction

One of the ways in which the EU conducts its external relations is by participating in international institutions. This includes both formal international organisations, such as the UN, and other 'institutionalised treaty regimes' such as the United Nations Framework Convention on Climate Change.[1] It also includes informal

[1] Schemers and Blokker define international organisations as: 'forms of cooperation (1) founded on an international agreement; (2) having at least one organ with a will of its own; and (3) established under international law.' HG Schermers and NM Blokker, *International institutional Law: Unity in Diversity*, 6th edn (Leiden, Brill/Nijhoff, 2018) 41.

bodies that are not founded in a treaty or other instrument, such as the G7 or G20. Among the changes that occurred with the entry into force of the Lisbon Treaty, the EU Treaties now include several references to international organisations and support for multilateralism, international law and the principles of the United Nations (Article 21 TEU).

International institutions play an important role in world affairs. It is difficult to find an area of international relations that is not regulated in some way by a relevant international organisation or treaty regime. Early in the life of the (then) European Economic Community, it became apparent that its external relations had to include relationships with, and in some cases, participation in, these international institutions. Most international institutions are made up of states. The participation of the EU, itself an international organisation (see discussion in Chapter 1), further complicates its participation in these bodies. The EU and its Member States are also increasingly influenced by the decisions of international organisations. For example, many EU (and national) rules find their origin in decision-making processes in other international organisations.

The EU has attained various positions in international institutions. These range from full membership to observer status. Participation in an international organisation includes, among other roles, the right to attend meetings, being elected for functions in the organs of the organisation and exercising voting and speaking rights. In addition to formal international institutions and regimes, the EU also participates in less formal ones, such as the G20. The EU also has close cooperation and partnership with several international institutions in areas of common interest.

II. Treaty Competences Related to the Participation of the EU in International Institutions

A. Implied and Express Competences

As discussed in Chapter 3, to be able to act externally, the EU needs to have the competence to do so. There are a number of provisions of the EU Treaties that deal with the EU's position in international institutions (discussed below). Generally, the EU's participation in an international institution depends on two factors.

The first relates to the division of competences between the EU and the Member States in the field covered by the international institution. Internal struggles between Member States or between Member States and EU institutions may form an obstacle to the accession of the EU to an international organisation. The EU Member States often prefer to remain present and visible in international institutions. This is even clearer in relation to international regimes that cannot be considered formal international organisations. The EU may nonetheless want to participate in such institutions. This may be based on legal arguments, for instance, where the EU exercises exclusive or significant competences in the field covered by the institution. EU presence may also be based on more political arguments, given the EU's priority in a given field. In both cases, the EU needs to ensure that both legal and political arrangements resulting from cooperation within a regime respect its competences and reflect the Union's political agenda. In these cases, the EU decision-making machinery is limited to providing the content of the EU-position (for instance, in relation to the EU's participation in the G20). This means that large parts of the EU's multilateral activities are not directly regulated by the Treaties but find their basis in decisions and declarations which aim to present a unified EU position. For example, see below an excerpt of a joint letter of the European Council President and Commission President to the Member States, meant to coordinate the 'European' stance in an upcoming G-20 Summit.

Joint letter of Presidents Donald Tusk and Jean-Claude Juncker on the upcoming G20 summit, 27 November 2018

Later this week we will be attending the G20 Summit in Argentina, on behalf of the EU. The outlook ahead of the summit is rather bleak. The rules-based international order is under increasing strain and global trade tensions remain unresolved, thereby negatively affecting the global economic outlook. We, therefore, want to focus our attention on convincing our partners that there is no better alternative than a coordinated multilateral cooperation, which should be aimed at security and prosperity of our People, ensuring a fair level playing field among all Nations in order to shape a globalised interconnected world in line with our shared interests and values.

We want to seek solutions for the defining struggles of our times: climate change, trade tensions, irregular migration, poverty and terrorism. In short, to make sure that our People will be safe in the ever-more globalised world. In this light, we would like to inform you about the key issues that we will discuss at the G20 Summit in Buenos Aires on 30 November–1 December.

The second issue relates to the whether the institution itself allows for the EU to become a member of that institution (or other forms of participation). Few international organisations allow other international organisations to be members. This reflects the fact that international organisations have traditionally been made up of states. For the EU to participate in an international organisation it must either (a) amend the constitutive instrument of the organisation to allow for EU membership, or (b) participate in the organisation without full membership.

Even where the EU has extensive competence, it may be prevented from full participation in the decision-making process within international organisations and bodies. For example, the EU is a party to the UN Convention on the Law of the Sea, but it is not able to participate in all areas of the UNCLOS institutional system.[2]

[2] See C Cinelli, 'Law of the Sea Framework: Is EU Engagement a *sine qua non* for Influence?' in RA Wessel and J Odermatt (eds) *Research Handbook on the EU and International Organizations* (Cheltenham, Edward Elgar, 2019).

Despite exercising significant competences in the fields dealt with by the bodies, the EU is neither a member of the International Maritime Organization (IMO) nor the International Civil Aviation Organization (ICAO).

For participation in informal regimes, the EU Treaty framework only sets the outer boundaries of the Union's actions: they may not conflict with EU or international law. However, when regimes do find their basis in an international agreement, the EU's formal participation depends on its legal competence to join a particular treaty. The case for a formal role of the EU in a given international institution is stronger in cases where the EU has competences related to the objectives and functions of that institution. This is particularly the case in areas in which the EU enjoys exclusive competence (eg, in the CCP), but also applies to situations where the competence is shared with the Member States (aviation, environment, etc.).

There is no specific Treaty provision that deals with the EU joining or establishing an international organisation. That process is covered by the Treaty provisions on the conclusion of international agreements, namely Articles 218 and 219(3) TFEU (see Chapter 4). This is the process by which the EU may be a founding member of a new international organisation or join an existing one. The EU does this by becoming a party to the organisation's 'constitutive treaty' (ie, the treaty establishing an international organisation).

Participation in, and membership of, international institutions is predominantly based on implied powers. The EU's competence to participate in a given institution is linked to the Union's general competence in different policy fields. For example, the Union's membership of the Food and Agricultural Organization (FAO) is based on the Articles 43 TFEU (agriculture and fisheries), 207 TFEU (commercial policy) and 209 TFEU (development cooperation).

In addition to the participation in international institutions, the EU Treaties also refer to specific policy areas where the EU is to cooperate with certain international institutions. Article 211 TEU is the closest to a general competence-conferring provision.

Article 211 TFEU

Within their respective spheres of competence, the Union and the Member States shall cooperate with third countries and with the competent international organisations.

This 'cooperation' may also lead to the establishment of legal relationships. This can be derived from the provisions creating a competence for the Union to conclude international agreements.

Article 216(1) TFEU

The Union may conclude an agreement with one or more third countries or international organisations where the Treaties so provide or where the conclusion of an agreement is necessary in order to achieve, within the framework of the Union's policies, one of the objectives referred to in the Treaties, or is provided for in a legally binding Union act or is likely to affect common rules or alter their scope.

Article 217 TFEU

The Union may conclude with one or more third countries or international organisations agreements establishing an association involving reciprocal rights and obligations, common action and special procedure.

In addition to the power to join the constitutive treaties of international institutions, the Court of Justice has recognised that the EU may also establish new international institutions.

Opinion 1/76 (*Draft Agreement establishing a European laying-up fund for inland waterway vessels*), ECLI:EU:C:1977:63, para 5

In order to attain the common transport policy, the contents of which are defined in Articles 74 and 75 of the treaty, the council is empowered to lay down 'any other appropriate provisions', as expressly provided in Article 75(1)(c) [now Article 91(1)(d) TFEU]. The Community is therefore not only entitled to enter into contractual relations with a third country in this connexion but also has the power, while observing the provisions of the treaty, to cooperate with that country in setting up an appropriate organism such as the public international institution which it is proposed to establish under the name of the 'European laying-up fund for inland waterway vessels'. The Community may also, in this connexion, cooperate with a third country for the purpose of giving the organs of such an institution appropriate powers of decision and for the purpose of defining, in a manner appropriate to the objectives pursued, the nature, elaboration, implementation and effects of the provisions to be adopted within such a framework.

Both the European Economic Area (EEA) and the 'associations' created by association agreements (see Chapters 4 and 13), are examples of international organisations created by what is now the European Union (now Article 217 TFEU). In *Opinion 1/94*, the Court implicitly accepted a role of the EU as one of the founding members of the WTO. Although not explicitly regulated, this also seems to imply a competence of the EU to fully participate in so-called 'treaty regimes' based on a formal accession to a treaty (eg, the UN Framework Convention on Climate Change and the Kyoto Protocol). As in formal international organisations, the EU participates either because the parties have granted it observer or full participant status or because the treaty includes a clause that allows for the participation of a Regional Economic Integration Organization (REIO). For example, Article II of the FAO Constitution was modified to allow for the accession of any 'regional economic integration organization'. An REIO is commonly defined in UN protocols and conventions as 'an organization constituted by sovereign states of a given region to which its Member States have transferred competence in respect of matters governed by … convention or its protocols and [which] has been duly authorised, in accordance with its internal procedures, to sign, ratify, accept, approve or accede to it [the instruments concerned]'.[3] In the 2010 United Nations Convention on the Rights of Persons with Disabilities, to which the EU is a party, the REIO clause (Article 44) had evolved to a RIO (Regional Integration Organisation) clause, which recognises the scope of the EU's activities beyond economic integration.

In most cases, the EU Member States will remain competent in certain areas covered by the multilateral agreement. This means that they are concluded as 'mixed agreements', which allow both the EU and Member States to participate in the institution (see Chapters 3 and 4).

As we have seen in Chapter 3, the EU does not always need an express competence to conclude an international agreement. This means that it can join international institutions or participate in a treaty regime (Opinion 1/94 *WTO*) based on the external dimension of internal competence. This is confirmed by Article 216(1) TFEU, which explicitly refers to international organisations: 'The Union may conclude an agreement with one or more third countries or international organisations …'. This provision gives the EU a broad mandate to also conclude international agreements in order to become a member of an international organisation or to join a treaty regime.

Questions relating to the division of competences are also dependent on international law. In Joined Cases C-626/15 and C-659/16, the CJEU found that in that situation, a shared competence should be exercised in a shared manner, based on international law and the notion that EU Member States should be able to live up to their own international obligations. The case concerned Union positions on the creation of several marine-protected areas in the Antarctic Seas by the Commission for the Conservation of Antarctic Marine Living Resources (CCAMLR).

[3] See for instance Articles 4.1, 4.2, 4.3 and 4.5, 21 and 22 of the Kyoto Protocol.

Joined Cases C-626/15 and C-659/16 *Antarctique*, ECLI:EU:C:2018:925

128 In the specific context of the system of Antarctic agreements, exercise by the European Union of the external competence at issue in the present cases that excludes the Member States would be incompatible with international law.

129 It is clear from reading Article VII(2)(c) of the Canberra Convention in conjunction with Article XXIX(2) thereof that a regional economic integration organisation, such as the European Union, can accede to that convention and become a member of the CCAMLR only if its Member States are members. On the other hand, no analogous condition is laid down tying the presence of those States within the CCAMLR to the fact that the regional organisation concerned is also a member of that commission.

130 Consequently, the Canberra Convention does not grant regional integration organisations, such as the European Union, a fully autonomous status within the CCAMLR.

131 That is all the more the case given that the set of treaties and international agreements applicable to the Antarctic forms an organised and coherent system, headed by the oldest and most general treaty among them, namely the Antarctic Treaty, a fact which is reflected by Article V of the Canberra Convention. It follows from Article V that even the parties to the Canberra Convention who are not parties to the Antarctic Treaty acknowledge the special obligations and responsibilities of the Antarctic Treaty consultative parties and, consequently, observe the various measures recommended by them. Therefore, the Antarctic Treaty consultative parties have primary responsibility for developing the aforesaid set of Antarctic agreements and for safeguarding its coherence.

B. Specific Areas Indicated in the Treaties

The Treaties also refer to specific policy fields or specific international organisations. Article 37 TEU allows the EU to conclude agreements 'with one or more states or international organizations' in the area of the common foreign and security policy (CFSP). Similar provisions can be found in relation to environmental policy (Article 191(4) TFEU), development cooperation (Article 209(2) TFEU), economic, financial and technical cooperation (Article 212(3) TFEU) and humanitarian aid (Article 214(4) TFEU). Regarding Union policy on the environment, the Treaties set out that '[w]ithin their respective spheres of competence, the Union and the Member States shall cooperate with third countries and with the competent international organisations'. (Article 191(4) TFEU). Regarding humanitarian aid, the Union must ensure that its operations 'are coordinated and consistent with those of international organisations and bodies, in particular, those forming part of the United Nations system' (Article 214(7) TFEU). Article 6(2) TEU also requires the Union to accede to the European Convention for the Protection of Human Rights and Fundamental

Freedoms, although it has not yet done so (see the discussion on *Opinion 2/13* in Chapters 5 and 10).

Article 208(2) TFEU

The Union and the Member States shall comply with the commitments and take account of the objectives they have approved in the context of the United Nations and other competent international organisations.

Article 210(1) TFEU adds to that an obligation of coordination between the EU and the Member States in the field of development cooperation. As discussed in Chapter 10, this means that the EU and Member States must take account of the UN Sustainable Development Goals.

Article 210(1) TFEU

In order to promote the complementarity and efficiency of their action, the Union and the Member States shall coordinate their policies on development cooperation and shall consult each other on their aid programmes, including in international organisations and during international conferences. They may undertake joint action. Member States shall contribute, if necessary, to the implementation of Union aid programmes.

In addition, there are references in relation to the European Central Bank and the European Investment Bank (see Protocols Nos 4 and 5 to the Treaty). The first provision in a specific Treaty Title on 'The Union's Relations with International Organisations and Third Countries and Union Delegations' sets out a more general provision:

Article 220(1) TFEU

The Union shall establish all appropriate forms of cooperation with the organs of the United Nations and its specialised agencies, the Council of Europe, the Organisation for Security and Cooperation in Europe and the Organisation for Economic Cooperation and Development.

The Union shall also maintain such relations as are appropriate with other international organisations.

KE Jørgensen and KV Laatikainen, 'Introduction' in KE Jørgensen and KV Laatikainen (eds) *Routledge Handbook on the European Union and International institutions: Performance, Policy, Power* (Abingdon, Routledge, 2013) 1–3

While the European Union's prolonged effort to address the debt crisis within Europe captured headlines through 2012, a broader perspective of the international institutional landscape revealed an EU very much at the centre of the twenty-first century multilateralism. Europeans congratulated themselves in May 2011 for successfully obtaining enhanced observer status in the UN General Assembly so that, in accordance with the Lisbon Treaty, the European Union delegation could represent the EU when there is a common position. While the modalities of this observer status are still being defined (eg, when the EU can speak among the major groups in the General Assembly meetings), the resolution conferring this status was passed only after an extensive diplomatic campaign that encountered resistance among other regional groups and small states within the UN. Yet is it not only the UN General Assembly that has seen EU attention …

[D]uring the same period that the EU has championed 'effective multilateralism' and experienced a dramatic internal reform process to improve its performance in external relations, broader multilateral processes have also undergone dramatic change, partly through negotiated reform processes and partly in ad hoc response to broader global crises. This book, therefore, attempts to capture how scholars have wrestled with two moving targets – the evolving role of Europe in international institutions and the transformations in international institutions themselves.

These two dynamics are playing out in a global environment of new emerging powers and a great deal of uncertainty. Europe and the post-Lisbon European Union contribute to this shifting terrain of global governance. While the Lisbon Treaty introduces reforms to enhance EU foreign policy, it has not clarified the long-standing question of whether the EU is a participant in or partner to other international institutions. Critical appraisals of the notion of 'effective multilateralism' have also cast a spotlight on how the EU interacts with a variety of international institutions: does 'effectiveness' require working through and empowering existing institutions, working against existing international institutions because they are ineffective, or working outside existing institutions and thereby consigning them to an indifferent fate. These questions lie at the heart of a growing body of scholarship that the present volume aims to review and summarise existing research, while also pointing to new avenues of inquiry.

This overview reveals that the competences of the EU in relation to international institutions are fragmented and scattered across the Treaties. Apart from these EU competences, many of the provisions relate to 'cooperation' or to the role of

Member States. Thus, the goal to foster cooperation with third countries and competent international organisations is evident in fields of education and sport (Article 165(3) TFEU), vocational training (Article 166(3) TFEU), culture (Article 167(3) TFEU) and public health (Article 168(3) TFEU). A similar promotion of cooperation with other international organisations is mentioned in relation to social policy (Article156 TFEU) and cooperation in Union research, technological development and demonstration (Article 180(b) TFEU). The Treaty articles on the Unions foreign and security policy (see below) also include specific rules on the EU's presence in international organisations.

III. Status of the EU in International Institutions

The EU can have a variety of legal positions in other international organisations or bodies. This can include: (i) membership, (ii) observer status or (ii) other forms of cooperation and participation.

A. Membership

The EU will have *membership* status in organisations that deal with fields where the EU has exclusive or extensive competences (such as trade, fisheries and largely harmonised dimensions of the internal market). However, this does not mean that the EU is a member of all organisations that deal with areas of exclusive EU competence. The EU is a member of only a limited number of bodies, including the Food and Agricultural Organization (FAO), the World Trade Organization (WTO), and the Hague Conference on Private International Law. It is also a *de facto* member of the World Customs Organization (WCO). Its participation in the Organization for Economic Cooperation and Development (OECD) comes quite close to full membership. Despite the more modest formal arrangement that the European Commission 'shall take part in the work' of the OECD (Article 13 of the 1960 Paris Convention in conjunction with Protocol 1), it has been observed that 'this participation goes well beyond that of a mere observer',[4] giving the Commission quasi-member status.

Full participation is also possible in the case of treaty regimes. Thus, the EU (as such) has joined a number of UN Conventions, including the Convention on the Rights of Persons with Disabilities, United Nations Convention against Corruption, the United Nations Convention against Transnational Organized Crime and the UN Framework Convention on Climate Change. The Northwest Atlantic Fisheries Organization (NAFO) reveals that it is even possible for the EU to become a member of a treaty regime without its Member States themselves being a member.[5]

[4] See 'European Union and the OECD'. Available at: www.oecd.org/eu/european-union-and-oecd.htm.
[5] France and Denmark are members, but on behalf of other territories not in the EU.

In most cases, the EU is party to these treaties alongside the Member States, meaning that they are concluded as mixed agreements (see Chapters 3 and 4) as, in many cases, competences are shared between the EU and the Member States or because the Member States wish to be participants in the organisation for political reasons. To avoid a situation whereby the EU and its Member States have competing or diverging policies in these bodies, they are subject to the 'duty of sincere cooperation' (Article 4(3) TEU), which may restrain the actions of the Member States in these bodies (see Chapter 2).

P Eeckhout, *EU External Relations Law*, 2nd edn (Oxford, Oxford University Press, 2011) 255

The ... case law on the duty of co-operation and the Community's experience with work in international organizations suggest that the principle's effectiveness is limited if it is not fleshed out. There is an obvious case for creating some ... EU treaty language on this crucial principle for mixed external action. There is also an obvious case for basic legal texts on how to conduct co-operation in the framework of international organizations.

The FAO and the WTO are examples of organisations in which the EU participates as a full member. The EU is excluded from joining the UN itself and in the Specialised Agencies (Article 4(1) of the UN Charter), but joined the FAO in 1991 after the provisions of the its Constitution were amended to allow for the accession of regional economic integration organisations. One of the difficult issues that arises from parallel membership of the EU and the Member States is the question of which entity is entitled to participate in the organisation on a given topic. This question is relevant to the other members, who wish to ensure that any obligations under the agreement in question are respected. To deal with this issue, the EU has been required to submit a 'declaration of competences', a formal document setting out the different areas of the agreement where the EU and the Member States are responsible for its implementation. This issue also relates to the speaking and other participation rights in the FAO. EU competences must be established before each FAO meeting and for each item on the agenda. Without that statement, the Member States are presumed to be competent (CFAO, Article II, paragraph 6). In cases where the EU is entitled to vote, its vote equals the number of votes of the Member States (CFAO, Article II, paragraph 10). This requirement to constantly provide statements of competences is an obstacle to the efficient functioning of the EU in the FAO.[6] In addition, the EU is excluded from the organisational and budgetary affairs of the FAO. Thus, it is 'not eligible for election or designation' to bodies with restricted membership, which include the Constitutional,

[6] P Eeckhout, *EU External Relations Law*, 2nd edn (Oxford, Oxford University Press, 2011) 229.

Legal, Financial and Planning Committees.[7] The actual and potential problems that this state of affairs raises will be addressed below. Following up on its FAO membership, the Community joined the Codex Alimentarius Commission (CAC) in 2003.

The EU's membership of the WTO (see further below) differs in the sense that the Community was one of the founders of the WTO and a major player in the Uruguay Round negotiations that led to the establishment of the WTO.[8] In this case, there is no real difference between EU and state membership. In the WTO, voting rights may either be exercised by the EU (in which case the EU vote has the weight of the number of its Member States) or by the individual EU Member States. As decisions are usually taken by consensus and voting rarely takes place, the application of the WTO voting rules remains rather theoretical. Nevertheless, the issue of competences remains a source for a complex participation of both the EU and its Member States in the WTO. In *Opinion 1/94*, the Court held that the Community did not have an exclusive competence to conclude agreements in the area of trade in services and trade-related aspects of intellectual property rights.[9] These are both areas that form part of the WTO system, in the form of the Agreement on Trade in Services (GATS) and the Agreement on Trade-Related Aspects of Intellectual Property Rights (TRIPS) (in addition to the modified General Agreement on Tariffs and Trade – GATT). This has not prevented the EU from playing an increasingly prominent role in relation to these areas. Billet points to two reasons for an active role of the Commission, which represents the EU at the WTO, even where competences are (mainly) in the hands of the Member States. First, the strongly institutionalised setting of the WTO, in particular the system of dispute settlement, strengthens the position of the Commission 'both internally – vis-à-vis the Member States – as well as internationally'.[10] The second reasons relate to the EU's own decision-making procedure (the 'Community method') as well as the Commission's expertise in the area of trade.[11]

B. Observer Status

The EU has *observer status* when it can attend meetings of a body or an organisation but does not have voting rights. The precise rights that can be exercised by the EU as an observer varies from organisation to organisation. Usually, the presence of an observer is limited to formal meetings. In addition, formal interventions may only be possible at the end of the interventions of formal participants. In areas where the EU does have formal competences, but where the statutes of the particular international institution do not allow for EU membership, this may lead to a complex form of EU involvement. A good example is the practice at the International Labour Organization (ILO), which

[7] CFAO, Art II, para 9.
[8] Art XI, para 1 of the 1994 Marrakesh Agreement.
[9] Opinion 1/94 (*WTO*), ECLI:EU:C:1994:384.
[10] S Billet, 'From GATT to WTO: Internal Struggle for External Competences in the EU' (2009) 44 *Journal of Common Market Studies* 899, 901.
[11] Ibid, 901–05.

does not allow for the membership of international organisations.[12] The existence of Community competences in the area of social policy nevertheless called for its participation in ILO Conferences. The Community was officially granted observer status in 1989, which allows it (represented by the Commission) to speak and participate in ILO Conferences, to be present at the meeting of the Committees of the Conference and to participate in discussions there. The status also allows a presence at the ILO Governing Body, where the Commission may participate in the Plenary as well as in the committees. However, it cannot become a party to any of the ILO Conventions. This complex division of powers between the EU and its Member States in the ILO was addressed by the Court in Opinion 2/91.

Opinion 2/91 (*ILO Convention No. 170*), ECLI:EU:C:1993:106, para 5

In any event, although, under the ILO Constitution, the Community cannot itself conclude Convention No 170, its external competence may, if necessary, be exercised through the medium of the Member States acting jointly in the Community's interest.

Hence, the Member States act as agents of the European Union to allow the latter to make use of its external competences in this field. Obviously, coordination issues arise, although both the EU and its Member States increasingly see the need for a joint approach to live up to the principle of consistency (see also Chapter 1). A similar situation is found in relation to other organisations where only states can become members, but which are involved in fields that deal with areas of EU competences such as the IMO or ICAO. The Court has made it clear, however, that Member States may not abuse the fact that the Union is not a member of a particular international organisation. In cases of exclusive competence, Member States are not free to act entirely on their own, even if the Union is not able to table proposals by itself. Here also, the principle of sincere cooperation (Article 4(3) TEU) must be observed.[13]

This may be prevented by granting the EU observer status and allowing it to act on behalf of its Member States in areas where it has assumed powers, rather than asking Member States to act on behalf of the Union in areas where they, perhaps, no longer have powers. Although it remains difficult for international organisations and third states (and occasionally even for Member States) to accept a role of the EU in international institutions, the extensive observer status enjoyed by the EU in the ILO is not unique and can be found in many Specialised Agencies and programs of the United Nations, as well as in the UN's General Assembly and in ECOSOC. With regard to a number of international institutions (including the ICAO, UNESCO, OECD, and the

[12] Art 1(2) Constitution of the International Labour (signed 28 June 1919, entered into force 10 January 1920, as amended 20 April 1948) 15 UNTS 40.

[13] Case C-45/07 *Commission v Greece (International Maritime Organization)*, ECLI:EU:C:2009:81.

Council of Europe), the arrangements have been referred to as 'full participant' status, indicating that the only real difference between membership and observer status is voting rights.[14]

Finally, the European Union may participate in treaty regimes or informal international networks in areas which are deliberately left to the Member States. Examples include the regimes on non-proliferation and export controls. On the basis of Article 347 TFEU, Member States have claimed their own competence in relation to commodities related to the maintenance of international peace and security. This provision calls upon the Member States to ensure that any measures taken in this respect do not prevent the functioning of the internal market and are in line with the common commercial policy. There is thus a reason for the European Commission (not the EU as such) to participate in some of these regimes, since they may have an effect on the functioning of the internal market. Its role can be that of a 'permanent observer' (eg, in the Zangger Committee to harmonise the interpretation of nuclear export control policies for parties to the Non-Proliferation Treaty (NPT)) or even as a 'full participant' (as in the Australia Group which aims to ensure that exports do not contribute to the development of chemical or biological weapons).

F Hoffmeister, 'Outsider or Frontrunner? Recent Developments under International and European Law on the Status of the European Union in International Organizations and Treaty Bodies' (2007) 44 *Common Market Law Review* 41, 54

... After the breakthrough of Community membership in the FAO in 1991, the status of the European Union has further advanced in other international organizations and treaty bodies. Despite some resistance, inter alia from the United States, the Union has achieved greater visibility within and influence over the activities over several important organizations on the global level (ICAO, WHO, UNESCO). It has also consolidated and further refined its participant status in the Council of Europe and the OECD. It became a member in such diverse organizations as the Hague Conference on international private law and the newly founded Energy Community. On the other hand, the Union also keeps on struggling with the reluctance of some Member States to accept such a role in the transport sector in particular (IMO, Rhine and Danube Commissions) and continues to face a deadlock in some important UN bodies (for example UNHCR).

Against the backdrop of this mixed picture of factual developments, some interesting questions under international law came to the forefront. It could be shown that decisions to grant the status of a 'full participant' to the European

[14] F Hoffmeister, 'Outsider or Frontrunner? Recent Developments under International and European Law on the Status of the European Union in International Organizations and Treaty Bodies' (2007) 44 *Common Market Law Review* 41, 54.

Union belong to the respective organs of an international organization, as long as they do not intend to regulate the overall status of the Union in the whole organization. In the latter scenario, the decision must be taken by the plenary organ. It also became clear that the Union's membership in treaty bodies will face new challenges when such bodies are not open to all contracting parties, but only to a certain number of elected members. ...

In a nutshell, the European Union is neither an outsider anymore nor has it become a frontrunner in the multilateral arena. Rather it turns into a respected actor in international organizations and treaty bodies with the same speed as the law develops. Under international law that needs years of skilful multilateral diplomacy, under European law the European Court of Justice may accelerate the process.

C. Status Other than Observer

Through membership and observer status, the EU is capable of having an actual presence in international institutions and bodies. Yet it is also capable of having a relationship with international institutions, even where it does not have any formal status in that body. This is the case, for example, with the International Atomic Energy Agency (IAEA). The EU is neither a member nor an observer at the IAEA, but nevertheless has had quite some influence upon the many international agreements with which the IAEA is involved.[15] The EU's relationship with the IAEA is one of cooperation and partnership, rather than EU representation. Similarly, the EU and Council of Europe are partners that cooperate in numerous fields, including human rights.[16]

IV. Representation in International Institutions

A. Coordination of Positions

According to Article 17(1) TEU, the Commission 'shall ensure the Union's external representation', with the exception of CFSP and other cases provided for in the Treaties. In areas related to CFSP, the Union's High Representative for Foreign Affairs and Security Policy has a special role in relation to international institutions.

[15] See A Södersten, 'International Atomic Energy Agency (IAEA): The EU's Role in International Nuclear Energy Policy' in RA Wessel and J Odermatt (eds) *Research Handbook on the EU and International Organizations* (Cheltenham, Edward Elgar, 2019). The EU was an active actor in the negotiations of the Convention on Nuclear Safety (1994) and the Joint Convention on the Safety of Spent Fuel Management and on the Safety of Radioactive Waste Management in (1997), among others.

[16] See R Lawson, 'The Council of Europe: Cooperation in the Field of Human Rights, Democracy and the Rule of Law' in RA Wessel and J Odermatt (eds) *Research Handbook on the EU and International Organizations* (Cheltenham, Edward Elgar, 2019).

Article 27(2) TEU

The High Representative shall represent the Union for matters relating to the common foreign and security policy. He shall conduct political dialogue with third parties on the Union's behalf and shall express the Union's position in international organisations and at international conferences.

Member States that are members of an international institutions have an obligation to coordinate their positions (under the guidance of the High Representative). Once a Union position has been established, the High Representative or Member States present will have to uphold that position.

Article 34(1) TEU

Member States shall coordinate their action in international organisations and at international conferences. They shall uphold the Union's positions in such forums. The High Representative of the Union for Foreign Affairs and Security Policy shall organise this coordination.

In international organisations and at international conferences where not all the Member States participate, those which do take part shall uphold the Union's positions.

To have its voice heard within a particular institution, the EU often needs the coordinated actions of the Member States. This explains why the TEU stresses the obligations of Member States to uphold the Union's positions in international organisations and at international conferences in which not all the Member States participate. This obligation to coordinate also applies to the diplomatic missions of the Member States and the Union delegations regarding the formulation and implementation of a common approach (Articles 32 and 35 TEU). The EU is represented by 'Union delegations in third countries and at international organizations' (Article 221(1) TFEU). However, Member States seem to be somewhat anxious about the developments in this area. In a special declaration to the Treaty (No 13) they stated the following:

Declaration No 13 concerning the common foreign and security policy [2010] OJ C83/343

... the creation of the office of High Representative of the Union for Foreign Affairs and Security Policy and the establishment of an External Action Service,

> do not affect the responsibilities of the Member States, as they currently exist, for the formulation and conduct of their foreign policy nor of their national representation in third countries and international organisations.

This declaration underlies the tension between, on one hand, the need to coordinate positions in international organisations and where possible have these presented by an EU representative and, on the other hand, the wish of many Member States to maintain their own visible presence in international institutions.

As explained in Chapter 1, the European External Action Service (EEAS) plays an important role in the coordination of positions, in particular through the 'Union delegations'. Union delegations have replaced the former Commission delegations, including to international institutions. They are responsible for representing the Union at various international bodies, including the UN in New York and the OSCE in Vienna. Article 220(1) TFEU requires the EU to 'establish all appropriate forms of cooperation' with various international organisations including, but not limited to, the UN, the Council of Europe, the OSCE and the OECD (Article 220(2) TFEU). On the basis of this provision, the Union has already begun to implement its ambitions in terms of presence in multilateral forums. It faced initial pushback from third states, and even some EU Member States, as it sought to enhance its role in international forums. One example of this was when the EU sought enhanced participation in the UN General Assembly (discussed below).

One particular legal question arises where the Union is not a member of an international organisation, but nonetheless has competence and interest in that field. Article 218(9) TFEU sets out that the Union may establish the positions to be adopted on its behalf in certain situations.

> **Article 218(9) TFEU**
>
> The Council, on a proposal from the Commission or the High Representative of the Union for Foreign Affairs and Security Policy, shall adopt a decision suspending application of an agreement and establishing the positions to be adopted on the Union's behalf in a body set up by an agreement, when that body is called upon to adopt acts having legal effects, with the exception of acts supplementing or amending the institutional framework of the agreement.

In 2012, the Council used Article 218(9) TFEU as a basis for a Decision 'establishing the position to be adopted on behalf of the European Union with regard to certain regulations to be voted in the framework of the International Organisation for Vine and Wine' (IOV).[17] Germany had been overruled in the Council when the Decision was adopted internally. It brought an action to annul the Decision, arguing that Article 218(9) TFEU does not apply to agreements to which the EU is not a party. The Council argued that Article 218(9) TFEU establishes a procedure by which the Union can establish a position in international organisations where the acts to be adopted are to be incorporated subsequently into EU law.

Case C-399/12 *Germany v Council (OIV)*, ECLI:EU:C:2014:2258

49 First of all, it should be noted that the provision in question makes reference to a body set up by 'an agreement' but does not specify whether the European Union must be a party to that agreement. Similarly, the reference in that provision to the positions to be adopted 'on the Union's behalf' does not mean that the European Union has to have been a party to the agreement which set up the international body in question.

50 It follows that there is nothing in the wording of Article 218(9) TFEU to prevent the European Union from adopting a decision establishing a position to be adopted on its behalf in a body set up by an international agreement to which it is not a party.

…

56 Next, it must be ascertained whether the recommendations to be adopted by the OIV which are under consideration in the present case constitute 'acts having legal effects' for the purposes of that provision.

57 In that regard, it can be seen from recitals 5, 6 and 7 to the contested decision and from the annex thereto that the OIV recommendations to be voted on at that organisation's General Assembly which are referred to in that decision relate to new oenological practices, methods of analysis for determining the composition of products of the wine sector, or purity and identification specifications of substances used in oenological practices.

58 Consequently, those recommendations fall within the areas indicated in Article 2(2)(b) of the OIV Agreement, which, moreover, is not disputed by any of the parties to these proceedings.

59 Under Article 2(1)(b) and (c) and Article 2(2) of the OIV Agreement, the aim of the recommendations adopted by the OIV in those areas is to help to achieve the objectives of that organisation, which include assisting other international organisations, especially those which carry out standardisation activities, and contributing to international harmonisation of existing practices and standards and, as necessary, to the preparation of new international standards …

[17] Council Document No 11436, 2012.

61 In addition, within the framework of the common organisation of the wine markets, the EU legislature incorporates those recommendations into the legislation adopted in that regard: Articles 120g and 158a(1) and (2) of Regulation No 1234/2007 and the first subparagraph of Article 9(1) of Regulation No 606/2009 explicitly compare OIV recommendations to rules of EU law as regards the methods of analysis for determining the composition of products of the wine sector, the special requirements applicable, in terms of oenological practices, to imports of wine originating from third countries, and the purity and identification specifications of substances used in such practices.

64 It follows from the findings set out in paragraphs 57 to 63 above that such recommendations, in particular by reason of their incorporation into EU law by virtue of Articles 120f(a), 120g and 158a(1) and (2) of Regulation No 1234/2007 and the first subparagraph of Article 9(1) of Regulation No 606/2009, have legal effects in that area for the purposes of Article 218(9) TFEU and that the European Union, while not a party to the OIV Agreement, is entitled to establish a position to be adopted on its behalf with regard to those recommendations, in view of their direct impact on the European Union's acquis in that area.

The Court dismissed Germany's action, finding that Article 218(9) TFEU was the correct legal basis of the Decision. Important in the Court's reasoning was the fact that the OIV's decisions have legal effects in the Union, despite it not being a party to the OIV Agreement.

The principle of sincere cooperation is a way to ensure a coherent position within international organisations, even when the EU is not a formal member (see Chapter 2). This principle also applies to representation before international dispute settlement bodies.[18] Case C-73/14 (ITLOS) concerned an action for annulment of a Commission decision to submit a '[w]ritten statement by the European Commission on behalf of the European Union' to the International Tribunal for the Law of the Sea (ITLOS) regarding an advisory opinion of the latter. The case involved the conservation of marine biological resources under the common fisheries policy, an exclusive Union competence. The case before the CJEU dealt with statements to be expressed on behalf of the Union before an international *judicial* body.

Case C-73/14 *Council v Commission (ITLOS)*, ECLI:EU:C:2015:663

84 Under Article 13(2) TEU, the European Union's institutions are to practise mutual sincere cooperation. That sincere cooperation, however, is exercised

[18] See C Hillion and RA Wessel, 'The European Union and International Dispute Settlement: Mapping Principles and Conditions' in M Cremona, A Thies and RA Wessel (eds) *The European Union and International Dispute Settlement* (Oxford, Hart Publishing, 2017) 7–30.

within the limits of the powers conferred by the Treaties on each institution. The obligation resulting from Article 13(2) TEU is therefore not such as to change those powers (judgment in *Parliament v Council*, C-48/14, ECLI:EU:C:2015:91, paragraphs 57 and 58).

85 In the present case, the main argument put forward by the Council and some of the intervening Member States in the context of the second plea in law is based on the premise that the determination of the content of the written statement submitted on behalf of the European Union to ITLOS in Case No 21 fell within the competence of the Council pursuant to Article 218(9) TFEU or the second sentence of Article 16(1) TEU. That was not the case, however, as can be seen from the examination of the first plea in law. Accordingly, it cannot be claimed that the Commission failed to fulfil its obligation of sincere cooperation by not taking the initiatives entailed in the application of those two provisions.

86 That being said, the principle of sincere cooperation requires the Commission to consult the Council beforehand if it intends to express positions on behalf of the European Union before an international court.

B. Delivery of EU Demarches on Behalf of the EU and/or its Member States

A recurring question relates to who is entitled to speak on behalf of the Union in international organisations. Some Member States have resisted the diplomatic presence of the Union in these bodies. The United Kingdom, for instance, resisted the explicit recognition of the Union's legal personality, which is now included in Article 47 TEU, arguing that this explicit legal personality meant that, rather than making statements on behalf of the European Union, they must be made on behalf of the 'the EU *and its Member States*'. This led to a situation in 2011 where several dozen EU statements and demarches were blocked because of a disagreement as to who was to deliver the statement: 'the European Union' or 'the European Union and its Member States'. A temporary ceasefire was agreed on 24 October 2011 in the form of a document entitled 'general arrangements for EU statements'.[19] Through this document, the EU wishes to keep competence battles 'internal and consensual' so that the EU can achieve 'coherent, comprehensive and unified external representation' in multilateral organisations.[20] This example shows how difficult and contentious it can be for the Union to achieve a unified diplomatic presence in international organisations and fora.

Another question is whether, since the Lisbon Treaty, Member States have acted 'outside' the EU framework in a number of policy fields.

[19] Council of the European Union, *General Arrangements for EU Statements in Multilateral Organisations*, 16901/11 (Brussels, 24 October 2011).

[20] Ibid, 2.

KE Smith, 'EU Member States at the UN: A Case of Europeanization Arrested?' (2017) 55 *Journal of Common Market Studies* 628, 641–42

The new institutions and decision-making procedures introduced by the Lisbon Treaty appear to have had a limited impact on the EU's activity in the UN's key intergovernmental human rights bodies, the General Assembly's Third Committee and the Human Rights Council. The level of EU activity has not changed much: the EU is issuing a steadily increasing number of statements in the Third Committee but about the same number in the HRC, and it sponsors the same number of resolutions on the same topics in both bodies. In the Third Committee, where the EU delegation has a stronger role than in the HRC, more Member States are issuing more statements. At the HRC, there has been a significant increase in activity by Member States acting outside the EU, on an individual basis or in cross-regional or other groups.

These findings contribute to the literature on Europeanization in the field of EU foreign policy co-operation. Firstly, the process of Europeanization does not always proceed clearly towards more convergence. What can be observed at the UN is not exactly a process of 'de-Europeanization' as the Member States have not generally reduced EU activity or defected from existing EU positions. Instead, it can be seen as a case of 'arrested Europeanization'. Member States are clearly still keen to protect their autonomy and capacity to act on a national basis.

Second, the external context matters. The reasons why the Member States are intent on acting outside the EU in the HRC are to be found both in dissatisfaction or frustration with 'internal' EU processes and institutions (too slow, too difficult to find agreement, and so on) and in awareness of the constraints and opportunities of the external UN context. Most Member States want to influence debates and outcomes in the HRC, and thus they act outside the EU, because acting within the EU is ineffective due to the dynamics of group politics at the UN. Rather than using the EU as an 'institutional repository of the second-order normative concerns', such as human rights, Member States are acting individually to pursue their normative goals in the HRC. If there is more cross-regional coalition-building in the Third Committee in the future, then it is likely that we will see EU Member States acting more outside the EU context – despite the EU delegation's enhanced role there.

Third, the lessons of the external context are paradoxical for the EU. On the one hand, in an increasingly multipolar, interconnected world, size matters, and the EU Member States would surely benefit from the 'politics of scale' if they acted collectively. On the other hand, acting collectively in the microcosm of UN human rights bodies backfires precisely because the EU is not quite big enough (EU Member States can easily be outvoted) and has struggled to gather enough supporters to win debates and outcomes. This tension between the imperatives of collective action in the wider international system and the imperative not to act as a bloc in the UN is likely to persist for some time and complicate any process of convergence on foreign policy issues.

Finally, the article contributes to our understanding of the impact that institutionalization can have in an intergovernmental framework: Member States still protect their capacity and freedom to act outside the EU, and they can 'box in' stronger central institutions so that they contribute to or take over policy-making only in prescribed areas. The Member States agreed to create the institutions in the first place but are clearly not keen to allow the institutions to take on much of 'a life of their own' – yet, at least.

V. The EU in Key International Institutions

This book cannot examine the Union's activity in all international organisations where it is present.[21] The following sections detail how the Union is active in two important organizations: the WTO[22] and the United Nations.[23] These two examples illustrate the very different ways that the Union can engage with international institutions.

A. The World Trade Organisation

Since 1968, the European Union constitutes a customs union and has been actively involved in the most important trade regime established since the 1960s, the GATT.[24] In 1995, the European Community became one of the founding members of the WTO.[25] The common commercial policy (CCP; see Chapter 7) falls within the scope of the exclusive competences of the Union, and the European Commission is endowed with extensive functions for the management of this important external policy field, including the negotiation of trade agreements with third countries.[26]

[21] For an overview, see RA Wessel and J Odermatt (eds) *Research Handbook on the EU and International Organizations* (Cheltenham, Edward Elgar, 2019) as well as C Kaddous (ed) *The European Union in International Organisations and Global Governance: Recent Developments* (Oxford, Hart Publishing, 2015).

[22] See M Hahn and L Danieli, 'You'll Never Walk Alone: The European Union and Its Member States in the WTO' (2013) 4 *European Yearbook of International Economic Law, Special Issue* 49; T Perišin, 'World Trade Organization (WTO): The EU's Influential Role in Global Trade Policy' in RA Wessel and J Odermatt (eds) *Research Handbook on the EU and International Organizations* (Cheltenham, Edward Elgar, 2019).

[23] See E Paasivirta and T Ramopoulos, 'UN General Assembly, UN Security Council and UN Human Rights Council: The EU in State-centred Multilateral Frameworks' in RA Wessel and J Odermatt (eds) *Research Handbook on the EU and International Organizations* (Cheltenham, Edward Elgar, 2019).

[24] Since the successful establishment of the customs union in 1968, the European Community has had a *de facto* institutional status in the *de facto* international organisation known as the GATT.

[25] For regional trade arrangements in the form of a customs union or free trade area, the relevant provision is Art XXIV of the GATT Agreement. See Art XI of the Agreement establishing the WTO.

[26] The substantive dimension of the WTO is dealt with in Chapter 9.

The EU is a full member of the WTO, along with its Member States. While the participation of the European Community in the GATT had already paved the way for EU Membership of the WTO, the Uruguay Round of multilateral trade negotiations revealed the complexities and sensitivities of formally including the EU. The key question concerned the division of competences between the EU and its Member States. The EU has exclusive competence in relation to trade in goods – but questions arose regarding its competence to conclude agreements covering trade in services (GATS) and intellectual property (TRIPS) (see Chapter 3).

One of the issues was how to regulate the voting rights within the WTO. Other WTO members did not want EU countries to increase their voting power through the addition of an extra 'EU vote'. The solution can be found in Article IX of the WTO Agreement.

Article IX of the WTO Agreement

1. The WTO shall continue the practice of decision-making by consensus followed under GATT 1947. Except as otherwise provided, where a decision cannot be arrived at by consensus, the matter at issue shall be decided by voting. At meetings of the Ministerial Conference and the General Council, each Member of the WTO shall have one vote. Where the European Communities exercise their right to vote, they shall have a number of votes equal to the number of their member States which are Members of the WTO. Decisions of the Ministerial Conference and the General Council shall be taken by a majority of the votes cast, unless otherwise provided in this Agreement or in the relevant Multilateral Trade Agreement.

1. The body concerned shall be deemed to have decided by consensus on a matter submitted for its consideration, if no Member, present at the meeting when the decision is taken, formally objects to the proposed decision.
2. The number of votes of the European Communities and their member States shall in no case exceed the number of the member States of the European Communities.
3. Decisions by the General Council when convened as the Dispute Settlement Body shall be taken only in accordance with the provisions of paragraph 4 of Article 2 of the Dispute Settlement Understanding.

The solution is quite simple: either the EU or the Member States vote. When the EU votes, it gets the number of votes equal to the number of its Members. This practice of alternative voting is used in some other multilateral agreements where the EU and the Member States are members.[27] As the WTO generally takes decisions by consensus, however, this issue of voting rarely arises in practice.

[27] Alternate voting arrangements also exist in Art II, FAO Constitution; Art 4(4) of Annex IX of UNCLOS, and Art XI, Statute of the International Renewable Energy Agency (IRENA).

There is very little regulation concerning the role of the Commission and the Member States in the WTO, either at the EU level or in the WTO. While there have been attempts to decide upon a code of conduct, no final document has been agreed upon. Article 207 TFEU recognises the central role of the EU in the WTO, based on the broad scope of the common commercial policy.

Article 207 TFEU

1. The common commercial policy shall be based on uniform principles, particularly with regard to changes in tariff rates, the conclusion of tariff and trade agreements relating to trade in goods and services, and the commercial aspects of intellectual property, foreign direct investment, the achievement of uniformity in measures of liberalisation, export policy and measures to protect trade such as those to be taken in the event of dumping or subsidies. The common commercial policy shall be conducted in the context of the principles and objectives of the Union's external action.

Given the exclusive competence of the EU in this area (see Chapter 3), the role of the individual Member States in the WTO is limited (with the notable exception of transport). In fact, the CJEU's broad definition of 'trade issues' was already made clear in *Opinion 1/78* when the question arose of who should negotiate a draft Agreement on Natural Rubber in 1978.

Opinion 1/78 (*International Agreement on Natural Rubber*), ECLI:EU:C:1979:224

50 Having regard to the specific nature of the provisions relating to commercial policy in so far as they concern relations with non-member countries and are founded, according to Article 113, on the concept of a common policy, their scope cannot be restricted in the light of more general provisions relating to economic policy and based on the idea of mere co-ordination. Consequently, where the organization of the Community's economic links with nonmember countries may have repercussions on certain sectors of economic policy such as the supply of raw materials to the Community or price policy, as is precisely the case with the regulation of international trade in commodities, that consideration does not constitute a reason for excluding such objectives from the field of application of the rules relating to the common commercial policy. Similarly, the fact that a product may have a political importance by reason of the building up of security stocks is not a reason for excluding that product from the domain of the common commercial policy. It is in the light of the same considerations

that the connexion between Article 113 and Article 116 must be determined in the context of the chapter of the Treaty devoted to the common commercial policy. Whilst those two provisions contribute to the same end inasmuch as their objective is the realization of a common policy in international economic relationships, as a basis for action the two articles are founded on different premises and consequently apply different ideas. According to Article 113 the common commercial policy is determined by the Community, independently, that is to say, acting as such, by the intervention of its own institutions; in particular, agreements entered into under that provision are, in the terms of Article 114, 'concluded … on behalf of the Community' and accordingly negotiated according to the procedures set out in those provisions and in Article 228. Article 116 on the other hand was conceived with a view to evolving common action by the Member States in international organizations of which the Community is not part; in such a situation the only appropriate means is concerted, joint action by the Member States as members of the said organizations.

51 In this case a problem relating to the demarcation of the sphere of application of Articles 113 and 114 on the one hand and 116 on the other hand arises from the fact that the agreements on commodities are at present being negotiated within UNCTAD. The Court has already given its views on this problem in its Opinion 1/75 which itself concerned an international agreement arrived at within the framework of an international organization (the OECD). In that opinion the Court stressed that what counts with regard to the application of the Treaty is the question whether negotiations undertaken within the framework of an international organization are intended to lead to an 'undertaking entered into by entities subject to international law which has binding force'. In such a case it is the provisions of the Treaty relating to then negotiation and conclusion of agreements, in other words Articles 113, 114 and 228, which apply and not Article 116.

Irrespective of the legal battles on the question of who should be at the international negotiating table, Member States seem to have accepted a leading role of the EU. The Member States rely on the considerable experience of the Commission on trade matters, and the Commission will take the lead in dispute settlement involving complaints against them.

Several fundamental questions arose when the WTO Agreement was being negotiated. It is one thing to accept the Commission's role on an *ad hoc* basis (as exemplified by the Court's Opinions during the 1970s and 1980s), but it is quite another thing to accept a structural and permanent limitation of traditional state powers in what was to become one of the leading international organisations in the world. During the Uruguay Round (discussed above) the Commission was the key negotiator, with the

Council and the Member States closely looking over its shoulder. The Commission in the end nevertheless requested the Court to confirm its exclusive competences in this area.[28]

In Opinion 1/94, the Court was asked whether the European Union (at the time the European Community) was exclusively competent to conclude the 1994 WTO Agreement. The argument was that all underlying agreements had trade policy objectives.[29] The WTO Agreement itself can be seen as an umbrella agreement, which – apart from establishing the WTO – tied together a number of different agreements. The Court agreed with the Commission with regard to the agreements related to the trade in goods (Annex 1A of the WTO Agreement), but that exclusivity of the Union in relation to the GATS (Annex 1B) could only be established as regards cross-border services. Transport was not considered part of the common commercial policy and could therefore also not be automatically included under the heading of exclusive competences. The TRIPs Agreement on intellectual property rights could not fully be seen as coinciding with the Union's treaty competences in trade policy. This led the Court to conclude that the Member States were also still competent to conclude the GATS and the TRIPs.[30]

J Bourgeois, 'The EC in the WTO and Advisory Opinion 1/94: An Echternach Procession' (1995) 32 *Common Market Law Review* 763, 763–64 and 786

On 22 December 1994 the Council of the European Union formally approved the conclusion of the Agreement establishing the WTO and the agreements and associate legal instruments including the annexes to the WTO Agreement. According to its Article XIV the WTO Agreement is open for acceptance, *inter alia*, by 'contracting parties to GATT 1947 and the European Communities, which are eligible to become original Members of the WTO'. Throughout the whole Uruguay Round negotiation, the European Community has acted as an entity with the European Commission negotiating, assisted by the usual committee of representatives of Member States, called 'the mothers-in-law', and reporting from time to time to the Council to obtain fresh negotiation directives. However, partly as a result of the dispute between the Commission and several Member States on the question whether all matters negotiated in the Uruguay Round come within the EC's exclusive powers under Article 113 EC [now Article 207 TFEU], the EC insisted itself that not only the EC but also its Member States be considered as members of the WTO.

[28] P Van den Bossche, 'The European Community and the Uruquay Round Agreements' in JH Jackson and AO Sykes (eds) *Implementing the Uruguay Round* (Oxford, Oxford University Press, 1997) 25–26.

[29] P Eeckhout, *EU External Relations Law*, 2nd edn (Oxford, Oxford University Press, 2011) 28. See also J Bourgeois, 'The EC in the WTO and Advisory Opinion 1/94: An Echternach Procession' (1995) 32 *Common Market Law Review* 763; M Hilf, 'The ECJ's Opinion 1/94 on the WTO – No Surprise, But Wise?' (1995) 6 *European Journal of International Law* 245.

[30] Opinion 1/94 (*WTO*), ECLI:EU:C:1994:384.

A similar line of reasoning was followed by the Court in Opinion 2/92 (*Re Third Revised Decision of the OECD on national treatment*), ECLI:EU:C:1995:83 and in Case C-360/93 *Parliament v Council*, ECLI:EU:C:1996:84.

This was admittedly the case in the GATT. Here was, however, a rational explanation for that: the EC Member States were contracting parties to the GATT before the creation of the EC. As the EC progressively took trade policy over from its Member States, this substitution of the Member States by the EC came to be recognized both within the EC and within the GATT. For all practical purposed the EC had become a GATT contracting party in the place of its Member States. The pragmatic acceptance by the other GATT contracting parties of the EC as a single entity replacing its Member States had been obtained without amending the GATT, inter alia, on the basis of the argument that one should not amend the GATT solely for the purposes of formally substituting the EC for its Member States; this could wait until the GATT was amended for other reasons. The creation of the WTO and the review of the GATT offered such opportunity. The EC missed it. This is the first reason for referring to the Echternach procession.

The second reason is Advisory Opinion 1/94 of the Court of Justice of the European Communities ... Opinion 1/94 is likely to have negative effects on the administration on the EC side of the WTO Agreement and its related agreements on the status of the EC within the WTO ... With a bit of negotiating skill, other WTO Members will have a field day in exploiting the situation ...

Despite these rather pessimistic forecasts, practice has revealed a workable situation, in which EU Member States entrust the Union to a large extent to take care of their interests. Such practice has been accepted for the most part by the other WTO members. The EU's position in the WTO can be contrasted with its role in another key international institution: the United Nations system. Whereas both institutions are of key importance to the Union, the state-driven nature of the UN system has meant the EU has encountered significant hurdles when seeking to play a greater role in the UN.

B. The United Nations

The EU Treaties present the United Nations and its Charter as the guiding legal framework for the EU in its external relations. Article 3(5) TEU mentions 'respect for the principles of the United Nations Charter' as part of 'the strict observance and the development of international law' which are to be pursued by the EU in its engagement with the world. Article 21(1) TEU sets out that the Union is to promote 'multilateral solutions to common problems *in particular* in the framework of the United Nations'.[31]

Soon after the entry into force of the Lisbon Treaty, it was decided that the EU should pursue an upgraded status within the UN General Assembly to achieve greater

[31] Art 21(1) TEU (emphasis added).

presence and have a more unified position.[32] The UN is an organisation of states, and remains a state-driven organisation.[33] The EU's attempts to pursue an 'enhanced observer' status were initially met with opposition. While the EU has had a status of 'enhanced observer' in the UNGA since 2011, it has faced difficulties translating this position into a meaningful role.[34]

The Union faces similar obstacles in the UN Security Council. Article 34(2) TEU aims to ensure that the EU Member States in the UN Security Council take into account the EU's CFSP.

Article 34(2) TEU

... Member States which are also members of the United Nations Security Council will concert and keep the other Member States and the High Representative fully informed. Member States which are members of the Security Council will, ... defend the positions and the interests of the Union, without prejudice to their responsibilities under the provisions of the United Nations Charter.

When the Union has defined a position on a subject which is on the United Nations Security Council agenda, those Member States which sit on the Security Council shall request that the High Representative be invited to present the Union's position.

The High Representative addresses the Security Council on issues where the Union has a defined position. For example, High Representative Mogherini addressed the UN Security Council on 12 March 2019, to discuss issues including the war in Syria and Yemen, climate change and the EU's support for multilateralism.[35] In order for the High Representative to speak, the EU Member States sitting in the UN Security Council need to request the Security Council to issue an invitation. The Union's presence at the UN Security Council further contributes to the EU's ability to speak with one voice on matters of peace and security.

[32] See J Wouters, J Odermatt and T Ramopoulos, 'The Status of the European Union at the United Nations General Assembly' in I Govaere, E Lannon, P Van Elsuwege, and S Adam (ed) *The European Union in the World Essays in Honour of Marc Maresceau* (Leiden, Martinus Nijhoff, 2013).

[33] Article 4(1) of the UN Charter sets out that membership 'is open to all other peace-loving states'. See E Paasivirta and T Ramopoulos, 'UN General Assembly, UN Security Council and UN Human Rights Council: The EU in State-centred Multilateral Frameworks' in RA Wessel and J Odermatt, *Research Handbook on the EU and International Organizations* (Cheltenham, Edward Elgar, 2019).

[34] See J Wouters, A Chané, J Odermatt, and T Ramopoulos, 'Improving the EU's Status in the UN and the UN System: An Objective without a Strategy?' in C Kaddous (eds) *The European Union in International Organisations and Global Governance: Recent Developments* (Oxford, Hart Publishing, 2015).

[35] Speech by High Representative/Vice-President Federica Mogherini at the United Nations' Security Council, New York, 12 March 2019.

In order to prevent these new diplomatic competences of the Union from affecting the Member States' own powers, a special Declaration was adopted during the Lisbon Intergovernmental Conference:

Declaration No 14 concerning the common foreign and security policy [2010] OJ C83/343

The Conference underlines that the provisions covering the Common Foreign and Security Policy including in relation to the High Representative of the Union for Foreign Affairs and Security Policy and the External Action Service will not affect the existing legal basis, responsibilities, and powers of each member state in relation to the formulation and conduct of its foreign policy, its national diplomatic service, relations with third countries and participation in international organisations, including a member state's membership of the Security Council of the United Nations.

Irrespective of the interpretative character of this type of Declarations, they can never be used to evade the actual Treaty provisions. Any further development will therefore depend on the use by Member States of the new treaty provisions allowing for a stronger diplomatic representation by the High Representative (see Chapter 1).

With the coming of age of the EU's Common Security and Defence Policy (CSDP), relations between the EU and the UN have also gained importance. As analysed in Chapter 9, Article 42(1) TEU provides that the Union may use its civilian and military assets missions outside the Union for peace-keeping, conflict prevention and strengthening international security, and again this should be done 'in accordance with the principles of the United Nations Charter'. In fact, the Treaties foresee the possibility of EU missions operating in a UN framework. The preamble of Protocol 10 to the Treaties refers to the fact that 'the United Nations Organisation may request the Union's assistance for the urgent implementation of missions undertaken under Chapters VI and VII of the United Nations Charter'. Article 1 of the Protocol considers a 'permanent structured cooperation' between able and willing EU Member States necessary 'in particular in response to requests from the United Nations Organisation'.

Development cooperation (a shared-complementary competence) is to be based on decisions taken by and in other international organisations, including the UN.

Article 208(2) TFEU

The Union and the Member States shall comply with the commitments and take account of the objectives they have approved in the context of the United Nations and other competent international organisations.

The same holds for humanitarian aid operations, which are to be 'coordinated and consistent with those of international organisations and bodies, in particular those forming part of the United Nations system' (Article 214(7) TFEU).

The EU Treaties clearly demonstrate the importance of the United Nations and its principles. They refer to the UN system 19 times (including the Protocols and Declarations). Irrespective of the CJEU's 2008 *Kadi* judgment, which emphasised the primacy of the EU Treaties over international law, including the UN Charter (see Chapter 5), the EU clearly regards many of its actions as being part of a global governance programme in which the UN has a central position. The EU Global Strategy also shows how the Union views the UN system as the 'bedrock of the multilateral rules-based order'.

Shared Vision, Common Action: A Stronger Europe – A Global Strategy for the European Union's Foreign and Security Policy, Brussels, June 2016, 39

Global Governance for the 21st Century

Without global norms and the means to enforce them, peace and security, prosperity and democracy – our vital interests – are at risk. Guided by the values on which it is founded, the EU is committed to a global order based on international law, including the principles of the UN Charter, which ensure peace, human rights, sustainable development and lasting access to the global commons. This commitment translates into an aspiration to transform rather than simply preserve the existing system. The EU will strive for a strong UN as the bedrock of the multilateral rules-based order and develop globally coordinated responses with international and regional organisations, states and non-state actors.

The Union is therefore committed to the principles in the UN Charter, but also to reform of the multilateral system, including the UN Security Council. The Treaty provisions on EU–UN relations aim to regulate substantive EU policy, rather than in an institutional manner. This emphasises that EU policy is to take place within the limits of the UN system.

J Odermatt and RA Wessel, 'The Challenges of Engaging with International institutions: The EU and Multilateralism under Strain' in RA Wessel and J Odermatt (eds) *Research Handbook on the European Union and International Organisations* (Cheltenham, Edward Elgar, 2019) 671–672

At the time of the creation of the EEC, the idea of the Community joining another international organization was not really envisaged. Today, it is difficult to find an international institution or multilateral setting where the EU has no presence or engagement whatsoever. Yet the EU's engagement with international institutions remains a 'patchwork', one where the EU's ability to engage effectively depends on multiple factors, including the EU's interests in the work of the organization, the EU's competence in the field in question, and the institutional environment in which the EU finds itself. This institutional environment is becoming the crucial issue. With the rise of other regional players, and the challenges to the multilateral system, the EU's presence in international institutions will come under strain. The EU must therefore do more to show how its presence in these bodies adds real value, and not to focus on entirely internal issues relating to EU competences and powers. Of course, competences matter – it remains the main compelling reason for the EU to engage in IOs – but they are unlikely to have much sway when seeking to persuade third states of the need for EU presence. The EU cannot be everywhere. There may be instances where it is still appropriate to allow EU Member States to take on an active international role, even where the EU Treaties may allow the EU to have a role. In the field of climate issues, one where the EU has been active and influential, the presence of the EU Member States has amplified, not diminished, the EU's influence ...

It is almost taken for granted that the EU, itself a form of international cooperation, would support other international institutions. Yet the EU may also find itself in competition with other institutions, especially when it feels that it has the 'better' approach to a certain issue, such as on climate change mitigation or human rights. At a time when multilateral bodies are under stress and states begin to adopt more unilateral measures, it might be tempting for the Union to similarly forge its own path, without the need to involve multilateral institutions. At a time when multilateral institutions are under threat, the EU is also presented with the question of how to support multilateralism. Does this mean that the EU must work through multilateral settings in every policy area, even if there is deadlock and a lack of meaningful progress? Does it mean that the EU should pursue unilateral measures to protect its interests and pursue these goals, even if this means jettisoning some multilateral institutions? The latter policy is fraught with pitfalls. Even if the EU can use its economic power and influence to produce such results, the methods of achieving them also have the effect of chipping away, not only at international intuitions, but the values that make multilateralism work. Moreover, such a policy may also invite other states or regions to pursue similar strategies, further undermining the coherence and effectiveness of global strategies. A renewed commitment to multilateralism will not only strengthen the international rules-based system, but also strengthen the Union.

VI. The Broader Picture of EU External Relations Law

This chapter focused on the extent to which EU external relations law regulates the Union's position in other international institutions. Although there is no specific article in the EU Treaties that regulates the Union's engagement with international organisations, the Treaties clearly demonstrate the importance of international institutions, especially the bodies in the UN system. In addition to the Treaties themselves, the EU's engagement with international institutions is also dependent on international law, most notably the constituent treaties establishing international organisations. EU engagement is also conditioned by political factors. Other states, international organisations, as well as EU Member States themselves, may be hesitant to allow active participation of the EU in its own right. A clear example of this is the EU's push to increase its participation at the United Nations. In addition to the question of the EU's membership and participation, there are legal issues about the *representation* in these bodies. When is the EU entitled to speak on its own behalf, and when should the EU Member States be present? This involves complex legal and political issues related to the division of competences and will continue to be litigated by the Court of Justice.

It is in the interests of the Union to be an active participant in international organisations and institutions. It is increasingly affected by the normative impact of decisions of international bodies. In many of the foreign policy areas that the EU prioritises, such as nuclear non-proliferation or climate change, these decisions are made in the context of international institutions and treaty bodies.[36] Internal disputes about competences and representation may make it more difficult for the EU to act effectively in such international bodies and detract from the goal in the EU Treaties to 'promote multilateral solutions to common problems'.

VII. Sources and Further Reading

Alvarez, J, *International Organizations as Law-Makers* (Oxford, Oxford University Press, 2005).

Billet, S, 'From GATT to WTO: Internal Struggle for External Competences in the EU' (2009) 44 *Journal of Common Market Studies* 899.

Birnberg, G, 'The Voting Behavior of the EU Member States in the UN General Assembly' (PhD Thesis LSE, LSE Theses online, 2009).

Bourgeois, J, 'The EC in the WTO and Advisory Opinion 1/94: An Echternach Procession' (1995) 32 *Common Market Law Review* 763.

[36] See eg EU Priorities at the United Nations and the 73rd United Nations General Assembly (September 2018–September 2019), adopted by the Council, 25 June 2018.

Chiti, E and RA Wessel, 'The Emergence of International Agencies in the Global Administrative Space: Autonomous Actors or State Servants?' in ND White and R Collins (eds) *International Organizations and the Idea of Autonomy: Institutional Independence in the International Legal Order* (Oxford/New York, Routledge, 2011) 142–59.

Costa, O and KE Jørgensen, 'The Influence of International Institutions on the EU: A Framework for Analysis' in O Costa and KE Jørgensen (eds) *The Influence of International Institutions on the EU: When Multilateralism Hits Brussels* (Basingstoke, Palgrave Macmillan, 2012) 1–22.

De Baere, G, 'EU Status in Other International Organizations' in T Tridimas and R Schütze (eds) *Oxford Principles of European Union Law – Volume 1: The European Union Legal Order* (Oxford, Oxford University Press, 2018) 1234–81.

Delarue, R, 'ILO-EU Cooperation on Employment and Social Affairs' in F Hoffmeister, J Wouters and T Ruys (eds) *The United Nations and the European Union: An Ever Stronger Partnership* (The Hague, TMC Asser Press, 2006) 93–114.

Eeckhout, P, *EU External Relations Law*, 2nd edn (Oxford, Oxford University Press, 2011).

Follesdal, A, RA Wessel, and J Wouters (eds) *Multilevel Regulation and the EU: The Interplay between Global, European and National Normative Processes* (Leiden, Brill/Nijhoff, 2008).

Frid, R, *The Relations between the EC and International Organizations* (The Hague, Kluwer Law International, 1995).

Hoffmeister, F, 'Of Presidents, High Representatives and European Commissioners: The External Representation of the European Union Seven Years after Lisbon' (2017) 1 *Europe and the World: A Law Review* 16.

Hoffmeister, F, 'Outsider or Frontrunner? Recent Developments under International and European Law on the Status of the European Union in International Organizations and Treaty Bodies' (2007) 44 *Common Market Law Review* 41.

Hoffmeister, F and PJ Kuijper, 'The Status of the European Union at the United Nations: Institutional Ambiguities and Political Realities' in F Hoffmeister, J Wouters and T Ruys (eds) *The United Nations and the European Union: An Ever Stronger Partnership* (The Hague, TMC Asser Press, 2006) 9–34.

Hoffmeister, F, J Wouters and T Ruys (eds) *The United Nations and the European Union: An Ever Stronger Partnership* (The Hague, TMC Asser Press, 2006).

Holdgaard, R, 'The European Community's Implied External Competence after the Open Skies cases' (2003) 8 *European Foreign Affairs Review* 365.

Jørgensen, KE (ed) *The European Union and International Organizations* (London, Routledge, 2008).

Jørgensen, KE and RA Wessel, 'The Position of the European Union in (Other) International Organizations: Confronting Legal and Political Approaches' in P Koutrakos (ed) *European Foreign Policy: Legal and Political Perspectives* (Cheltenham, Edward Elgar Publishing, 2011) 261–86.

Kaddous C (ed) *The European Union in International Organisations and Global Governance: Recent Developments* (Oxford, Hart Publishing, 2015).

Marchisio, S, 'EU's Membership in International Organizations' in E Cannizzaro (ed) *The European Union as an Actor in International Relations* (The Hague, Kluwer Law International, 2002) 231–60.

Pauwelyn, J, RA Wessel and Wouters, J (eds) *Informal International Lawmaking* (Oxford, Oxford University Press, 2012).

Rasch, MB, *The European Union at the United Nations: The Functioning and Coherence of EU External Representation in a State-centric Environment* (Leiden, Brill/Nijhoff, 2008).

Sack, J, 'The European Community's Membership of International Organizations' (1995) 32 *Common Market Law Review* 1227.

Schermers, HG and NM Blokker, *International Institutional Law: Unity in Diversity*, 6th edn (Leiden, Brill/Nijhoff, 2018).

Van den Bossche, P, 'The European Community and the Uruguay Round Agreements' in JH Jackson and AO Sykes (eds) *Implementing the Uruguay Round* (Oxford, Oxford University Press, 1997) 23–102.

Van den Bossche, P, *The Law and Policy of the World Trade Organization: Text, Cases and Materials* (Cambridge, Cambridge University Press, 2008).

Van Vooren, B and RA Wessel, 'The EEAS' Diplomatic Dreams and the Reality of European and International Law' (2013) *Journal of European Public Policy* 1.

Wessel, RA and Blockmans, S (eds) *Between Autonomy and Dependence: The EU Legal Order Under the Influence of International Organisations* (The Hague, TMC Asser Press, 2013).

Wessel, RA and Blockmans, S, 'The Legal Status and Influence of Decisions of International Organizations and other Bodies in the European Union' in P Eeckhout, M Lopez-Escudero (eds) *The European Union's External Action in Times of Crisis* (Oxford, Hart Publishing, 2016) 223–48.

Wessel, RA and Odermatt, J (eds) *Research Handbook on the EU and International Organizations* (Cheltenham, Edward Elgar, 2019).

Wouters J, Chané, A, Odermatt, J, Ramopoulos T, 'Improving the EU's Status in the UN and the UN System: an Objective Without a Strategy?' in C Kaddous (ed) *The European Union in International Organisations and Global Governance* (Oxford, Hart Publishing, 2015) 45–74.

7

Common Commercial Policy

Central Issues

- This chapter deals with a policy area that is traditionally seen as being at the heart of EU external relations law. The Common Commercial Policy (CCP) was not only at the start of the development of EU external relations, it remains a key example of how internal and external policies are inextricably linked.
- The chapter starts with an overview of the relation between the internal market and external trade and addresses the question of how this relationship influenced the development of CCP.
- Subsequently, we analyse the principles and instruments of the CCP. Building on the references in primary law, the Union has developed several instruments to shape this policy area. Moreover, we look at the roles of the Union institutions and the applicable decision-making procedures, which differ in some respects from the EU's other policy areas.

I. Introduction

The Common Commercial Policy (CCP) 'remains the centre-piece of the EU's external policies'.[1] In the early days, many authors would even have a tendency to equate EU external relations law to the CCP and, even today, academic treatises explain basic notions underlying EU external relations law with extensive references to the CCP.[2]

[1] See P Eeckhout, *EU External Relations Law*, 2nd edn (Oxford, Oxford University Press, 2011) 439.
[2] See ibid; and P Koutrakos, *EU International Relations Law*, 2nd edn (Oxford, Hart Publishing, 2015), who both start with the CCP in the first chapter.

The existence, nature and scope of external competences (see Chapter 3) have for a long time largely been defined by reference to early cases in the area of the CCP.

The CCP is not just a key external relations policy but, in substantive terms, it is at the heart of the European integration project and a logical consequence of the interaction between internal and external developments, in particular between the EU's customs union and the rules of free trade laid down in the General Agreement on tariffs and Trade (GATT). Also, in quantitative terms, the CCP cannot be ignored. According to the European Commission, the 'EU is the world's largest exporter and importer of goods and services taken together, the largest foreign direct investor and the most important destination for foreign direct investment (FDI)'.[3] This makes the EU the 'largest trading partner of about 80 countries and the second most important partner for another 40'.[4] Moreover, many of the agreements concluded between the EU and third states concern trade or at least deal with trade-related issues. Since the CCP has been part and parcel of the European integration process from the outset, a vast amount of legislation and case law exists in this area. In addition, despite the fact that the CCP competences are exclusively in the hands of the EU (see Chapter 3), issues of demarcation with Member State powers continue to flare up. Related to the last point, there is more to external relations than just trade and combinations and tensions with other policy areas (such as CFSP or development cooperation) do occur.

It is indeed difficult to overestimate the trade dimensions of the EU's external relations. In order to enable a solid understanding of the CCP, this chapter first provides a brief overview of the development of the CCP at the intersection of the European integration process and the international trade agenda. This is followed by the CCP's main instruments and the interplay between the EU's institutions in this policy area.

II. Development of the CCP: The Internal Market and International Trade

The development of the CCP can only be properly understood when taking into account that it was being shaped from the very outset by, on the one hand, the evolution of the international trade regime and, on the other, by the process of economic integration in Europe, most notably the advances in the completion of the internal market. Thus, the CCP is at the same time the EU's voice in the international trading order as well as 'a necessary corollary for the maintenance of its internal market'.[5] Arguably more than any other EU policy, the CCP exemplifies that, in the contemporary world, internal and external policies are inextricably intertwined.

[3] European Commission, *Trade for All: Towards a More Responsible Trade and Investment Policy* (European Union, 2015) 7.

[4] Ibid.

[5] J Larik, 'Much More Than Trade: The Common Commercial Policy in a Global Context' in M Evans and P Koutrakos (eds) *Beyond the Established Legal Orders: Policy Interconnections Between the EU and the Rest of the World* (Oxford, Hart Publishing, 2011) 16.

A. The Internal Market and GATT/WTO

The establishment and further evolution of the CCP reflects the strong relationship between internal and external aspects of economic integration. This was explicitly acknowledged by the Court in in Opinion 1/75.

Opinion 1/75 (*Re Understanding on a Local Costs Standard*), ECLI:EU:C: 1975:145, 1362–63

[C]oncerning the common commercial policy, the Community is empowered, pursuant to the powers which it possesses, not only to adopt internal rules of Community law, but also to conclude agreements with third countries pursuant to Article 113(2) and Article 114 of the Treaty [Articles 206 and 207 TFEU].

A commercial policy is in fact made up by the combination and interaction of internal and external measures, without priority being taken by one over the others. Sometimes agreements are concluded in execution of a policy fixed in advance, sometimes that policy is defined by the agreements themselves.

Such agreements may be outline agreements, the purpose of which is to lay down uniform principles … Furthermore, the implementation of the export policy to be pursued within the framework of a common commercial policy does not necessarily find expression in the adoption of general and abstract rules of internal or Community law. The common commercial policy is above all the outcome of a progressive development based upon specific measures which may refer without distinction to 'autonomous' and external aspects of that policy and which do not necessarily presuppose, by the fact that they are linked to the field of the common commercial policy, the existence of a large body of rules, but combine gradually to form that body.

It was indeed the 'combination and interaction of internal and external measures' which turned the CCP into one of the key policy areas of the Union. In this context, it should be recalled that 'European integration itself was launched in the shadow of the pre-existing General Agreement on Tariffs and Trade (GATT)'.[6] When the original six Member States signed the Treaty of Rome in 1957, the GATT had been in existence for a decade, and the Six were already parties to it. In fact, 'the EEC's common market was modelled partly on the GATT, and many of the EC Treaty provisions clearly reflect this'.[7] The EU (at the time still the Communities) came to succeed the Member States, by virtue of the CCP, in exercising the rights and duties under the GATT, as confirmed by the CJEU in *International Fruit Company*.[8]

[6] Ibid.

[7] G De Búrca and J Scott, 'The Impact of the WTO on EU Decision-making' in G De Búrca and J Scott (eds) *The EU and the WTO: Legal and Constitutional Issues* (Oxford, Hart Publishing, 2001) 2.

[8] Joined Cases 21/72-24/72 *International Fruit Company and Others v Produktschap voor Groenten en Fruit*, ECLI:EU:C:1972:115, paras 16–18.

While the origins of the CCP can be found in the liberalisation of trade in goods, which was also the object of the GATT, gradually the scope of the CCP expanded to trade in services and trade-related aspects of intellectual property rights, in lockstep with the expansion of the international trade agenda. Yet, competences in the latter areas were shared with the Member States. In Opinion 1/94 on the WTO Agreements, the CJEU held that the EU could conclude the General Agreement on Services (GATS) and the Agreement on Trade-Related Aspects of Intellectual Property Rights (TRIPS) only together with its Member States (see Chapter 3). This explains why the EU Member States are still members of the WTO in addition to the Union.

With regard to the links between the internal market and the WTO, the successive enlargements of the EU are also a noteworthy development. Enlargement can well be considered the area in which the EU has had the most tangible impact on domestic policy. Using the attraction of access to the prosperous EU market, it has incentivised candidate states to effect wide-ranging reforms to comply with the *acquis communautaire* (see Chapter 14). This has an important trade dimension. By virtue of pre-accession agreements with the candidate countries, which usually include the granting of trade preferences to them and their subsequent integration into the Union, trade is reinforced within the Union, which expands the EU's combined market leverage further but is, at the same time, diverted from the rest of the world. In addition to enlarging the EU, it has also partially extended the internal market beyond its own Member States, for instance through the European Economic Area (EEA) and a partial customs union with Turkey (see Chapter 13 on the EU's neighbourhood policy).

B. The Scope of the CCP

The scope of the CCP has been drastically expanded over time by amendments to the EU Treaties as well as through interpretations of the Court of Justice. As early as 1975, the Court of Justice ruled that the CCP had been devised in the Treaties 'in the context of the operation of the Common Market, for the defence of the common interests of the Community, within which the particular interests of the Member States must endeavour to adapt to each other'.[9] Its external nature is reflected in the Preamble to the TFEU, which explicitly refers to *international* trade as opposed to trade between the Member States.

Preamble TFEU

DESIRING to contribute, by means of a common commercial policy, to the progressive abolition of restrictions on international trade ...

[9] Opinion 1/75 (*Re Understanding on a Local Costs Standard*), ECLI:EU:C:1975:145, 1363–64.

As we will see, the contribution of the EU to the 'progressive abolition of restrictions' is not always clear when we take into account the protection of certain industries or consumers in the Member States, as well as the preferences granted only to certain external partners (eg, in development cooperation, see Chapter 8). Nonetheless, the definition of the CCP starts out in the TFEU with an emphasis on liberalisation.

Article 206 TFEU

By establishing a customs union in accordance with Articles 28 to 32, the Union shall contribute, in the common interest, to the harmonious development of world trade, the progressive abolition of restrictions on international trade and on foreign direct investment, and the lowering of customs and other barriers.

This 'liberalisation objective' is also reflected in Article 21(2)(e) TEU, which commits the EU to 'the integration of all countries into the world economy'. Article 206 TFEU points to the direct relationship between the establishment of an internal 'customs union' and the objective of replicating this, at least to some extent, at a global level. This explains why from the outset it was clear that the core of the CCP needed to be based on an exclusive competence. Any discretion on the side of Member States to enter into trade agreements on an individual basis could seriously harm the very foundations of the internal market and the customs union. Furthermore, in comparison to its pre-Lisbon predecessor, Article 206 TFEU not only mentions international trade, but also foreign direct investment (FDI) as forming part of the CCP, which indeed turns it into a more full-fledged 'commercial policy'.

The underlying principles and the scope of the CCP are set out in Article 207 TFEU (the only other provision specifically on the CCP).

Article 207(1) TFEU

The common commercial policy shall be based on uniform principles, particularly with regard to changes in tariff rates, the conclusion of tariff and trade agreements relating to trade in goods and services, and the commercial aspects of intellectual property, foreign direct investment, the achievement of uniformity in measures of liberalisation, export policy and measures to protect trade such as those to be taken in the event of dumping or subsidies. The common commercial policy shall be conducted in the context of the principles and objectives of the Union's external action.

The first sentence refers to the so-called principle of uniformity, requiring the adoption of common rules throughout the EU in the field of the CCP in order to prevent distortions of the internal market and to preserve the unity of the EU's position with respect to third countries. The scope of the CCP was expanded significantly by the

Lisbon Treaty. Now, Article 207(1) TFEU underlines that the CCP covers all trade aspects, eliminating previous uncertainties beyond trade in goods. Together with the references to services and 'commercial aspects of intellectual property', the CCP not only covers the GATT, but also to the two other key WTO agreements, the GATS and the TRIPS. This was confirmed by the CJEU in its later case law.[10] However, transport services remain a notable exception not covered by the CCP, which are part of the EU's transport policy, which is a shared competence (Article 4(2)(g) TFEU).

Like Article 206 TFEU, Article 207 underlines that foreign direct investment falls within the scope of the CCP. FDI usually involves long-term investments with an interest in having a degree of control over the management of the enterprise in question. It is to be distinguished from so-called 'portfolio investments' (eg, investments through stock), which are more short-term and which are not included in the scope of the CCP as defined in Article 207 TFEU. International investment operates in a different way than traditional trade. International trade agreements deal with the exchange of goods and cross-border services between two or more states (or the EU and third states for that matter), whereas international investment agreements aim to protect foreign investment in a specific country. However, it is often difficult to separate the two areas, which makes it important that both are covered by the CCP. Most interestingly, perhaps, is that, following the reforms introduced by the Lisbon Treaty, FDI has been turned into an exclusive competence of the Union. This has serious consequences for the many existing Bilateral Investment Treaties (BITs) which over the years have been concluded between Member States and third states. By contrast, where investment agreements or trade agreements with investment chapters also cover portfolio investments, that remains a shared competence and will require the conclusion of mixed agreements, as the CJEU confirmed in Opinion 2/15 (see also Chapters 3 and 4).[11]

Being 'a world power in trade and through trade',[12] the CCP also serves as an instrument of foreign policy through which a wider normative agenda and interests can be pursued by the EU. It should therefore come as no surprise that the CCP is an integral part of 'The Union's External Action' (Part Five TFEU) and finds its basis in Title II of that Part. Article 207(1) TFEU makes explicit that the CCP 'shall be conducted in the context of the principles and objectives of the Union's external action'. These are expressed, next to Article 21 TEU, in Article 3(5) TEU.

A Dimopoulos, 'The Effects of the Lisbon Treaty on the Principles and Objectives of the Common Commercial Policy' (2010) 15 *European Foreign Affairs Review* 153, 169

[T]he Lisbon Treaty marks a new era for the orientation of the CCP. It signals the transformation of the CCP from an autonomous field of EU external

[10] Case C-414/11 *Daiichi Sankyo*, ECLI:EU:C:2013:520 regarding TRIPs; and Case C-137/12 *Commission v Council (Conditional Access Convention)*, ECLI:EU:C:2013:675 regarding trade in services.

[11] Opinion 2/15 (*Singapore*), ECLI:EU:C:2017:376, paras 225–44.

[12] S Meunier and K Nicolaïdis, 'The EU as a Trade Power' in C Hill and M Smith (eds) *International Relations and the European Union*, 3rd edn (Oxford, Oxford University Press, 2017) 211.

action, subject to its own rules and objectives, into an integrated part of EU external relations, characterized by common values that guarantee unity and consistency in the exercise of Union powers. Within this framework, uniformity and liberalization are no longer the only principles determining the formation of the CCP. EU action in the field shall take into account and pursue the general objectives of EU external relations, thus legitimizing the current practice of adopting CCP measures for achieving other trade and non-trade goals. In particular, the references to fair trade and integration to the world economy next to liberalization illustrate that trade liberalization should not be seen any longer as a self- determining objective, but it should be regarded within the broader context of economic and social development objectives.

Article 207(2) TFEU provides the legal basis for the adoption of 'measures for the implementation' of the CCP.

Article 207(2) TFEU

The European Parliament and the Council, acting by means of regulations in accordance with the ordinary legislative procedure, shall adopt the measures defining the framework for implementing the common commercial policy.

This empowers the EU's institutions 'by means of regulations' to adopt measures for the implementation of the CCP. A degree of flexibility is reflected in the phrase 'defining the framework'. As we have seen in Chapter 3, CCP competences are exclusive, which implies that the Member States have now transferred their powers in this (extended) area entirely to the Union. These wide-ranging exclusive powers notwithstanding, two safeguards have been introduced.

Article 207(6) TFEU

The exercise of the competences conferred by this Article in the field of the common commercial policy shall not affect the delimitation of competences between the Union and the Member States, and shall not lead to harmonisation of legislative or regulatory provisions of the Member States in so far as the Treaties exclude such harmonisation.

The first safeguard merely states the obvious and is in line with the principle of conferral. The second aims to make sure that trade agreements in services do not lead to a harmonisation 'through the backdoor'. The exclusive competence of the European Union to negotiate and conclude international agreements within the scope of the CCP brings about the need to allow the Union to implement these agreements internally. However, this may lead to an extension of the European Union's competence to act internally in those areas where competence lies with the Member States. At the same time, allowing the EU to act internationally only to the extent that it has the competence to legislate at the internal level would restrict the external competence of the European Union as it could only implement international agreements to the extent that it has the internal power. Consequently, the European Union needs to enjoy the power to negotiate and conclude international agreements which fall within the scope of the CCP even if it does not have the power to legislate internally in this respect. This means that the EU's competence can be exclusive at the external level in the areas where it has internally shared competence with the Member States. Obviously, the duty of sincere cooperation between the European Union and Member States (see Chapter 2) should minimise the EU's lack of power to implement international agreements in this regard. In addition, the responsibility of the European Union to implement these agreements under public international law should encourage the Member States to implement them.[13]

III. Instruments and Tools of the Common Commercial Policy

The institutional and substantive rules that make up the CCP have been formalised in different instruments and tools that have placed some flesh on the skeleton presented in the Treaties. These instruments relate, inter alia, to tariffs, trade barriers, market access, and trade defence mechanisms. These are unilateral measures set by the EU, though they should be exercised in accordance with international law. Moreover, the CCP is carried out through negotiating and concluding trade agreements, which requires the consent of one or more external parties. Finally, the EU also engages in dispute settlement at the WTO as part of the CCP.

A. Common Custom Tariff

The Common Customs Tariff (CCT) dates back to 1968 and follows the logic of the internal market: once internal tariffs are removed one needs to agree on a common

[13] See G Villalta Puig and B Al-Haddab, 'The Common Commercial Policy after Lisbon: An Analysis of the Reforms' (2011) 36 *European Law Review* 289.

external tariff to prevent goods entering the internal market through the Member State with the lowest import tariff. The CCT can be found in Regulation 2658/87, which is frequently updated.[14] This Regulation makes a difference between so-called autonomous rates of duty, which were fixed in 1968, and conventional rates that are the result of the negotiations in the WTO.

Domestic authorities are in charge of the application of the CCT. Its application is quite technical and complex and finds its basis in Council Regulation 952/2013 laying down the Union Customs Code.[15] The EU's Customs Union needs to be distinguished from (partial) customs unions which the EU maintains with a number of surrounding countries. Andorra and San Marino have joined the customs union, as well as Monaco, which is part of the EU customs territory through an agreement with France. A customs union also exists between the EU and Turkey, but here agricultural products, inter alia, are excluded.

B. Trade Barriers and Market Access

Rules concerning market access and trade liberalisation find their basis in a number of regulations, the most general one being Regulation 2015/478, which lays down the basic rules on imports from third countries;[16] while general rules on exports are specified in Regulation 2015/479 establishing common rules for exports.[17] Next to this, separate regulations deal with specific (groups of) countries or specific products (eg, textiles).

Monitoring of the global rules on free trade is done above all on the basis of the Dispute Settlement system of the WTO. Yet, this system is only accessible to WTO members, not individuals or companies. However, by virtue of the Trade Barriers Regulation (TBR), first adopted in 1994, EU enterprises, industries or their associations (as well as the EU Member States) can lodge a complaint with the European Commission, which then investigates and determines whether there is evidence of a violation of international trade rules which has resulted in either adverse trade effects or injury. It is aimed at opening third country markets by eliminating obstacles to trade for the benefit of EU exporters. It not only relates to goods but also to services and intellectual property rights, when the rules concerning these rights have been violated and had an impact on trade between the EU and a third country. Hence, the TBR is designed to ensure that the rights of the EU under international trade agreements can be enforced in cases where third countries adopt or maintain barriers to trade.

[14] Council Regulation (EEC) No 2658/87 of 23 July 1987 on the tariff and statistical nomenclature and on the Common Customs Tariff [1987] OJ L 256/1.

[15] Regulation (EU) No 952/2013 of the European Parliament and of the Council of 9 October 2013 laying down the Union Customs Code [2013] OJ L 269/1.

[16] Regulation (EU) 2015/478 of the European Parliament and of the Council of 11 March 2015 on common rules for imports [2015] OJ L 83/16.

[17] Regulation (EU) 2015/479 of the European Parliament and of the Council of 11 March 2015 on common rules for exports [2015] OJ L 83/34.

Regulation (EU) 2015/1843 of the European Parliament and of the Council of 6 October 2015 laying down Union procedures in the field of the common commercial policy in order to ensure the exercise of the Union's rights under international trade rules, in particular those established under the auspices of the World Trade Organization (codification) [2015] OJ L 272/1

Article 1

This Regulation provides for Union procedures in the field of the common commercial policy in order to ensure the exercise of the Union's rights under international trade rules, in particular those established under the auspices of the World Trade Organization ('WTO') which, subject to compliance with existing international obligations and procedures, aim to:

(a) respond to obstacles to trade that have an effect on the market of the Union, with a view to removing the injury resulting therefrom;
(b) respond to obstacles to trade that have an effect on the market of a third country, with a view to removing the adverse trade effects resulting therefrom.

The procedures referred to in the first paragraph shall be applied in particular to the initiation and subsequent conduct and termination of international dispute settlement procedures in the area of common commercial policy.

In addition, the Regulation makes clear that the rules are not intended to protect the interests of individual companies (or even Member States). Instead, there needs to be evidence that a Union-wide interest is at stake.

In relation to Development Policy (see Chapter 8), the CCP and the facilitation of access to the EU market has always played a role in creating leverage for improving for instance human rights or environmental standards. In this vein, CCP allows for special trade benefits for developing countries. This can be seen as specific steps to the 'eradication of poverty and the protection of human rights' (Article 3(5) TEU) as elements forming the context in which CCP should be implemented. Although the current EU Treaties do not make a distinction between different developing countries, the CCP had a history of treating the African, Caribbean and Pacific (ACP) countries differently. It is with these countries that the EU had a special relationship on the basis of a series of international agreements, most recently the Cotonou Agreement of 2000; see further Chapter 8). This special relationship has caused some controversies in the trade relationships with some other countries, including a longstanding dispute regarding bananas.

The WTO disputes on bananas arose from the fact that the EU differentiated between the ACP countries and other third countries, some of which were also producers of bananas. Through Regulation 404/93 the European Community at the time aimed at protecting both the domestic banana production and the imports of bananas from the ACP countries. The result was that it was much easier for ACP countries to have access to the European market than, say, for Latin American countries, where large American corporation operate.

J Larik, 'Much More Than Trade: The Common Commercial Policy in a Global Context' in M Evans and P Koutrakos (eds) *Beyond the Established Legal Orders: Policy Interconnections Between the EU and the Rest of the World* (Oxford, Hart Publishing, 2011) 26

It is in this context that the *Bananas* dispute arose, which would become the EU's longest-lasting trade dispute. The United States and several Latin American countries challenged the EU's regime for the import, sale and distribution of bananas favouring ACP countries. The [WTO] Appellate Body repeatedly found that the EU's preferential treatment, even after several reconfigurations, violated WTO rules. The EU had exceeded the derogations introduced in the GATT/WTO system favouring developing countries, as well as the special waiver granted to the EU in 1994 for the Lomé Agreement. Recently, the EU agreed to reduce the overall import tariffs for bananas in exchange for a no-litigation commitment from the Latin American countries. Consequently, an eroded preferential banana market organisation for the ACP countries will remain, but in order to adjust to the stiffer competition, the EU decided to pay additional financial aid to the ACP countries. While this is arguably a positive move in terms of WTO compliance, it also appears an implicit acknowledgement of the failure of this particular example of development through trade. More generally, the EU has abandoned its ACP-wide approach for granting trade preferences and has moved to negotiate WTO compatible bi-regional agreements.

In addition to challenges from third countries, the banana regime was also the subject of litigation within the EU. Germany, in an action it had brought before the CJEU challenged, among other things, Title IV of the Regulation, which referred to traditional imports of bananas form ACP countries into the Union and the absence of customs duties. Germany also argued that the Regulation was adopted in breach of GATT as well as the Banana Protocol. While the case was relevant in the context of determining the direct (non-)applicability of GATT provisions in EU and Member State courts (see further below and Chapter 5), in a more substantive sense it also clarified the subdivision of the tariff quota in favour of importers of EU and ACP bananas. These issues had been brought up by Germany by referring to the principle of non-discrimination.

Case C-280/93 *Germany v Council*, ECLI:EU:C:1994:367

72 It is therefore clear that before the Regulation was adopted the situations of the categories of economic operators among whom the tariff quota was subdivided were not comparable.

73 It is true that since the Regulation came into force those categories of economic operators have been affected differently by the measures adopted. Operators traditionally essentially supplied by third-country bananas now find their import possibilities restricted, whereas those formerly obliged to market essentially Community and ACP bananas may now import specified quantities of third-country bananas.

74 However, such a difference in treatment appears to be inherent in the objective of integrating previously compartmentalized markets, bearing in mind the different situations of the various categories of economic operators before the establishment of the common organization of the market. The Regulation is intended to ensure the disposal of Community production and traditional ACP production, which entails the striking of a balance between the two categories of economic operators in question.

75 Consequently, the complaint of breach of the principle of non-discrimination must be rejected as unfounded.

Apart from the preferential treatment of ACP countries (which has now been replaced by bi-regional agreements), there are other ways the EU can offer preferential access to its market. A so-called Generalised System of Preferences (GSP) provides such preferential access to developing countries. While such differential treatment would normally be at odds with the WTO's most-favoured national principle, the GSP is covered by the WTO's 1979 'enabling clause' regarding developing countries.[18]

In addition, rules for more wide-ranging market access were laid down by the EU in two special schemes.[19] First, the 'Special incentive arrangement for sustainable development and good governance', known as GSP+, incentivises third countries to comply with a range of international agreements, covering issues from labour standards and human rights to environmental protection, through preferential trade with the EU. Secondly, the 'Special arrangement for the least-developed countries', known as 'Everything but Arms' (EBA) is aimed specifically at helping the world's poorest countries through duty-free access to the EU market. As of January 2019, 15 developing countries fall under the standard GSP, which is now restricted to low and lower-middle income countries since 2014,[20] 48 under EBA, while only eight countries have qualified for GSP+. In general, the effects of these arrangements have been said to be limited, not least due to their complexity.[21] In the *EC-Tariff Preferences* dispute, the WTO

[18] GATT, *Decision on Differential and More Favourable Treatment, Reciprocity and Fuller Participation of Developing Countries*, Decision of 28 November 1979, L/4903.

[19] Regulation (EU) No 978/2012 of the European Parliament and of the Council of 25 October 2012 applying a scheme of generalised tariff preferences and repealing Council Regulation (EC) No 732/2008 [2012] OJ L 303/1, ch III and ch IV.

[20] S Gstöhl and D De Bièvre, *The Trade Policy of the European Union* (London, Palgrave Macmillan, 2018) 160.

[21] L Bartels, *Human Rights Conditionality in the EU's International Agreements* (New York, Oxford University Press, 2005) 155–56.

Appellate Body determined that certain forms of its conditionality were not covered by the enabling clause, which underlines that also these EU preferential treatment regimes run the risk of being at odds with by the international trade rules.[22]

Next to development, the issue of environmental protection has received more heightened attention, not least in view of climate change. Both are linked through the notion of sustainable development, which features in the EU Treaties[23] and in the Preambles to the WTO Marrakech Agreement and the Doha Ministerial Declaration.[24] Noteworthy trade-related environmental protection measures adopted by the EU include the Regulation on waste shipment,[25] which transposes into EU Law the Basel Convention on the Control of Transboundary Movements of Hazardous Wastes and their Disposal and the adherence of the Union to the Rotterdam Convention on the Prior Informed Consent Procedure for Certain Hazardous Chemicals and Pesticides in International Trade.[26] This serves to show that the CCP is not always about liberalising trade, but can indeed also be used to regulate and, if necessary, restrict it, if this is in the interest of the Union.[27] Another area where the EU has combined trade with environmental protection is through the establishment of a regional emissions trading scheme, linked on the global level to the Kyoto Protocol. Finally, we can recall that environmental conventions also figure among the agreements to be ratified to qualify for GSP+.[28]

C. Trade Defence Instruments

At first sight, trade defence seems to go against the idea of a free market. However, perhaps ironically, to reach the objective of free trade adequate regulation and protection are needed. The EU's three principal trade defence instruments concern anti-dumping and countervailing (against subsidies) measures and safeguards.

The purpose of anti-dumping measures is to prevent the domestic market from being distorted by products that are sold below their so-called 'normal value' by imposing special duties. Determining whether sales are made below value is a complex

[22] WTO, *European Communities – Conditions for the Granting of Tariff Preferences to Developing Countries*, Appellate Body Report (adopted 20 April 2004), WT/DS246/AB/R.

[23] See Art 3(3) TEU on 'sustainable development of Europe'; Art 3(5) TEU on 'sustainable development of the Earth'; and Art 21(2)(d) TEU on 'sustainable economic, social and environmental development of developing countries'.

[24] WTO, *Ministerial Declaration*, adopted on 14 November 2001, WT/MIN(01)/DEC/1, Pt 6; see also Pts 31–33.

[25] Regulation 1013/2006/EC of the European Parliament and of the Council of 14 June 2006 on shipments of waste [2006] OJ L 190/1.

[26] Council Decision 2006/730/EC of 25 September 2006 on the conclusion, on behalf of the European Community, of the Rotterdam Convention on the Prior Informed Consent Procedure for certain hazardous chemicals and pesticides in international trade [2006] OJ L299/23.

[27] See, to this effect, Case C-94/03 *Commission v Council (Rotterdam Convention)*, ECLI:EU:C:2006:2, para 49. See also Chapter 9, which addresses the relation between CCP and 'restrictive measures' (economic sanctions) established on the basis of the Common Foreign and Security Policy (CFSP).

[28] Regulation (EU) No 978/2012 of the European Parliament and of the Council of 25 October 2012 applying a scheme of generalised tariff preferences and repealing Council Regulation (EC) No 732/2008 [2012] OJ L 303/1, Art 9(1)(b) and Annex VIII Part B.

yet (politically) highly contested process, since it depends on an accurate comparison of data that is inherently hard to compare. The EU's commitment to the liberalisation of international trade depends on a level playing field between domestic and foreign producers based on genuine competitive advantages. Hence, like other markets, the EU is keen on using the possibilities to defend free trade that find their basis in Article VI GATT and issued Regulation 2016/1036 on protection against dumped imports from countries not members of the European Union.[29] The Commission monitors the application of these instruments, follows up the enforcement of measures and negotiates future international rules with EU trading partners.

Regulation (EU) 2016/1036 of the European Parliament and of the Council of 8 June 2016 on protection against dumped imports from countries not members of the European Union OJ [2016] L 176/21

Article 1 (Principles)

1. An anti-dumping duty may be imposed on any dumped product whose release for free circulation in the Union causes injury.
2. A product is to be considered as being dumped if its export price to the Union is less than a comparable price for a like product, in the ordinary course of trade, as established for the exporting country.
3. The exporting country shall normally be the country of origin. However, it may be an intermediate country, except where, for example, the products are merely transhipped through that country, or the products concerned are not produced in that country, or there is no comparable price for them in that country.
4. For the purposes of this Regulation, 'like product' means a product which is identical, that is to say, alike in all respects, to the product under consideration, or, in the absence of such a product, another product which, although not alike in all respects, has characteristics closely resembling those of the product under consideration.

The following extract is an example whereby the European Commission decided to impose provisional anti-dumping duties on imports of solar panels and key components such as solar cells and wafers from China. An investigation by the Commission found that Chinese solar panels were sold to Europe far below their normal market value. This decision, taken by the Commission, was particularly sensitive for Germany. That Member State has the largest solar panel industry in the Union and feared that EU-level action would spark a trade war with China with commensurate impact on its industry. The Commission argued that international trade relations are to be conducted

[29] Regulation (EU) 2016/1036 of the European Parliament and of the Council of 8 June 2016 on protection against dumped imports from countries not members of the European Union [2016] OJ L 176/21.

based on law, rather than political strong-arming and divide-and-rule tactics by third countries. The day after publication of the extract below, China opened anti-dumping proceedings against European wine imports into that country, which made up two-third of its imports in 2012.

European Commission, *EU Imposes Provisional Anti-dumping Duties on Chinese Solar Panels*, 4 June 2013, MEMO/13/497

Whereas the dumping rate is at 88% on average, the anti-dumping duties imposed will only be set at an average of 47.6%, which is required to remove the harm caused by the dumping to the European industry … The duty will have to be paid as an 'ad valorem' duty; in other words, as a percentage of the import value. It is provisional and imposed in total for a period of maximum six months …

The investigation was initiated on 6 September 2012 following a complaint lodged by EU ProSun, an industry association, which claims solar panels from China are being dumped in the EU at prices below market value and causing material injury to the EU photovoltaic industry.

The investigation was carried out within a strict legal framework covering a full analysis of dumping by Chinese exporting companies, injury suffered by the EU photovoltaic industry as a result of that dumping, and the interest of all EU players (Union producers, suppliers of components such as silicon, installers, importers, users and consumers). It showed that:

- there is dumping by the exporting producers in China: Chinese solar panels are sold on the European market far below their normal market value, resulting, on average, in dumping margins of 88%, which means that the fair value of a Chinese solar panel sold to Europe should actually be 88% higher than the price to which it is sold. In some cases, dumping margins of up to 112.6% were found;
- material injury has been suffered by the Union industry concerned translated in loss of market shares in the EU, decrease in sales prices and decrease in profitability leasing [sic] to a number of insolvencies of Union producers;
- there is a causal link between the dumping and injury found;
- the imposition of measures is not against the Union interest …

How has the duty been calculated?

In general, duty rates are set by reference to the 'lesser duty rule'. The 'lesser duty rule' is a so-called 'WTO-plus' commitment of the EU, ie, which allows the Commission to set a duty at a level lower than the dumping margin when this lower level is sufficient to remove the injury suffered by the Union industry. This fair approach benefits the exporters and goes beyond what is required by

> our WTO obligations. In practice, the injury margin is the amount 'removing the injury' ie, it aims at increasing prices to a level allowing EU industry to sell at a reasonable profit …
>
> Since the EU does not recognise China as a 'market economy', India has been chosen as the most appropriate and reasonable analogue country. This choice is not disputed by the Chinese side. In effect, a number of parties – including Chinese – have proposed India and expressed a clear preference over other alternatives such as the USA …
>
> By 5 December 2013, the European Commission may propose to the Council (a) to terminate the case without measures or (b) to impose definitive anti-dumping measures for a duration of five years. According to the current rules, the Council can reject the Commission's proposal by simple majority …

In addition, Regulation 2016/1037 aims to protect the internal market and its industries from subsidised imports from third states.[30] The EU can do so by imposing so-called countervailing duties to neutralise the benefit of such subsidies if the latter are 'specific to an enterprise or industry or group of enterprises or industries'.[31] Export subsidies and subsidies contingent on the use of domestic over imported goods are deemed to be specific.[32] Subsidies can be used for different purposes eg, pursuing domestic and social policies, boosting production or exports, creating jobs, facilitating the creation and expansion of new industries, supporting economic activities that might otherwise fail, etc. However, they may distort competition by making subsidised goods artificially competitive against non-subsidised goods. In parallel to the aforementioned solar panel anti-dumping investigation, the Commission has, since the end of 2012, also carried out an anti-subsidy investigation.

The third category of trade defence instruments concerns so-called safeguards. Safeguards are intended for situations in which an EU industry is affected by an unforeseen, sharp and sudden increase of imports from third countries. The objective is to give the industry a temporary breathing space to make necessary adjustments. Safeguards always come with an obligation to restructure. Unlike anti-dumping and anti-subsidy measures, they do not focus on whether trade is fair. Hence, the conditions for imposing them are more stringent. A safeguard investigation may lead to quantitative restrictions on imports of the investigated product (import or tariff quota) from any non-EU country and surveillance (a system of automatic import licensing). The legal basis for safeguards is different for measures against WTO members

[30] Regulation (EU) 2016/1037 of the European Parliament and of the Council of 8 June 2016 on protection against subsidised imports from countries not members of the European Union [2016] OJ L 176/55.

[31] Ibid, Art 4(2).

[32] Ibid, Art 4(4).

(Regulation 2015/478) and non-WTO members (Regulation 2015/755).[33] The results of the Trade Defence Instruments are presented to the European Parliament on a yearly basis.

D. Trade Agreements

The EU has a decades-long history and expertise in the negotiation and conclusion of Free Trade Agreements (FTAs) with third parties. It has built a dense web of FTAs around the world, which continues to expand and evolve. Trade agreements serve as a tool for acquiring access to foreign markets and for promoting the EU's values and interests. Moreover, they go further in terms of collaboration than the multilateral framework of the WTO with specific partners, for instance by providing a framework for closer regulatory cooperation. The procedural specificities that apply to the CCP are outlined below in section IV, while the EU's international treaty-making in general is discussed in Chapter 4. Here, we consider the substance of these agreements, which illustrates how they are used by the EU.

There is no one-size-fits-all model for trade agreements. In most cases, the EU tends to negotiate comprehensive FTAs. While bilateral trade agreements may – at first sight – not contribute to a global trade liberalisation regime, they are often used as alleged 'stepping stones' to multilateral liberalisation. The rules for FTAs are set out in the WTO, specifically in Article XXIV of the GATT and Article V of the GATS. FTAs are designed to create opportunities by: opening new markets for goods and services; increasing investment opportunities; making trade *cheaper* (by eliminating substantially all customs duties); making trade *faster* (by facilitating the transit of goods through customs and setting common rules on technical and sanitary standards); and making the policy environment more *predictable* (by taking joint commitments on areas that affect trade such as intellectual property rights, competition rules and the framework for public purchasing decisions).

Free Trade Agreement between the European Union and its Member States, of the one part, and the Republic of Korea, of the other part [2011] OJ 127/6

HAVE AGREED AS FOLLOWS:

CHAPTER ONE

OBJECTIVES AND GENERAL DEFINITIONS

Article 1.1

Objectives

1. The Parties hereby establish a free trade area on goods, services, establishment and associated rules in accordance with this Agreement.

[33] Regulation (EU) 2015/755 of the European Parliament and of the Council of 29 April 2015 on common rules for imports from certain third countries [2015] OJ L 123/33.

2. The objectives of this Agreement are:

   (a) to liberalise and facilitate trade in goods between the Parties, in conformity with Article XXIV of the General Agreement on Tariffs and Trade 1994 (hereinafter referred to as 'GATT 1994');
   (b) to liberalise trade in services and investment between the Parties, in conformity with Article V of the General Agreement on Trade in Services (hereinafter referred to as 'GATS');
   (c) to promote competition in their economies, particularly as it relates to economic relations between the Parties;
   (d) to further liberalise, on a mutual basis, the government procurement markets of the Parties;
   (e) to adequately and effectively protect intellectual property rights;
   (f) to contribute, by removing barriers to trade and by developing an environment conducive to increased investment flows, to the harmonious development and expansion of world trade;
   (g) to commit, in the recognition that sustainable development is an overarching objective, to the development of international trade in such a way as to contribute to the objective of sustainable development and strive to ensure that this objective is integrated and reflected at every level of the Parties' trade relationship; and
   (h) to promote foreign direct investment without lowering or reducing environmental, labour or occupational health and safety standards in the application and enforcement of environmental and labour laws of the Parties …

As this excerpt shows, the coverage is comprehensive, going far beyond traditional trade in goods and tariff issues. The reference to 'sustainable development' serves as an example of the wider normative 'context of the principles and objectives of the Union's external action'. As confirmed by the CJEU in Opinion 2/15 concerning the EU's FTA with Singapore, 'the objective of sustainable development henceforth forms an integral part of the common commercial policy'.[34]

Widening of the substance of trade agreements, however, brings back the question of 'mixity' (see Chapter 4). This means that if issues are included in an FTA which exceed the scope of the exclusive CCP competence, then the participation of the Member States as parties in their own right may become necessary. This issue flared up in the context of investor-state dispute settlement mechanisms in FTAs. As noted above, while foreign direct investment is now covered by the CCP, portfolio investment is not. According to the CJEU, therefore, an envisaged agreement with Singapore that would have covered non-direct investments and a dispute settlement mechanism to rule

[34] Opinion 2/15 (*Singapore*), ECLI:EU:C:2017:376, para 147.

on investment disputes 'cannot be approved by the European Union alone'.[35] As the CJEU clarified in a later judgment, however, this meant that there was no *legal duty* to conclude such an agreement as an EU-only agreement. By contrast, if there had been the political will within the Council to make it an EU-only agreement, that would have been an option.[36]

Concluding trade agreements as mixed agreements slows down the process leading to ratification, as the FTA needs to be approved by all Member States according to their constitutional requirements, in addition to the EU itself. A prominent example for the repercussions of mixity is the Comprehensive Economic and Trade Agreement (CETA) with Canada. After seven years of negotiations, the agreement was ready for signature by the parties. However, this was delayed due to Wallonia (one of the three federal states of Belgium) withholding its consent which, in turn, was necessary for Belgium to agree under its own constitutional law. The crisis was overcome by a compromise, though all Member States are needed to ratify the agreement. In order to bridge this waiting period (parts of) trade agreements are being applied 'provisionally' (see further on that below).

A way to avoid mixity is to 'split' the comprehensive agreement into two separate parts, one of which can be concluded as an EU-only agreement. This was done, for instance, in the case of the EU–Japan Economic Partnership Agreement. The part on investment protection, which remains a shared competence, was split into an agreement of its own, while the EU-only agreement was concluded in December 2018 by the Union and entered into force in February 2019.[37]

E. Trade Dispute Settlement

The EU is also one of the most active participants in WTO dispute settlement (on the EU's position in the WTO generally see Chapter 6). It has been a complainant in over 100 cases and had to defend the EU as respondent in more than 80 cases.

Unlike most other international dispute settlement mechanisms, dispute settlement at the WTO is quasi-compulsory thanks to the so-called 'reverse consensus principle'. This means that *unless* there is a consensus *not* to establish a panel, it will be established.[38] Similarly, *unless* there is a consensus *not* to adopt a panel report or Appellate Body report, they will be adopted.[39] The same applied to the authorisation of 'suspensions of concessions' (often called 'trade sanctions' in the media) to encourage the responding party to comply with its obligations.[40] Hence, as long as at least one WTO member votes in favour, the procedure moves ahead.

[35] Ibid, para 244.
[36] Case C-600/14 *Germany v Council (COTIF)*, ECLI:EU:C:2017:935, para 68.
[37] Council Decision (EU) 2018/1907 of 20 December 2018 on the conclusion of the Agreement between the European Union and Japan for an Economic Partnership [2018] OJ L 330/1.
[38] Understanding on rules and procedures governing the settlement of disputes (DSU), Annex 2 of the WTO Agreement, Art 6(1).
[39] Art 16(4) and Art 17(14) DSU, respectively.
[40] Art 22(6) DSU.

Even though the EU and the Member States are both represented at the WTO, only the EU brings cases against other WTO members. Moreover, the EU takes up the defence, even if cases are occasionally brought against individual Member States. When the EU is authorised to adopt 'suspensions of concessions' against WTO members who have violated their obligations towards it, it can use the entire weight of its internal market to make them effective. However, as a whole, the EU also represents a larger target.

A Delgado Casteleiro and J Larik, 'The "Odd Couple": The Responsibility of the EU at the WTO' in M Evans and P Koutrakos (eds) *The International Responsibility of the European Union* (Oxford, Hart Publishing, 2013) 253

The combined result of this particular enforcement mechanism and the position the EU has assumed in the WTO is that the Union can be targeted as a whole, and not the individual Member States in which the violation was committed. This makes sense, since the Union is the bigger target providing a wider selection of vulnerable sectors and companies to single out in the quest for inducing compliance. This is confirmed by practice, as there is no instance thus far in which a WTO Member has requested suspension of concessions against a single EU Member State. As shown earlier, in the cases where Member States have been targeted either individually or alongside the EU for complaints, in most cases a mutually agreed solution was reached by the EU. At the same time, suspensions have been applied against the EU in its entirety. Prominent examples include suspensions by the US in the course of the bananas and hormones disputes. These targeted a range of products from various Member States, with specific targets such as Italian pecorino cheese in the former case, and French Roquefort cheese in the latter.

As we have seen from the discussion of trade defence instruments such as anti-dumping measures, the CCP also plays a crucial role in defending the internal market from external influences which are seen as harmful to it, also at the WTO. In attempting to maintain a level playing field also with respect to the outside world, these instruments can be understood as complementing competition and state aid policy within the Union. For example, in the *Large Civil Aircraft* disputes between the United States and the EU, both sides accused the other of subsidising their major civil aviation companies in violation of WTO Agreement on Subsidies and Countervailing Measures.[41] In view of the fact that Boeing and Airbus are also involved in the production of defence equipment, ie military aircraft, and given that awarding

[41] WTO, *United States – Measures Affecting Trade in Large Civil Aircraft*, Request for consultations by the European Communities of 12 October 2004, WT/DS317/1; WTO, *European Communities and Certain Member States – Measures Affecting Trade in Large Civil Aircraft*, Request for Consultations by the United States of 12 October 2004, WT/DS316/1.

such projects to them might be seen as masked subsidies, it cannot be denied that 'this matter is all but exclusively civil, and relates to the EU's efforts for armaments cooperation',[42] and thus, albeit indirectly, to the CSDP (see Chapter 9).

To take another example, the EU market is also to be protected from products which are considered harmful to European consumers, which other WTO members can see as protectionism. The issue of trade restrictions based on health concerns is addressed in the WTO framework by the Agreement on the Application of Sanitary and Phytosanitary Measures (SPS). Under this agreement, the EU found itself being sued by its trading partners, notably the US, in widely publicised disputes such as *Beef Hormones*[43] and those concerning genetically modified organisms (GMOs).[44] These disputes raise fundamental questions about the interpretation of the 'precautionary principle' and the use of scientific evidence by the WTO Appellate Body. These controversies show that the internal market and its relations with the outside world are far from being matters of only technical relevance and can become highly politicised.

IV. The Role of the Institutions and Decision-making

The main actors and instruments of EU external relations were introduced in Chapters 1 and 4. In the framework of the CCP, there are a number of important deviations from the general rules and procedures which are explained in this section.

A. The Commission

International agreements concluded in the area of the CCP follow the single procedure laid down in Article 218 TFEU (see Chapter 4). However, Article 207(3) TFEU adds a few particularities, which point to a somewhat different position of the institutions.

> **Article 207(3) TFEU**
>
> Where agreements with one or more third countries or international organisations need to be negotiated and concluded, Article 218 shall apply, subject to the special provisions of this Article.
>
> The Commission shall make recommendations to the Council, which shall authorise it to open the necessary negotiations. The Council and the Commission

[42] Larik (n 5) 20.
[43] WTO, *European Communities – Measures Concerning Meat and Meat Products (Hormones)*, Appellate Body Report (adopted 13 February 1998) WT/DS26/AB/R, WT/DS48/AB/R.
[44] WTO, *European Communities – Measures Affecting the Approval and Marketing of Biotech Products*, Panel Report (adopted 21 November 2006) WT/DS291/R, WT/DS292/R, WT/DS293/R.

> shall be responsible for ensuring that the agreements negotiated are compatible with internal Union policies and rules.
>
> The Commission shall conduct these negotiations in consultation with a special committee appointed by the Council to assist the Commission in this task and within the framework of such directives as the Council may issue to it. The Commission shall report regularly to the special committee and to the European Parliament on the progress of negotiations.

It is explicitly mentioned that the Council and the Commission need to make sure that the agreements are compatible with internal policies. There is no choice in the selection of the 'Union negotiator' or the 'negotiating team' (see Article 218 TFEU). Trade negotiations are, by definition, in the hands of the Commission. However, the Commission must act in consultation with a special committee. Whereas Article 218 TFEU gives some freedom to the Council to establish such committees, it is mandatory in relation to the CCP. Through this 'Trade Policy Committee' the Council can maintain its influence on the negotiations. The European Parliament is to be regularly informed during the negotiations (see below).

Despite the expressly mentioned roles of the Council and the European Parliament in the final decision-making, the role of the Commission in CCP cannot be overstated. Over the years, the Commission has built-up an extensive (technical) expertise and has been the main Union representative at the WTO (previously the GATT). It is the negotiator of trade agreements and executes the EU's trade policy. On the basis of the adapted comitology rules of 2011, which define the role of the various Member States driven committees in the Commission's decision-making procedure,[45] the Commission – and no longer the Council – takes final trade defence measures in the important CCP fields of anti-dumping, anti-subsidy and safeguards. Finally, the Commission's general competence to initiate an infringement procedure against a Member State is also applicable in relation to CCP matters.[46]

B. The Council

> **Article 207 TFEU**
>
> 2. The European Parliament and the Council, acting by means of regulations in accordance with the ordinary legislative procedure, shall adopt the measures defining the framework for implementing the common commercial policy …

[45] Regulation 182/2011/EU of the European Parliament and of the Council of 16 February 2011 laying down the rules and general principles concerning mechanisms for control by Member States of the Commission's exercise of implementing powers [2011] OJ L 55/13.

[46] See for instance, Case C-173/05 *Commission v Italy*, ECLI:EU:C:2007:362.

4. For the negotiation and conclusion of the agreements referred to in paragraph 3, the Council shall act by a qualified majority.

For the negotiation and conclusion of agreements in the fields of trade in services and the commercial aspects of intellectual property, as well as foreign direct investment, the Council shall act unanimously where such agreements include provisions for which unanimity is required for the adoption of internal rules.

The Council shall also act unanimously for the negotiation and conclusion of agreements:

(a) in the field of trade in cultural and audiovisual services, where these agreements risk prejudicing the Union's cultural and linguistic diversity;
(b) in the field of trade in social, education and health services, where these agreements risk seriously disturbing the national organisation of such services and prejudicing the responsibility of Member States to deliver them.

Together with the European Parliament, the Council is the main decision-making institution – this time in the formation as the 'Trade Council'. Article 207(2) TFEU refers to the application of the ordinary legislative procedure for the adoption of 'the measures defining the framework for implementing the common commercial policy'. As the Member States are represented in the Council and the Trade Policy Committee, they can discuss and influence all trade matters also in non-mixed contexts.

In terms of voting modalities, the two paragraphs are clear: the Council decides by qualified majority voting (QMV). This follows from the application of the ordinary legislative procedure. Yet, Article 207(4) TFEU also mentions an exception to the rule: the Council acts unanimously in the negotiation and conclusion of international agreements in the areas of trade in services, commercial aspects of intellectual property, as well as FDI, 'where such agreements include provisions for which unanimity is required for the adoption of internal rules'.

In the areas mentioned in paragraphs 4(a) and (b), the Council always decides by unanimity. These concerns areas that are particularly sensitive for the Member States, such as 'cultural and audio-visual services and health services. Pre-Lisbon, FTAs addressing these issues would be concluded as mixed agreements to accommodate this sensitivity. With former Article 133 TEC having been modified and replaced by Article 207 TFEU, these sensitivities are now catered to by more burdensome procedures and voting prerogatives of the Member States within the Council, while the CCP as a whole has become an exclusive Union competence.

This pre-Lisbon practice is one factor explaining the large number of mixed agreements (see Chapter 2) in an area which is considered to be the prime example of exclusivity. At the same time, it puts the relevance of the principle of parallelism (see Chapter 3) into perspective, as harmonisation is not possible in areas not foreseen by the Treaty. These days, this is clearly laid down in paragraph 6 of Article 207. This excludes the conclusion of international agreements once these would lead to internal harmonisation in areas where this was not meant to happen, such as the areas mentioned in Article 6 TFEU, even in the area of the CCP.

C. The European Parliament

As in most other areas of Union policy, the European Parliament is a co-decider in relation to the CCP. As we have seen, according to Article 207(2) TFEU, the ordinary legislative procedure applies here, which implies that internal measures on CCP issues need the support of a majority in the EP. Moreover, the EP must be kept informed on the negotiations of trade agreements by the Commission on the basis of Article 207(3) TFEU.

Article 207(3) TFEU

The Commission shall report regularly to the special committee and to the European Parliament on the progress of negotiations.

This allows for parliamentary scrutiny over trade negotiations. Irrespective of these specific provisions, Article 207(3) TFEU points to the applicability of the general procedure in Article 218 TFEU, which, inter alia, includes the following in relation to the negotiation and conclusion of international agreements (see also Chapter 4):[47]

Article 218 TFEU

6. … the Council shall adopt the decision concluding the agreement:

(a) after obtaining the consent of the European Parliament in the following cases: …

 (v) agreements covering fields to which either the ordinary legislative procedure applies, or the special legislative procedure where consent by the European Parliament is required.

The European Parliament and the Council may, in an urgent situation, agree upon a time-limit for consent. …

10. The European Parliament shall be immediately and fully informed at all stages of the procedure.

[47] The arrangements are further specified in the Framework Agreement on relations between the European Parliament and the European Commission [2010] OJ L 304/47.

Article 218(6)(a)(v) TFEU implies that the consent of the EP is also necessary for international agreements concluded under the CCP. This is an important change to the situation pre-Lisbon, where the EP's consent was not necessary for the conclusion of trade agreements.[48] Yet, while the requirement of final consent may certainly be helpful, the EP has only a limited role to play during the negotiation process. Obviously, it will be very difficult for the EP to deny its consent or call for amendments after (usually) difficult and complex negotiations have ended. This makes consulting the EP during the negotiation process all the more important, thereby giving the Parliament the possibility of indicating some possible obstacles for its final consent.

The EP's consent is not needed for provisional application of international agreements. Council decisions to authorise the provisional application of an agreement can be taken following a proposal from the Commission alone without the need to ask for prior parliamentary consent (Article 218(3) TFEU). The latter rule is of particular importance in relation to CCP, as indicated by the 'Banana Agreement' between the EU and a number of Latin-American States which effectively ended that long trade dispute. The EU was only able to conclude this deal with the possibility to put it into early provisional application in late 2009. The Latin American countries dropped their WTO cases against the EU in return for easier access to the EU market. On 3 February 2011, the European Parliament then gave its consent to the text. The agreement was officially signed in November 2012.

The extract below illustrates the proactive role the European Parliament plays in the CCP. In this legally non-binding resolution, the EP sets out its views on trade negotiations conducted by the Commission with Australia. It stresses the promotion of common values, the interest of the European agricultural sector and the wide-ranging scope of EU trade agreements. Moreover, it references important developments in the case law – here Opinion 2/15 – and its implications for democratic scrutiny. Last, but not least, the EP does not fail to remind the other institutions of its prerogatives, ie, the requirement of its consent to such an agreement and, therefore, to have its positions 'duly taken into account at all stages'.

European Parliament Resolution of 26 October 2017 containing the Parliament's recommendation to the Council on the proposed negotiating mandate for trade negotiations with Australia, 2017/2192(INI)

The European Parliament …

A. whereas the EU and Australia work together in tackling common challenges across a broad spectrum of issues and cooperate in a number of international fora, including on trade policy issues in the multilateral arena; …

F. whereas the European agricultural sector and certain agricultural products, such as beef, lamb, dairy products, cereals and sugar – including special sugars – are particularly sensitive issues in these negotiations; …

[48] Villalta Puig and Al-Haddab (n 13) 299.

K. whereas Australia is among the EU's oldest and closest partners, sharing common values and a commitment to promoting prosperity and security within a global rules-based system; …

1. Underlines the importance of deepening relations between the EU and the Asia-Pacific region, among other things, in order to foster economic growth within Europe and stresses that this is reflected in the EU's trade policy; …

9. Calls on the Council to fully respect the distribution of competences between the EU and its Member States, as can be deduced from CJEU Opinion 2/15 of 16 May 2017, in its decision on the adoption of the negotiating directives; …

14. Emphasises that an ambitious agreement must address, in a meaningful way, investment, trade in goods and services (drawing on recent European Parliament recommendations as regards policy space reservations and sensitive sectors), customs and trade facilitation, digitalisation, e-commerce and data protection, technology research and support for innovation, public procurement, energy, state-owned enterprises, competition, sustainable development, regulatory issues, such as high-quality sanitary and phytosanitary standards and other norms in agricultural and food products without weakening the EU's high standards, robust and enforceable commitments on labour and environmental standards, and the fight against tax avoidance and corruption while remaining within the scope of the Union's exclusive competence, all while giving special consideration to the needs of micro-enterprises and SMEs; …

20. Stresses that following CJEU Opinion 2/15 on the EU–Singapore FTA, Parliament should see its role strengthened at every stage of the EU-FTA negotiations from the adoption of the mandate to the final conclusion of the agreement; … reminds the Commission of its obligation to inform Parliament immediately and fully at all stages of the negotiations (before and after the negotiating rounds); is committed to examining the legislative and regulatory issues that may arise in the context of the negotiations and the future agreement without prejudice to its prerogatives as a co-legislator; reiterates its fundamental responsibility to represent the citizens of the EU, and looks forward to facilitating inclusive and open discussions during the negotiating process;

21. Recalls that Parliament will be asked to give its consent to the future agreement, as stipulated by the TFEU, and that its positions should therefore be duly taken into account at all stages; calls on the Commission and the Council to request the consent of the Parliament before its application, while also integrating this practice into the interinstitutional agreement;

22. Recalls that Parliament will monitor the implementation of the future agreement; …

D. The Court of Justice

This sub-section differs from those addressing the other institutions in the sense that we will use it to highlight several issues on which the role of the Court of Justice has been quite decisive with regard to the definition and development of the CCP. Because of the inextricable relationship between the CCP and the European integration process, a broad range of actors may be affected by CCP measures or hope to be able to rely on WTO agreements before EU courts (including Member State courts). In principle, the EU Courts are competent to deal with CCP on the basis of the general judicial procedures: the action for annulment (Article 263 TFEU), the preliminary reference procedure (Article 267 TFEU) and an action to invoke the contractual liability of the Union (Articles 268 and 340 TFEU). Furthermore, the Member States and the institutions can request the *ex ante* review of a trade agreement by the Court under Article 218(11) TFEU, as was the case with the WTO agreements of 1994 or CETA.[49] The extensive case law may be divided in cases related to commercial policy measures and cases on the effects of GATT/WTO law in the EU legal order, both reflecting the internal/external interface which is so characteristic for the CCP.

(i) CCP Measures

The possibility for individuals to bring an action for annulment against a CCP measure was confirmed by the Court in *Allied Corporation and Others*, which concerned an anti-dumping measure.[50] Irrespective of their general legislative nature, the fact that the exporters (of fertilizers) were expressly named in the regulation caused the Court to rule that the provisions of anti-dumping regulations could be of direct and individual concern to the producers and exporters. Indeed, many CCP cases concern anti-dumping measures. In *Timex*,[51] a watch producer successfully argued that anti-dumping duties on imports of mechanical wrist watches originating from the (then) Soviet Union were insufficient to protect its interests on the EU market. In this case, the measure in question was of direct and individual concern to Timex as this company was involved in initiating the proceedings and was in fact the only producer that was affected by the dumping of Soviet watches.

Anti-dumping duties are paid by the importers of dumped products and obviously they may disagree with the duties themselves or with their amount. However, proving to be directly and individually concerned has proven difficult for importers. In *Alusuisse*,[52] the Court found the anti-dumping measure to be of general application as the importers were not listed in the regulation. Exceptions have been noted when importers were associated with the mentioned exporters, or in very specific situations,[53]

[49] Opinion 1/94 (*WTO*), ECLI:EU:C:1994:384; Opinion 1/17 (*CETA*), ECLI:EU:C:2019:341.
[50] Joined Cases 239/82 & 275/82 *Allied Corporation and Others v Commission*, ECLI:EU:C:1984:68.
[51] Case 264/82 *Timex v Council and Commission*, ECLI:EU:C:1985:119.
[52] Case 307/81 *Alusuisse v Council and Commission*, ECLI:EU:C:1982:337.
[53] Case C-358/89 *Extramet Industrie v Council*, ECLI:EU:C:1991:214.

but the general rule seems to be that anti-dumping measures apply generally and hence cannot be challenged in court by individual importers.

Nevertheless, the fact that current Article 263(4) TFEU allows individuals to initiate proceeding against a 'regulatory act' when it is 'of direct concern to them and does not entail implementing measures', may allow for some flexibility. After all, once anti-dumping measures can be qualified as 'regulatory acts' there is no need for individuals to state their individual concern. As explained by the CJEU in the judgment below (concerning anti-dumping duties applied to iron or steel fasteners originating in the People's Republic of China or consigned from Malaysia), this happens because otherwise the private party would first need to violate the measure to cause 'individual concern'.

Case C-145/17 P *Internacional de Productos Metálicos SA v Commission*, ECLI:EU:C:2018:839, para 49

Where a regulatory act directly affects the legal situation of a natural or legal person without requiring implementing measures, that person could be denied effective judicial protection if he did not have a legal remedy before the European Union judicature for the purpose of challenging the legality of the regulatory act. In the absence of implementing measures, natural or legal persons, although directly concerned by the act in question, would be able to obtain a judicial review of that act only after having infringed its provisions, by pleading that those provisions are unlawful in proceedings initiated against them before the national courts …

(ii) Effects of WTO Law

The effects of international law in the EU legal order have been addressed in Chapter 5. In this sub-section, we highlight some specific aspects of the role of the CJEU in relation to the CCP and, above all, the effects of WTO rules in the Union's legal order. In principle, the competence of the Court extends to CCP issues and in terms of legal scrutiny and protection the whole regime of Article 263 TFEU annulment proceedings applies.

However, challenging EU acts on the basis of violations of the GATT and later on WTO law has proved difficult due to the CJEU's stance. In *International Fruit Company*, the Court found that the then Community was bound by the GATT as it had assumed the rights previously exercised by the Member States. Nevertheless, the Court ruled that individuals could not rely on the GATT 1947 to call into question the validity of EU measures in either national courts or the EU courts. It did so for the reasons set out below.

Joined Cases 21/72-24/72 *International Fruit Company and Others v Produktschap voor Groenten en Fruit*, ECLI:EU:C:1972:115

19 It is also necessary to examine whether the provisions of the general agreement confer rights on citizens of the Community on which they can rely before the courts in contesting the validity of a Community measure.

20 For this purpose, the spirit, the general scheme and the terms of the General Agreement must be considered.

21 This agreement which, according to its preamble, is based on the principle of negotiations undertaken on the basis of 'reciprocal and mutually advantageous arrangements' is characterized by the great flexibility of its provisions, in particular those conferring the possibility of derogation, the measures to be taken when confronted with exceptional difficulties and the settlement of conflicts between the contracting parties.

22 Consequently, according to the first paragraph of Article XXII [GATT] 'each contracting party shall accord sympathetic consideration to, and shall afford adequate opportunity for consultation regarding, such representations as may be made by any other contracting party with respect to … all matters affecting the operation of this agreement'.

23 According to the second paragraph of the same Article, 'the contracting parties' – this name designating 'the contracting parties acting jointly' as is stated in the first paragraph of Article XXV – 'may consult with one or more contracting parties on any question to which a satisfactory solution cannot be found through the consultations provided under paragraph (1)'.

24 If any contracting party should consider 'that any benefit accruing to it directly or indirectly under this agreement is being nullified or impaired or that the attainment of any objective of the agreement is being impeded as a result of', inter alia, 'the failure of another contracting party to carry out its obligations under this agreement', Article XXIII lays down in detail the measures which the parties concerned, or the contracting parties acting jointly, may or must take in regard to such a situation.

25 Those measures include, for the settlement of conflicts, written recommendations or proposals which are to be 'given sympathetic consideration', investigations possibly followed by recommendations, consultations between or decisions of the contracting parties, including that of authorizing certain contracting parties to suspend the application to any others of any obligations or concessions under the General Agreement and, finally, in the event of such suspension, the power of the party concerned to withdraw from that agreement.

26 Finally, where by reason of an obligation assumed under the General Agreement or of a concession relating to a benefit, some producers suffer or are

threatened with serious damage, Article XIX gives a contracting party power unilaterally to suspend the obligation and to withdraw or modify the concession, either after consulting the contracting parties jointly and failing agreement between the contracting parties concerned, or even, if the matter is urgent and on a temporary basis, without prior consultation.

27 Those factors are sufficient to show that, when examined in such a context, Article XI of the General Agreement is not capable of conferring on citizens of the Community rights which they can invoke before the courts ...

However, the CJEU has carved out some exceptions to this general rule of no direct applicability in the EU legal order. In *Fediol*, the Court established that the flexibility of the GATT rules did not prevent it from interpreting the Agreement to assess the consistency of a specific commercial practice with its provisions. In the case the applicant had a right to challenge a Commission Decision in view of the GATT by virtue of the very detailed procedure laid down in the regulation which provided the framework for the contested decision, and its explicit reference to the GATT.[54] Moreover, in *Nakajima*, the Court was asked whether a Council Regulation (the 1988 'Basic Regulation'[55] against dumped or subsidised imports from third countries) violated the Anti-Dumping Code annexed to GATT 1947. Court ruled that 'direct effect' of international legal commitments was not the issue, as the Basic Regulation was clearly intended to implement the relevant commitment within the EU.[56] *Fediol* and *Nakajima* did not change the principle set out in *International Fruit*, but rather pointed to the fact that, in these strictly defined cases, the GATT rules were to be seen as part of the Community legal order, which made it unnecessary to address the question of whether international trade law could be relied upon by individuals. Finally, the Court has argued that the provisions of international agreements should be taken into account as far as possible when reading EU legislation by virtue of the principle of 'consistent interpretation' (see also Chapter 5).[57]

The establishment of the WTO (1994) and, in particular, its quasi-judicial dispute settlement system laid down in the Understanding on Rules and Procedures Governing the Settlement of Disputes (or 'Dispute Settlement Understanding', DSU), turned the rather 'member-driven' GATT 1947 trade regime into a more sophisticated, and 'rules-based' system. Reports are prepared by panels and an Appellate Body, but ultimately adopted by the 'Dispute Settlement Body' (DSB) in which all WTO Member States are represented. However, the crucial novelty was the applicable voting procedure called 'reverse consensus'. As noted above, this means panel reports will be

[54] Case 70/87 *Fediol v Commission*, ECLI:EU:C:1989:254.

[55] Regulation 2423/88/EEC of 11 July 1988 on protection against dumped or subsidized imports from countries not members of the European Economic Community [1988] OJ L 209/1.

[56] Case C-69/89 *Nakajima v Council*, ECLI:EU:C:1991:186.

[57] Case C-61/94 *Commission v Germany* (*International Dairy Arrangement*), ECLI:EU:C:1996:313.

adopted unless they are appealed by a party to the dispute.[58] Appellate Body reports, in turn, will always be adopted 'unless the DSB decides by consensus not to adopt the Appellate Body report'.[59] In other words, as long as at least one Member State (the winning party) votes in favour of adopting the report, it shall be deemed to have been adopted.

This development sparked several cases before the CJEU, as it was expected that it might depart from its approach in *International Fruit*. However, this was not the case. The leading case is *Portuguese Textiles*,[60] in which Portugal challenged a Council Decision concerning the conclusion of Memoranda of Understanding between the Community and Pakistan and India on arrangements in the area of market access for textile products. In this case the CJEU was asked to decide on the direct applicability of WTO law in the EU legal order, which the Court denied. While this case was brought to the Court by a Member State, two years later it came to a similar conclusion in *Parfums Dior* concerning the question of whether individuals could challenge the legality of EU secondary legislation by invoking a WTO agreement.[61]

Case C-149/96 *Portugal v Council*, ECLI:EU:C:1999:574

36 While it is true that the WTO agreements, as the Portuguese Government observes, differ significantly from the provisions of GATT 1947, in particular by reason of the strengthening of the system of safeguards and the mechanism for resolving disputes, the system resulting from those agreements nevertheless accords considerable importance to negotiation between the parties.

37 Although the main purpose of the mechanism for resolving disputes is in principle, according to Article 3(7) of the [DSU], to secure the withdrawal of the measures in question if they are found to be inconsistent with the WTO rules, that understanding provides that where the immediate withdrawal of the measures is impracticable compensation may be granted on an interim basis pending the withdrawal of the inconsistent measure.

38 According to Article 22(1) of that Understanding, compensation is a temporary measure available in the event that the recommendations and rulings of the dispute settlement body provided for in Article 2(1) of that Understanding are not implemented within a reasonable period of time, and Article 22(1) shows a preference for full implementation of a recommendation to bring a measure into conformity with the WTO agreements in question.

39 However, Article 22(2) provides that if the member concerned fails to fulfil its obligation to implement the said recommendations and rulings within a

[58] Annex 2 of the WTO Agreement: Understanding on rules and procedures governing the settlement of disputes, Art 14(4).

[59] Ibid, Art 17(4).

[60] Case C-149/96 *Portugal v Council*, ECLI:EU:C:1999:574.

[61] Joined Cases C-300/98 and C-392/98 *Parfums Christan Dior*, ECLI:EU:C:2000:688.

reasonable period of time, it is, if so requested, and on the expiry of a reasonable period at the latest, to enter into negotiations with any party having invoked the dispute settlement procedures, with a view to finding mutually acceptable compensation.

40 Consequently, to require the judicial organs to refrain from applying the rules of domestic law which are inconsistent with the WTO agreements would have the consequence of depriving the legislative or executive organs of the contracting parties of the possibility afforded by Article 22 of that memorandum of entering into negotiated arrangements even on a temporary basis.

41 It follows that the WTO agreements, interpreted in the light of their subject-matter and purpose, do not determine the appropriate legal means of ensuring that they are applied in good faith in the legal order of the contracting parties.

42 As regards, more particularly, the application of the WTO agreements in the Community legal order, it must be noted that, according to its preamble, the agreement establishing the WTO, including the annexes, is still founded, like GATT 1947, on the principle of negotiations with a view to 'entering into reciprocal and mutually advantageous arrangements' and is thus distinguished, from the viewpoint of the Community, from the agreements concluded between the Community and non-member countries which introduce a certain asymmetry of obligations, or create special relations of integration with the Community, such as the agreement which the Court was required to interpret in *Kupferberg*.

43 It is common ground, moreover, that some of the contracting parties, which are among the most important commercial partners of the Community, have concluded from the subject-matter and purpose of the WTO agreements that they are not among the rules applicable by their judicial organs when reviewing the legality of their rules of domestic law.

…

46 To accept that the role of ensuring that Community law complies with those rules devolves directly on the Community judicature would deprive the legislative or executive organs of the Community of the scope for manoeuvre enjoyed by their counterparts in the Community's trading partners.

47 It follows from all those considerations that, having regard to their nature and structure, the WTO agreements are not in principle among the rules in the light of which the Court is to review the legality of measures adopted by the Community institutions.

48 That interpretation corresponds, moreover, to what is stated in the final recital in the preamble to Decision 94/800 [concerning the conclusion of the WTO agreements], according to which 'by its nature, the Agreement establishing the

World Trade Organisation, including the Annexes thereto, is not susceptible to being directly invoked in Community or Member State courts'.

[The CJEU goes on to explain that the above-mentioned *Fediol* and *Nakajima* exceptions do not apply in this case.]

The sentence in paragraph 47 is particularly important: 'The WTO agreements are not in principle among the rules in the light of which the Court is to review the legality of measures adopted by the Community institutions.' Hence, the changes introduced to the international trade regime by the WTO agreements, notwithstanding the arguments noted by the Court, continue to highlight the strong element of 'negotiation' between the parties, the reciprocal and mutually advantageous nature of the WTO and the fact that allowing for direct effect in the EU legal order would lead to putting the EU at a disadvantage with regard to the application of WTO rules, given the fact that other WTO members would not allow it.

But what about decisions by the WTO's Dispute Settlement Body? After all, a report by the WTO Appellate Body is 'as final a pronouncement on compatibility with WTO law as a party can possibly get',[62] providing a clear illustration of the legalisation process within that international organisation. In *Van Parys*, the Court was confronted with this question.

Case C-377/02 *Van Parys v BIRB*, ECLI:EU:C:2005:121

39 It is settled case-law in that regard that, given their nature and structure, the WTO agreements are not in principle among the rules in the light of which the Court is to review the legality of measures adopted by the Community institutions ...

40 It is only where the Community has intended to implement a particular obligation assumed in the context of the WTO, or where the Community measure refers expressly to the precise provisions of the WTO agreements, that it is for the Court to review the legality of the Community measure in question in the light of the WTO rules ...

41 In the present case, by undertaking after the adoption of the decision of the [WTO's Dispute Settlement Body] of 25 September 1997 to comply with the WTO rules and, in particular, with Articles I(1) and XIII of GATT 1994, the Community did not intend to assume a particular obligation in the context of the WTO, capable of justifying an exception to the impossibility of relying on

[62] Koutrakos (n 2) 288.

WTO rules before the Community Courts and enabling the Community Courts to exercise judicial review of the relevant Community provisions in the light of those rules.

42 First, it should be noted that even where there is a decision of the DSB holding that the measures adopted by a member are incompatible with the WTO rules, as the Court has already held, the WTO dispute settlement system nevertheless accords considerable importance to negotiation between the parties (*Portugal* v *Council*, paragraphs 36 to 40).

43 Thus, although, in the absence of a resolution mutually agreed between the parties and compatible with the agreements in question, the main purpose of the dispute settlement system is in principle, according to Article 3(7) of the understanding, to secure the withdrawal of the measures in question if they are found to be inconsistent with the WTO rules, that provision provides, however, that where the immediate withdrawal of the measures is impracticable, compensation may be granted or the application of concessions or the enforcement of other obligations may be suspended on an interim basis pending the withdrawal of the inconsistent measure ....

44 It is true that, according to Articles 3(7) and 22(1) of the understanding, compensation and the suspension of concessions or other obligations are temporary measures available in the event that the recommendations and rulings of the DSB are not implemented within a reasonable period of time, the latter of those provisions showing a preference for full implementation of a recommendation to bring a measure into conformity with the WTO agreements in question (*Portugal* v *Council*, paragraph 38).

45 However, Article 22(2) [of the DSU] provides that, if the Member concerned fails to enforce those recommendations and decisions within a reasonable period, if so requested, and within a reasonable period of time, it is to enter into negotiations with any party having invoked the dispute settlement procedures with a view to agreeing compensation. If no satisfactory compensation has been agreed within 20 days after the expiry of the reasonable period, the complainant may request authorisation from the DSB to suspend, in respect of that member, the application of concessions or other obligations under the WTO agreements ...

47 Where there is no agreement as to the compatibility of the measures taken to comply with the DSB's recommendations and decisions, Article 21(5) of the understanding provides that the dispute shall be decided 'through recourse to these dispute settlement procedures', including an attempt by the parties to reach a negotiated solution.

48 In those circumstances, to require courts to refrain from applying rules of domestic law which are inconsistent with the WTO agreements would have the

consequence of depriving the legislative or executive organs of the contracting parties of the possibility afforded by Article 22 of that memorandum of reaching a negotiated settlement, even on a temporary basis ...

49 In the dispute in the main proceedings, it is apparent from the file that:

- after declaring to the DSB its intention to comply with the DSB's decision of 25 September 1997, the Community amended its system for imports of bananas upon the expiry of the period allocated to it for that purpose; ...

[The judgment goes on to summarise further steps in the dispute and efforts by the EU to adapt its system with a view to making it compatible with WTO law.]

50 Such an outcome, by which the Community sought to reconcile its obligations under the WTO agreements with those in respect of the ACP States, and with the requirements inherent in the implementation of the common agricultural policy, could be compromised if the Community Courts were entitled to judicially review the lawfulness of the Community measures in question in light of the WTO rules upon the expiry of the time-limit, in January 1999, granted by the DSB within which to implement its decision of 25 September 1997.

51 The expiry of that time-limit does not imply that the Community had exhausted the possibilities under the understanding of finding a solution to the dispute between it and the other parties. In those circumstances, to require the Community Courts, merely on the basis that that time-limit has expired, to review the lawfulness of the Community measures concerned in the light of the WTO rules, could have the effect of undermining the Community's position in its attempt to reach a mutually acceptable solution to the dispute in conformity with those rules. ...

Key elements are to be found in paragraphs 50 and 51, where the Court concludes that a judicial review possibility at EU-level would undermine the negotiating position of the Community, also with regard to reports of the Appellate Body that clearly find that the EU is violating its obligations under the WTO agreements.

In both *Portuguese Textiles* and *Van Parys*, the Court refers to earlier case law of the pre-WTO era denying the direct applicability of the GATT in the EU legal order and expanding it to WTO law as a whole. The argumentation has been criticised quite extensively over the years[63] and mainly related to the specific nature of the agreement which was characterised by the Court to exhibit 'great flexibility'. This idea of flexibility was based on a number of specific characteristics of the original GATT, such as the duty of contracting parties to engage in consultations on any issue pertaining to the operation of GATT and their right to engage in further consultation if a satisfactory

[63] See T Cottier and K Schefer, 'The Relationship between World Trade Organization Law, National and Regional Law' (1998) 1 *Journal of International Economic Law* 83, 91–106.

solution was not reached and the possibility of derogation by means of unilateral suspension of GATT obligations in the event or the threat of serious damage. This precluded individuals and even Member States to challenge the legality of EU legislation in the light of GATT.

Moreover, as the Court found in *FIAMM*,[64] companies or individuals in the EU cannot claim damages for being adversely affected by 'suspensions of concessions' imposed by third countries authorised by the DSB for WTO law-inconsistent behaviour on the part of the EU.

The effects of WTO law in the EU legal order can be summarised as follows: As the general rule, the provisions of WTO Agreements cannot be invoked by either Member States (*Portuguese Textiles*) or individuals (*Parfums Dior*) to challenge the legality of EU secondary legislation. This general rule holds even when the DSB has decided that an EU measure is incompatible with the WTO rules (*Van Parys*). However, by way of exception, EU measures may be challenged in the light of a WTO rule if it can be established that the latter was to be implemented by that particular EU measure (*Nakajima*) or when an EU measure makes an express reference to that WTO rule (*Fediol*).

Obviously, the limited role the Court can play here may be criticised as it excludes parts of the exercise of the CCP from scrutiny by the Court and may be seen to condone certain violations of international law by the EU, which is at odds with its self-imposed pledge to the 'strict observance' of international law (Article 3(5) TEU).

V. The Broader Picture of EU External Relations Law

This chapter addressed the key role of the CCP in the EU's external relations regime, which also has shaped EU external relations law from the beginning. This role as a 'driving force' behind the development of the Union's external relations flows from the fact that internal market issues were – and still are – closely related to external trade issues. Both the existence and further development of the GATT and later the WTO, have had a large impact on the CCP – and *vice versa*.

Meanwhile, with the Lisbon Treaty and through the case law of the CJEU, the CCP has not only expanded in scope but has also been integrated more fully into the EU's external action, while democratic oversight over it was strengthened by requiring the EP's consent for the conclusion of trade agreements. However, stressing the need for political manoeuvring space in international trade, the CJEU continues to severely limit the extent to which individuals, companies and even Member States can rely on WTO law in EU courts.

[64] Joined Cases C-120/06 & C-121/06 *FIAMM and Others v Council and Commission*, ECLI:EU:C:2008:476.

VI. Sources and Further Reading

Bartels, L, *Human Rights Conditionality in the EU's International Agreements* (New York, Oxford University Press, 2005).

Bartels, L, 'Human Rights and Sustainable Development Obligations in EU Free Trade Agreements' (2013) 40 *Legal Issues of Economic Integration* 297.

Cottier, T and Schefer, K, 'The Relationship between World Trade Organization Law, National and Regional Law' (1998) 1 *Journal of International Economic Law* 83.

Cremona, M, 'The External Dimension of the Internal Market: Building (on) the Foundations' in C Barnard and J Scott (eds) *The Law of the Single European Market: Unpacking the Premises* (Oxford, Hart Publishing, 2002) 351–94.

Cremona, M, 'The Internal Market and External Economic Relations' in P Koutrakos and J Snell (eds) *Research Handbook on the Law of the EU's Internal Market* (Cheltenham, Edward Elgar, 2017) 479–99.

De Búrca, G and Scott, J, 'The Impact of the WTO on EU Decision-making' in G De Búrca and J Scott (eds) *The EU and the WTO: Legal and Constitutional Issues* (Oxford, Hart Publishing, 2001) 1–30.

Delgado Casteleiro, A and Larik, J, 'The "Odd Couple": The Responsibility of the EU at the WTO' in M Evans and P Koutrakos (eds) *The International Responsibility of the European Union* (Oxford, Hart Publishing, 2013) 233–55.

Dimopoulos, A, 'The Effects of the Lisbon Treaty on the Principles and Objectives of the Common Commercial Policy' (2010) 15 *European Foreign Affairs Review* 153.

Eeckhout, P, *EU External Relations Law*, 2nd edn (Oxford, Oxford University Press, 2011).

Gstöhl, S and D De Bièvre, *The Trade Policy of the European Union* (London, Palgrave Macmillan, 2018).

Koutrakos, P, *EU International Relations Law*, 2nd edn (Oxford, Hart Publishing, 2015).

Larik, J, 'Much More Than Trade: The Common Commercial Policy in a Global Context' in M Evans and P Koutrakos (eds) *Beyond the Established Legal Orders: Policy Interconnections Between the EU and the Rest of the World* (Oxford, Hart Publishing, 2011) 13–45.

Meunier, S and Nicolaïdis, K, 'The EU as a Trade Power' in C Hill and M Smith (eds) *International Relations and the European Union*, 3rd edn (Oxford, Oxford University Press, 2017) 209–34.

Petersmann, E-U and Pollack, M (eds) *Transatlantic Economic Disputes: The EU, the US, and the WTO* (Oxford, Oxford University Press, 2003).

Villalta Puig, G and Al-Haddab, B, 'The Common Commercial Policy after Lisbon: An Analysis of the Reforms' (2011) 36 *European Law Review* 289.

8

EU Development Policy

Central Issues

- EU development policy is as old as the European integration project itself. Objectives in this policy area have evolved from associating EEC Member States' colonies with a focus on trade and aid to a progressively broader development agenda incorporating human rights, sustainable development, and most recently links to common foreign and security policy. EU development policy can be defined through the three C's which are expressly incorporated into the competence conferring provisions of the TFEU: complementarity, coherence and coordination.
- Complementarity implies that the exercise of EU and Member State competences shall complement and reinforce each other. From the perspective of the nature of the EU's development competence, it means that EU action does not pre-empt Member State action, thereby making coherence and coordination between the two levels crucial.
- Coherence is composed of three aspects: first, coherence of EU development cooperation with the more general principles and objectives of EU external relations; secondly, poverty reduction as the primary policy objective, providing intra-policy focus as to how diverse development initiatives cohere with the central goal; thirdly, the obligation to take account of development objectives in other policies which are likely to affect developing countries.
- Coordination entails that EU and Member States must proactively collaborate and consult in order to ensure complementarity and coherence of their respective EU development policies. Article 210 TFEU gives the Commission a central role in ensuring coordination of EU and Member State development cooperation initiatives.

I. The Three C's of EU Development Policy: Complementary, Coherent and Coordinated

Article 208 TFEU

1. Union policy in the field of development cooperation shall be conducted within the framework of the principles and objectives of the Union's external action. The Union's development cooperation policy and that of the Member States *complement* and reinforce each other.

   Union development cooperation policy shall have as its primary objective the reduction and, in the long term, the eradication of poverty. *The Union shall take account of the objectives of development cooperation in the policies that it implements which are likely to affect developing countries.*
2. The Union and the Member States shall comply with the commitments and take account of the objectives they have approved in the context of the United Nations and other competent international organisations.

Article 210 TFEU

1. In order to promote the *complementarity* and efficiency of their action, the Union and the Member States shall *coordinate* their policies on development cooperation and shall consult each other on their aid programmes, including in international organisations and during international conferences. They may undertake joint action. Member States shall contribute if necessary to the implementation of Union aid programmes.
2. The Commission may take any useful initiative to promote the *coordination* referred to in paragraph 1.

Article 211 TFEU

Within their respective spheres of competence, the Union and the Member States shall cooperate with third countries and with the competent international organisations.

[emphasis added]

The essential features of EU development policy are traditionally captured in the so-called *three C's*: complementarity, coherence and coordination.[1] They imply

[1] For the results of the EU initiative evaluating the three C's of EU development policy, see www.three-cs.net.

'(1) that the policy *vis-à-vis* developing countries and other policies must be coherent, (2) that Union policy and Member State policies in the area of development cooperation must be complementary, and (3) that the Union and the Member States are obliged to coordinate their efforts in the field of development cooperation'.[2] The three C's have legal significance since the articles conferring development competence on the EU have been drafted incorporating them as fundamental legal and policy dimensions of EU development cooperation:

- *Complementarity:* Article 208(1) TFEU expresses that EU and Member State competences shall complement and reinforce each other. This provision is closely linked to Article 4(4) TFEU which states that in the areas of development cooperation and humanitarian aid, the Union shall have competence to carry out activities and conduct a common policy; but that the exercise of that competence shall not result in Member States being prevented from exercising theirs. In other words, complementarity to a large extent concerns the *nature* of EU competence in the areas of development policy (and humanitarian aid) and more generally views the EU and national levels as positively and mutually reinforcing. Complementarity is different from subsidiarity because, in the case of complementarity, the two levels are equally appropriate to exercise competences in the same area simultaneously.
- *Coherence:* Article 208(1) and (2) TFEU both express the need for coherence in different ways: it makes a link to the general principles and objectives of EU external action (eg, Article 21 TEU) states that other EU policies likely to affect developing countries must take account of development policy, and Article 208(2) requires that the EU and its Member States 'shall' take account of objectives approved at the UN and other competent international organisations. Defining coherence in the abstract is notoriously difficult as much depends on the perspective of the viewer.[3] In general, it may be seen as avoidance of conflicts and creation of positive synergy within EU development policy itself, between development and other policies, and between all relevant norms actors and instruments active in these domains.[4]
- *Coordination:* Article 210 TFEU lays down the obligation of coordination between the EU and Member States in the implementation of their development policies, with a specific right of initiative for the Commission to attain this objective. Coordination is the action-oriented dimension towards ensuring coherent and complementary policies, and can be defined as 'activities of two or more development partners that are intended to mobilise aid resources or to harmonise their policies, programmes, procedures and practices so as to maximise the development effectiveness of aid resources'.[5] The coordination dimension thus focuses on

[2] M Broberg, 'What is the Direction for the EU's Development Cooperation after Lisbon? A Legal Examination' (2011) 16 *European Foreign Affairs Review* 539, 543.

[3] B Van Vooren, *EU External Relations Law and the European Neighbourhood Policy: A Paradigm for Coherence* (Abingdon, Routledge, 2012) 289.

[4] Ibid, 69.

[5] P Hoebink (ed) *The Treaty of Maastricht and Europe's Development Co-operation, Studies in European Development Co-operation Evaluation No 1* (Amsterdam, Aksant Academic Publishers, 2005) 5.

various forms of consultation, cooperation and collaboration at all levels, from the international to the sub-national in setting out priorities, good practices, policies etc.

The objectives of EU development policy are explicit in the second indent of Article 208(1) TFEU. It states that the primary objective is to reduce and, in the long term eradicate, poverty. Prior to the Lisbon Treaty, the objectives of EU development policy were actually formulated more elaborately in Article 177 of the EC Treaty.[6] The objectives of EU development policy that were previously found in Article 177 EC Treaty have now been moved to Article 21 of the TEU, namely 21(2) paragraphs (b), (d), (e), and to a certain extent paragraph (f). These textual interventions in EU primary law were made exactly because of the increased emphasis on coherence. On the one hand, placing poverty reduction at the centre of EU development policy provides coherence by focusing on one single target, rather than a more diffuse set of 'issues which are all important'. On the other hand, placing objectives such as sustainable development and incorporation of developing countries into the world economy into the general provision of Article 21 TEU implies that the EU must not only pursue them through development cooperation, but through all its policies, including common commercial policy, transport policy, agricultural policy, and so on.

The principles, scope and substance of EU development policy have grown and evolved organically over the past six decades, and a brief historic introduction starting from the Treaty of Rome is indispensable to understand the operation of the 3 C's in EU development policy today.

II. A Brief History of EU Development Policy

A. A Succession of Treaties and Conventions: Rome, over Yaoundé, to Lomé and Cotonou

The Schuman Declaration of 9 May 1950 underlined that the proposed integration project had a calling in the field of development cooperation. It stated that the pooling of coal and steel would free up resources which would allow the Community 'to pursue the achievement of one of its essential tasks, namely, the development of the African continent'. Whereas the subsequent Treaty on the European Coal and Steel Community had no such provisions, the 1957 Rome Treaty – under French pressure, which viewed France and its colonies as a cultural unity ('Eurafrica'[7]) – stated in Article 3(r) that one of the activities of the Community was 'the association of

[6] M Broberg and R Holdgaard, 'EU Development Co-operation Post-Lisbon: Main Constitutional Challenges' (2015) 3 *European Law Review* 349, 351.

[7] L Bartels, 'The Trade and Development Policy of the European Union' in M Cremona (ed) *Developments in EU External Relations Law* (Oxford, Oxford University Press, 2008) 130; M Broberg, *The EU's Legal Ties with its Former Colonies – When Old Love Never Dies*, DIIS Working Paper 2011/01, 10.

the overseas countries and territories (OCTs) in order to increase trade and promote jointly economic and social development'. Subsequently, the gradual elimination of duties and quantitative restrictions which characterised the creation of the common market was largely applied to the associated entities as well.[8] Beyond the trade aspect of the relationship, the Member States made commitments in the field of investments and notably the provision of development aid. In terms of its scope, development cooperation in the early years had a highly narrow focus on trade and aid.[9]

Decolonisation of the African continent took place in the years immediately following the entry into force of the Rome Treaty. As a consequence, relations with the newly sovereign nations could no longer be conducted on the basis of Part IV of the Rome Treaty, but would be founded on a succession of multilateral framework treaties instead.

M Broberg, *The EU's Legal Ties with its Former Colonies – When Old Love Never Dies*, DIIS Working Paper 2011/01, 10

... in the years following the creation of the EEC most of these [Overseas Countries and Territories (OCTs)] gained independence requiring a redefinition of the framework regulating the relationship between the former colonies and the EEC. Hence, in 1964 the first Yaoundé Convention came into force. This was followed, first, by the second Yaoundé Convention and, subsequently, by the so-called Lomé Conventions. In 2000, the fourth Lomé Convention was replaced by the Cotonou Partnership Agreement which will remain in force until 2020. Since the first Yaoundé Convention the number of (non-European) countries covered by the legal scheme has grown from 18 originally to 79 today. The majority are former French and British colonies in Africa, but former colonies in the Caribbean and the Pacific are also parties to the Agreement – hence the name African, Caribbean and Pacific countries (widely referred to as ACP countries).

The first and second Yaoundé Conventions were based on two fundamental principles: free trade[10] and 'financial and technical co-operation' (eg, development aid).[11] In Title I concerning trade, it was made clear that the first Yaoundé Convention continued the direction taken with the Rome Treaty on customs duties and quantitative restrictions, with specific treatment for coffee, bananas and the Common Agricultural Policy.[12]

[8] Bartels (n 7) 133.
[9] Broberg (n 7) 540.
[10] Title I Yaoundé Convention.
[11] Title II Yaoundé Convention. See Commission of the European Communities, *The Second Yaoundé Convention – Great Possibilities for Private Investment in Africa* (Commission Working Document, 1971) 5.
[12] See First Yaoundé Convention, Arts 2 and 11. Art 2(3) of the First Yaoundé Convention reads: 'Imports from third countries of unroasted coffee into the Benelux countries on the one hand, and of bananas into

L Bartels, 'The Trade and Development Policy of the European Union' in M Cremona (ed) *Developments in EU External Relations Law*, (Oxford, Oxford University Press, 2008) 137

One of the striking features of these trade arrangements [Yaoundé] was their emphasis on reciprocal trade liberalization. In modern times, reciprocity in trade relations is justified on both economic and political economy grounds: put simply, it gives the country granting the trade concessions a means of extracting trade concessions from the other party ... At the time of the Yaoundé Conventions, however, the main reasons given for reciprocity were ideological. First, it was said that only with mutual obligations could Africa negotiate as an 'equal' with Europe; second that these obligations went 'beyond' more contractual relations; and third, that these obligations were essential to ensure that Africa did not fall under the sway of a (non-French) economic power ... A practical effect to these preferences ... was to benefit the (mainly) French exporters, who tended to be monopolists, and therefore able to keep prices high despite their low exports costs. [Reciprocity] was a concept hard to identify in practice.

In an institutional sense, the first Yaoundé Convention set up an Association Council,[13] a Parliamentary Conference[14] and a Court of Arbitration.[15] Development aid commitments were carried out through the first European Development Fund (EDF), to which the Member States provided the necessary funds[16] and the European Investment Bank (EIB) undertook to provide loans out of its own resources.[17] All economic sectors could benefit from aid under these instruments but funds were primarily directed at industry, tourism, agriculture, socio-economic infrastructure (schools, roads, hospitals etc.) and export promotion.[18] Development cooperation under the Yaoundé regime was still very much characterised by a 'government-to-government' nature, which would slowly change in subsequent conventions in line with evolving perceptions of development policy and cooperation.[19]

the Federal Republic of Germany on the other hand, shall be subject to the terms set out respectively, as to unroasted coffee, in the Protocol this day concluded between the Member States and. as to bananas, in the Protocol concluded on 25 March 1957 between the Member States and in the Declaration annexed to this Convention.'

[13] Ibid, Arts 39–49.

[14] Ibid, Art 50.

[15] Ibid, Art 51. No case was ever decided before this tribunal. See Bartels (n 7) at 135.

[16] The EDF was kept separate from the EC budget because of lack of enthusiasm on the part of other Member States to fund French former colonies. In principle, the EDF allows each Member State to decide how much it is willing to contribute under the applicable convention (see further Section IV below). To the EDF, France and Germany contributed roughly one-third each. See Commission of the European Communities, *The Second Yaoundé Convention – Great Possibilities for Private Investment in Africa* (Commission Working Document, 1971) 7.

[17] First Yaoundé Convention, Art 16.

[18] Commission (n 16) at 7.

[19] Ibid, 18.

The two Yaoundé Conventions were subsequently replaced by four consecutive Lomé conventions entering into force in 1975, 1981, 1986 and 1990 which, like Yaoundé, were concluded as mixed agreements. The backdrop to these new agreements is important: the first EEC enlargement which included the United Kingdom and thus a new perspective on international development, the oil crisis which created a fear of shortages of raw materials, all combined with a desire to hold on to valued overseas markets and a sense of responsibility for the colonial past.[20] In terms of market access, the central change with the preceding Yaoundé legal regime was the inclusion of the principle of *non-reciprocal* trade preferences, mainly under the pressure of the 27 other nations joining the Yaoundé associates, of which 21 were Commonwealth nations due to the UK's accession to the EEC.[21]

European Commission, *Information Note, Development and Cooperation*, 1975, 99/75 F (Translated from French)

... Title I of the Convention concerning commercial cooperation has certainly posed the most arduous problems to the negotiators, with the EEC and ACP countries being each other's primary commercial partners ... The diversity of situations, traditions and wishes of the different partners, including that of the Community, seemed a priori in opposition. In the end the negotiators succeeded in surmounting these difficulties and to base – in spite of everything – their future commercial relations on a just and certain basis, with the needed flexibility for ensuring an application without ambiguity of the provisions of the Convention.

1. The non-reciprocity of the commercial obligations.

This principle has been one of the major innovations of the Lomé Convention. Justified by the different levels of development, it implies that the ACP Countries are not held to subscribe to obligations corresponding to those of the Community in relation to products originating in the latter ... Nevertheless, the ACP Countries, as regards their commercial relations with the Community, have committed to not discriminate between the Member States, and to accord to the Community a treatment not less favourable to that which they give to the most favoured nation ... However, the Community has accepted that MFN [Most Favoured Nation principle] shall not apply between the ACP nations, or between them and other developing nations. For example, when a Caribbean Country concludes an agreement with a Latin American Nation, it is free to accord commercial advantages which it does not provide to the Community.

[20] European Commission, *Green Paper on Relations between the EU and the ACP Countries on the Eve of the 21st Century – Challenges and Options for a New Partnership*, COM(96) 570 final, Brussels, 20 November 1996, 9.

[21] Bartels (n 7) 147. Certain East African countries had already entered into an agreement with the EEC in 1968.

Non-reciprocity therefore means that with Lomé, the Community demanded that it be treated equally to other non-developing nations, but that no obligations of reciprocity existed as regards other developing nations. Under Lomé, the Community continued to provide financial and technical assistance to the ACP countries on the basis of EDF and EIB funding.[22] The list of types of projects which could be covered by Community aid had a similar focus to that under Yaoundé[23] but was, in fact, wider and more diverse: rural development, industrialisation, energy, mining, tourism, socio-economic infrastructure, structural improvement to agriculture, technical cooperation, sales promotion, support to SME's, and grassroots micro projects. institutionally, Lomé reformed the previous governing bodies into an EEC-ACP Council of Ministers, a Committee of Ambassadors, and a Consultative Assembly.[24]

Between Lomé I and II little changed, but a notable shift occurred in Lomé III and IV: the incorporation of human rights into EEC relations with the ACP countries, and a general broadening of development cooperation beyond trade and aid. Compared to Lomé II, the third Lomé Convention now included a reference to human rights in the preamble: 'Reaffirming their adherence to the principles of the [UN Charter] and their faith in fundamental human rights, in the dignity and worth of the human person, in the equal rights of men and women and of nations large and small.' Lomé III was also different in the sense that its first part was no longer trade, followed by investment, technical cooperation etc. Instead, it had an introductory part which described in more general terms the political objectives and underlying principles of cooperation.[25] Article 1 of Chapter 1 of Lomé III thus made explicit that the agreement was to promote and expedite the economic, cultural and social development of ACP states. Both elements were indicative of a broadening scope of development cooperation beyond trade and aid, and towards a broader notion of sustainable development which implied focus on areas such as environmental protection and debt relief.[26] Lomé IV continued that re-orientation, in particular with its new Article 5 which stated that 'cooperation shall be directed towards development centred on man, the main protagonist and beneficiary of development, which thus entails respect for and promotion of all human rights'. In 1995, Lomé IV bis was the result of a review of the earlier agreement, placing further emphasis on political, security and social content as well as cooperation in a decentralised fashion with a greater role for civil society.

By the mid-1990s, it was argued that the various agreements which regulated the EC-ACP relationship for around 35 years were mostly significant in principle rather than in practice.[27] In particular, as regards trade, the significance of these agreements was progressively diminished through successive tariff reductions following from

[22] Commission of the European Communities, *Information Note, The Convention of Lomé, Europe/Africa, Caribbean, Pacific*, 1976, No. 129/76, 31; Commission of the European Communities, *Information Note, The ACP-EEC Convention of Lomé: One Year after its Entry into Force*, Brussels, March 1977, 6 (on the Stabex system, which was meant to stabilise export earnings and which was introduced with the Lomé Conventions).

[23] Lomé Convention, Art 46.

[24] Commission of the European Communities (n 22) 69.

[25] Commission of the European Communities, *Information Note, The Third Lomé Convention – Improvements and Innovations in Relation to Lomé II*, Brussels, November 1984, 1.

[26] Broberg (n 2) 542.

[27] M Sissoko, L Osuji and W Cheng, 'Impacts of the Yaoundé and Lomé Conventions on EC-ACP Trade' (1998) 1 *The African Economic and Business Review* 21.

multilateral GATT negotiations. The Cotonou agreement, which replaced Lomé IV, was signed in 2000 and was concluded between the Union and its Member States and 77 ACP countries for a period of 20 years.[28] Disappointed in the results of Lomé and due to a host of other reasons, the EU clearly sought a radical change to what existed beforehand.[29] This was initially not well received by ACP countries. Even if most still belonged to the category of 'Least-Developed Countries' after decades of Lomé, most ACP States argued that they would have been worse off without Lomé cooperation.[30]

K Arts, 'ACP-EU Relations in a New Era: The Cotonou Agreement' (2003) 40 *Common Market Law Review* 95, 96

The end of the Cold War, the creation of the World Trade Organization (WTO), a stronger emphasis on privatization, liberalization and on the need to allow for full participation of non-State actors in development (cooperation) processes, the challenges posed by the concept of sustainable development, and the outburst of armed conflict and humanitarian crises in a considerable number of ACP countries drastically changed the (largely external) environment within which ACP-EU cooperation found itself ... For the European Union, the combination of the disappointing Lomé performance record until then, the changes in the external environment ... and a number of internal circumstances provided strong incentives in favour of drastic modification of the traditional Lomé arrangements. These internal circumstances included, most notably: the overall declining political priority for maintaining a highly favourable package for the ACP, given the enlargement process and security and migration challenges closer to home in Central and Eastern Europe and around the Mediterranean; a certain degree of 'aid fatigue' in traditional donor countries; and the serious managerial and competence problems in the European Commission ...

The Cotonou agreement entailed significant changes in at least four important areas:

1. It further strengthened the political dimension of the new partnership which among others led to a strengthened conditionality and the incorporation of broader objectives such as peace and stability and a stable and democratic environment.[31]
2. Poverty alleviation was made the cornerstone of the new partnership. Legally this involved entrenching the wider focus on sustainable development (as reflected in

[28] Cuba was an ACP member country in 2000 but did not sign the Cotonou Agreement. Timor Leste became an ACP member country in 2003 and subsequently acceded to the Cotonou Agreement.

[29] Commission Communication, *Guidelines for the Negotiation of New Cooperation Agreements with the African, Caribbean and Pacific (ACP) countries*, COM (97) 537 final, Brussels, 29 October 1997, 3–5.

[30] K Arts, 'ACP-EU Relations in a New Era: The Cotonou Agreement' (2003) 40 *Common Market Law Review* 95, 96.

[31] Cotonou Agreement, Art 98.

the new EU development competence introduced by the Maastricht Treaty[32]) by including social, human, and environmental objectives alongside the more traditional focus on trade and aid.

3. This certainly did not diminish the importance of trade in the relationship with ACP, but a qualitative change did take place. As a consequence of the limited impact of Lomé to stimulate economic development, and due to the WTO-incompatibility of the EU's unilateral preferential trade regime for ACP countries, Cotonou was based on a new footing of progressive re-introduction of reciprocal preferences for all but the least-developed ACP's.[33] Cotonou would function as the framework agreement, and the ACP's were expected to negotiate free trade-oriented Economic Partnership Agreements with the Community.[34]
4. Cotonou would introduce a considerable element of geographical differentiation. This reflected an acceptance that there were significant differences among the 77 ACP nations, combined with an EU-centric view that regional integration is key to stimulating long-lasting and stable economic growth. As a consequence, so-called Economic Partnership Agreements (EPA's) would be negotiated with specific regional groupings. However, large question marks existed over the ACP countries' institutional capacity to support such comprehensive trade agreements. Furthermore, there has been significant disagreement between EU and ACP countries as to the link between trade liberalisation and the need for financial aid in these agreements. Finally, the EU has been subject to significant critique for its artificial creation of regional groupings which do not necessarily reflect actual reality as regards regional integration.[35]

The Cotonou agreement was negotiated for a period of 20 years, with a revision every five years. It was set to expire in February 2020. Therefore, already in 2015 the Commission and the High Representative initiated a process of reflection leading to a Joint Communication in November 2016 on the EU-ACP partnership post-Cotonou.[36] According to this Joint Communication the new partnership shall build upon the UN Sustainable Development Goals (SDGs), on the Global Strategy for the European Union's Foreign and Security Policy (see Chapter 9) and on the New European Consensus on Development.[37] Negotiations between the ACP group and the European Union began in September 2018, but since the new Agreement would not be ready to be applied by the expiry date in February 2020 the parties decided to adopt transitional measures to extend the application of the provisions of the Cotonou Agreement.

[32] EC Treaty, Art 177.

[33] The Least Developed Countries (LDCs) are a group of particularly vulnerable developing countries identified by the United Nations. The list of LDCs is revised every three years. As of June 2019, it contains 47 countries.

[34] Arts (n 30) at 111.

[35] M Meyn, 'Economic Partnership Agreements: An "Historic Step" towards a 'Partnership of Equals'?' (2008) 26 *Development Policy Review* 515, 519.

[36] Joint Communication to the European Parliament and the Council, A renewed partnership with the countries of Africa, the Caribbean and the Pacific, JOIN(2016) 52 final.

[37] The New European Consensus on Development 'Our World, Our Dignity, Our Future', Joint Statement by the Council and the Representatives of the Governments of the Member States Meeting within the Council, the European Parliament and the European Commission [2017] OJ C210/1. The New European Consensus on Development is discussed in Section IV.B below.

GR Olsen, 'Coherence, Consistency and Political Will in Foreign Policy: The European Union's Policy towards Africa' (2008) 9 *Perspectives on European Politics and Society* 157, 167

... the motives and reasons for launching the ideas to establish the EPAs were closely related to a political wish of the EU to be in line with the WTO and to be in agreement with its aim to promote trade liberalisation. WTO compliance is 'at the very centre of the present post-Lomé negotiations because the EU puts them there ... [T]he use of the WTO is a "strategic attempt by the EU to externalise responsibility for its own policy"'. On the other hand, the European Union sees the regional trade arrangements as a mechanism to promote development via trade liberalisation. It is an assumption that trade liberalisation will result in more trade and thus contribute to increase economic growth, which may lead to reduced poverty. At least, it is worth noting that one of the topics which were dealt with during the negotiations on establishing the EPAs was exactly how to promote development by means of trade. So if the future will show that the EPAs and free trade promote development, it is possible to argue that the trade policy of the Union buttresses the aim of its development aid policy. If on the other hand, the critics show to be right in their negative evaluation of the possible consequences of the EPAs, it is necessary to conclude that the trade policy is inconsistent and incoherent with the aims of several of the other policy instruments.

The historical overview is important to keep in mind when analysing the legal aspects of the three C's in EU development cooperation policy. In the preceding paragraphs, we have highlighted the intimate linkage between development and trade. However, as time progressed, the scope of development policy became progressively wider to include human rights, social and environmental concerns. The objectives of EU development policy and the instruments to implement them have evolved significantly: the oscillation of reciprocal and non-reciprocal trade arrangements, the shift in focus from governments to civil society, and so on. Finally, the relationship with the Member States is important too: the Member States upload their interests to the EU level while they simultaneously maintain their own individual development policies. To this day, these and other concerns are captured by the notions of complementarity, coherence and coordination.

B. Complementarity of EU Development Policy: Position of the Member States

As indicated in Chapter 3, non-pre-emptive and complementary shared competences are the exception and their effect is defined in Article 4(3) TFEU for research, technological development and space policy and, in Article 4(4) TFEU for development and humanitarian aid. The difference between these provisions is that the latter indicates that the EU can develop a 'common policy and carry out activities' whereas Article 4(3) TFEU merely points to 'carrying out activities'. In both cases, these paragraphs indicate that 'the exercise of that competence shall not result in Member States being prevented from exercising theirs'. In the sphere of development policy and humanitarian aid respectively, Articles 208(1) and 214(1) TFEU define this co-existence in a more positive, constructive fashion as 'complementing and reinforcing' each other. The purpose of defining these policy areas in this fashion is that there is a 'bias towards action', or even a 'the more the better' approach in these fields. The consequence of this peculiar legal nature of EU external competence – sometimes referred to as a 'parallel competence' – is that EU and Member State co-existence in development takes on a form rather different from that in pre-emptive shared competences. This is specifically reflected in the approach taken by the Court of Justice to EU and Member State action in this policy domain. In *Bangladesh* and *EDF*, the Court expressly exhibited a tolerant approach to the interconnection between intergovernmental and supranational approaches to organising and exercising the complementary competences of the Union and the Member States.

In *Bangladesh*, Parliament sought the annulment of an act adopted by the Council which was to grant special aid to Bangladesh[38] and of the means adopted by the Commission for the implementation of that act. This had not been adopted by the Council as an institution of the Union, but as 'the Member States meeting in Council', even though they decided 'on the basis of a Commission proposal' to grant aid to Bangladesh, which it would execute 'under a Community action'.[39] This meant that the Member States were not acting in their capacity as members of the Council, but as representatives of their governments collectively exercising the powers of the Member States.[40] The European Parliament submitted that the act really constituted an act of the Council since the document was entitled 'Council conclusions' and since all foreign ministers were present when the document was adopted. Therefore, it infringed the budgetary prerogatives conferred on Parliament. Parliament submitted several arguments to underline the 'Community'-nature of the act, which the Court all refuted. The CJEU founded its reasoning upon the nature of the competence as complementary, and gave the Member States and institutions a good amount of freedom to organise development policy:

Cases C-181/91 and C-248/91 *Parliament v Council and Commission (Bangladesh)*, ECLI:EU:C:1993:271

16 … it should be pointed out that the Community does not have exclusive competence in the field of humanitarian aid, and that consequently the Member

[38] This case concerned what is presently Art 214 TFEU, the EU's competence in humanitarian aid, as no distinct competence existed at the time of that judgment. Given the identical complementary nature of EU development and humanitarian competencies, the findings apply equally to the former competence.

[39] Cases C-181/91 & C-248/91 *Parliament v Council and Commission (Bangladesh)*, ECLI:EU:C:1993:271, para 2.

[40] Ibid, para 12. The Council argued that therefore the action was inadmissible, but the Court maintained that an action for annulment is available in the case of all measures adopted by the institutions, whatever their nature or form, which are intended to have legal effects. See para 13 and Case 22/70 *Commission v Council (ERTA)*, ECLI:EU:C:1971:32.

States are not precluded from exercising their competence in that regard collectively in the Council or outside it.

17 In support of its application, Parliament relies firstly on the reference made in the contested act to the Commission's proposal. In its opinion, that reference shows that, in view of the procedure which led to the act's adoption, it was the Council, not the Member States, which acted in this case.

18 That argument is not conclusive. Not all proposals from the Commission necessarily constitute proposals within the meaning of Article 149 of the Treaty [now Article 293 TFEU]. Their legal character must be assessed in the light of all the circumstances in which they were made. They may just as well constitute mere initiatives taken in the form of informal proposals.

19 Secondly, Parliament observes that, according to the description of the act, the special aid was to be administered by the Commission. According to the fourth indent of Article 155 of the Treaty [now Article 17 TEU], however, powers of implementation may be conferred on the Commission only by a decision of the Council.

20 That argument cannot be accepted either. The fourth indent of Article 155 of the Treaty does not prevent the Member States from entrusting the Commission with the task of coordinating a collective action undertaken by them on the basis of an act of their representatives meeting in the Council.

The objective of the Parliament's arguments was to more fully 'communautarise' action in development policy and thereby ensure its own (budgetary) role in the process. In this case, the Commission had made a proposal on aid to Bangladesh and Member States could either choose to provide contributions to the EC which the Commission would then administer or to provide contributions bilaterally to Bangladesh. The Court found that such a proposal does not necessarily 'start up' a Union (legislative) process. They may also be informal policy proposals whose legal consequences ought to be assessed in their own right.[41] More generally, the Court found that the role of the Commission was not limited by the Treaty. It could function as an institution of the EU as a legal person, but the Treaties did not exclude that it provided services which were more akin to that of a 'secretariat of an international organization' being requested to support a collective of Member States. This approach of the Court can be seen as an expression of the idea of 'mutually reinforcing and complementary' EU and Member State competence, and the corollary need for coordination. The relevant actors are free to exercise and coordinate their respective powers on a supranational or intergovernmental basis as they deem most appropriate.

[41] For more on soft law and its role in developing EU external relations, see Chapters 4 and 13.

A few months after the *Bangladesh* judgment, in *EDF*, Parliament sought the annulment of a Financial Regulation of July 1991 applicable to development finance cooperation under the Fourth Lomé Convention.[42] To implement financing commitments under that Convention, the Member States meeting within the Council had adopted the instrument setting up a seventh European Development Fund (EDF)[43] which, in turn, would be implemented through a financial Regulation adopted according to a procedure which did not include Parliament. The latter institution thus sought a declaration from the Court that development aid under the Lomé Convention was Community expenditure and therefore had to be governed by financial regulations implemented according to the applicable EEC Treaty procedure which required consultation of Parliament.[44] In short, the Parliament argued that the institutional balance within the Treaties had been impinged. The Court tackled this question by first examining who had undertaken financial commitments towards third countries under the Lomé Convention (EC or Member States) and, secondly, who was subsequently responsible for the performance of those obligations. In both instances, the answer was essentially derived from the complementary nature of EU competence in the area of development cooperation. The EU and the Member States can choose which of them, or both jointly, undertakes an international commitment in this sphere and subsequently they can choose which of them, or both jointly, is responsible for carrying out their financing obligations. In this instance they chose to do so through the EDF.

Case C-316/91 *Parliament v Council (EDF)*, ECLI:EU:C:1994:76

21 The Parliament argues that it follows from the very words of Article 231 of the [Lomé Convention] that the Community as such has undertaken vis-à-vis the ACP States ... an obligation of international law distinct from those undertaken by the Member States ...

24 The question as to who has entered into a commitment vis-à-vis the ACP States must be dissociated from the question whether it is for the Community or its Member States to perform the commitment entered into. The answer to the first question depends on an interpretation of the Convention and on how in Community law powers are distributed between the Community and its Member States in the relevant field, while the answer to the second question depends only on how those powers are distributed.

25 It is appropriate first to consider the distribution of powers between the Community and its Member States in the field of development aid.

26 The Community's competence in that field is not exclusive. The Member States are accordingly entitled to enter into commitments themselves vis-à-vis

[42] Case C-316/91 *Parliament v Council (EDF)*, ECLI:EU:C:1994:76, para 1.
[43] Ibid, para 2.
[44] Ibid, para 4.

non-member States, either collectively or individually, or even jointly with the Community ...

28 It is appropriate next to interpret the Convention in order to identify the parties which have entered into commitments.

29 The Convention was concluded, according to its preamble and Article 1, by the Community and its Member States of the one part and the ACP States of the other part. It established an essentially bilateral ACP-EEC cooperation. In those circumstances, in the absence of derogations expressly laid down in the Convention, the Community and its Member States as partners of the ACP States are jointly liable to those latter States for the fulfilment of every obligation arising from the commitments undertaken, including those relating to financial assistance.

30 Although Article 231 of the Convention, like Article 1 of the Financial Protocol, uses the phrase 'the Community's financial assistance', it is nonetheless the case that several other provisions use the term 'Community' in order to denote the Community and its Member States considered together ...

33 It follows from the above that, in accordance with the essentially bilateral character of the cooperation, the obligation to grant 'the Community's financial assistance' falls on the Community and on its Member States, considered together.

34 As for the question whether it is for the Community or for its Member States to perform that obligation, it should be noted, as stated above at paragraph 26, that the competence of the Community in the field of development aid is not exclusive, so that the Member States are entitled collectively to exercise their competence in that field with a view to bearing the financial assistance to be granted to the ACP States.

III. Coherence in EU Development Policy: Evolving Scope and Links with other Policies

A. 'Policy Coherence for Development': Legal and Policy Dimensions

In development cooperation, coherence has significant legal and political implications. The principle has a firm footing in Article 208(1) TFEU. According to this provision there are three distinct aspects to coherence in this policy area: first, coherence of EU development cooperation with the more general principles and objectives of EU external relations (eg, linking to Article 21 TEU); secondly, poverty reduction as the primary policy objective providing intra-policy focus as to how different initiatives cohere to the central goal; thirdly, the obligation to take account of development objectives in other policies which are likely to affect developing countries.

These legal obligations attract regular and significant attention in EU policy making through the process called 'Policy Coherence for Development (PCD)'.[45] PCD was formalised in the 2005 European Consensus[46] as a way of strengthening work towards achieving the Millennium Development Goals (MDGs).[47] In 2017 the first consensus was replaced by the 'New European Consensus'.[48] These 'consensuses' particularly focus on linkages between development and other EU policies since 'the impact of EU non-aid policies on developing countries should not be underestimated, and neither should their potential to make a positive contribution to the development process in these countries. EU policies in areas such as trade, agriculture, fisheries, food safety, transport and energy have a direct bearing on the ability of developing countries to generate domestic economic growth' as duly observed by the Commission.[49]

The New European Consensus on Development: 'Our World, Our Dignity, Our Future', Joint Statement by the Council and the Representatives of the Governments of the Member States Meeting within the Council, the European Parliament and the European Commission [2017] OJ C210/1

Policy coherence for development to achieve the SDGs

108. Sustainable development is at the heart of the EU project and firmly anchored in the Treaties, including for its external action. The EU and its Member States are committed to ensuring development that meets the needs of the present without compromising the ability of future generations to meet their own needs. Ensuring policy coherence for sustainable development as embedded in the 2030 Agenda requires taking into account the impact of all policies on sustainable development at all levels – nationally, within the EU, in other countries and at global level …

111. Delivering on the new universal framework for sustainable development in the field of development cooperation is a shared responsibility of

[45] Communication from the Commission, *Policy coherence for Development – Accelerating progress towards attaining the Millennium Development Goals*, COM (2005) 134 final, Brussels, 12 April 2005.

[46] 'The European Consensus, Joint statement by the Council and the representatives of the governments of the Member States meeting within the Council, the European Parliament and the Commission on European Union [2006] OJ C46/1.

[47] In 2015 the MDGs were replaced by the Sustainable Development Goals (SDGs). After 2015, PCD continues to play a significant role given the breadth in scope of current-day development policy.

[48] The New European Consensus on Development: 'Our World, Our Dignity, Our Future'. The New European Consensus on Development is treated in Section IV.B below.

[49] Communication from the Commission, *Policy Coherence for Development – Accelerating Progress towards Attaining the Millennium Development Goals*, COM (2005) 134 final, Brussels, 12 April 2005, 3–4.

> all stakeholders. Sustainable development requires a holistic and cross-sector policy approach and is ultimately an issue of governance which needs to be pursued in partnership with all stakeholders and on all levels. The EU and its Member States will therefore promote whole-of-government approaches and ensure political oversight and coordination efforts at all levels for SDG implementation. In order to better support policy formulation and decision-making, they will ensure the evidence base of policy impacts on developing countries through consultations, stakeholder engagement, ex-ante impact assessments and ex-post evaluations of major policy initiatives. Ongoing EU action towards sustainable global supply chains, such as in the timber and garment sectors, illustrate the added value of pursuing a coherent approach …

The main legal implications of PCD are found in the scope of EU competence and the choice of legal basis. In Chapter 3 we have seen that in the Treaty of Rome, the EEC was only conferred two substantive competences in the external field, namely CCP[50] and Association agreements.[51] As the nature of international trade relations began to change, the EEC sought to incorporate development concerns into its international trade policies which led to early case law on the scope of CCP, and the expansive approach of the Court of Justice. With new competences being conferred from the Single European Act onwards, the CJEU more carefully worked towards a 'balance of competences'. In Chapter 3 we examined the intricate relationship between diverse competence conferring provisions, the scope of these competences, the obligation to take into account objectives from other policy areas and the challenges with regard to establishing the appropriate legal basis. In the following subsections, we will build on this knowledge, and highlight two legal aspects of coherence as they apply in relation to development policy: First, the incorporation of human rights conditionality in development policy and secondly, the relationship between development policy and security (CFSP) concerns.

B. EU Development Policy and Human Rights Conditionality

Human rights represent an important aspect of the EU's external action (see Chapter 10), including in the context of development policy. In the succession of treaties from Yaoundé over Lomé to Cotonou, a progressive dynamic of politicisation and broadening the scope of the agreements beyond aid and trade has taken place. The inclusion of human rights first happened in 1986 with their addition to the preamble of Lomé III, subsequently included in the body of Lomé IV in Article 5 in 1990. With the Maastricht Treaty, respect and promotion of human rights was made one of

[50] TEC, Art 113 TEC (original Rome Treaty version).
[51] Ibid, Art 238.

the general objectives of the EU's development cooperation policy (Article 130u TEC (Maastricht version)).[52]

This treaty-based obligation served as foundation to the Commission's efforts to elevate the respect for human rights by the parties to its international agreements to an essential element of that agreement. The 'essential' reference was taken from Article 60(3)(b) of the Vienna Convention on the Law of Treaties, which lays down that '[t]he violation of a provision essential to the accomplishment of the object or purpose' of a given treaty constitutes a material breach of that treaty. A 'material breach' of a bilateral treaty by one party 'entitles the other to invoke the breach as a ground for terminating the treaty or suspending its operation in whole or in part'. In other words, if a developing country breaches a human rights clause in a treaty with the European Union and this clause is an 'essential element' of that treaty, the EU will be empowered to terminate or suspend the operation of whole or parts of the treaty. The European Union's development of 'essential element clauses' meant that effective observance of human rights and real progress towards democracy became a pre-condition for commitments contained in that EU trade or association treaty with the third country.[53] It is therefore generally referred to as 'conditionality'.[54] The question then arose as to whether that meant that the EU *de facto* pursued 'an external human rights policy' through incorporation of such clauses, or whether the incorporation of human rights into external development instruments could indeed be said to simply be an element of EU development competence.

The inclusion of essential element clauses in agreements which could be used to suspend the other provisions it contains, gave rise to the 1994 *Portugal v Council* case.[55] Portugal argued that the EC–India Partnership and Development Agreement, which had been founded on trade and development legal bases, required the inclusion of the flexibility clause (current Article 352 TFEU) because the development competence allegedly did not suffice to support the inclusion of human rights as an essential element of the agreement. Portugal considered that respect for human rights could at most be a general objective of the cooperation agreement if based on the development competence alone. Conversely, the Council argued that action could be taken without using the flexibility clause provision. The Court sided with the Council, drawing on an argument that reflects the coherence rationale of EU development policy as embedded in the Treaties. The fact that respect for human rights in development must be 'taken into account' (ex Article 177(2) TEC, current Article 208(1) TFEU) entails that it is possible for the EU to give substantive meaning to that provision without needing recourse to the flexibility clause. As we have seen in Chapter 3, the Court's approach

[52] See M Cremona, 'Human Rights and Democracy Clauses in the EC's Trade Agreements' in D O'Keeffe and N Emiliou (eds) *The European Union and World Trade Law: After the GATT Uruguay Round* (Chichester, Wiley, 1996).

[53] Ibid, 64. The European Union's human rights clauses have undergone extensive developments over the years so that a distinction is made between the 'basic clause', the 'essential elements clause', the 'Baltic clause' and the 'Bulgarian clause'. See further N Hachez, 'Essential Elements' Clauses in EU Trade Agreements: Making Trade Work in a Way that Helps Human Rights?' (2015) 53 *Cuadernos europeos de Deusto* 81.

[54] A method which is now more generally applicable in EU external relations, extending beyond fundamental rights.

[55] Case C-268/94 *Portugal v Council*, ECLI:EU:C:1996:46.

was one of seeking to guarantee the *effet utile* of the competences conferred upon the EU: it would not make sense for the drafters of the Treaties to refer to human rights in the competence conferring provision, if no real-world action could be taken on their basis.

Case C-268/94 *Portugal v Council*, ECLI:EU:C:1996:461

23 By declaring that 'Community policy (...) shall contribute to the general objective of developing and consolidating democracy and the rule of law, and to that of respecting human rights and fundamental freedoms', [current equivalent is Article 21 TEU] requires the Community to take account of the objective of respect for human rights when it adopts measures in the field of development cooperation.

24 The mere fact that Article 1(1) of the Agreement provides that respect for human rights and democratic principles 'constitutes an essential element' of the Agreement does not justify the conclusion that that provision goes beyond the objective stated in [Article 208 TFEU]. The very wording of the latter provision demonstrates the importance to be attached to respect for human rights and democratic principles, so that, amongst other things, development cooperation policy must be adapted to the requirement of respect for those rights and principles.

In Chapter 3 we have seen that there is a fine line between 'taking into account' a given policy objective and pursuing such an objective in its own right which requires a separate legal basis. We have seen that the Court approaches this question both in the context of establishing the scope of a given EU competence and in the closely related issue of 'correct legal basis'. In EU development policy, the Court has been faced with this question most recently in the context of the security-development nexus.

C. The Relationship Between Development and Security Policy

M Broberg, 'EU Development Cooperation and the CFSP: Mutual Encroachment?' in S Blockmans and P Koutrakos (eds) *Research Handbook on the EU's Common Foreign and Security Policy* (Cheltenham, Edward Elgar, 2018) 274

Even though the Lisbon Treaty has made poverty eradication a primary objective of the Union's development cooperation policy, ... in practice other objectives are attributed very considerable weight in the development cooperation policy;

this is particularly so with regard to security and migration. To some extent this may be explained by the Lisbon Treaty's revamping of the European Union's external relations framework; in particular the streamlining of objectives provided by Article 21 TEU and the creation of the High Representative/the EEAS. In other words, in the fields of security and migration, the EU development cooperation policy encroaches upon the CFSP …

Similarly … the European Union's CFSP pursues objectives that in principle fall within the development cooperation objectives – both at the general level and when we turn to the implementation of the CFSP. This is particularly so in the areas of security and migration, where the CFSP is used to further objectives that also have a clear development or humanitarian aspect.

In other words, it is clear that there is mutual encroachment of the European Union's development cooperation policy and its CFSP – first of all with regard to security and migration.

The security-development nexus has a policy and a legal dimension. From the policy side, the question revolves around the two-way relationship between a safe and secure environment and long-term progressive socio-economic development. From a legal perspective, the security-development relationship raises the question as to whether the EU ought to adopt a given initiative within the context of CFSP or its development competence – each with significantly different EU institutional structures, financial resources and diverse roles for the Member States. To summarise, stabilising or preventing armed conflict in the short term is commonly addressed through the EU's CFSP (see Chapter 9), whereas longer-term socio-economic development falls within the realm of Article 208 TFEU. Quite evidently, however, initiatives that stimulate security will aid long-term development; initiatives that support development will aid security in a given region. In light of this need for coherent development initiatives (PCD), the question which arises is similar to that on human rights above: to which extent do security initiatives fall within the scope of EU development competence? In pre-Lisbon case law, the Court of Justice has affirmed the wide scope of EU development policy in relation to a dispute on a border management project in the Philippines[56] and in a case concerning EU support to ECOWAS to combat the illegal dissemination of small arms and weapons (see also Chapters 3 and 9).[57] In these cases of 2007 and 2008, the Court of Justice confirmed that development cooperation has developed to a very broad policy field which meant that security-oriented measures could also be adopted by the Union under its development competence, as long as they were focused on the socio-economic objectives of EU development policy, in particular the eradication of poverty.

[56] Case C-403/05 *Parliament v Commission (Philippine Border Mission)*, ECLI:EU:C:2007:624.
[57] Case C-91/05 *Commission v Council (Small Arms/ECOWAS)*, ECLI:EU:C:2008:288.

With the *Philippine Border Mission* Case, the Parliament sought to annul the Commission Decision approving a project concerning the security of the borders of the Philippines. The contested Decision was based on Regulation No 443/92 organising financial and technical cooperation with the Asian and African countries, predating the entry into force of the Maastricht Treaty by little over a year. This regulation was subsequently replaced by Regulation (EC) 1905/2006.[58] The 2006 regulation stated that the old Regulation continued to apply for legal acts and commitments of the pre-2007 budget years and the contested decision was to be financed from the 2004 budget. As regards objectives, the contested decision clearly stated that 'the overall objective of the proposed project is to assist in the implementation of the UNSCR 1373 (2001) in the fight against terrorism and international crime'.[59] Parliament submitted that the Commission exceeded its implementing powers because the reasons for that decision were clearly based on considerations connected with the fight against terrorism and international crime, thereby going beyond the framework set out by Regulation No 443/92 which served as its basis.[60] The Commission made two counter-arguments: one as regards the specific objective of the instrument,[61] and one as regards the general scope of EU development policy. For present purposes the second is solely pertinent.

Case C-403/05 *Parliament v Commission (Philippine Border Mission)*, ECLI:EU:C:2007:624

45 Relying on the general framework and evolution of development policy over recent years the Commission then explains that the strengthening of institutions, which is one of the horizontal aspects essential to sustainable development, henceforth forms an integral part of Community cooperation policies. That follows also from a reading of Articles 177 EC [current Article 208 TFEU] and 181a EC [current Article 212 TFEU], in which the terms employed show that assistance may be given in fields not expressly referred to, such as, in particular, mine-clearance or the decommissioning of light weapons.

46 Whilst recognising that it has no independent powers in respect of anti-terrorism, the Commission points out that Regulation No 443/92 is a financial instrument at the service of a global policy, so that, in determining its scope, it

[58] Regulation 1905/2006 of the European Parliament and of the Council of 18 December 2006 establishing a financing instrument for development cooperation [2006] OJ L378/41. Regulation 1905/2006 has since been replaced by Regulation 233/2014 of the European Parliament and of the Council of 11 March 2014 establishing a financing instrument for development cooperation for the period 2014-2020 [2014] OJ L77/44.

[59] Case C-403/05 *Parliament v Commission (Philippine Border Mission)*, ECLI:EU:C:2007:624, para 16. United Nations Security Council Resolution 1373 (2001) of 28 September 2001 was adopted immediately in the wake of the 9/11 terrorist attacks.

[60] Case C-403/05 *Parliament v Commission (Philippine Border Mission)*, ECLI:EU:C:2007:624, para 39.

[61] See paras 43 and 44. Essentially, the Commission sought to argue that combating international terrorism was not the dominant aim of the contested Decision, but combating trafficking in drugs and human beings, which more generally creates conditions conducive to economic development. It thereby sought to steer the objectives of the instrument away from a predominant 'security-focus' to ensure that the instrument remained within the scope of Regulation 443/92.

is appropriate to show a certain flexibility and to take account, in particular, of the general policy framework.

The Court thus had to answer the question whether the scope of EU development policy of the early 2000's had developed and widened to the extent that EU development measures can support and 'take into account' international efforts combating terrorism.

Case C-403/05 *Parliament v Commission (Philippine Border Mission)*, ECLI:EU:C:2007:624

55 In order to rule upon the Parliament's action, it is appropriate, therefore, to determine whether an objective such as that pursued by the contested decision, relating to the fight against terrorism and international crime, comes within the scope of Regulation No 443/92.

56 Admittedly, Articles 177 EC to 181 EC [current Articles 208 to 211 TFEU], inserted by the EU Treaty and dealing with cooperation with developing countries, refer not only to the sustainable economic and social development of those countries, their smooth and gradual integration into the world economy and the campaign against poverty, but also to the development and consolidation of democracy and the rule of law, as well as to respect for human rights and fundamental freedoms, whilst complying fully with their commitments in the context of the United Nations and other international organisations.

57 In addition, it follows from the Joint statement of the Council and the representatives of the governments of the Member States meeting within the Council, the European Parliament and the Commission on European Union Development Policy entitled 'The European Consensus' (OJ 2006, C 46, p. 1) that there can be no sustainable development and eradication of poverty without peace and security and that the pursuit of the objectives of the Community's new development policy necessarily proceed via the promotion of democracy and respect for human rights.

58 The Community legislature thus decided … to strengthen the development policy framework in order to improve its effectiveness. In that respect, Regulation (EC) No 1717/2006 of the European Parliament and of the Council of 15 November 2006 establishing an Instrument for Stability (OJ 2006 L 327, p. 1) establishes Community assistance, complementary to that provided for under external assistance, by contributing, among other things, to preventing the fragility of the States concerned. Under the sixth recital in the preamble to that regulation, account must be taken of the European Council Declaration on Combating Terrorism of 25 March 2004, in which it called for counter-terrorist objectives to be integrated into external assistance programmes …

> 59 The fact remains that it is common ground that Regulation No 443/92 contains no express reference to the fight against terrorism and international crime. In that same respect, it must be pointed out that the proposal for amendment of Regulation No 443/92, presented by the Commission in 2002 (COM 2002/0340 final of 2 July 2002) and intended to insert in the scope of that regulation, among other things, the fight against terrorism, failed. ...
>
> 68 It follows from all the foregoing that the contested decision pursues an objective concerning the fight against terrorism and international crime which falls outside the framework of the development cooperation policy pursued by Regulation No 443/92, so that the Commission exceeded the implementing powers conferred by the Council in Article 15 of that regulation.

The Court starts from the observation that the competences inserted into the EC Treaty in Maastricht are quite broad. They also include objectives relating to democracy, rule of law and human rights although the connection of development to security is not explicit in EU primary law as it stood in 1992. Given that the contested instrument was adopted in the implementation of the old Regulation based on the Treaties as they stood then, the scope of EU development policy should be read in light of its specific point in time, and security objectives did not fall within the scope of EU development competence. It is then important that the CJEU expressly accepts that the scope of EU powers has since developed. In the excerpt above, it supports this evolutive interpretation of the scope of EU development powers with reference to a number of political and legal developments. Importantly, the CJEU does not accept that the Commission, as an implementing institution, can independently establish the evolving scope of EU development powers. Instead, this clearly falls to the EU legislative bodies. Although the Lisbon Treaty has since reshuffled the objectives of EU external relations (see Chapter 1), the principle still stands: EU development policy is wide in scope, and can take into account security-related initiatives in function of eradicating poverty (Article 208 (1) TFEU).[62]

In the *ECOWAS* (or *Small Arms and Light Weapons – SALW*) judgment, the Court was again faced with having to establish the scope of EU development policy, confirming its wide scope established in the Philippine Border Mission case. The case nonetheless deserves attention, since it was a politically high-profile clash between the Member States on the one hand, and the Commission and Parliament on the other.

The dispute originated between the Commission and the Council concerning financial and technical assistance to the Economic Community of West African States (ECOWAS). From a policy perspective, the objective was to legally formalise into a binding treaty, a pre-existing moratorium on the trade of small arms and light weapons. The Council adopted a Decision providing funds to ECOWAS with that objective

[62] See also Case C-377/12 *Commission v Council (Philippines)*, ECLI:EU:C:20141903 and the examination of this ruling in M Broberg and R Holdgaard, 'Demarcating the Union's Development Cooperation Policy after Lisbon: *Commission v. Council (Philippines PCFA)*' (2015) 52 *Common Market Law Review* 547.

in mind and did so on a CFSP legal basis. However, the Commission was of the opinion that such action fell within the sphere of development cooperation. In *ECOWAS*, the Court similarly defined the broad scope of EU development policy, utilising the (old) European Consensus,[63] a statement of the Development Council on the threat of small arms to global stability, and a statement of the European Council on combating the illicit spread of small arms and light weapons.[64]

Case C-91/05 *Commission v Council (Small Arms/ECOWAS)*, ECLI:EU: C:2008:288, para 69

For example, on 21 May 1999, the 'development' Council of the European Union adopted a resolution on small arms in which it presented the proliferation of those weapons as a problem of global proportions which, in particular in crisis zones and countries where the security situation is unstable, has been an obstacle to peaceful economic and social development. More recently, in the European Union strategy to combat illicit accumulation and trafficking of small arms and light weapons adopted by the European Council on 15 and 16 December 2005 (Council document No 5319/06 PESC 31 of 13 January 2006), the European Council referred, among the consequences of the illicit spread of small arms and light weapons, in particular to those relating to the development of the countries concerned, that is, the weakening of State structures, displacement of persons, collapse of health and education services, declining economic activity, reduced government resources, the spread of pandemics, damage to the social fabric and, in the long term, the reduction or withholding of development aid, while adding that those consequences constitute, for sub-Saharan Africa, the region principally affected, a key factor in limiting development.

In delineating CFSP from EU development policy, the Court thus found that the intimate relationship between socio-economic development and security and stability of developing nations means the following: a concrete measure aiming to combat the proliferation of small arms and light weapons may be adopted by the Union under its development cooperation competence, if that measure by virtue both of its aim and its content falls within the socio-economic objectives of development policy and it does not pursue a security objective in itself (see also Chapter 9).[65]

While the broadening scope of development cooperation stands, the Treaty of Lisbon has made significant changes to the Treaty structure which also impact EU development competence. We refer to Chapter 3 for the analysis of how Lisbon has

[63] Case C-91/05 *Commission* v *Council (Small Arms/ECOWAS)*, ECLI:EU:C:2008:288, para 66.
[64] Ibid, paras 69–70.
[65] Case C-91/05 *Commission* v *Council (Small Arms/ECOWAS)*, ECLI:EU:C:2008:288, para 71.

reoriented established case law on scope and choice of legal basis, including on the possibility of using a dual legal basis. Notably, the Lisbon Treaty placed greater emphasis on coherence by linking various external objectives in Article 21 TEU (see Chapter 1), aiming to avoid competence conflicts and instead focus energy on the substance of policy making.

Evidently, the question of legal basis is but a narrow aspect of the security-development nexus in EU development cooperation. The fact that dual legal bases may be utilised for an international instrument implies a policy connection between development and security matters. Still, the present treaty-basis is likely to continue to constitute a challenge to EU policy makers as well as to institutions and the judiciary.

H Merket, *The EU and the Security-Development Nexus: Bridging the Legal Divide* (Leiden, Brill/Nijhoff, 2016) 356–65

The Union's gradual constitutional changes followed the rhythm of pragmatics rather than grand design, successively adding new layers and subsystems; new dividing lines and bridges across them. The complex system that ensued, sets out the legal boundaries within which the rising commitment to the security-development nexus has matured. While the challenges of insecurity, fragility, poverty and development are ruthlessly cross-cutting, the Union's means to cut across the competence boundaries between them are regulated and restricted by primary law. This makes efforts to align and integrate EU security and development policies legally complex as it requires difficult choices of legal basis between divided policy toolboxes. At the same time, it raises administrative challenges as these choices have to be made across very distinct policy-making communities. These are moreover politically sensitive as they affect the division of competences and balance of power between EU institutions. …

In sum, the EU's commitment to enhance the security-development nexus has incited an impressive activation of instruments, expansion of institutions and unceasing embracement of new spheres of action. However, largely due to the decades-old constitutional insulation of the CFSP, this is not the result of a unified endeavour, but of separate and often independent development cooperation and CFSP/CSDP efforts …

In essence, the [development-CFSP] integration-delimitation paradox implies that the last word with regard to the enhancement of coherence between development cooperation and CFSP/CSDP was not said with the entry into force of the Lisbon Treaty. Its drafters ensured that the balance with delimitation would develop on its own pace … If the current trends endure, this could gradually flatten out many differences between the policy, institutional and legal regimes of CFSP and development cooperation. This will, however, change nothing to the Treaty-rooted delimitation itself, which will continue to challenge EU policy-makers, institutions and the judiciary, and require them to come up with innovative solutions.

IV. Vertical and Horizontal Coordination in EU Development Policy

A. Introduction

Coordination is the operative arm of the other two C's: complementarity and coherence. The conferral of a complementary EU development competence implies that the Member States remain fully competent to deploy initiatives in this domain alongside the EU, without one excluding the other. This 'bias towards action' makes vertical coordination of EU and Member State action all the more imperative. It is for that reason that Article 210 TFEU contains an explicit obligation to coordinate and consult, with a distinct role for the Commission to promote complementarity and efficiency of EU and Member State action. The notion of coherence then overlaps with complementarity in that it evidently implies positive synergies between the EU and national levels. Coherence is, however, more than that, as it also has an important horizontal component. As we have seen, the scope of EU development policy is wide and legal obligations exist to take into account objectives from other EU policies as well. Thus, intra-EU coordination between different institutions and bodies or within institutions is crucial. This includes a range of relationships such as the Council-Commission-Parliament relationship in legislative work (Article 209 TFEU) but, most crucially, the Commission-EEAS relationship at the implementing level and also intra-organisational relations such as those between Commission DG's (eg, DG Trade – DG DEVCO). In sum, complementarity and coherence in practice requires coordination between all actors involved. We will examine the vertical and horizontal dimensions by looking at the way EU development policy is financed and implemented in practice.

B. Multi-Track Financing of Development Cooperation: EDF and EU Budget

The challenge to coordinate EU and Member State efforts is best illustrated through the important non-legally binding document from 2017 known as the New European Consensus on Development. The full name of this soft legal document is: '*Joint statement by the Council and the representatives of the governments of the Member States meeting within the Council, the European Parliament and the Commission on European Union Development Policy: The New European Consensus on Development 'Our World, Our Dignity, Our Future.*'[66] The stated objective of this document is to provide the framework for a common approach to development policy that will be applied by the EU institutions and the Member States while fully respecting each other's distinct roles and competences. From a legal perspective, the title of the document indicates that

[66] Title as quoted [2017] OJ C210/1.

the Member States participated as the Council – an institution of the EU – as well as sovereign nations exercising their retained competence. They signed up to the New European Consensus to set out a common vision together with the Commission and European Parliament as institutions of the EU as an international organisation. By rising above legal dividing lines, this document meant to coordinate the three dominant streams of development assistance that make up *European* (as opposed to EU) development cooperation: funds from Member State budgets disbursed in accordance with national rules and policy priorities; funds from the EU budget disbursed in accordance with EU development policy priorities (208 TFEU); funds from the Member State budgets which are pooled in a 'European Development Fund' (EDF) and disbursed in accordance with the priorities jointly agreed in the Cotonou Agreement with the ACP countries.

M Broberg, *Governing by 'Consensuses' – On the Legal Regulation of the EU's Development Cooperation Policy*, DIIS Working Paper 2010/23, 6–7

As a rule, the Union's expenses are financed via its budget. Such expenditure presupposes the prior adoption of a legally binding Union act forming the legal basis for the expenditure in accordance with the Union's financial regulation. However, the Union's development cooperation policy only partially follows this scheme, since to a large extent, development assistance to the ACP countries is financed via the European Development Fund (EDF) instead of via the Union's budget. There are historical reasons for this and on several occasions the Commission has proposed integrating all development assistance in the budget. Such integration would lead to a different allocation of the Member States' financing of assistance to the ACP countries and would give the Commission greater power in this field. Perhaps this is part of the explanation why the EDF continues to exist. The EDF is financed by the Member States, has its own financial rules and is governed by a special committee. The continuing existence of the EDF means that the European Union's development assistance flows via two main channels, namely the budget and the EDF.

The EDF is funded outside the EU budget, consisting of financial contributions by the EU Member States proportionally to contribution keys which represent a certain percentage of the entire value of the EDF. For example, the eleventh EDF for 2014–2020 amounts to €30.5 billion,[67] of which Germany contributes about 20 per cent, and Bulgaria contributes around 0.2 per cent.[68] The funds are provided

[67] With an additional €2.6 billion that will be made available by the European Investment Bank in the form of loans from its own resources.

[68] Cf Article 1 of Internal agreement between the Representatives of the Governments of the Member States of the European Union, meeting within the Council, on the financing of European Union aid under the multiannual financial framework for the period 2014 to 2020, in accordance with the ACP-EU Partnership Agreement, and on the allocation of financial assistance for the Overseas Countries and Territories to which Part Four of the Treaty on the Functioning of the European Union applies [2013] OJ L210/1.

on an intergovernmental basis, yet the Commission has a significant role; it is responsible for administering the Fund in line with an implementing Regulation which is adopted for each EDF period. The Member States play a role in EDF governance through a committee which consists of representatives of the Member States set up at the Commission. This EDF committee is chaired by a Commission representative and, for each EDF it adopts rules of procedure, which specify when it meets and renders decisions in line with the pertinent implementing Regulation.[69] While the EDF has been in existence since the early days of the EEC, incorporation into the EU budget has been on the agenda for some time. The first EDF was launched in 1959, with the eleventh and possibly last EDF running until 2020. With respect to the negotiations for the 2021–2027 multi-annual financial framework, the Commission has proposed to integrate the EDF into the EU budget ('EDF budgetisation').[70] This would then coincide with the expiry of the Cotonou Agreement. However, at the time of writing, the outcome of these negotiations are not clear.

The second channel through which the EU provides financing for its development policy is the EU budget. Here the EU adopts a set of legally binding instruments via the ordinary legislative procedure (Article 209 TFEU), through which funds are administered in accordance with the general budgetary rules of the EU's Financial Regulation.[71] These legally binding acts – usually Regulations – are adopted for the duration of the seven-year multi-annual financial framework (MFF) (eg, 2014–2020)[72] in parallel to the EDF. In their scope of application and objectives for which funds are allocated, a distinction is made between geographic and thematic instruments. For the present MFF, the EU has adopted the following instruments:[73]

- *Geographic*: Development cooperation Instrument (DCI), Instrument for Pre Accession Assistance (IPA II), Instrument for Greenland (IfG), and European Neighbourhood Instrument (ENPI).
- *Thematic*: European Instrument for Democracy and Human Rights Worldwide (EIDHR), Instrument contributing to Stability and Peace (IcSP), Instrument for Nuclear Safety Cooperation (INSC) and the Partnership Instrument (PI).

[69] For the eleventh EDF: Council Decision 2015/355 of 2 March 2015 adopting the rules of procedure for the European Development Fund Committee [2015] OJ L61/17.

[70] Proposal for a Council Regulation laying down the multiannual financial framework for the years 2021 to 2027, COM(2018) 322 final.

[71] M Broberg, *Governing by 'Consensuses' – on the Legal Regulation of the EU's Development Cooperation Policy*, DIIS Working Paper 2010/23, 6–7.

[72] Regulation 1311/2013 of 2 December 2013 laying down the multiannual financial framework for the years 2014–2020 [2013] OJ L347/884.

[73] Regulation 233/2014 of 11 March 2014 establishing a financing instrument for development cooperation for the period 2014–2020 [2013] OJ L77/44; Regulation 232/2014 of 11 March 2014 establishing a European Neighbourhood Instrument [2014] OJ L77/27; Regulation 231/2014 of 11 March 2014 establishing an Instrument for Pre-Accession Assistance (IPA II) [2014] OJ L77/11; Regulation 230/2014 of 11 March 2014 establishing an Instrument contributing to Stability and Peace (IcSP) [2014] OJ L77/1; Regulation 235/2014 of 11 March 2014 establishing a financing instrument for democracy and human rights worldwide [2014] OJ L77/85; Council Regulation 237/2014/Euratom of 13 December 2013 establishing an Instrument for Nuclear Safety Cooperation, [2014] OJ L77/109; Regulation 234/2014 of 11 March 2014 establishing a Partnership Instrument for cooperation with third countries [2014] OJ L77/77; and Council Decision 2014/137 of 14 March 2014 on relations between the European Union on the one hand, and Greenland and the Kingdom of Denmark on the other (IfG) [2014] OJ L76/1.

These instruments illustrate how coordination, coherence and complementarity are intertwined in the day-to-day practice of EU development cooperation.

Joint Communication of the Commission and High Representative, *Global Europe: A new Approach to Financing EU External Action*, COM(2011) 865 final, Brussels, 7 December 2011

The emphasis for the post-2013 period will be on adapting the EU's methods of designing, programming and delivering external assistance to the new political, economic and institutional realities while building on what has proven to be successful so far. Addressing short-, mid- and long-term challenges on a variety of issues and mobilising a mix of external instruments at EU and Member State level will require particular efforts ensuring overall policy coherence in our engagement with our partners in the pursuit of a comprehensive EU approach. The proposed revision of the programming process will ensure greater consistency between the different areas of EU external action and a more result-driven approach, while allowing flexibility to respond to political priorities.

The new generation of external instruments will facilitate political dialogue, negotiations and implementation of existing and future agreements with our partners in support of an overall political strategy for that country. In this framework, policy coherence for development remains a key priority …

The EU must seek to target its resources where they are needed most and where they could make the most difference. A more differentiated approach to partnerships and aid allocation driven by the country context is a core principle of this proposal. The EU should continue to recognise the particular importance of supporting development in its own neighbourhood and in Sub-Saharan Africa. On the other hand, many countries are graduating from EU development assistance because they are capable of funding their own development. Assistance will be allocated on the basis of country needs, capacities, commitments, performance and potential EU impact. The specific needs of countries in vulnerable, fragile, conflict-affected and crisis situations will be a priority …

Overall, EU external instruments will take greater account of human rights, democracy and good governance when it comes to allocating external assistance to partner countries. With enlargement and neighbouring countries, country allocations and delivery of assistance should be more closely linked to progress in implementing reforms. For developing countries, the EU will strengthen mutual accountability in respect of commitments and the fulfilment of objectives as agreed with partner countries … In line with the Lisbon Treaty provisions, the new instruments will implement new mechanisms to ensure more democratic debate on EU external assistance through a stronger involvement of the European Parliament. An example of this is the use of delegated acts, which can increase the flexibility of external instruments. Democratic scrutiny over the European Development Fund (EDF) will also be improved by bringing it into line with the Development Cooperation Instrument, while taking into account the specificities of the instrument.

C. Executing EU Development Policy: Commission and EEAS

The financing instruments to support EU development are adopted for a seven-year window covering the multi-annual financial framework. Thereafter, the Union must utilise these macroscopically oriented financing instruments to set more specific policy priorities and targets with shorter timespans. In turn, these are to be concretised and implemented through on-the-ground projects. This process of EU development policy making encompasses three phases: (1) management, (2) programming and (3) implementing EU development policy. In the pre-Lisbon context, the Commission oversaw this process. In the post-Lisbon era, a complex division of tasks exists between the EEAS and the Commission (specifically the Directorate-General for International Cooperation and Development (DevCo)). This is based on their respective roles as laid down in Articles 17 and 27(3) TEU, and has been specified in Article 9 of the Council Decision establishing the European External Action Service (see also Chapter 1).

Article 9, Council Decision 2010/427/EU establishing the organisation and functioning of the European External Action Service [2010] OJ L201/30

1. The management of the Union's external cooperation programmes is under the responsibility of the Commission without prejudice to the respective roles of the Commission and of the EEAS in programming as set out in the following paragraphs.

2. The High Representative shall ensure overall political coordination of the Union's external action, ensuring the unity, consistency and effectiveness of the Union's external action, in particular through the following external assistance instruments:

- the Development Cooperation Instrument,
- the European Development Fund,
- the European Instrument for Democracy and Human Rights,

- the European Neighbourhood and Partnership Instrument,
- the Instrument for Cooperation with Industrialised Countries,
- the Instrument for Nuclear Safety Cooperation,
- the Instrument for Stability, regarding the assistance provided for in Article 4 of Regulation (EC) No 1717/2006.

3. In particular, the EEAS shall contribute to the programming and management cycle for the instruments referred to in paragraph 2, on the basis of the policy objectives set out in those instruments. It shall have responsibility for preparing the following decisions of the Commission regarding the strategic, multiannual steps within the programming cycle:

(i) country allocations to determine the global financial envelope for each region, subject to the indicative breakdown of the multiannual financial framework. Within each region, a proportion of funding will be reserved for regional programmes;
(ii) country and regional strategic papers;
(iii) national and regional indicative programmes.

In accordance with Article 3, throughout the whole cycle of programming, planning and implementation of the instruments referred to in paragraph 2, the High Representative and the EEAS shall work with the relevant members and services of the Commission without prejudice to Article 1(3). All proposals for decisions will be prepared by following the Commission's procedures and will be submitted to the Commission for adoption.

[The article continues to set out specific modi operandi for each listed instrument.]

In the three execution phases of development policy, the Commission is responsible for the 'management' of external development cooperation, whereas the EEAS and Commission share roles in the 'programming' phase. The 'implementation' phase again falls to the Commission. The line between management and programming can be difficult to draw, whereas implementation is perhaps the most straightforward to delineate: The implementation phase concerns the actual delivery of aid in an efficient and effective way, usually through a project or sector approach,[74] or straightforward budget support. The line between management and programming, and the role of the EEAS and Commission therein, is explained in the extract below.

[74] The project approach entails funding projects of civil society or private actors with a clearly specified objective in a given time period. The sector approach is broader by focusing on working with partner governments and other donors or stakeholders to coordinate longer term outcomes and financing for a given sector.

S Blockmans et al, *EEAS 2.0 – A Legal Commentary on Council Decision 2010/427/EU establishing the organisation and functioning of the European External Action Service*, SIEPS Working Paper 2013/1, 92–93

In the context of (business) administration, 'management' is the process of dealing with or controlling things or people; the responsibility for and control of a company or organisation. Management in all business and organisational activities is the act of getting people together to accomplish desired goals and objectives using available resources efficiently and effectively. Management comprises designing, planning, organising, staffing, leading or directing, and controlling an organisation (a group of one or more people or entities) or effort for the purpose of accomplishing a goal.

According to Article 9(1) [of the Council Decision establishing the EEAS], the management of the EU's external cooperation programmes is 'under' the responsibility of the Commission 'without prejudice to the respective roles of the Commission and of the EEAS in programming'. Thus, the Commission retains overall responsibility for dealing with and controlling the Union's external cooperation programmes, whereas it shares the role of 'programming' ie designing, scheduling or planning the EU's external cooperation programmes (only an element of the wider concept of 'management') with the EEAS. In short, the basic prescript, namely that during the whole process of planning and implementation both parts of the organisation should work together and that all proposals for decision have to be prepared through the Commission procedures and submitted to the Commission (Article 9(3) [of the Council Decision establishing the EEAS]), has remained unchanged ... In its contribution to the Union's external cooperation programmes, the EEAS is expected to work towards ensuring that the programmes fulfil the objectives for external action as set out in Article 21 TEU, in particular in paragraph (2)(d) thereof, and that they respect the objectives of the Union's development policy in line with Article 208 TFEU.

Programming is the decision-making process whereby strategy, budget and priorities for spending aid in non-EU countries is drawn up. During the MFF 2014–2020 this occurred through three kinds of instruments: first, the general strategy papers per country or region covering the whole period of seven years; second the more detailed indicative programmes (national or regional); and third the detailed annual action programmes for each year of the programming period. Looking to the 2014–2020 MFF and new development cooperation instruments, the joint EEAS-Commission Instructions for the Programming of the 11th European Development Fund (EDF) and the Development Cooperation Instrument (DCI) – 2014–2020, has made a number of proposals to strengthen the three C's throughout the forthcoming programming cycle.

Instructions for the Programming of the 11th European Development Fund (EDF) and the Development Cooperation Instrument (DCI) – 2014–2020, Brussels, 15 May 2012, 4–7

2.2 Programming process

A simplified process

One of the main purposes of the present instructions is to simplify the process of programming the EU's bilateral development cooperation with partner countries and regions, making use, wherever possible, of existing national or regional policy documents as the main reference documents for the programming process. Consequently, the multiannual indicative programme should become the central document of the programming process and EU specific strategy papers) should in most cases no longer be needed and should only be used where no other option is available. Instead, the existing national or regional development plans (or their equivalents) should from now on be used as the point of departure for the programming process, and as the main basis for coordination and dialogue with EU Member States and other donors. …

A second element of simplification is the aim to have succinct programming documents. In the same spirit, there will no longer be a standard obligation for EU Delegations to prepare various technical annexes to the programming documents on specific issues (such as migration).

[at p. 7 under the heading 'Comprehensiveness and coherence' the Instructions continue by observing:]

Such a vision also should be the basis for a greater coherence at four levels:

- between the country programmes and the regional programmes which are managed by/in cooperation with regional bodies within the context of specific regional cooperation or integration frameworks (such as ASEAN or COMESA);
- between these country and regional programmes, on the one hand, and HQ managed regional multi-country programmes (eg, EDF Intra-ACP) and DEVCO- or FPI- managed thematic programmes (DCI) and instruments (EIDHR, Instrument for Stability, Nuclear Safety, and Partnership Instrument), on the other;
- between development and other cross-cutting or sectoral EU policies and programmes (eg security, disaster risk reduction, migration, environment, climate change, energy, trade, agriculture, fisheries, drugs) to ensure an effective EU external action and promote Policy Coherence for Development (PCD);
- between policies, instruments and actions of the EU, and those of EU Member States and/or the EIB and other European Development Finance institutions.

The previously discussed security-development nexus provides good insight into the impact of the EEAS on policy making in EU development cooperation policy as is reflected in the excerpt below.

H Merket, *The EU and the Security-Development Nexus: Bridging the Legal Divide* (Leiden, Brill/Nijhoff, 2016) 176 and 200

While the optimisation of the security-development nexus may not have shaped the debate on the creation of the EEAS, its aims of enhanced effectiveness and consistency indirectly raise hopes for this particular interface …

In sum, as a central policy interlocutor with a heterogeneous composition the EEAS could finally put the rhetoric of coordination across the security-development nexus in practise. Its setting enables a decentralised and cross-fertilising exchange of experience-based knowledge in a network of security and development-oriented actors. Yet, as with the High Representative, the EEAS' design gives the impression of a halfway solution that is still in an experimental phase. In spite of all the faith put in this new body, its 'hands are tied to the competences attributed to the political masters it is supposed to serve'. Consequently, the old challenges of delimitating CFSP and development cooperation seeped through in the EEAS' constellation. This causes considerable hurdles of duplication, coordination, accountability and institutional solidarity, which at present prevent the EEAS from collecting the full gains in terms of efficiency and coherence. Besides the challenges of delimitation there are also risks attached to increased integration of both policy fields. The development-related responsibilities of the EEAS have intensified the long-standing concern about the potential instrumentalisation of aid. However, the fears that this would lead to an increased exposure to short-term political and economic pressures appear unfounded at this stage. Ironically, this is less due to a commonality of objectives than to the limited interest of the EEAS to make its imprint on development cooperation.

V. The Broader Picture of EU External Relations Law

EU development policy is a mature policy field as old as the European integration process itself. As a result, the legal principles, institutions and instruments that underpin it have been progressively shaped through the interaction between European integrative processes, concrete policy needs, and law as a structuring element. The complementary nature of EU development policy is exemplary of this interaction and the broader context of EU external relations law. During the early years of the Treaty of Rome, mainly France pushed its development interests through the supranational level in the form of associating certain third States with the EEC. This did not pre-empt Member State development initiatives and EU development policy's complementary nature created the basis for 'the other two C's', namely the need for coherence and coordination between the two levels. The European Development Fund soon became an interesting peculiarity of EC development cooperation exhibiting all three C's: funds of the Member States were being pooled on an intergovernmental basis (complementarity), with a central management role for the Commission (coordination), with jointly agreed policy objectives but without actually integrating the funds into the EU budget (coherence). In the early 1990s Parliament sought to push 'budgetisation' through judicial means, which would also have extended its role in EU budgetary matters over (the quantitatively significant) EDF funds. However, the Court was unreceptive and expressly confirmed the complementary nature of this competence. Eventual 'budgetisation' is likely however. During the negotiations on the 2014–2020 multi-annual financial framework, the Commission certainly would have wished to propose the integration of EDF funding into the EU budget structures, arguing that this would streamline funding procedures, ease coordination efforts and substantive coherence between initiatives and increase transparency in the provision of EU development aid, but chose not to make such a proposal at that time. Therefore, only in 2018 the Commission has put forward a proposal for the budgetisation of the EDF funding in connection with the revision of the Cotonou agreement.

VI. Sources and Further Reading

Arts, K, 'ACP-EU Relations in a New Era: The Cotonou Agreement' (2003) 40 *Common Market Law Review* 95.

Arts, K and AK Dickson (eds) *EU Development Cooperation – From Model to Symbol* (Manchester, Manchester University Press, 2004).

Bartels, L, 'The Trade and Development Policy of the European Union' in M Cremona (ed) *Developments in EU External Relations Law* (Oxford, Oxford University Press, 2008) 128–71.

Blockmans, S, M Cremona, D Curtin, G De Baere, S Duke, C Eckes, C Hillion, B Van Vooren, R Wessel and J Wouters, *EEAS 2.0 – A Legal Commentary on Council Decision 2010/427/EU Establishing the Organisation and Functioning of the European External Action Service*, SIEPS Working Paper 2013/1.

Broberg, M, 'EU Development Cooperation and the CFSP: Mutual Encroachment?' in S Blockmans and P Koutrakos (eds) *Research Handbook on the EU's Common Foreign and Security Policy* (Cheltenham, Edward Elgar, 2018) 254–275.

Broberg, M, *Governing by 'Consensuses' – on the Legal Regulation of the EU's Development Cooperation Policy*, DIIS Working Paper 2010/23.

Broberg, M, *The EU's Legal Ties with its Former Colonies – When Old Love Never Dies*, DIIS Working Paper 2011/01.

Broberg, M, 'What is the Direction for the EU's Development Cooperation after Lisbon? A Legal Examination' (2011) 16 *European Foreign Affairs Review* 539.

Broberg, M and R Holdgaard, 'Demarcating the Union's Development Cooperation Policy after Lisbon: *Commission v Council (Philippines PCFA)*' (2015) 52 *Common Market Law Review* 547.

Broberg, M and R Holdgaard, 'EU Development Co-operation Post-Lisbon: Main Constitutional Challenges' (2015) 3 *European Law Review* 349.

Carbone, M, 'Au-delà de l'aide: la cohérence des politiques de développement de l'Europe' (2012) 3 *Revue Internationale de Politique de Développement* 197.

Carbone, M, 'Preserving Policy Autonomy: EU Development Cooperation from Maastricht to Lisbon' in F Laursen (ed) *The EU's Lisbon Treaty: Institutional Choices and Implementation* (Farnham, Ashgate, 2012) 229–42.

Carbone, M (ed) *Policy Coherence and EU Development Policy* (Abingdon, Routledge, 2009).

Cremona, M, 'Human Rights and Democracy Clauses in the EC's Trade Agreements' in D O'Keeffe and N Emiliou (eds) *The European Union and World Trade Law: After the GATT Uruguay Round* (Chichester, Wiley, 1996) 62–77.

Hachez, N, 'Essential Elements' Clauses in EU Trade Agreements: Making Trade Work in a Way that Helps Human Rights?' (2015) 53 *Cuadernos europeos de Deusto* 81.

Hadfield, A, 'Janus Advances? An Analysis of EC Development Policy and the 2005 Amended Cotonou Partnership Agreement' (2007) 12 *European Foreign Affairs Review* 39.

Hoebink, P (ed) *The Treaty of Maastricht and Europe's Development Co-operation, Studies in European Development Co-operation Evaluation No 1* (Amsterdam, Aksant Academic Publishers, 2005).

McMahon, JA, 'Negotiating in a Time of Turbulent Transition: The Future of Lomé' (1999) 36 *Common Market Law Review* 599.

Merket, H, *The EU and the Security-Development Nexus: Bridging the Legal Divide* (Leiden, Brill/Nijhoff, 2016).

Meyn, M, 'Economic Partnership Agreements: An 'Historic Step' Towards a 'Partnership of Equals'?' (2008) 26 *Development Policy Review* 515.

Olsen, GR, 'Coherence, Consistency and Political Will in Foreign Policy: The European Union's Policy towards Africa' (2008) 9 *Perspectives on European Politics and Society* 157.

Sissoko, M, Osuji, L and Cheng, W, 'Impacts of the Yaoundé and Lomé Conventions on EC-ACP Trade' (1998) 1 *The African Economic and Business Review* 6.

Van Vooren, B, *EU External Relations Law and the European Neighbourhood Policy: A Paradigm for Coherence* (Abingdon, Routledge, 2012).

Ward, A, 'Community Development Aid and the Evolution of the Inter-institutional Law of the European Union' in A Dashwood and C Hillion (eds) *The General Law of EC External Relations* (London, Sweet and Maxwell, 2000) 42–47.

Youngs, R, 'Fusing Security and Development: Just Another Euro-platitude?' (2008) 30 *Journal of European Integration* 419.

9

Common Foreign, Security and Defence Policy

Central Issues

- The EU's foreign and security policy is based on a set of compromises. From the outset, Member States have been hesitant to hand-over powers in this area. Yet, the strong links with other policies as well as the single institutional structure, caused an integration of CFSP into the Union legal order and a further 'normalisation' of this policy field. While its distinct nature remains clearly visible, CFSP has become part and parcel of the EU's external relations regime.
- In this chapter we will address the obligations of the Member States under CFSP as well as the role of the EU institutions, including the CJEU, and the legal nature and function of the CFSP instruments.
- Part of CFSP is the Common Security and Defence Policy (CSDP). The CSDP provisions not only allow the EU to be active as a global military actor, but new rules increasingly commit the EU members to work closer together in what is termed the Permanent Structured Cooperation (PESCO).

I. Foreign Policy as an Integral Part of EU External Relations

The Common Foreign and Security Policy (CFSP) of the EU has for decades been the 'odd one out'. It emerged separate from the European Economic Community in an incremental, pragmatic fashion in the beginning of the 1970s. The process was stimulated through the realisation that the coordination of the different foreign policies of the (six, then nine etc.) Member States was helpful and occasionally even necessary for the Community to pursue its goals. At present, CFSP objectives have become an integral part of the overall external objectives of the Union as laid down in Article 21 TEU (see Chapter 1).

L Lonardo, 'Common Foreign and Security Policy and the EU's External Action Objectives: An Analysis of Article 21 of the Treaty on the European Union' (2018) 14 *European Constitutional Law Review* 584, 607

The retention of the CFSP's legal distinctiveness might be a response to the Member State's need to maintain power 'when it matters': foreign policy is a domain at the core of state functions. But, as the rationale of Article 21(2) TEU suggests and the analysis of institutional behaviour has shown, there are no objectives exclusive to CFSP. All objectives specified under the eight letters of Article 21(2) have been used to pursue non-CFSP competences. Yet the same eight letters could have been CFSP objectives: as has been shown, there is a credible link between each of them and political or defence matters. While this is consistent with the desire to enhance the coherence of Union external actions, it also adds to the difficulty in delimitating the scope of CFSP.

Thus, this policy area has developed from a more intergovernmental form of information exchange, coordination, and cooperation in the days of the European Political Cooperation (EPC), to an EU competence in its own right and an area in which the Member States have accepted significant forms of institutionalisation and legalisation. The integration of CFSP policy goals is clearly visible in the Treaty when we look at the general statement of the EU's objectives in Article 3(5) TEU (see Chapter 1), which includes peace and security, and the protection of EU citizens. Over the years, the 'normalisation' of CFSP – in the sense that it fully belongs to the Union's legal order and is subject to most of its rules and principles – has become more accepted in scholarly work. Yet, the distinct development of CFSP in the early days that seems to be at the source of a 'tradition of otherness' sometimes blurs its present-day constitutionalisation.

PJ Cardwell, 'On "Ring-Fencing" the Common Foreign and Security Policy in the Legal Order of the European Union' (2015) *Northern Ireland Legal Quarterly*, 443–63, 445

This 'otherness' of the CFSP within the constitutional order is expressed in the ring-fencing metaphor. But it does not explain why the CFSP should be exceptional within the EU's legal order. In one sense there is an obvious answer: the tradition of otherness of the CFSP and legal expression of the Member States' fear of the encroachment on their sovereignty if the Court of Justice was able to extend supranational EU legal principles to foreign policy. The Treaty seems to stem the 'Brusselsization' of the CFSP where 'the member states have in practice entered a slippery slope of integration with decision-making competence 'creeping' to Brussels' with the Court in Luxembourg filling in the gaps. But given that other areas have been 'communitarianised' in the most recent Treaty, is the ring-fence likely to prove effective in keeping the CFSP separate from the rest of the EU's legal order? ... this is highly unlikely ...

Admittedly, the integration is not complete. The CFSP maintains a certain 'distinctiveness' from the general former 'Community logic'. Most notably, CFSP (with CSDP and the European Neighbourhood Policy) is the only substantive policy domain found in the Treaty on European Union, whereas other policies are found in the TFEU.

In some respects, the nature of CFSP still differs significantly from other 'common' policies, such as the Common Commercial Policy (Article 207 TFEU) or the Common Agricultural Policy (Article 38 TFEU). In the early years in particular, Member States showed a willingness to cooperate in CFSP, but remained reluctant to actually transfer competences. This makes it difficult to establish the *nature* of competence the EU has under CFSP (see Chapter 3). Nevertheless, the existence of a *Union* competence is beyond any doubt.

Article 2(4) TFEU

The Union shall have competence, in accordance with the provisions of the Treaty on European Union, to define and implement a common foreign and security policy ...

This provision indicates that CFSP has moved beyond intergovernmentalism. An actual competence has been *conferred* upon the Union rather than existing as a mere cooperative framework for the Member States. CFSP is not mentioned in Articles 3–6 TFEU under either of the categories: exclusive competences, shared competences or supporting, coordinating or supplementing competences. It would probably come closest to the field of complementary or parallel competence as observed in the field of development: both the Union and the Member States have roles to play, strong coordination is both legally required and politically desirable. At the same time, it remains somewhat unclear to what extent activities of the Union would pre-empt Member State action. Although most textbooks would present CFSP as a non-pre-emptive competence the present chapter will highlight Member States' obligations. The *sui generis* nature of CFSP is usually related to a number of elements which are lacking when compared to most other Union policy areas: the different roles of the European Commission and the European Parliament in the decision-making process, the impossibility of the Court to rule on most CFSP decisions and Treaty provisions, the different effects of CFSP decisions in the domestic legal orders of the Member States, and the different nature of the instruments themselves.

II. The Nature of CFSP

On 7 February 1992, the Member States of the European Economic Community (EEC) entered a new phase in the ongoing process of intensifying their political cooperation. In signing the TEU they officially embraced foreign and security cooperation as an inextricable component of what from that moment on was to be referred to as the 'European Union' (see Chapter 1). CFSP was – from entry into force of the Treaty on 1 November 1993 – to be seen as one of the areas that would serve as the justification for the establishment of that Union.

The CFSP did not, however, appear out of the blue. Its origins date back to the 1950s.[1] The history of CFSP reveals an ongoing struggle to reach an agreement between the members of the EEC on political cooperation alongside their economic cooperation and, above all, on the legal-institutional relationship between the economic and political policy domains.

A. The Position of CFSP in the Treaty

The 2009 Lisbon Treaty made an end to the so-called 'pillar-structure'. Since the entry into force of that Treaty and the resulting amended Treaty on European Union, CFSP is no longer 'the second pillar' of the Union, but an integral part of the single legal person that is the EU. While CFSP is occasionally referred to in the first parts of the TEU in relation to the role of the institutions, the main provisions are to be found in Title V of the TEU, entitled 'General Provisions on the Union's External Action and Specific Provisions on the Common Foreign and Security Policy'. The 'specific provisions' to which the Treaty refers, are laid down in Chapter 2 of this Title V. CFSP has a wide scope and, at first glance, seems to cover all foreign policy dimensions of the Union.

[1] One may even go back as far as 19 September 1946, when Winston Churchill stressed the need to establish 'a kind of United States of Europe'; or to 7 May 1948 when the so-called 'Congress of Europe' called for the establishment of a Political and Economic Union in Europe. See, on some of the history, G Butler, *Constitutional Law of the EU's Common Foreign and Security Policy: Competence and Institutions in External Relations* (Oxford, Hart Publishing, 2019) and RA Wessel, *The European Union's Foreign and Security Policy: A Legal institutional Perspective* (The Hague, Kluwer Law International, 1999).

Article 24(1) TEU

The Union's competence in matters of common foreign and security policy shall cover all areas of foreign policy and all questions relating to the Union's security, including the progressive framing of a common defence policy that might lead to a common defence ...

In principle, nothing in foreign affairs is excluded. At the same time, reference is made to the fact that the regular decision-making procedures that are applicable to other policy areas do not apply to CFSP. Chapter 2 of Title V thus provides its *lex specialis*. The key differences as regards the institutional balance and the role of the CJEU in CFSP are also spelled out in Article 24 TEU.

Article 24(1) TEU

The common foreign and security policy is subject to specific rules and procedures. It shall be defined and implemented by the European Council and the Council acting unanimously, except where the Treaties provide otherwise. The adoption of legislative acts shall be excluded. The common foreign and security policy shall be put into effect by the High Representative of the Union for Foreign Affairs and Security Policy and by Member States, in accordance with the Treaties. The specific role of the European Parliament and of the Commission in this area is defined by the Treaties ...

CFSP is thus characterised by different voting rules, different instruments, a different role for the institutions and, in particular, a more limited role for the Court of Justice. The subsequent sections in this chapter will analyse these aspects in more detail.

B. The Choice for the Correct Legal Basis

With a view to the many political questions underlying CFSP decisions, it remains important to underline that, from a legal perspective, CFSP is subject to legal rules and procedures. Its formulation is spelled out in detail in the Treaties and, in adopting CFSP decisions and actions, the Union is bound by the principles of EU law. As clearly emphasised by Article 23(1) TEU: 'The Union's action on the international scene, pursuant to this Chapter, shall be guided by the principles, shall pursue the objectives of, and be conducted in accordance with, the general provisions laid down in Chapter 1.'

G Butler, *Constitutional Law of the EU's Common Foreign and Security Policy: Competence and Institutions in External Relations* (Oxford, Hart Publishing, 2019) 5

Despite seeming to be the contrary, CFSP matters are a legalised field. For lawyers, everything in EU external relations begins with a discussion on the legal basis for supporting actions. As the Union strives for more coordination, consistency and cooperation, the choice of legal basis is of profound importance. The law is only one element of EU external relations, but it is an integral component that caters for the execution of external action. This is even more so in CFSP matters where strict conditions for the procedural issues are set down in the treaties. This is not only in EU external relations law, but for all EU acts or measures, which must have a legal basis.

Chapter 3 examined the legal complexity that results from the principle of conferred powers: any and all EU action must find a legal basis in the TEU or TFEU. The centre of gravity test was developed to make the 'correct' choice as to whether an initiative falls within one or the other policy domain. However, in policy reality, such neat separations are often very difficult to make: trade and environmental issues can be interlinked, as can development and security. In fact, as we have seen in Chapter 8 on Development, the Treaty-mandated consistency requirement actually calls for a proactive approach to combining different areas of external action. Yet, especially in the field of CFSP, the diverging decision-making procedures make it difficult to combine a CFSP legal basis with a legal basis in another (TFEU) policy area. This is a significant legal obstacle to comprehensive external action.

In the pre-Lisbon version of the TEU, choices for the correct legal basis were to be made based on (former) Article 47 TEU. This so-called 'non-affect clause' had as its main purpose to 'protect' the so-called *acquis communautaire* from incursion by the special CFSP method, and provided that 'nothing in [the TEU] shall affect the Treaties establishing the European Communities or the subsequent Treaties and Acts modifying and supplementing them'. The landmark case at that time clarifying the application of the 'non-affect clause' was *ECOWAS* (or *Small Arms and Light Weapons*). The result of this case was that the Council CFSP Decision was annulled because it also included aspects of development cooperation, an area not covered by the CFSP legal basis. Post-Lisbon, the pillars no longer exist and Article 47 has been replaced by Article 40 TEU. This provision reflects the current focus on coherent EU external relations and is therefore more balanced between CFSP and the other Union policies now compiled in the TFEU. In substantive terms, it essentially reflects the method whereby the correct legal basis is found through establishing the 'centre of gravity' of the decision at stake (see Chapter 3).

Article 40 TEU

The implementation of the common foreign and security policy shall not affect the application of the procedures and the extent of the powers of the institutions laid down by the Treaties for the exercise of the Union competences referred to in Articles 3 to 6 of the Treaty on the Functioning of the European Union.

Similarly, the implementation of the policies listed in those Articles shall not affect the application of the procedures and the extent of the powers of the institutions laid down by the Treaties for the exercise of the Union competences under this chapter.

In other words, in adopting CFSP decisions, the Council should be aware of the external policies in the TFEU *and vice versa*. Despite its 'balanced' approach, Article 40 implies that EU CFSP measures are excluded once they start to interfere with the exclusive powers of the Union, for instance in the area of Common Commercial Policy. This may seriously limit the freedom of the Member States in the area of restrictive measures (see below) or the export of 'dual goods' (commodities which can also have a military application). At the same time, the question may rightfully be asked what the current value of Article 40 is, since it mainly seems to repeat a general legal requirement in EU law: the correct legal basis is chosen on the basis of the centre of gravity test.

In Case C-130/10, the European Parliament challenged a Council Regulation imposing certain specific restrictive measures directed against certain persons and entities associated with Usama bin Laden. The Court confirmed the following:

Case C-130/10 *Parliament v Council (Smart Sanctions)*, ECLI:EU:C:2012:472

44 With regard to a measure that simultaneously pursues a number of objectives, or that has several components, which are inseparably linked without one's being incidental to the other, the Court has held that, where various provisions of the Treaty are therefore applicable, such a measure will have to be founded, exceptionally, on the various corresponding legal bases (see, in particular, *Parliament v Council*, paragraph 36 and case-law cited).

45 None the less, the Court has held also, in particular in paragraphs 17 to 21 of Case C-300/89 *Commission v Council* [1991] ECR I-2867 ('Titanium dioxide'), that recourse to a dual legal basis is not possible where the procedures laid down for each legal basis are incompatible with each other (see, in particular, *Parliament v Council*, paragraph 37 and case-law cited).

The different decision-making procedures and legal instruments render combinations of CFSP and other legal bases difficult.

In a more recent case from September 2018, the Court was given a chance to clarify how to deal with decisions or agreements that cover both CFSP and other policy areas. The 'Enhanced Partnership and Cooperation Agreement' is a bilateral mixed agreement between the EU and its Member States and the Republic of Kazakhstan. It was based on both CFSP (Articles 31(1) and 37 TEU) and TFEU provisions (Articles 91 and 100(2) TFEU (transport), and Articles 207 and 209 TFEU (trade and development cooperation)). The case was about the correct legal basis for the adoption of an EU position in the Cooperation Council that was created based on the Agreement. The Council felt that Article 31(1) TEU was to be included as a substantive legal basis of the decision, as it had also been included in the decision approving the provisional application of the Agreement with Kazakhstan. The Court thus had to apply its 'gravity test'.

Case C-244/17 *Commission v Council (PCA with Kazakhstan)*, ECLI:EU:C:2018:662

42 It is true that, as the Advocate General has noted in points 64 to 68 of her Opinion, the Partnership Agreement displays certain links with the CFSP. Thus, Article 6 of that agreement, in Title II headed 'Political dialogue, cooperation in the field of foreign and security policy', is specifically devoted to that policy, the first paragraph of Article 6 providing that the parties are to intensify their dialogue and cooperation in the area of foreign and security policy and are to address, in particular, issues of conflict prevention and crisis management, regional stability, non-proliferation, disarmament and arms control, nuclear security and export control of arms and dual-use goods. Furthermore, Articles 9 to 12 of the Partnership Agreement, which define the framework of the cooperation between the parties regarding conflict prevention and crisis management, regional stability, countering the proliferation of weapons of mass destruction and the fight against illicit trade in small arms and light weapons, may also be linked with the CFSP.

43 However, it is clear that, as the Advocate General has observed in essence in point 69 of her Opinion, those links between the Partnership Agreement and the CFSP are not sufficient for it to be held that the legal basis of the decision on the signing of that agreement, on behalf of the European Union, and its provisional application had to include Article 37 TEU.

44 First, most of the provisions of the Partnership Agreement, which contains 287 articles, fall within the common commercial policy of the European Union or its development cooperation policy.

45 Second, the provisions of the Partnership Agreement displaying a link with the CFSP and cited in paragraph 42 of the present judgment, apart from being

> few in number in comparison with the agreement's provisions as a whole, are limited to declarations of the contracting parties on the aims that their cooperation must pursue and the subjects to which that cooperation will have to relate, and do not determine in concrete terms the manner in which the cooperation will be implemented (see, by analogy, judgment of 11 June 2014, *Commission v Council*, C-377/12, ECLI:EU:C:2014:1903, paragraph 56).
>
> 46 Those provisions, which fall fully within the objective of the Partnership Agreement, set out in Article 2(2) thereof, of contributing to international and regional peace and stability and to economic development, are not therefore of a scope enabling them to be regarded as a distinct component of that agreement. On the contrary, they are incidental to that agreement's two components constituted by the common commercial policy and development cooperation.
>
> 47 Therefore, in the light of all those considerations, the Council was wrong to include Article 31(1) TEU in the legal basis of the contested decision and that decision was wrongly adopted under the voting rule requiring unanimity.

In other words, it not necessary to include a CFSP basis merely because there are CFSP elements in a certain agreement or decision. This line of reasoning is consistent with views held earlier by the Court in judgments relating to the agreements bringing Somali pirates before courts in *Mauritius* and *Tanzania*.[2]

III. Member State Obligations under CFSP

A. The Information and Consultation Obligation

> **Article 25 TEU**
>
> The Union shall conduct the common foreign and security policy by: ...
>
> (c) strengthening systematic cooperation between Member States in the conduct of policy.

The concept of *systematic cooperation* directly builds on the system of European Political Cooperation (EPC), in which it was agreed that the participating states

[2] See, respectively, Case C-658/11 *Parliament v Council (Mauritius)*, ECLI:EU:C:2014:2025 and Case C-263/14 *European Parliament v Council (Tanzania)*, ECLI:EU:C:2016:435.

'undertake to inform and consult each other on any foreign policy matters of general interest'.[3] It is this systematic cooperation that formed the core of EPC from 1970–1993. In CFSP it still serves as the key notion, in the absence of which it would be impossible for the Union to define and implement a foreign and security policy. Article 32 contains the actual procedural obligations. In principle, the scope of issues to which the systematic cooperation applies is not subject to any limitation regarding time or space.

Article 32 TEU

Member States shall inform and consult one another within the European Council and Council on any matter of foreign and security policy …

While this is indeed a very broad obligation, Article 32 TEU immediately puts this into perspective by adding a few important extra words (emphasis added):

Article 32 TEU

… on any matter of foreign and security policy *of general interest*.

The European Council has not provided any further specification of 'general interest' in Article 32 TEU. This seriously limits the strong information and consultation obligation in the first part of this Article. On the one hand, Member States are obliged to inform and consult one another, whereas, on the other hand, they are given the individual discretion to decide whether a matter is of 'general interest'. Hence, once Member States do not agree that a matter is of general interest (eg, because one Member States considers it to be of national interest only) it becomes very hard for the Union to develop a policy in that area.

However, today there are very few foreign policy issues that really do only concern a single Member State. Therefore, it can be asserted that the Member States are indeed under a broad obligation to inform and consult one another. Through the information and consultation obligation the Member States ordered themselves to use it as one of the means to attain the CFSP objectives in Article 24 and 21 TEU. The procedures stipulated in Article 32 TEU only reflect the methods by which the Member States implement CFSP. Moreover, as we have seen, the content of the norm does not provide any other conditions than that the issue should be of general interest.

Taking into account the nature of the information and consultation obligation, it is rather unfortunate that the Treaty does not further define the obligation. Yet, there

[3] See the Single European Act (1986), Art 30, para 2(a).

are no reasons to assume that the notion of consultation as used in Article 32 TEU deviates from more general definitions, which leads us to conclude that the EU Member States are to refrain from making national positions on CFSP issues of general interest public before they have discussed these positions in the framework of the CFSP cooperation. Informing and consulting one another should take place 'within the European Council and the Council' (Article 32 TEU). Keeping in mind the requirement of *systematic* cooperation, this should not be interpreted as only being within those institutions. Cooperation within the preparatory organs (Political and Security Committee, COREPER, and working parties – see below), as well as bilateral and multilateral consultations and cooperation (both in Brussels, in third states, or international organisations such as the UN) are equally covered by this obligation. In fact, as we will see, it is in these bodies that the actual systematic cooperation takes place. A second reason not to limit the cooperation to meetings of the Member States in the Council, may be found in Article 34 TEU. According to this provision, Member States shall coordinate their action in international organisations and at international conferences as well. Even when not all Member States are represented in an international organisation or an international conference, those that do participate are to keep the absent states informed of any matter of common interest (see also Chapter 6).

Over the years, CFSP cooperation at all levels has become more intense, automatic and systematic. The flipside, however, is that the larger Member States tend to ignore the information and consultation procedures whenever sensitive policy issues are at stake (eg, in Libya in 2011 and in Syria in 2012–2013). In these cases they take individual positions and diplomatic initiatives or opt for cooperation in the framework of another international organisation. This paradoxical situation reveals that CFSP may have become part of the day-to-day policy making in the national ministries as well as in Brussels, but that important or sensitive issues may also still be dealt with nationally or in other fora.

B. The Loyalty Obligation

The conclusions in the previous section bring us to the so-called 'loyalty obligation', which clearly formulates what is expected of Member States in this regard:

Article 24(3) TEU

The Member States shall support the Union's external and security policy actively and unreservedly in a spirit of loyalty and mutual solidarity and shall comply with the Union's action in this area.

The Member States shall work together to enhance and develop their mutual political solidarity. They shall refrain from any action which is contrary to the

> interests of the Union or likely to impair its effectiveness as a cohesive force in international relations.
>
> The Council and the High Representative shall ensure compliance with these principles.

To further define the kinds of action this requires of the Member States, we may find inspiration in the comparable and more general provision in Article 4(3) TEU, which lays down the 'duty of sincere cooperation' (see Chapter 2). Like Article 4(3) TEU, the specific CFSP provision contains a *positive* obligation for the Member States to actively develop the Union's policy in the indicated area. In addition, the loyalty obligation contains the *negative* obligation not to undertake 'any action which is contrary to the interests of the Union or likely to impair its effectiveness as a cohesive force in international relations' (Article 24(3) TEU). The comparison of the CFSP loyalty obligation with the duty of sincere cooperation in Article 4(3) TEU reveals its potential impact. The latter Article is often seen as part of the basis of the constitutional nature of Union law and has been frequently used by the Court of Justice in its case law. As seen in Chapter 2, the Commission has utilised the duty of sincere cooperation very effectively to ensure that Member States do not deviate from 'the Union interest' in their own external relations.[4]

IV. CFSP Decision Making and the Role of the Institutions

The institutions responsible for CFSP do not differ from those in other policy areas (see Chapter 1). Indeed, the preamble of the TEU refers to a 'single institutional framework' and Article 13 TEU on the institutions does not exclude any policy area. Yet, the role of the institutions and the balance between them is clearly different in CFSP.

The provision in Article 24(1)(2) TEU that 'the adoption of legislative acts shall be excluded' implies that CFSP decisions are not adopted on the basis of the legislative procedure, which is, inter alia, characterised by the Commission's right of initiative, co-decision by the European Parliament, and qualified majority voting (QMV) in the Council as a default rule. As we will see, neither of these elements form part of CFSP decision-making.

A. The European Council

Apart from its general role described in Article 15 TEU, the European Council has a leading role in the formulation of CFSP.

[4] See also RA Wessel, 'General Principles in CFSP Law' in V Moreno Lax, P Neuvonen, K Ziegler (eds) *Research Handbook on General Principles of EU Law* (Cheltenham, Edward Elgar, 2020).

Article 22(1) TEU

… the European Council shall identify the strategic interests and objectives of the Union …

The European Council shall act unanimously on a recommendation from the Council, adopted by the latter under the arrangements laid down for each area. Decisions of the European Council shall be implemented in accordance with the procedures provided for in the Treaties.

Article 26(1) TEU

The European Council shall identify the Union's strategic interests, determine the objectives of and define general guidelines for the common foreign and security policy, including for matters with defence implications. It shall adopt the necessary decisions …

The competences of the European Council in implementing CFSP are thus indirect: they make possible or facilitate the decision-making by the Council. Its strategic decisions form the basis for the CFSP decisions taken by the Council.

The permanent President of the European Council, an office introduced by the Lisbon Treaty, has an important role to play in CFSP.

Article 15(6) TEU

The President of the European Council shall, at his level and in that capacity, ensure the external representation of the Union on issues concerning its common foreign and security policy, without prejudice to the powers of the High Representative of the Union for Foreign Affairs and Security Policy.

This person may convene an extraordinary meeting of the European Council to define the strategic lines of the Union's policy if international developments so require (Article 26(1) TEU).

B. The Council

The Council can be regarded as the main CFSP decision-making institution.

Article 26(2) TEU

The Council shall frame the common foreign and security policy and take the decisions necessary for defining and implementing it on the basis of the general guidelines and strategic lines defined by the European Council.

More specific provisions (Articles 28 and 29 TEU) stipulate that '[t]he Council shall adopt decisions'. Furthermore, the Council decides on the voting procedures and reviews the national positions and actions Member States take pursuant to a CFSP decision. Usually CFSP decisions will be taken by the Foreign Affairs Council (FAC), consisting of the Ministers for Foreign Affairs of the Member States and chaired by the High Representative (see below).

Unanimity continues to form the basis for CFSP decisions, 'except where the Treaties provide otherwise' (Article 24(1) TEU). Yet, a number of exceptions are provided by the TEU, allowing for the use of qualified majority voting under CFSP. Some exceptions already existed pre-Lisbon and reappear in Article 31(2) TEU, which allows for QMV:

- when adopting a decision defining a Union action or position on the basis of a decision of the European Council relating to the Union's strategic interests and objectives, as referred to in Article 22(1) TEU;
- when adopting any decision implementing a decision defining a Union action or position; or
- when appointing a special representative in accordance with Article 33 TEU.

In addition, it is possible for the Council to adopt measures by QMV following a proposal submitted by the High Representative (Article 31(2) TEU). Such proposals should, however, follow a specific request from the European Council, in which, of course, Member States can foreclose the use of QMV. Moreover, QMV may be used for setting up, financing, and administering a start-up fund to ensure rapid access to appropriations in the Union's budget for urgent financing of CFSP initiatives (Article 41(3) TEU). This start-up fund may also be used for crisis management initiatives, which would potentially speed up the financing process of operations. Overall, however, it is clear that any action on the part of the EU will in the end continue to depend on the consent of its Member States.

In most cases CFSP Decisions are adopted without any debate in the Council; they have been prepared by the Council's subsidiary organs and a consensus has already been established between the representatives of the Ministers for Foreign Affairs. When decisions are taken by the Council, the issues do not appear on the agenda out of the blue. In most cases the draft decisions have already followed a long path through the various subsidiary organs of the Council. Some of these preparatory and implementing organs have an express treaty basis, others have been set up by the Council itself. According to Article 240 TFEU, the Committee of Permanent Representatives of the Member States (Coreper)[5] is responsible for preparing the work of the Council and for carrying out the tasks assigned to it by the Council. Regardless of the fact that Coreper is not explicitly mentioned in the provisions on CFSP, its competences in this area are beyond any doubt since Article 38(1) TEU provides that the Political and Security Committee shall act '[w]ithout prejudice to Article 240 TFEU'. As we have seen in Chapter 1, there are two Coreper configurations. While Coreper I consists of deputy heads of mission and deals largely with social and economic issues, Coreper II consists of EU Member State representatives at ambassadorial level and deals with political, financial and foreign policy issues.

Over the years, the Political and Security Committee (PSC) has developed into the key preparatory and implementing organ for CFSP and CSDP. This body has its origin in European Political Cooperation (EPC), where a 'Political Committee' was created.[6] The PSC is a standing committee, composed of representatives from the Member States.

Article 38(1) TEU

... a Political and Security Committee shall monitor the international situation in the areas covered by the common foreign and security policy and contribute to the definition of policies by delivering opinions to the Council at the request of the Council or of the High Representative of the Union for Foreign Affairs and Security Policy or on its own initiative. It shall also monitor the implementation of agreed policies, without prejudice to the powers of the High Representative.

The PSC is also a key actor in the Union's security and defence policy (see below).

As in all other areas, CFSP decisions are prepared in working groups or working parties (composed of representatives of the Member States and the Commission). These preparatory bodies are installed by the Council and have an important function during the first phase of the decision-making process. According to Article 19(3) of the Council's Rules of Procedure, the main task of the working groups is to carry out certain preparatory work or studies defined in advance. These may include all possible 'CFSP output', ranging from *démarches* to decisions in the form of Joint Actions. The Council secretariat prepares reports of the discussions of the working group meetings, which are circulated to all delegations through the so-called COREU/CORTESY network. On all CFSP matters the working groups report to the PSC.

[5] This French abbreviation (*Comité des représentants permanents*) is used in English texts as well.

[6] The Political Committee was introduced by the *Davignon Report* in 1970 and gained a legal treaty basis in the Single European Act (1986) Art 30, para 10(c). Usually the French abbreviation of *Comité Politique* is used.

C. The High Representative and the EEAS

As indicated in Chapter 1, unlike other Council configurations, in its configuration as 'Foreign Affairs Council' the Council is chaired not by Member State representatives, but by the High Representative (Article 18(3) TEU). Mitigating the original dominant role of the Member States in CFSP, Article 30(1) TEU lays down the general rule that '[a]ny Member State, the High Representative of the Union for Foreign Affairs and Security Policy, or the High Representative with the Commission's support, may refer any question relating to the common foreign and security policy to the Council and may submit to it initiatives or proposals as appropriate'.

Article 27 TEU

1. The High Representative of the Union for Foreign Affairs and Security Policy, who shall chair the Foreign Affairs Council, shall contribute through his proposals to the development of the common foreign and security policy and shall ensure implementation of the decisions adopted by the European Council and the Council.
2. The High Representative shall represent the Union for matters relating to the common foreign and security policy. He shall conduct political dialogue with third parties on the Union's behalf and shall express the Union's position in international organisations and at international conferences.
3. In fulfilling his mandate, the High Representative shall be assisted by a European External Action Service. This service shall work in cooperation with the diplomatic services of the Member States and shall comprise officials from relevant departments of the General Secretariat of the Council and of the Commission as well as staff seconded from national diplomatic services of the Member States. The organisation and functioning of the European External Action Service shall be established by a decision of the Council. The Council shall act on a proposal from the High Representative after consulting the European Parliament and after obtaining the consent of the Commission.

The pivotal position of the HR is strengthened by the fact that the person holding the position at the same time acts as a vice-president of the Commission (Article 17(4) and (5)). The potential impact of this combination on the role of the EU in international affairs lies in the fact that there could be more coherence between the different external policies, in particular where borders between policies are fuzzy, such as in crisis management. At the same time – as indicated above – the continued separation between CFSP and other Union issues may very well lead to a need for different procedures and hence for the use of distinct CFSP and other Union instruments. This holds true not only for the outcome of the decision-making process, but also for the process itself, in which sincere cooperation between the Council and the Commission, supported by the HR/VP and the hybrid European External Action Service (see Chapter 1), will remain of crucial importance. While extensively referring to the role of the EEAS in relation to CFSP, the 2010 EEAS Decision is clearly aimed at combining the different dimensions of the EU's external relations.

Council Decision 2010/427/EU of 26 July 2010 establishing the organisation and functioning of the European External Action Service [2010] OJ L201/30

Article 2 – Tasks

1. The EEAS shall support the High Representative in fulfilling his/her mandates as outlined, notably, in Articles 18 and 27 TEU:
   - in fulfilling his/her mandate to conduct the Common Foreign and Security Policy ('CFSP') of the European Union, including the Common Security and Defence Policy ('CSDP'), to contribute by his/her proposals to the development of that policy, which he/she shall carry out as mandated by the Council and to ensure the consistency of the Union's external action …

Indeed, a successful CFSP depends on effective leadership and the position of the High Representative has clearly been strengthened by the Lisbon reform (see also Chapter 1). The EEAS – a sort of 'EU Foreign Ministry' in all but name – has proven its value in consolidating the EU's external relations, but functions at the 'service' of the EU institutions, the rotating Presidency, and the Member States.

Mauro Gatti, *European External Action Service: Promoting Coherence through Autonomy and Coordination* (Leiden, Brill/Nijhoff, 2017) 304

Overall, the analysis shows that the legislator designed the EEAS in a way that should enable it to effectively discharge its function, ie promoting coherence. This does not mean that the Service can single-handedly ensure synergy among the different foreign policies of the EU and of its Members. The EEAS operates in cooperation (and integration) with other administrations. Even when it can impose its views *de facto* – for instance, in the management of certain international cooperation instruments – it cannot entirely ignore the views of other actors … In summary, the EEAS is a useful tool for the promotion of coherence in the present institutional framework of the Union, but its power is limited.

D. The European Commission

The limited formal competences of the Commission in the CFSP area have not led to the Commission being completely passive in this field. From the outset, the Commission has been represented at all levels in the CFSP structures. Within the negotiating process in the Council, the Commission is a full negotiating partner as in any working party or Committee (including the PSC). The President of the Commission attends European Council and other *ad hoc* meetings at that level. The Commission can be considered another 'Member State' at the table; it safeguards the *acquis communautaire* and ensures the consistency of the action of the Union other than CFSP. In the implementation of CFSP Decisions, however, the Commission's role is formally non-existent as delegation of executive competences from the Council to the Commission is prevented by the fact that CFSP acts are not legislative acts (Article 29 TFEU). Nevertheless, practice from the outset showed an involvement of the Commission in the implementation of CFSP Decisions, not least because other measures were, in some cases, essential for an effective implementation of CFSP policy decisions. Regardless of these competences of the Commission under CFSP, it is not difficult to conclude that this institution is nowhere near the pivotal position it occupies in the other policy areas of the Union. Although it is not formally excluded by Article 17 TEU, the Commission lacks its classic function as a watchdog under CFSP. The absence of an exclusive right of initiative also denies the Commission the indispensable role it has in other areas.

E. The Role of the European Parliament: A Democratic Deficit in CFSP?

The Single European Act (1986) already provided for the right of Parliament to be closely associated with European Political Cooperation and to be informed by the Presidency.[7] This provision found its way into the post-Lisbon TEU:

Article 36 TEU

The High Representative of the Union for Foreign Affairs and Security Policy shall regularly consult the European Parliament on the main aspects and the basic choices of the common foreign and security policy and the common security and defence policy and inform it of how those policies evolve. He shall ensure that the views of the European Parliament are duly taken into consideration.

Special representatives may be involved in briefing the European Parliament.

The European Parliament may address questions or make recommendations to the Council or the High Representative. Twice a year it shall hold a debate on progress in implementing the common foreign and security policy, including the common security and defence policy.

Here, too, the differences with regard to most other Union policy areas are obvious. The main difference lies in the fact that, with regard to CFSP, parliamentary influence

[7] Single European Act (1986), Art 30(4).

is not directed towards a concrete decision (as is the case in other procedures), but only towards 'the main aspects and the basic choices' of CFSP. Moreover, it is not the decision-making institution (the Council) that is ordered to consult the EP, but the High Representative.

Yet, as outlined in Chapter 1, the European Parliament is an active player in CFSP and external relations in general and is perhaps the single most active parliament in foreign policy given the many reports it produces in this area. Through these reports, debates and crucially, by using its budgetary powers, it has been able to influence CFSP on critical occasions.[8] Even more important, perhaps, is that the European Parliament's role in relation to CFSP was clarified by the Court of Justice in a number of cases. The Treaty provides the EP with an important right in the procedure to conclude international agreements:

Article 218(10) TFEU

The European Parliament shall be immediately and fully informed at all stages of the procedure.

Despite the limited role of the Court in relation to CFSP (see the following section), it held that democratic scrutiny is essential in the case of a CFSP international agreement. In other words, the CFSP context cannot form a reason to deprive the European Parliament of one of its essential functions. With regard to Article 218(10) the Court argued the following:

Case C-658/11 *Parliament v Council (Mauritius)*, ECLI:EU:C:2014:2025, para 81

That rule is an expression of the democratic principles on which the European Union is founded. In particular, the Court has already stated that the Parliament's involvement in the decision-making process is the reflection, at EU level, of the fundamental democratic principle that the people should participate in the exercise of power through the intermediary of a representative assembly (see, to that effect, Case 138/79 *Roquette Frères v Council* ECLI:EU:C:1980:249, paragraph 33, and *Parliament v Council* ECLI:EU:C:2012:472, paragraph 81).

F. The Court of Justice of the European Union

The role of the Court has proven to be essential in underlining that, despite its special nature, the CFSP is part of the Union's legal order. However, some powers of the

[8] J Santos Vara and SR Sánchez-Tabernero (eds) *The Democratisation of EU International Relations through EU Law* (Abingdon, Routledge, 2018).

Court of Justice are excluded by Treaty provisions. The reason is that most Member States argued that foreign policy be shielded from what some perceived to be 'judicial activism', which resulted in a partial denial of the Court's competences in the area of CFSP. *Prima facie*, Articles 24 TEU and 275 TFEU seem to fully exclude the Court's role in CFSP:

Article 24(1) TEU

... The Court of Justice of the European Union shall not have jurisdiction with respect to these provisions, with the exception of its jurisdiction to monitor compliance with Article 40 of this Treaty and to review the legality of certain decisions as provided for by the second paragraph of Article 275 of the Treaty on the Functioning of the European Union ...

Article 275 TFEU

The Court of Justice of the European Union shall not have jurisdiction with respect to the provisions relating to the common foreign and security policy nor with respect to acts adopted on the basis of those provisions ...

The exclusion of the Court has been part and parcel of CFSP from the outset.[9] This is not to say that today the CFSP provisions are not at all relevant for the Court of Justice. The second part of Article 275 TFEU mentions two situations in which the Court shall have jurisdiction.

Article 275 TFEU

...

However, the Court shall have jurisdiction to monitor compliance with Article 40 of the Treaty on European Union and to rule on proceedings, brought in accordance with the conditions laid down in the fourth paragraph of Article 263 of this Treaty, reviewing the legality of decisions providing for restrictive measures against natural or legal persons adopted by the Council on the basis of Chapter 2 of Title V of the Treaty on European Union [the specific provisions on CFSP].

[9] It was affirmed by the Court almost immediately in Case C-167/94 *Grau Gomis and Others*, ECLI:EU:C:1995:113.

In addition, as we have seen above, Article 40 TEU regulates the relation between CFSP and the other areas of external action.

Irrespective of the focus on demarcation, earlier cases have already made clear that, in certain constitutional areas, the Court opted for a Union-wide application of certain fundamental rules and principles. The Court made clear that wherever access of information is concerned, no distinction is made on the basis of the content of the requested document (*Swedish Union of Journalists* case).[10] Similarly, the Court argued that judicial protection was to be applied Union-wide. It referred to Article 6 TEU and concluded: 'the Union is founded on the principle of the rule of law and it respects fundamental rights as general principles … It follows that the institutions are subject to review of the conformity of their acts with the treaties and the general principles of law, just like the Member States when they implement the law of the Union.'[11] These cases underline the possibility of what may be termed 'indirect scrutiny' (we addressed this in Chapter 5 in discussing the *Kadi* case).

The Treaties also provide for an additional situation in which the Court enjoys jurisdiction in relation to CFSP. It is competent to rule on proceedings brought in accordance with the conditions laid down in the fourth paragraph of Article 263 TFEU, reviewing the legality of decisions providing for restrictive measures against natural or legal person.

Article 263(4) TFEU

Any natural or legal person may, under the conditions laid down in the first and second paragraphs, institute proceedings against an act addressed to that person or which is of direct and individual concern to them, and against a regulatory act which is of direct concern to them and does not entail implementing measures.

This provision, which gives the Court the possibility to *directly* scrutinise a CFSP measure, is the result of the proliferation of sanctions targeted at individuals in the (global) fight against terrorism. The implication is that, even if the restrictive measure are only laid down in CFSP measures, the Court has jurisdiction once the applicant is directly and individually concerned.

More recent case law confirms the notion that the exclusion of the Court's jurisdiction in relation to CFSP is to be put in perspective and is perhaps to be seen as the exception rather than as the rule. The case law that has developed since the entry into force of the Lisbon Treaty displays the Court's broader conception of its CFSP-related jurisdiction.

[10] Case T-174/95 *Svenska Journalistförbundet v Council*, EU:T:1998:127. More implicitly, this had already been accepted by the Court in Case T-194/94 *Carvel and Guardian Newspapers v Council*, ECLI:EU:T:1995:183.

[11] Case C-355/04 *P Segi and Others v Council*, EC:C:2007:116, para 51.

Case C-658/11 *Parliament v Council (Mauritius)*, ECLI:EU:C:2014:2025, para 70

[T]he final sentence of the second subparagraph of Article 24(1) TEU and the first paragraph of Article 275 TFEU introduce a *derogation* from the rule of the general jurisdiction which Article 19 TEU confers on the Court to ensure that in the interpretation and application of the Treaties the law is observed, and they must, therefore, *be interpreted narrowly* [emphasis added].[12]

Articles 24(1) TEU and 275(2) TFEU are thus not interpreted as establishing a distinct jurisdiction of the Court for the purpose of CFSP. Rather, the judicial control the Court intends to perform in relation to that policy appears to be the same as the one it exercises generally, as envisaged in Article 19 TEU, albeit within the specific limits spelled out for CFSP.

This 'generalist' conception of the Court's jurisdiction in the area of CFSP led it to consider that its legality control over CFSP restrictive measures is not limited to annulment proceedings envisaged in Article 263(4) TFEU, but includes the possibility for it to give a preliminary ruling on their validity.

Case C-72/15 *Rosneft*, ECLI:EU:C:2017:236

75 Since the purpose of the procedure that enables the Court to give preliminary rulings is to ensure that in the interpretation and application of the Treaties the law is observed, in accordance with the duty assigned to the Court under Article 19(1) TEU, it would be contrary to the objectives of that provision and to the principle of effective judicial protection to adopt a strict interpretation of the jurisdiction conferred on the Court by the second paragraph of Article 275 TFEU, to which reference is made by Article 24(1) TEU …

76 In those circumstances, provided that the Court has, under Article 24(1) TEU and the second paragraph of Article 275 TFEU, jurisdiction *ex ratione materiae* to rule on the validity of European Union acts, that is, in particular, where such acts relate to restrictive measures against natural or legal persons, it would be inconsistent with the system of effective judicial protection established by the Treaties to interpret the latter provision as excluding the possibility that the courts and tribunals of Member States may refer questions to the Court on the validity of Council decisions prescribing the adoption of such measures.

[12] See also Case C-439/13P *Elitaliana*, ECLI:EU:C:2015:753, para 41; Case C-455/14P *H v Council*, ECLI:EU:C:2016:569, para 40.

While *Rosneft* does not perhaps open the preliminary procedure to all kinds of CFSP questions – as it relates to economic sanctions that were already singled out in the Treaty – recent case law points to an interesting observation, keeping in mind the distinctive nature of CFSP as highlighted in the introduction to this chapter: in principle, the Court's legality control over certain CFSP acts is similar to the one it exercises over other EU acts whenever fundamental EU rules and principles are at stake. It is an expression of its general mandate as established in Article 19 TEU; it is governed by the same principles, in particular the principle of effective judicial remedies enshrined in Article 47 of the Charter of Fundamental Rights. The application of the general EU rules on legality control to the CFSP context illustrates that the Court considers CFSP as firmly embedded in the EU legal order, despite its procedural specificity mentioned in Article 24(1) TEU.

This development is further illustrated by several cases with a CFSP dimension. First – as we have seen in relation to the European Parliament – the Court has made clear that since international agreements in the area of CFSP are concluded on the basis of the general provisions of Article 218 TFEU, albeit subject to some specific arrangements, the Court would exercise judicial control to ensure compliance with the terms of that procedure. Second, and in the same vein, the Court has considered that it would have jurisdiction to control the legality of a decision awarding a public service contract in the context of an EU CSDP Mission given that the contract concerned involved an expenditure to be allocated to the EU budget, and thereby subject to the provisions of the EU Financial Regulation.[13] Third, the EU judicature has applied a similar approach in *H v Council and Commission* – a case brought by a staff member of the EU Police Mission in Bosnia and Herzegovina (EUPM), established under CFSP.

Case C-455/14P *H v Council*, ECLI:EU:C:2016:569, para 55

[T]he scope of the limitation, by way of derogation, on the Court's jurisdiction … cannot be considered to be so extensive as to exclude the jurisdiction of the EU judicature to review acts of staff management relating to staff members seconded by the Member States the purpose of which is to meet the needs of that mission at theatre level, when the EU judicature has, in any event, jurisdiction to review such acts where they concern staff members seconded by the EU institutions.

The above-mentioned rulings confirm that the Court of Justice considers CFSP as part and parcel of the Union's constitutional set-up.[14] Yet, it remains clear that the current regime regarding legal protection reveals several shortcomings. The most obvious

[13] Case C-439/13P *Elitaliana*, ECLI:EU:C:2015:753, para 49.

[14] C Hillion and RA Wessel, 'The Good, the Bad and the Ugly: Three Levels of Judicial Control over the CFSP', in S Blockmans and P Koutrakos (eds) *Research Handbook in EU Common Foreign and Security Policy* (Cheltenham, Edward Elgar, 2018) 65–87.

lack of judicial control is apparent when competences and decision-making procedures *within* the CFSP legal order are at stake. Keeping in mind the Member States' preference for 'intergovernmental' cooperation where CFSP is concerned, it may be understandable that they had the strong desire to prevent a body of 'CFSP law' coming into being by way of judicial activism on the part of the Court of Justice. However, it is less understandable that they were also reluctant to allow for judicial control over the *procedural* arrangements they explicitly agreed upon, although it is acknowledged that it may be difficult to unlink procedures and content and that political questions easily emerge. Similarly, it remains unclear why the CJEU should not have general jurisdiction to rule on the question of whether CFSP acts respect human rights.[15]

V. The CFSP Instruments

Article 26(2) TEU entails a general competence for the Council to 'frame the common foreign and security policy and take the decisions necessary for defining and implementing it on the basis of the general guidelines and strategic lines defined by the European Council'. A combination of this provision and the more specific legal bases allows the Council to adopt different CFSP legal and political instruments.

Article 25 TEU

The Union shall conduct the common foreign and security policy by:

(a) defining the general guidelines;
(b) adopting decisions defining:
    (i) actions to be undertaken by the Union;
    (ii) positions to be taken by the Union;
    (iii) arrangements for the implementation of the decisions referred to in points (i) and (ii);

and by

(c) strengthening systematic cooperation between Member States in the conduct of policy.

The *general guidelines* are adopted by the European Council to lay down the strategies of the Union in relation to a particular third state, region, or theme (Article 26(1) TEU). Based on the same provisions, Decisions may also be adopted

[15] See also M Brkan, 'The Role of the European Court of Justice in the Field of Common Foreign and Security Policy after the Treaty of Lisbon: New Challenges for the Future' in PJ Cardwell (ed) *EU External Relations Law and Policy in the Post-Lisbon Era* (The Hague, TMC Asser Press, 2012) 100.

by the European Council, but in relation to CFSP issues these usually take the form of 'Conclusions'.

A. Informal Instruments

CFSP is often shaped based on 'Declarations', which are often issued on behalf of the European Union by the HR. Declarations are usually reactions to world events (natural disasters, conflicts, or serious human rights violations) and are relatively easy to draft and to agree on. Although they lack a specific legal basis, the Council confirmed that the political impact of Declarations may go beyond that of formal decisions. The difference with some generally phrased decisions is not always easy to establish. Although Declarations may be used for policy orientations *vis-à-vis* a third state, they lack an operational framework, which ultimately calls for a formal legal act to implement that policy. At the same time, Declarations are often used to present the EU's view on a certain situation and to call on others to support that view.

Declaration by the High Representative Federica Mogherini on behalf of the EU on the support to the UN facilitated political process in Libya, 2 August 2019

The European Union and its Member States are united in demanding that all Libyan parties commit to a permanent ceasefire and return to a UN facilitated political process. The European Union and its Member States welcome the proposal by Special Representative of the Secretary-General of the United Nations Ghassan Salame for a truce on the occasion of the Eid al-Adha as an important step in this regard. These measures could constitute a first step towards peace …

The European Union and its Member States urge all parties to protect civilians, including migrants and refugees, by allowing and facilitating a safe, rapid and unimpeded delivery of humanitarian aid and services to all those affected, as stipulated under International Humanitarian Law and International Human Rights Law. The indiscriminate attacks on densely populated residential areas may amount to war crimes and those breaching International Humanitarian Law must be brought to justice and held to account. The European Union and its Member States demand all parties to cease the targeting of humanitarian workers and medical staff as well as hospitals and ambulances and protect national infrastructure.

In practice, CFSP systematic cooperation has also proved important with regard to the so-called 'political dialogues' with third countries. Political dialogues as such cannot be found in the Treaty on European Union but are established on the basis of general association treaties, decisions, declarations, or simply on the basis of an exchange of letters. Political dialogues take place in the framework of CFSP.

B. Legal Acts

(i) CFSP Decisions as Legal Acts?

The adoption of CFSP legal acts is a relatively rare phenomenon. In many cases the minutes of the Council meetings contain the decisions of the Council, without these being adopted as formal CFSP Decisions. CFSP legal acts cannot be adopted in the form of Regulations or Directives, but indeed only as 'Decisions'. This is again a striking difference compared to other Union policy areas. Although they are qualified as 'legal acts' (or 'actes juridiques' in, for instance, the CFSP Annual Reports), unlike the 'Decisions' in Article 288 TFEU, they cannot be adopted on the basis of a legislative procedure.

Article 25 TEU makes a distinction between decisions defining: (i) actions to be undertaken by the Union; and (ii) positions to be taken by the Union. Hence, both actions and positions can be laid down in the form of a CFSP Decision. At the same time Decisions can be used for '(iii) arrangements for the implementation of the decisions referred to in points (i) and (ii)'. Again, this follows the practice that all implementing, modifying, or repealing decisions take the shape of a CFSP Decision.

Over the years, CFSP Decisions have been used to regulate various issues. Regardless of some failed attempts to include a list of possible issue areas to be covered by CFSP in the text of the Treaty, the 'common interests' which were to be a source of CFSP Decisions, were to some extent defined by the European Council in the early days of CFSP.[16] These days, a substantive orientation can perhaps best be derived from the EU's 'Global Strategy for the European Union's Foreign and Security Policy', which was adopted in 2016, but is followed up by yearly reports.[17] When we take a first look at the contents of actual CFSP Decisions, the main objectives seem to be 'political' (eg, reinforcing democracy and respect for human rights) and 'diplomatic' (eg, preventing and solving conflicts, coordinating emergency situations). 'Economic' objectives (eg, support of economic reforms, regional development) and 'legal' objectives (eg, supporting the development of the rule of law and good governance) can also be found.

From the outset, the binding nature of CFSP Decisions has puzzled academics and practitioners alike. Yet, their normative force is quite clear, even if the text does not use the word 'bind' but rather 'commit':

Article 28(2) TEU

Decisions referred to in paragraph 1 shall commit the Member States in the positions they adopt and in the conduct of their activity.

[16] Lisbon European Council (1992), 26 and 27 June, Annex 1.

[17] Shared Vision, Common Action: A Stronger Europe – A Global Strategy for the European Union's Foreign and Security Policy, Brussels, June 2016.

Hence, CFSP Decisions, once adopted, limit the freedom of Member States in their individual policies. Member States are not allowed to adopt positions or otherwise act contrary to the Decisions. They have committed themselves to adapting their national policies to the agreed Decisions. Apart from Article 28(2) TEU, their binding nature may be derived from Article 29 TEU, which forms the legal basis for most CFSP Decisions.

Article 29 TEU

The Council shall adopt decisions which shall define the approach of the Union to a particular matter of a geographical or thematic nature. *Member States shall ensure that their national policies conform to the Union positions* [emphasis added].

The nature of Article 29 TEU Decisions as specific norms of conduct demanding a certain unconditional behaviour from the Member States, is underlined by the strict ways in which exceptions are allowed. A first possibility to depart from adopted CFSP Decision is offered by Article 28(1) TEU and concerns a change in circumstances.

Article 28(1) TEU

Where the international situation requires operational action by the Union, the Council shall adopt the necessary decisions. They shall lay down their objectives, scope, the means to be made available to the Union, if necessary their duration, and the conditions for their implementation.

If there is a change in circumstances having a substantial effect on a question subject to such a decision, the Council shall review the principles and objectives of that decision and take the necessary decisions.

Consequently, even if the original circumstances constitute an essential basis of the consent of the parties to be bound, or the effect of the change is radically to transform the extent of obligations still to be performed, Member States may not invoke the change in circumstances as a ground for not living up to the particular Decision.

The idea that CFSP Decisions, which are adopted by the Council, can only be modified or terminated by that institution, is further emphasised by the subsequent paragraphs of Article 28 TEU.

Article 28(3) TEU

Whenever there is any plan to adopt a national position or take national action pursuant to a decision as referred to in paragraph 1, information shall be provided by the Member State concerned in time to allow, if necessary, for prior consultations within the Council. The obligation to provide prior information shall not apply to measures which are merely a national transposition of Council decisions.

The rationale behind this provision is obvious: it creates a procedure to identify potential conflicting national policies at an early stage. The procedure is in the interest of the Member States themselves; it prevents the adoption of national policies which, because of a conflict with a CFSP Decision, would run the risk of being in violation of Article 28(2) TEU.

Member States are not obliged to refer national implementation measures to the Council. However, when they have major difficulties in implementing a CFSP Decision, paragraph 5 stipulates that these should be referred to the Council, which shall discuss them and seek appropriate solutions.[18] The inviolability of adopted CFSP Decisions is underlined by the rule, formulated in the last sentence of paragraph 5, that '[s]uch solutions shall not run counter to the objectives of the decision … or impair its effectiveness'. While the wording of paragraph 5 is in general quite clear, the question emerges why this procedure is related to 'major' difficulties only. What if a Member State encounters problems with the implementation of a minor part of the Decision only? Obviously, there would be no obligation to refer the case to the Council. Nevertheless, we have seen that a Decision commits the Member States; there is no ground for reading paragraph 2 as 'Decisions commit the Member States *to the largest possible extent*'. This, together with the loyalty obligation discussed above, leads to the conclusion that the discretion offered to the Member States to decide whether their implementation problems need to be brought to the attention of the Council, is limited. In case of any controversy concerning this issue, it seems to be up to the Council, to seek an appropriate solution.

Does it follow from the fact that CFSP Decisions are binding that Member States may *never* avoid the obligations laid down in the Decision in question? The CFSP provisions include one quite explicit exception:

Article 28(4) TEU

In cases of imperative need arising from changes in the situation and failing a review of the Council decision as referred to in paragraph 1, Member States

[18] The United Kingdom initially proposed a withdrawal clause in case of vital national interests. The majority of the Member States, however, were against such a clause, which would certainly erode the very nature of the Joint Action. The provision in the Luxembourg Draft Treaty of 1991 already reflected the current provision (Art K, para 4).

may take the necessary measures as a matter of urgency having regard to the general objectives of that decision. The Member State concerned shall inform the Council immediately of any such measures.

(ii) International Agreements

To engage in legal relationships with *third* states or international organisations, the European Union needs to conclude international agreements. As we have seen in Chapter 4 these agreements can also be concluded in relation to CFSP issues. Whereas the Treaties reveal one procedure only, Article 218 TFEU lists several modifications to the standard procedure that apply to agreements that 'relate exclusively to the CFSP'. Such CFSP agreements are authorised, adopted and concluded by unanimity, rather than by QMV (the default voting procedures for other agreements). Secondly, in case of CFSP agreements, the role of the European Parliament is limited to being informed, its increased role in relation to other international agreements notwithstanding. Thirdly, the opening of negotiations is not recommended by the Commission but proposed by the High Representative. And, finally, the CJEU's jurisdiction in relation to CFSP agreements is limited to situations where they influence non-CFSP provisions and where they are called upon to check the role of the EP in the procedure to conclude international agreements (see above).

These diverging procedural requirements make it difficult for the Union to combine CFSP and other issues in one single international agreement. At the same time, as underlined by, for instance, *Kazakhstan* (above), it is possible for international agreements to include CFSP elements without having to add a CFSP legal basis.

Most international agreements in the area of foreign policy fall under the Common Security and Defence Policy (see below).

(iii) Restrictive Measures

Article 215 TFEU

1. Where a decision, adopted in accordance with Chapter 2 of Title V of the Treaty on European Union, provides for the interruption or reduction, in part or completely, of economic and financial relations with one or more third countries, the Council, acting by a qualified majority on a joint proposal from the High Representative of the Union for Foreign Affairs and Security Policy and the Commission, shall adopt the necessary measures. It shall inform the European Parliament thereof.
2. Where a decision adopted in accordance with Chapter 2 of Title V of the Treaty on European Union so provides, the Council may adopt restrictive

measures under the procedure referred to in paragraph 1 against natural or legal persons and groups or non-State entities.

3. The acts referred to in this Article shall include necessary provisions on legal safeguards.

Restrictive measures – usually referred to as 'sanctions' – form a classic example of substantive CFSP and form the bulk of the CFSP Decisions. They are a combination of economic and political policies in the sense that a political goal is being achieved by economic means. The two-step system is reflected in the wordings of Article 215 TFEU: first a CFSP Decision is adopted, providing for sanctions. This is then (to be) followed by a measure adopted by the Council, following the procedure in Article 215. While this procedure involves many other actors (the High Representative, the Commission, and the European Parliament) it is interesting to note that the Council nevertheless seems to be under an obligation to deliver ('the Council shall adopt'). This may put a certain pressure on those involved, but obviously there may be some freedom to decide on the exact content of the 'measures'.

Article 215 TFEU makes clear that sanctions can be directed both towards states and towards natural or legal persons, and groups or non-State entities. If sanctions against non-state entities or persons are envisaged, this should already be made clear in the CFSP Decision (see Article 215(2) TFEU).

Apart from these types of sanctions, the Treaty foresees another situation in Article 75 TFEU, which relates to the Area of Freedom, Security and Justice (AFSJ, see Chapter 12).

Article 75 TFEU

Where necessary to achieve the objectives set out in Article 67, as regards preventing and combating terrorism and related activities, the European Parliament and the Council, acting by means of regulations in accordance with the ordinary legislative procedure, shall define a framework for administrative measures with regard to capital movements and payments, such as the freezing of funds, financial assets or economic gains belonging to, or owned or held by, natural or legal persons, groups or non-State entities.

The Council, on a proposal from the Commission, shall adopt measures to implement the framework referred to in the first paragraph.

The acts referred to in this Article shall include necessary provisions on legal safeguards.

This provision explicitly relates to 'the objectives set out in Article 67', which lists the goals and background of the AFSJ (see Chapter 12). Furthermore, Article 75 makes clear that the sanctions are directed at natural or legal persons, groups or non-state entities, in other words: not towards states. The provision is therefore the correct legal basis for financial or administrative sanctions against (potential) terrorists or individuals or groups facilitating terrorism. The available separate procedure allows for anti-terrorism measures to be adopted fast and without delay (based on a one-step procedure).

The distinction between Article 75 and Article 215 TFEU was clarified by the Court in 2012 when it held that Article 215(2) may constitute the legal basis of restrictive measures, including those designed to combat (international) terrorism, taken against natural or legal persons, groups or non-State entities by the Union when the decision to adopt those measures is part of the Union's action in the sphere of CFSP.[19]

VI. Common Security and Defence Policy

During the 1950s and 1960s far-reaching proposals were tabled to establish a common defence policy with supranational features. These proposals were never accepted and a security and defence policy developed partly as part of the Common Foreign and Security Policy (CFSP) and partly autonomously. Since 2003, the EU has launched over 30 civilian missions and military operations on three continents, deployed in response to crises ranging from post-tsunami peacebuilding in Aceh, to protecting refugees in Chad, to fighting piracy in and around Somalian waters. The Common Security and Defence Policy (CSDP) has developed into a major policy area in EU external relations. Like CFSP, it is formed on the basis of specific rules and procedures but, at the same time, we have witnessed a development from a largely intergovernmental policy area to a 'Brussels-based' cooperation in which EU preparatory organs play a leading role and Member States increasingly accept commitments.

The 'Provisions on the Common Security and Defence Policy' are laid down in Section 2 of Chapter 2 TEU on the 'Specific Provisions on the Common, Foreign and Security Policy'. This underlines that CSDP can be seen as forming part of CFSP.

Since the first drafts of the TEU the objectives included a reference to the eventual framing of a defence policy, this strengthens the idea that the security concept is also directed at security between the Member States. After all, this security would be ultimately guaranteed by a common defence policy. This holistic approach to security seems to be confirmed by the Treaty.

Article 24(1) TEU

The Union's competence in matters of common foreign and security policy shall cover … all questions relating to the Union's security, including the progressive framing of a common defence policy that might lead to a common defence.

[19] Case C-130/10 *Parliament v Council (Smart Sanctions)*, ECLI:EU:C:2012:472.

In light of this broad, yet vague, definition by the Treaties, practice reveals that CFSP is linked mostly to the practice of 'Foreign Affairs Ministries' which includes diplomacy, political dialogues and the like, whereas CSDP would be the responsibility of the Defence Ministries. This would also draw a relative clear line of division between 'military security' (CSDP) and other forms of security (CFSP).

A. The Substantive CSDP Treaty Provisions

Title V, Chapter 2, Section 2 of the TEU lists the 'Provisions on the Common Security and Defence Policy'. The 'external' nature of this policy is underlined by the first provision in this section.

Article 42(1) TEU

The common security and defence policy shall be an integral part of the common foreign and security policy. It shall provide the Union with an operational capacity drawing on civilian and military assets. The Union may use them on missions outside the Union for peace-keeping, conflict prevention and strengthening international security in accordance with the principles of the United Nations Charter. The performance of these tasks shall be undertaken using capabilities provided by the Member States.

The way CSDP functions, is that Member States provide the Union with certain civil and military assets, which may then be used for missions outside the Union. CSDP is thus intended to allow the Union to play a distinct role as a regional and global security actor, separate from that of the Member States. This is underlined by Article 43 TEU, which outlines more specifically for what the CSDP can be used. The references to 'joint disarmament operations', 'military advice and assistance tasks', 'post-conflict stabilisation', and 'the fight against terrorism' in Article 43(1) TEU were introduced by the Lisbon Treaty and allow the Union to further develop its security and defence policy beyond what was previously possible. Though some of this terminology is relatively wide, it is clear that the purposes for which the Union may use military assets are limited and are by no means equal to that of a State.

Article 43(1) TEU

The tasks referred to in Article 42(1), in the course of which the Union may use civilian and military means, shall include joint disarmament operations, humanitarian and rescue tasks, military advice and assistance tasks, conflict prevention and peace-keeping tasks, tasks of combat forces in crisis management, including peace-making and post-conflict stabilisation. All these tasks may contribute to the fight against terrorism, including by supporting third countries in combating terrorism in their territories.

Crisis management may also be needed in response to an attack on the Union itself. However, with regard to the 'defence' part of CSDP, the Treaty remains ambiguous.

Article 42(2) TEU

The common security and defence policy shall include the progressive framing of a common Union defence policy. This will lead to a common defence, when the European Council, acting unanimously, so decides.

Despite the careful wording of this provision in line with earlier versions, the Treaty does offer reasons to conclude that something has changed. First of all – and despite the claim that a 'common defence' is not yet included in CSDP – another paragraph in this Article is suddenly quite clear on the defence dimension of CSDP.

Article 42(7) TEU

If a Member State is the victim of armed aggression on its territory, the other Member States shall have towards it an obligation of aid and assistance by all the means in their power, in accordance with Article 51 of the United Nations Charter. This shall not prejudice the specific character of the security and defence policy of certain Member States. ...

Taking into account that according to the Helsinki (1999) and Laeken (2001) Declarations by the European Council 'the development of military capabilities does not imply the creation of a European army', it is unclear what the European Council will have to decide on (Article 42(2) TEU). After all, Article 42(7) comes quite close to what is usually understood by 'common defence'.

Yet, these provisions also need to be read in the context of the notion that the development of the Union's CSDP is not meant to duplicate NATO:

Article 42(7) TEU

... Commitments and cooperation in this area shall be consistent with commitments under the North Atlantic Treaty Organisation, which, for those States which are members of it, remains the foundation of their collective defence and the forum for its implementation.

While this would indeed allow the certain states (Austria, Finland, Ireland, and Sweden) not to participate in measures of collective self-defence taken in accordance with Article 51 UN Charter, the EU's collective defence obligation does not really differ from Article 5 of the NATO Treaty.[20] The special position of Member States with a neutrality/non-alignment history is also reflected in Article 42(2), which provides that CSDP 'shall not prejudice the specific character of the security and defence policy of certain Member States'.

Article 42(7) TEU was invoked by France after the Paris terrorist attacks in 2015.[21] Interestingly enough, France did not choose to invoke the so-called 'solidarity clause', which could have been more appropriate. This clause flowed from the 'Declaration on Solidarity Against Terrorism',[22] which was issued by the European Council after the Madrid terrorist attacks in March 2004, although the Declaration does not refer to a role for the Union as such, but to the 'Member States acting jointly'. It is somewhat peculiar that this solidarity clause is separated from the collective defence clause and is included in the TFEU rather than together with the CSDP provisions in the TEU. The solidarity clause does not restrict common defence to 'armed aggression', but in fact extends the obligation to terrorist attacks.

Article 222 TFEU

1. The Union and its Member States shall act jointly in a spirit of solidarity if a Member State is the object of a terrorist attack or the victim of a natural or man-made disaster. The Union shall mobilise all the instruments at its disposal, including the military resources made available by the Member States, to:

    (a)
    - prevent the terrorist threat in the territory of the Member States;
    - protect democratic institutions and the civilian population from any terrorist attack;
    - assist a Member State in its territory, at the request of its political authorities, in the event of a terrorist attack;

    (b) assist a Member State in its territory, at the request of its political authorities, in the event of a natural or man-made disaster.

[20] Art 5 of the North Atlantic Treaty reads: 'The Parties agree that an armed attack against one or more of them in Europe or North America shall be considered an attack against them all and consequently they agree that, if such an armed attack occurs, each of them, in exercise of the right of individual or collective self-defence recognised by Article 51 of the Charter of the United Nations, will assist the Party or Parties so attacked by taking forthwith, individually and in concert with the other Parties, such action as it deems necessary, including the use of armed force, to restore and maintain the security of the North Atlantic area …'

[21] 3426th Council meeting Foreign Affairs, Brussels, 16 and 17 November 2015.

[22] Brussels European Council 25–26 March 2004, Presidency Conclusions.

2. Should a Member State be the object of a terrorist attack or the victim of a natural or man-made disaster, the other Member States shall assist it at the request of its political authorities. To that end, the Member States shall coordinate between themselves in the Council.
3. The arrangements for the implementation by the Union of the solidarity clause shall be defined by a decision adopted by the Council acting on a joint proposal by the Commission and the High Representative of the Union for Foreign Affairs and Security Policy. The Council shall act in accordance with Article 31(1) of the Treaty on European Union where this decision has defence implications. The European Parliament shall be informed.

While the wording of the solidarity clause leaves room for both the Member States and the Council regarding the type and scope of their reaction, it may be seen as an innovation to the previous legal regime, where no obligations for the Member States or competences of the Council formed part of the Treaties.

B. The Institutionalisation of CSDP

As CSDP can be seen as forming part of CFSP, the decision making takes place along similar lines. Decisions are taken by the Council.

Article 42(4) TEU

Decisions relating to the common security and defence policy, including those initiating a mission as referred to in this Article, shall be adopted by the Council acting unanimously on a proposal from the High Representative of the Union for Foreign Affairs and Security Policy or an initiative from a Member State. The High Representative may propose the use of both national resources and Union instruments, together with the Commission where appropriate.

Both the HR and the Member States may take the initiative for a decision. A difference with CFSP is that the HR cannot work together with the Commission on an initiative; nor is it possible to decide on the basis of QMV (not even in the case of implementing decisions). These rules underline the preference of most Member States to keep CSDP as intergovernmental as possible. Yet, the role of some organs no doubt points to a serious institutionalisation of this policy area. Apart from the HR, which according to Article 43(2) TEU 'shall ensure coordination of the civilian and military aspects of [the Petersberg] tasks', the Political and Security Committee (PSC) has been granted a pivotal role in CSDP. Irrespective of the fact that it is hardly mentioned in the CSDP section, the PSC has developed into the centre around which all CSDP actions converge. It meets at the ambassadorial level as the preparatory body for the Council to keep track of the international situation, help to define policies within CFSP and CSDP, and prepare a coherent EU response to a crisis.

AE Juncos and C Reynolds, 'The Political and Security Committee: Governing in the Shadow' (2007) 12 *European Foreign Affairs Review* 127, 136

In the event of … a crisis, the PSC constitutes the key strategic actor leading the formulation and implementation of a [CSDP] operation. According to the EU's crisis management procedures, all available information relating to the ongoing crisis should be forwarded to the PSC which will subsequently be convened in order to agree on a Crisis Management Concept. At this stage, coordination with the Member States, NATO, the Commission and other institutional actors such as the EU Military Committee is crucial. The PSC is also at the core of the process leading to the drafting of the relevant Decision, Concept of Operations and Operational Plan which together constitute the key documents guiding the implementation of the operation on the ground. Given the nature of crisis management, these phases often take place simultaneously. Once agreed at the PSC, these documents are forwarded to the Council essentially to be rubber-stamped since it is rare that the Council will reopen issues that have been already approved by the PSC.

The institutionalisation of CSDP included the creation of several specific organs, some of which do not have an explicit Treaty basis. The European Council (Nice, December 2000) decided to establish permanent political and military structures. Apart from the PSC, CSDP depends on a number of other bodies, which are partly embedded in the EEAS.

The European Union Military Committee (EUMC) is the highest military body set up within the Council. It is composed of the Chiefs of Defence of the Member States, who are regularly represented by their permanent military representatives. The EUMC provides the PSC with advice and recommendations on all military matters within the EU.

In parallel with the EUMC, the PSC is advised by a Committee for Civilian Aspects of Crisis Management (CIVCOM) which provides information, drafts recommendations and gives its opinion to the PSC on civilian aspects of crisis management.

The Crisis Management and Planning Directorate (CMPD) contributes to the objectives of the European External Action Service, the Common Security and Defence Policy and a more secure international environment by the political-strategic planning of CSDP civilian missions and military operations, ensuring coherence and effectiveness of those actions as part of the EU comprehensive approach to crisis management and developing CSDP partnerships, policies, concepts, and capabilities.

The European Union Military Staff is a Directorate-General at the EEAS and composed of both military and civilian experts seconded to the EEAS by Member States and officials of the EEAS. The EUMS is the source of military expertise within the EEAS and works under the direction of the Military Committee and Member States' Chiefs of Defence and under the direct authority of the High Representative/Vice-President of the European Commission.

The Civilian Planning and Conduct Capability (CPCC), which is also part of the EEAS, is the permanent structure responsible for an autonomous operational conduct of civilian CSDP operations. Under the political control and strategic direction of the Political and Security Committee and the overall authority of the High Representative, the CPCC ensures the effective planning and conduct of civilian CSDP crisis management operations, as well as the proper implementation of all mission-related tasks.

Apart from these bodies, the Satellite Centre and the Institute for Security Studies were taken over from the Western European Union by taking over the personnel contracts and the agreements with other organisations. The Satellite Centre (in Torrejón de Ardoz, Spain) supports CSDP by supplying satellite images; the Institute for Security Studies (EUISS in Paris) does academic research on topics relevant for the development of CSDP.

One body is explicitly mentioned in the Treaty, the European Defence Agency (EDA). Its role is defined as follows:

Article 42(3) TEU

The European Defence Agency shall identify operational requirements, shall promote measures to satisfy those requirements, shall contribute to identifying and, where appropriate, implementing any measure needed to strengthen the industrial and technological base of the defence sector, shall participate in defining a European capabilities and armaments policy, and shall assist the Council in evaluating the improvement of military capabilities.

It is further defined in Protocol No 10 On Permanent Structured Cooperation Established by Article 42 TEU and has been given a central role in defining and coordinating the available military capabilities.

C. CSDP Decisions and International Agreements

In legal terms, CSDP takes shape in the form of decisions and international agreements. As according to Article 42(1) TEU '[t]he common security and defence policy shall be an integral part of the common foreign and security policy', most CFSP rules apply to CSDP as well and Article 28 TEU can be used as a legal basis for CSDP Decisions.

Article 28(1) TEU

Where the international situation requires operational action by the Union, the Council shall adopt the necessary decisions. They shall lay down their objectives, scope, the means to be made available to the Union, if necessary their duration, and the conditions for their implementation ...

In addition, the adoption of CSDP Decisions is regulated in Articles 42(4) and 43(2) TEU, which serve as specific legal bases.

Article 42(4) TEU

Decisions relating to the common security and defence policy, including those initiating a mission as referred to in this Article, shall be adopted by the Council acting unanimously on a proposal from the High Representative of the Union for Foreign Affairs and Security Policy or an initiative from a Member State. The High Representative may propose the use of both national resources and Union instruments, together with the Commission where appropriate.

Article 43(2) underlines the role of the Council and point to a specific task of the HR.

Article 43(2) TEU

The Council shall adopt decisions ... defining their objectives and scope and the general conditions for their implementation. The High Representative of the Union for Foreign Affairs and Security Policy, acting under the authority of the Council and in close and constant contact with the Political and Security Committee, shall ensure coordination of the civilian and military aspects of such tasks.

As CSDP is part of CFSP it is clear that other EU legal instruments such as Regulations and Directives cannot be used for CSDP issues. Yet – as in CFSP – the legal nature of CSDP Decisions is beyond any doubt and all Decisions are published in the L (Legislation) version of the Official Journal of the EU.

As CSDP is mainly intended to establish missions outside the EU (and so far, no CSDP mission has operated in one of the Member States), many Decisions have the purpose of adopting international agreements. For the conclusion of agreements, the CFSP procedures apply (see above), which implies that not only Article 37 TEU serves as the general legal basis, but also that the procedure in Article 218 TFEU applies to the negotiation and conclusion of the agreements.

CSDP agreements are concluded for a variety of different purposes. Most agreements concern the *participation of third states in CSDP operations*. These not only regulate the legal issues surrounding the participation of non-EU members but also ensure the autonomy of the Union's decision making. Thus, irrespective of the participation of third states (ranging from Switzerland to New Zealand and the USA) the operations remain a true EU mission which are covered by the EU legal order and follow the specific CSDP procedures. With a limited number of third states (including Ukraine, Canada, Bulgaria, Iceland, Norway, Romania, Turkey, Montenegro, the USA, Serbia, New Zealand and Albania), so-called *Framework Participation Agreements* have been concluded. These agreements facilitate the participation of those states in operations to which they are invited.

A second category concerns the Status of Forces Agreements (SOFAs) and Status of Missions Agreements (SOMAs). These agreements regulate the legal rights and duties of the forces/missions and their personnel in the third country where the operation is established. On the basis of these agreements, the CSDP mission enjoys the status of a diplomatic mission under the 1961 Vienna convention on Diplomatic Relations and privileges and immunities of personnel are unusually regulated in detail.

A Sari, 'Status of Forces and Status of Mission Agreements Under the ESDP: The EU's Evolving Practice' (2008) 19 *European Journal of International Law* 67, 97

The EU's practice in negotiating status agreements with third parties has evolved along two main lines over the past fifteen years. First, the status agreements concluded by the EU have become increasingly more sophisticated. The most recent agreements regulate a broader range of matters and do so in greater detail than most of their predecessors, including the first [CSDP] status agreement, the EUPM SOMA, did. Second, the process of concluding status agreements under the [CSDP] has been simplified. The experiences gained during the first few [CSDP] missions have clearly demonstrated that the procedures governing the conclusion of international agreements under [the former] Article 24 TEU were unwieldy and therefore unsuited for keeping up with the fast pace of international crisis management operations. In response, the Council adopted the EU Model SOFA and SOMA to eliminate the need to issue a fresh negotiating mandate to the Presidency in the course of future EU crisis management operations.

A specific set of agreements deal with security procedures for the exchange of information. EU operations depend on classified information which needs to be secured once it is shared with third states.

Finally, in the context of Operation Atalanta in Somalian waters, a new category of CSDP international agreements emerged: transfer agreements. Transfer agreements have, inter alia, been concluded with Kenya, the Seychelles, Mauritius and Tanzania. The agreements are meant to lay down the conditions of transfer of suspected pirates and associated seized property from the EU force to the partner country as well as the treatment of the suspects.

D. Flexible and Permanent Structured Cooperation

Some of the shortcomings in early EU crisis management seemed to relate to the *ad hoc* implementation of CSDP. The current legal framework aims to counter this with the introduction of some form of institutionalisation of procedures, formats, and (civil and military) capabilities. First, the Lisbon Treaty introduced a new form of *ad hoc* flexibility:

Article 44(1) TEU

... the Council may entrust the implementation of a task to a group of Member States which are willing and have the necessary capability for such a task. Those Member States, in association with the High Representative of the Union for Foreign Affairs and Security Policy, shall agree among themselves on the management of the task.

This allows the Union to implement CSDP by sub-contracting it to so-called 'coalitions of the able and willing'. An example of this arrangement can be found in Operation Artemis, in which France took the initiative to form a group of EU Member States and other states to assist the UN operation MONUC in the Democratic Republic of Congo.

A second form of enhanced cooperation may be found in relation to the notion of 'permanent structured cooperation' or 'PESCO'.[23]

Article 42(6) TEU

Those Member States whose military capabilities fulfil higher criteria and which have made more binding commitments to one another in this area with a view to the most demanding missions shall establish permanent structured cooperation within the Union framework.

[23] S Biscop, 'Permanent Structured Cooperation and the Future of the ESDP: Transformation and Integration' (2008) 13 *European Foreign Affairs Review* 431.

The permanent structured cooperation is further elaborated upon by Article 46 TEU and by Protocol No 10. According to this Protocol, permanent structured cooperation can be seen as an institutionalised form of cooperation in the field of defence policy between able and willing Member States. In that sense it may be regarded as a special form of enhanced cooperation, although the term is not used.

Nowhere a reference is made to the creation of a 'European army'. Any explicit hints in that direction would have been unacceptable for certain Member States (in particular Denmark). Nevertheless, PESCO was formally launched in 2017.

Council Decision (CFSP) 2017/2315 of 11 December 2017 establishing permanent structured cooperation (PESCO) and determining the list of participating Member States [2017] OJ L 331/57

THE COUNCIL OF THE EUROPEAN UNION,

...

Article 1

Establishment of permanent structured cooperation

Permanent structured cooperation (PESCO) within the Union framework is hereby established between those Member States whose military capabilities fulfil higher criteria as referred to in Article 1 of Protocol No 10, and which have made commitments to one another in this area as referred to in Article 2 of that Protocol, with a view to the most demanding missions, and contributing to the fulfilment of the Union level of ambition.

...

On the basis of Article 2 of this Decision, the vast majority of Member States have agreed to participate. PESCO is implemented based on so-called 'projects' (Article 5), the first 17 of which were defined in 2018, ranging from the establishment of a European Medical Command, an EU Training Mission Competence Centre, Cyber Rapid Response Teams and Mutual Assistance in Cyber Security, to Military Disaster Relief and an upgrade of Maritime Surveillance.

S Blockmans, 'The EU's Modular Approach to Defence Integration: An Inclusive, Ambitious and Legally Binding PESCO?' (2018) 55 *Common Market Law Review* 1785, 1825

In light of the generally ad hoc nature of the CFSP/CSDP, the EU's efficiency as an international actor in security and defence matters is being increased in function of the objective to contribute to the maintenance of international peace and security (Art. 21(2)(c) TEU). At the same time, politicians and policy-makers should not promise to the public what PESCO cannot deliver: an *avant garde* able to carry out the most demanding missions. Both concepts have been diluted in the inception phase as a result of the drive to launch this unique form of differentiated integration in as inclusive a format as possible. In fact, the modular approach to structured cooperation may end up serving as a permanent vehicle for opt-outs and exemptions in the area of defence. Going by Member States' past experience in other EU policy fields, the 'Just do it!' attitude that many stakeholders and observers seem to rely on will simply not do, especially if the big Member States that should lead by example persist in their bad habits. The absence of legally binding commitments and supranational enforcement mechanisms imply that national sovereign decisions will remain the norm. And structural differences between Member States' strategic cultures (threat assessments, national postures to taking risks, operational experiences) and institutional preferences (NATO) are likely to impede the emergence of a 'common defence' in the sense of Article 24(1) TEU for some time to come.

VII. CSDP Missions and Operations

FRANCO-BRITISH SUMMIT

JOINT DECLARATION ON EUROPEAN DEFENSE

Saint-Malo, 4 December 1998

The Heads of State and Government of France and the United Kingdom are agreed that:

1. The European Union needs to be in a position to play its full role on the international stage. This means making a reality of the Treaty of Amsterdam, which will provide the essential basis for action by the Union. It will be important to achieve full and rapid implementation of the Amsterdam provisions on CFSP. This includes the responsibility of the European Council to decide on the progressive framing of a common defence policy in the framework of CFSP. The Council must be able to take decisions on an intergovernmental basis, covering the whole range of activity set out in Title V of the Treaty of European Union.
2. To this end, the Union must have the capacity for autonomous action, backed up by credible military forces, the means to decide to use them and a readiness to do so, in order to respond to international crises …

Both military and civilian missions may be established on the basis of the CSDP provisions. On 1 January 2003, the EU launched the European Union Police Mission in Bosnia and Herzegovina (EUPM) as its first-ever civilian crisis management operation within the framework of the CSDP.[24] On 31 March 2003, the EU deployed Operation Concordia, its inaugural military mission, to follow up on NATO's efforts to contribute to a stable and secure environment in FYROM.[25]

The EU has never acted in the capacity of enforcer of the peace (eg, like NATO in Kosovo in 1999) nor in defence against an armed attack on its territory. While, as we have seen, Article 42(7) was invoked by France after the terrorist attacks in Paris in 2015, the implementation of the aid and assistance by other Member States very much took place on an *ad hoc* basis.

VIII. The Broader Picture of EU External Relations Law

The image of CFSP as a purely 'intergovernmental' form of international cooperation is not supported by the Treaty provisions. Regardless of the *prima facie* broad scope of CFSP on the basis of its objectives (which indeed seem to cover almost every conceivable area of foreign and security policy) it is not to be seen as a *common policy* in the same way as the concept is used in, for instance, the Common Commercial Policy. The non-exclusive nature of CFSP is paramount. The competences of the institutions, the obligations of the Member States, and the decision-making procedures all reflect the intention of the Member States to create a common policy that would not unconditionally *replace* the national policies of the individual states, but that would only emerge *where and when possible*. Despite specific obligations aiming at the establishment of a common policy, a number of vague notions ('important common interests', 'general interest', 'reasons of national policy') allow for a considerable margin of appreciation on the part of the Member States. Whenever a common policy does not prove possible, Member States are free to pursue their own national foreign policies.

This chapter further outlined the emergence and further development of the Union's security and defence policy. In a relatively short period, the EU has developed into a global security actor. While the number and size of civilian and military missions may not be that impressive, CSDP has become an important policy area and is a key element of the Union's foreign and security policy.

[24] See Council Decision 2002/968/CFSP of 10 December 2002 concerning the implementation of Joint Action 2002/210/CFSP on the European Union Police Mission [2002] OJ L335/1.

[25] See Council Decision 2003/202/CFSP of 18 March 2003 relating to the launch of the EU military operation in the Former Yugoslav Republic of Macedonia [2003] OJ L76/43. For an up-to-date list, see the website of the Council of the EU, CSDP operations. Available at: https://eeas.europa.eu/topics/military-and-civilian-missions-and-operations/430/military-and-civilian-missions-and-operations_en.

IX. Sources and Further Reading

Bátora, J and D Spence (eds) *The European External Action Service: European Diplomacy Post-Westphalia* (Basingstoke, Palgrave MacMillan, 2015).

Butler, G, *Constitutional Law of the EU's Common Foreign and Security Policy: Competence and Institutions in External Relations* (Oxford, Hart Publishing, 2019).

Blockmans, S and P Koutrakos (eds) *Research Handbook in EU Common Foreign and Security Policy* (Cheltenham, Edward Elgar Publishing, 2018).

Blockmans, S and RA Wessel, 'The European Union and Peaceful Settlement of Disputes in its Neighbourhood: The Emergence of a New Regional Security Actor?' in A Antoniadis, R Schütze and E Spaventa (eds) *The European Union and Global Emergencies: A Law and Policy Analysis* (Oxford, Hart Publishing, 2011) 73–103.

Blockmans, S, J Wouters and T Ruys (eds) *The European Union and Peacebuilding: Policy and Legal Aspects* (The Hague, TMC Asser Press, 2010).

Cardwell, PJ, 'On "Ring-Fencing" the Common Foreign and Security Policy in the Legal Order of the European Union' (2015) 64 *Northern Ireland Legal Quarterly* 443.

Gatti, M, *European External Action Service: Promoting Coherence through Autonomy and Coordination* (Leiden, Brill/Nijhoff, 2017).

Koutrakos, P, *The EU Common Security and Defence Policy* (Oxford, Oxford University Press, 2013).

Wessel, RA, *The European Union's Foreign and Security Policy: A Legal Institutional Perspective* (The Hague, Kluwer Law International, 1999).

Wessel, RA, 'General Principles in CFSP Law' in V Morena, P Neuvonen and K Ziegler (eds) *Research Handbook on General Principles of EU Law* (Cheltenham, Edward Elgar Publishing, 2020).

Wessel, RA, 'Resisting Legal Facts: Are CFSP Norms as Soft as They Seem?' (2015) 20 *European Foreign Affairs Review* 123.

10

EU External Human Rights Policy

Central Issues

- The Union is founded on a number of values which includes respect for human rights. Successive Treaty amendments have made increasingly explicit that respect for human rights has both an internal and external dimension.
- While the EU regularly proclaims its ambition to remain at the forefront of the protection and promotion of human rights worldwide, there are significant differences between the internal and external dimension of Union action in the context of human rights, particularly in terms of the lack of legislative competence and role of specific Union institutions.
- In its external dimension, respect for human rights is one of the core objectives of the EU's external action. This means, inter alia, that the EU must define and pursue common policies and actions and cooperate to pursue objectives including the consolidation and support of human rights. The EU is furthermore under a Treaty *obligation to act consistently with international law, including customary international law and, by extension, international human rights obligations.*
- To promote and protect human rights in its relations with the wider world and fulfil its regularly proclaimed ambition to be the leading global actor when it comes to the universal protection and promotion of human rights, the EU relies on multiple instruments, and mechanisms. To ensure and enhance the clarity, coherence, and effectiveness of its external human rights policy, the EU has adopted inter alia its first Strategic Framework and Action Plan on Human Rights and Democracy in 2012, with a second Action Plan adopted in 2015.

- Four cross-cutting challenges may be identified when it comes to the EU's external promotion of its values, including respect for human rights: the delivery challenge; the coherence challenge; the effectiveness challenge, and the credibility challenge.

I. Introduction

The promotion and protection of human rights, democracy and the rule of law is regularly presented as a core priority of the EU's foreign and security policy by the main EU institutions such as the European Commission, the European Parliament or the Council of the EU (see Chapters 1 and 9). It is not unusual in this context to see EU institutions claiming that the EU strives to be 'the leading global actor in the universal promotion and protection of human rights'.[1]

As recalled by the Preamble to what is now the Treaty on European Union and further made clear by several provisions within the Treaty, the EU was established by countries who subscribe to the principles of liberty, democracy, respect for human rights and the rule of law; the EU itself is said to be based on these principles. Legal consequences and commitments flow from this understanding. To exclusively focus on respect for human rights, this first essentially means that both the EU and its Member States, when national authorities act within the scope of EU Law, must comply with EU human rights standards as respect for human rights is a condition of the lawfulness of EU measures. In addition, the Treaties compel the EU to consolidate and support human rights in its relations with the wider world.

The fact that the EU Treaties refer to both human and fundamental rights may be a source of confusion. The terms of 'human rights' or 'fundamental rights' are, however, used by the Treaties as equivalent to one another.

European Union Agency for Fundamental Rights (2019) 'What is the difference between human rights and fundamental rights?'[2]

The term 'fundamental rights' is used in European Union (EU) to express the concept of 'human rights' within a specific EU internal context. Traditionally, the term 'fundamental rights' is used in a constitutional setting whereas the term 'human rights' is used in international law. The two terms refer to

[1] European Parliament Resolution of 12 December 2018 on the annual report on human rights and democracy in the world 2017 and the European Union's policy on the matter, 2018/2098(INI), para A.

[2] 'Frequently Asked Questions' (*European Union Agency for Fundamental Rights*, 2019). Available at: http://fra.europa.eu/en/about-fundamental-rights/frequently-asked-questions.

similar substance as can be seen when comparing the content in the Charter of Fundamental Rights of the European Union with that of the European Convention on Human Rights and the European Social Charter.

II. Legal Framework

A. Key Primary Law Provisions

Respect for human rights did not feature in the earliest treaties of the European Community, which was primarily envisioned as an economic entity. Neither the Treaty of Paris nor the Treaty of Rome, which established the European Economic Community, precursor to the European Union, made human rights either a general principle or an objective to be pursued by the Community, though the European Court of Justice quickly recognised respect for human rights as a general principle of (then EEC) law in 1969.[3]

In their capacity as Masters of the Treaties, EU Member States were arguably slow to recognise this judicial development. When they did so in 1992, their recognition was limited, beginning with ex-Article F(2) TEU which merely provided that the EU 'shall respect fundamental rights, as guaranteed by the European Convention for the Protection of Human Rights and Fundamental Freedoms … and as they result from the constitutional traditions common to the Member States, as general principles of Community law'. This provision was subsequently replaced via the Amsterdam Treaty by ex-Article 6 TEU which provided that the EU is founded, inter alia, on the principle of respect for human rights before reiterating the text first introduced in 1992. The Amsterdam Treaty also made respect for human rights a justiciable transversal Treaty principle in so far as the European Court of Justice was granted jurisdiction.[4]

Following the entry into force of the Lisbon Treaty in 2009, radical changes were made to the EU's human rights architecture.[5] After recalling in the new Article 2 TEU that respect for human rights is not only one of the values which is common to the EU Member States but also one of the foundational values on which the EU is based, the Lisbon Treaty gave for the first time legally binding force to the provisions of

[3] C-29/69 *Erich Stauder v City of Ulm – Sozialamt*, ECLI:EU:C:1969:57. For an historical overview of the Court of Justice's case law before the Lisbon Treaty, see eg, H Abbott, 'The European Court of Justice and the Protection of Fundamental Rights' (2008) 15 *Irish Journal of European Law* 79.

[4] For further analysis, see K Lenaerts (President of the CJEU 2015–2021), 'Respect for Fundamental Rights as a Constitutional Principle of the European Union' (2000) 6 *Columbia Journal of European Law* 1, 4 *et seq*.

[5] For more details on the historical overview of the evolution of the EU's commitment to human rights when acting externally, see A Egan and L Pech, 'Respect for Human Rights as a General Objective of the EU's External Action' in S Douglas-Scott and N Hatzis (ed) *Research Handbook on EU Law and Human Rights* (Cheltenham, Edward Elgar Publishing, 2017).

the EU Charter of Fundamental Rights while also simultaneously empowering and committing the EU to seek accession to the ECHR.

Article 2 TEU

The Union is founded on the values of respect for human dignity, freedom, democracy, equality, the rule of law and respect for human rights, including the rights of persons belonging to minorities. These values are common to the Member States in a society in which pluralism, non-discrimination, tolerance, justice, solidarity and equality between women and men prevail.

Article 6 TEU

1. The Union recognises the rights, freedoms and principles set out in the Charter of Fundamental Rights of the European Union of 7 December 2000, as adapted at Strasbourg, on 12 December 2007, which shall have the same legal value as the Treaties. The provisions of the Charter shall not extend in any way the competences of the Union as defined in the Treaties.
2. The Union shall accede to the European Convention for the Protection of Human Rights and Fundamental Freedoms. Such accession shall not affect the Union's competences as defined in the Treaties.
3. Fundamental rights, as guaranteed by the European Convention for the Protection of Human Rights and Fundamental Freedoms and as they result from the constitutional traditions common to the Member States, shall constitute general principles of the Union's law.

The Lisbon Treaty also brought about a greater and clearer emphasis on the importance of respect for human rights as regards the EU's external relations, which is also a common feature in national constitutions.[6] The first reference to human rights provisions which directly relate to the external affairs of the Union is Article 3(5) TEU, which summarises the objectives of the EU in its relations with the 'wider world' (see also Chapter 1). This reference to the promotion of values and interests to the 'wider world' can be understood to widen the scope of relevance to more than that strictly related to the EU's external policy under CFSP, development cooperation or humanitarian aid, and instead refer to all policy areas which could have external impact.

Article 3(5) TEU

In its relations with the wider world, the Union shall uphold and promote its values and interests and contribute to the protection of its citizens. It shall

[6] J Larik, *Foreign Policy Objectives in European Constitutional Law* (Oxford, Oxford University Press, 2016) 108–10.

contribute to peace, security, the sustainable development of the Earth, solidarity and mutual respect among peoples, free and fair trade, eradication of poverty and the protection of human rights, in particular the rights of the child, as well as to the strict observance and the development of international law, including respect for the principles of the United Nations Charter.

Article 3(5) TEU obligates the EU to uphold and promote Union values, including human rights and the rule of law in its external action. By reference to 'contributing' to the wider world, Article 3(5) TEU reflects the positioning of the EU as a force for multilateralism by connecting the protection of human rights with international law and the principles of the UN Charter. In *Air Transport Association of America* (analysed in Chapter 5) the Court held that Article 3(5) TEU establishes an obligation to act consistently with international law, including customary international law, and by extension the international human rights obligations contained there (see also below).[7]

Article 21 TEU directs the conduct of the EU's external action to be systematically guided by the 'principles which have inspired its own creation' and obligates the Union to define and pursue common policies and actions, and cooperate to pursue objectives including the consolidation and support of human rights.

Article 21 TEU

1. The Union's action on the international scene shall be guided by the principles which have inspired its own creation, development and enlargement, and which it seeks to advance in the wider world: democracy, the rule of law, the universality and indivisibility of human rights and fundamental freedoms, respect for human dignity, the principles of equality and solidarity, and respect for the principles of the United Nations Charter and international law. …
2. The Union shall define and pursue common policies and actions, and shall work for a high degree of cooperation in all fields of international relations, in order to:
   (a) safeguard its values, fundamental interests, security, independence and integrity;
   (b) consolidate and support democracy, the rule of law, human rights and the principles of international law;

   …

[7] Case C-366/10 *Air Transport Association of America*, ECLI:EU:C:2011:864, para 101.

Article 21(1) TEU has the effect of mainstreaming human rights and the rule of law as objectives of the external relations of the Union. Reference to the 'universality and indivisibility of human rights and fundamental freedoms', an echo of the United Nations Vienna Declaration of 1993, embraces a universalist vision of human rights. By requiring coherence between internal and external dimensions as regards human rights policies, it interlinks commitment to human rights at an internal level and external level. This is further supported by Article 21(3) TEU which refers to the respect of these principles and pursuit of objectives 'in the development and implementation … of the external aspects of its other policies', implying the external aspect of its internal policies.

There are, however, significant differences between the internal and external dimension of Union action in the context of human rights, particularly in terms of the lack of legislative competence and role of specific Union institutions. For example, while the Court of Justice has played a significant, if not crucial, role in the internal development of human rights protection against EU action and Member State action (when national authorities act within the scope of EU law), the Court of Justice has not yet contributed to a similar degree to the development of human rights as regards external action policies. This is due to a number of factors such as its limited jurisdiction over CFSP matters (see Chapter 9).[8]

Looking beyond CFSP matters, it is important to recall that the European Court of Justice has taken into account the 'guidelines supplied by international treaties for the protection of human rights on which the Member States have collaborated or of which they are signatories'[9] when it had to identify, interpret and protect fundamental rights within the EU legal order as general principles of EU law prior to the entry into force of the EU Charter of Fundamental Rights. In this task, the Court has repeatedly emphasised the 'special significance' of the ECHR. However, to this day, the ECHR is not itself part of EU law in the absence of EU accession to the ECHR that was blocked by the Court of Justice when it concluded in its Opinion 2/13 that the draft EU-ECHR accession agreement is not compatible with the EU law, noting, inter alia, that the draft agreement 'fails to have regard to the specific characteristics of EU law with regard to the judicial review of acts, actions or omissions on the part of the EU in CFSP matters'.[10]

[8] J Wouters, 'The EU's Post-Lisbon Legal and Institutional Architecture on Human Rights and Democracy' in F Gómez Isa, C Churruca Muguruza and J Wouters (eds) *EU Human Rights and Democratization Policies: Achievements and Challenges* (Abingdon, Routledge, 2018) 31. For a rapid overview and critique, see L Pech, '"A Union Founded on the Rule of Law": Meaning and Reality of the Rule of Law as a Constitutional Principle of EU Law' (2010) 6 *European Constitutional Law Review* 359, 393–94.

[9] See eg Opinion 2/94 (*ECHR*), ECLI:EU:C:1996:140, para 33.

[10] Opinion 2/13 (*ECHR II*), ECLI:EU:C:2014:2454, para 257. In a resolution adopted on 12 February 2019, the European Parliament asked the 'Commission to take the necessary steps to eliminate the legal barriers that prevent the conclusion of the accession process, and to present a new draft agreement for the accession of the Union to the ECHR providing positive solutions to the objections raised by the CJEU in Opinion 2/13 of 18 December 2014'. See European Parliament Resolution on the implementation of the Charter of Fundamental Rights of the EU in the EU institutional framework, 2017/2089(INI), para 29. For further analysis of the Court's limited jurisdiction over CFSP matters in the light of Opinion 2/13, see C Hillion, 'Decentralised Integration? Fundamental Rights Protection in the EU Common Foreign and Security Policy' (2016) 1 *European Papers* 55.

Following the entry into force of the EU Charter of Fundamental Rights, the EU is furthermore under an explicit obligation laid down in Article 53 of this document to maintain the level of protection afforded by human rights instruments to which 'the Union or all the Member States are party'. Other provisions of EU primary law refer explicitly to some international treaties: for instance, Article 78 of the TFEU refers to the Geneva Convention of 28 July 1951 and the Protocol of 31 January 1967 relating to the status of refugees.

Main international human rights instruments taken into account by the Court of Justice of the EU when interpreting and applying EU fundamental rights

- European Convention for the Protection of Human Rights and Fundamental Freedoms (ECHR)
- International Covenant on Civil and Political Rights (ICCPR)
- International Covenant on Economic, Social and Cultural Rights (ICESCR)
- Convention on the Elimination of all Forms of Discrimination against Women (CEDAW)
- International Convention on the Elimination of Racial Discrimination (CERD)
- Convention against Torture (UNCAT)
- Convention on the Rights of the Child (CRC)
- Convention on the Rights of Persons with Disabilities (CRPD)

Beyond Articles 3(5) and 21 TEU, one may briefly mention Article 49 TEU which provides, inter alia, that countries seeking to accede to the EU must respect the values on which the EU is founded as well as commit themselves to promoting them.

B. Key Legal and Political Issues

A key legal issue concerns the legal basis. As we have seen in Chapters 2 and 3, in the absence of any legal basis provided for in the Treaties the EU cannot act. With respect to the EU's external policy on human rights, political actors have also repeatedly sought via diverse initiatives to enhance its consistency. These two aspects will be briefly examined below.

(i) Legal Bases for EU's External Action in the Area of Human Rights

As noted above, Article 21(1) TEU sets out the principles which drive Union policy, while Articles 3(5) TEU and 21(2) TEU provide the objectives to be pursued by the Union when acting externally. Similar to Article 2 TEU, which does not in and of itself create any new competences for the EU to act, Articles 3 and 21 TEU do not automatically create or automatically extend the competences of the EU. Any external policy or action in pursuit of these objectives must rely on other legal bases in the Treaties. For example, the 2014 Regulations laying down the European Instrument for Democracy and Human Rights (EIDHR) could be adopted by the EU because Articles 209 TFEU (on development cooperation) and Article 212 TFEU (on economic, financial and technical cooperation) provided the EU with the power to do so.

Regulation (EU) No 235/2014 of 11 March 2014 establishing a financing instrument for democracy and human rights worldwide [2014] OJ L77/ 85

THE EUROPEAN PARLIAMENT AND THE COUNCIL OF THE EUROPEAN UNION,

Having regard to the Treaty on the Functioning of the European Union, and in particular Articles 209 and 212 thereof,

...

HAVE ADOPTED THIS REGULATION:

Article 1

Subject-matter and objectives

This Regulation establishes a European Instrument for Democracy and Human Rights (EIDHR) for the period 2014-2020 under which the Union shall provide assistance to the development and consolidation of democracy and the rule of law and of respect for all human rights and fundamental freedoms.

Similarly, the EU can only become a party to an international human rights treaty if it has been empowered to do so. With respect to the ECHR, as previously noted, the TEU explicitly provides the EU with the power, if not an obligation, to seek accession to the ECHR.

Article 6(2) TEU

The Union shall accede to the European Convention for the Protection of Human Rights and Fundamental Freedoms. Such accession shall not affect the Union's competences as defined in the Treaties.

EU accession to the ECHR has been a topic which has been on and off the EU agenda since 1979.[11] The post-Lisbon Treaty version of Article 6(2) TEU itself is the direct, albeit belated, result of an opinion given by the CJEU in 1996 in which the Court concluded that the (then) EC had no competence to accede to the ECHR.[12] Following some painstaking negotiations, with the Commission acting on behalf of the entire EU following the negotiating mandate it secured from the meeting of EU Justice Ministers in the Council, a draft accession treaty and explanatory report was agreed and published on 14 October 2011.[13] The European Court of Justice has, however, since held that EU accession could not happen until the problems of compatibility with EU law it identified with respect to the draft accession treaty were resolved by amending the draft text.[14] One of the multiple problems identified by the Court in its Opinion 2/13 concerns judicial review in matters of CFSP. As we have seen in Chapters 5 and 9, for the Court, it would not be compatible with EU law to empower a non-EU body, the ECtHR, to rule on the compatibility with the ECHR of CFSP acts, actions or omissions in a context where the same CFSP acts, actions or omissions fall outside the ambit of judicial review by the Court of Justice.[15]

The first time the EU became a party to an international human rights treaty was in 2010 when the EU ratified the UN Convention on the Rights of Persons with Disabilities (UNCRPD).[16] The signature and ratification of the UNCRPD was justified on the basis of the following combination of (pre-Lisbon Treaty) legal bases: Articles 13 and 95 of the Treaty establishing the European Community (now Articles 19 and 114 TFEU) in conjunction with the second sentence of the first paragraph of Article 300(2), and the first subparagraph of Article 300(3) TEC (now Article 218 TFEU).

(ii) Enhancing the Clarity, Coherence and Effectiveness of the EU's External Policy on Human Rights

Provisions such as Articles 3 and 21 TEU, while not extending the competences of the EU, have created a new impetus to reform EU external action with the view in particular of better ensuring 'consistency between the different areas of its external action and between these and its other policies' (Article 21(3) TEU).

[11] See, in particular, the European Commission's memorandum of 4 April 1979, Supplement no 2/79, Bulletin of the EC and the Commission communication published on 19 November 1990 (Sec(90)2087 final).

[12] Opinion 2/94 (*ECHR*).

[13] Council of Europe, Report of the Steering Committee for Human Rights (CDDH) to the Committee of Ministers on the elaboration of the legal instruments for the accession of the EU to the ECHR, CDDH(2011)009, 14 October 2011.

[14] Opinion 2/13 (*ECHR II*).

[15] For further analysis, see T Lock, 'The Future of the European Union's Accession to the European Convention on Human Rights after Opinion 2/13: Is It Still Possible and Is It Still Desirable?' (2015) 11 *European Constitutional Law Review* 239.

[16] Council Decision of 26 November 2009 concerning the conclusion, by the European Community, of the United Nations Convention on the Rights of Persons with Disabilities, 2010/48/EC [2010] OJ L 23/35.

Soon after the entry into force of the Lisbon Treaty, the Commission and the High Representative adopted a joint communication:

Joint Communication by the European Commission and the High Representative of the Union for Foreign Affairs and Security Policy, 'Human Rights and Democracy at the heart of EU External Action – Towards a More Effective Approach', COM(2011) 886 final, 12 December 2011, 6

The EU has not always been as effective or joined up as it might have been. The task in hand is to ensure the clarity, coherence and effectiveness of policy, by being smarter and more strategic. The promise of the Lisbon Treaty to put human rights, democracy and the rule of law at the centre of all external action and to ensure consistency between the different areas of its external action and the implementation of the principles of the EU's foreign policy make this even more pressing.

The aim of the communication was therefore 'to open a discussion with the other European institutions on how to make the EU's external policy on human rights and democracy more active, more coherent and more effective' (p 4). By reference to Article 21 TEU, action in four (transversal) areas was proposed: delivery mechanisms, integrating policies, building partnerships and speaking with one voice. The joint communication was followed up soon after by the adoption in 2012 of the first ever EU Strategic Framework and Action Plan on Human Rights and Democracy along with the 2015 Action Plan. These were rightly described by Wouters as 'important breakthroughs' which reflected the changes brought about by the Lisbon Treaty when it came to the EU's commitment to human rights and democracy and the EU's continuing ambition to be the leading actor when it comes to advancing them both 'in the wider world'.

J Wouters, 'The EU's Post-Lisbon Legal and Institutional Architecture on Human Rights and Democracy' in F Gómez Isa, C Churruca Muguruza and J Wouters (eds) *EU Human Rights and Democratization Policies: Achievements and Challenges* (Abingdon, Routledge, 2018) 43–44

The Union has been in rough waters ever since the entry into force of the Lisbon Treaty, with a set of parallel or quickly succeeding crises: the financial crisis, the Eurozone sovereign debt crisis, the refugee crisis, internal rule of law backsliding, terrorist attacks in multiple Member States and the challenges posed by Brexit. Still, it is fair to say that, overall, the legal and institutional framework of the EU with regard to human rights and democracy has proven to be stable. Important breakthroughs have been the 2012 EU Strategic Framework for Human Rights and Democracy and the related Action Plan, renewed in 2015.

The case-law of the CJEU has given an active application and interpretation of the Charter. Permanent actors have replaced the EU for its representation in the wider world, and this has generally led to more recognition, deeper engagements and the building of trust. Still, much remains to be done. The EU–Turkey Statement of 18 March 2016 shows a Union that is much less caring about human rights of refugees than those of its own citizens. Member States continue to pursue interests which stand at odds with a unified international position of the Union in the field of human rights. Above all, the EU institutions – the European Council on top – are in need of a renewed commitment to human rights at the highest political level, both for the internal policies of the EU and its Member States, and for the Union's actions in the wider world.

Before offering an outline of the content of the EU Strategic Framework and the two connected EU action plans adopted respectively in 2012 and 2015, the main features of the EU's post-Lisbon institutional architecture will be described below so as to better understand 'who does what' when it comes to the EU's external policy on human rights.

III. Institutional Framework

With respect to the EU's institutional framework, the Lisbon Treaty did not bring about any radical change. The most important institutional change, as far as the external objective of consolidating and supporting human rights is concerned (Article 21(2)(b) TEU) was the creation of a new post of High Representative of the Union for Foreign Affairs and Security Policy (HR) (see Chapter 1). This change notwithstanding, responsibility for determining the formulation, implementation and monitoring of external action policy continues to remain primarily shared between the Council and the European Commission under the supervision of the European Parliament. The respective roles of additional key EU institutions such as the European Council and one EU agency (the Fundamental Rights Agency) will be also outlined below.[17]

A. European Council and Council

While the European Council may deal with human rights related matters, the Council is the institution, which regularly does so in practice. For instance, it is the Council rather than the European Council, which sets out the EU priorities in UN human rights fora every year.[18] An Annual Report on Human Rights and Democracy is also adopted

[17] This section borrows from Egan and Pech (n 5) 246–50.

[18] See Council Conclusions on EU Priorities in UN Human Rights Fora in 2019, 6339/19, 18 February 2019.

by the Council each year.[19] The production of this report is significantly aided by the Working Party on Human Rights (COHOM), which was established in 1987 by the Council and has responsibility for the human rights aspects of external relations and supports the decision-making process of the Council in this area. COHOM is constituted of experts from each Member State and chaired by a delegate of the Member State holding presidency of the Council. It examines proposals from the Commission based on its expertise, before they are sent to the Foreign Affairs Council. Preparatory 'day-to-day' affairs are in the hands of the Working Party on Human Rights (COHOM).

Mandate of the Working Party on Human Rights (COHOM), 16510/14, Brussels, 10 December 2014

COHOM's main task is to promote the development and to oversee the worldwide implementation of the EU's policy in the field of human rights and democracy, including EU human rights guidelines and human rights dialogues and consultations with third countries. In particular, COHOM assists in identifying the EU's strategic priorities and coordinating the positions of the EU and its Members States with regard to specific thematic or geographic issues in multilateral human rights fora, in particular the UN General Assembly (Third Committee) and the UN Human Rights Council.

In addition, the COHOM also organises regular joint meetings with the Council working group which deals with the *internal* dimension of fundamental rights known as FREMP (Fundamental Rights, Citizens Rights and Free Movement of Persons). In practice, FREMP is responsible, inter alia, for preparatory work in the legislative procedures of the Council in the relevant areas and is also involved in the negotiations in respect to EU accession to the ECHR. The joint meetings between COHOM and FREMP aim to guarantee as much coherence as possible as regards the external promotion and internal delivery of human rights protection.

B. European Commission and High Representative

As we have seen in Chapter 1, the Commission represents the EU externally, with the exception of CFSP and where otherwise provided for by the Treaties (Article 17 TEU). Prior to the entry into force of the Treaty of Lisbon, the Directorate General with primary responsibility for the EU's external relations policy and, as a result, its global human rights policy, was the Directorate General for External Relations. It is also worth emphasising that the Commission, even prior to Lisbon, has been repeatedly pushing for the EU to promote respect for human rights in its external relations together with the promotion of pluralistic democracy and the rule of law.

[19] See Council of the EU, *EU Annual Report on Human Rights and Democracy in the World 2017*, 9122/18, 28 May 2018.

European Commission, *The European Union's Role in Promoting Human Rights and Democratisation in Third Countries*, COM(2001) 252 final, 8 May 2001, 3–6

The European Commission (EC) has adopted a number of Communications relating to human rights and democratisation in the last decade. This Communication does not seek to rewrite the fundamental policy. Rather it seeks to set this policy in the context of the Commission's overall strategic approach in external relations for the coming years. Changes in the external environment, as well as internal Commission reforms, require a re-focusing of human rights and democracy strategies, in particular to ensure that these issues permeate all Community policies, programmes and projects. Prioritisation, focus, delivery and impact are the main threads running throughout the document. The Commission wants to be judged on its performance in meeting the EU's policy goals.

... With the Council and Member States, the Commission is uniquely placed to promote consistency between Community activity, EU activity, and that of member states ... The Commission also ensures through its input into Council discussions and the development of positions in international human rights forums that these reflect Community action, as well as CFSP. The Commission contributes a Community input to the drafting of the Council's Annual Report on Human Rights, established in 1999.

Post-Lisbon, the Directorate General for External Relations was abolished and its functions transferred in large part to the newly created European Union External Action service (EEAS), with the Commission's Directorate General for International Cooperation and Development (DG DEVCO) remaining however in place – strictly speaking, DG DEVCO is the result of the merger of EuropeAid Cooperation Office (AIDCO) and the Directorate General for Development and Relations with ACP States – to formulate and implement EU development policy with the view, inter alia, of promoting 'democracy, the rule of law, good governance and respect for human rights, notably through external cooperation'[20] (see also Chapter 8).

The EEAS must work in cooperation with the diplomatic services of the EU Member States and is responsible, among other things, for presenting an annual report on EU performance in meeting the objectives of its human rights strategy in the annual report on human rights and democracy in the world. Within the EEAS, the Human Rights Division within the Human Rights, Global and Multilateral Issues Managing Directorate (MD GLOBAL) is a focal point for supporting structure and coherence in the EU's external human rights policy. However, as a transversal issue, it also features in the work of other departments and divisions.

[20] European Commission, International Cooperation and Development, Mission Statement. Available at: https://ec.europa.eu/europeaid/mission-statement_en.

2018 Annual Activity Report of the EEAS, 1 July 2019, 4–7

During 2018 the EU continued to enhance its role as a security provider and reliable international partner through concerted action, in line with the EU Global Strategy ... The EU continued to take the lead in promoting human rights and democracy across the globe ... The EU also pursued its efforts to secure its uninterrupted access to critical technologies, such as space and cyber. In this respect, the EU and its Member States support a global, open, safe and secure cyberspace where human rights and fundamental freedoms and the rule of law fully apply, with a view to societal wellbeing, economic growth, prosperity and the integrity of free and democratic societies ... In parallel, proactive strategic communications remained a priority activity for the EEAS. We ran a number of high-profile communications and outreach campaigns on thematic foreign policy priorities (eg human rights, security and defence), and in key geographical areas.

C. European Parliament

The European Parliament has been a significant advocate of human rights protection over the course of its development[21] and it works to include consideration of human rights on nearly all issues of debate. The 2012 Action Plan on Democracy and Human Rights recognised that the democratic mandate of the Parliament gives it 'particular authority and expertise in the field of human rights' and plays a significant role in the promotion of human rights, particularly through its resolutions. The Parliament has exercised its powers to highlight human rights issues, for example through emergency debates in plenary, parliamentary resolutions, third-country visits from parliamentary delegations and also through the annual awarding of the Sakharov Prize for Freedom of Thought.

European Parliament resolution of 12 December 2018 on the annual report on human rights and democracy in the world 2017 and the European Union's policy on the matter (2018/2098(INI))

The European Parliament,

- having regard to the Universal Declaration of Human Rights and other UN human rights treaties and instruments, notably the International Covenant on Civil and Political Rights (ICCPR) and the International Covenant

[21] R Rack and S Lausegger, 'The Role of the European Parliament: Past and Future' in P Alston (ed) *The EU and Human Rights* (Oxford, Oxford University Press, 1999); G Harrris, 'The Role of the European Parliament in Human Rights Protection' (2009) *European Yearbook of Human Rights* 109.

on Economic, Social and Cultural Rights (ICESCR), both adopted on 16 December 1966 by the United Nations General Assembly in New York,

- having regard to the European Convention on Human Rights,
- having regard to the Charter of Fundamental Rights of the European Union,
- having regard to the UN Convention on the Rights of the Child (UNCRC),
- having regard to Articles 2, 3, 8, 21 and 23 of the Treaty on European Union (TEU),
- having regard to Article 207 of the Treaty on the Functioning of the European Union,
- having regard to the Action Plan on Human Rights and Democracy 2015-2019, adopted by the Council on 20 July 2015, and to its mid-term review of June 2017,

…

A. whereas respect for and the promotion, indivisibility and safeguarding of the universality of human rights, as well as the promotion of democratic principles and values including the rule of law, respect for human dignity and the principle of equality and solidarity, are the cornerstones of the EU's ethical and legal *acquis* and its common foreign and security policy (CFSP), as well as of all its external action; whereas the EU should continue to strive to be the leading global actor in the universal promotion and protection of human rights, including on the level of multilateral cooperation, in particular through an active and constructive role in diverse UN bodies and in compliance with the UN Charter, the Charter of Fundamental Rights of the European Union and international law, as well as the obligations in the area of human rights and of the commitments assumed under the 2030 Agenda for Sustainable Development and the Sustainable Development Goals;

…

General considerations

1. Expresses profound concern at the pushback against democracy, human rights and the rule of law worldwide in 2017, and urges the EU and its Member States to pursue unconditionally the mainstreaming of the European and international standards regarding human rights, the rule of law, democracy and the rights of minorities to which they are bound, and to ensure increased coherence between the EU's internal and external human rights policies and greater coordination between the external policies of the Member States, in fields such as migration, counter-terrorism and trade …

The work of the European Parliament on external human rights policy is supported by the Foreign Affairs Committee and the subcommittee on Human Rights which is additionally responsible for the protection of minorities and the promotion of democratic values while its geographical remit covers countries outside the EU. These committees are comprised of representatives of the political groups in the European Parliament.

D. Fundamental Rights Agency

The Fundamental Rights Agency (FRA) is an EU agency established on the basis of a regulation adopted in 2007 and tasked with providing independent and evidence-based expertise on fundamental rights to EU institutions and Member States when implementing EU law.[22] The work of the FRA can, however, inform the policies of the EU institutions where it has been requested to do so. The agency does not have any mandate in the area of external relations and its role is limited to an advisory, internal dimension. The FRA is not empowered to provide information and analysis on human rights issues in third countries with which the EU cooperates, or in which it operates. It does, however, work with international organisations, including the Council of Europe, the UN and the Organisation for Security and Co-operation in Europe (OSCE) on matters related to human rights. It is furthermore open for participation of EU candidate countries as observers and countries with which the EU has concluded a stabilisation and association agreement may also be invited to participate in the work of the FRA. For example, Serbia joined the FRA as observer on 1 July 2018. In practical terms, this meant the appointment by Serbia of an observer to take part in FRA Management Board meetings and a National Liaison Officer to act as the main point of contact between FRA and Serbia.[23]

The current limited geographical scope of the FRA – it can only focus on the situation of fundamental rights in the EU and its Member States when they implement EU law – has been a source of recurring debate ever since the Commission submitted its draft proposal establishing an EU FRA in 2005 which initially foresaw a more ambitious role for the FRA.

House of Lords, EU Committee, 29th Report of Session 2005-06, *Human Rights Protection in Europe: The Fundamental Rights Agency*, Report with Evidence, HL Paper 155	**Article 3 in the draft proposal of 30 June 2005:**
56. Our witnesses had divergent views regarding whether the Agency should look at fundamental rights protection in third countries. Amnesty International was in favour of a remit which would allow the Agency to provide information and analysis on third countries …	3. When pursuing its activities, the Agency shall concern itself with the situation of fundamental rights in the European Union and in its Member States when implementing Community law …

(continued)

[22] Council Regulation 168/2007 of 15 February 2007.

[23] European Union Agency for Fundamental Rights, Serbia Joins FRA As Observer' (2019). Available at: https://fra.europa.eu/en/news/2018/serbia-joins-fra-observer.

(Continued)

House of Lords, EU Committee, 29th Report of Session 2005-06, *Human Rights Protection in Europe: The Fundamental Rights Agency*, Report with Evidence, HL Paper 155	**Article 3 in the draft proposal of 30 June 2005:**
57. The Commission for Racial Equality, on the other hand, considered that the Agency should be restricted to the EU. It argued that 'An extra-EU remit would direct resources away from its primary function: to ensure better fundamental rights in the European Union' and that 'there would no doubt be serious duplication should the EU begin to play a human rights function in wider Europe' … 131. Where the Agency can add value to the Commission's role in monitoring accession countries it should be permitted, although not obliged, to do so. The decision to make use of the Agency's resources should only be made after full consideration of the information already available …	4. … the Agency shall, at the request of the Commission, provide information and analysis on fundamental rights issues identified in the request as regards third countries with which the Community has concluded association agreements or agreements containing provisions on respect of human rights, or has opened or is planning to open negotiations for such agreements, in particular countries covered by the European Neighbourhood Policy. **Article 3 in the adopted version of 15 February 2017:** 3. The Agency shall deal with fundamental-rights issues in the European Union and in its Member States when implementing Community law. [original paragraph 4 was not adopted]

IV. Strategic Framework

On 25 June 2012, the Council of the EU adopted the first EU's Strategy Framework on Human Rights and Democracy. To implement this Strategy Framework, an Action Plan was also adopted for the period 2012–2014. As explained by Catherine Ashton, then High Representative for Foreign and Security Policy, human rights is 'a silver thread that runs through everything that we [ie the EU] do in external relations. With this comprehensive package we want to enhance the effectiveness and visibility of EU human rights policy'.[24] A second Action Plan was adopted in 2015 and covers the period until 31 December 2019. The EU's Global Strategy adopted in 2016 is also worth noting to the extent that it does explicitly commit the EU, inter alia, to 'champion the indivisibility and universality of human rights' when acting globally.[25]

[24] Council of the EU, 'EU Adopts Strategic Framework on Human Rights and Democracy', 11737/12, 25 June 2012.

[25] Shared Vision, 'Common Action: A Stronger Europe – A Global Strategy for the EU's Foreign and Security Policy', Brussels, June 2016, 18.

As it is not, however, specifically dedicated to the consolidation of and support for human rights – respect for human rights is not mentioned as one of the priorities of the EU's external action while Article 21 TEU is not cited once – the EU's Global Strategy will not be subject to further developments.[26]

A. The 2012 Strategic Framework on Human Rights and Democracy and the 2012–2014 Action Plan

With the adoption of the Lisbon Treaty, the EU sought to reframe itself as a 'community of values' defined and determined by Article 2 TEU. As part of an early initiative, the newly created High Representative for Foreign and Security Policy pushed for a major review of human rights actions. This resulted in the first independent assessment of EU-funded human rights programming in third countries, over the period 2000–2010. Published in 2011, the report identified significant failings in Commission leadership and 'systemic constraint' which had 'structurally hampered' the impact of EU action in the promotion of human rights.[27] As a result of this report, an ambitious initiative was developed by the High Representative, with significant input from the Member States, which resulted in the adoption, in 2012, of the first ever EU Strategic Framework on Human Rights and Democracy and the first ever Action Plan on Human Rights and Democracy.

Reminiscent of Article 2 TEU, the first edition of the EU's Action Plan declared its commitment to human rights promotion and identified key thematic issues which would be pursued in the plan:

EU Strategic Framework and Action Plan on Human Rights and Democracy, Luxembourg, 25 June 2012, 11855/12

The EU will promote human rights in all areas of its external action without exception. In particular, it will integrate the promotion of human rights into trade, investment, technology and telecommunications, Internet, energy, environmental, corporate social responsibility and development policy as well as into Common Security and Defence Policy and the external dimensions of employment and social policy and the area of freedom, security and justice, including counter-terrorism policy. In the area of development cooperation, a human rights-based approach will be used to ensure that the EU strengthens

[26] For a discussion of whether the Global Strategy adds any new significance to the EU's human rights commitment set out in the Treaties and other documents, see C Altafin, V Haász, K Podstawa, 'The New Global Strategy for the EU's Foreign and Security Policy at a Time of Human Rights Crises' (2017) 35 *Netherlands Quarterly of Human Rights* 122.

[27] PARTICIP GmbH Consortium (2011) 'Thematic evaluation of the European Commission support to respect of human rights and fundamental freedoms' (including solidarity with victims of repression) EuropeAid/122888/C/SER/Multi, December 2011, Part I, 12.

its efforts to assist partner countries in implementing their international human rights obligations.

The 2012–2014 Action Plan on Human Rights and Democracy identified 97 actions under 36 headings, assigning joint responsibility to the European Commission and EU Member States for their implementation. While embodying an innovative, more comprehensive approach by comparison to the situation before the entry into force of the Lisbon Treaty, both the Strategic Framework and Action Plan have been criticised on multiple grounds.

C Churruca Muguruza, 'Human Rights and Democracy at the Heart of the EU's Foreign Policy? An Assessment of the EU's Comprehensive Approach to Human Rights and Democratization' in F Gómez Isa, C Churruca Muguruza and J Wouters (eds) *EU Human Rights and Democratization Policies: Achievements and Challenges* (Abingdon, Routledge, 2018) 60–62

Still what the [Strategic Framework (SF)] and [Action Plan (AP)] did not set is a comprehensive approach to human rights and democracy as a strategy which combines objectives with ways and means of reaching these objectives. The Action Plan listed actions and expected outcomes and highlighted the responsible institution to achieve them. What the AP did not do is to consider the instruments and resources necessary to achieve those objectives within a specified time frame. It did not acknowledge the decisions that had to be taken to direct the necessary resources to their fulfilment or indicated the specific instruments or the policies and actors that had to be mobilized to implement these decisions. Moreover, the AP was not a plan to order priorities within the objectives, taking into consideration the available resources …

Neither the SF nor the AP consider democracy in the same comprehensive way as human rights and, in particular, do not give sufficient space to outcomes related to democracy. Instead, it clearly puts the focus on legal aspects of human rights rather than a practice that ensures democratic participation. Yet 'issues such as freedom of association and assembly, freedom of expression, the rights of minorities or women's rights and their participation in the political process are essential areas linked to democratic governance' (European Partnership for Democracy 2015: 1). The second is the lack of internal and external consistency. Although respect for human rights is a strict prerequisite for becoming a member, many European governments are taking an authoritarian turn and discriminating against minorities such as the Roma among other questions (European Partnership for Democracy 2015: 10–12). The lack of concern and respect for economic and social rights at a time of economic hardship and the prioritization of security cooperation and migration deterrence instead of putting human rights protection at the front of the agenda are some examples of these inconsistencies. In addition, there is no uniformity in the way that the EU promotes human rights externally. With regard to individual human rights issues, the EU places a stronger focus on the promotion of civil and political rights, to the detriment of economic, social and cultural rights. With regard to individual third country partners, the EU has been criticized for addressing human rights violations in 'economically weak and politically isolated countries, while being less vocal about comparable incidents in allied or partner countries' (EPD 2014: 13).

B. The 2015–2019 Action Plan on Human Rights and Democracy

The second Action Plan on Human Rights and Democracy 2015–2019 was adopted by the Council in July 2015. Identifying the 'considerable progress in improving the impact and coherence of its actions on human rights and democracy' made by the 2012–2014 Action Plan, the EU 'further developed guidelines on key human rights issues, enhanced the effectiveness of bilateral human rights and democracy work, successfully promoted action at the multilateral level, and improved the mainstreaming of human rights across the EU's external action'.[28]

Following the framework of the 2012–2014 Action Plan, the 2015–2019 Action plan identified five strategic areas of action: (i) boosting ownership of local actors; (ii) addressing human rights challenges; (iii) ensuring a comprehensive human rights approach to conflicts and crises; (iv) fostering better coherence and consistency; and (v) a more effective EU human rights and democracy support policy. Each of these areas were then categorised into certain objectives and subdivided into actions to be taken by identified EU actors. For example, in order to pursue objective 29 'Increasing the effectiveness of Human Rights Dialogues', the EEAS, and Council were expected to:

(a) develop, share and build upon the best practices identified for human rights dialogues, including follow-up processes. Responsibility for the implementation of the Plan was given jointly to the EEAS, the Commission and the EU Member States, in 'close consultation' with the European Parliament and civil society; and
(b) ensure that human rights and democracy considerations are factored in to the different sectorial dialogues with a partner country and as such form part of the overall bilateral strategy.

[28] Council of the EU, 'Action Plan on Human Rights and Democracy' (December 2015) 7.

While in pursuit of the same objective, the EEAS, Commission, Council and Member States were jointly required by 2017 to:

(a) ensure internal-external coordination in the context of human rights dialogues, including the annual EU-CSO dialogue; define and address a number of human rights and democracy priority issues in the context of external human rights dialogues on which a better EU response can be provided.

An innovation of the 2015–2019 Action Plan is the introduction of a mid-term review of the implementation, to make such adjustments as required to achieve the aims of EU policies and financial assistance. This mid-term review was published in June 2017.[29] With respect to human rights dialogues, it offers a rather upbeat assessment speaking of 'an encouraging trend overall, with the dialogues gaining in legitimacy and exerting a more positive impact on third countries'.[30]

Despite many improvements and the positive features identified in the context of the mid-term review mentioned above, the 2015–2019 Action Plan may be said to continue to suffer from a number of shortcomings. To merely cite two identified by the FRAME research project:[31] the EU Charter of Fundamental Rights 'is only mentioned once in passing in the *Strategic Framework for Human Rights and Democracy*, and not at all in the *Action Plan 2015–2019* (a departure from the previous action plan)'[32] and while ESC rights figure more prominently in the Action Plan, concrete implementation by the EU of its commitment to ESC rights has yet to be observed'.[33] While the European Commission and High Representative of the Union for FA and SP did accept that 'more work is needed to fulfil' some of the guiding principles that underpin the Action Plan, especially when it comes to 'strengthening internal-external coherence; improving communication; and enhancing the EU's capacity to measure and evaluate the human rights impacts of its actions',[34] their mid-term review offers a predominantly positive assessment of the Action Plan. In its conclusions on the mid-term review, the Council was similarly if not more positive with the Council merely inviting 'all partners to continue to contribute to further achievements' and stating that the 'EU will continue to work to further improve the evaluation of the human rights impact of its actions and to enhance its communication'.[35]

[29] European Commission and High Representative of the Union for Foreign Affairs and Security Policy (2017), Joint Staff Working Document, EU Action Plan on Human Rights and Democracy (2015–2019): Mid-Term Review June 2017, SWD(2017) 254 final, 2017. Available at: http://data.consilium.europa.eu/doc/document/ST-11138-2017-INIT/en/pdf.

[30] Ibid, 19.

[31] 'How to Better Foster Human Rights Among EU Policies – FRAME Final Recommendation' (*Fp7-frame.eu*, 2017). Available at: www.fp7-frame.eu/.

[32] Ibid, 16.

[33] Ibid, 59.

[34] Joint Staff Working Document, EU Action Plan on Human Rights and Democracy (2015–2019): Mid-Term Review June 2017, 22.

[35] Council conclusions on the mid-term review of the action plan on human rights and democracy, Foreign Affairs Council, 16 October 2017, annex to Council document 12815/17.

JOINT STAFF WORKING DOCUMENT, EU ACTION PLAN ON HUMAN RIGHTS AND DEMOCRACY (2015–2019): MID-TERM REVIEW[36]	SOME KEY ACHIEVEMENTS ACCORDING TO THE COUNCIL[37]
Though the situation for human rights and democracy globally remains deeply worrying, this mid-term review has highlighted achievements in implementing the EU Action Plan since 2015 and demonstrates that human rights are a core concern of EU foreign policy. Like its predecessor in 2012–2015, the Action Plan has proved its value as a policy and planning instrument: it has defined clear areas of focus, and provides flexibility to respond to new challenges as they arise. It is also aligned with new policies and strategies adopted since 2015 … The April 2015 Joint Communication set out several guiding principles to underpin the Action Plan, which the EU has generally upheld well. EU human rights and democracy policy has increasingly been orientated towards empowering third country actors and regional bodies. The EU has continued to demonstrate leadership in multilateral fora, even in a confrontational and polarised context. EU instruments have also been increasingly well-aligned, especially in the case of human rights dialogues … Overall, good progress has been made in implementing all five chapters of the Action Plan	• During challenging times, the EU and its Member States have promoted consistent actions in support of human rights and democracy. • The Action Plan has been instrumental in fostering and delivering a more coherent approach to mainstreaming human rights in all areas of EU external action. • The EU human rights and democracy policy in external action has progressively been orientated towards empowering third-country actors and regional bodies and to a model that empowers individuals to understand their rights. • The EU continues to be a leading supporter of inclusive, transparent and credible elections as well as the fundamentals of democratic pluralism. • EU instruments have been increasingly coordinated and well-aligned, especially in the case of human rights dialogues, guidelines and Human Rights and Democracy Country Strategies. • The EU has continued to promote and defend the universality and indivisibility of all human rights.

V. Main Instruments Used to Promote Human Rights

Union action in the field of human rights policy in external action is characterised by a strong preference for positive measures to support and encourage respect for human rights.[38] In practice, the EU relies on a 'broad range of policies, tools and external

[36] Ibid, 21–22.
[37] Ibid, 4.
[38] For a comprehensive overview, see Egan and Pech (n 5) at 254–63.

financing instruments at its disposal to promote and defend human rights. These include public diplomacy, such as EU statements and declarations, more discreet diplomacy tools including démarches and political dialogues, but also human rights guidelines and human rights country strategies, regular human rights dialogues, and financial cooperation projects'.[39]

A. Soft Law Instruments

(i) Human Rights Guidelines

The EU has adopted 12 Guidelines on Human Rights, which are designed to signal priorities areas from the point of view of the EU when acting externally while also serving 'as a practical tool to guide EU actors throughout the world when implementing EU human rights priorities at local level'.[40]

EU Guidelines on Human Rights

- EU Human Rights Guidelines on Non-discrimination in External Action (2019).
- EU Guidelines on the Promotion and Protection of the Rights of the Child – Leave no Child Behind (2017).
- EU Human Rights Guidelines on Freedom of Expression Online and Offline (2014).
- EU Guidelines on the promotion and protection of freedom of religion or belief (2013).
- Guidelines to promote and protect the enjoyment of all human rights by lesbian, gay, bisexual, transgender and intersex (LGBTI) persons (2013).
- EU Guidelines on Death Penalty: revised and updated version (2013).
- Guidelines to EU Policy towards third countries on torture and other cruel, inhuman or degrading treatment or punishment – an update of the guidelines (2012).
- EU Guidelines on promoting compliance with International Humanitarian Law (IHL) (2009).
- EU guidelines on human rights dialogues with third countries – update (2008).

[39] *EU Annual Report on Human Rights and Democracy in the World 2017* (n 19) 79.
[40] *EU Annual Report on Human Rights and Democracy in the World 2018*, 9024/19, 13 May 2019, 97.

- EU Guidelines on Children and Armed Conflict (2008).
- Ensuring protection – European Union Guidelines on Human Rights Defenders (2008)
- EU guidelines on violence against women and girls and combating all forms of discrimination against them (2008)

These guidelines are addressed to EU institutions and Member States to promote internal-external coherence in human rights policy, as well as to third countries and other external stakeholders. While the guidelines provide legal guidance on the understanding of their respective areas, they are not legally binding and are not internally applicable.

J Wouters and M Hermez, 'EU Guidelines on Human Rights as a Foreign Policy Instrument: An Assessment' in S Poli (ed) *Protecting Human Rights in the European Union's External Relations*, CLEER Working Papers 2016/5, 81

EU Human Rights Guidelines emerge as valuable policy instruments with the potential to strengthen EU human rights diplomacy and to provide EU representatives on the ground with the tools to intensify and steer human rights-related aspects of their work. Considering their lack of legally binding force but importance as steering instruments for the EU's external human rights objectives, the Guidelines are to be considered mere policy instruments. This is in line with the EU's preference for positive measures in pursuing its human rights objectives in relation to third countries. However, as has been pointed out by several scholars, the question of how and when to resort to negative measures has not been comprehensively addressed in the EU's official discourse, rendering the EU an easy target for accusations of incoherence and selectivity in the choices it has made. This can also apply to the Guidelines: there are certain fields in which the EU has not (yet) adopted any Guidelines, arguably because of pragmatic considerations based on self-interest rather than ideological convictions in terms of human rights protection. Despite the fact that EU Human Rights Guidelines are considered valuable steering policy instruments, they need to be implemented more rigorously, especially by EU Member States in their external action, in order to unlock their full potential. Lack of awareness, lack of training and lack of capacities are the main hurdles for effective implementation.

Two additional guidelines are under preparation for adoption in 2019.

(ii) Bilateral and Multilateral Diplomacy

Human rights issues are also pursued by the Council in its conclusions, as well as declarations and both public and private démarches. Responsibility for issuing these declarations and démarches has been given to the High Representative, where previously it was exercised by the Member State holding the rotating presidency of the Council. The creation of a High Representative has strengthened the position of the EU on bilateral human rights diplomacy through establishing continuity and consistency of diplomatic effort. The appointment in 2012 of the first ever EU Special Representative for Human Rights also aimed to increase the effectiveness, cohesion and visibility of human rights in EU foreign policy. EU delegations have also assumed a coordinating role between Member States' national embassies, though this has enabled Member States to 'hide behind' a collective position as expressed by the EU, which is critical of a human rights standard without compromising their own bilateral relations with third countries.[41]

EU Annual Report on Human Rights and Democracy in the World 2018, 51–52

The issue of capital punishment was consistently raised with third countries still using it and featured on the EU agendas of political dialogues or dedicated human rights dialogues. Based on the minimum standards defined by international law and the EU Guidelines on the Death Penalty, the EU issued a number of public statements deploring the use of the death penalty, and called on those countries to consider a moratorium …

The EU continued to raise its opposition to the death penalty in all relevant multilateral fora, in particular at the UN, the OSCE and the Council of Europe. The Global Alliance for Torture-Free Trade also takes measures to control and restrict trade in death penalty instruments.

To mark the European Day against the Death Penalty and the World Day against the Death Penalty on 10 October 2018, the EU and the Council of Europe issued a joint statement reaffirming their opposition to the use of capital punishment in all circumstances, and their commitment to the abolition of the death penalty worldwide. Numerous EU delegations marked this significant date by organising debates, publishing op-eds, and conducting other public awareness activities.

As part of its commitment to effective multilateralism and as shown by the example above, the EU also engages with several international organisations. As we have seen in Chapter 6, at the core of its multilateralist diplomacy is the United Nations. The EU

[41] See R Balfour and K Raik (eds) *The European External Action Service and National Diplomacies*, European Policy Centre, Issue Paper No 73 (2013).

is involved in the work of the UN human rights system through its participation in the UN General Assembly and the Human Rights Council. The EU has presented country-specific statements and resolutions, commissions of inquiry, fact-finding missions, the Universal Periodic Review within this framework. For example, in March 2017, the EU presented a resolution on Myanmar/Burma, which was adopted without a vote, to establish an international fact-finding mission and extend the mandate of the Special Rapporteur.

The EU and Council of Europe also cooperate on a number of human rights initiatives, for example, joint programmes covering cooperation in the EU enlargement region, the Eastern Partnership and Southern Mediterranean countries. One example of cooperation is the Horizontal Facility for the Western Balkans and Turkey, launched in 2016, which assists target third countries with challenges pertaining to the rule of law and human rights. It funds support by ensuring justice through judicial reform, fighting economic crime including corruption and organised crime, and combatting discrimination and protecting the rights of vulnerable groups.

Similar to the Council of Europe, all EU Member States are participating states of the OSCE. The EU and the OSCE cooperate in several key areas, including human rights and democracy. Through a number of partnership and cooperation or stabilisation and association agreements in regions including the Balkans and Eastern Europe, the EU and OSCE work with third countries to improve areas including judicial and public administration reform; democratisation and human rights institution building and election oversight.

B. Unilateral Trade, Technical and Financial Instruments

(i) Generalised System of Preferences

As indicated in Chapter 7, since 1971, the Generalised System of Preferences (GSP) gives developing countries access to EU markets with unilateral and non-reciprocal trade preferences. It currently consists of three different trade arrangements: (1) The so-called Standard GSP; (2) the so-called GSP+; and (3) the special arrangement known as Everything But Arms (EBA). These arrangements are regularly presented by the EU as a key aspect of its trade policy when it comes to encouraging sustainable development and respect for human rights.

European Commission, Factsheet on the Three-pronged GSP, 19 January 2018

- **Standard GSP** beneficiaries benefit from reduced customs duties on 66% of all EU product categories. In 2016, the EU imported goods worth **€32 billion** from the 23 Standard GSP beneficiaries.
- **GSP+** beneficiaries export around 66% of all product categories duty-free in return for their commitment to effectively implement 27 international core conventions covering labour rights, human rights, good governance and

environmental concerns. In 2016, the EU imported goods worth **€7.5 billion** from the 10 GSP+ beneficiaries.

- **The least developed countries under the Everything but Arms (EBA)** arrangement of GSP are granted duty-free access to the EU for all products except arms and ammunition. In 2016, EU imports from the 49 EBA beneficiaries amounted to **€23.5 billion.**

Serious and systemic violation of the principles laid down in a number of human rights and labour rights conventions can lead to the provisional withdrawal of standard GSP or EBA preferences. All GSP countries must, for instance, comply with core international human rights and labour conventions, listed in an annex to Regulation 978/2012. With respect to GSP+, the EU requires third countries to accept monitoring and reporting requirements under the international conventions, and regular monitoring by the European Commission via onsite visits. The GSP+ compliance dialogue with the EU is furthermore based on a list of issues drawn up for each GSP+ beneficiary and the 'EU assessment relies primarily assessment relies primarily on the most recent reports and recommendations from international monitoring bodies, such as the ILO and the UN' with the EU also making 'use of a wide range of other information and meets with civil society organisations (CSOs), including trade unions, human rights defenders, businesses and employers before and during monitoring missions, both in the EU and in the beneficiary country'.[42]

The European Parliament has underlined the need for closer monitoring of the GSP+ regime 'including by the use of detailed Human Rights Impacts Assessments, a consistent and fair benchmarking system, and open consultations when the preference is being awarded' and advocated giving such preferences only to 'countries that have ratified and effectively implemented key international conventions on sustainable development, human rights – particularly child labour – and good governance'.[43] Subsequently, the European Parliament, while expressing 'a positive view of the GSP+ preference system as a means to stimulate the effective implementation of 27 core international conventions on human rights and labour standards' has, however, called 'for the genuine enforcement of GSP+' and for 'the Commission to report back to Parliament and to the Council on the status of its ratification and the progress made under this scheme'.[44]

A 2017 study offered a more mixed assessment of the social and human rights impact of the 2012 GSP Regulation, but the main conclusion remains that overall, it

[42] European Commission, *Report on the Generalised Scheme of Preferences Covering the Period 2016–2017* COM(2018) 36 final, 19 January 2018, 8.

[43] European Parliament resolution of 16 December 2010 on the Annual Report on Human Rights in the World 2009 and European Union's policy on the matter (2010/2202(INI)), para 112.

[44] European Parliament resolution of 13 December 2017 on the Annual Report on Human Rights in the World 2016 and European Union's policy on the matter (2017/2122(INI), para 30.

has had 'a positive impact on social and human rights in the beneficiary country'.[45] However, the study notes that while 'the EU may decide to withdraw trade preferences in case of severe and systematic violations of fundamental rights, which creates an incentive for governments to better guarantee these rights for their people', in practice it is 'perceived as not having consistently applied this approach in cases of labour and human rights violations. Instead of withdrawing preferences, which could severely harm the beneficiary's economy, the Commission has engaged in a structured dialogue where feasible. The EU could potentially have a bigger impact on adherence to fundamental rights by more consistently invoking the possibility of applying the temporary withdrawal mechanism'.[46]

(ii) Other Trade-related Measures

Trade-related restrictive measures for human rights violations can be imposed by the EU where there is unanimous agreement among all the EU states acting within the CFSP framework (see Chapter 9). A range of options including economic and financial sanctions and military sanctions (such as the imposition of arms embargoes) are available measures. In all cases, such measures must respect the EU's international obligations. In practice, the EU tends to prioritise the adoption of 'smart sanctions' targeting particular individuals, rather than, for instance, withdrawing standard GSP or EBA preferences. Such smart sanctions often combine freezing assets, denying visas, and the imposition of arms embargoes. While measures/sanctions of this nature may be justified in the name of safeguarding EU's values, in particular the objective of consolidating and supporting human rights, they must themselves respect human rights standards.

Council of the EU, *Guidelines on Implementation and Evaluation of Restrictive Measures (Sanctions) in the Framework of the EU Common Foreign and Security Policy*, 11205/12, 15 June 2012

2. Within the framework of the Common Foreign and Security Policy, the Council may decide to impose restrictive measures against third countries, entities or individuals. These measures must be consistent with CFSP objectives, as set out in Article 21 of the Treaty on European Union (TEU) ...

9. The introduction and implementation of restrictive measures must always be in accordance with international law. They must respect human rights and fundamental freedoms, in particular due process and the right to an effective remedy. The measures imposed must always be proportionate to their objective.

[45] European Commission, Mid-Term Evaluation of the EU's Generalised Scheme of Preferences (GSP), Final Interim Report, prepared by Development Solutions, 21 September 2017, Section 11.2, 277.

[46] Ibid.

10. As indicated above, the restrictive measures should, in particular, be drafted in light of the obligation under Article 6(3) TEU for the EU to respect fundamental rights, as guaranteed by the European Convention on Human Rights and as they result from the constitutional traditions common to the Member States, as general principles of Union law.

The EU has also introduced a number of trade-related human rights measures which regulate, for example, the trade in arms and products which could be used for capital punishment, torture or other inhuman cruel and degrading treatment.[47] Restrictions on the trade of medicinal materials used in executions, of which the EU is a major producer, have expanded to include the commercial marketing, brokering or transit of such substances through EU territory.[48]

(iii) Technical and Financial Assistance Instruments

Between 2014 and 2020, the EU allocated €1.3 billion as part of the Multiannual Indicative Programme to the European Instrument for Democracy and Human Rights (EIDHR). The EIDHR supports non-governmental organisations promoting human rights, democracy and the rule of law, and observes elections throughout the world, in addition to the other thematic areas identified as priorities by the EU. Established by Regulation 1889/2006 the EIDHR is the only financial instrument whose primary aim is to promote democracy and human rights through the EU's external action. It is intended to support other EU programmes, for example the European Neighbourhood Instrument (ENI) and the Development Co-operation Instrument (DCI).

The EIDHR is often presented as one of the most successful financial instruments of the EU when it comes to the external promotion of human rights. For instance, in its annual report on human rights for the year 2017, the Council presents the EIDHR as 'one of the key external financing instruments used to promote and support democracy and human rights worldwide. Building on its key strength, which is the ability to operate without the need for host government consent, the EIDHR is able to focus on sensitive issues and innovative approaches, and to cooperate directly with isolated or marginalised civil society organisations'.[49] Similarly, the European Parliament offered a rather positive assessment of the EIDHR in its annual report for the same year

[47] Council Regulation (EC) 1236/2005 concerning the trade in certain good which could be used for capital punishment, torture or other cruel, inhuman or degrading treatment of punishment [2005] OJ L220/1.

[48] Commission Implementing Regulation (EU) No 1352/2011 of 20 December 2011 amending Council Regulation (EC) No 1236/2005 concerning trade in certain goods which could be used for capital punishment, torture or other cruel, inhuman or degrading treatment or punishment [2011] OJ L338/31; and Commission Implementing Regulation (EU) No 775/2014 of 16 July 2014 amending Council Regulation (EC) No 1236/2005 concerning trade in certain goods which could be used for capital punishment, torture or other cruel, inhuman or degrading treatment or punishment [2014] OJ L210/1.

[49] *EU Annual Report on Human Rights and Democracy in the World 2017* (n 19) 83.

and spoke of it as constituting 'the flagship instrument of the EU in implementing its external human rights policy'.[50]

In October 2018, new strategic priorities were adopted for the EIDHR for the period 2018–2020 with enhanced emphasis to be placed 'on the protection of at-risk human rights defenders and on actions addressing shrinking democratic, civic and civil society spaces, while strong support for democracy and the key actors of worldwide human rights architecture will be maintained'.[51]

C. Bilateral External Agreements

Human rights clauses have been included as 'conditionality clauses' in all cooperation and association agreements concluded by the EU since 1995. The so-called 'standard human rights clauses' traditionally include two elements: (1) a reference to respect for democratic principles, the rule of law and human rights as an essential foundation of the agreement; and (2) a non-execution clause, allowing for the suspension or termination of the agreement where a violation of an essential element represents so material a breach of its terms even in the absence of consultation with the third country. To mention some examples, human rights clauses have been included in the 2014 Association Agreements with Ukraine, Georgia and Moldova, under Article 217 TFEU as part of the larger context of the European Neighbourhood Policy.[52]

L Bartels, *A Model Human Rights Clause for the EU's International Trade Agreements*, German Institute for Human Rights, 2014, 28

The conclusion is that there is, therefore, a need for a specific human rights clause that enables the parties to such agreement to adopt appropriate measures when necessary. This raises the question whether the standard human rights clause is adequate to this task. For two main reasons, it is not.

First, the standard human rights clause does not allow a party to protect human rights in its own territory. The general exceptions that are found in trade agreements permit measures to protect human health and life, but, as noted above, this is barely sufficient. For this reason, all trade agreements should contain clauses permitting exceptional measures to be adopted to protect human rights domestically. For both the EU and the third country, this is necessary in order

[50] European Parliament resolution of 13 December 2017 (n 44) para 51.

[51] *EU Annual Report on Human Rights and Democracy in the World 2018* (n 40) 101.

[52] Association Agreement between the European Union and its Member States, of the one part, and Ukraine of the other part [2014] OJ L161/3 (EU–Ukraine AA); Association Agreement between the European Union and the European Atomic Energy Community and their Member States, of the one part, and Moldova of the other part [2014] OJ L260/4 (EU-Moldova AA); Association Agreement between the European Union and the European Atomic Energy Community and their Member States, of the one part, and Georgia of the other part [2014] OJ L261/4 (EU–Georgia AA).

for them to be able to comply with their own obligations to ensure the protection of human rights in areas for which they are primarily responsible. …

The second problem is that the standard human rights clause is triggered by a violation by the other party. This is too limited. As has been shown, the EU has an independent obligation to ensure that it respects human rights in a third country, regardless of the obligations of the third country. Indeed, this obligation may require the EU to act even when the third country is itself not responsible, due to a lack of capacity. It is therefore legally necessary, under EU law, for the EU to be able to adopt measures under a human rights clause without having to demonstrate that a third state is responsible for human rights violations.

To answer the criticism levelled at the 'standard human rights clause', a 'model human rights clause' was incrementally developed and is supposed to stand alongside the standard clause and commits the parties to the agreement to cooperate on human rights, and explicitly recognises the need for positive engagement on both sides. By identifying human rights as an issue of common concern and commitment, it specifies human rights as a topic for discussion with the context of bilateral political dialogue. The model represents an effort to make human rights transversal in all communications, rather than isolating such dialogue to single focus human rights dialogue. It was used for the first time in the EU partnership and cooperation agreement with Indonesia signed in 2009, which entered into force in 2014.

Framework Agreement on Comprehensive Partnership and Cooperation between the EC and its Member States and the Republic of Indonesia [2014] OJ L 125/17

Article 1 General Principles

1. Respect for democratic principles and fundamental human rights, as laid down in the Universal Declaration of Human Rights and other international human rights instruments applicable to both Parties underpins the internal and international policies of both Parties and constitutes an essential element of this Agreement.

Article 26 Human Rights

1. The Parties agree to cooperate in the promotion and protection of human rights.

…

3. The Parties agree that a dialogue between them on this matter would be beneficial.

Article 44 Settlement mechanism

...

3. If either Party considers that the other Party has failed to fulfil any of its obligations under this Agreement it may take appropriate action. Before doing so, except in cases of special urgency, it shall present to the Joint Committee all the relevant information required for a thorough examination of the situation with a view to seeking a solution acceptable to the Parties.

4. The Parties agree that for the purpose of the correct interpretation and practical application of this agreement the term 'cases of special urgency' in paragraph 3 means a case of the material breach of the Agreement by one of the Parties. A material breach consists in:

(i) repudiation of the agreement not sanctioned by the general rules of international law, or
(ii) violation of an essential element of the Agreement, as described in Articles 1(1) ...

A consistent criticism of the human rights clause is their inconsistent use by the EU with weak third states having committed grave breaches of human rights 'more likely to suffer suspension of aid than states that enjoy a more secure bargaining position with the EU.'[53] To address this criticism, action 33(a) of the 2012 EU Action Plan on Human Rights and Democracy called for the development of working methods to 'ensure the best articulation between dialogue, targeted support, incentives and restrictive measures', while action 33(b) calls for the development of 'criteria for application of the human rights clause' by 2013 and 2014, respectively. Little progress was made on these two fronts and the 2015 EU Action Plan on Human Rights and Democracy reiterated the need to 'improve coherence in the application of human rights clauses' which are to be 'systematically included in all new EU international agreements' (action 33(e)), a recurrent demand of the European Parliament.

European Parliament Resolution of 13 December 2017 on the Annual Report on Human Rights and Democracy in the World 2016 and the European Union's Policy on the Matter (2017/2122(INI))

30. Reiterates its support for the systematic introduction of human rights clauses in international agreements between the EU and third countries, including

[53] A Ward, 'Framework for Cooperation between the European Union and Third States: A Viable Matrix for Uniform Human Rights Standards?' (1998) 3 *European Foreign Affairs Review* 505, 505–06.

trade and investment agreements; recalls that all human rights must be considered of equal value, being indivisible, interdependent and interrelated; calls on the Commission to monitor the implementation of such clauses effectively and systematically and to provide Parliament with regular reports on partner countries' respect for human rights; …

70. Recalls the EU's commitment to placing human rights and democracy at the centre of its relations with third countries; stresses, therefore, that the advancement of human rights and democratic principles, including human rights conditionality clauses in international agreements, needs to be supported through all EU policies with an external dimension, such as enlargement and neighbourhood policy, the CSDP, and environment, development, security, counter-terrorism, trade, migration, justice and home affairs policies; …

VI. The Broader Picture of EU External Relations Law

Three cross-cutting challenges may be identified when it comes to the external promotion of its values by the EU: the delivery challenge; the coherence challenge and the effectiveness challenge.[54] With increasing democratic and rule of law backsliding within the EU itself, one may also add the 'credibility challenge' to this list.

A. The Delivery Challenge

By delivery challenge, one must understand 'the difficulties that the Union may have in going from the theory of its commitment to the practice arising from factual policy'[55] considering how bold and unconditional the EU's commitment to human rights is on paper. Several problems may be highlighted in this respect.

Manifestations of the Delivery Challenge according to the FRAME research project[56]

- Concrete applications of EU human rights standards to be found, inter alia, in the EU Charter often poses problems with for instance economic, social

[54] See 'How to Better Foster Human Rights Among EU Policies' (n 31) 8.
[55] Ibid.
[56] Ibid, 8–9.

and cultural rights often given less priority than civil and political rights while also being considered by the EU less enforceable than civil and political rights both in its internal and external policies;
- Concrete delivery of the EU's commitment to human rights depends to a large extent on the EU Member States' willingness to coordinate and use their resources when it comes to fulfilling the EU's international agenda;
- Concrete implementation of the EU's commitment to human rights also depends on EU officials whose knowledge of the EU's priorities and agenda in this area may be relatively low when human rights are not at the core of their official tasks.

B. The Effectiveness Challenge

Closely related to the criticisms inherent within the delivery challenge, the EU has been confronted with allegations of ineffectiveness when it comes to its commitment to promote and protect human rights when it acts externally. The EU is aware of this issue and has repeatedly sought to make its external policy on human rights (and democracy) more effective.[57] Indeed, one of the five strategic areas of action priorities of the EU Action Plan 2015–2019 is to deepen the effectiveness and results culture of EU action so as to increase its impact on human rights via a 'better use of existing instruments, activities and policies' in a context 'of increasing challenges and limited resources'.[58] However, one of the problems faced by the EU is how to measure effectiveness.

F Gómez Isa et al, 'Challenges to the Effectiveness of EU Human Rights and Democratisation Policies', FRAME research report[59]

While the field of development cooperation has a long tradition of well-established methodologies to conduct evaluations and impact assessments, that is not the case in the area of human rights and democratization support. The main methodological constraints are the problem of attribution; the multi-dimensional and multi-level character of democratization processes; and the so-called counterfactual, given that one cannot know what would have happened in a given process of democratization without the external support. As it was stressed by the members of the research team that conducted the case study on

[57] Joint communication of the European Commission and the High Representative for FA and SP, Human Rights and Democracy at the heart of EU External Action – Towards a More Effective Approach, COM(2011) 886 final, 12 December 2011.

[58] Action Plan on Human Rights and Democracy 2015–2019, 6.

[59] 'Challenges to the Effectiveness of EU Human Rights and Democratisation Policies | FRAME' (*Fp7-frame.eu*, 2016). Available at: www.fp7-frame.eu/frame-reps-12-3/.

Peru and Bolivia, the impact evaluation of human rights and democratization policies is an under-researched area. There is a need for more systematic impact evaluation and more scholarly work on it, preferably in collaboration with local researchers and institutions.

C. The Consistency Challenge

A challenge for the EU in both its external and internal aspects has been ensuring consistency (coherence is also often used in this context and understood as synonymous with consistency) in its policy, implementation and review of external human rights policy. There is complex matrix of sources which underlie the (in)consistency challenge. One important reason is the fragmentation of human-rights related powers and competences between EU institutions and the EU Member States. While the creation of a permanent representation improved the external face of external policy, the Lisbon Treaty also introduced new roles with overlapping competences in the High Representative and the President of the European Council.

D Morondo Taramundi, 'The Search for Coherence in the EU's Human Rights Policy and Discourse' in F Gómez Isa, C Churruca Muguruza and J Wouters (eds) *EU Human Rights and Democratization Policies: Achievements and Challenges* (Abingdon, Routledge, 2018) 73–74

Incoherence and inconsistent policies are liable to produce a faulty or inefficient delivery of policy processes, and a waste or inefficient use of the (scarce) resources allocated; exhibit divergent positions by EU institutions, agencies and bodies, and the Member States; undermine the effectiveness of human rights policies; and impair the legitimacy and credibility of the EU as a global human rights actor. It is thus generally considered that lack of coherence or low levels of consistency should be avoided, but no clear definition has been provided of lack of coherence or incoherencies. Therefore, what the problem of coherence is, or seems to be, is less of concern than the means to achieve coherence.

The recognition of the need for separate policies and actions tailored to each individual state was lauded as a constructive step, but it also lays bare the lack of benchmarks, and the inconsistent treatment of third countries, leading to repeated accusations of 'double standards'. The perception is that EU sanctions are applied only to comparatively 'weak' third countries where there is a breach of human rights commitments, whereas legally binding human rights clauses are not included in agreements with comparatively 'powerful' countries. Equally, there is justified criticism of the failure of the EU to address major and systemic human rights abuses in third countries where it would be politically or economically inconvenient to do so.[60]

This problem is also increasingly, and critically, apparent in the discrepancy between the comprehensive and increasingly demanding monitoring imposed on EU candidate countries when it comes to Article 49 TEU conditions for accession to the EU and in particular the condition of respecting EU human rights standards, and the lack of a similar permanent, systematic and demanding monitoring scheme once countries have joined the EU. At a time of serious democratic and rule of law backsliding within the EU, this discrepancy is not only undermining the coherence of the EU's human right policy, it is undermining its credibility as will be outlined below.

Editorial Comments, 'Fundamental Rights and EU Membership: Do as I say, not as I do!' (2012) 49 *Common Market Law Review* 481, 485 and 487–88

As the Union strengthens the promotion of fundamental rights in relation to candidates for membership, it displays some discomfort in addressing internal contentious situation. The obvious case in point these days is Hungary, though it is certainly not alone ... Such a discrepancy, which undermines the credibility of the EU fundamental rights policy, is multifarious. It finds its first expression in the scope of fundamental rights to be respected by candidates and by Member States, respectively ... Beyond this substantive discrepancy, the obligation to respect fundamental rights appears to vary depending on the pre or post accession contexts. In principle, EU fundamental rights only bite Member States when they act in the context of EU law, whereas *any* conduct of a candidate is considered for the purpose of evaluating progress in assimilating EU fundamental rights ... A third level of incongruity concerns the *monitoring* of EU fundamental rights. The latter significantly differs whether operating in the context of pre-accession, or within the Union. In the former case, monitoring is systematic, based as it is on the regular reporting by the Commission, and involving a considerable leverage on the candidates' behaviour. By contrast, EU monitoring of Member States' compliance with the Union's fundamental rights appears circumspect ...

D. The Credibility Challenge

The EU's regularly advertised ambition to act as a global normative power has been seriously undermined by its relative passivity when it came to addressing obvious signs of increased authoritarianism in a number of EU countries. As noted by the European Parliament, 'the EU's influence as a credible and legitimate international actor is greatly shaped by its ability to advance respect for human rights and democracy, both

[60] See generally U Khaliq, *Ethical Dimensions of the Foreign Policy of the EU: A Legal Analysis* (Cambridge, Cambridge University Press, 2009).

internally and externally'.[61] Faced with serious and seemingly spreading democratic and rule of law backsliding, that is the deliberate and systematic undermining of internal checks on power with the view of dismantling the liberal democratic state, within the EU itself,[62] the EU institutions have since reacted by activating, inter alia, the so-called Article 7 TEU procedure first against Poland in December 2017 and subsequently against Hungary in September 2018.[63]

To date, the EU's inability to contain, let alone roll back this process can only undermine the credibility of the EU institutions when urging third countries to respect, for instance, the independence of the judiciary or emphasising the significance of free and fair elections for democratic processes at a time where at least one EU country is engaged in an unprecedented process of undermining judicial independence and the submission of judges to political control,[64] while another has been criticised for the unfairness of its legislative elections to the extent that 'the main governing party enjoyed an undue advantage because of a pervasive overlap between state and ruling party resources, biased media coverage and opaque campaign financing regulations'.[65]

European Parliament resolution of 12 December 2018 on the annual report on human rights and democracy in the world 2017

25. Reaffirms that the independence of the judiciary and the absolute transparency of a system for the administration of justice in which all operators are required to carry out their roles in an upright and independent manner are prerequisites for the development of a democratic state and legal protection for human rights; condemns roundly all attempts to place restrictions on the freedom of judges, public prosecutors and lawyers, and all forms of direct and indirect violence employed against them; calls on the EU to pay the utmost attention to this point in the context of its diplomatic relations with non-EU countries.

…

40. Emphasises the significance of free and fair elections for democratic processes and is concerned at the growing number of illegitimate elections around the world; recalls that independent media and diversity of opinion are essential in guaranteeing free and fair elections; calls for the EU not to recognise the results of rigged or falsified elections and to use all the diplomatic, economic and policy tools at its disposal to uphold the credibility of elections around the

[61] European Parliament resolution of 12 December 2018 (n 1) para 1.

[62] See L Pech and KL Scheppele, 'Illiberalism within: Rule of Law Backsliding in the EU' (2017) 19 *Cambridge Yearbook of European Law* 3.

[63] For further information, see L Pech and J Grogan, Article 7 EU, Dem-Dec. Available at: www.democratic-decay.org/article-7-eu.

[64] European Commission, Rule of Law: European Commission launches infringement procedure to protect judges in Poland from political control, Brussels, IP/19/1957, 3 April 2019.

[65] 'Hungary: Parliamentary Elections 8 April 2018' (*Osce.org*, 2018). Available at: www.osce.org/odihr/elections/hungary/385959?download=true, accessed 21 June 2019. ODIHR final report on Hungary's parliamentary elections points to inadequate separation between party and state activities and offers recommendations to improve the electoral process.

world and compel countries to meet the free and fair election criteria; considers that the support the EU provides for electoral processes and democracy around the world – its electoral missions and subsequent follow-up, its electoral assistance and, in particular, the active role played by Parliament in this regard – is of the utmost importance;...

When one compares, for instance, EU support for electoral processes and democracy around the world with the lack of support for and monitoring of the EU Member States' elections so as to guarantee their integrity, it is not merely the EU's credibility as a global promoter of human rights which becomes at risk but, more broadly, its own legitimacy. To avoid such an indictment, the EU must, in practice, be as committed to the protection of human rights, democracy and the rule of law within its borders as it claims to be in the promotion of these same principles beyond them.

VII. Sources and Further Reading

Altafin, C, V Haász, V and K Podstawa, 'The New Global Strategy for the EU's Foreign and Security Policy at a Time of Human Rights Crises' (2017) 35 *Netherlands Quarterly of Human Rights* 122.

Bartels, L, *Human Rights Conditionality in the EU's International Agreements* (Oxford, Oxford University Press, 2005).

Búrca, G de, 'The Road Not Taken: The EU as a Global Human Rights Actor' (2011) 105 *American Journal of International Law* 649.

Egan, A and L Pech, 'Respect for Human Rights as a General Objective of the EU's External Action' in S Douglas-Scott (ed) *Research Handbook on EU Law and Human Rights* (Cheltenham, Edward Elgar, 2017) 243–66.

Gómez Isa, F, C Churruca Muguruza and J Wouters (eds) *EU Human Rights and Democratization Policies: Achievements and Challenges* (Abingdon, Routledge, 2018).

Khaliq, U, *Ethical Dimensions of the Foreign Policy of the EU: A Legal Analysis* (Cambridge, Cambridge University Press, 2009).

Larik, J, 'Shaping the International Order as an EU Objective' in D Kochenov and F Amtenbrink (eds) *The European Union's Shaping of the International Legal Order* (Cambridge, Cambridge University Press, 2014) 62–86.

Larik, J, *Foreign Policy Objectives in European Constitutional Law* (Oxford, Oxford University Press, 2016).

Marx, A, B Natens, D Geraets and J Wouters 'Global Governance Through Trade: An Introduction' in J Wouters, A Marx, D Geraets and B Natens (eds) *Global Governance Through Trade* (Cheltenham, Edward Elgar, 2015) 1–18.

Neframi, E, 'Vertical Division of Competences and the Objectives of the European Union's External Action' in Cremona M, Thies A (eds) *The European Court of Justice and External Relations Law* (Oxford, Hart Publishing, 2014) 73–94.

Wouters, J, 'The EU's Post- Lisbon Legal and Institutional Architecture on Human Rights and Democracy' in FG Isa, CC Muguruza and J Wouters (eds) *EU Human Rights and Democratization Policies: Achievements and Challenges* (London, Routledge, 2018) 27–45.

11

EU External Environmental Policy

Central Issues

- Since it was attributed external powers over environmental matters in the late 1980s, the EU has gradually developed a mature external environmental policy using a plethora of multilateral, regional, bilateral and unilateral instruments. Moreover, it has increasingly aspired to play a leadership role in international environmental affairs, and most notably in the global fight against climate change.
- In this chapter, we examine the constitutional framework that underpins the formulation and conduct of the EU's external environmental policy and expose the reader to the key legal and policy challenges stemming from the EU's external environmental practice through the lens of selected case-studies.
- The EU's environmental policy is constitutionally linked to other external policies in a number of Treaty provisions and, in particular, the environmental integration requirement (Article 11 TFEU) and the common set of objectives for the Union's external action (Article 21 TEU). However, this constitutional imperative will often confront the EU legislator with a delicate balancing and trade-offs between environmental and other (economic, social) policy objectives.
- A common thread running through the various EU external environmental measures examined in the Chapter is whether the Union can and should use its market size and structural power to promote – or one could even say to force – third-party and global environmental action.

I. The Constitutional Framework on EU External Environmental Policy

A. EU External Competence for Environmental Matters

The constitutional core of EU external environmental policy is found in Title XX TFEU dealing specifically with the environment, which was first introduced by the Single European Act (SEA) of 1986[1] and has undergone several amendments by the Treaty of Maastricht, the Treaty of Amsterdam and the Treaty of Lisbon.[2] These provisions first lay down a set of objectives and principles for EU environmental policy which, pursuant to the principle of conferral,[3] determine the substantive scope of EU competence (whether internal or external) in this field. The TFEU requires EU environmental policy to contribute to the pursuit of a number of objectives.

Article 191(1) TFEU

Union policy on the environment shall contribute to pursuit of the following objectives:

- preserving, protecting and improving the quality of the environment,
- protecting human health,
- prudent and rational utilisation of natural resources,
- promoting measures at international level to deal with regional or worldwide environmental problems, and in particular combating climate change.

Article 191(2) TFEU further provides a number of principles that are specifically applicable to the exercise of EU environmental competence (both internally and externally)[4] as a guide for law-making and for interpretation, namely: a high level of environmental protection, prevention, precaution, rectification at the source and the polluter pays.[5] At first sight, these provisions may appear relatively elaborated when compared to

[1] Single European Act [1987] OJ L169/24, Art130r(5).

[2] For an overview of this historical evolution, see G Marín Durán and E Morgera, *Environmental Integration in the EU's External Relations – Beyond Multilateral Dimensions* (Oxford, Hart Publishing, 2012) 9–13.

[3] TEU, Art 5(2).

[4] In addition, this is subject to the general principles of proportionality (TFEU Art 5(4)) and subsidiarity (TEU Art 5(3)).

[5] For a more detailed discussion, see Marín Durán and Morgera (n 2) 15–16. Note that TFEU Art 191(3) further lists a number of criteria that the EU legislator 'shall take into account' in environmental policy making, including: available scientific and technical data; environmental conditions in various regions of the

those of other EU external policies, such as the Common Commercial Policy (see further Chapter 7).[6] Yet, the objectives and principles enshrined in Article 191 TFEU are broadly defined, rendering it almost impossible to clearly delineate the substantive boundaries of EU environmental policy. EU primary law does not, in fact, seek to (unduly) restrict the substantive scope of EU environmental competence, but leaves the EU legislator a wide margin of appreciation in deciding what action and measures, if any, are necessary to achieve the environmental objectives and principles stipulated in Article 191 TFEU.[7] This seems a desirable approach, given the need for flexibility and adaptation in formulating a policy that can address a range of environmental issues and adjust to new developments and specific circumstances. As to the territorial scope of EU environmental competence, reference to 'regional and worldwide environmental problems' in Article 191(1) TFEU indicates that the EU can also take measures targeting the environment beyond its borders, in the same way in which its Member States can do so, within the limits imposed by international law on the extraterritorial application of domestic environmental measures.

Therefore, the substantive content of the EU external environmental policy has evolved considerably over the past four decades, driven by changes in the international environmental landscape as well as by the EU's own policy priorities. Among the environmental issues prioritised by the EU in its external action,[8] the fight against climate change has undoubtedly taken the lion's share, as could be anticipated from the prominent attention it receives in Article 191(1) TFEU.[9] In fact, the EU has aspired to play a leadership role in the global battle against climate change since the late 1980s, both by attempting to influence and strengthen the multilateral framework for climate change mitigation and by seeking to 'lead by example' through internal climate policies and legislation.[10] In this regard, the EU's overarching objective of becoming an 'energy-efficient, green and competitive low-carbon economy' by 2020[11] led to the adoption in May 2007 of the 2020 Climate and Energy Package, whereby the EU set for itself the targets of: reducing its greenhouse gas (GHG) emissions by 20% from 1990 levels; increasing the share of renewable energy to at least 20% in EU final energy consumption and to at least 10% of energy used in the transport sector; and improving energy

EU; potential benefits and costs of action or lack of action; and the economic and social development of the EU as a whole.

6 See TFEU, Arts 206–207.

7 Ibid, Art 192(1).

8 See Decision No 1386/2013/EU of the European Parliament and of the Council of 20 November 2013 on a General Union Environment Action Programme to 2020 [2013] OJ L354/171 (Seventh Environment Action Programme); and its predecessor Decision (EC) 1600/2002 of 22 the European Parliament and of the Council laying down the Sixth Environment Action Programme [2002] OJ L242/1.

9 This is also evident from the setting up of a specific Directorate General (DG) within the European Commission (DG Climate Action) in 2010 to deal with climate change matters, which were previously handled by DG Environment.

10 K Kulovesi, 'Climate Change in EU External Relations: Please Follow My Example (or I Might Force You To)' in E Morgera (ed) *The External Environmental Policy of the European Union: EU and International Perspectives* (Cambridge, Cambridge University Press, 2013) 118–38.

11 European Commission, 'Communication on Europe 2020. A Strategy for Smart, Sustainable and Inclusive Growth' COM (2010) 2020, endorsed by the European Council, 'Conclusions' (EUCO13/10), 17 June 2010.

efficiency by 20%.[12] In October 2014, EU leaders further committed to new and more ambitious targets under the 2030 Climate and Energy Framework.[13]

K Kulovesi, 'Climate Change in EU External Relations: Please Follow My Example (or I Might Force You To)' in E Morgera (ed) *The External Environmental Policy of the European Union: EU and International Perspectives* (Cambridge, Cambridge University Press, 2013) 115–17

Over the years, the EU has attempted to use its international influence to strengthen the multilateral framework for climate change mitigation under the United Nations Framework Convention on Climate Change (UNFCCC), albeit with modest results. Its efforts to 'lead by example' through internal climate policies and legislation have been somewhat more successful ... However, few developed countries have chosen to follow the EU's footsteps and introduce equivalent, national, climate change legislation ... Given the lack of success of its cooperative international efforts, the EU has recently taken certain steps to force the direction of international climate policy. It has included international aviation emissions in the ETS [Emissions Trading Scheme] and banned credits from controversial industrial gas projects under the Kyoto Protocol's Clean Development Mechanism (CDM). It has also introduced sustainability criteria for biofuels and considered the possibility of trade measures against imports of energy-intensive products from countries lacking effective climate policies.

The EU's global climate change leadership has also been affected by broader trends around multilateralism and international law. Europeans have traditionally sought to promote international law, hoping to model international relations on domestic legalism. This stands in contrast to Americans, who tend to see international legalisation as merely 'a policy choice, a matter of costs and benefits with no *a priori* reason to believe that the latter would outweigh the former' ... [T]hese general attitudes have had a discernible influence on international climate change cooperation and the EU's outlook in terms of guiding the international community towards a strong international legal regime has tended to oscillate between optimism and pessimism.

[12] European Council, 'Presidency Conclusions – Brussels, 8/9 March 2007' (7224/1/07), 2 May 2007, 10–12 and 19–18. For a discussion, see, inter alia, K Kulovesi, E Morgera and M Muñoz, 'Environmental Integration and Multi-Faceted International Dimensions of EU Law: Unpacking the EU's 2009 Climate and Energy Package' (2011) 48 *Common Market Law Review* 829.

[13] European Commission, 'Communication on a Policy Framework for Climate and Energy in the period from 2020 to 2030' COM(2014) 15 final, 22 January 2014; and European Council, 'Conclusions – Brussels, 23–24 October 2014' (EUCO 169/14), 24 October 2014, namely: (i) 40% reduction in GHG emissions from 1990 levels by 2030; (ii) 27% share of renewable energy in EU energy consumption by 2030; (iii) 27% improvement in energy efficiency by 2030.

Aside from climate change, the Seventh Environment Action Programme (2014–2020) also highlights other thematic priorities for the EU's external environmental policy, and notably: the protection of biodiversity, sustainable forest management, sound management of chemicals and of hazardous waste and air and water quality.[14] In terms of approach, the Action Plan reaffirms the EU's multifaceted role as a global environmental actor: a commitment to multilateralism wherever possible, while calling for EU action at regional, bilateral and unilateral levels where deemed appropriate.

Seventh Environment Action Programme (2014–2020)

98. Many of the priority objectives set out in the 7th EAP can only be fully achieved as part of a global approach and in cooperation with partner countries, and overseas countries and territories. That is why the Union and its Member States should engage in relevant international, regional and bilateral processes in a strong, focused, united and coherent manner ... The Union and its Member States should continue to promote an effective, rules-based framework for global environment policy, complemented by a more effective, strategic approach in which bilateral and regional political dialogues and cooperation are tailored towards the Union's strategic partners, candidate and neighbourhood countries, and developing countries, respectively, supported by adequate finance.

103. The Union should also leverage its position as one of the largest markets in the world to promote policies and approaches that decrease pressure on the global natural resource base. This can be done by changing patterns of consumption and production, including by taking the steps necessary to promote sustainable resource management at international level and to implement the 10-year Framework of Programmes on Sustainable Consumption and Production, as well as ensuring that trade and internal market policies support the achievement of environment and climate goals and provide incentives to other countries to upgrade and enforce their environmental regulatory frameworks and standards, with a view to preventing environmental dumping.

EU external environmental policy is included in the list of shared competences in Article 4(2) TFEU,[15] but it arguably belongs to the special sub-category of *non-pre-emptive* shared competence (see further Chapter 3) – that is, the exercise of EU external competence should not, in principle, prevent the Member States from acting in the environmental field at the international level.

[14] European Commission, 'A General Union Environment Action Programme to 2020: Living Well, within the Limits of our Planet' (2014) 81–84.

[15] TFEU, Art 4(2)(e).

Article 191(4) TFEU

Within their respective spheres of competence, the Union and the Member States shall cooperate with third countries and with the competent international organisations. The arrangements for Union cooperation may be the subject of agreements between the Union and the third parties concerned. [This] shall be without prejudice to Member States' competence to negotiate in international bodies and to conclude international agreements.

Moreover, the classic *ERTA* pre-emptive effect (see Chapter 3) would seem of limited relevance in the environmental sphere, where the EU often adopts legislation establishing minimum standards, rather than aimed at substantial harmonisation of rules. Thus, Member States are allowed to adopt more stringent measures domestically and assume more stringent obligations internationally.

Article 193 TFEU

[EU environmental legislation and action programmes] shall not prevent any Member State from maintaining or introducing more stringent protective measures.

However, this possibility can be significantly curtailed in the context of 'mixed' agreements by the duty of sincere cooperation (Article 4(3) TEU), which will be discussed later in the chapter.

B. Instruments and Institutional Actors

As any other international actor, the EU conducts its external environmental policy through two main types of instruments: international agreements (multilateral, regional, bilateral) and autonomous (or unilateral) measures. In terms of institutional actors, the Council, the European Parliament and the European Commission exercise most direct influence in EU external environmental policy making.

Autonomous EU environmental legislation (Regulations or Directives) is generally adopted following the ordinary legislative procedure, that is: the Council (by qualified majority voting) and the European Parliament act on a legislative proposal from the Commission, after consulting the Economic and Social Committee and the Committee of Regions. This procedure also applies to the adoption of general action programmes (as Decisions), which are the key tool for setting out the priority objectives for EU environmental policy, such as the Seventh Environment Action Programme (2014–2020) mentioned above. However, decision-making on a number of specific matters is still subject to unanimity in the Council:

Article 192(2) TFEU

By way of derogation from the decision-making procedure provided for in paragraph 1 and without prejudice to Article 114, the Council acting unanimously in accordance with a special legislative procedure and after consulting the European Parliament, the Economic and Social Committee and the Committee of the Regions, shall adopt:

(a) provisions primarily of a fiscal nature;
(b) measures affecting:
- town and country planning,
- quantitative management of water resources or affecting, directly or indirectly, the availability of those resources,
- land use, with the exception of waste management;

(c) measures significantly affecting a Member State's choice between different energy sources and the general structure of its energy supply.

The conclusion of agreements with third countries and international organisations based on Article 191(4) TFEU is undertaken in accordance with the general procedure laid down in Article 218 TFEU. The Council, usually based on a recommendation from the Commission, will authorise the opening of negotiations. The Commission usually acts as the negotiator for the EU side, based on directives set by the Council and often in consultations with a committee of national representatives set up jointly with the Member States for this purpose. The Council, after obtaining the consent of the European Parliament, will then take a decision authorising the signing of the agreement and another decision on the conclusion of the agreement on behalf of the EU, which is equivalent to an authorisation to ratify the agreement (see further Chapter 4). The Council generally acts by qualified-majority voting throughout this procedure, except in cases where unanimous decision-making is required internally (as per Article 192(2) TFEU seen above). However, given the 'mixed' nature of most environmental agreements, EU Member States will also take part in the negotiation process, as well as conclude and ratify the agreement in accordance with their respective constitutional requirements.

II. EU External Environmental Policy in Practice

Since it was bestowed with an express external competence for environmental matters by the 1986 SEA, the European Union (then European Economic Community) has increasingly sought to assert itself as an ever more influential player in global environmental governance. This is hardly surprising given that a worthwhile environmental policy necessarily implicates an external dimension, which the EU has gradually developed using a plethora of multilateral, bilateral and unilateral instruments. Furthermore, the EU has a clear potential – and one could even argue responsibility – as a global environmental actor, speaking on behalf of its (presently) 28 Member States and being the world's largest trading bloc and major provider of official development aid (ODA) and contributions to the United Nations (UN) budgets.[16]

A. Multilateral Environmental Agreements: Legal Issues from Mixity

The EU is presently a party to over 30 international environmental agreements,[17] including key multilateral environmental agreements (MEAs) negotiated under the auspices of the UN, such as:

The EU as a party to MEAs

- *In the area of climate change and ozone depletion:* the 1985 Convention for the Protection of the Ozone Layer (Ozone Convention)[18] and its 1987 Montreal Protocol;[19] the 1992 UN Framework Convention on Climate Change,[20] its 1997 Kyoto Protocol[21] and the 2015 Paris Agreement.[22]
- *In the area of conservation and biodiversity:* the 1973 Convention on International Trade in Endangered Species of Wild Fauna and Flora (CITES);[23] 1979 Convention on the Conservation of Migratory Species of Wild Animals;[24] the 1992 Convention on Biological Diversity (CBD),[25] its 2003 Cartagena Protocol on Biosafety[26] and its 2010 Nagoya Protocol on

[16] In 2017, EU and Member States' collective ODA amounted to €75.7 billion, constituting 57% of global ODA. However, only four EU Member States met the UN target of 0.7% GNI. See http://europa.eu/rapid/press-release_IP-18-3002_en.htm.

[17] European Commission, 'Multilateral Environmental Agreement to which the EU is a Contracting Party' (August 2017). Available at: http://ec.europa.eu/environment/international_issues/agreements_en.htm.

[18] Vienna Convention for the Protection of the Ozone Layer, 22 March 1985, 1513 UNTS 293, entered into force for the EU on 22 September 1988.

[19] Montreal Protocol on Substances that Deplete the Ozone Layer, 16 September 1987, 1522 UNTS 3, entered into force for the EU on 1 January 1989.

[20] United Nations Framework Convention on Climate Change, 4 June 1992, 1771 UNTS 107, entered into force for the EU on 21 March 1994.

[21] Kyoto Protocol, 11 December 1997, 37 ILM. 22 (1998), entered into force for the EU on 16 February 2005.

[22] Paris Agreement, 12 December 2015, entered into force for the EU on 4 November 2016.

[23] Convention on International Trade in Endangered Species of Wild Fauna and Flora, 3 March 1973, 993 UNTS 243, entered into force for the EU 8 July 2015.

[24] Convention on the Conservation of Migratory Species of Wild Animals, 23 June 1979, 1651 UNTS 333 entered into force for the EU on 1 November 1983.

[25] Convention on Biological Diversity, 5 June 1992, 1760 UNTS 79, entered into force for the EU on 29 December 1993.

[26] Cartagena Protocol on Biosafety, 29 January 2000, 2226 UNTS 208, entered into force for the EU on 11 September 2003.

Access to Genetic Resources;[27] and the 2001 International Treaty on Plant Genetic Resources for Food and Agriculture.[28]

- *In the area of hazardous substances*: the 1989 Basel Convention on the Control of Transboundary Movements of Hazardous Wastes and their Disposal;[29] the 1998 Rotterdam Convention on the Prior Informed Consent Procedure for Certain Hazardous Chemicals and Pesticides in International Trade (Rotterdam Convention);[30] the 2001 the Stockholm Convention on Persistent Organic Pollutants (POPs Convention);[31] and the 2013 Minamata Convention on Mercury.[32]
- *In the area of soil*: the 1994 Convention to Combat Desertification.[33]

In addition, the EU is a party to multilateral agreements with an important environmental dimension, such as the 1982 UN Convention on the Law of Sea (UNCLOS)[34] and its implementing agreements on fish stocks[35] and seabed mining,[36] as well as to several international environmental agreements negotiated at regional level (eg, in the context of the UN Economic Commission for Europe)[37] and sub-regional level (eg, for the management of seas or transboundary rivers).[38]

[27] Nagoya Protocol on Access to Genetic Resources and the Fair and Equitable Sharing of the Benefits Arising from their Utilization, 29 October 2010, UNEP/CBD/COP/DEC/X/1, entered into force for the EU on 12 October 2014.

[28] International Treaty on Plant Genetic Resources for Food and Agriculture, 3 November 2001, 2400 UNTS 303, entered into force for the EU on 29 June 2004.

[29] Basel Convention on the Control of Transboundary Movements of Hazardous Wastes and their Disposal, 22 March 1989, 1673 UNTS 57, entered into force for the EU on 5 May 1992.

[30] Rotterdam Convention on Prior Informed Consent for Certain Hazardous Chemicals and Pesticides, 10 September 1998, 2244 UNTS 337, entered into force for the EU on 24 February 2004.

[31] Stockholm Convention on Persistent Organic Pollutants, 22 May 2001, 2256 UNTS 119, entered into force for the EU on 17 May 2004.

[32] Minamata Convention on Mercury, 10 October 2013, entered into force for the EU 18 May 2017.

[33] Convention to Combat Desertification in Countries Experiencing Serious Drought and/or Desertification, particularly in Africa, 14 October 1994, 1954 UNTS 3, entered into force for the EU on 26 December 1996.

[34] United Nations Convention on the Law of the Sea, 10 December 1982, 1833 UNTS 3, entered into force for the EU on 16 November 1994.

[35] Agreement for the Implementation of the Provisions of the United Nations Convention on the Law of the Sea relating to the Conservation and Management of Straddling Fish Stocks and Highly Migratory Fish Stocks, 4 August 1995, 2167 UNTS 3, entered into force for the EU on 11 December 2001.

[36] Agreement relating to the Implementation of Part XI of the United Nations Convention on the Law of Sea of 10 December 1982, 28 July 1994, 1836 UNTS 3, entered into force for the EU on 28 July 1996.

[37] Eg, the UNECE Convention on Long-range Transboundary Air Pollution, 13 November 1979, 1302 UNTS 217, entered into force for the EU on 16 March 1983; and the UNECE Convention on Access to Information, Public Participation in Decision-Making and Access to Justice in Environmental Matters, 25 June 1998, 2161 UNTS 447, entered into force for the EU on 30 October 2001.

[38] Eg, the Barcelona Convention for the Protection of the Mediterranean Sea against Pollution, 16 February 1976, 1102 UNTS 16908, entered into force for the EU on 15 April 1978 (as amended and its protocols).

Nevertheless, the Seventh Environment Action Programme (2014–2020) recognises that:

Seventh Environment Action Programme (2014–2020)

101. The Union has a good track-record when it comes to membership of multilateral environmental agreements (MEAs), although a number of Member States have still not ratified key agreements. This compromises the Union's credibility in related negotiations. Member States and the Union should ensure the ratification and approval, respectively, in a timely manner, of all MEAs to which they are signatories.

In the vast majority of these MEAs, the EU's participation has been accommodated through so-called 'regional economic integration organization' (REIO) clauses. In the case of CITES, the 1983 Gaborone Amendment permitting REIO membership took several decades to enter into force and the EU could only accede to this treaty in April 2015. By way of illustration, the REIO participation clause in CITES provides:

Article XXI CITES – Accession

1. The present Convention shall be open indefinitely for accession. Instruments of accession shall be deposited with the Depositary Government.
2. This Convention shall be open for accession by regional economic integration organizations constituted by sovereign States which have competence in respect of the negotiation, conclusion and implementation of international agreements in matters transferred to them by their Member States and covered by this Convention.

…

These MEAs have been concluded as 'mixed' agreements and this joint participation of the EU and its Member States poses several internal and external challenges. Internally, the practice of mixed agreements demands close cooperation between the EU and its Member States throughout the conclusion, negotiation and implementation phases with a view to ensuring 'the unity in the international representation of the [Union]'.[39] This has been addressed to a large extent by the duty of sincere

[39] Opinion 2/91 (*ILO Convention No. 170*), ECLI:EU:C:1993:106, para 36; Opinion 1/94 (*WTO*), ECLI:EU:C:1994:384, paras 108–9.

cooperation set out in Article 4(3) TEU, which has been gradually interpreted by the Court as entailing for the Member States not only a procedural 'best-endeavours' obligation to consult and cooperate with the EU institutions, but also a more substantive duty of abstention (see Chapter 2). In fact, it is in the context of an MEA (the POPs Convention) that the Court adopted this stricter reading of the duty of sincere cooperation. In *Commission v Sweden*, it found Sweden in breach of Article 4(3) TEU for unilaterally proposing the inclusion of PFOS (perfluorooctane sulfonates) in Annex A of the POPs Convention, even though it had consulted the EU institutions on the possibility of a common proposal to list PFOS but no formal decision was taken on the matter within Council. The Court, however, held:

Case C-246/07 *Commission v Sweden (PFOS)*, ECLI:EU:C:2010:203

76 In the present case, it is settled ground that, at the time when the Kingdom of Sweden submitted the proposal for the listing of PFOS in Annex A to the Stockholm Convention on 14 July 2005, the Council had not adopted any formal decision as regards a proposal to list substances in that annex. However, the Court must examine whether, as the Commission maintains, there was at the time a Community strategy in that regard which was not to propose the listing of PFOS immediately in the context of that convention, inter alia, for economic reasons.

…

87 Contrary to what the Kingdom of Sweden and the interveners maintain, it appears that there was no 'decision-making vacuum' or even a waiting period equivalent to the absence of a decision. A number of factors lend support to the argument that the Council's Working Party on International Environmental Issues did not intend to reach a decision on 6 July 2005 – but certainly thereafter – on the substances to be proposed under the Stockholm Convention in addition to those already proposed in May 2005. The urgency of deciding first on the substances to be proposed under the Aarhus Protocol and the economic considerations connected with proposals under that convention may be mentioned in that regard.

…

89 In any event, it may be regarded as established that, in 2005, there was a common strategy not to propose, at that time, to list PFOS in Annex A to the Stockholm Convention, since, as is apparent from the Council's conclusions of March 2005, the experts of the Member States and of the Community were to choose the substances to be proposed from among those already covered by the Aarhus Protocol and that, as is apparent from the minutes of the meeting of the Council's Working Party on International Environmental Issues of 6 July 2005, PFOS was not one of those substances.

…

> 91 It follows that, in unilaterally proposing the addition of PFOS to Annex A to the Stockholm Convention, the Kingdom of Sweden dissociated itself from a concerted common strategy within the Council.
>
> 92 Moreover, as is apparent from examination of the decision-making process provided for by that convention, the Kingdom of Sweden's unilateral proposal has consequences for the Union.
>
> …
>
> 98 That argument is, however, based on the assumption that the Union would be in a position to make a declaration of non-acceptance of an amendment proposed and voted for by one or more Member States. Under Article 25(2) of the Stockholm Convention, the Union and its Member States are not entitled to exercise rights under the Convention concurrently.
>
> 99 However, even supposing, despite Article 25(2) of the Stockholm Convention, that the Union could still notify a declaration of non-acceptance of an amendment proposed and voted for by several Member States, such a situation could give rise to legal uncertainty for the Member States, the Secretariat of the Stockholm Convention and non-member countries which are parties to that convention.
>
> …
>
> 104 Such a situation is likely to compromise the principle of unity in the international representation of the Union and its Member States and weaken their negotiating power with regard to the other parties to the Convention concerned.

In the circumstances of this specific case, there were seemingly genuine reasons for safeguarding a united Union position under the Stockholm Convention, particularly since it was not clear whether the EU would have been able to opt-out from an amendment unilaterally proposed and voted for by one (or more) of its Member States. Nonetheless, this case law raises broader questions as to which course of Union action triggers the application of duty of sincere cooperation and when would EU Member States be allowed to act in areas of shared external competences, such as environmental policy.

> **A Delgado Casteleiro and J Larik, 'The Duty to Remain Silent: Limitless Loyalty in EU External Relations?' (2011) 36 *European Law Review* 524, 540**
>
> … whereas previously the duty seemed to be triggered from the moment a concerted Union position had been launched by a positive legal act (giving the Commission a mandate or at least an official Commission proposal), now, after

> these cases, it has become unclear until which point Member States would still be free to act. They must now be silent even before the Union has made up its own mind about whether and when it is going to speak. The concept of a Union position has been broadened by the Court so as to include situations in which the EU institutions have not reached a decision ... One might even say that, according to the ECJ, indecisiveness constitutes a valid Union position or strategy ...
>
> [T]he scope of the 'duty to remain silent' seems to make the distinction between exclusive and shared competence virtually irrelevant. Simply because a Member State still is competent about a matter, it does not mean that it can speak up about it outside the European Union. As the recent case law shows, it seems that Member States need a kind of EU authorisation in order to exercise 'their share' of shared competence. Therefore, what is left for Member States to do on the world stage? Is there any situation in which a Member State could open its mouth in the presence of Union competence (and ECJ jurisdiction) but in the absence of Union authorisation?

From an international law perspective, the mixed character of MEAs inevitably prompts the question as to who – the EU, the Member States, or both – is responsible towards third parties for the performance of obligations assumed under these agreements, and hence for remedying any alleged breach (see further Chapter 5).[40] In an attempt to address this question, a common practice has been for the EU to make a 'Declaration of Competence' in MEAs that explicitly demand clarification as to the distribution of competences between the REIO and its Member States.[41] However, these declarations have generally failed to offer much legal clarity to other contracting parties as to who is responsible on the EU side for the performance of mixed MEAs.[42] In most cases, such declarations are very short and merely indicate the existence of EU external competence for environmental matters on the basis of Article 191 TFEU and its responsibility for the performance of obligations resulting from the MEA which 'are covered by [EU] law in force' without further specification.[43] In addition,

[40] See generally, A Nollkaemper, 'Joint Responsibility between the EU and Member States for Non-Performance of Obligations under Multilateral Environmental Agreements' in E Morgera (ed) *The External Environmental Policy of the European Union: EU and International Perspectives* (Cambridge, Cambridge University Press, 2013).

[41] See eg, UNCLOS, Annex IX, Article 5.1. Subsequent MEAs to which the EU has made a 'Declaration of Competence' include: 1985 Ozone Convention and its Montreal Protocol; the 1992 UNFCCC, its Kyoto Protocol and Paris Agreement; 1998 Rotterdam Convention; the 2001 POPs Convention; 1992 CBD and its Cartagena and Nagoya Protocols.

[42] See generally, A Delgado Casteleiro, 'EU Declarations of Competence to Multilateral Agreements: A Useful Reference Base?' (2012) 17 *European Foreign Affairs Review* 491.

[43] See eg, Council Decision of 19 December 2002 concerning the approval, on behalf of the European Community, of the Rotterdam Convention on the Prior Informed Consent Procedure for certain hazardous chemicals and pesticides in international trade [2003] OJ L 63/27, Annex B.

the declarations often signal that '[t]he exercise of [EU] competence is, by its nature, subject to continuous development.'[44] In light of this, the EU undertakes to update the relevant declarations, but this has hardly happened in practice: for instance, the declaration under UNCLOS has never been updated since 1982 and refers to several pieces of EU legislation that have been amended or indeed fully repealed.[45] Admittedly, given the complex and dynamic nature of the EU's external competences, drafting a legally accurate and clear declaration, and keeping it up-to-date, is a nearly impossible endeavour. This being so, a more suitable approach has been adopted under UNCLOS which, however, is exceptional among the multilateral agreements jointly concluded by the EU and its Member States in the sphere of environmental protection. A procedural mechanism has been established under UNCLOS to provide third parties with the possibility of requesting further clarification about the EU and Member States' respective responsibility on a case-by-case basis and, ultimately, with the legal certainty that somebody on the EU side will be responsible.

UNCLOS, Annex IX, Article 6.2

Any State Party may request an international organisation or its member States which are States Parties for information as to who has responsibility in respect of any specific matter. The organisation and the member States concerned shall provide this information. Failure to provide this information within a reasonable time or the provision of contradictory information shall result in joint and several liability.

B. Bilateral Environmental Instruments: FLEGT Voluntary Partnership Agreements

Alongside participating in multilateral environmental agreements, the EU has also advanced environmental protection goals through *bilateral* instruments, not only to promote the implementation of existing MEAs and on-going multilateral environmental negotiations,[46] but also in the absence thereof. One significant example of the latter is in the area of sustainable forest management, which has long been a priority of the EU's external environmental policy and where the Union has been supporting the development of an international convention.[47] In the lack thereof, the EU has

[44] See eg, Council Decision of 14 October 2004 concerning the conclusion, on behalf of the European Community, of the Stockholm Convention on Persistent Organic Pollutants [2006] OJ L 209/1, Annex.

[45] Council Decision of 23 March 1998 concerning the conclusion by the European Community of the United Nations Convention of 10 December 1982 on the Law of the Sea and the Agreement of 28 July 1994 relating to the implementation of Part XI thereof [1998] OJ L179/129, Annex II.

[46] See Section III.B for examples.

[47] A Savaresi, 'EU External Action on Forest: FLEGT and the Development of International Law' in E Morgera (ed) *The External Environmental Policy of the European Union – EU and International Law Perspectives* (Cambridge, Cambridge University Press, 2013) 150–53.

concluded so-called 'Voluntary' Partnership Agreements (VPA) with (thus far) seven timber-producing countries[48] in the framework of its 2003 Forest Law Enforcement, Governance and Trade (FLEGT) Action Plan aimed at fighting illegal logging and associated trade.[49] These VPAs are based on the 2005 FLEGT Regulation, which sets up a licensing scheme for controlling the legality of timber imported into the EU.[50] To ensure that only legally produced timber is shipped to the EU, VPAs provide for the establishment of a legality assurance system in the third country concerned addressing the following basic elements: a clear definition of 'legal' timber, sophisticated mechanisms for verifying compliance throughout the production and supply chain, issuance of FLEGT licences by the competent national authority and independent audits.

Voluntary Partnership Agreement between the European Union and Viet Nam

Article 1 – Objectives

1. The objective of this Agreement, consistent with the Parties' common commitment to the sustainable management of all types of forest, is to provide a legal framework aimed at ensuring that all imports into the Union from Viet Nam of timber and timber products covered by this Agreement have been legally produced and, in doing so, to promote trade in timber products from sustainably managed forests and harvested in accordance with the domestic legislation in the country of harvest.
2. This Agreement also provides a basis for dialogue and cooperation between the Parties to facilitate and promote the full implementation of this Agreement and enhance forest law enforcement and governance.

...

Article 3 – FLEGT Licensing Scheme

1. A Forest Law Enforcement, Governance and Trade Licensing Scheme (hereinafter referred to as 'the FLEGT licensing scheme') is hereby established between the Parties. It establishes a set of procedures and requirements aimed at verifying and attesting, by means of FLEGT licences, that timber products shipped to the Union were legally produced. In accordance with Regulation (EC) No 2173/2005 and this Agreement, the Union shall accept such shipments from Viet Nam for import into the Union only if they are covered by FLEGT licences.

[48] These are: Cameroon, Central African Republic, Ghana, Indonesia, Liberia, Republic of Congo and Vietnam. Negotiations are ongoing with Côte d'Ivoire, Gabon, Guyana, Honduras, Laos, Malaysia and Thailand.

[49] European Commission Communication, 'Forest Law Enforcement, Governance and Trade (FLEGT) – Proposal for an EU Action Plan' COM(2003)251 final, dated 21 May 2003.

[50] Council Regulation (EC) No 2173/2005 of 20 December 2005 on the Establishment of a FLEGT Licensing Scheme for Imports of Timber into the European Community [2005] OJ L347/1.

2. The FLEGT licensing scheme shall apply to the timber products listed in Annex 1.
3. Each Party agrees to take all measures necessary to implement the FLEGT licensing scheme.

Article 4 – Licensing Authorities

1. Viet Nam shall designate the FLEGT Licensing Authority and notify its contact details to the European Commission. Both Parties shall make this information available to the public.
2. The Licensing Authority shall verify that timber products have been legally produced in accordance with the legislation identified in Annex II. The Licensing Authority shall issue FLEGT licences covering shipments of timber products that are legally produced in Viet Nam for export to the Union.

Article 5 – Competent Authorities

1. The European Commission shall inform Viet Nam of the contact details of the competent authorities designated by the Member States of the Union. Both Parties shall make this information available to the public.
2. The competent authorities shall verify that each shipment is covered by a valid FLEGT licence before releasing that shipment for free circulation in the Union. The release of the shipment may be suspended and the shipment may be held if there are doubts regarding the validity of the FLEGT licence.

…

Article 7 – Definition of Legally Produced Timber

For the purposes of this Agreement, a definition of legally produced timber is given in Paragraph (j) of Article 2 of this Agreement and specified in Annex II. This Annex describes Vietnamese legislation that must be complied with in order for timber products to be covered by a FLEGT licence. It also includes documentation containing the principles, criteria, indicators and verifiers serving to prove compliance with such legislation.

Article 8 – Verification of Legally Produced Timber

1. Viet Nam shall establish and implement a Viet Nam Timber Legality Assurance System (VNTLAS) to verify that timber and timber products have been legally produced and to ensure that only shipments verified as such are exported to the Union. The VNTLAS shall include compliance checks and procedures to ensure that timber of illegal or unknown origin does not enter the supply chain.
2. The system for verifying that shipments of timber products have been legally produced is set out in Annex V.

…

Article 10 – Independent Evaluation

1. The purpose of the Independent Evaluation is to assess the implementation, effectiveness and credibility of the Viet Nam Timber Legality Assurance System and FLEGT licensing scheme, as set out in Annex VI.
2. Viet Nam, in consultation with the Union, shall engage the services of the Independent Evaluation to implement the tasks as set out in Annex VI.
3. The Independent Evaluator shall be a body with no conflict of interest resulting from an organisational or commercial relationship with the Union or with the Vietnam forestry sector regulatory authorities, its licensing authority or anybody given the responsibility of verifying the legality of timber production, or any operator exercising a commercial activity in its forestry sector. ...

The FLEGT initiative has been praised as being markedly partnership-orientated, where the EU 'acts as a co-creator of [environmental] norms rather than an exporter' of its own rules,[51] as well as a 'novel experimentalist architecture in transnational forest governance'.[52] This is partly because the national legislation of the partner country is the starting point for assessing the legality of timber products, albeit this is as set out in the VPA and, hence, as agreed by the EU. In addition, VPAs emphasise dialogue and cooperation between the Parties with a view to enhancing forest law enforcement and governance, as well as stakeholder involvement in the implementation of the agreement.[53] Under VPAs, the EU also commits to support partner countries in upgrading their legal and administrative frameworks on forest management through financial and technical assistance, and to implement measures promoting FLEGT-licensed timber within the EU market (eg, private and public procurement).[54]

As progress towards concluding VPAs remained somewhat limited, in 2010, the EU strengthened its bilateral approach with the (unilateral) Timber Due Diligence Regulation, which prohibits the placing of illegally harvested timber in the EU market and economic operators are required to exercise due diligence in ensuring the legal origin of timber products.[55] The Regulation creates an additional incentive for third

[51] E Morgera, 'Ambition, Complexity and Legitimacy of Pursuing Mutual Supportiveness through the EU's Environmental External Action' in B van Vooren and S Blockmans (eds) *The EU's Role in Global Governance – The Legal Dimension* (Oxford, Oxford University Press, 2013) 207.

[52] C Overdevest and J Zeitlin, 'Experimentalism in Transnational Forest Governance: Implementing European Union Forest Law Enforcement, Governance and Trade (FLEGT) Voluntary Partnership Agreements in Indonesia and Ghana' (2018) 12 *Regulation & Governance* 64.

[53] See eg, Voluntary Partnership Agreement between the European Union and the Republic of Indonesia on Forest Law Enforcement, Governance and Trade in Timber Products into the European Union [2014] OJ L150/252, Art 11.

[54] Ibid, Arts 13 and 16.

[55] Council and European Parliament Regulation (EU) No 995/2010 of 20 December 2010 laying down obligations of operators who place timber and timber products on the market [2010] OJ L295/23, Arts 1 and 4.

countries to enter into VPA negotiations with the Union, by providing a presumption of compliance with the due diligence requirements for FLEGT-licensed timber originating in VPA partner countries.[56] This is undoubtedly a powerful inducement, considering the EU is the largest importer of wood from Africa, Russia and South America and the second-largest from Asia.[57] At the same time, it may raise questions as to the truly 'voluntary' nature of these FLEGT-led partnerships. In addition, the interaction between VPAs and the Timber Due Diligence Regulation exemplifies that EU external action on a given environmental issue may involve a complex mix of policy tools and, hence, cannot always be placed into neat categories of 'multilateralism' or 'bilateralism' or 'unilateralism'.

C. Unilateral Environmental Instruments: ETS Aviation Directive

Aside from bilateral agreements, the Union has also used its market size and structural power to leverage global or third-party environmental action through *unilateral* instruments. One controversial example in the field of climate change is the EU's attempt to include international aviation emissions into its Emissions Trading System (ETS), which is the world's largest carbon trading scheme covering greenhouse gas emissions from approximately 11,000 energy-intensive power stations and industrial plants, as well as from commercial aviation, in 31 countries (ie, 28 EU Member States, plus Iceland, Liechtenstein and Norway). Against the backdrop of global inaction to address rapidly growing GHG emissions from aviation, and particularly within the International Civil Aviation Organization (ICAO),[58] the EU adopted the ETS Aviation Directive in 2008. It was intended to apply to *all* aircraft operators (including foreign-based airlines) with flights to/from an airport located in the European Economic Area (EEA), thus including GHG emissions from flights between EEA airports and airports *outside* the EEA.[59] Essentially, the ETS sets a cap for aviation emissions (95% of historical emissions from 2013 to 2020)[60] and requires all airlines included in the scheme to surrender allowances each year corresponding to their total (reported and verified) GHG emissions, irrespective of where these took place (ie, within or outside the EU airspace).[61] Failure to do so may lead the imposition of financial penalties and operating bans in the EU territory.

[56] Ibid, Art 3.

[57] European Commission Communication, (n 49) 9–10 and Annex 2.

[58] K Kulovesi, 'Addressing Sectoral Emissions outside the United Nations Framework Convention on Climate Change: What Roles for Multilateralism, Minilateralism and Unilateralism?' (2012) 21 *Review of European Community and International Environmental Law* 193, 195–98.

[59] Directive 2008/101/EC of the European Parliament and of the Council of 19 November 2008 amending Directive 2003/87/EC so as to include aviation activities in the scheme for greenhouse gas emission allowance trading within the Community OJ [2009] L8/3 (ETS Aviation Directive), Art 3(a) and Annex I.

[60] Ibid, Art 3(c)(2).

[61] Ibid, Art 3(d)–(e), whereby only 15% of these allowances are to be auctioned, while the rest are to be issued free of charge.

Directive 2008/101/EC of 19 November 2008 amending Directive 2003/87/EC so as to include aviation activities in the scheme for greenhouse gas emission allowance trading within the Community [2009] OJ L 8/3

THE EUROPEAN PARLIAMENT AND THE COUNCIL OF THE EUROPEAN UNION,

...

(9) ... Appendix L to Resolution A36-22 of the ICAO's 36th Assembly held in September 2007 urges Contracting States not to implement an emissions trading system on other Contracting States' aircraft operators except on the basis of mutual agreement between those States. Recalling that the Chicago Convention recognizes expressly the right of each Contracting Party to apply on a non-discriminatory basis its own air laws and regulations to the aircraft of all States, the Member States of the European Community and fifteen other European States placed a reservation on this resolution and reserved the right under the Chicago Convention to enact and apply market-based measures on a non-discriminatory basis to all aircraft operators of all States providing services to, from or within their territory.

(10) The Sixth Community Environment Action Programme ... provided for the Community to identify and undertake specific actions to reduce greenhouse gas emissions from aviation if no such action were agreed within the ICAO by 2002.

(16) In order to avoid distortions of competition and improve environmental effectiveness, emissions from all flights arriving at and departing from Community aerodromes should be included from 2012.

(17) The Community and its Member States should continue to seek an agreement on global measures to reduce greenhouse gas emissions from aviation. The Community scheme may serve as a model for the use of emissions trading worldwide. The Community and its Member States should continue to be in contact with third parties during the implementation of this Directive and to encourage third countries to take equivalent measures.

(25) In its Conclusions, the European Council meeting in Brussels on 13 and 14 March 2008 recognised that in a global context of competitive markets the risk of carbon leakage is a concern that needs to be analysed and addressed urgently in the new Emissions Trading System Directive, so that if international negotiations fail appropriate measures can be taken. An international agreement remains the best way of addressing this issue.

...

Article 16

3. Member States shall ensure that any operator or aircraft operator who does not surrender sufficient allowances by 30 April of each year to cover its emissions

during the preceding year shall be held liable for the payment of an excess emissions penalty. The excess emissions penalty shall be EUR 100 for each tonne of carbon dioxide equivalent emitted for which the operator or aircraft operator has not surrendered allowances. Payment of the excess emissions penalty shall not release the operator or aircraft operator from the obligation to surrender an amount of allowances equal to those excess emissions when surrendering allowances in relation to the following calendar year.

5. In the event that an aircraft operator fails to comply with the requirements of this Directive and where other enforcement measures have failed to ensure compliance, its administering Member State may request the Commission to decide on the imposition of an operating ban on the aircraft operator concerned.

...

While seeking to serve as a model for global/third-country action, the ETS Aviation Directive was initially faced with hostility from China, India and the United States among other countries, whereby the EU was accused of using unilateral measures and exercising extraterritorial jurisdiction in violation of international law. In addition, the validity of the ETS Aviation Directive was challenged by a group of American airlines before British courts and led to a preliminary ruling request before the EU Court. One of the key questions concerned the territorial scope of the Directive, and more specifically whether it infringed the principles of national sovereignty and territoriality under international law by requiring foreign airlines to surrender emission allowances also for those segments of their flights that take place outside the airspace of the EU Member States. The Court, however, rejected such a claim.

Case C-366/10 *Air Transport Association of America and Others v The Secretary of State for Energy and Climate Change*, ECLI:EU:C:2011:864

125 In laying down a criterion for Directive 2008/101 to be applicable to operators of aircraft registered in a Member State or in a third State that is founded on the fact that those aircraft perform a flight which departs from or arrives at an aerodrome situated in the territory of one of the Member States, Directive 2008/101 ... does not infringe the principle of territoriality or the sovereignty which the third States from or to which such flights are performed have over the airspace above their territory, since those aircraft are physically in the territory of one of the Member States of the European Union and are thus subject on that basis to the unlimited jurisdiction of the European Union.

127 It is only if the operator of such an aircraft has chosen to operate a commercial air route arriving at or departing from an aerodrome situated in the territory

> of a Member State that the operator, because its aircraft is in the territory of that Member State, will be subject to the allowance trading scheme.
>
> 128 As for the fact that the operator of an aircraft in such a situation is required to surrender allowances calculated in the light of the whole of the international flight that its aircraft has performed or is going to perform from or to such an aerodrome, it must be pointed out that, as European Union policy on the environment seeks to ensure a high level of protection in accordance with Article 191(2) TFEU, the European Union legislature may in principle choose to permit a commercial activity, in this instance air transport, to be carried out in the territory of the European Union only on condition that operators comply with the criteria that have been established by the European Union and are designed to fulfil the environmental protection objectives which it has set for itself, in particular where those objectives follow on from an international agreement to which the European Union is a signatory, such as the Framework Convention and the Kyoto Protocol.
>
> 129 Furthermore, the fact that, in the context of applying European Union environmental legislation, certain matters contributing to the pollution of the air, sea or land territory of the Member States originate in an event which occurs partly outside that territory is not such as to call into question, in the light of the principles of customary international law capable of being relied upon in the main proceedings, the full applicability of European Union law in that territory …

Ultimately, the EU decided to limit the geographic reach of the ETS to intra-EEA flights until 31 December 2023,[62] following recent progress in ICAO negotiations and in particular the commitment to implement a global market-based measure to tackle GHG emissions from international aviation by 2021[63] – failing which the EU may revert back to the full territorial scope of the ETS in relation to aviation activities.[64] From this perspective, the ETS Aviation Directive can be seen as a catalyst for global climate change action and, indeed, as an example of what Scott and Rajamani have termed the EU's 'contingent unilateralism'.

[62] Regulation (EU) No 421/2014 of the European Parliament and of the Council of 16 April 2014 amending Directive 2003/87/EC establishing a scheme for greenhouse gas emission allowance trading within the Community, in view of the implementation by 2020 of an international agreement applying a single global market-based measure to international aviation emissions [2014] OJ L129/1; and Regulation (EU) No 2017/2392 of the European Parliament and of the Council of 13 December 2017 amending Directive 2003/87/EC to continue current limitations of scope for aviation activities and to prepare to implement a global market-based measure from 2021 [2017] OJ L350/7, Art 1(6).

[63] International Civil Aviation Organization (ICAO) Assembly (39th Session), 'Resolution A39-3: Consolidated statement of continuing ICAO policies and practices related to environmental protection – Global Market-based Measure (MBM) scheme', adopted 6 October 2016.

[64] Regulation (EU) No 2017/2392, Art 28(b).

J Scott and L Rajamani, 'Contingent Unilateralism – International Aviation in the European Emissions Trading Scheme' in B Van Vooren and S Blockmans (eds) *The EU's Role in Global Governance – The Legal Dimension* (Oxford, Oxford University Press, 2013) 209

Fuelled by both environmental and competitiveness concerns, the EU is acting to extend the global reach of its 'domestic' climate change law. It is engaging in climate change unilateralism, albeit unilateralism of a particular and interesting kind. The EU's climate change unilateralism is 'contingent' in the sense that the global extension of EU climate change law depends upon there being no adequate international agreement or third country climate action in place. As such the EU should be viewed as a reluctant unilateralist and as deploying contingent unilateralism as a means of incentivizing urgently needed climate action elsewhere … [T]he EU is shaping the legal structures of global governance in a multi-polar world by testing the boundaries of permissible unilateral action and by experimenting with a form of action-forcing contingent unilateralism that conceives unilateralism as a necessary policy option but one which, ultimately, is second best.

At a broader normative level, the EU aviation scheme raises interesting questions as to whether clear-cut distinctions between 'multilateral' and 'unilateral' action can still be properly drawn in today's global environmental law landscape, and the extent to which 'minilateralism' should play a role in addressing global environmental challenges.

K Kulovesi, 'Addressing Sectoral Emissions outside the United Nations Framework Convention on Climate Change: What Roles for Multilateralism, Minilateralism and Unilateralism?' (2012) 21 *Review of European Community and International Environmental Law* 193, 201–02.

[T]he choice is no longer between unilateralism, multilateralism or 'doing nothing' but rather between a wider array of more or less collaborative forms of minilateral support to multilateralism. The point that I thus wish to make here is that where agreement on specific multilateral measures is hard to find – as tends to be the case with respect to climate change mitigation in general and sectoral emissions from international aviation and maritime transport in particular – minilateral efforts can play a role in advancing the implementation of multilaterally agreed treaty objectives.

[T]he key question is therefore not whether European countries were entitled to take minilateral action on aviation emissions, but whether the occupation of the regulatory space took place in such a way that violates international rules and principles. Here, I would argue that – by and large – it did not do so. While divergent views will remain, there is a sound legal justification for the territorial scope of the scheme, as also affirmed by the CJEU … [M]ore problematic may be the role of the principle of CBDRRC [Common But Differentiated Responsibilities and Respective Capabilities] in the design of the scheme; including the questions as to whether and how the EU should have taken this principle more carefully and explicitly into account. For this reason, it would be useful for the debate to turn away from the traditional focus on the permissibility of extraterritoriality and unilateralism towards international rules, principles and procedures that curtail EU-type 'minilateral' action that seeks to advance multilateral objectives in the absence of a global agreement.

III. EU Environmental Policy and Other External Policies

A. Environmental Integration as a Treaty Requirement

The interplay between EU environmental policy and other external policies is explicitly recognised in several provisions of the EU Treaties, and most prominently in Article 11 TFEU which stipulates the requirement of environmental integration as a general principle of EU law.

Article 11 TFEU

Environmental integration requirements must be integrated into the definition and implementation of the Union's policies and activities, in particular with a view to promoting sustainable development.

This provision is not the only mainstreaming requirement in EU treaty law, but forms part of a series of other policy-linking clauses progressively introduced as part of the Union's broader efforts to ensure 'horizontal coherence' across its various internal and external policies.[65] Nonetheless, it is the oldest of such clauses and has been steadily strengthened within the EU's constitutional setting.[66] The rationale behind Article 11

[65] See TFEU, Arts 7–13.

[66] Marín Durán and Morgera (n 2) 25–28; and J Nowag, 'Article 11 TFEU and Environmental Rights' in S Bogojevi and R Rayfuse (eds) *Environmental Rights in Europe and Beyond* (Oxford, Hart Publishing, 2018) 157–61.

TFEU lies in the realisation that the furtherance of the EU's environmental objectives may be hindered, or conversely facilitated, by developments in other policy fields, hence the requirement for a continuous 'greening' of all Union policies and activities. In the case of EU external policies, this environmental integration requirement has been reinforced by the Lisbon Treaty and, in particular, by Article 3(5) TEU and Article 21 TEU which lay down the objectives and principles of the Union's external action.[67] In this common set of non-prioritised objectives, environmental protection and sustainable development figure prominently.

Article 21(2) TEU

The Union shall define and pursue common policies and actions, and shall work for a high degree of cooperation in all fields of international relations, in order to: …

- foster the sustainable economic, social and environmental development of developing countries, with the primary aim of eradicating poverty;
- help to develop international measures to preserve and improve the quality of the environment and the sustainable management of global natural resources, in order to ensure sustainable development;
- assist populations, countries and regions confronting natural and man-made disasters;

…

It is largely undisputed that Article 11 TFEU is not merely programmatic, but imposes a legal obligation upon the EU institutions to integrate environmental protection requirements when defining and implementing all Union policies, as well as upon the Member States when implementing and applying EU law.[68] Even though EU legislation infringing Article 11 TFEU is thus liable for annulment by the EU courts, such a breach may be difficult to prove in practice. This is first because the Court has generally accorded a wide margin of discretion to the EU political institutions when implementing and striking a balance between environmental concerns and other (at times, competing) policy objectives set forth in the EU Treaties. In this respect, the exercise of judicial review is usually restricted to verifying that the EU legislator did not clearly exceed the bounds of its discretion (by committing a 'manifest error of appraisal') or misuse its powers.[69] In fact, no EU measure has yet been struck down by the EU courts on the sole basis

[67] Art 3(5) TEU, inter alia, provides that, in its external relations, the EU shall contribute to the 'sustainable development of the Earth'.

[68] Case C-379/98 *PreussenElektra v Schleswag*, Opinion of AG Jacobs, ECLI:EU:C:2000:585, para 231; Marín Durán and Morgera (n 2) 28–32.

[69] See notably Case C-341/95 *Gianni Bettati v Safety Hi-Tech Srl*, ECLI:EU:C:1998:353, paras 32–35 and 53; and for a discussion, Marín Durán and Morgera (n 2) 32–33.

of an infringement of Article 11 TFEU, nor of other Treaty integration clauses.[70] In addition, the environmental integration requirement in Article 11 TFEU is closely tied to the broader notion of 'sustainable development', which is an overarching objective in EU treaty law[71] and itself calls for advancing the three interdependent pillars of economic development, social development and environmental protection in an holistic and non-hierarchical manner.[72] This is also evident in the renewed EU's Sustainable Development Strategy,[73] which was recently adopted in response to the UN 2030 Agenda for Sustainable Development and addresses all internationally agreed 17 Sustainable Development Goals together.[74] In sum, Article 11 TFEU does not entail a strictly enforceable obligation for the EU legislator to effectively integrate, or give precedence to, environmental considerations within the Union's external policy making[75] – whether and how this is done is largely a matter of political appreciation.

M Montini, 'The Principle of Integration' in L Krämer and E Orlando (eds) *Principles of Environmental Law* (Cheltenham, Edward Elgar, 2016) 145–46

In the literature, it has been argued that the principle of integration 'calls for a permanent, continuous greening' of all European Union policies. However, this 'does not allow priority to be given to environmental requirements over other requirements'. It simply means that environmental considerations should be ranked at the same level as other interests and that an adequate balancing of the possibly competing needs should be pursued on a case-by-case basis. This view is also supported by other authors, who argue that the Treaty does not support the view that environmental requirements should be given priority over other policy areas. In fact, as it has been correctly argued, 'the integration principle is designed to ensure that protection of the environment is at least taken into consideration' in the definition and implementation of other EU policies. In sum, it may be concluded that the most correct interpretation of the scope of the principle of integration under TFEU is the following one: wherever any policy and activity of the Union is planned and undertaken 'full consideration must be given to protecting the environment'.

[70] Nowag, (n 66) 163. Exceptionally in Case T-229/04 *Sweden v Commission*, ECLI:EU:T:2007:217, para 262, the General Court did find that the challenged Commission decision was in breach of the integration principle, together with the precautionary and high level of protection principles. However, its reasoning on the breach of the integration principle is succinct and appears largely to rely on finding that the other environmental principles have been infringed: for further discussion, see E Scotford, *Environmental Principles and the Evolution of Environmental Law* (Oxford, Hart Publishing, 2017) 145–46.

[71] TEU Art 3(3).

[72] 'Political Declaration of the World Summit on Sustainable Development' (UN Doc A/CONF.199/20), 4 July 2002, Resolution 1, para 5.

[73] European Commission Communication, 'Next Steps for a Sustainable European Future – European Action for Sustainability' COM(2016) 739 final, dated 22 November 2016.

[74] UN General Assembly, 'Transforming Our World: the 2030 Agenda for Sustainable Development' (UN Doc/A/RES/70/1), 25 September 2015, providing the global blueprint for global sustainable development, with 17 SDGs and 169 associated targets.

[75] Similarly, see Case C-161/04 *Austria v Parliament and Council*, Opinion AG Geelhoed, ECLI:EU:C:2006:512, para 59.

Giving effect to the environmental integration imperative in Article 11 TFEU will often involve complex trade-offs between environmental and other (economic, social) policy objectives, and views are likely to diverge as to whether the EU legislator reached an appropriate balance in each particular case. In this regard, the Seventh Environment Action Programme (2014–2020) provides:

Seventh Environment Action Programme (2014–2020)

85 Although integrating environmental protection concerns into other Union policies and activities has been a Treaty requirement since 1997, the overall state of Europe's environment indicates that progress made to date, while commendable in some areas, has not been sufficient to reverse all negative trends. The achievement of many of the priority objectives of the 7th EAP will demand even more effective integration of environmental and climate-related considerations into other policies, as well as more coherent, joined up policy approaches that deliver multiple benefits. This should help to ensure that difficult trade-offs are managed early on, rather than in the implementation phase, and that unavoidable impacts can be mitigated more effectively.

…

89 In order to improve environmental integration and policy coherence, the 7th EAP shall ensure that by 2020:

(a) sectoral policies at Union and Member State level are developed and implemented in a way that supports relevant environment and climate-related targets and objectives.

This requires, in particular:

(i) integrating environmental and climate-related conditionalities and incentives in policy initiatives, including reviews and reforms of existing policy, as well as new initiatives, at Union and Member State level;
(ii) carrying out ex-ante assessments of the environmental, social and economic impacts of policy initiatives at appropriate Union and Member State level to ensure their coherence andeffectiveness;
(iii) fully implementing the Strategic Environmental Assessment Directive and the Environmental Impact Assessment Directive;
(iv) using ex-post evaluation information relating to experience with implementation of the environment acquis in order to improve its consistency and coherence;
(v) addressing potential trade-offs in all policies in order to maximize synergies and avoid, reduce and, if possible, remedy unintended negative effects on the environment.

B. Environmental Integration in Practice

When looking at practice in the area of external relations, environmental protection requirements have been integrated into both the EU's trade and the development policies.[76] From an international law standpoint, the integration of environmental concerns into development cooperation is less controversial than for trade policy, not least because of the constraints imposed by WTO law on the use of trade measures to promote environmental protection objectives. Conversely, an important aspect of the international environmental law's principle of CBDRRC is international assistance, including financial aid and technology transfer, in recognition of the fact that, historically, developed countries have played the greatest role in creating most of today's global environmental problems, and also have greater capacity to address them.[77]

Since the 2001 Environmental Integration Strategy,[78] the mainstreaming of environmental considerations into the EU's development policy has increasingly gained importance, and environment-related financial and technical support to third countries or regions, or to international bodies (eg, MEA secretariats), has been provided through various channels. The most visible one is the so-called 'thematic' programme specifically targeting climate change and environment for EU assistance under the Development Cooperation Instrument (DCI).[79] In quantitative terms, EU thematic funding for the environment raised considerably in absolute terms from the 2000–2006 period (€342 million), to the 2007–2013 period (€987 million) and current 2014–2020 period (€1.8 billion).[80] Nonetheless, these figures remain relatively modest when compared to the financial resources allocated to other EU thematic instruments.[81] This may be partly explained by the subsidiary character of the climate change/environment programme as a source of EU funding, which is meant to address 'global public goods and challenges' and to complement environment-related assistance provided to individual countries or regions under the various EU geographic financing instruments.[82]

Aside from these quantitative considerations, the international legitimacy and credibility of EU environment-related assistance ultimately depends on the uses to which it is put. In this regard, environmental integration into EU development cooperation reflects a complex mixture of support for environmental multilateralism (eg, implementation of MEAs and strengthening global environmental governance) and the

[76] Environmental integration has also taken place in EU internal policies with an important external dimension: see eg, in the Common Fisheries Policy, Council Regulation (EC) No 1005/2008 of 29 September 2008 establishing a Community system to prevent, deter and eliminate illegal, unreported and unregulated fishing [2008] OJ L286/1, including an import ban on fish products from non-cooperating countries (Art 38).

[77] Rio Declaration, Principle 7 and, for example, CBD, Art 20(4).

[78] European Commission, 'Working Paper on Integrating the Environment into economic and Development Cooperation', SEC (2001) 609; Council, 'Conclusions on strategy for the integration of Environmental Considerations into Development Policy to Promote Sustainable Development', 31 May 2001.

[79] Regulation (EU) No 433/2014 of the European Parliament and of the Council of 11 March 2014 establishing a financing instrument for development cooperation for the period 2014–2020 [2014] OJ L17/44.

[80] Ibid, Annex IV.

[81] For example, the Instrument for Stability and Peace with an indicative financial envelope of €2.3 billion.

[82] Regulation (EU) No 433/2014, Art 1(b).

Union's own policy priorities (including the FLEGT initiative previously examined).[83] This is hardly surprising, even if not satisfactory, given the essentially unilateral nature of development aid and the limited direct input from recipient countries and interested stakeholders in process of allocating EU funding. However, their increased participation in the programming of EU aid ought not necessarily to be equated with a greater weight for the environment and/or stronger support for multilateral environmental processes within EU development assistance.

G Marín Durán, 'Environmental Integration in EU Development Cooperation: Responding to International Commitments or its own Policy Priorities' in E Morgera (ed) *The External Environmental Policy of the European Union: EU and International Perspectives* (Cambridge, Cambridge University Press, 2013) 232–33

[T]he thematic programme for the environment allows for little direct input from interested stakeholders ... and the responsibility for ensuring environmental integration thus falls largely on the EU, and more particularly the Commission ... In the case of geographic funding, the allocation of resources is instead determined – albeit to varying degrees – on the basis of a dialogue with the aid recipients concerned, which is more in line with the ownership and partnership principles embedded in the Paris Declaration on Aid Effectiveness. This may serve to make EU aid more responsive to the particular environmental needs and priorities jointly identified with each country or region ... The responsibility for ensuring environmental integration through geographic instruments is thus 'shared' to some extent, although the bargaining position vis-à-vis the EU certainly differs across beneficiaries. However, increased participation from interested stakeholders in the programming of EU aid ought not necessarily to be equated with a greater weight for the environment and/or stronger support for multilateral environmental processes within EU development assistance. In fact, the levels of attention paid to the environment within [jointly drafted] CSPs [Country Strategy Papers] and RSPs [Regional Strategy Papers] is likely to differ and environmental protection goals may at times be 'squeezed out' in favour of other short- to medium-term sustainable development priorities, such as poverty reduction, food security or health issues.

Turning to the EU's external trade policy, environmental integration has similarly manifested itself in a variety of measures. At the unilateral level, a notable example is the 'Special Arrangement for Sustainable Development and Good Governance' (also known as 'GSP-plus'),[84] which has been part of the EU's generalised scheme of preferences since 2005. This special arrangement provides additional and non-reciprocal

[83] Ibid, Annex II.

[84] Regulation (EU) No 978/2012 of the European Parliament and of the Council of 25 October 2012 applying a scheme of generalised tariff preferences [2012] OJ L303/1, chapter III.

tariff preferences to developing countries that are considered 'vulnerable' by the EU and which are required to ratify and effectively implement a total of 27 international conventions, including seven core MEAs.

Regulation (EU) No 978/2012 of the European Parliament and of the Council of 25 October 2012 applying a scheme of generalised tariff preferences [2012] OJ L 303/1

THE EUROPEAN PARLIAMENT AND THE COUNCIL OF THE EUROPEAN UNION, ...

(11) The special incentive arrangement for sustainable development and good governance is based on the integral concept of sustainable development, as recognised by international conventions and instruments such as the 1986 United Nations (UN) Declaration on the Right to Development, the 1992 Rio Declaration on Environment and Development, the 1998 International Labour Organisation (ILO) Declaration on Fundamental Principles and Rights at Work, the 2000 UN Millennium Declaration, and the 2002 Johannesburg Declaration on Sustainable Development. Consequently, the additional tariff preferences provided under the special incentive arrangement for sustainable development and good governance should be granted to those developing countries which, due to a lack of diversification and insufficient integration within the international trading system, are vulnerable, in order to help them assume the special burdens and responsibilities resulting from the ratification of core international conventions on human and labour rights, environmental protection and good governance as well as from the effective implementation thereof.

...

Article 9

1. A GSP beneficiary country may benefit from the tariff preferences provided under the special incentive arrangement for sustainable development and good governance referred to in point (b) of Article 1(2) if:
    (a) it is considered to be vulnerable due to a lack of diversification and insufficient integration within the international trading system, as defined in Annex VII;
    (b) it has ratified all the conventions listed in Annex VIII (the 'relevant conventions') and the most recent available conclusions of the monitoring bodies under those conventions (the 'relevant monitoring bodies') do not identify a serious failure to effectively implement any of those conventions;
    (c) in relation to any of the relevant conventions, it has not formulated a reservation which is prohibited by any of those conventions or which is for the purposes of this Article considered to be incompatible with the object and purpose of that convention.

(d) it gives a binding undertaking to maintain ratification of the relevant conventions and to ensure the effective implementation thereof;
(e) it accepts without reservation the reporting requirements imposed by each convention and gives a binding undertaking to accept regular monitoring and review of its implementation record in accordance with the provisions of the relevant conventions; and
(f) it gives a binding undertaking to participate in and cooperate with the monitoring procedure referred to in Article 13.

Article 10

1. The special incentive arrangement for sustainable development and good governance shall be granted if the following conditions are met:
   (a) a GSP beneficiary country has made a request to that effect; and
   (b) examination of the request shows that the requesting country fulfils the conditions laid down in Article 9(1).

…

ANNEX VIII

PART B – Conventions related to the environment and governance principles

16. Convention on International Trade in Endangered Species of Wild Fauna and Flora (1973)

17. Montreal Protocol on Substances that Deplete the Ozone Layer (1987)

18. Basel Convention on the Control of Transboundary Movements of Hazardous Wastes and Their Disposal (1989)

19. Convention on Biological Diversity (1992)

20. The United Nations Framework Convention on Climate Change (1992)

21. Cartagena Protocol on Biosafety (2000)

22. Stockholm Convention on persistent Organic Pollutants (2001)

…

At the bilateral level, a more recent and significant example is the 'Trade and Sustainable Development' (TSD) chapter, which has been systematically included in all free trade agreements (FTA) which the EU has concluded since 2010, whether with developing countries (eg, 2012 EU–Central America Association Agreement),[85] emerging

[85] EU–Central America Association Agreement, signed 29 June 2012, provisionally applied 1 August 2013. Available at: http://ec.europa.eu/trade/policy/countries-and-regions/regions/central-america/.

economies (eg, 2016 EU–Vietnam Free Trade Agreement and Investment Protection Agreement)[86] or developed countries alike (eg, EU–Canada Comprehensive Economic and Trade Agreement).[87] While there is some variation across agreements, all TSD chapters share three basic provisions. First, each FTA party is required to comply with the MEAs (and ILO conventions) to which each it is already a party, thus establishing a minimum protection floor whereby these international environmental standards cannot be departed from under any circumstance. Secondly, FTA parties undertake to improve their domestic laws and provide 'high levels' of environmental (and labour) protection – albeit this commitment is couched in 'best-endeavour' terms. Thirdly, the TSD chapters contain a non-derogation clause, whereby an FTA party shall not derogate or fail to effectively enforce its domestic environmental (and labour) laws in manner affecting bilateral trade and investment.

EU–Singapore Free Trade Agreement [2019] OJ L294/3

CHAPTER TWELVE – TRADE AND SUSTAINABLE DEVELOPMENT

...

Article 12.2 – Right to Regulate and Levels of Protection

1. The Parties recognise the right of each Party to establish its own levels of environmental and labour protection, and to adopt or modify accordingly its relevant laws and policies, consistent with the principles of internationally recognised standards or agreements, to which it is a party, referred to in Articles 12.3 (Multilateral Labour Standards and Agreements) and 12.6 (Multilateral Environmental Standards and Agreements).
2. The Parties shall continue to improve those laws and policies, and shall strive towards providing and encouraging high levels of environmental and labour protection.

...

Article 12.6 – Multilateral Standards and Agreements

1. The Parties recognise the value of international environmental governance and agreements as a response of the international community to global or regional environmental problems and they stress the need to enhance the mutual supportiveness between trade and environment policies, rules and measures. In this context, they will consult and cooperate as appropriate

[86] EU–Vietnam Free Trade Agreement and Investment Protection Agreement, initialled 1 February 2016. Available at: http://ec.europa.eu/trade/policy/countries-and-regions/countries/vietnam/.

[87] Comprehensive Economic and Trade Agreement (CETA) between Canada, of the one part, and the European Union and its Member States, of the other part [2017] OJ L 11/23.

with respect to negotiations on trade-related environmental issues of mutual interest.

2. The Parties shall effectively implement in their respective laws, regulations or other measures and practices in their territories, the multilateral environmental agreements to which they are party.

...

Article 12.12 – Upholding Levels of Protection

1. A Party shall not waive or otherwise derogate from, or offer to waive or otherwise derogate from, its environmental and labour laws, in a manner affecting trade or investment between the Parties.
2. A Party shall not fail to effectively enforce its environmental and labour laws, through a sustained or recurring course of action or inaction, in a manner affecting trade or investment between the Parties.

...

It is noteworthy that, in both these initiatives, the EU has sought to distance itself from US practice and adopted an innovative model for integrating environmental protection standards into trade policy. This has been so, in particular, at the level of implementation where decision-making by the Commission (in the GSP-plus context)[88] or by joint committees (in the case of TSD chapters)[89] has been linked to the evaluations and expertise of MEA supervisory bodies, as well as at the level of enforcement where the EU has generally favoured a cooperative and non-confrontational approach rather than recourse to sanctions. While the European Parliament and some scholars have questioned the effectiveness of such a 'carrot'-based approach,[90] the Commission has expressed a number of pertinent reservations towards moving to a sanctions-based model.

[88] For an examination, see Marín Durán and Morgera (n 2) 162–65.

[89] For an examination, see G Marín Durán, 'Innovations and Implications of the Trade and Sustainable Development Chapter in the EU–Korea Free Trade Agreement' in J Harrison (ed) *The European Union and South Korea: The Legal Framework for Strengthening Trade, Economic and Political Relations* (Edinburgh, Edinburgh University Press, 2013) 136–38.

[90] European Parliament, 'Resolution on Human Rights and Social and Environmental Standards in International Trade Agreements of 25 November 2010' (2009/2219(INI), para 22(a); 'Resolution on Implementation of the 2010 Recommendations of Parliament on Social and Environmental Standards, Human Rights and Corporate Responsibility of 5 July 2016' (2015/2038(INI)), para 21(c) and (d). See also, M Bronckers and G Gruni, 'Improving the Enforcement of Labour Standards in the EU Free Trade Agreements' in D Prévost, I Alexovicova, JH Pohl (eds) *Restoring Trust in Trade – Liber Amicorium in Honour of Peter van den Bossche* (Oxford, Hart Publishing, 2018); B Wardhaugh, 'GSP+ and Human Rights: Is the EU's Approach the Right One?' (2013) 16 *Journal of International Economic Law* 827.

European Commission, 'Non-Paper on Trade and Sustainable Development (TSD) Chapters in EU Free Trade Agreements (FTAs)', 11 July 2017, 8–9

The idea behind this model is that providing for sanctions encourages partners to comply more fully with TSD provisions. Partners would be more willing to strengthen legislation or improve effective implementation of labour and environmental standards if there was a risk of economic consequences … This aspect of effectiveness of sanctions in the context of an FTA would require further analysis. To date, sanctions have never been applied to respond to a violation of labour and environment chapters … The only panel established under the US FTAs covers labour violations in Guatemala. The panel [found] no violations of the FTA between the US and Guatemala could be determined. One of the reasons was that no trade impact of the non-compliance with the labour provisions could be established … In the case of the EU, the majority of complaints about TSD implementation concern violations that are relevant in a trade context but have not had a measurable direct impact on bilateral exchanges … Proving the economic injury necessary for sanctions may be a challenge and the question is whether this may not lead to narrowing the scope of the EU's TSD work.

There is also a question as to what extent a sanctions-based approach would allow the EU to stick to its current strategy of reinforcing the multilateral bodies dealing with sustainable development, taking into account ongoing process and efforts within the multilateral system.

There may be an issue of perception with our negotiating partners, who may consider that the specific nature of trade sanctions in FTAs makes them a more confrontational tool when it concerns implementation of labour and environment commitments … and so a move to adopt such a model in the EU's FTAs could overall jeopardise long-term links with partners to improve capacity and effect changes. There is also a question about the role of civil society groups and international experts in enforcement, since the use of such an approach would increase national sensitivities. In practice sanctions mechanisms on labour and environment issues have only been triggered in exceptional circumstances. And there seems, so far, to be only very limited evidence to demonstrate a positive impact on the issues in question.

IV. The Broader Picture of EU External Relations Law

Environmental degradation knows no borders and, hence, the development of the EU's environmental policy has inevitably entailed a marked external dimension from the outset. Climate change mitigation has been the front-runner of the EU's external environmental policy and has exerted considerable influence on the directions of EU international action in the environmental field. Today, it goes largely undisputed that the EU is an important and influential global environmental actor, both within multilateral environmental processes and at other levels of environmental governance. In fact, over the past three decades, there has been a gradual shift in leadership style from the EU 'leading by example' towards using more assertively its market size and structural power to affect environmental action elsewhere, whether in support of existing MEAs (eg, TSD chapters), of ongoing multilateral environmental objectives or negotiating processes (eg, ETS Aviation Directive and UNFCCC/ICAO), or in the absence thereof (eg, FLEGT Initiative). In doing so, EU external environmental action has both cut across and invited us to critically reconsider the traditional divisions between multilateralism, bilateralism and unilateralism in global environmental affairs.

Nevertheless, the making of the EU's external environmental policy has encountered legal and practical challenges that are common to other areas of the Union's external relations. First, we have seen the usual legal complexities emerging in the sphere of shared competences, including the issue of *vertical coherence* between EU and Member States' environmental action on the international scene, which has been to a large extent addressed by the duty of sincere cooperation (Article 4(3) TEU) and its strict interpretation by the Court (*Commission v Sweden (PFOS)*). Second, there is the question of *horizontal coherence* and of how the EU political institutions should go about balancing environmental protection objectives and other (potentially competing) policy goals, as demanded by the environmental integration requirement (Article 11 TFEU). Third, questions have been raised over the *legality and legitimacy* of EU external environmental action, even more so when it involves unilateral measures. Is such unilateralism really confined to promoting multilaterally agreed environmental standards or objectives and within the permissible boundaries under international law (eg, ETS Aviation Directive and *ATA & Others* case or GSP-plus and WTO law), as the EU often claims? Last but not least, the *credibility* of the Union as a global environmental actor in the eyes of third parties will ultimately rest on its own environmental performance and that of its Member States, including with regards to the ratification and effective implementation of key MEAs.

V. Sources and Further Reading

Delgado Casteleiro, A and J Larik, 'The Duty to Remain Silent: Limitless Loyalty in EU External Relations?' (2011) 36 *European Law Review* 524.

Hadjiyianni, I, *The EU as a Global Regulator for Environmental Protection* (Oxford, Hart Publishing, 2019).

Kulovesi, K, 'Addressing Sectoral Emissions Outside the United Nations Framework Convention on Climate Change: What Roles for Multilateralism, Minilateralism and Unilateralism?' (2012) 21 *Review of European Community and International Environmental Law* 193.

Kulovesi, K, 'Climate Change in EU External Relations: Please Follow My Example (or I Might Force You To)' in E Morgera (ed) *The External Environmental Policy of the European Union: EU and International Perspectives* (Cambridge, Cambridge University Press, 2013) 115–48.

Marín Durán, G, 'Environmental Integration in EU Development Cooperation: Responding to International Commitments or its own Policy Priorities' in E Morgera (ed) *The External Environmental Policy of the European Union: EU and International Perspectives* (Cambridge, Cambridge University Press, 2013) 204–34.

Marín Durán, G, 'Innovations and Implications of the Trade and Sustainable Development Chapter in the EU-Korea Free Trade Agreement' in J Harrison (ed) *The European Union and South Korea: The Legal Framework for Strengthening Trade, Economic and Political Relations* (Edinburgh, Edinburgh University Press, 2013) 124–48.

Marín Durán, G and E Morgera, *Environmental Integration in the EU's External Relations – Beyond Multilateral Dimensions* (Oxford, Hart Publishing, 2012).

Montini, M, 'The Principle of Integration' in L Krämer and E Orlando (eds) *Principles of Environmental Law* (Cheltenham, Edward Elgar, 2016) 139–49.

Morgera, E, 'Ambition, Complexity and Legitimacy of Pursuing Mutual Supportiveness through the EU's Environmental External Action' in B Van Vooren and S Blockmans (eds) *The EU's Role in Global Governance – The Legal Dimension* (Oxford, Oxford University Press, 2013) 194–208.

Nollkaemper, A, 'Joint Responsibility between the EU and Member States for Non-Performance of Obligations under Multilateral Environmental Agreements' in E Morgera (ed) *The External Environmental Policy of the European Union: EU and International Perspectives* (Cambridge, Cambridge University Press, 2013) 304–46.

Nowag, J, 'Article 11 TFEU and Environmental Rights' in S Bogojevi and R Rayfuse (eds) *Environmental Rights in Europe and Beyond* (Oxford, Hart Publishing, 2018) 155–74.

Overdevest, C and J Zeitlin, 'Experimentalism in Transnational Forest Governance: Implementing European Union Forest Law Enforcement, Governance and Trade (FLEGT) Voluntary Partnership Agreements in Indonesia and Ghana' (2018) 12 *Regulation & Governance* 64.

Savaresi, A, 'EU External Action on Forest: FLEGT and the Development of International Law' in E Morgera (ed) *The External Environmental Policy of the European Union – EU and International Law Perspectives* (Cambridge, Cambridge University Press, 2013) 149–73.

Scott, J and L Rajamani, 'Contingent Unilateralism – International Aviation in the European Emissions Trading Scheme' in B Van Vooren and S Blockmans (eds) *The EU's Role in Global Governance – The Legal Dimension* (Oxford, Oxford University Press, 2013) 209–23.

12

The External Dimension of the Area of Freedom, Security and Justice

Central Issues

- The Area of Freedom, Security and Justice (AFSJ) is, arguably, the second largest integration project after the internal market and was introduced to facilitate cooperation amongst national authorities in the fields of migration, judicial cooperation in civil and criminal matters and policing. Today, the EU promotes the integration of the Member States *qua* AFSJ by harmonising national legislation, adopting common policies and coordinating operational activities in the different fields of the AFSJ. Moreover, in a number of fields such as the fight against certain types of transnational crimes, border controls and asylum, the consolidations of the AFSJ has led to the creation of a number of specialised agencies such as Europol, Frontex and Eurojust and the European Asylum Support Office (EASO).
- The development of the external dimension of the AFSJ is an example of the implied external powers doctrine discussed in Chapter 3: the internal policies revealed their external aspects and the Union soon found itself concluding international agreements and developing external policies on a wide range of issues covered by the AFSJ. Moreover, the relatively fast coming of age of the external dimension of the AFSJ was triggered by a number of external events and developments, including international terrorism, transnational organised crimes and the inflow of migrants to the EU.
- In all main areas of the AFSJ (immigration, judicial cooperation in civil and criminal matters, approximation of criminal law, police cooperation) the EU has enacted legislation and concluded international agreements revealing the strong link between internal and external policies. One of the elements distinguishing external relations in the field of the AFSJ from other areas is that the external measures and initiatives adopted often relate to fundamental rights and constitutionally protected rights in the Member States. This chapter will address these developments and these challenges.

I. The External Dimension of an Internal Concept

A. The AFSJ as an Internal, Organisational Concept

The Area of Freedom Security and Justice was primarily created at the time of the adoption of the 1997 Amsterdam Treaty to replace cooperation under the Justice and Home Affairs umbrella as framed under the 1992 Maastricht Treaty. At the time of its inception, the AFSJ's focus was internal and, therefore, its connection to EU external relations may not have been self-evident. The core Treaty provisions in the TEU and the TFEU still reflect the inward-focused nature of the AFSJ.

Article 3(2) TEU

The Union shall offer its citizens an area of freedom, security and justice without internal frontiers, in which the free movement of persons is ensured in conjunction with appropriate measures with respect to external border controls, asylum, immigration and the prevention and combating of crime.

Article 67 TFEU

1. The Union shall constitute an area of freedom, security and justice with respect for fundamental rights and the different legal systems and traditions of the Member States.
2. It shall ensure the absence of internal border controls for persons and shall frame a common policy on asylum, immigration and external border control, based on solidarity between Member States, which is fair towards third-country nationals. For the purpose of this Title, stateless persons shall be treated as third-country nationals.
3. The Union shall endeavour to ensure a high level of security through measures to prevent and combat crime, racism and xenophobia and through measures for coordination and cooperation between police and judicial authorities and other competent authorities, as well as through the mutual recognition of judgments in criminal matters and, if necessary, through the approximation of criminal laws.
4. The Union shall facilitate access to justice, in particular through the principle of mutual recognition of judicial and extrajudicial decisions in civil matters.

These provisions confirm that the AFSJ is offered to the *citizens of the Union* as a complement to the policies that have established and consolidated free movement within the EU. From this perspective, the fields covered by the AFSJ do not aim to substitute national systems; rather, the AFSJ was created to enhance, albeit indirectly, national cooperation to preserve and enhance freedom, security and justice in an open and larger EU.

Twenty years on, the AFSJ is being confronted with a plurality of challenges, many of which relate to its constitutional design. Indeed, whilst the AFSJ has expanded its scope and now covers operational tasks in fields such as the protection of the EU's financial interests through criminal law[1] or external border controls,[2] the mixture of negative integration and *de minimis* approximation of laws in the various AFSJ fields has caused constitutional conflicts, both within te EU and in its relations with the Member States;[3] often in cases with a clear external dimension.[4]

Because the AFSJ covers policies such as criminal law, asylum and migration and judicial cooperation in civil and criminal matters, the legal questions that need to be addressed in this chapter go beyond the classical institutional or competence questions of EU external relations. They often directly relate to fundamental questions of constitutional law such as the balance between human rights protection standards on the one hand, and the adoption and enforcement of coercive measures by public authorities on the other. Prior to addressing the birth and the evolution of the external dimension of the AFSJ, however, the next section will further reflect on a number of key constitutional characteristics of the AFSJ itself.

B. Scope of the AFSJ and Position of the Member States

From a formal perspective, the AFSJ falls within the category of shared competences under Article 4(2)(j) TFEU. This means that, in principle, also AFSJ measures can trigger pre-emption entailing the exclusionary effect that was first upheld in the *ERTA* judgment[5] and is now codified in Article 3(2) TFEU (see Chapter 3). However, because of the specific nature of the AFSJ, the reality is more nuanced. The first characteristic

[1] TFEU, Art 86. For An analysis of the challenges related to the establishment of the European Public Prosecutor's Office, see G Conway, 'The Future of a European Public Prosecutor', in the Area of Freedom Security and Justice' in M Fletcher, E Herlin-Karnell and C Matera (eds) *The European Union as an Area of Freedom, Security and Justice* (New York, Routledge, 2016) 176–200.

[2] Regulation (EU) 2016/1624 of the European Parliament and of the Council of 14 September 2016 on the European Border and Coast Guard [2016] OJ L251/1. For an assessment of the future of border controls see JJ Rijpma, 'Frontex and the European System of Border Guards: The Future of European Border Management' in M Fletcher, E Herlin-Karnell and C Matera (eds) *The European Union as an Area of Freedom, Security and Justice* (New York, Routledge, 2016) 217–45.

[3] With a focus on the conceptual flaws of the AFSJ integration project, see S Lavanex and W Wagner, 'Which European Public Order? Sources of Imbalance in the European Area of Freedom, Security and Justice' (2007) 16 *European Security* 225.

[4] See Opinion 1/15 (*Draft Agreement between Canada and the European Union – Transfer of Passenger Name Record Data from the European Union to Canada*), ECLI:EU:C:2016:656. For an analysis see Section III.D of this chapter.

[5] Case 22/70 *Commission v Council (ERTA)*, ECLI:EU:C:1971:32.

that needs to be addressed is the specific role that Member States maintain in the AFSJ in relation to enforcement and operational action. While other EU policies also require Member States' action for their implementation and enforcement, in the fields of the AFSJ, the role of the Member States is more than purely instrumental: after all, it is Member States who remain competent to confer asylum, arrest, detain, and adjudicate family law disputes. The protection of these prerogatives is codified in the Treaties.

Article 72 TFEU

This Title shall not affect the exercise of the responsibility's incumbent upon Member States with regard to the maintenance of law and order and the safeguarding of internal security.

Article 4(2) TEU

The Union shall respect the equality of Member States before the Treaties as well as their national identities, inherent in their fundamental structures, political and constitutional, inclusive of regional and local self-government. It shall respect their essential State functions, including ensuring the territorial integrity of the State, maintaining law and order and safeguarding national security. In particular, national security remains the sole responsibility of each Member State.

As we will see, however, it is questionable whether Member States' responsibilities are not affected at all by the integration process in AFSJ fields. However, it is difficult to identify where the boundaries of internal security and public order reside in the EU context. Notwithstanding the fact that it is not clear what exactly these provisions cover, the Court always interprets derogations from the Treaties restrictively; therefore, these provisions should be interpreted as preserving ample discretion for Member States only in relation to the implementation and enforcement of EU measures with coercive clauses.[6] Conversely, the two provisions above should not be interpreted as granting to Member States a sort of leeway from EU legislation in all matters pertaining to national security and public order.[7]

The second characteristic that must be considered is the fact that the broad and ambiguous objective enshrined in Article 3(2) TEU must be read in the light of Article 67 TFEU and subsequent policy-specific provisions. Irrespective of the widely defined objectives in Article 3(2) TEU (inter alia, related to the maintenance of public

[6] Of course, the EU integration process has been confronted with the notions of public order and public security in other fields, such as in the Internal Market; however, these have special significance for the AFSJ. The broad interpretation of TFEU Art 72 seems to be upheld by the CJEU in Case C-278/12 *PPU Adil*, ECLI:EU:C:2012:508.

[7] A Lang, 'Articolo 72 TFEU' in A Tizzano (ed) *Trattati dell'unione Europea*, 2nd edn (Milano, Giuffré, 2014).

order and public security), the Union's AFSJ powers are limited by the sector-specific provisions. This means that similarly to the Internal Market concept and contrary to fields such as the Common Commercial Policy (Chapter 7) or Development Cooperation (Chapter 8), the AFSJ is a complex legal construction that is highly diverse and where the EU exercises different regulatory roles for each policy field. This means that, both internally and externally, one cannot analyse the scope of EU powers using the AFSJ as the object of study, but must address each specific sector (border controls, visa, migration, asylum, judicial cooperation in civil and criminal matters, and police cooperation) independently. For this reason alone, it would be more appropriate to speak of external *dimensions* of the AFSJ rather than using the singular version of the noun. To illustrate this diversity, Section III of this chapter will analyse a number of initiatives adopted in various AFSJ domains.

Furthermore, notwithstanding the formal difficulties to streamline and unify a field of EU action which maintains a high degree of fragmentation, an analysis of the AFSJ cannot ignore the reactive nature of public order as a policy. Contrary to areas such as the internal market or the common currency, the AFSJ introduced an objective that did not need to be established from scratch. Instead, the AFSJ led to the introduction of an objective that calls for the preservation of something familiar, namely public order and internal security. The predominant reactive nature of the policies of the AFSJ is arguably best reflected in the very wording of the Treaties when it calls upon the Union's institutions to build measures to combat crime and build a common policy on asylum and immigration. In both cases the EU is tasked to react to societal phenomena which relate to public order and security. However, 'the reactive, security-centred approach may have an in-built tendency to marginalise familiar constitutional constraints, such as the proper balancing of fundamental values, the primacy of democratic decision, due process in individual cases, and a robust system of separation and diversification of powers and of institutional checks and balances'.[8]

Finally, related to the reactive nature of the AFSJ, its relation to fundamental rights and civil liberties must also be addressed. While the name of the policy field at hand refers to 'freedom' as the first of its three main features, the AFSJ should not be confused with a 'human rights protection'-type of competence. In fact, the EU legal order, like the legal orders of its Member States, is bound to respect human rights and civil liberties, but the EU does not have a competence on human rights in the strict sense (see also Chapter 10).[9] This is to say that while AFSJ action has to respect Article 6 TEU and other specific international instruments such as the Geneva Convention of 28 July 1951 on the Rights of Refugees, AFSJ powers on human rights and civil liberties are restricted to those identified by specific provisions such as the protection of victims of crime ex Article 82 TFEU, or the adoption of measures enhancing access to (civil) justice under Article 81 TFEU. However, these internal restrictions are at odds with the broad and ambitious goal of promoting EU values as

[8] N Walker, 'In Search of the Area of Freedom, Security and Justice: A Constitutional Odyssey' in N Walker (ed), *Europe's Area of Freedom, Security, and Justice* (Oxford, Oxford University Press, 2004) 13.

[9] Note in this context that the EU Fundamental Rights Agency was created on the basis of the residual powers ex Art 352 (then 308 EC), Council Regulation (EC) No 168/2007 of 15 February 2007 establishing a European Union Agency for Fundamental Rights [2007] OJ L53/1.

codified in Articles 3(5) and 21 TEU. One of the main criticisms of the developments concerning the AFSJ over the past years, including in its external dimension, has been that it has disregarded fundamental rights concerns either by adopting measures in violation of said standards or by failing to provide adequate remedies or procedural guarantees for those whose rights had been (allegedly) violated as a consequence of the enforcement of an AFSJ measure.[10]

The characteristics of the AFSJ addressed in this section strengthen the image of the AFSJ as a thorny policy domain for the EU integration project. Moreover, we have seen that Articles 3(2) TEU and 67 TFEU frame an inward-looking policy domain, aimed at protecting internal freedoms by enhancing cooperation mechanism in the fields of security and justice amongst the Member States. Yet, a systematic reading of the Treaties suggests that the AFSJ has, like other policy fields of the EU, also an external vocation; the next section will address this last aspect.

C. The Relation between the Internal and External Dimension

As we have seen, the key provisions of the Treaties on the AFSJ paint an inward-looking picture. More specifically, the provisions in question suggest that the creation of the AFSJ is instrumental to the creation of the internal market and the protection of the freedoms associated with it. In this regard, it was also noticed that the protection of EU citizens played an important role in the framing and the justification of the AFSJ. Similarly, 'protection of [the EU's] citizens' is equally reflected by the first sentence of Article 3(5) TEU on the objectives of EU external relations (see Chapter 1).

Whilst it is difficult to make conclusive assertions over the characterisation of the AFSJ independently from adopted legislation in the various AFSJ fields, a systematic reading of the provision above with Articles 3(2) TEU and 67 TFEU suggests that the objectives of EU external relations and of the AFSJ converge in the protection of the EU citizens. Teleologically, this suggests that citizens' protection is a vehicle for the externalisation of the AFSJ under the doctrine of implied powers. In other words, while the AFSJ is a rather ambiguous term that covers a diverse set of sector-specific goals and tools, immaterial notions such as freedom, security and justice find a common denominator with external relations in relation to the pursuit of citizens' protection.

At the same time, it would be wrong to characterise the provisions in question and their focus on protection as being directed solely at contributing to a 'fortress Europe' in a globalised world: the protection of EU citizens in not the only link between the AFSJ and external relations. Indeed, EU external relations objectives permeate the Union as whole and, as Article 21(3) TEU suggests, internal and external policies

[10] As an example of the first type of violation see the Opinion of the Court in relation to the Passenger Name Record (PNR) agreement with Canada, Opinion 1/15 (*PNR*), ECLI:EU:C:2016:656; as an example of the second type of challenge see the approach of the General Court in relation to the EU–Turkey Deal, in T-192/16 *NF v European Council*, Order of the Court 28 February 2017 ECLI:EU:T:2017:128, and Case C-638/16 *PP X, X v État Belge*, Opinion of AG Mengozzi, para 157 in relation to the scope of EU visa rules and access to EU territory.

should be pursued in a consistent manner. Therefore, just as EU external relations must contribute to the protection of EU citizens, the development of the AFSJ must also be consistent with the values and objectives that characterise the EU as global actor promoting multilateralism, the development of international law and the protection of human rights. Therefore, it could be argued that the externalisation of the AFSJ widens EU action to cover AFSJ-related cooperation at the international level. Examples of the practical implications of the integration of the AFSJ with external relations objectives can be found in numerous bilateral and multilateral agreements concluded by the EU with one or more third countries.

Partnership and Cooperation Agreement between the European Union and its Member States, of the one part, and the Republic of Iraq, of the other part … [2012] OJ L 204/20

Article 106 Combatting Organised Crime and Corruption

The Parties agree to cooperate on and contribute to the fight against organised, economic and financial crime and corruption, counterfeiting and illegal transactions, through full compliance with their existing mutual international obligations in this area including on effective cooperation in the recovery of assets or funds derived from acts of corruption. The Parties will promote the implementation of the UN Convention on Transnational Organised Crime and its supplementing Protocols and the UN Convention against Corruption.

Similarly, but in the field of migration, the EU–Armenia Enhanced Partnership Agreement contains provisions such as the following on asylum and refugees.

Comprehensive and Enhanced Partnership Agreement between the European Union and the European Atomic Energy Community and their Member States, of the one part, and the Republic of Armenia, of the other part [2018] OJ L 23/4

Article 14 Cooperation on migration, asylum and border management

1. The Parties reaffirm the importance of the joint management of migration flows between their territories and shall establish a comprehensive dialogue on all migration-related issues, including legal migration, international protection and the fight against illegal migration, smuggling and trafficking in human beings.
2. Cooperation will be based on a specific needs assessment conducted through mutual consultation between the Parties and will be implemented

in accordance with their relevant legislation in force. It will, in particular, focus on: ...

(b) the development and implementation of national legislation and practices as regards international protection, with a view to satisfying the provisions of the Geneva Convention relating to the status of refugees of 1951, the Protocol relating to the Status of Refugees of 1967 and other relevant international instruments, such as the European Convention on Human Rights, and to ensuring respect for the principle of 'non-refoulement'; ...

The first observation that we can make from the two examples above is that the systematic reading of Articles 3(2) and 3(5) and 21 TEU shows its practical implications when the EU inserts AFSJ-related clauses in agreements it concludes with third countries. Secondly, the clauses above show that they serve two distinct, but connected, objectives. The first is to identify a field and an objective in relation to which the parties agree to cooperate in the future. In this sense, such clauses are *enabling clauses* as they provide a first framework upon which future initiatives will be based on.

Whilst a specific clause represents a common interest, there can be no doubt that where the EU manages to do so, some clauses reflect the interests of the EU more than those of a specific third country.

Framework Agreement on Partnership and Cooperation between the European Union and its Member States, of the one part, and the Republic of the Philippines, of the other part [2017] OJ L 343/3

Article 26 Cooperation on Migration and Development

...

3. Within the framework of cooperation in this area and without prejudice to the need to protect victims of human trafficking, the Parties further agree that:

(a) The Philippines shall admit back any of its nationals as defined under paragraph 2, point (e) of this Article present in the territory of a Member State upon request by the latter, without undue delay once nationality has been established and due process in the Member State carried out.
(b) Each Member State shall readmit any of its nationals as defined under paragraph 2, point (e) of this Article present in the territory of the Philippines upon request by the latter, without undue delay once nationality has been established and due process in the Philippines carried out.
(c) The Member States and the Philippines will provide their nationals with required documents for such purposes. Any request for admission or

> readmission shall be transmitted by the requesting state to the competent authority of the requested state …
>
> 4. The Parties agree to conclude as soon as possible an agreement for the admission/readmission of their nationals, including a provision on the readmission of nationals of other countries and stateless persons.

Thus, while both excerpts of the agreements with Armenia and Iraq show how the AFSJ agenda can be integrated with the broader external relations objectives of the EU and the promotion of international law and multilateralism in AFSJ-related matters (paragraph 2(b) of the EU–Armenia agreement above), at other times the EU may take the opportunity of negotiating a framework agreement to insert clauses that prioritise its agenda by inserting detailed provisions on the repatriation of irregular migrants, including third-country nationals (EU–Philippines agreement above). As we have seen, in both cases, the agreements in question frame cooperation on asylum law (the one with Armenia) and on the fight against transnational organised crime (the one with Iraq) within the normative and policy context of the relevant UN conventions as a further proof of the EU's commitment to multilateralism and the promotion of international law.

The clauses of the agreements considered in this section also tell us something about the relationship between the internal and the external AFSJ. While we have argued that these clauses show how the AFSJ objectives are related to the broader objectives of EU external action, the clauses must also be considered from the viewpoint of EU external relations law. In this regard, the case law of the Court on the point is quite unequivocal: the centre of gravity test determines the correct legal basis of an agreement (see Chapter 3). For the AFSJ clauses of the agreements analysed above, this means that, from a formal perspective, each of them belongs to the (broad) notion of EU Development Policy as defined in Article 209 TFEU (see Chapter 8).[11] This was confirmed by the Court of Justice in relation to the identification of the legal basis for the EU–Philippines Agreement.

> **Case C-377/12 *Commission v Council (Philippines)*, ECLI:EU:C:2014:1903**
>
> 58 Whilst Article 26(3) of the Framework Agreement does admittedly contain wording stating how requests for readmission are to be dealt with, the fact remains that, as is apparent from Article 26(2)(f), the readmission of persons residing

[11] The agreements in question were principally concluded based on Art 209 TFEU on Development Cooperation and Art 207 TFEU on Trade.

without authorisation is included in Article 26 as one of the matters upon which cooperation on migration and development will have to focus, without it being covered at this stage by detailed provisions enabling its implementation, such as those contained in a readmission agreement. It cannot therefore be considered that Article 26 of the Framework Agreement prescribes in concrete terms the manner in which cooperation concerning readmission of nationals of the contracting parties is to be implemented, a conclusion which is reinforced by the commitment, in Article 26(4), to conclude a readmission agreement very soon.

59 It is consequently apparent that the provisions of the Framework Agreement relating to readmission of nationals of the contracting parties, to transport and to the environment do not contain obligations so extensive that they may be considered to constitute objectives distinct from those of development cooperation that are neither secondary nor indirect in relation to the latter objectives.

In light of the excerpt above it can be concluded that, from a formal perspective, the insertion of AFSJ clauses in agreements concluded under the aegis of broad external policies such as Development Cooperation do not belong to the external dimension of the AFSJ. As implicitly noted by the Court in paragraph 58 of the judgment excerpted above, only the necessary bilateral agreement(s) to implement the readmission clause will require an AFSJ legal basis. In addition, other agreements such as Association Agreements contain AFSJ clauses without being considered AFSJ agreements in the strictest sense. For instance, the EU–Georgia Association Agreement was concluded on the sole basis of Articles 217 and 218 TFEU even though it contained a plurality of AFSJ-related clauses.[12]

At the beginning of this section attention was drawn to the shared goals between the AFSJ and EU external action. The convergence of these objectives brought us to look at how such convergence works in practice not only substantively, but also from a procedural perspective. We have seen that AFSJ objectives and clauses are absorbed by the centre of gravity test when it comes to identifying the correct legal basis for the conclusion of an international agreement that is predominantly anchored to broad external instruments (Association Agreements) or broad external policies (such as Development Cooperation).

However, the externalisation of AFSJ objectives does not occur solely in conjunction with the negotiation and conclusion of umbrella and framework agreements such as those mentioned above; the externalisation of the AFSJ actually occurs whenever the EU concludes an international agreement on the basis of a provision contained in Title V of Part Three of the TFEU (ie on the basis of one of the AFSJ provisions). In the next section, the substantive and institutional aspects of the external dimension of the AFSJ will be addressed.

[12] See Council Decision of 16 June 2014 on the signing, on behalf of the European Union, and provisional application of the Association Agreement between the European Union and the European Atomic Energy Community and their Member States, of the one part, and Georgia, of the other part [2014] OJ L261/1.

II. External Competences in the AFSJ

A. The Rationale for the Development of AFSJ External Action

The objective of ensuring 'a high level of security' within the AFSJ provided for by Article 67(3) TFEU must be understood as incorporating external threats into the AFSJ. Europol reports have assessed the most serious challenges and have, inter alia, pointed to a serious increase in criminal activities originating from many countries in the EU's neighbourhood or further away.[13] Apart from general forms of crime, the identified security threats relate to phenomena such as terrorism and mass migration flows. All these challenges 'have in common that the EU's capacity to respond effectively to them depends crucially on cooperation with third countries'.[14] However, external factors alone cannot explain the development of the external AFSJ and, in the excerpt below, Jörg Monar further elaborates on the reasons why the external dimension of the AFSJ has gained momentum in EU external relations in recent years.

J Monar, 'The EU's Growing External Role in the AFSJ Domain: Factors, Framework and Forms of Action' (2014) 27 *Cambridge Review of International Affairs* 147, 148–49

The development of the external dimension of the AFSJ can be explained by two separate but interrelated categories of factors: external challenges, which have acted as 'driving' factors and internal 'enabling' factors. External challenges to internal AFSJ objectives have clearly been the primary 'driving' factors, as they have both necessitated and justified the use of external instruments to complement purely internal measures …

External pressures on their own, however, would not have been sufficient to ensure the development of a significant external dimension of the AFSJ without a range of internal 'enabling' factors. The extension of EU internal action possibilities through the Maastricht (1993), Amsterdam (1999) and Lisbon (2009) Treaty reforms, the growth of the internal legal acquis and the establishment and strengthening of the special agencies Europol, Eurojust and Frontex have all contributed to a parallel growth of the rationale, possibilities and needs for EU external action.

[13] For a study on the transnational nature of security threats in the EU see Europol, *Serious and Organised Crime Assessment. SOCTA 2017* (The Hague, Europol, 2017), and Frontex, *Annual Risk Analysis for 2019* (Warsaw, Frontex, 2019).

[14] J Monar, 'The EU's Growing External Role in the AFSJ Domain: Factors, Framework and Forms of Action' (2014) 27 *Cambridge Review of International Affairs* 147, 148.

While external push factors such as international terrorism, human trafficking and mass migration have placed a significant pressure on the institutions of the EU to develop and strengthen the AFSJ, including its external dimension, the measures adopted have often been controversial from both substantive and institutional perspectives. In the sections that follow, we will look at questions concerning the existence and the nature of EU external competences with regard to the AFSJ. Secondly, this section will look at the institutional dimension of the external dimension of the AFSJ since various organs have a distinctive role to play in the different aspects of the AFSJ and, finally, we will look at the thorny issue of opt-outs.

B. AFSJ External Competences in the Treaties

As we have seen before, the AFSJ belongs to the domain of EU shared competences that can be pre-empted (see also Chapter 3). However, because of the role that Member States maintain in the AFSJ on the one hand, and because of the different mandates that the EU has received to deliver the AFSJ, it is impossible to draw general conclusions on the nature of EU external powers in this area. Yet, before addressing this last aspect, this section will first consider the existence of an AFSJ external competences in the Treaties.

To date, the AFSJ comprises only one express external competence, Article 79(3) TFEU.

Article 79(3) TFEU

The Union may conclude agreements with third countries for the readmission to their countries of origin or provenance of third-country nationals who do not or who no longer fulfil the conditions for entry, presence or residence in the territory of one of the Member States.

In relation to the other AFSJ policies, the EU can only act externally through the application of the implied powers doctrine now codified in Article 216(1) TFEU.

Article 216(1) TFEU

The Union may conclude an agreement with one or more third countries or international organisations where the Treaties so provide or where the conclusion of an agreement is necessary in order to achieve, within the framework of the Union's policies, one of the objectives referred to in the Treaties, or is provided for in a legally binding Union act or is likely to affect common rules or alter their scope.

Indeed, as indicated in Chapter 3, the *ERTA* doctrine has become an explicit part of this new provision, which implies that AFSJ international agreements could be based on an AFSJ provision linked to Article 3(2) TEU, on a decision adopted in the area of AFSJ or to protect the AFSJ *acquis*.

While the existence of external implied powers in the AFSJ fields cannot be questioned, the nature of EU external action in these domains is a more intricate issue to address. Indeed, as the AFSJ is a shared, pre-emptive competence of the EU, it is possible to envisage the emergence of exclusive external competences as the internal integration develops. However, several factors position the AFSJ outside the traditional dichotomy between exclusive and shared competences.

The first issue to address is the ambiguity of several Treaty provisions. As stated, the AFSJ is, formally speaking, a shared, pre-emptive, competence of the EU. However, we have also seen that EU action in the AFSJ fields cannot affect the prerogatives of the Member States in relation to public order and public security per Article 72 TFEU. In this regard, it has been argued that rather than placing a limit on the exercise of EU competences, Article 72 TFEU should be interpreted as preserving the leeway of Member States on policing measures with the caveat that Member States must make sure that national norms do not hinder the effectiveness of EU measures. Nevertheless, notwithstanding the nebulous scope of Article 72 TFEU, it is a fact that with the exception of a convention on judicial cooperation in civil matters (see below, section III.B), no exclusive competence of the EU has emerged thus far.[15]

Additionally, other elements militate against the emergence of exclusive external competences of the EU in the AFSJ fields. For instance, the possibility for the Member States to conclude international agreements in various AFSJ domains is confirmed in a special Declaration on Article 218 TFEU, the procedure pertaining to the conclusion of international agreements by the EU.

36. Declaration on Article 218 of the Treaty on the Functioning of the European Union concerning the negotiation and conclusion of international agreements by Member States relating to the area of freedom, security and justice [2010] OJ C 83/349

The Conference confirms that Member States may negotiate and conclude agreements with third countries or international organisations in the areas covered by Chapters 3, 4 and 5 of Title V of Part Three in so far as such agreements comply with Union law.

In Part Three, Title V TFEU, Chapter 3 concerns 'judicial cooperation in civil matters', Chapter 4 'judicial cooperation in criminal matters' and Chapter 5 deals with 'police cooperation'. Interestingly, the protection of national external prerogatives does not seem to be covering border checks, asylum and migration (ie, Chapter 2).

[15] For an analysis of the *Lugano Convention* Opinion see Section III.B.

However, this does not mean that Member States have stopped concluding bilateral agreements, as well as soft law commitments, covering the policy fields of Chapter 2 of the AFSJ.[16] At the same time, it would equally be wrong to assume that the external prerogatives of the Member States are left untouched, as the excerpt of the EU-Cape Verde Readmission Agreement suggests.

Agreement between the European Union and the Republic of Cape Verde on the readmission of persons residing without authorisation, [2013] OJ L 282/15

Article 20

Relation to bilateral readmission agreements or arrangements of Member States

The provisions of this Agreement shall take precedence over the provisions of any legally binding instrument on the readmission of persons residing without authorisation which, under Article 19, have been or may be concluded between individual Member States and Cape Verde, in so far as the provisions of any such legally binding instrument are incompatible with those of this Agreement.

In relation to policy fields falling under Chapter 2 and left out of the Declaration mentioned above, the nature of the competence on border checks also has to consider Protocol 23 to the Treaties.[17] Protocol 23 affirms that the measures on the crossing of external borders included in Article 77(2)(b) TFEU are without prejudice to the competence of Member States to negotiate or conclude agreements with third countries as long as they respect Union law and other relevant international agreements. This provision confirms the previous consideration according to which, in the AFSJ fields, it is often difficult to find spheres of exclusive external action even where the EU has fully harmonised a field, as is the case of the Schengen Borders Code.[18]

Thus far, the question about the nature of EU external competences in the AFSJ suggests that Member States have preserved a certain portion of external powers for themselves. However, it is not entirely clear from the existing practice what such portion may cover. We have seen that for readmission agreements there seems to be a parallel shared competence with an exclusionary effect against Member States, but only to the effect that their bilateral agreement with a third country on re-admission cannot contradict the substance of the agreement that the EU has concluded with the same third party. Yet, the portion of national discretion left to Member States

[16] J-P Cassarino, 'Informalizing EU Readmission Policy' in A Ripoll-Servent and F Trauner (eds) *The Routledge Handbook of Justice and Home Affairs* (New York, Routledge, 2017) 83–98.

[17] See Protocol (23) to the Treaties on External relations of the Member States with regard to the crossing of the external borders.

[18] Regulation (EU) 2016/399 of the European Parliament and of the Council of 9 March 2016 on a Union Code on the rules governing the movement of persons across borders (Schengen Borders Code) [2016] OJ L 77/1.

hardly resembles autonomy since national agreements will essentially cover only those procedural aspects related to enforcing the repatriation of irregular migrants.

Considering the complexity of the AFSJ provisions and their constitutional limits, one could imagine that in opposition to exclusive external competence, most AFSJ agreements are concluded as mixed ones. Yet, this is not the case. Whilst there are a number of AFSJ mixed agreements that have been concluded, most of them are actually concluded by the Union alone. We have already seen that the EU can include AFSJ clauses within agreements that cover a broad range of topics. This is the case with Association Agreements or Development Cooperation agreements. In any of these cases, the agreement covering, inter alia, AFSJ clauses will be concluded as a mixed agreement – but not necessarily *because* of the AFSJ clauses present. However, key agreements such as readmission agreements, mutual legal assistance agreements and data exchange agreements for security purposes have all been concluded exclusively by the EU. As we shall see in greater detail in the last section of this chapter, the reason for this is that the EU has acquired in many of the AFSJ fields an exclusive competence as norm setter, and because of this it has also acquired the capacity to engage autonomously with third countries.

C. The Role of the Institutions

(i) The European Council

The European Council has a leading and strategic position in the development of the AFSJ, this evidenced by Article 68 TFEU. This provision is somehow unique because only in relation to the AFSJ, the role of the European Council has a dedicated Treaty provision in addition to Article 15 TEU; possibly this provision further reflects the key role that Member States have maintained in the development of the AFSJ.

Article 68 TFEU

The European Council defines the strategic guidelines for legislative and operational planning within the area of freedom, security and justice.

Over the years the European Council made use of this competence also to further strengthen the external relations of the AFSJ. This is partly based on the general competence of the European Council to take strategic decisions, including those with a foreign affairs dimension.[19] The European Council has exercised its prerogatives by adopting pluriannual programmes in 1999 (Tampere Conclusions),[20] 2004 (The Hague

[19] Article 22(1) TEU: '... Decisions of the European Council on the strategic interests and objectives of the Union shall relate to the common foreign and security policy and to other areas of the external action of the Union.'

[20] See the Presidency conclusions of the Tampere European Council (15–16 October 1999).

Programme), and the Stockholm Programme in 2009. During the Italian presidency of 2014, the practice was interrupted and no sign of adopting programmatic documents was manifested at the beginning of the Finish presidency in the summer of 2019.[21] Nevertheless, also in 2014, the European Council adopted a number of strategic guidelines addressed to the other institutions concerning the development of the AFSJ and its external dimension.[22] Over the past 20 years, European Council conclusions have placed an emphasis on linking different external policy measures in a coherent and integrated manner, including CFSP and CSDP (see Chapter 9).[23]

(ii) The Council

Key decisions are taken by the Council in its configuration as Justice and Home Affairs (JHA) Council. As a general observation, the Council in its JHA configuration, follows the same rules and procedures established for other policy fields under Articles 16 TEU, the provisions of Section 3, Chapter 1 of Part Six of the TFEU and, in relation to external initiatives, Article 218 TFEU. Thus, the JHA Council approves all programming documents for the JHA's external dimension, adopts all relevant legislative acts, and takes the decisions on the opening, signing and conclusion of international agreements in the AFSJ domain. It approves the Commission's negotiation mandates, decides on external risk assessments and defines action priorities regarding specific third-countries or regions. Given the original internal focus of the AFSJ, policy preparation in the Working Groups often needs input from a special Group on External JHA Issues (JAIEX), which gathers experts on international AFSJ issues from the national ministries, and the respective regional CFSP working groups.[24]

Decisions are taken on the basis of the 'ordinary legislative procedure' (Article 294 TFEU) with qualified majority voting in the Council and co-decision by the European Parliament. In relation to the external dimension, this means that agreements based on an AFSJ legal basis will require, in principle, the consent of the EP ex Article 218(6)(v) TFEU (see also Chapter 4).[25]

Furthermore, an EU Counter-terrorism Coordinator (CTC) works under the authority of the High Representative but takes their instructions from and reports primarily to the JHA Council. The CTC coordinates counter-terrorism activities within the Council and monitors the implementation of EU counter-terrorism measures.

[21] See the Finnish Presidency programme Available at: https://eu2019.fi/documents/11707387/14346258/EU2019FI-EU-puheenjohtajakauden-ohjelma-en.pdf/3556b7f1-16df-148c-6f59-2b2816611b36/EU2019FI-EU-puheenjohtajakauden-ohjelma-en.pdf.pdf.

[22] European Council Conclusions 26/27 June 2014, EUCO 79/14. Available at: www.consilium.europa.eu/uedocs/cms_Data/docs/pressdata/en/ec/143478.pdf.

[23] P Koutrakos, 'The Nexus between CFSP/CSDP and the Area of Freedom, Security and Justice' in S Blockmans and P Koutrakos (eds) *Research Handbook on the EU's Common Foreign and Security Policy* (Cheltenham, Edward Elgar, 2018) 296–311.

[24] See Council document 144319/1/08, Creation of an Ad Hoc Support Group concerning the external dimension of JHA questions, 28/10/2008. Available at: http://data.consilium.europa.eu/doc/document/ST-14431-2008-REV-1/en/pdf.

[25] A number of AFSJ policies are subject to special legislative procedures such as family law matters ex Art 81(3) TFEU with only the consent of the EP and unanimity of the Council. Naturally, for such cases, the different procedures codified in Art 218 TFEU will apply.

In relation to external initiatives, the CTC can be described as the Union's 'chief counter-terrorism diplomat',[26] as they have the task of ensuring the effective communication of EU objectives and cooperation offers to third countries.

(iii) The Commission, the High Representative and the European External Action Service

Given the application of the ordinary legislative procedure, the role of the Commission follows the general rules of that procedure. The composition of the JHA Council (Ministers for Justice and Ministers for Home Affairs) is mirrored in the involvement of the Commission, with two responsible Directorates Generals (DGs): 'Home Affairs' (HOME) and 'Justice' (JUST). The still somewhat hybrid nature of the AFSJ is reflected in the non-exclusive right of initiative of the Commission in the fields of judicial cooperation in criminal matters (AFSJ Chapter 4) and police cooperation (AFSJ Chapter 5).

Article 76 TFEU

The acts referred to in Chapters 4 and 5, together with the measures referred to in Article 74 which ensure administrative cooperation in the areas covered by these Chapters, shall be adopted:

(a) on a proposal from the Commission, or
(b) on the initiative of a quarter of the Member States.

In the external domain, the negotiation and conclusion of AFSJ agreements follows the general rules laid down in Article 218 TFEU. This implies that the Commission is normally responsible for submitting the negotiation recommendation to the Council (Article 218(3) TFEU), except where the agreement relates exclusively or principally to CFSP (see further Chapters 4 and 9).

As we have seen in Chapter 1, the scope of the European External Action Service (EEAS) covers all areas of the EU's external action. It has been argued that the EEAS can play a significant role in the external dimension of the AFSJ, through contributions to the coherence of the EU's external action law-making, and through its ambivalent position within the Council and the Commission.[27] Given the strong link between a number of AFSJ and CFSP issues such as countering international terrorism, a similar role can be foreseen for the High Representative.

[26] See J Monar, 'The EU's Growing External Role in the AFSJ Domain: Factors, Framework and Forms of Action' (2014) 27 *Cambridge Review of International Affairs* 147, 154.

[27] M Gatti, 'The Role of the European External Action Service in the External Dimension of the Area of Freedom Security and Justice' in C Flaesch-Mougin and LS Rossi (eds) *La Dimension Externe de l'Espace de liberté sécurité et justice de l'Union Européenne après le traite de Lisbonne* (Brussels, Bruylant, 2012) 171–93.

(iv) The European Parliament

Again, through the general application of the ordinary legislative procedure, the position of the European Parliament is comparable to what it can do in most other areas of Union action: co-decision (legislation is finally adopted together by the Council and the European Parliament) and consent for the conclusion of international agreements have made the European Parliament a serious player in this area.[28]

The European Parliament has been given a role that is in line with the potential effects of the AFSJ decisions on EU citizens and individuals in general. This is a fundamental matter: as the powers conferred on the EU in the AFSJ fields have the power to affect fundamental rights of individuals such as the right to privacy and data protection (Articles 16 TFEU and Articles 7 and 8 of the Charter of Fundamental Rights of the European Union) or the right to ask for asylum (Article 18 Charter of Fundamental Rights of the European Union), it is imperative that the only directly and democratically elected law maker in the Union be a decisive player. In the field of external relations, an example for the EP exercising its prerogatives, as laid down in Article 218(6)(a) TFEU, was its refusal to give its consent to the interim agreement between the EU and the USA on bank data transfers via the SWIFT network in February 2010. This vote prevented the agreement from entering into force.

However, on other occasions, the EP has obtained significant, but marginal successes. This is the case n the two actions brought before the Court of Justice against the procedure and the legal bases adopted to conclude agreements with third countries for the purpose of arresting and trying and detaining suspected pirates arrested in the framework of Operation Atlanta (see Chapter 9).[29]

(v) AFSJ-related Agencies

In order to support and enhance the Union's activities to pursue the establishment and development of the AFSJ, a number of specialised European agencies were created: Europol, Eurojust, Frontex and EASO.[30] These bodies respectively cover the following main domains of the AFSJ: police cooperation (Europol), judicial cooperation in criminal matters (Eurojust), the management of the external border of the Union

[28] Exception do persist in certain aspects of AFSJ decision making; thus, in some fields, the EP may be merely consulted (TFEU, Art 81(3)) or more simply asked to give its consent (TFEU Art 86(1)).

[29] For an analysis of the cases see C Matera and RA Wessel, 'Context or Content? A CFSP or AFSJ Legal Basis for EU International Agreements' (2014) 49 *Revista de Derecho Comunitario Europeo* 1047 and, for the second judgement, SR Sánchez-Tabernero, 'The Choice of Legal Basis and the Principle of Consistency in the Procedure for Conclusion of International Agreements in CFSP Contexts: Parliament v. Council (Pirate Transfer Agreement with Tanzania) (2017) 54 *Common Market Law Review* 899.

[30] Respectively, Regulation (EU) 2016/794 of the European Parliament and of the Council of 11 May 2016 on the European Union Agency for Law Enforcement Cooperation (Europol) [2016] OJ L 135/53; Regulation (EU) 2018/1727 of the European Parliament and of the Council of 14 November 2018 on the European Union Agency for Criminal Justice Cooperation (Eurojust) [2018] OJ L 295/183; Regulation (EU) 2016/1624 of the European Parliament and of the Council of 14 September 2016 on the European Border and Coast Guard and amending Regulation (EU) 2016/399 of the European Parliament and of the Council and repealing Regulation (EC) No 863/2007 of the European Parliament and of the Council, Council Regulation (EC) No 2007/2004 and Council Decision 2005/267/EC [2004] OJ L 251/1; Regulation 439/2010 establishing a European Asylum Support Office [2010] OJ L132/11.

(Frontex) and support to national authorities in the application of the common asylum system (EASO).

In each case, these agencies have been given legal personality and have been conferred with express treaty-making powers. That these competences have been used is reflected, for instance, in the agreements concluded between Europol and a large number of third countries on the sharing of strategic data (regarding the fight against organised crime and terrorism, in particular) and on the sharing of personal data (so-called 'operational agreements'). Eurojust, for example, has agreements with the US, Norway and Switzerland on the posting of liaison magistrates, whereas legal cooperation agreements have also been concluded with a number of other countries. These agencies also conclude agreements with other international organisations such as Interpol or the World Customs Organisation.[31]

While the actual wording of the different founding instruments of the agencies differs, it is possible to affirm, in principle, that the agencies of the AFSJ have been conferred a limited external competence with a specific purpose: that is to say that these agencies have the power to conclude agreements with external partners 'in so far as necessary for the performance of [their] tasks'.[32] The teleological nature of external powers for AFSJ agencies serves two purposes. First, it identifies the objectives that the agencies must pursue when negotiating agreements with their external partners and, secondly, it serves as a limiting tool to prevent abuses of powers.

In the light of the current legal framework we can classify the agreements that the AFSJ agencies can conclude in two categories: cooperation agreements and operational agreements. Under the first type of agreements, AFSJ agencies are given the power to establish stable frameworks in order to work together with external partners. For instance, the Europol–Russia agreement of 2003 creates a platform for cooperation in the following ways: (1) by enabling the exchange technical and strategic information such as crime situations and development reports, threat assessments; (2) by enabling the exchange of law enforcement experience including the organisation of scientific and practice-oriented conferences, internships, consultations and seminars; (3) by enabling the exchange of legislation, manuals, technical literature and other law enforcement materials; and (4) by promoting common trainings.[33] In order to give effect to the agreement, a cooperation agreement usually identifies contact points for each party to facilitate direct contacts for cooperation and coordination.

Operational agreements are distinguished from cooperation agreements for two related reasons. Substantially, operational agreements are those concluded by one of the AFSJ agencies that include a mechanism to share personal data between the parties and/or that foresee concrete operational mechanisms such as joint patrolling of borders or the coordination of investigations. Procedurally, in order to conclude an agreement that envisages the exchange of personal data, the EU agency will have to go through a number of authorisations.[34] Due to their material scope, operational

[31] For an overview, C Matera, 'International Organizations and the Area of Freedom, Security and Justice' in A Ripoll-Servent and F Trauner (eds) *Crime within the Area of Freedom, Security and Justice: A European Public Order* (Cambridge, Cambridge University Press, 2011) 468–79.

[32] Art 23(1) of the Europol Regulation (n 30) and Art 47(1) of the Eurojust Regulation (n 30).

[33] Art 5 Europol–Russia Agreement of 6 November 2003. Available at: www.europol.eu.

[34] See Art 25 of the Europol Regulation (n 30).

agreements require a thorough scrutiny and an assessment of the international partner with which the agency wants to conclude it to make sure that EU standards on rights protection and rule of law are respected.[35] While the European Parliament always strives to scrutinise the activities of the agencies, their democratic and substantive accountability has been put into question because these bodies are connected to the Council and the Member States.[36]

Other than the possibility to exchange personal data, operational agreements concluded by the agencies may even go so far as to establish hosting officials from third countries (so-called liaison desks) and foresee the participation of third-country officials in border control operations. Thus, depending on the agency's mandate, an operational agreement concluded by an AFSJ agency is an agreement that goes beyond the establishment of cooperative tools and that establishes means of cooperation at the enforcement moment.

Therefore, while the different tasks assigned to the different agencies should be taken into due account, the lack of coherence and consistency in relation to the respect of the rule of law, human rights and international law have, in the past, raised serious concerns. Considering the persistent challenges related to the management of migratory flows in the Mediterranean, the excerpt below is still relevant to this date.

E Papastravridis, '"Fortress Europe" and FRONTEX: Within or Without International Law?' (2010) 79 *Nordic Journal of International Law* 75, 110–11

FRONTEX was established in 2004 to help Member States in implementing community legislation on the surveillance of EU borders and to coordinate their operational cooperation in order to strengthen security at external borders. No matter how efficient it has been in the attainment of these objectives, there appear to be sound reasons for concluding that many of its operations, especially in the maritime domain, are not in full consistency with international law. Moreover, as was recognized by the European Commission, there is 'disunity within the EU over which obligations arises from EU fundamental rights and international human rights and refugee law, and how these obligations relate to the law of the sea'. This ambiguity over the relevant legal obligations of the Member States is significantly enhanced by the secrecy and non-transparency governing the Agency's operations ...

Of specific interest is the application of the principle of *non-refoulement* in the present context, which appears to be especially problematic in the majority of

[35] V Mitsilegas, *EU Criminal Law* (Oxford, Hart Publishing, 2009); and C Matera, 'The Influence of International Organisations on the EU's Area of Freedom, Security and Justice: A First Inquiry' in RA Wessel and S Blockmans (eds) *Between Autonomy and Dependence: The EU Legal Order Under the Influence of International Organisations* (Berlin, TMC Asser Press/Springer, 2013) 269–96.

[36] J Santos Vara, 'The External Activities of AFSJ Agencies: The Weakness of Democratic and Judicial Controls' (2015) 20 *European Foreign Affairs Review* 118.

these operations since it is very likely that the persons on board the intercepted vessels would be forced to return to their countries of origin where they may face prosecution or be subjected to torture or inhuman or degrading treatment. This has been very recently acknowledged by the European Commission with regard to Member States, in particular when engaged in joint operations or in operations taking place within the territorial waters of another State or in the high seas.

However, the recent conclusion of a working arrangement between FRONTEX and UNHCR shows the way forward and, if coupled with other relevant initiatives, would not only 'strengthen the security and freedom of the citizens of the EU', but also the security and freedom of all human beings in need of protections. It is apt to conclude by recalling Article 1 of the European Convention on Human Rights: 'The High Contracting Parties shall secure to everyone within their jurisdiction the rights and freedoms defined in Section I of the Convention.' It is for FRONTEX and EU Member States, which are all parties to the latter Convention, to assume that responsibility and bring it to fruition.

(vi) The Court of Justice

Given the subject area, the CJEU's contribution to the AFSJ is facilitated by certain special procedures that allow certain cases to be dealt with more rapidly when required. Article 267 TFEU allows for the usually lengthy preliminary procedure to be applied more swiftly in case it concerns a person in custody.

Article 267 TFEU

If such a question is raised in a case pending before a court or tribunal of a Member State with regard to a person in custody, the Court of Justice of the European Union shall act with the minimum of delay.

Such questions may also be raised in relation to international agreements concluded in the AFSJ area. In general, however, most AFSJ cases before the Court concern internal issues; although the 'external dimension' is almost always visible in the background (eg, international treaties on asylum, migration or fundamental rights).

The Court is fully competent to scrutinise all AFSJ legislative activity by the Council and the European Parliament. Unlike CFSP (see Chapter 9), no exceptions have been made for certain acts or procedures and both direct and indirect actions are allowed, although a number of quite complicated transitional rules were formulated at the time of the move of the AFSJ from the EC-Treaty to the TFEU. This distinction between pre-existing acts and acts adopted after the entry into force of the Lisbon Treaty is also relevant for the current external AFSJ actions.

D. Opt-outs

The opt-outs negotiated by certain Member States in relation to the AFSJ affect the external competences of the Union in this area. With the adoption of Protocol No 21 on the position of the United Kingdom and Ireland in respect of the Area of Freedom, Security and Justice annexed to the Treaty of Lisbon, the two Member States claimed far-reaching exceptions relating to all matters falling under Title V of Part Three of the TFEU.[37] While external relations are not mentioned explicitly, Protocol 21 refers to 'measures pursuant to Title V of Part Three of the Treaty on the Functioning of the European Union' in general, including the AFSJ. This implies that the UK and Ireland have also opted-out of acts adopting international agreements in this area. Article 2 of the protocol explicitly refers to the fact that 'no provision of any international agreement concluded by the Union … shall be binding upon or applicable' in those Member States. In fact, it would be difficult to see the two countries be bound by international agreements in an area in which they do not participate.

In addition to the UK and Irish opt-outs, Denmark has a special relationship with the EU's AFSJ and its external relations (see Protocol 22). However, because Denmark participates in the Schengen rules on the free movement of persons, the opt-out of this country complicates EU external action by requiring additional procedural steps to reflect its special position. Therefore, in fields such as EU visa policy, in which Denmark participates by the means of public international law, an EU visa facilitation agreement with a third country will have to be concluded separately by Denmark.[38]

Variable geometry and different opt-out regimes have characterised the evolution of AFSJ integration.[39] To this date, however, the impact has been predominantly internal since external action reflects the internal distribution of powers and architecture. In terms of substantive coherence, studies have argued that variable geometry has not compromised the coherence of EU action either internally or externally, but has predominantly impacted the procedural and formal architecture EU external action.[40]

[37] Protocol (No 21) On the Position of the United Kingdom and Ireland in Respect of the Area of Freedom, Security and Justice [2010] OJ C83/295.

[38] See, for example, the EU's Agreement between the European Community and the Russian Federation on the facilitation of the issuance of visas to the citizens of the European Union and the Russian Federation [2007] OJ L 129/1, and the Danish one of 2008 which is, as the preamble expressly states, based on the EU one. Available from this source with an English translation: https://nyidanmark.dk/en-GB/Words%20and%20Concepts%20Front%20Page/US/Visum/Visa_facilitations_agreements.

[39] B Martenczuk, 'Variable Geometry and the External Relations of the ECLI:EU: The Experience of Justice and Home Affairs' in B Martenczuk and S van Thiel (eds) *Justice, Liberty, Security: New Challenges for EU External Relations* (Brussels, Brussels University Press, 2008) 493–523.

[40] See J Santos Vara and E Fahey, 'Variable Geometry and International Relations within the Matrix of the AFSJ: A Practice-Based Case Study of Opting-in and Out in EU–US Relations' in S Blockmans and B Van Vooren (eds) *How to Legally Accommodate Variable Geometry in EU External Action* (Brussels, Centre for European Policy Studies, 2013); and C Matera, 'Much Ado about "Opt-outs"? The Impact of 'Variable Geometry' in the AFSJ on the EU as a Global Security Actor' in Blockmans and Van Vooren, ibid).

III. The External Dimension of the Main AFSJ Policy Areas

The following section will provide a short overview of some key initiatives and elements that have characterised the development of the external dimension of the AFSJ. As a comprehensive analysis of substantive, procedural and institutional aspects would go beyond the scope of this Chapter, a handful of examples covering the different AFSJ fields have been selected.

A. Policies on Border Checks, Asylum and Immigration

Chapter 2 of Title V TFEU contains primary law provisions on border checks (Article 77 TFEU), asylum (Article 78 TFEU) and immigration (Article 79 TFEU). Thus, Article 77(2) TFEU is dedicated to internal and external borders and mandates the EU to adopt measures relating to: (i) a common policy on visas and other short-stay permits, (ii) the checks at the external borders of the EU, (iii) the establishment of the conditions upon which third country nationals can move freely within the EU, (iv) the establishment of an integrated management system of the external borders and, finally (v) the absence of controls at the crossing of the internal borders of the EU. Secondly, Article 78 TFEU on asylum, subsidiary protection and temporary protection mandates the Union to develop a common policy in these domains in paragraph 1 and identifies the different specific legal bases in paragraph 2. Article 79 in relation to the development of a common immigration policy further confers on the EU the necessary powers to (i) determine the conditions of entry and residence for third-country nationals, (ii) define the rights conferred to third-country nationals residing within the EU, (iii) adopt measures to fight illegal migrations and unauthorised residence, including removal and repatriation and (iv) combatting human trafficking.

In relation to the external dimension of these policies, this section looks at three issues possessing particular importance: border controls, the short-stay visa policy and readmission agreements.

(i) Local Border Traffic

The management of EU borders is built upon the Schengen Border Code (SBC) on the one hand, and the establishment of a network of national and EU bodies vested with the operational tasks linked to border controls, on the other hand. Whilst the normative framework of border management is centrally provided by the EU, the 2000 Schengen Convention held that the peculiar geographic and economic context of some regions at the external borders of the EU required exceptional rules. Today, Article 40 of the Schengen Border Code provides for the adoption of special rules for local border traffic (LBT).[41] As Dubowski has argued, '[l]ocal border traffic could be described in a nutshell as a mechanism balancing the need for strict protection of Union's external borders and the necessity of holding the Union open to the cooperation with third countries'.[42] To implement this provision of the SBC, the EU has adopted Regulation 1931/2006 on the rules on local border traffic to allow for a smoother management of the external borders of the EU in certain specific contexts.[43]

The Regulation thus established a specialised regime and a specific permit concerning local border traffic to exclude the strict applicability of the controls normally prescribed by the Schengen Borders Code; and to this end it created an authorisation mechanism through which Member States are empowered to conclude bilateral agreements with neighbouring third countries for the purpose of facilitating the crossing of borders for individuals living in an area next to the external border of an EU Member State.[44] More specifically, the Regulation allows for derogations from the SBC for residents of an area that extends no more than 30 kilometres from the border and, for this purpose, defines LBT as the regular crossing of an external land border by residents for societal, cultural, family or substantiated economic reasons.[45]

Leaving the analysis of the rules on border checks aside, the LBT is a good example of how the dichotomy between exclusive and shared competences does not describe the reality of EU external action within the AFSJ, as the excerpt below shows.

Regulation (EC) No 1931/2006 of the European Parliament and of the Council of 20 December 2006 laying down rules on local border traffic at the external land borders of the Member States and amending the provisions of the Schengen Convention [2006] OJ L 405/1

Article 13

Bilateral Agreements between Member States and neighbouring third countries

1. For the purposes of implementing the local border traffic regime, Member States shall be authorised to conclude bilateral Agreements with neighbouring third countries in accordance with the rules set out in this Regulation.

[41] Art 40 Schengen Border Code: 'This Regulation shall be without prejudice to Community rules on local border traffic and to existing bilateral agreements on local border traffic.' Regulation (EU) 2016/399 of the European Parliament and of the Council of 9 March 2016 on a Union Code on the rules governing the movement of persons across borders (Schengen Borders Code) [2016] OJ L 77/1.

[42] T Dubowski, 'Local Border Traffic – European Union and Member States' Perspective (based on Polish Experience)' (2012) 14 *European Journal of Migration and Law* 367.

[43] Regulation (EC) No 1931/2006 of the European Parliament and of the Council of 20 December 2006 laying down rules on local border traffic at the external land borders of the Member States and amending the provisions of the Schengen Convention [2006] OJ L 405/1.

[44] Ibid, Art 1.

[45] Ibid, Art 3.

Member States may also maintain existing bilateral Agreements with neighbouring third countries on local border traffic. To the extent that such Agreements are incompatible with this Regulation, the Member States concerned shall amend the Agreements in such a way as to eliminate the incompatibilities established.

2. Before concluding or amending any bilateral Agreement on local border traffic with a neighbouring third country, the Member States concerned shall consult the Commission as to the compatibility of the Agreement with this Regulation.

   If the Commission considers the Agreement to be incompatible with this Regulation, it shall notify the Member State concerned. The Member State shall take all appropriate steps to amend the Agreement within a reasonable period in such a way as to eliminate the incompatibilities established.

3. Where the Community or the Member State concerned has not concluded a general readmission Agreement with a third country, the bilateral Agreements on local border traffic with that third country shall provide for the readmission of persons found to be abusing the local border traffic regime as established by this Regulation to be facilitated.

This provision created a new mechanism according to which, in an area in which the EU has attained the harmonisation of rules governing the controls and the management of borders, Member States are authorised to conclude bilateral agreements with their neighbouring countries so as to derogate from EU rules where historical, societal or geographical reasons exist. In this case, the LBT Regulation affirms that before concluding or amending any bilateral agreement on LBT, Member States must consult the Commission as to the compatibility of the agreement with the Regulation and, if the Commission considers that the agreement envisaged is incompatible with the Regulation, the Member State concerned must amend the incompatible rules. Moreover, the Regulation also provides that, should there be no readmission agreement between the parties of an LBT agreement, then that agreement must contain rules and procedures on readmission.

Since the Regulation was adopted, nine agreements have been concluded: three between EU Member States and Belarus (Poland, Latvia and Lithuania), one between Poland and the Russian Federation in relation to Kaliningrad and one between Norway and the Russian Federation. This is relevant because Norway is a Schengen-associated country and must also comply with Schengen rules in the exercise of its foreign relations.[46] Moreover, Hungary, Slovakia and Poland have concluded LBT

[46] Communication of the Commission on the implementation and functioning of the LBT regime COM (2011) 47 final and Report from the Commission on the bilateral agreement concluded by Poland with the Russian Federation COM (2014) 74 final.

agreements with Ukraine and Romania has concluded one with Moldova.[47] While the Commission has considered that most agreements were not fully in compliance with the LBT Regulation to date, the only dispute that has been brought to the attention of the CJEU concerned the time limitations linked to the LBT permits.[48]

(ii) Visa Facilitation, Visa Waiver and Readmission Agreements

In addition to initiatives directly pertaining to the management and surveillance of external borders, the EU has made use of its powers to conclude visa-related agreements and readmission agreements. Concerning visa policy,[49] it must be borne in mind that, because the EU is an area without internal borders, it plays a key role in establishing the rules concerning the documents necessary to enter the EU as well as conditioning the timeframe in which third-country nationals are allowed to enter and move within the EU. EU visa policy comprises a list with the countries whose citizens need a visa to enter the EU,[50] a visa code regulating the procedural aspects of issuing a visa and,[51] finally, a visa format (ie the rules establishing what the document should look like).[52] Bearing in mind the level of harmonisation reached internally, the short-term visa policy (ie visas valid for three months within the Schengen area) is one of the few domains in which it seems appropriate to speak of an exclusive external competence of the Union: in relation to short-term stays, the EU alone establishes visa requirements and, consequently, the EU alone can negotiate and conclude agreements that relate to those measures such as visa facilitation agreements (ie agreements that soften the bureaucratic hurdles connected to obtaining a visa).[53] Because agreements of this type do not impact prerogatives related to national security, but merely set administrative standards and have a regulatory function, questions about the interference with national prerogatives are absent.

In relation to visas and where the risks for irregular migration are considered acceptable by the institutions in Brussels, the EU may also conclude 'short-stay visa waiver treaties' whereby the EU and the third country in question decide to reciprocally stop requiring short-term visas. The EU has concluded this type of agreements with key partner countries such as Brazil[54] or with countries that are not perceived to

[47] Ibid.

[48] Case C-254/11 *Szabolcs-Szatmár-Bereg Megyei Rendőrkapitányság Záhony Határrendészeti Kirendeltsége v Oskar Shmodi*, ECLI:EU:C:2013:182.

[49] In a nutshell, a visa is a document issued by the border offices of a country authorising entry and stay to a given individual.

[50] Regulation (EU) 2018/1806 of the European Parliament and of the Council of 14 November 2018 listing the third countries whose nationals must be in possession of visas when crossing the external borders and those whose nationals are exempt from that requirement [2018] OJ L 303/39.

[51] Regulation (EC) No 810/2009 of the European Parliament and of the Council of 13 July 2009 establishing a Community Code on Visas (Visa Code) [2009] OJ L 243/1.

[52] Regulation (EU) 2017/1370 of the European Parliament and of the Council of 4 July 2017 amending Council Regulation (EC) No 1683/95 laying down a uniform format for visas [2017] OJ L198/24.

[53] For example, see the agreement between the EU and the Republic of Azerbaijan on the facilitation of the issuance of visas [2014] OJ L128/49.

[54] Agreement between the European Union and the Federative Republic of Brazil on short-stay visa waiver for holders of ordinary passports [2012] OJ L 255/4.

be a source of mass irregular migration. A recent example of the latter type of visa waiver agreement is that with the Solomon Islands concluded in 2016.[55]

To open negotiations on visa facilitation or visa waiver agreements, the EU will likely demand the conclusion of a readmission agreement. Similar to what was observed for the EU's visa policy, in this case EU external action comes as a result of a number of legislative acts adopted by the EU internally. The EU has adopted a Directive on the mutual recognition of expulsion decisions for third-country nationals[56] and a number of other operational instruments to enhance cooperation amongst Member States. Externally, the EU can benefit from the only express external power of the AFSJ in Article 79(3) TFEU regarding the conclusion of international agreements in this regard. We have already seen that despite the level of internal harmonisation, the nature of this external competence has never been considered exclusive. This is probably because, contrary to visa policy and visa agreements, return and readmission demand the exercise of public authority and directly impact the involvement of bodies such as police forces and judicial authorities that have the power to restrict the freedom of individuals and thus fall within the scope of Article 72 TFEU.

B. Judicial Cooperation in Civil Matters

Paragraph 2 of Article 81 TFEU on judicial cooperation in civil law identifies eight fields of competence for the EU, ranging from the cross-border service of judicial and extra-judicial documents to the training of the judiciary of the Member States and their staff. Moreover, paragraph 3 of Article 81 TFEU contains a mandate for action in the field of family law but in this case the EU institutions will have to follow the special legislative procedure and the Council will act unanimously. However, the core of this provision is related to conferral of legislative powers to the EU in relation to 'mutual recognition of and enforcement between Member States of judgements and of decisions in extrajudicial case' and in relation to 'the compatibility of the rules applicable in the Member States concerning conflict of laws and jurisdiction'.

Judicial cooperation in civil matters, together with judicial cooperation in criminal matters and police cooperation, distinguishes itself from the role the EU is called upon to exercise by the Treaty. Contrary to areas in which the EU is called to substitute, to lead or to support Member States in the decision-making process, in these cases the Union is primarily asked to adopt legislative instruments to facilitate direct cooperation amongst the judicial authorities of the Member States without having to make use of diplomatic channels and central governmental authorities. In this sense, the EU is a normative hub which supports direct cooperation amongst national judicial authorities and extends the validity of decisions adopted by national judges beyond national borders in matters of private international law.

[55] Agreement between the European Union and Solomon Islands on the short-stay visa waiver [2016] OJ L292/3.

[56] Council Directive 2001/40/EC of 28 May 2001 on the mutual recognition of decisions on the expulsion of third country nationals [2001] OJ L 149/34.

The history of judicial cooperation in civil law, however, does not solely rely on the principle of mutual recognition and the impact of the Amsterdam Treaty and the *Tampere* decision; rather, this dimension of the AFSJ is built upon the successful history of negative integration that can be traced back to the Brussels Convention of 1968 on jurisdiction and the enforcement of judgments in civil and commercial matters.[57] Whilst the scope of that Convention has been absorbed by the integration of judicial cooperation in civil matters as a EU competence, because the EU internal market is connected with non-EU Member States such as Norway, Iceland and Switzerland, those rules on judicial cooperation in civil matters became the object of an international treaty: the Lugano Convention, the only AFSJ-related treaty in relation to which the CJEU recognised an exclusive competence for the EU in Opinion 1/03.[58]

The Opinion of the CJEU in relation to the Lugano Convention and the resulting exclusive external competence of the EU to negotiate and conclude the Convention is only one aspect of the type of external action in the field of private international law. Both Opinion 1/03 and Article 3(2) TEU confirm that the jurisdiction and the enforcement of judgements in civil and commercial matters fall under the exclusive competence of the EU.

In the light of the *Lugano* Opinion the EU has either concluded or has acceded to a number of agreements in this field. Yet, because the scope of these agreements was often broader than the sphere of competence that the Court found to be exclusive in relation to the Lugano Convention, only a few have been concluded exclusively by the EU: this is the case, for example, with the Hague convention on the choice of court agreements[59] and the Protocol on the Hague convention on maintenance obligations concerning the choice of law.[60]

At the centre of the external activities of the EU in this field resides the cooperation with the Hague Conference on Private International Law. The EU joined the Conference in 2007[61] and since then has consolidated its role as a proactive member in the field of private international law. In this respect, having participated to the negotiation of covenants within the framework of activities of the Conference since the 1960s, and having proactively worked for the adoption of a number of conventions in that context, EU membership to this international organisation came as a natural development of the EU's role in the field of private international law. EU participation in this forum should be read as a means for the EU to coordinate with the Member States the rules on conflicts of law and jurisdiction adopted at EU level with the

[57] 1968 Brussels Convention on jurisdiction and the enforcement of judgments in civil and commercial matters (consolidated version) [1998] OJ C27/1, for the consolidated version after the accession to the EU of Austria, Finland and Sweden.

[58] Opinion 1/03 (*Lugano Convention*), ECLI:EU:C:2006:81.

[59] Council Decision of 26 February 2009 on the signing on behalf of the European Community of the Convention on Choice of Court Agreements [2009] OJ L133/1.

[60] Council Decision of 30 November 2009 on the conclusion by the European Community of the Hague Protocol of 23 November 2007 on the Law Applicable to Maintenance Obligations [2009] OJ L 331/1.

[61] Council Decision 2006/719/EC of 5 October 2006 on the accession of the Community to the Hague Conference on Private International Law [2006] OJ L297/1.

'acquis de la Haye' (ie the bulk of conventions on private international law that has been adopted under the aegis of the Hague Conference).

Another aspect of the external dimension of judicial cooperation in civil matters is the adoption, by the EU, of authorisations for Member States to conclude international conventions falling within this AFSJ domain as 'trustees' of EU law.[62] The Council has adopted a number of these decisions on matters such as parental responsibility for children.[63] Lastly, it must be emphasised that, in the aftermath of the *Lugano* Opinion, the Council has adopted two separate Regulations where the EU disciplines the conditions under which, in spite of *Lugano*, Member States are allowed to conclude their own treaties in civil and commercial matters linked to Article 81 TFEU.[64]

For the purpose of this chapter, the most interesting aspect of the external dimension of judicial cooperation in civil matters is how the classic dichotomy between exclusive and shared competences is not fully applicable to the EU's AFSJ and that the relation between EU external powers and those of the Member States is more fluid and dynamic than in other fields. In this regard, the *Lugano* Opinion emerges more as an exception rather than the rule.[65] Rather, this section shows that in the AFSJ fields, the EU is mostly a facilitator of cooperation and a framework setter. It promotes coherence whilst respecting the roles and prerogatives of Member States.

C. Judicial Cooperation in Criminal Matters

The provisions on judicial cooperation in criminal matters (JCCM) present more nuances than those concerned with civil justice cooperation and they best portray the ambivalent role that 'judicial cooperation' is really called to play within the European integration process. Chapter 3 of Title V on the AFSJ contains both bridging norms, aiming to create direct cooperation mechanisms between national judicial authorities; and provisions reflecting the general interest of the EU, thus allowing the Union to develop a genuine European policy in criminal law and in criminal procedural law. In this perspective, it is possible to refer to the objectives and measures envisaged in Article 82(1) TFEU as bridging measures aiming to establish cooperation based on mutual recognition; whereas in paragraph (2) of the same Article the EU has been granted powers to introduce some degree of (instrumental) approximation in order to supersede the shortcomings of the application of the mutual recognition. This means

[62] M Cremona, 'Member States as "Trustees" of the Community Interest: Participating in International Agreements on Behalf of the European Community', EUI Working Paper 17/2009, 17.

[63] Council Decision of 19 December 2002 authorising the Member States, in the interest of the Community, to sign the 1996 Hague Convention on Jurisdiction, Applicable Law, Recognition, Enforcement and Cooperation in respect of Parental Responsibility and Measures for the Protection of Children [2003] OJ L 48/1.

[64] See, for instance, Regulation (EC) No 662/2009 of the European Parliament and of the Council of 13 July 2009 establishing a procedure for the negotiation and conclusion of agreements between Member States and third countries on particular matters concerning the law applicable to contractual and non-contractual obligations, [2009] OJ L200/25.

[65] See P Franzina, *The External Dimension of EU Private International Law after Opinion 1/13* (Mortsel, Intersentia, 2016).

that paragraph (2) can only be used to facilitate the application of the mutual recognition principle and the instruments adopted under paragraph (1).

Although the Treaty provisions seem focused on internal matters, also in this case the EU has developed an external dimension because it is engaged in fighting transnational forms of crime such as organised crime (including international terrorism), human trafficking and drug trafficking. To do so, the EU has to act on two fronts: contribute to the development of multilateral instruments that promote the criminalisation of certain activities at the global level and, on the other side, develop mechanisms with third countries and international organisations which foster the cooperation of judicial authorities for the purpose of investigating and suppressing such forms of crime.

In relation to the first front, the EU has ratified instruments such as the UN Convention on Transnational Organised Crime[66] and its two protocols: the Protocol Against the Smuggling of Migrants by Land, Sea and Air and the Protocol to Prevent, Suppress and Punish Trafficking in Persons, Especially Women and Children.[67] Interestingly enough, at that time the EU did so on the basis of a plurality of Treaty provisions raging from former Article 95 TEC on the approximation of laws to provisions on migration and development cooperation. This type of (fragmented) solution was the result of two main factors: the broad range of EU competences covered by the international instruments in question and a certain prejudice against the use of the criminal law legal basis under the former third pillar since, at that time, using Article 37 TEU (pre-Lisbon) would have imposed the application of CFSP rules and not the community method. The same rationale also explains why at the time of concluding the United Nations Convention against Corruption, the EU opted for an internal market rationale.[68] Should those negotiations and conventions be concluded today, then it would be impossible to ignore the relevant AFSJ provisions and, with the extension of the ordinary legislative procedure, to convincingly conclude such multilateral treaties without using the relevant articles of the Treaties on criminal law and justice.

In relation to the second front mentioned above, the EU has concluded two main sets of agreements that directly fall within the scope of judicial cooperation in criminal

[66] Council Decision 2004/579/EC of 29 April 2004 on the conclusion, on behalf of the European Community, of the United Nations Convention against Transnational Organised Crime [2004] OJ L261/69.

[67] See, respectively, Council Decision 2006/617/EC of 24 July 2006 on the conclusion, on behalf of the European Community, of the Protocol Against the Smuggling of Migrants by Land, Sea and Air, supplementing the United Nations Convention Against Transnational Organised Crime concerning the provisions of the Protocol, in so far as the provisions of the Protocol fall within the scope of Part III, Title IV of the Treaty establishing the European Community, [2006] OJ L262/34, Council Decision 2006/618/EC of 24 July 2006 on the conclusion, on behalf of the European Community, of the Protocol to Prevent, Suppress and Punish Trafficking in Persons, Especially Women and Children, supplementing the United Nations Convention against Transnational Organised Crime concerning the provisions of the Protocol, in so far as the provisions of this Protocol fall within the scope of Articles 179 and 181a of the Treaty establishing the European Community, [2006] OJ L262/44 and Council Decision 2006/619/EC of 24 July 2006 on the conclusion, on behalf of the European Community, of the Protocol to Prevent, Suppress and Punish Trafficking in Persons, Especially Women and Children, supplementing the United Nations Convention against Transnational Organised Crime concerning the provisions of the Protocol, in so far as the provisions of the Protocol fall within the scope of Part III, Title IV of the Treaty establishing the European Community [2006] OJ L262/51.

[68] Council Decision 2008/801/EC of 25 September 2008 on the conclusion, on behalf of the European Community, of the United Nations Convention against Corruption [2008] OJ L 287/1.

matters: the Mutual Legal Assistance (MLA) and Extradition agreements with the USA and Japan. Moreover, it has also concluded MLA agreements with Norway, Iceland Switzerland and Lichtenstein as a result of the special association position these countries have with Schengen and the EU.

MLA and extradition agreements are instruments that aim to discipline cooperation in criminal affairs. MLA agreements discipline judicial and administrative cooperation in a number of fields such as transmission and collection of evidence between two different States and establishment of joint investigation teams; extradition agreements discipline the conditions concerning the surrendering of individuals suspected of having committed a crime with a view to making the suspect stand trial or the surrendering of convicted individuals for the purpose of executing a sentence.

The USA–EU MLA and extradition agreements[69] are the first examples of criminal law-based international treaties concluded by the EU. The agreements work as a 'framework agreement' or 'umbrella agreement' (Articles 14 MLA and 18 Extradition Agreement), providing a common framework and content for MLA and extradition rules in relation to individual agreements existing between individual Member States and the USA. In other words, the EU-USA agreement sets minimum and common rules that must be respected by the USA and the Member States when negotiating their respective bilateral instruments. This type of agreement is a clear expression of the division of tasks between Member States and the EU in respect of many AFSJ fields: the EU as a norm-setting authority, with enforcement-related rules are carried out by Member States. In contrast, the MLA agreement with Japan[70] contains no clause on bilateral agreements and must therefore be understood as a self-standing agreement which, nonetheless, authorises Japan and the Member States to 'request and provide assistance on the basis of other applicable international conventions' and even to conclude agreements 'confirming, supplementing, extending or amplifying' the provisions of the EU–Japan agreement.[71]

Also in this field, the least-developed field of EU external action under the AFSJ, we observe how the dichotomy between exclusive and shared competences is misleading. Whilst the EU may conclude an agreement exclusively, this does not necessarily mean that it has replaced the Member States: the enforcement and operational prerogatives of Member States remain intact in a renewed context in which the EU provides for the reference framework.

D. Data protection in international agreements

The external dimension of the AFSJ raises complex questions from a legal-constitutional perspective and, specifically, the capacity of the EU to maintain in its

[69] Agreement on extradition between the European Union and the United States of America [2003] OJ L181/27; and Agreement on mutual legal assistance between the European Union and the United States of America [2003] OJ L181/34.

[70] Agreement between the European Union and Japan on mutual legal assistance in criminal matters [2010] OJ L39/20.

[71] Article 27 of the Agreement between the European Union and Japan on mutual legal assistance in criminal matters [2010] OJ L39/20.

external relations the constitutional standards that have been agreed upon within the EU. These constitutional concerns relate to the impact that these agreements may have on the life of individuals and on the relations between the international community and the EU. In the CFSP area, an example of this type of concern emerged with the *Kadi* saga (see Chapter 5) and the externalisation of the AFSJ has raised numerous similar concerns in relation to data protection and privacy standards.

The protection of EU standards on data protection and privacy have acquired particular significance for two main reasons. The first is that, since the terrorist attacks of 9/11, national and international authorities have been striving to share as much information as possible to prevent, investigate and punish criminal activities such as terrorism. The second reason is that data protection and privacy are considered as fundamental rights within the European Union and the legal standards adopted within the EU have extraterritorial relevance.[72] The ambition of combining the protection and promotion of EU standards whilst sharing sensitive data with third countries to prevent and fight against crime meant that on top of existing databases such as the Schengen Information System (SIS),[73] the EU has concluded a number of agreements aiming at exchanging information with third countries and international organisations. Other than within the framework of the external activities of its specialised agencies an example directly related to the AFSJ are the Passenger Name Record (PNR) cases, which concern the transfer of personal data by airlines to border and police authorities of a third country with which the EU has concluded a specific agreement.

A PNR agreement sets the conditions for the transfer and use of PNR data, originally collected for commercial purposes by airlines, with national police authorities for public order and public safety purposes. More specifically, transfers of data are framed as contributing to 'preventing, detecting, investigating or prosecuting terrorist offences or serious transnational crime'.[74] The PNR agreements are a good example of the struggle the EU faces when having to combine the respect for internal standards on fundamental rights and civil liberties with the necessity to cooperate internationally to tackle security concerns. After a first set of agreements concluded in 2004 and 2006 with the USA and Canada respectively, and annulled by the CJEU on grounds that the incorrect legal basis had been chosen,[75] the EU concluded another strand of such agreements with the USA (2012), Australia (2012), and Canada (2014).

[72] See Arts 3, 44 and 45 Regulation (EU) 2016/679 of the European Parliament and of the Council of 27 April 2016 on the protection of natural persons with regard to the processing of personal data and on the free movement of such data, and repealing Directive 95/46/EC, OJ 2016 L 119/1. The standards of the EU need to be respected by partners the EU shares data with also in the AFSJ fields: see Article 35 Directive (EU) 2016/680 of the European Parliament and of the Council of 27 April 2016 on the protection of natural persons with regard to the processing of personal data by competent authorities for the purposes of the prevention, investigation, detection or prosecution of criminal offences or the execution of criminal penalties, and on the free movement of such data, and repealing Council Framework Decision 2008/977/JHA [2016] OJ L 119/89.

[73] Regulation (EC) No 1987/2006 of the European Parliament and of the Council of 20 December 2006 on the establishment, operation and use of the second-generation Schengen Information System (SIS II) [2006] OJ L381/4.

[74] See Article 3 of the EU-Canada Agreement. Available at: http://data.consilium.europa.eu/doc/document/ST-12657-2013-REV-5/en/pdf.

[75] Joined Cases C-317/04 and C-318/04 *Parliament v Commission (European Network and Information Security Agency)*, ECLI:EU:C:2006:346.

After the conclusion of the negotiations with Canada, this PNR agreement was referred to the Court of Justice by the European Parliament in 2015 for an *ex ante* Opinion by virtue of Article 218(11) TFEU to ascertain whether it was compatible with the right to data protection and privacy as safeguarded by Article 16 TFEU and Articles 7 and 8 of the Charter of Fundamental Rights. This was the first time in the history of EU law that an international agreement was tested against the provisions of the Charter. The Court was asked to assess the draft agreement on both procedural matters (the choice of the correct legal basis) and on substantive grounds (the respect for the right to data protection and the right to private and family life). With its Opinion 1/15 of 2017, the Court held that, because of its dual nature (protecting data and sharing data for anti-crime purposes), the agreement had to be based on Articles 16 and 87 TFEU and not on Article 82 TFEU since the agreement does not promote or affect judicial cooperation between the EU and Canada. Substantively, the Court held that for several reasons, the agreement was not upholding EU internal standards on data and privacy protection.[76] The excerpt below explains its constitutional significance.

C Kuner, 'International Agreements, Data Protection, and EU Fundamental Rights on the International Stage: Opinion 1/15, EU-Canada PNR' (2018) 55 *Common Market Law Review* 857, 880–82

The case displays strikingly the changes that have taken place in EU law since the Court's first PNR judgment. That judgment resulted in a determination that a PNR agreement with the US had been concluded under the wrong 'pillar' of the EU legal structure, without any discussion of fundamental rights issues. Changes under the Lisbon Treaty mean that the pillar structure is no more and a measure in the Area of Freedom, Justice and Security such as a PNR agreement is subject to a fundamental rights review by the Court. In this way, EU law has come far in the last few years.

The Opinion takes the standards that the Court applied to data protection in other key judgments such as *Digital Rights Ireland*, *Schrems*, and *Tele2* and applies them to international agreements. The Court made it clear that it was aware of the international implications of the case, but also affirmed that this did not affect its strict standard of review. The EU will, in the future, seek to conclude further international agreements concerning data transfers, not only with regard to PNR data but also in a myriad of other areas as well (such as Brexit). The Opinion shows that it will not hesitate to strike them down if they do not meet the standards of the Charter.

The case demonstrates the vitality of the Article 218(11) [TFEU] procedure to obtain an Opinion of the Court, and the Parliament's power to invoke it

[76] Opinion 1/15 (*PNR*), ECLI:EU:C:2016:656.

to challenge international agreements on fundamental rights grounds. It also shows how the Opinion procedure has evolved: the Court's Opinions used to be viewed as directed mainly at questions of external competence, but Opinion 1/15 deals with substantive legal issues, such as the compatibility of the Draft Agreement with the Charter. One can expect the Parliament to make other requests for Opinions in the future in cases involving fundamental rights.

A final point concerns the Opinion's effect on the negotiation of international agreements by the EU. There is no doubt that it has made it more difficult for the EU to negotiate agreements involving international data sharing. The detailed scrutiny that the Court gave the Draft Agreement may be necessary to ensure that international agreements comply with primary EU law, in particular the Charter. However, it seems to present the EU with a quandary: a strict level of fundamental rights protection requires detailed analysis of international agreements, but third countries may prove unwilling to enter into them in the first place if they may later be picked apart by the Court. If not carefully considered, the unilateral assertion of EU fundamental rights on the international stage may lead to less, rather than more, data protection in practice (such as by causing third countries to resort unilaterally to increased data processing or surveillance). The implications of Opinion 1/15 will thus resonate not only in EU law, but also around the world.

IV. The Broader Picture of EU External Reactions Law

The existing challenges of global governance have pushed for the AFSJ to acquire an important external dimension. In that sense, it can be concluded that internal integration and external developments mutually reinforced the expansion of the AFSJ domain.

However, the external dimension has added more complexity to an already highly sensitive area. While 'respect for fundamental rights' is referred to in the first AFSJ provision (Article 67(1) TFEU), this principle is even more difficult to respect once norms are not merely decided on within the EU legal order, but are found in international agreements or decisions by other international organisations, such as the United Nations. Balancing security and fundamental rights appears to be one of the biggest constitutional challenges the EU faces with the further development of the AFSJ and its external dimension.

Furthermore, the challenges related to the complex issues covered by the AFSJ fields require institutional and political coordination to guarantee the adoption of norms that respect the canons of the consistency principle between internal and external EU action. Indeed, whilst the Stockholm Programme stated that '[t]he external dimension is crucial to the successful implementation of the objectives of this programme',[77] this chapter has shown that, on a number of occasions, the externalisation of the AFSJ agenda has raised serious concerns of constitutional legitimacy precisely because external initiatives were not abiding by internal constitutional standards either from a institutional or substantive perspective.

For instance, while the Lisbon Treaty has conferred an active role on the European Parliament and the Court, the coming years will also have to clarify the extent to which the plurality of institutions and bodies responsible for the external AFSJ are capable of not only striking the right balance between the different elements of the AFSJ (free movement, security and justice), but also of upholding this balance in a globalising world in which both territorial borders and borders between legal orders are increasingly fuzzy. Upholding the values and principles of Article 2 TEU is of existential importance for the EU both externally and internally. Externally, because its credibility as a normative power depends on the consistent prioritisation of the highest standards in human rights, democracy and transparency when cooperating with third countries and international organisations; internally, because it is precisely on the respect of those values that the European integration process depends.

V. Sources and Further Reading

Blockmans, S and P Koutrakos (eds) *Research Handbook on the EU's Common Foreign and Security Policy* (Cheltenham, Edward Elgar Publishing, 2018).

Cassarino, J-P, 'Informalizing EU Readmission Policy' in A Ripoll-Servent and F Trauner (eds) *The Routledge Handbook of Justice and Home Affairs* (Abingdon, Routledge, 2017) 83–98.

Conway, G, 'The Future of a European Public Prosecutor' in the Area of Freedom Security and Justice' in M Fletcher, E Herlin-Karnell and C Matera (eds) *The European Union as an Area of Freedom, Security and Justice* (Abingdon, Routledge, 2016) 176–200.

Cremona, M, 'Member States as "Trustees" of the Community Interest: Participating in International Agreements on Behalf of the European Community', EUI Working Papers 17/2009.

Cremona, M, J Monar and S Poli (eds) *The External Dimension of the European Union's Area of Freedom, Security and Justice* (Bruxelles, Peter Lang, 2011).

Dony, M (ed) *La dimension Externe de l'Espace de Libérté sécurité et Justice au Lendemain de Lisbonne et de Stockholm: un bilan à mi-parcours* (Brussels, Editions de l'Université Libre de Bruxelles, 2012).

Dubowski, T, 'Local Border Traffic – European Union and Member States' Perspective (Based on Polish Experience)' (2012) 14 *European Journal of Migration and Law* 367.

Flaesch-Mougin, C and LS Rossi (eds) *La Dimension Externe de l'Espace de liberté sécurité et justice de l'Union Européenne après le traite de Lisbonne* (Brussels, Bruylant, 2013).

[77] Council Document No 17024/09, *The Stockholm Programme – An Open and Secure Europe Serving and Protecting the Citizen*, 73.

Fletcher, M, E Herlin-Karnell and C Matera (eds) *The European Union as an Area of Freedom, Security and Justice* (New York, Routledge, 2016).
Franzina, P, *The External Dimension of EU Private International Law after Opinion 1/13* (Cambridge, Intersentia, 2016).
Gatti, M, 'The Role of the European External Action Service in the External Dimension of the Area of Freedom Security and Justice' in C Flaesch-Mougin and LS Rossi (eds) *La Dimension Externe de l'Espace de liberté sécurité et justice de l'Union Européenne après le traite de Lisbonne* (Brussels, Bruylant, 2013) 171–93.
Koutrakos, P, 'The Nexus between CFSP/CSDP and the Area of Freedom, Security and Justice' in S Blockmans and P Koutrakos (eds) *Research Handbook on the EU's Common Foreign and Security Policy* (Cheltenham, Edward Elgar, 2018) 296–330.
Kuner, C, 'International Agreements, Data Protection, and EU Fundamental Rights on the International Stage: Opinion 1/15, EU–Canada PNR' (2018) 55 *Common Market Law Review* 857.
Lang, A, 'Articolo 72 TFEU' in A Tizzano (ed) *Trattati dell'Unione Europea* (Milano, Giuffré, 2014) 819–20.
Lavanex, S and W Wagner, 'Which European Public Order? Sources of Imbalance in the European Area of Freedom, Security and Justice' (2007) 16 *European Security* 225.
Martenczuk, B and S van Thiel (eds) *Justice, Liberty, Security. New Challenges for EU External Relations* (Brussels, Brussels University Press, 2008).
Matera, C, 'Much Ado about "Opt-outs"? The Impact of "Variable Geometry" in the AFSJ on the EU as a Global Security Actor' in S Blockmans and B Van Vooren (eds) *Differentiated Integration in the EU. From the Inside Looking Out* (Brussels, Centre for European Policy Studies, 2013) 75–103.
Matera, C, 'The Influence of International Organisations on the EU's Area of Freedom, Security and Justice: A First Inquiry' in RA Wessel and S Blockmans (eds) *Between Autonomy and Dependence: The EU Legal Order Under the Influence of International Organisations* (The Hague, TMC Asser Press/Springer, 2013) 269–96.
Matera, C and RA Wessel, 'Context or Content? A CFSP or AFSJ Legal Basis for EU International Agreements' (2014) 49 *Revista de Derecho Comunitario Europeo* 1048.
Mitsilegas, V, *EU Criminal Law* (Oxford, Hart Publishing, 2009).
Monar, J, 'The EU's Growing External Role in the AFSJ Domain: Factors, Framework and Forms of Action' (2013) 1 *Cambridge Review of International Affairs* 147.
Papastravridis, E, '"Fortress Europe" and FRONTEX: Within or Without International Law?' (2010) 79 *Nordic Journal of International Law* 75.
Peers, S, *EU Justice and Home Affairs Law*, 4th edn (Oxford, Oxford University Press, 2016).
Rijpma, JJ, 'Frontex and the European System of Border Guards: The Future of European Border Management' in M Fletcher, E Herlin-Karnell and C Matera (eds) *The European Union as an Area of Freedom, Security and Justice* (New York, Routledge, 2016) 217–45.
Ripoll-Servent, A and Trauner, F (eds) *The Routledge Handbook of Justice and Home Affairs* (New York, Routledge, 2017).
Sánchez-Tabernero, R, The Choice of Legal Basis and the Principle of Consistency in the Procedure for Conclusion of International Agreements in CFSP Contexts: Parliament v Council (Pirate-Transfer Agreement with Tanzania)' (2017) 54 *Common Market Law Review* 899.
Santos Vara, J, 'The External Activities of AFSJ Agencies: The Weakness of Democratic and Judicial Controls' (2015) 20 *European Foreign Affairs Review* 118.
Santos Vara, J and E Fahey, 'Variable Geometry and International Relations within the Matrix of the AFSJ: A Practice-Based Case Study of Opting-in and out in EU–US Relations' in S Blockmans and B Van Vooren (eds) *Differentiated Integration in the EU. From the Inside Looking Out* (Brussels, Centre for European Policy Studies, 2013) 103–25.
Walker, N, 'In Search of the Area of Freedom, Security and Justice: A Constitutional Odyssey' in N Walker (ed) *Europe's Area of Freedom Security and Justice* (Oxford, Academy of European Law–European University Institute, 2004) 3–40.

13

The EU and its Neighbours

Central Issues

- This chapter examines the wide range of policies and means through which the EU engages with the countries in its neighbourhood. First, the EU's relations with the Western Balkan countries and Turkey, both formally involved in the EU's enlargement policy, will be addressed. Second, specific attention will be devoted to the European Neighbourhood Policy (ENP), launched in 2004 for those countries who are not eligible for membership either permanently or in the short to medium term. Third and finally, EU relations with neighbouring countries not taking part in the ENP or the enlargement process will be discussed.
- The *ENP* was formally launched in 2004, against the background of the fifth enlargement, and aims to create a special relationship with those neighbouring countries to the South and East that are not included in the enlargement process. From an instrumental perspective, this policy provides an excellent case study on the use of soft law in EU external relations law. From a methodological perspective, it illustrates how the EU has drawn on objectives and processes from EU enlargement policy and applied them in a non-accession context, with commensurate difficulties. As regards instruments it builds on binding bilateral frameworks and then utilises a plethora of soft legal documents to re-orientate them towards new neighbourhood objectives.
- The *Russian Federation* preferred not to take part in the ENP. Attempts to develop a 'Strategic Partnership', including an upgrade of the bilateral legal framework, faced significant legal and political hurdles. In particular, Russia's annexation of Crimea and the conflict in Eastern Ukraine seriously affected bilateral relations and resulted in the adoption of sanctions and the freezing of some policy dialogues and cooperation mechanisms.

- With the *countries of the European Free Trade Association (EFTA)*, the EU has attained a depth of integration that is so extensive that, should these countries wish, they could accede to the EU rather rapidly. However, for most of these countries there is no such desire and alternative legal structures are presently in place: the so-called 'bilaterals' with Switzerland, and the European Economic Area (EEA) with Iceland, Liechtenstein and Norway. These legal relationships present the Union with a specific challenge of 'legal homogeneity' in the application of the EU *acquis* beyond the EU legal space.

I. Neighbours with an Accession Perspective: Western Balkans and Turkey

Without analysing the procedural aspects of the EU's enlargement policy, which is discussed in Chapter 14, it is clear that the perspective of membership is a significant tool in designing the EU's relations with its (European) neighbours. Such a perspective is formally granted to the countries of the Western Balkans in the framework of the so-called Stabilisation and Association Process (SAP) and to Turkey, which is a long-standing associated country of the EU.

A. The Stabilisation and Association Process in the Western Balkans

The EU's policy towards the Western Balkans started in 1999 with the Stability Pact for South-Eastern Europe, launched in Cologne on 10 June 1999. Initiated in the context of the EU's CFSP,[1] it was not an EU foreign policy instrument but rather a multilateral political declaration and framework agreement including alongside the EU and its Member States. The G-8 countries and a wide range of international organisations including the international financial institutions, as well as the UN, OSCE, OECD, NATO and others were involved. A crucial aspect of that initiative was that the Union provided an express accession perspective to the Western Balkan countries, applying the methodology which had been developed earlier in relation to the CEECs: the conclusion of bilateral Stabilisation and Association Agreements (SAAs) with a strong element of conditionality and exporting of the EU *acquis* as a means of preparing the associated countries for EU accession. Despite the considerable similarities with the old Europe Agreements, a distinct type of association was nevertheless deemed necessary to tackle the particular challenges regarding the Western Balkans.[2] The most significant

[1] Common Position 1999/345/CFSP concerning a Stability Pact for South- Eastern Europe [1999] OJ L133/1; S Blockmans, *Tough Love: The European Union's Relations with the Western Balkans* (The Hague, TMC Asser Press, 2007) 248.

[2] D Phinnemore, 'Stabilisation and Association Agreements: Europe Agreements for the Western Balkans?' (2003) 8 *European Foreign Affairs Review* 77, 81.

difference was the focus on stabilisation on the basis of regional cooperation and good neighbourliness within the framework of the so-called Stabilisation and Association Process (SAP) covering Bosnia-Herzegovina, Croatia, the Former Yugoslav Republic of Macedonia, Albania and the Federal Republic of Yugoslavia (which later became Montenegro, Serbia and Kosovo according to resolution 1244 of the United Nations Security Council).[3]

The central objective of the SAP is to foster a process of regional reconciliation and cooperation based on common political and economic goals. Of particular significance is the offer of a so-called 'European perspective', implying that the participating countries are recognised as potential candidates for EU membership. This is confirmed in so many words in the preamble of the bilateral SAAs, creating an explicit link between the successful implementation of the agreement and progress towards the objective of membership.

The latest SAA with Kosovo is a special case in the sense that it is concluded as an EU-only agreement and with the explicit proviso that this does not constitute recognition of Kosovo as an independent state.[4] This reality has some implications regarding the formulation of certain provisions and the scope of the agreement. For instance, the preamble to the SAA with Kosovo carefully avoids the words 'potential candidate Member State', which can be found in all other SAAs. Alternatively, it uses the more diplomatic formula that implementation of the SAA 'will lead to progress in Kosovo's European perspective and rapprochement with the EU, should objective circumstances so permit and Kosovo fulfil the criteria defined by the European Council in Copenhagen on 21–22 June 1993 and the aforementioned conditionalities'.[5] The abundant use of the caveat 'should objective circumstances so permit' in the preamble, but also in several provisions of the SAA, reveals the uncertainties regarding the development of EU-Kosovo relations and thus prompted some legal creativity.

P Van Elsuwege, 'Legal Creativity in EU External Relations: The Stabilisation and Association Agreement between the EU and Kosovo' (2017) 22 *European Foreign Affairs Review* 393, 408

The EU–Kosovo SAA cannot be disconnected from the broader political context, in particular the SAP for the Western Balkans and the process of reconciliation between Serbia and Kosovo. So far, the EU has been quite successful in brokering bilateral deals between Kosovo and Serbia. In return, both Kosovo and Serbia could make significant steps forward in their process

[3] On the principle of 'good neighbourliness' as a condition for EU membership, see further Chapter 2 and P Van Elsuwege, 'Good Neighbourliness as a Condition for Accession to the European Union: Searching the Balance between Law and Politics' in D Kochenov and E Basheska (eds) *Good Neighbourly Relations in the European Legal Context* (Leiden, Brill/Nijhoff, 2015) 217–34.

[4] Stabilisation and Association Agreement between the European Union and the European Atomic Energy Community, of the one part, and Kosovo, of the other part [2016] OJ L71/3, Art 2.

[5] Ibid, Preamble.

of rapprochement with the EU. The opening of accession negotiations with Serbia and the conclusion of the SAA with Kosovo are significant landmarks on the long and difficult journey towards stabilisation of the Western Balkans region. The EU used this opportunity to codify its leadership role in this process and to operationalise the principle of good neighbourliness as a key condition for further progress … Be that as it may, the unresolved issue of Kosovo's international legal status implies that the EU-Kosovo SAA is an example of legal creativity. The EU stretched the limits of its competence to conclude an agreement that, to the extent possible, reflects the SAAs concluded with the other Western Balkan countries without recognising Kosovo as a sovereign state. Accordingly, the EU–Kosovo SAA is fully in line with the official policy of 'diversity on recognition but unity in engagement'. Nevertheless, this approach is not without consequences … Despite the incorporation of Kosovo in the SAP and numerous declarations about its 'European vocation', it is no coincidence that the SAA carefully avoids the explicit qualification of Kosovo as a 'potential candidate for EU membership'. Concluding a bilateral agreement with a country with an asterisk is one thing but accepting a potential Member State with an asterisk is something completely different. In other words, the asterisk solution is an interesting tool to proceed with the development of EU-Kosovo relations in the short term, but it is not tenable in the middle to long term, at least as far as the granting of EU membership perspectives is concerned.

In February 2018, the Commission confirmed the accession perspective of the Western Balkan countries. Moreover, it linked the future of the EU's enlargement strategy to the general reform of the EU by 2025 and envisaged the possible membership for Serbia and Montenegro by this date.

European Commission, A Credible Enlargement Perspective for an Enhanced EU Engagement with the Western Balkans, COM (2018) 65 final, 17

The EU has long supported the European perspective of the Western Balkans. The future of the region as an integral part of the EU is in the *Union's very own political, security and economic interest.* The EU's enlargement policy is part and parcel of the larger strategy to strengthen the Union by 2025. With strong political will, delivery of real and sustained reforms, and definitive solutions to disputes with neighbours, Serbia and Montenegro *could potentially be ready for membership by this date.* Accession is and will *remain a merit-based process* fully dependent on the objective progress achieved by each country.

B. Turkey: A Long-standing Associated Country

The EEC and Turkey signed an association agreement in 1963.[6] An additional protocol, signed in 1970 and which entered into force in 1973, introduced more specific commitments regarding the gradual establishment of a customs union and the envisaged introduction of free movement of persons and services. For this purpose, the association council had to adopt the necessary implementing decisions. Even though the latter failed to take the measures required for the introduction of a free movement regime in the relations between the EU and Turkey, this institutional body played a crucial role in the deepening of the bilateral relations. It significantly strengthened the legal position of Turkish workers inside the Union[7] and provided for the establishment of the customs union with the adoption of Association Decision No 1/95 in December 1995.[8] The EU–Turkey association *acquis*, including the association agreement, the additional protocol and the association council decisions, has been the subject of multiple proceedings before the Court of Justice of the European Union (CJEU).[9] Despite this close relationship, Turkey's bid for accession has thus far been unsuccessful (see Chapter 14).

II. The European Neighbourhood Policy

A. Article 8 TEU: Competence or Objective?

The Lisbon Treaty introduced a new legal basis for developing the EU's relations with its neighbouring countries in Article 8 TEU. The first proposals for such a specific 'neighbourhood clause' were launched within the European Convention during the preparation of the Draft Treaty establishing a Constitution for Europe in 2002/03 and coincided with the emerging European Neighbourhood Policy (ENP).[10] In this way, the Treaty constitutionalises the special relationship with the neighbourhood that was considered politically expedient to avoid new dividing lines between those nations that were part of the fifth enlargement in 2004, and those that were not.

[6] Agreement establishing an association between the European Economic Community and Turkey [1977] OJ L361/1.

[7] In this respect, Association Council decisions 2/76, 1/80 and 3/83 turned out to be particularly important. For comments, see M Maresceau, 'Turkey: A Candidate State Destined to Join the Union' in N Niamh Shuibhne and L Gormley (eds) *From Single Market to Economic Union. Essays in Honour of John A Usher* (Oxford, Oxford University Press, 2012) 321–22.

[8] Decision No 1/95 of the EC-Turkey Association Council on implementing the final phase of the Customs Union [1996] OJ L35/1.

[9] For an analysis of this case law see, eg, K Groenendijk, 'The Court of Justice and the Development of EEC-Turkey Association Law' in D Thym and M Zoeteweij-Turhan (eds) *Rights of Third-country Nationals under EU Association Agreements. Degrees of Free Movement and Citizenship* (Leiden, Brill/Nijhoff, 2015) 39–64.

[10] P Van Elsuwege and R Petrov, 'Article 8 TEU: Towards a New Generation of Agreements with the Neighbouring Countries of the European Union?' (2011) 36 *European Law Review* 688, 689.

Article 8 TEU

1. The Union shall develop a special relationship with neighbouring countries, aiming to establish an area of prosperity and good neighbourliness, founded on the values of the Union and characterised by close and peaceful relations based on cooperation.
2. For the purposes of paragraph 1, the Union may conclude specific agreements with the countries concerned. These agreements may contain reciprocal rights and obligations as well as the possibility of undertaking activities jointly. Their implementation shall be the subject of periodic consultation.

The first paragraph of Article 8 corresponds with Article 21 TEU in that it sets out an objective for the Union, specific to its neighbourhood. Importantly, however, the provision is strongly worded. First of all, the Union 'shall' develop special relations with the neighbours, meaning that the EU can therefore not choose not to have a neighbourhood policy.[11] Secondly, the policy aims at creating an 'area of prosperity and good neighbourliness' implying a multilateral dimension of the neighbourhood policy. Thirdly, the relationship must be based on the values of the Union, thereby referring back to Article 3(5) TEU and injecting the latter provision into the relationship with the neighbours.

The second paragraph of this provision pertains to the instrument through which to attain the objective set out in relation to the neighbourhood: 'specific' agreements with the neighbours. The striking similarity with the wording of Article 217 TFEU on association raises questions about the relationship between both provisions. Given the absence of specific procedural guidelines under Article 218 TFEU, Article 8(2) TEU may be viewed in a similar vein to Articles 3(5) and 21 TEU: stating an objective, but not providing a substantive legal basis. Article 8 TEU indicates the key features and objectives of EU engagement with its neighbours but does not confer new or distinct powers upon the Union. This is supported by the fact that the Commission proposal for the ENP funding Regulation from 2014 onwards views Article 8 TEU as 'providing the general thrust and basis for the ENP', but that the actual legal basis for the financing instrument would be Articles 209(1) and 212(2) TFEU.[12] Similarly, the association agreements with Ukraine, Moldova and Georgia do not include a single reference to Article 8 TEU and have been concluded on the substantive legal basis of Articles 37 TEU (CFSP) and 217 TFEU (association).[13]

[11] C Hillion, 'Anatomy of EU Norm Export Towards the Neighbourhood. The Impact of Article 8 TEU' in P Van Elsuwege and R Petrov (eds) *Legislative Approximation and Application of EU Law in the Eastern Neighbourhood of the European Union. Towards a Common Regulatory Space?* (Abingdon, Routledge, 2014) 16.

[12] European Commission, *Proposal for a Regulation of the European Parliament and of the Council establishing a European Neighbourhood Instrument*, Brussels 7 December 2011, COM(2011) 839 final, 7.

[13] See eg Council Decision of 16 June 2014 on the signing, on behalf of the European Union, and provisional application of the Association Agreement between the European Union and the European Atomic Energy Community and their Member States, of the one part, and the Republic of Moldova, of the other part [2014] OJ L260/1.

P Van Elsuwege and R Petrov, 'Legal Perspectives on the Study of the European Neighbourhood Policy' in T Schumacher, A Marchetti and T Demmelhuber (eds) *The Routledge Handbook on the European Neighbourhood Policy* (Abingdon, Routledge, 2018) 108

Rather than providing a new type of integration arrangement, which stops short of accession but goes beyond existing forms of partnership and association, Article 8 TEU only institutionalises the ambiguity that also characterises the ENP. Apart from the uncertain procedural requirements for the application of this provision, it appears that most of the neighbouring countries are not interested in such a formula ... Moreover, the special relationship envisaged under Article 8 TEU lacks exclusivity. It is not at all clear what kind of specific benefits it offers to neighbouring countries in comparison to traditional association or even partnership agreements ... Finally, it remains to be seen to what extent the objective of creating 'reciprocal rights' would allow the neighbouring countries to contribute effectively to the development of the bilateral relationship. As a result, the neighbourhood clause may be regarded as a largely symbolic or 'utopian' provision which does not solve the complexities relating to the search of an appropriate legal basis for the conclusion of international agreements with neighbouring countries ...

B. Key Features of the European Neighbourhood Policy

Before the formal launch of the ENP, the EU had already developed a framework for cooperation with its Southern Mediterranean neighbours through the 'Euro-Mediterranean Partnership' (EMP or Euromed). The latter, also known as the Barcelona process, started in 1995 and aimed to establish a regular dialogue on political and security matters; economic, trade and financial cooperation including the creation of a free trade area as well as cooperation on social, cultural and human affairs.[14] Within this context, the EU concluded bilateral Euro-Mediterranean Association Agreements (EMAAs) with seven countries of the Southern Mediterranean (Tunisia, Morocco, Israel, Jordan, Egypt, Algeria and Lebanon)[15] and a special 'Euro-Mediterranean Interim Association Agreement on trade and co-operation' with the Palestine Liberation Organisation (PLO).[16] With countries of the former Soviet

[14] See E Philippart and G Edwards, 'The Euro-Mediterranean Partnership: Fragmentation and Reconstruction' (1997) 4 *European Foreign Affairs Review* 465, 465–89.

[15] A Euro-Mediterranean Association Agreement with Syria was initialled in 2004 and, after a revision, in 2008 but it was never signed. Libya is the other country from the Southern Mediterranean which has no association agreement with the EU.

[16] See, on this particular agreement, E Lannon, 'L'accord d'association intérimaire: Communauté européenne-OLP: l'institutionnalisation progressive des relations euro-palestiniennes' (1997) 1 *Revue des affaires européennes* 169.

Union, a network of bilateral Partnership and Cooperation Agreements (PCAs) was concluded in the second half of the 1990s. In its famous Agenda 2000 Communication published in 1997, the European Commission already briefly reflected about the consequences of the EU's eastward enlargement for relations with countries such as Russia, Ukraine, Belarus and Moldova.[17] However, it was only with the 2002 reflection paper written by the, at that time, High Representative for the CFSP, Javier Solana and Commissioner for external relations, Chris Patten, that the debate about a new neighbourhood policy really kicked off.[18] The Solana-Patten Joint Letter sketched four key issues the Union would have to consider in designing the European neighbourhood policy and outlined some tentative answers:

- The geographic scope of policy: which neighbours to include and not to include?
- What would the EU hope to achieve with the new initiative: its interests, values and objectives?
- How to ensure there is no ambiguity on the (absence of) link with further enlargement?
- What method and instruments would be used to carry out the policy: full application of conditionality?

Javier Solana and Chris Patten, *Joint Letter, Wider Europe*, 7 August 2002 (extracts – emphasis in original)

1. What should be *the geographical coverage* of this exercise? The enlarged Union's neighbours fall into three main regional groupings: the Mediterranean (Barcelona Process); the Western Balkans (Stabilisation and Association Process); and Russia and the other eastern neighbours (Partnership and Co-operation Agreements) ... The imminent enlargement presents an opportunity to develop a more coherent and durable basis for relations with our immediate neighbours. The pace and scope of this process will have to be flexible – there can be no one-size-fits-all approach ... Looking to the medium and longer term, we could foresee a gradually evolving framework surrounding the Union, which would nevertheless stop short of full membership or creating shared institutions.
2. How do we want to *develop our relations* with present and future neighbours? The three main geographical groupings above can be distinguished by what we say about their prospect of accession to the EU. For the Balkans it is an explicit goal ... in the Mediterranean (apart from current candidates) membership is explicitly excluded ... our future eastern neighbours fall somewhat uncomfortably in between. Making their

[17] European Commission, *Agenda 2000: For a Stronger and Wider Union* [1997] COM(1997) 2000.
[18] J Solana and C Patten, *Joint Letter, Wider Europe*, 7 August 2002, on file with the author.

situation less ambivalent … particularly for Ukraine which is most actively seeking more concrete recognition of her European aspirations is probably the most immediate challenge for our neighbourhood policy. This requires the delineation of an ambitious but workable policy framework for the next ten years or so, without closing any options for the more distant future.

3. *What are our interests* and what do we want to achieve? There are a number of overriding objectives for our neighbourhood policy? Stability, prosperity, shared values and rule of law … failure in any of these will lead to increased risks of negative spill-over on the Union. …
5. Do we need to create *new contractual arrangements such as Neighbourhood or Proximity Agreements*? There is already scope to upgrade relations within the existing agreements with the countries concerned and we must guard against cosmetic changes … becoming a substitute for substantive measures. The debate needs careful handling to avoid unrealistic expectations over the prospects of future enlargement. On the other hand, if we decide to set out specific and qualitatively enhanced objectives for our policy, this could justify a relabeling of our relations. Moreover, the strong symbolism of a new label that marks a strengthened commitment of the Union could help to raise the profile of relations with the EU and thus unlock additional political will and administrative capacity.

On the basis of this joint letter, we can examine the key choices which were subsequently made in in designing the ENP, in particular as far as the geographical scope, objectives and methodology are concerned. It is noteworthy that individual Member State foreign policy priorities, as well as third-country demands and external geopolitical events have progressively shaped the outlook of the ENP. Of particular relevance are two major revisions which took place against the background of significant geopolitical evolutions in the EU's neighbourhood: the Arab Spring (2011) and the conflict in Ukraine (2015).

C. Geographic Scope: Confluence of Geopolitics and Member State Interests

In line with Agenda 2000 and the later Solana-Patten Joint Letter, the 'New Neighbours Initiative' discussed in the Council in October 2002 focused only on the Eastern Neighbours and was bilateral in nature: an upgrade in relations with Ukraine, Moldova and Belarus, as well as Russia.[19] However, in 2003, the Russian Federation refused to be treated on an equal basis with the other three countries, so the Union instead

[19] Conclusions of the General Affairs and External Relations Council, *New Neighbours Initiative*, 30 September 2002.

decided to create a bilateral 'strategic partnership' with that country. Subsequently, under pressure from Member States such as Italy, France and Spain who did not want to see the Southern nations receive less attention in EU external policy, the Mediterranean rim was also included in the ENP.[20] As the 'Rose Revolution' unfolded in Georgia in 2003, by 2005 the ENP also came to encompass the Southern Caucasus: the EU wished to reward that country for its return to democracy and also included Georgia's neighbours Azerbaijan and Armenia. As a result, the ENP covered relations with Algeria, Armenia, Azerbaijan, Belarus, Egypt, Georgia, Israel, Jordan, Libya, Lebanon, Moldova, Morocco, Palestine Authority, Tunisia, Syria and Ukraine. Four countries (Algeria, Belarus, Libya and Syria) were not actively involved because legal and political reasons stood in the way of developing 'standard' ENP relations: the EU did not have an Association Agreement or, in the case of Belarus, a Partnership and Cooperation Agreement due to the absence of compliance with EU values on rule of law and democracy.

The single geographic scope was rather artificial, which was all the clearer when the French EU Presidency in 2008 strongly pushed for the launch of a 'Union for the Mediterranean' (UMed). Former President Sarkozy saw it as a distinct regional component separate from the ENP, but other Member States and the Commission strongly objected to France moving ahead with this proposal.[21] Thus, as a compromise this Southern dimension was 'latched on' to the ENP as a regional dimension to the ENP, named 'Barcelona Process – Union for the Mediterranean'. However, a lack of enthusiasm from the EU institutions and Member States, and because of events in the Middle East in early 2009, the UMed broadly failed to deliver. Subsequently, the idea of carving out a clearer Eastern dimension to the ENP was floated in a Polish-Swedish non-paper of May 2008, partially in response to the French MedU proposal. On the basis of this initiative, the European Council of 19–20 June 2008 invited the Commission to prepare a proposal on the Eastern Partnership (EaP) and the Extraordinary European Council of 1 September 2008 asked this work to be accelerated in the wake of the Russian-Georgian war of August 2018.[22] The EaP, formally launched with the adoption of a Joint Declaration on the occasion of a special 'Eastern Partnership Summit' in Prague on 7 May 2009, combines the ambition of deeper bilateral engagement, including the prospect of association and visa liberalisation, with a regional framework for cooperation with the Eastern ENP countries. Hence, an increasing differentiation between the Eastern and Southern dimension of the ENP can be observed. Moreover, an increased differentiation within each geographical sub-group can be observed as a result of diverging ambitions among the partners countries. However, the term ENP remains in existence as a political umbrella: it encompasses all initiatives which share the neighbourhood as their geographic focus, and which have certain methodological and financial approaches in common.

[20] Conclusions of the General Affairs and External Relations Council, *European Neighbourhood Policy*, 14 June 2004.

[21] *Déclaration commune du sommet de Paris pour la Méditerranée*, Paris, 13 juillet 2008. Available at: www.diplomatie.gouv.fr/IMG/pdf/Declaration_commune_UPM_bis.pdf.

[22] Communication from the Commission to the European Parliament and the Council, *Eastern Partnership* Brussels, 8 December 2008, COM(2008) 823/4, 2.

State of play ENP	South	East
Regional/Multilateral dimension	Union for the Mediterranean	Eastern Partnership
Bilateral dimension	Maghreb and Mashreq countries	Ukraine Moldova, Georgia, Armenia, Azerbaijan, Belarus

D. Objectives: A Stable and Prosperous Neighbourhood for a Secure Union

The Council has described the objectives of the ENP as sharing 'the benefits of an enlarged EU with neighbouring countries in order to contribute to increased stability, security and prosperity of the European Union and its neighbours'.[23] This mirrored the Commission's formulation which was 'to avoid drawing new dividing lines in Europe and to promote stability and prosperity within and beyond the new borders of the Union'.[24] These formulations indicated the logic on which the ENP was constructed. In essence, the ENP was to be considered a security policy because, following the 2004 enlargement, the EU would have very different countries and challenges right outside its borders. Thus, with this policy, the EU wished to create stable and prosperous neighbours to ensure its own security. This approach is still valid, as can be derived from the 2016 Global Strategy.[25]

Shared Vision, Common Action: A Stronger Europe – A Global Strategy for the European Union's Foreign and Security Policy, Brussels, June 2016, 14 and 25

Internal and external security are ever more intertwined: our security at home entails a parallel interest in peace in our neighbouring and surrounding regions. It implies a broader interest in preventing conflict, promoting human security, addressing the root causes of instability and working towards a safer world …

State and societal resilience is our strategic priority in the neighbourhood. Many people within the scope of the European Neighbourhood Policy (ENP) both to the east and to the south wish to build closer relations with the Union. Our enduring power of attraction can spur transformation and is not aimed against any country.

[23] Conclusion of the GAER Council, 14 June 2004, 11–14.

[24] Communication from the Commission, *Wider Europe – Neighbourhood: A New Framework for Relations with our Eastern and Southern Neighbours*, Brussels, 11 March 2003, COM(2003) 104 final, 4 (hereafter: Wider Europe Communication).

[25] The full text of the EU Global Strategy is available at: https://eeas.europa.eu/archives/docs/top_stories/pdf/eugs_review_web.pdf (last consulted 20 January 2019). On the link between the security dimension of the ENP and the 2003 European Security Strategy, see the first edition of this book.

The fact that the ENP is a security policy should not be understood as meaning that this policy falls squarely within the remit of the Union's CFSP competence. Rather, the ENP and the Global Strategy reflect a broad consensus that security in the twenty-first century is 'comprehensive' and must bring together all the instruments, capabilities and policies of the EU and its Member States. This means that the ENP is very much an 'umbrella policy' which aims to coalesce all aspects of EU external relations in a coherent whole: CFSP, but also trade, migration, environment, energy and so on; encompassing both EU and Member State external policies.

Joint Communication of the European Commission and the High Representative of the Union for Foreign Affairs and Security Policy, Review of the European Neighbourhood Policy, Joint (2015) 50 final, 3–4

The ENP is a long-term engagement with the EU's neighbours, but it also needs to take account of the most pressing needs. In the next three to five years, the most urgent challenge in many parts of the neighbourhood is stabilisation. The causes of instability often lie outside the security domain alone. The EU's approach will seek to comprehensively address sources of instability across sectors. Poverty, inequality, a perceived sense of injustice, corruption, weak economic and social development and lack of opportunity, particularly for young people, can be roots of instability, increasing vulnerability to radicalisation. The new ENP will make a determined effort to support economies and improve prospects for the local population. The policy should help make partner countries places where people want to build their future, and help tackle uncontrolled movement of people.

E. Methodology: Inspiration from Enlargement

The objectives of stability and prosperity are clearly inspired by the EU's pre-accession policy, but the parallels between the ENP and enlargement do not stop there. Both policies are horizontal in nature in the sense that they do not belong to any of the EU's specific competences. This explains why the soft law instruments developed within the enlargement context proved very useful tools that could be easily adopted and adapted without falling into the pitfalls of competence-related struggles. From a legal perspective, it therefore made sense to transplant the instruments and methodologies of what was perceived to be a very successful enlargement policy to the ENP.

B Van Vooren, *EU External Relations Law and the European Neighbourhood Policy: A Paradigm for Coherence* (Abingdon, Routledge, 2012) 178

The ENP was constructed in a focused effort to provide synergies between different policies towards the Southern and Eastern neighbourhood and sought to upgrade Union action across the board in light of the security, stability and prosperity objectives. In constructing the ENP towards these ends, we can observe a skeleton of hard legal instruments co-existing with a plethora of soft (legal) instruments which are not specifically connected to competences or policy areas. ... the true innovation of the ENP's policy framework [is] its legal and political construction in comparison to other policies such as trade or development [ie] its use of 'soft law' to attain a coherent external policy for the European Union as a whole.

Mirroring the accession partnerships developed within the framework of the EU's enhanced pre-accession strategy, ENP Action Plans defining short and medium-term objectives for political, economic and legal reform constituted the key instrument of the ENP. Based upon Commission monitoring reports analysing the progress in meeting the defined priorities, the Council would then define the scope for new contractual arrangements with each ENP partner country.

The two revisions of the ENP gradually developed the ENP instruments and methodology. The first revision of 2011 introduced the 'more for more' principle, implying that additional reform efforts by partner countries were to be rewarded with additional financial and other support.

European Commission, High Representative of the EU for Foreign Affairs and Security Policy, *A New Response to a Changing Neighbourhood*, COM (2011) 303 final, 28

Increased EU support will depend on progress in building and consolidating democracy and respect for the rule of law. The more and the faster a country progresses in its internal reforms, the more support it will receive from the EU. This enhanced support will come in various forms, including increased funding for social and economic development, larger programmes for institution-building (CIB), greater market access, increased EIB financing in support of investments; and greater facilitation of mobility. These preferential commitments will be tailored to the needs of each country and to the regional context. They will recognise that meaningful reform comes with significant upfront costs. For countries where reform has not taken place, the EU will reconsider or even reduce funding.

The second revision of 2015 introduced additional changes, which reflect the growing flexibility and differentiation of the ENP with an increased focus on tailor-made approaches for each neighbour without however abandoning the overarching policy framework.

Joint Communication of the European Commission and the High Representative of the Union for Foreign Affairs and Security Policy, *Review of the European Neighbourhood Policy*, Joint (2015) 50 final, 5

There will no longer be a single set of progress reports on all countries simultaneously. Instead the EU will seek to develop a new style of assessment, focusing specifically on meeting the goals agreed with partners. These reports will be timed to provide the basis for a political exchange of views in the relevant high-level meetings with partner countries, such as Association/Cooperation Councils. For those partners who prefer to focus on a more limited number of strategic priorities, the reporting framework will be adjusted to reflect the new focus. In addition to the country-specific reporting, regular reports will track developments in the neighbourhood. These reports will contain the elements required under the Regulation on the European Neighbourhood Instrument, including information on fundamental freedoms, the rule of law, gender equality and human rights issues.

The new ENP should be the focus for a more coherent effort by the EU and the Member States. The EU is more influential when united in a common approach and communicating a single message. It offers partners more when using its resources in a strategic and well-coordinated way. Therefore, alongside discussions with partners, there will be a greater role for the Council and Member States in identifying priorities and in supporting their implementation. This will include joint programming. Member States will be invited to play the role of lead partner for certain initiatives or to accompany certain reform efforts.

In the absence of an accession perspective, the upgrading of the bilateral legal relations was devised a major carrot for the ENP countries. The initial Commission documents referred to the prospect of new 'European Neighbourhood Agreements',[26] but it soon became clear that not all ENP partner countries were interested in the negotiation of such a new type of agreement. Ukraine, for instance, strongly opposed the use of the 'neighbourhood' label and insisted on a classical association agreement instead. The offer of association was explicitly included in the design of the EaP whereas, for the Southern neighbours, a modernisation of their existing EMAAs was put on the agenda.

The Association Agreements concluded with Ukraine, Georgia and Moldova within the framework of the EaP replace the old PCAs and provide for a significant upgrade of the bilateral relations with the countries concerned. They establish an enhanced institutional framework and include innovative provisions on regulatory and legislative approximation. Of particular significance is the ambition to establish

[26] Communication from the Commission, *European Neighbourhood Policy Strategy Paper*, COM (2004) 373 final, 12 May 2004.

Deep and Comprehensive Free Trade Areas (DCFTAs), leading to the associated countries' gradual (but partial) integration into the EU internal market. This implies a far-reaching liberalisation of trade in goods and services and the abolition of non-tariff barriers through regulatory convergence with regard to issues such as the protection of intellectual property rights, competition law, rules of origin, labour standards and environmental protection.

G Van der Loo, P Van Elsuwege and R Petrov, '*The EU–Ukraine Association Agreement: Assessment of an Innovative Legal Instrument*', EUI Working Paper Law 2014/09, 2–3

[T]he EU–Ukraine AA is unique in many respects and, therefore, provides a new type of integration without membership. The agreement can be characterised by three specific features: *comprehensiveness*, *complexity* and *conditionality*.

First, the AA is a *comprehensive framework agreement* covering the entire spectrum of EU-Ukraine relations. Hence, it includes provisions dealing with the whole array of EU activities, including cooperation and convergence in the field of common foreign and security policy (CFSP) as well as cooperation in the area of freedom, security and justice (AFSJ). Moreover, due to the inclusion of provisions on nuclear energy and areas falling within Member State competences, the European Atomic Energy Community (Euratom) and all EU Member States are also contracting parties to the agreement …

Second, the *complexity* of the AA is not only related to its comprehensive scope but also to its level of ambition, in particular the aim to achieve Ukraine's economic integration in the EU internal market through the establishment of a DCFTA. The objective of 'deep' integration requires extensive legislative and regulatory approximation including sophisticated mechanisms to secure the uniform interpretation and effective implementation of relevant EU legislation.

Last but not least, the EU-Ukraine AA is based on a strict *conditionality* approach. The preamble to the agreement explicitly states that 'political association and economic integration of Ukraine within the European Union will depend on progress in the implementation of the current agreement as well as *Ukraine's track record in ensuring respect for common values, and progress in achieving convergence with the EU in political, economic and legal areas*.' This link between the third country's performance and the deepening of the EU's engagement is a key characteristic of the European Neighbourhood Policy (ENP) and the Eastern Partnership (EaP). Whereas this principle has so-far been applied on the basis of soft-law instruments such as Action Plans and the Association Agenda, it is now encapsulated in a legally binding bilateral agreement.

It is noteworthy that Armenia decided not to conclude an association agreement with the EU in 2013 in light of the country's later accession to the Eurasian Economic Union.[27] Alternatively, a Comprehensive and Enhanced Partnership Agreement (CEPA) was signed in November 2017.[28] The latter does not aim at the gradual integration of the country in the EU internal market by setting up a DCFTA but rather seeks to establish enhanced trade cooperation and regulatory cooperation in compliance with the rights and obligations arising from WTO membership.

In the EU's southern neighbourhood, the ENP resulted in a further broadening and deepening of the EU's relations with certain southern neighbours. For instance, bilateral agreements on agricultural, processed agricultural and fisheries products have been concluded in the form of an exchange of letters and then added as protocols to the EMAAs with Israel, Egypt, Morocco and Jordan. In addition, new dispute settlement protocols have been concluded with Tunisia, Jordan, Egypt, Lebanon and Morocco. Negotiations on the further liberalisation of trade with a view to the establishment of a DCFTA have been launched with Tunisia and Morocco but did not yet result in a further amendment of the EMAAs.[29] With Morocco, the dispute concerning the right to self-determination of the Western Sahara further complicates the negotiations.[30]

P Van Elsuwege and G Van der Loo, 'Continuity and Change in the Legal Relations between the EU and its Neighbours: A Result of Path Dependency and Spill-over Effects' in D Bouris and T Schumacher (eds) *The Revised European Neighbourhood Policy: Continuity and Change in EU Foreign Policy* (London, Palgrave, 2017) 107–08

Also the legal framework of the EU's (trade) relations with the Mediterranean ENP countries is under revision. The initial EMAAs provided only for a liberalisation of trade in goods over a transitional period of up to 12 years. More sensitive agricultural, fishery and processed agricultural products are

[27] On 1 January 2015, the Eurasian Economic Union (EAEU) started as a new international organisation with Russia, Belarus, Kazakhstan and Armenia as its Member States. Taking into account the fact that the EAEU forms a customs union, the elaboration of bilateral DCFTAs with the EU is excluded. This is one of the reasons why Armenia decided to terminate the preparations for the conclusion of an AA with the EU in the summer of 2013.

[28] Council Decision (EU) 2018/104 on the signing, on behalf of the Union, and provisional application of the Comprehensive and Enhanced Partnership Agreement between the European Union and the European Atomic Energy Community and their Member States, of the one part, and the Republic of Armenia, of the other part [2018] OJ L 23/1.

[29] G Van der Loo, 'Mapping out the Scope and Contents of the DCFTAs with Tunisia and Morocco' (2016) 28 *EuroMesco Paper*. Available at: www.ceps.eu/publications/mapping-out-scope-and-contents-dcftas-tunisia-and-morocco.

[30] In a series of judgments, the CJEU concluded that the EU-Morocco Association Agreement nor the EU's fisheries agreement with Morocco apply to the territory of the Western Sahara, which is a non-self-governing territory in accordance with Art 73 of the UN Charter. See Case C-104/16 *Council v Front Polisarsio*, ECLI:EU:C:2016:973 and Case C-266/16 *Western Sahara Campaign UK*, ECLI:EU:C:2018:118. For comments see, eg, P Van Elsuwege, 'The Principle of Self-determination between the EU and its Neighbours: between *Realpolitik* and Respect for International Law' (2018) 1 *Zeitschrift für öffentliches Recht*, 747, 747–65.

largely left outside the scope of these agreements and most EMAAs contain little services liberalisation. Also the EMAAs' provisions on TBT, SPS, IPR, public procurement, competition, transparency and movement of capital are limited or absent. However, already from the very outset (ie the 1995 Barcelona Declaration), the parties agreed to further broaden and deepen the EMAA FTAs and to gradually establish a free-trade area covering most goods and services by 2010. Although this deadline was missed, several bilateral EMAA FTAs were gradually updated and broadened to match with the revamped trade objectives of the ENP and the Union for the Mediterranean. Remarkably, DCFTAs were initially only offered to the EaP countries, and not to the Mediterranean ENP partners. Instead, the Commission stated that the existing EMAAs had to be 'deepened and expanded to include other regulatory areas such as … SPS, IPR, public procurement, trade facilitation and competition'. In this view, additional bilateral agreements on agricultural products were concluded and added as a Protocol to the respective EMAAs with Morocco, Egypt, Jordan, Israel, the Palestinian Authority and supplementary agreements on dispute settlement have been concluded with Tunisia, Jordan, Egypt, Lebanon and Morocco. Negotiations were also launched with several partner countries to further liberalise trade in services. Nevertheless, even these 'broadened' EMAA FTAs are still a far cry from the three EaP DCFTAs.

It was only after the Arab Spring that DCFTAs were offered to the Mediterranean neighbours … The Council adopted negotiating directives for DCFTAs with Morocco, Jordan, Egypt and Tunisia in December 2011 and the first negotiations were launched with Morocco in March 2013. Contrary to the EaP DCFTAs, the envisaged DCFTAs with these four Mediterranean countries will not be included as a separate title in a new framework (association) agreement. Instead, these DCFTAs will be added as a protocol to the existing EMAAs.

Evidently, in the light of the ENP's differentiation policy, the 'Mediterranean' DCFTAs will differ from the three EaP DCFTAs, depending on the economic situation and political will of the associated countries. In this view, the scope and the depth of trade liberalisation will vary. Nevertheless, the overall structure and objectives of the DCFTAs will most likely be similar. The Mediterranean DCFTAs are developed in the same ENP policy framework and have the same objective of 'progressive economic integration with the EU Internal Market … through progressive approximation of EU rules and practices' (European Commission/High Representative, 2011). The Council even explicitly stated that certain aspects of the EU-Ukraine DCFTA 'can serve as a model for other ENP partners in the future' (Council, 2007). Although several elements of the EaP DCFTAs can be taken over in the Mediterranean DCFTAs, tailored to the needs and political will of the partner countries, it remains to be seen whether the Mediterranean partners, in the absence of EU membership ambitions, will accept the same explicit forms of market access conditionality and will commit themselves to similar far-reaching legislative approximation commitments.

III. EU Relations with other Neighbouring Countries

The geographic scope of the ENP does not encompass the countries included in the EU's enlargement policy (see above), the Russian Federation or the so-called 'Western European Neighbours of the EU'. The latter group includes the EFTA countries (Iceland, Liechtenstein, Norway and Switzerland) and the micro-states (Andorra, San Marino, Monaco). Because of political expediency, economic differences, and diverse accession perspectives, the EU engages these countries through a different set of policies. With Russia, instead of the ENP, the EU aimed to set a strategic partnership which, however, largely failed to materialise as a result of (geo)political conflicts in the shared neighbourhood with the Russia-Georgia war of August 2008 and Russia's annexation of Crimea in 2014 as the most obvious examples. With Norway, Iceland and Liechtenstein, relations are conducted through the European Economic Area (EEA) and, with Switzerland, through a large number of bilateral agreements. Finally, the EU's relations with the micro-states Andorra, Monaco and San Marino are 'extended but fragmented'.[31] Therefore, the conclusion of one or several association agreements is on the agenda. In this final section it is difficult to do justice to the full scope of EU legal relations with these countries and regions and exigencies of space merely permit a limited overview of core legal and policy questions.

A. EU Relations with the Russian Federation

Relations between the European Union and Russia are still conducted on the basis of a PCA which was concluded in 1994 and entered into force in 1997 for a period of 10 years, with automatic annual renewal.[32] In May 2006, both parties agreed that a new framework agreement would be negotiated to replace the PCA.

However, due to political obstacles such as the Russia-Georgia conflict of August 2008, the launch of the negotiations was postponed and later suspended as part of the EU's sanctions adopted in the wake of Russia's annexation of Crimea and the destabilisation of eastern Ukraine. In addition, the EU gradually imposed other types of sanctions such as asset freezes and travel restrictions, targeted economic sanctions and restrictions on economic cooperation. On 14 March 2016, the EU Foreign Ministers and High Representative Mogherini agreed on 'five guiding principles of the EU's policy towards Russia', which are still the foundation of contemporary EU–Russia relations.[33]

[31] Council of the European Union, *Council Conclusions on EU Relations with EFTA Countries* (2010). Available at: www.consilium.europa.eu/uedocs/cms_data/docs/pressdata/EN/foraff/118458.pdf.

[32] Agreement on partnership and cooperation establishing a partnership between the European Communities and their Member States, of one part, and the Russian Federation, of the other part [1997] OJ L327/3.

[33] Council of the EU, Foreign Affairs Council, Meeting no 3457, Brussels, 14 March 2016.

Remarks by High Representative/Vice-President Mogherini at the press conference following the Foreign Affairs Council, 14 March 2016

Let me stress that we had, among the 28, unanimity on five guiding principles of the European Union's policy towards Russia:

The first of these guiding principles is the full implementation of the Minsk agreements as a key element for any substantial change in our relations …

The second principle is strengthening relations with our Eastern Partners and other neighbours, in particular in Central Asia, and we had very good discussions on how to proceed in this respect.

Third, strengthening internal European Union resilience, in particular in view of energy security, hybrid threats and strategic communication, but not only.

The Fourth principle we all agreed on is the need for selective engagement with Russia, both on foreign policy issues – this is clear, when it comes to Iran or the Middle East Peace Process or Syria, but also DPRK, migration or counter-terrorism, climate change – but also in other areas where there is a clear European Union interest.

The fifth of our guiding principles is the willingness to support more and more the Russian civil society and engage and invest in people-to-people contacts and exchanges and policies that are related to that, with a particular view to the youth of Russia and the youth of the European Union because we see the future of our countries as something we need to invest into.

B. EU Relations with Western European Neighbours

On a two-yearly basis, the Council reviews the state of EU relations with its Western European neighbours. The following extract of the conclusions of December 2018 illustrates the EU's interest in developing close relations in a wide variety of areas. With respect to economic integration, ensuring the integrity and homogeneity of the internal market is a key concern.

Council Conclusions on a Homogenous Extended Internal Market and EU Relations with non-EU Western European Countries, doc. 15561/18, Brussels, 13 December 2018

The non-EU Western European countries are the EU's closest partners in building a stronger, safer, more competitive and prosperous Europe. The Council emphasises the weight and importance the EU attaches to relations with all these special, like-minded partners. Our long-standing cooperation is based on shared fundamental values and interests and underpinned by our common heritage and history, as well as strong cultural and geographical ties. Economic integration within the framework of the extended EU internal market brings us together even more and frames the inter-dependency of our future prosperity and competitiveness. In the last two years, our close relations have been further enhanced by a number of initiatives across a wide range of strategic areas.

The Council reiterates that the strength of our economic integration depends on full respect for the four freedoms of the internal market. It is, therefore, the responsibility of all the States which already participate or wish to increase their level of participation in the extended internal market to ensure its integrity and homogeneity, as well as full respect for equal rights and obligations for both citizens and businesses.

The Council notes the excellent cooperation in areas of EU external action such as development aid, human rights and the rule of law, and the common foreign and security policy. The Council expresses its strong appreciation for the alignment of its closest Western European partners to the EU's foreign policy instruments and positions. The Council looks forward to the consolidation and strengthening of this alignment. Cooperation in international fora underpins the determination of the EU and its non-EU Western European partners to further strengthen multilateralism.

The EU's relations with the Western European countries can be further divided in several sub-categories. The most-far reaching relationship is based on the 1994 Agreement creating the European Economic Area (EEA).[34] The objective of this agreement is to extend the EU internal market and competition rules as well as a number of so-called 'flanking policies' such as research and development, the environment, education and social policy to the participating EFTA States (Norway, Iceland and Liechtenstein). For this purpose, the EEA involves a sophisticated institutional structure ensuring the homogenous interpretation and application of the shared legal rules.[35] Switzerland was originally meant to participate in the EEA, but in a 1992 referendum only 49.7% of the Swiss people voted in favour of that country's participation.[36] Instead of the EEA, in subsequent years the EU and Switzerland concluded a large number of bilateral agreements establishing cooperation between the partners in a large number of specific sectors. On several occasions, the EU criticised this approach of sectoral bilateralism since it creates legal uncertainty for citizens and businesses.

[34] Agreement on the European Economic Area [1994] OJ L1/3.

[35] C Baudenbacher, 'The Goal of Homogeneous Interpretation of the Law in the European Economic Area' (2008) 1 *The European Legal Forum* 22, 22–31.

[36] C Kaddous, 'The Relations between the EU and Switzerland' in A Dashwood and M Maresceau (eds) *Law and Practice of EU External Relations – Salient Features of a Changing Landscape* (Cambridge, Cambridge University Press, 2008) 228.

Council Conclusions on EU Relations with the Swiss Confederation, doc. 6767/17, Brussels, 28 February 2017

The Council takes note of the reconfirmation by Switzerland of its attachment to the sectoral approach. However, the Council recalls that a precondition for further developing the sectoral approach remains the establishment of a common institutional framework for existing and future agreements through which Switzerland participates in the EU's Single Market, in order to ensure homogeneity and legal certainty for citizens and businesses. The Council stresses the common understanding between the EU and Switzerland about the need to finalise the negotiations on the institutional framework agreement as soon as possible. Its conclusion will allow the EU-Swiss comprehensive partnership to develop to its full potential.

A draft institutional framework agreement was made public by the Swiss government in December 2018 as part of a broad internal consultation process. Hence, the fate of this agreement was highly uncertain when this Chapter was finalised. A similar remark can be made with respect to the post-Brexit relations between the EU and the UK. A political declaration adopted in the framework of the withdrawal negotiations only reveals that the new agreement, to be concluded after the UK is no longer a member of the EU, should be based on an overarching institutional framework that could take the form of an association agreement.[37] Finally, the EU is also reviewing its relations with three small-sized states (Andorra, San Marino and Monaco) in order to conclude one or several association agreement(s) providing for the participation of these countries in the single market and cooperation in other policy areas.[38]

IV. The Broader Picture of EU External Relations Law

The legal relations between the EU and its neighbours cannot be disconnected from the politics of European integration and the search for effective and coherent EU external policies covering the entire scope of EU and Member State competences.

First and foremost, notice the diverse roles of law in EU enlargement policy, the ENP and the differentiated approaches towards the other neighbours. In all these

[37] European Commission, Political declaration setting out the framework for the future relationship between the European Union and the United Kingdom. Available at: https://ec.europa.eu/commission/publications/political-declaration-setting-out-framework-future-relationship-between-european-union-and-united-kingdom_en (last accessed 21 January 2019).

[38] Council of the EU, *Council Adopts Mandate to Negotiate Association Agreement(s) with Andorra, Monaco and San Marino* (2014) Press Release 659. The negotiations opened in March 2015 but were not finalised as this book went to press.

policies, a complex legal toolbox is used, tailor-made to the specific situation at issue. In all these legal relationships, an international agreement is the core framework used to establish relations with the EU: a Europe Agreement, a SAA, a PCA, a set of bilateral agreements or a multilateral legal framework such as the EEA. Surrounding this legal core, there is then a whole set of instruments and methodologies which are employed in diverse ways: soft legal accession partnerships, action plans, progress reports, communications, MoU's, among others. A constant methodological choice in all these policies is then the idea of law as an EU export product, in pursuit of certain objectives. The EU will work with third countries for them to adopt the EU *acquis*, for them to prepare for EU membership or to create a form of integration without membership. In this sense, law has a dual function: it organises EU external relations with its entire neighbourhood and it is also the substance itself of EU policies. Thus, the EU certainly lives up to the chapeau of Article 21 TEU (mirrored in Article 8 TEU) that its 'action on the international scene shall be guided by the principles which have inspired its own creation, development and enlargement, and which it seeks to advance in the wider world'.

Second, there is the issue of coherence between all these policies. At their core, they follow a similar methodology and toolbox consisting of soft and hard legal instruments. However, their objectives are different and this raises questions as to the efficacy and applicability of certain methodologies with certain countries or regions. For instance, the ENP developed from a comprehensive framework based upon a methodology borrowed from enlargement policy into a more differentiated policy with distinct legal and political instruments for different types of neighbours as a reflection of their own ambitions and capacities.

Third, the evolution of the legal frameworks between the EU and its neighbours is largely determined by the broader political context. For instance, the EU's enlargement policy is essentially an instrument to ensure political stability in the fragile region of the Western Balkans; the differentiation in the EU's eastern neighbourhood and the largely frozen relations with Russia is the result of (geo)political frictions and conflicts. Last, but not least, the Brexit process implies a search for a new and innovative legal framework with a former Member State. Whereas the divergent political situations require tailor-made responses, key legal principles such as the autonomy of the EU legal order and the integrity of the internal market define the margins of the political debate.

V. Sources and Further Reading

Baudenbacher, C, 'The Goal of Homogeneous Interpretation of the Law in the European Economic Area' (2008) 1 *The European Legal Forum* 22.

Blockmans, S, *Tough Love: The European Union's Relations with the Western Balkans* (The Hague, TMC Asser Press, 2007).

Blockmans, S, 'European Neighbourhood Policy: CFSP in disguise?' in S Blockmans and P Koutrakos (eds) *Research Handbook on the EU's Common Foreign and Security Policy* (Cheltenham, Edward Elgar, 2018) 312–30.

Cremona, M, 'The European Neighbourhood Policy: More than a Partnership?' in M Cremona (ed) *Developments in EU External Relations Law* (Oxford, Oxford University Press, 2008) 244–99.

Groenendijk, K, 'The Court of Justice and the Development of EEC–Turkey Association Law' in D Thym and M Zoeteweij-Turhan (eds) *Rights of Third-Country Nationals under EU Association Agreements. Degrees of Free Movement and Citizenship* (Leiden, Brill/Nijhoff, 2015) 39–64.

Hillion, C, 'Anatomy of EU Norm Export Towards the Neighbourhood. The Impact of Article 8 TEU' in P Van Elsuwege and R Petrov (eds) *Legislative Approximation and Application of EU Law in the Eastern Neighbourhood of the European Union. Towards a Common Regulatory Space?* (Abingdon, Routledge, 2014) 13–20.

Kaddous, C, 'The Relations between the EU and Switzerland' in A Dashwood and M Maresceau (eds) *Law and Practice of EU External Relations – Salient Features of A Changing Landscape* (Cambridge, Cambridge University Press, 2008) 227–69.

Lauhlé Shaelou, S, *The EU and Cyprus: Principles and Strategies of Full Integration* (Leiden, Brill/Nijhoff, 2010).

Leino, P and R Petrov 'Between "Common Values" and Competing Universals – The Promotion of the EU's Common Values through the European Neighbourhood Policy' (2009) 15 *European Law Journal* 654.

Maresceau, M, 'Turkey: A Candidate State Destined to Join the Union' in N Niamh Shuibhne and L Gormley (eds) *From Single Market to Economic Union. Essays in Honour of John A Usher* (Oxford, Oxford University Press, 2012) 315–40.

Philippart, E and G Edwards, 'The Euro-Mediterranean Partnership: Fragmentation and Reconstruction' (1997) 4 *European Foreign Affairs Review* 465.

Phinnemore, P, 'Stabilisation and Association Agreements: Europe Agreements for the Western Balkans?' (2003) 8 *European Foreign Affairs Review* 77.

Van der Loo, G, *The EU–Ukraine Association Agreement and Deep and Comprehensive Free Trade Area* (Leiden, Brill/Nijhoff, 2016).

Van der Loo, G, P Van Elsuwege and R Petrov 'The EU-Ukraine Association Agreement: Assessment of an Innovative Legal Instrument', EUI Working Paper Law 2014/09.

Van Elsuwege, P, 'Good Neighbourliness as a Condition for Accession to the European Union: Searching the Balance between Law and Politics' in D Kochenov and E Basheska (eds) *Good Neighbourly Relations in the European Legal Context* (Leiden, Brill/Nijhoff, 2015) 217–34.

Van Elsuwege, P, 'Legal Creativity in EU External Relations: The Stabilisation and Association Agreement between the EU and Kosovo' (2017) 1 *European Foreign Affairs Review* 393.

Van Elsuwege, P, 'The Principle of Self-determination between the EU and its Neighbours: Between *Realpolitik* and Respect for International Law' (2018) 1 *Zeitschrift für öffentliches Recht*, 747.

Van Elsuwege, P and R Petrov 'Article 8 TEU: Towards a New Generation of Agreements with the Neighbouring Countries of the European Union?' (2011) 36 *European Law Review* 688.

Van Elsuwege, P and R Petrov 'Legal Perspectives on the Study of the European Neighbourhood Policy' in T Schumacher, A Marchetti and T Demmelhuber (eds) *The Routledge Handbook on the European Neighbourhood Policy* (Abingdon, Routledge, 2018) 105–16.

Van Elsuwege, P and G Van der Loo 'Continuity and Change in the Legal Relations between the EU and its Neighbours: A Result of Path Dependency and Spill-over Effects' in D Bouris and T Schumacher (eds) *The Revised European Neighbourhood Policy. Continuity and Change in EU Foreign Policy* (Basingstoke, Palgrave Macmillan, 2016) 94–116.

Van Vooren, B, *EU External Relations Law and the European Neighbourhood Policy: A Paradigm for Coherence* (Abingdon, Routledge, 2012).

14

The External Dimension of Joining and Leaving the EU

Central Issues

- The EU's membership has expanded from the 'original six' countries that founded the European Coal and Steel Community to more than two dozen countries from across the continent during the course of the past decades. At the same time, as the referendum in the United Kingdom from June 2016 and the ensuing events show, a Member State may also decide to leave the European Union.
- Neither joining nor leaving the EU are easy tasks. Both have not only wide-ranging internal legal and political consequences for the Union; they also have important external repercussions. Acceding to the EU provides access to its large internal market but requires candidate countries to adapt their legal systems to conform with the EU's values and *acquis communautaire* of legislation. Hence, the prospect of membership is an important tool of the EU's external action. At the same time, disentangling a withdrawing Member State from the Union not only turns it from subject to object of EU external action; it also, to a large extent, redefines that state's relations with the rest of the world.
- This chapter outlines the legal dimension of joining and leaving the EU from the point of view of EU external relations. Given that the EU has a decades-long history of accessions, but much more recent experience with a Member State willing to leave, the former will be addressed in greater detail than the latter.

I. Joining the EU

A. The History of the EU's Enlargement

Since the High Contracting Parties to the Treaty of Rome came together in 1957, the original Community of six Members has gone through seven rounds of enlargement, with the last in July 2013.

- First enlargement – 1 January 1973: Denmark, Ireland and the United Kingdom
- Second enlargement – 1 January 1981: Greece
- Third enlargement – 1 January 1986: Portugal and Spain
- Fourth enlargement – 1 January 1995: Austria, Finland and Sweden
- Fifth enlargement – 1 May 2004: Cyprus, Czech Republic, Estonia, Latvia, Lithuania, Hungary, Malta, Poland, Slovakia and Slovenia
- Sixth enlargement – 1 January 2007: Bulgaria and Romania
- Seventh enlargement – 1 July 2013: Croatia

That EU membership also has implications for a country's place in the wider world was well captured in 1975 by Margaret Thatcher, then leader of the British Conservative Party, in a speech that launched her party's campaign to remain in the then European Economic Community:

M Thatcher, *Speech to Conservative Group for Europe (opening Conservative referendum campaign)*, 16 April 1975

And as Harold Macmillan, who made Britain's first application to join the Community, said: 'We are European, geographically and culturally and we cannot, even if we would, disassociate ourselves from Europe.'

That vision of Europe took a leap into reality on the 1st of January 1972 when, Mr. Chairman [Edward Heath], due to your endeavours, enthusiasm and dedication Britain joined the European Community.

- The Community gives us peace and security in a free society, a peace and security denied to the past two generations.
- The Community gives us access to secure sources of food supplies. This is vital to us, a country which has to import half of what we need.
- The Community does more trade and gives more aid than any group in the world.
- The Community gives us the opportunity to represent the Commonwealth in Europe. The Commonwealth want us to stay in and has said so. The Community wants us.

The largest and in many ways most significant enlargement remains that of 2004, when no fewer than ten countries, eight of which were formerly communist Central and Eastern European countries (CEECs), became Member States of the EU. As noted by then European Commission President Romano Prodi, it was an important step in overcoming the division of Europe imposed by the Iron Curtain during the second half of the twentieth century and redefined the EU's role in the world:

R Prodi, President of the European Commission, *Accession Day*, Press Conference, Dublin Castle, 1 May 2004, SPEECH/04/221

This is truly an historic and a happy day ... For many long years we have been preparing the ground for the accession to the European Union of these 10 countries from central and eastern Europe and the Mediterranean. The negotiations we have conducted, while difficult at times, bear witness to our common commitment to unify our continent and finally to end the artificial division the Iron Curtain imposed on us for more than half a century.

First, I want to pay tribute to the peoples of Europe who are joining us today. Even in the darkest days of Stalinism, they never lost hope. Since the fall of the Berlin Wall, they have carried out a quiet revolution based on the democratic values that are our common heritage today.

I also want to pay tribute to the leaders of these countries – to the Governments and Parliaments that have followed since the fall of the Berlin Wall. Despite difficulties of all sorts, they have managed to mobilise the whole population in their countries and implement courageous reforms. And I also want to pay tribute to the peoples of the 15 older members for welcoming in the new countries and sharing their area of prosperity and security with them ...

In an increasingly complex world, the enlarged Union, based on democratic values, economic openness and a strong social model, can achieve far more than any country can ever hope to achieve on its own.

It can provide a reference for all those across the world who seek their own path, from Latin America to Africa and to Asia.

This does not mean that Europeans want to impose their model on others. Particularly as our 'model' is based on the recognition and safeguarding of our diversity.

But Europe has a great responsibility to help build a world based on the principles of partnership, fairness and justice.

B. The Legal Framework

The legal framework for joining the EU is laid down in Article 49 TEU.

Article 49 TEU

Any European State which respects the values referred to in Article 2 and is committed to promoting them may apply to become a member of the Union. The European Parliament and national Parliaments shall be notified of this application. The applicant State shall address its application to the Council, which shall act unanimously after consulting the Commission and after receiving the consent of the European Parliament, which shall act by a majority of its component members. The conditions of eligibility agreed upon by the European Council shall be taken into account.

The conditions of admission and the adjustments to the Treaties on which the Union is founded, which such admission entails, shall be the subject of an agreement between the Member States and the applicant State. This agreement shall be submitted for ratification by all the contracting States in accordance with their respective constitutional requirements.

Thus, both the conditions for accession and the necessary amendments to the EU treaties are set out in accession agreements. Although the European Union – and in particular the Commission – is the key negotiator, the final agreement is concluded 'between the Member States and the applicant State' and requires the ratification by each state. Accession agreements are thus not concluded by the Union (in contrast to withdrawal agreements, as we will see later). For these reasons, they form a special category of international agreements under EU law, as opposed to 'normal' international agreements concluded by the EU, which follow the procedure laid down in Article 218 TFEU (see Chapter 4).

The procedure in Article 49 TEU can be described as predominantly intergovernmental with significant supranational aspects. First, there is the unanimity requirement in the Council at the outset to decide whether a third country can indeed receive applicant status. At the end of the procedure, it is the 'contracting' parties (to the EU Treaties) that must all ratify the Treaty of Accession with the new Member State. Upon ratification, the accession agreement becomes part of EU primary law.

What is now Article 49 TEU has changed through successive treaty changes: notably, consent of the European Parliament is now required, and the provision speaks of 'consulting' the Commission. Additionally, the article now also includes a few substantive requirements. In the Treaty of Rome, the only substantive accession condition was that a *European State* can apply to become a member, but in the post-Lisbon version we find the explicit need for a commitment to the values stated in Article 2 TEU, as well as respect for the 'conditions of eligibility agreed upon by the European Council'.

The latter sentence is important, as it opens the door to the application of an extensive 'EU accession *acquis*' which has been elaborated in a piecemeal fashion through successive enlargements. This occurred predominantly during the 1990s, where we saw various European Council meetings laying the bricks of a pre-accession policy in preparation for the fifth enlargement in 2004. This also explains why the Commission is 'to be consulted': it indicates that over time enlargement has become a *policy* in its own right, whereby the Commission plays a crucial policy function in ensuring convergence and compliance with the criteria set out by the Member States reunited in the European Council. Thus, Article 49 TEU provides the general framework, but not the full picture of the steps a third country must take to become a member of the European Union.

C. Procedure for Accession to the EU: A Sketch

In what follows we provide an overview of the path towards EU accession for a third country. The description below is at a relative level of abstraction, since the path towards accession of any third country will be specific to the political, socio-economic, historical and cultural background of the applicant country.

- A third country first presents its application to the Council of the EU. This is a highly political act and usually, such an application will already have been preceded by (extensive) political discussions. This formal request is not quite unlike a proposal for marriage: it will usually not occur until it is relatively certain that a positive reply will follow, and this within a reasonable time period.
- Once the third country has submitted its application, the Council requests the opinion of the Commission. A response of the Council may then come rather swiftly, or it may not. In the case of Morocco, the rejection came soon after its application in 1987, but Turkey received its formal candidate status only in 1997 – ten years after its application. In any case, when the third country has presented its application, the Council will request the Commission to submit its opinion on this application in line with Article 49 TEU.
- The Commission's opinion is published rather quickly after the request by the Council. For example, Serbia presented its application on 22 December 2009, the Council requested the Commission's opinion on 25 October 2010, and the Commission delivered this opinion one year later in October 2011.[1] In this opinion, one will find a macroscopic overview of the extent to which the applicant lives up to the accession criteria at that moment in time (see further below on the accession criteria). The granting of the status of 'candidate country' based on this report is not automatic. It is an important hurdle to be overcome. Granting such status may be conditional upon continued efforts in certain problematic areas. In the case of Serbia, the Commission's positive recommendation was predicated 'on the understanding that Serbia re-engages in the dialogue with Kosovo'.[2]

[1] Communication from the Commission to the European Parliament and the Council, *Commission Opinion on Serbia's Application for Membership to the European Union*, COM(2011) 668 final, Brussels, 12 October 2011.

[2] Ibid, 12.

- Contrary to Article 49 TEU, the practice is such that the final decision on granting candidate status is made by the European Council, rather than the Council. Thus, in the case of Serbia, on 28 February 2012, the General Affairs Council stated that it 'recommends to grant Serbia candidate status and looks forward to the confirmation of this decision by the European Council'.[3] This confirmation followed in March of that year.[4]
- The fact that the applicant is granted candidate status does not mean that formal accession negotiations are immediately opened. That decision is again taken by the Council and European Council on the basis of strict conditionality. For Serbia, the 11 December 2012 Council outlined the need for further progress on Kosovo – among other issues – as precondition for opening accession negotiations. In these conclusions, the Council invited the Commission to report on progress in 2013, stating that a positive recommendation from that institution would lead to opening formal negotiations during the following rotating Presidency.
- Once the Council – again as confirmed by the European Council – agrees, negotiations are opened based on a negotiation framework proposed by the Commission. For Serbia, this step at European Council level occurred in June 2013, with the first round of negotiations starting in January 2014. Such negotiations concern the adoption, implementation and enforcement of the EU *acquis* which is composed of 35 chapters divided according to policy field.[5] One should not understand these 'negotiations' in the traditional sense of negotiating an international agreement between equal sovereign nations. In fact, it concerns a lengthy process of agreeing on how and when to adopt and implement EU rules, without flexibility on defining the substance of the rules themselves. In these negotiations, chapters are not taken all at once, imposing further hurdles of conditionality in the pre-accession process: the Council may politically prioritise which to open first, before it is possible to move to other areas of the *acquis*. For instance, it has become common practice to tackle the chapters on 'judiciary and fundamental rights' and 'justice, freedom and security' early in the negotiations to allow maximum time to establish the necessary legislation, institutions and solid track records of implementation before the negotiations are closed.[6] The negotiations take place between representatives of the EU and the candidate country in so-called intergovernmental conferences.

[3] General Affairs Council, *Conclusions on Enlargement and the Stabilisation and Association Process*, Brussels, 28 February 2012.

[4] Conclusions of the European Council, 1/2 March 2012, EUCO 4/3/12 REV 3.

[5] These are: (1) free movement of goods, (2) free movement of workers, (3) right of establishment and freedom to provide services, (4) free movement of capital, (5) public procurement, (6) company law, (7) intellectual property law, (8) competition policy, (9) financial services, (10) information society and media, (11) agriculture and rural development, (12) food safety, veterinary and phytosanitary policy, (13) fisheries, (14) transport policy, (15) energy, (16) taxation, (17) economic and monetary policy, (18) statistics, (19) social policy and employment, (20) enterprise and industrial policy, (21) trans-European networks, (22) regional policy and coordination of structural instruments, (23) judiciary and fundamental rights, (24) justice freedom and security, (25) science and research, (26) education and culture, (27) environment, (28) consumer and health protection, (29) customs union, (30) external relations, (31) foreign, security and defence policy, (32) financial control, (33) financial and budgetary provisions, (34) institutions, and (35) other issues.

[6] Council of the EU, First Accession Conference with Serbia, Brussels, 21 January 2014, doc 5486/14.

For each chapter, the European Commission first carries out a detailed examination (called 'screening') to determine the level of preparedness of the candidate country. On this basis, the Commission either recommends the opening of the negotiations or requires certain conditions to be fulfilled: the so-called 'opening benchmarks'. During the negotiations – which can take many years – the EU then provides extensive support to the candidate country for the effective incorporation of the *acquis*. Overall, this 'negotiation' is a constant back and forth between the third country, the Commission and the Council consisting of regular progress reports, strategy papers etc in order to progressively 'close' the chapters and prepare the applicant for membership. For most chapters, the Council will set 'closing benchmarks' which need to be met by the candidate country before negotiations in the policy field concerned can be closed. The pace of negotiations thus depends upon the progress in complying with the relevant benchmarks. This implies that the accession negotiations are an open-ended process the outcome of which cannot be guaranteed beforehand.

Conclusions of the General Affairs Council, 25 June 2013, 11443/13, 7

The Council recommends to the June European Council [held three days later], with a view to holding the first intergovernmental conference with Serbia in January 2014 at the very latest, to invite the Commission to submit without delay a proposal for a framework for negotiations in line with the European Council's December 2006 conclusions and established practice, also incorporating the new approach to the chapters on the judiciary and fundamental rights and justice, freedom and security. The steps leading to the normalisation of relations between Belgrade and Pristina will also be addressed in the framework. Prior to the first intergovernmental conference, this negotiating framework will be adopted by the Council and confirmed by the European Council. The Council also recommends to the June European Council to invite the Commission to carry out the process of analytical examination of the *acquis communautaire* with Serbia, starting with the above-mentioned chapters to facilitate rapid early progress in these negotiations.

- Once the negotiations and accompanying reforms have been completed, the country can join the Union. This will be signalled by a 'Commission Opinion on the application for accession to the EU' by the third country. For Croatia, this 'favourable opinion' addressed to the Council was given on 12 October 2011.[7]
- A candidate country accedes to the Union once it and all the Member States have ratified the accession agreement between them and that country. This agreement

[7] Commission Opinion on the application for accession to the European Union by the Republic of Croatia, COM(2011) 667 final, Brussels 12 October 2011.

is specific in that the EU itself is not a party, and the agreement is ratified by all EU Member States as contracting parties. The accession treaties are nevertheless part of the primary law of the EU. The content is rather technical as it will usually make adjustments to the TEU and the TFEU which are largely of an institutional nature (allocation of seats in the EP etc) so as to prepare the Union (institutions) to welcome the new Member State.

D. The 'Conditions of Eligibility': The Copenhagen Criteria

Article 49 TEU states that any *European* state may apply to become a member, a criterion which is open to interpretation. In the run-up to the June 1993 Copenhagen European Council, the Commission captured the difficulty of defining what it means to fulfil this condition for eligibility.

European Commission, *Europe and the Challenge of Enlargement*, 24 June 1992, Bulletin of the EC, supplement 3/92, para 7

The term 'European' has not been officially defined. It combines geographical, historical and cultural elements which all contribute to the European identity. The shared experience of proximity, ideas, values, and historical interaction cannot be condensed into a simple formula, and is subject to review each succeeding generation. The Commission believes that it is neither possible nor opportune to establish now the frontiers of the European Union whose contours will be shaped over many years to come.

In 1987, Morocco submitted an application to become a member of the (then) European Communities but was rejected by the Council on the grounds that it was not a European state.[8] Turkey also applied in 1987 and it received candidate status a decade later. However, its accession negotiations have been significantly hampered by the political debate in Member States over whether this criterion has indeed been fulfilled. The EU institutions and Member States have never explicitly defined what it means to be 'European'. At the 1993 Copenhagen European Council, which authoritatively codified the essential conditions for accession, the focus was entirely political and economic in nature. These 'Copenhagen criteria' have been incorporated into the Article 49 TEU procedure in the statement 'the conditions of eligibility agreed upon by the European Council shall be taken into account'.

[8] European Parliament Legal Service, *Briefing No 23 Legal Questions of Enlargement*, Luxembourg, 19 May 1998, PE 167.617, 5.

Presidency Conclusions, Copenhagen European Council, 21–22 June 1993, 13 (numbering added)

Membership requires that the candidate country has **[1]** achieved stability of institutions guaranteeing democracy, the rule of law, human rights and respect for and protection of minorities, **[2]** the existence of a functioning market economy as well as the capacity to cope with competitive pressure and market forces within the Union. Membership presupposes **[3]** the candidate's ability to take on the obligations of membership including adherence to the aims of political, economic and monetary union.

[4] The Union's capacity to absorb new members, while maintaining the momentum of European integration, is also an important consideration in the general interest of both the Union and the candidate countries.

The first criterion is one of political conditionality, the second is an economic criterion, the third entails the need to fully adopt the *acquis* and the fourth pertains to the Union's own 'absorption capacity' and the debate over widening versus deepening the EU. We will discuss these 'Copenhagen criteria' in turn.

(i) First Criterion: Political Conditionality and Stability of Institutions

Article 49 TEU refers to the need for applicant countries to respect and show commitment to the values listed in Article 2 TEU. These include human dignity, freedom, democracy, equality, the rule of law and respect for human rights, including the rights of persons belonging to minorities. This reference was not present in the pre-Amsterdam version of the accession procedure, hence this inclusion represents the constitutionalisation of the political conditionality embedded in the first Copenhagen criterion.[9] The notion of a European community based on free and democratic European states was already stated in the Treaty of Rome itself and was explicitly taken up as a criterion during the second and third enlargements of 1981 and 1986 applied to countries transitioning from non-democratic regimes.

C Hillion, 'The Copenhagen Criteria and their Progeny' in C Hillion (ed) *EU Enlargement: A Legal Approach* (Oxford, Hart Publishing, 2004) 4–5

[T]he political conditionality first materialised in the context of the EEC relations with Greece, Portugal and Spain. Discussions on their potential membership were made conditional to their acceptance and establishment of democracy.

[9] C Hillion, 'The Copenhagen Criteria and their Progeny' in C Hillion (ed) *EU Enlargement: A Legal Approach* (Oxford, Hart Publishing, 2004) 3.

Indeed, the development of Greece's relations with the EEC was frozen following the coup of the 'Colonels', while Spain and Portugal had to free themselves of their dictatorships before they could eventually be regarded as admissible states … the Preamble of the Commission's opinions on the applications of the three southern candidates … underlined that: the principles of pluralist democracy and respect for human rights form part of the common heritage of the peoples of the States brought together in the European communities and are therefore essential elements of membership of the said Communities.

The concrete implementation of the political conditionality criterion means that the Commission carries out a systematic examination of the main ways in which the applicant country's public authorities are organised and operate, as well as the mechanisms for the protection of fundamental rights. Therefore, it aims to assess the extent to which democracy and the rule of law operate *in practice*, and indeed this is not merely a formal or abstract requirement. This examination, therefore, includes a substantive assessment of the structure, powers and functioning of the legislative, executive and judicial branches; and a close look at the actual exercise of civil and political rights and the protection of minorities.

During later European Councils, political conditionality was fleshed out further due to specific (geo)political requirements. In particular, the requirement to solve all bilateral disputes before accession, if needed through involvement of the International Court of Justice, has become an increasingly important condition for membership. Whereas this is sometimes considered to be part of the general political conditions for membership, it may also be regarded as part of a separate condition of 'good neighbourliness'.

(ii) Second Criterion: Functioning Market Economy

Membership of the Union requires a functioning and competitive market economy. If an applicant acceded without it, membership would be more likely to harm than benefit the economy of such a country, but it would also disrupt the good functioning of the internal market.[10] The reasoning goes that in the absence of flexibility in the economy and without a sufficient level of human and physical capital and infrastructure, competitive pressures upon entering could soon be considered too intense by some sections of society. The consequence could be calls for protective measures and a national reflex which, if implemented, would undermine the internal market.

[10] European Commission, *Europe and the Challenge of Enlargement*, 24 June 1992, Bulletin of the EC, supplement 3/92, 9.

(iii) Third Criterion: Taking on the Obligations of Membership

Membership equally implies the acceptance of the EU *acquis* (eg, the rights and obligations, actual and potential, of the Union legal and political system, and its institutional framework). The *acquis* is a broad notion which includes (1) the principles and political objectives of the Treaties, (2) the secondary legislation adopted to implement the Treaties as well as the case law of EU Courts, (3) soft legal documents such as declarations and resolutions adopted in the Union framework as well as (4) international agreements concluded by the Union and its Member States in relation to Union policies. The criterion that an applicant must take on the obligations of membership then has two predominant implications, which essentially mean that if a country wishes to accede, the *acquis* is very much a take-it-or-leave-it affair.

First, the applicant must *accept the entire acquis*. This obligation of full legal approximation means that any difficulties on the side of the applicant should be resolved through transitional measures in the third country rather than by adapting EU rules.[11] During the Maastricht Treaty negotiations, both Denmark and the UK had negotiated opt-outs to the third stage of Economic and Monetary Union, and Britain also to the Social chapter. In relation to the subsequent fifth enlargement, the Commission thus strongly expressed its view that the *acquis* must be accepted as a whole to safeguard the achievements of European integration.[12] The possibility of past opt-outs becoming the rule rather than the exception was to be severely limited. This implies that new Member States are expected to work towards joining the Euro and that they must accept and implement the CFSP as it stands upon accession and its subsequent evolution. If an applicant country's stance in international affairs does not permit this, it cannot be satisfactorily integrated into the Union. For CFSP, this was particularly relevant for the accession of Austria, Finland and Sweden in 1995, due to their long-standing policies of neutrality or non-alignment. This was resolved with the phrase in the Treaty on European Union that the European (now Common) Security and Defence Policy (CSDP) 'shall not prejudice the specific character of the security and defence policy of certain member States'[13] (current Article 42(2) TEU; see Chapter 9).

Second, taking on the obligations of membership also means that the applicant state needs to *effectively apply and implement* the *acquis*. In this sense, it means that the applicant state should have the legal and administrative framework in the public and private sectors to implement and enforce all aspects of the acquis (and thus also the first two Copenhagen criteria).[14] This consideration was particularly acute in relation to the CEECs during the fifth enlargement. It is for that reason that the 1995

[11] Hillion (n 9) 9.
[12] European Commission (n 10) 12.
[13] K Smith, 'The Evolution and Application of EU Membership Conditionality' in M Cremona (ed) *The Enlargement of the European Union* (Oxford, Oxford University Press, 2003) 112.
[14] European Commission (n 10) 9.

Madrid European Council expanded on this third Copenhagen criterion by stating the EU pre-accession strategy should also include the 'adjustment of their administrative structures'. Below we expand on how EU enlargement *policy* has been devised exactly to guarantee that countries fulfil what is essentially a horizontal accession requirement: the institutional capacity to *in concreto* apply, support and implement the legal, political and economic obligations of EU membership.

(iv) Fourth Criterion: Integration (or Absorption) Capacity

The 1993 Copenhagen European Council added a fourth accession criterion which applies to the Union itself. Namely, it is important to take into consideration the general interest of the Union in terms of 'absorption capacity' to ensure the momentum of European Integration. In its 2006–2007 enlargement strategy paper, the Commission introduced the concept 'integration capacity' to point at the EU's ability to function effectively after enlargement.

European Commission, *Enlargement Strategy and Main Challenges 2006–2007*, COM(2006) 649 Brussels, 8 November 2006, 17

The EU's absorption capacity, or rather integration capacity, is determined by the development of the EU's policies and institutions, and by the transformation of applicants into well-prepared Member States. The capacity of would-be members to accede to the Union is rigorously assessed by the Commission on the basis of strict conditionality. Integration capacity is about whether the EU can take in new members at a given moment or in a given period, without jeopardizing the political and policy objectives established by the Treaties. Hence, it is first and foremost a functional concept.

E. The Condition of 'Good Neighbourliness'

The enlargement policy of the EU aims to create security, stability and prosperity on the European continent. It is, therefore, no coincidence that the promotion of regional cooperation and good neighbourly relations constitutes an essential part of the EU's pre-accession strategy. This was explicitly recognized for the first time in the Presidency Conclusions of the 1994 Essen European Council[15] and later developed in subsequent European Council meetings.[16]

[15] Presidency Conclusions, Essen European Council 9/10 December 1994, Pt 12.
[16] See, eg, Presidency Conclusions Helsinki European Council 10–11 December 1999, Pt 4.

P Van Elsuwege, 'Good Neighbourliness as a Condition for Accession to the European Union: Searching the Balance between Law and Politics' in D Kochenov and E Basheska (eds) *Good Neighbourly Relations in the European Legal Context* (Leiden, Brill/Nijhoff, 2015) 217

... the 1993 Copenhagen European Council ignored the principle of good neighbourliness when it defined the political, economic and legal conditions for accession to the EU. It was only one year later, at the 1994 Essen European Council, that the promotion of good neighbourly relations formally entered the EU's pre-accession strategy. This evolution cannot be disconnected from the so-called *Pact on Stability in Europe*. The latter had been initiated in 1993 on the initiative of the French Foreign Minister Eduard Balladur and became the first EU Joint Action within the framework of the Common Foreign and Security Policy (CFSP). The main objective was to bring together all Central and Eastern European countries into a pan-European conference in order to discuss outstanding issues related to the protection of minorities and the delimitation of borders ... The work conducted within the context of the Stability Pact for Europe helped to operationalize the principle of good neighbourliness as a precondition for EU accession. Derived from the UN Charter, the 1975 CSCE Helsinki Final Act and the 1990 CSCE Charter [of Paris for a New Europe], it requires the candidate countries' respect for ten principles, including (1) sovereign equality of states, (2) refraining from the threat or use of force, (3) inviolability of frontiers, (4) territorial integrity of states, (5) peaceful settlement of disputes, (6) non-intervention in internal affairs of other countries, (7) human rights and fundamental freedoms, including the freedom of thought, conscience, religion and belief, (8) equal rights and self-determination of peoples, (9) cooperation among states and (10) fulfilment in good faith of obligations under international law.

Good neighbourliness has gained particular importance during the EU accession preparations of the Western Balkan countries. The obligation to foster cooperation and good neighbourly relations with the other countries of the region is included in all Stabilisation and Association Agreements (SAAs) and has become a standard item in the annual Commission monitoring reports assessing the preparedness of candidate countries for accession to the European Union. Moreover, it found its way into the process of EU accession negotiations. For instance, the negotiating framework with Serbia explicitly refers to the normalisation of relations with Kosovo, which should lead to a legally binding agreement by the end of Serbia's accession negotiations. This issue is addressed as a specific item under chapter 35 on 'other issues'.[17]

[17] Council of the EU (n 6).

The Prespa Agreement settling the name dispute between Greece and the Former Yugoslav Republic of Macedonia, based on which the latter officially became the Republic of North Macedonia, may be regarded as an example of good neighbourliness. It removed an important obstacle towards the possible start of accession negotiations, which had been recommended by the European Commission since 2009. Following the conclusion of the Prespa Agreement, as well as the Treaty on Good Neighbourly Relations with Bulgaria, the Council envisaged it would decide on this question no later than October 2019.[18]

II. EU Enlargement Policy in Practice

In this section, we examine the development of a fully-fledged EU enlargement *policy* in preparation for the 2004, 2007 and 2013 enlargements. As a starting point it is notable that there is a world of difference between the latest three rounds and the preceding rounds of enlargement because, beforehand, one could not speak of a strategy or 'policy of pre-accession'. We have seen that acceding to the Union requires the aspiring Member State to make numerous legislative, institutional, economic and political adaptations. During the first four enlargements, difficulties for the applicant to adapt to the *acquis* were commonly resolved during transitional periods included in the accession agreement, therefore taking place *after* accession. However, in the lead-up to the 2004 enlargement of the Central and Eastern European countries, a true strategic pre-accession process unfolded based on the 1993 Copenhagen criteria. This was a consequence of the fact that the complexity and volume of the *acquis* had grown significantly between the 1970s and the 1990s, but more importantly because greater convergence between the EU and the aspiring CEECs was required to ensure a successful enlargement for both sides.

The EU's general enlargement policy *vis-à-vis* the countries of Central and Eastern Europe basically started with the formulation of the 1993 Copenhagen criteria and the formal proclamation of a 'pre-accession strategy' at the December 1994 Essen European Council.[19] The latter involved a bilateral and multilateral dimension. At the bilateral end, it meant a substantive re-orientation of the Europe Agreements from association to pre-accession instruments, without actually renegotiating the texts of these agreements. It was rather through a pragmatic policy process that the Europe Agreements and its institutions became the bilateral conduit for intensified, tailor-made pre-accession collaboration.[20] On the multilateral side, there was the creation of a so-called 'Structured Dialogue'. This relationship covered all areas of the *acquis* and was meant to familiarize the candidate countries with the various activities of the Union by allowing CEECs representatives to meet with their EU counterparts, mostly

[18] Council conclusions on enlargement and stablisation and association process, 18 June 2019. The final decision on opening accession negotiations with North Macedonia (and Albania) still had to be taken when this manuscript was finished.

[19] European Council Conclusions, Essen, 9–10 December 1994, Annex IV.

[20] K Inglis, 'The Europe Agreements Compared in the Light of their Pre-Accession Reorientation' (2000) 37 *Common Market Law Review* 1173, 1182.

in the margins of formal Council meetings.[21] Finally, it is important to recall that the launch of the pre-accession strategy was also meant to prepare the EU itself in line with the fourth Copenhagen criterion. Thus, the European Council announced as part of its strategy that the institutional conditions for ensuring the proper functioning of the Union must be created at the 1996 Intergovernmental Conference (ICG), in what became known as the Amsterdam Treaty.

Meanwhile, Malta and Cyprus had also submitted applications for EU membership and were also included in the pre-accession process. In December 1995, the Madrid European Council decided that accession negotiations could start six months after the end of the 1996 IGC. In June 1997, the European Council reached the following conclusions:

European Council Conclusions, Amsterdam, 16–17 June 1997

The European Council notes that, with the successful conclusion of the Intergovernmental Conference, the way is now open for launching the enlargement process in accordance with the conclusions of the Madrid European Council.

It welcomes the Commission's intention to present by mid-July its opinions on the accession applications as well as a comprehensive communication ('Agenda 2000') covering the development of Union policies including the agricultural and structural policies, the horizontal questions related to enlargement and finally the future financial framework beyond 1999.

The European Council notes that the Commission in its Agenda 2000 communication will draw the main conclusions and recommendations from the opinions and give its views on the launching of the accession process including proposals on reinforcing pre-accession strategy and further developing pre-accession assistance building on ongoing reforms of PHARE.

The Commission Communication entitled 'Agenda 2000: For a stronger and wider union' was published in July 1997[22] and contained Commission opinions on each application for membership. The individual country opinions were contentious, as the Commission stated that only five CEECs were ready to open accession negotiations: Poland, Hungary, the Czech Republic, Slovenia and Estonia. The Commission opinion on Cyprus was positive, whereas Malta had excluded itself by freezing its application for membership. The December 1997 Luxembourg European Council confirmed the choice for the five CEECs made by the Commission and agreed upon Agenda 2000's *enhanced* pre-accession strategy which – sensitive to negative political responses from excluded applicants – was applied to all CEECs. Enhanced pre-accession was applied to Cyprus and Malta from 2000 onwards.

[21] M Maresceau, 'Pre-accession' in M Cremona (ed) *The Enlargement of the European Union* (Oxford, Oxford University Press, 2003) 20.

[22] European Commission, *Agenda 2000: For a stronger and wider Union*, 15 July 1997, COM(97) 2000 final.

The enhanced pre-accession strategy established a comprehensive legal framework for supporting and monitoring the situation in the applicant countries, with the introduction of Accession Partnerships (APs) as the core instrument. For each candidate country, an individual AP laid down, in a single framework, the priority areas for further progress towards accession, the financial assistance available for implementing these priorities and the conditions applicable to that assistance. The priorities were identified on the basis of the Commission's opinions and, later on, its annual progress reports. Consequently, the Commission played a crucial role in the preparation of the APs even though, from a legal point of view, they took the form of unilateral Council decisions.

The December 2002 European Council in Copenhagen confirmed the conclusion of accession negotiations with the CEECs (minus Romania and Bulgaria), Cyprus and Malta. The Accession Treaty between the candidates and the (then) 15 Member States was signed in April 2003 and entered into force on 1 May 2004. However, the fifth accession did not come without its caveats. Significant transitional arrangements were included in the accession agreement, including post-accession conditionality.

K Inglis, 'The Union's Fifth Accession Treaty: New Means to Make Enlargement Possible' (2004) 41 *Common Market Law Review* 937, 971–72

The current Accession Treaty distinguishes itself from previous accession treaty practice for a number of reasons. While this is the first enlargement where the in-comers are not acceding to the entirety of the Union's activities, the new Member States are given no option to permanently derogate from the *acquis* nor to opt out from those chapters where certain of the Fifteen have opted out – Schengen and EMU. Also, the trust of the Fifteen Member States in the new Member States' capacity and willingness to meet the obligations of membership has arisen in the current enlargement. Trust arises as an issue because of the lack of proven performance of the ex-communist countries. In the context of an enlarged Union, expectations with respect to the incoming Member States' future behaviour is put under further strain due to the dramatic increase in the number of Member States combined with the deepening and widening of EU integration, and the consequent intensification of monitoring and enforcement efforts to ensure the integrity of the *acquis* in a Union of twenty-five ...

Perhaps the single most controversial topic in the months that preceded enlargement was that of the movement of workers. Public fears of mass migration to the Fifteen led most of them to make use of the transitional arrangements for workers in respect of workers from the eight CEEC Member States.

The EU's sixth accession treaty regarding the enlargement towards Bulgaria and Romania introduced new mechanisms of conditionality. For instance, it included a 'membership postponement safeguard clause' giving the Council the possibility to postpone the envisaged date of accession by twelve months should the acceding countries fail to fulfil their commitments following the end of accession negotiations. This unique clause was not used in practice. Both countries could join the EU on 1 January 2007.

A Łazowski, 'And Then They were Twenty-Seven... A Legal Appraisal of the Sixth Accession Treaty' (2007) 44 *Common Market Law Review* 401, 416

The membership postponement safeguard clause was not used; nevertheless, it can be argued that its mere existence played an important political role. It served as a stick to discipline the forthcoming members in their last-minute pre-accession efforts. Had it been used, its potential benefits would have been rather limited. The postponement of membership by 12 months would not have saved the European Union from admitting the two countries struggling with their accession commitments.

In addition, the European Commission set up a Cooperation and Verification Mechanism (CVM) on the legal basis of the internal market and justice and home affairs safeguard clauses.[23] This allowed the Commission to continue assessing the two countries' progress in relation to judicial reform, corruption and (only for Bulgaria) organised crime on the basis of a benchmarking procedure. The Commission issued its first assessment report on 27 June 2007 and, more than ten years after the Romania's and Bulgaria's accession, this practice still exists.[24] The Commission reports are discussed and endorsed by the Council. In practice, the Schengen accession of Romania and Bulgaria has been tied to removal of the CVM.

Council Conclusions on the Cooperation and Verification Mechanism, Brussels, 12 December 2018, doc 15187/18

The Council reiterates that the Cooperation and Verification Mechanism continues to be instrumental for progress. It remains an appropriate tool to assist Bulgaria and Romania in their respective reform efforts, in order for each of them to achieve a record of concrete and lasting results required to fulfil the objectives of the Mechanism. The Council recalls its continued readiness to support efforts of Bulgaria and Romania in this regard through EU and bilateral assistance. Pending the satisfactory fulfilment of all respective benchmarks through a substantial and lasting reform process, which the Council expects in this framework, the Mechanism stays in place.

[23] Commission Decision 2006/928/EC of 13 December 2006 establishing a mechanism for cooperation and verification of progress in Romania to address specific benchmarks in the areas of judicial reform and the fight against corruption [2006] OJ L 354/56; Commission Decision 2006/929/EC of 13 December 2006 establishing a mechanism for cooperation and verification of progress in Bulgaria to address specific benchmarks in the areas of judicial reform and the fight against corruption and organized crime [2006] OJ L354/58.

[24] The annual CVM reports are available at: https://ec.europa.eu/info/policies/justice-and-fundamental-rights/effective-justice/rule-law/assistance-bulgaria-and-romania-under-cvm_en.

The EU's seventh accession agreement was signed on 9 December 2011 between Croatia and the, at that time, 27 EU Member States. It includes a new monitoring mechanism based on conditionality and benchmarking particularly (but not exclusively) in the area of the judiciary and fundamental rights. Apart from the 'membership postponement safeguard clause', it also covers a set of safeguard clauses known from previous accession treaties (ie, the general economic safeguard clause, the economic market safeguard clause and the Justice and Home Affairs safeguard clause).[25] Hence, it seems fair to conclude that the evolution of the EU's pre-accession conditionality since the preparation of the EU's fifth enlargement goes hand in hand with increased attention for post-accession conditionality in the treaties of accession.

III. The Future of EU Enlargement Policy

Each year, the European Commission adopts its 'enlargement package', setting out the state of play of the EU's enlargement policy together with country reports assessing the situation in each candidate country and potential candidate.

European Commission, *2018 Communication on EU Enlargement Policy*, COM(2018) 450 final, Strasbourg, 17 April 2018, 1

The enlargement process continues to be built on established criteria and fair and rigorous conditionality. Each country is assessed on the basis of its own merits. The assessment of progress achieved and the identification of shortcomings aim to provide incentives and guidance to the countries to pursue the necessary far-reaching reforms. For the prospect of enlargement to become a reality, a firm commitment to the principle of 'fundamentals first' remains essential. Structural shortcomings persist, notably in the key areas of the rule of law and the economy. Accession candidates must deliver on the rule of law, justice reform, fight against corruption and organised crime, security, fundamental rights, democratic institutions and public administration reform, as well as on economic development and competitiveness. Given the complex nature of the necessary reforms, it is a long-term process.

The EU's enlargement process currently includes the countries of the Western Balkans, which are all given the prospect of EU membership in the framework of the so-called Stabilisation and Association Process (SAP), and Turkey, which has been recognised as a candidate country at the December 1999 Helsinki European Council. For a substantive analysis of the EU's relations with these countries, see Chapter 13 on 'The EU and its neighbours'.

[25] A Łazowski, 'European Union Do Not Worry, Croatia is Behind You: A Commentary on the Seventh Accession Treaty' (2012) 8 *Croatian Yearbook of European Law and Policy* 1.

A. Accession Prospects for the Western Balkans

The EU remains committed to ensure a credible enlargement perspective for the Western Balkans. In this respect, the European Commission envisaged an enhanced engagement with the region, based upon the well-known principles of conditionality and differentiation.

European Commission, *A credible enlargement perspective for an enhanced EU engagement with the Western Balkans*, COM(2018) 65 final, 2

Accession negotiations are already well underway with Montenegro and Serbia. With strong political will, the delivery of real and sustained reforms, and definitive solutions to disputes with neighbours, they could potentially be ready for membership in a 2025 perspective. This perspective is extremely ambitious. Whether it is achieved will depend fully on the objective merits and results of each country.

...

The Western Balkan countries now have a **historic window of opportunity** to firmly and unequivocally bind their future to the European Union. They will have to act with determination. Accession is and will remain a merit-based process fully dependent on the objective progress achieved by each country. The countries may catch up or overtake each other depending on progress made.

The Commission is ready to prepare recommendations to open accession negotiations with Albania and the former Yugoslav Republic of Macedonia, on the basis of fulfilled conditions. With sustained effort and engagement, Bosnia and Herzegovina could become a candidate for accession. Kosovo* has an opportunity for sustainable progress through implementation of the Stabilisation and Association Agreement and to advance on its European path once objective circumstances allow.

The Commission's ambitious strategy for the Western Balkans implied, amongst others, a road map for Montenegro and Serbia to complete their accession process in a 2025 perspective and the opening of accession negotiations with Albania and North Macedonia. In its 2019 Communication on the EU's enlargement policy, the Commission explicitly asked the EU Member States to take 'concrete and fast action' in order to ensure the EU's credibility in the region and beyond.

European Commission, *Communication on EU Enlargement Policy* COM(2019) 260 final, 1–2

The EU's enhanced engagement with and commitment to the region over the last year is already yielding concrete and significant **results**. North Macedonia not only continued its ambitious reform agenda, but also reached a historic agreement with Greece resolving a 27-year old name dispute. This, together with the bilateral agreement with Bulgaria, is an example of how to strengthen good neighbourly relations for the entire region, and testimony to the power of attraction of the European perspective. Similarly, Albania is pursuing profound reforms, in particular a major transformation of its justice system, including an unprecedented re-evaluation of judges and prosecutors.

This welcome progress achieved now calls for the Union's concrete and fast action. The EU has the opportunity, and a strong self-interest, to lock in long-term positive momentum across the region. The Union must live up to its commitments and give credit where credit is due. Failure to reward objective progress by moving to the next stage of the European path would damage the EU's credibility throughout the region and beyond. A tepid response to historic achievements and substantial reforms would undermine stability, seriously discourage much needed further reforms and affect work on sensitive bilateral issues like the Belgrade-Pristina dialogue. Strategically, it would only help the EU's geopolitical competitors to root themselves on Europe's doorstep.

However, the 17–18 October 2019 European Council failed to reach a consensus on the next steps. France, in particular, opposed the start of accession negotiations with Albania and North Macedonia and requested a fundamental revision of the EU's enlargement policy. The French position was clarified in a non-paper, published in November 2019.

Non-Paper on Reforming the European Union Accession Process, November 2019

Twenty years after recognizing the European perspective of the Western Balkan countries, despite the reforms undertaken and the courageous acts of reconciliation undertaken (such as the Prespa Agreement), the profound political, economic and social transformations required for a future accession to the European Union continue to be too slow and the concrete benefits for citizens in candidate countries remain insufficient.

A renewed approach to the accession process is therefore necessary to support the Western Balkan countries in concrete terms with regard to the reforms necessary to fully comply with the rule of law and generally to apply the European acquis. This approach should be accompanied by a strong commitment by the European Union in order to help them to confront the numerous and complex challenges related to their economic and social development, to have command of the competences regarding their territory, and confront their migration and security challenges.

A renewed approach should be based on 4 principles: gradual association; stringent conditions; tangible benefits; reversibility

- Negotiations organized around policy blocks, in which candidate countries would gradually be included;
- Stringent conditions, in order to effectively converge towards European norms and standards over the long term, in the field of the rule of law, but also economic and social convergence;
- Concrete benefits during the process (which are currently lacking and prevent migratory movements from being stemmed, posing problems for both parties), particularly through increased financial support;
- A reversible process to ensure its credibility and incentive nature.

This new approach would also be based on enhanced political governance

B. Turkey: A Candidate Destined to Join the Union?

Turkey occupies a special place in the EU's enlargement policy. Already the 1963 EU-Turkey association agreement (see Chapter 13) provides that the contracting parties 'shall examine the possibility of the accession of Turkey to the Community' as soon as the operation of the agreement had advanced far enough.[26] In 1987, Turkey formally applied for EEC membership. In its 1989 opinion, the Commission concluded that it was not the appropriate moment for starting accession negotiations taking into account the difficult economic and political situation in Turkey. Nevertheless, it confirmed Turkey's eligibility for membership and suggested that the completion of the customs union would be helpful to deepen the bilateral relationship.[27] After the adoption of association council Decision No 1/95 and against the background of the EU's enlargement policy including the CEECs, Malta and Cyprus, the 1999 Helsinki European Council significantly upgraded the position of Turkey within the EU enlargement process when it concluded that 'Turkey is a candidate state destined to join the Union on the basis of the same criteria as applied to the other candidate countries.'[28]

The opening of accession negotiations started in October 2005 but rather quickly the Council blocked the opening of a series of important negotiating chapters in reaction to Turkey's refusal to open its air and sea ports to planes and vessels from the Republic of Cyprus. This, in turn, is the direct result of Turkey's refusal to recognise the authorities of the Republic of Cyprus as the legitimate representatives of the entire island.[29] Despite several attempts to re-energise the negotiations, Turkey's accession process has been stalled since the failed coup attempt of July 2016.

[26] Agreement establishing an association between the European Economic Community and Turkey [1977] OJ L361/1, Art 28.

[27] Commission Opinion on Turkey's request for accession to the Community, SEC (1989) 2290 final, 8.

[28] Presidency Conclusions Helsinki European Council, 10–11 December 1999, para 12.

[29] S Lauhlé Shaelou, *The EU and Cyprus: Principles and Strategies of Full Integration* (Leiden, Martinus Nijhoff, 2010) 62–68.

European Commission Staff Working Document, Turkey 2018 Report, SWD (2018) 153 final, 3

Turkey remains a key partner for the European Union. ... Within the framework of accession negotiations, 16 chapters have been opened so far and one of these was provisionally closed. The Turkish government reiterated its commitment to EU accession but this has not been matched by corresponding measures and reforms. On the contrary, Turkey has been moving away from the European Union. The Presidency conclusions of December 2016 stated that under the currently prevailing circumstances, no new chapters are considered for opening.

In March 2019, the European Parliament recommended the formal suspension of accession negotiations with Turkey and suggested a redefinition of the existing relationship based upon a modernisation of the customs union.[30] The Parliament's resolution is non-binding and requires further initiatives from the Commission and the Council.

IV. Leaving the EU

A. The Legal Framework

Before 2009, there was no clause setting out a procedure for leaving the Union. This changed with the entry into force of the Lisbon Treaty, which introduced Article 50 TEU.

Article 50 TEU

1. Any Member State may decide to withdraw from the Union in accordance with its own constitutional requirements.
2. A Member State which decides to withdraw shall notify the European Council of its intention. In the light of the guidelines provided by the European Council, the Union shall negotiate and conclude an agreement with that State, setting out the arrangements for its withdrawal, taking account of the framework for its future relationship with the Union. That agreement shall be negotiated in accordance with Article 218(3) of the Treaty on the Functioning of the European Union. It shall be concluded on behalf of the Union by the Council, acting by a qualified majority, after obtaining the consent of the European Parliament.

[30] European Parliament Resolution of 13 March 2019 on the 2018 Commission Report on Turkey, P8_TA(2019)0200.

3. The Treaties shall cease to apply to the State in question from the date of entry into force of the withdrawal agreement or, failing that, two years after the notification referred to in paragraph 2, unless the European Council, in agreement with the Member State concerned, unanimously decides to extend this period.
4. For the purposes of paragraphs 2 and 3, the member of the European Council or of the Council representing the withdrawing Member State shall not participate in the discussions of the European Council or Council or in decisions concerning it.
A qualified majority shall be defined in accordance with Article 238(3)(b) of the Treaty on the Functioning of the European Union.
5. If a State which has withdrawn from the Union asks to rejoin, its request shall be subject to the procedure referred to in Article 49.

B. The Procedure for Leaving the Union

Article 50 TEU calls upon the Union to negotiate and conclude 'an agreement with that State, setting out the arrangements for its withdrawal, taking account of the framework for its future relationship with the Union'. Reference is made to Article 218(3) TFEU, which is part of the EU's general procedure for the negotiation and conclusion of international agreements with third states (see Chapter 4). According to Article 50(2) TEU, such a withdrawal agreement 'shall be concluded on behalf of the Union by the Council, acting by a qualified majority, after obtaining the consent of the European Parliament'. It is interesting to note that to join the Union a legal relationship with the current Member States needs to be established but to leave the Union, a State will have to settle the issue with the organisation of which it has become a member, which is a complex endeavour.

A Łazowski, 'Withdrawal from the European Union and Alternatives to Membership' (2012) 37 *European Law Review* 523, 539–41

This analysis demonstrates that a departure is politically and legally possible; at the same time it will be an extremely complex and controversial exercise. Article 50 TEU provides only a general legal framework for withdrawal and a lot of additional decisions would be required in order to develop this into a fully-fledged withdrawal *acquis*. Although theoretically one can come to the conclusion that art. 50 TEU allows for a unilateral withdrawal, the analysis above shows that this is rather illusory. It is argued that to facilitate an exit the European Union will have to negotiate an agreement with the departing State which will not only outline the terms of departure but also regulate future relations between the two sides. Such an agreement would be concluded in accordance with art. 218 TFEU, and therefore would fall fully under the jurisdiction of the Court of Justice. Furthermore, lacunae left by the legislator will have to be filled by the decision-makers when the departure of a particular Member State from the European Union becomes a reality …

The best arrangement for future relations between a divorcée and the European Union remains uncertain. The two existing models of integration without membership may be tempting for those whose understanding of the idiosyncrasies of the European Economic Area and the Swiss model is limited. But as soon as the basic issues in these models are explored, it becomes clear that neither would now be acceptable for a former Member State of the European Union (or the European Union itself). Furthermore, one should also remember that if a country decides to leave the European Union, art. 50(5) TEU must be taken into account. In order to return to the European Union such a country would have to go through the entire accession process from scratch. In the case of a country like the United Kingdom, the renegotiation of existing opt-outs and budgetary rebate would be politically very difficult, if not impossible. One has to remember that any new entrant is obliged to accept participation in the Economic and Monetary Union and the Schengen Conventions.

In conclusion, a divorce from the European Union should not be the triumph of the imagination over intelligence or hope over experience, but a decision based on a very thorough political, economic and legal analysis – as the consequences in all possible respects will be profound.

In the wake of the referendum in the United Kingdom of June 2016, which resulted in a 52 percent overall majority in favour of leaving the EU, a number of developments have started to clarify how the process of withdrawal operates.

According to Article 50(1) TEU, the decision to leave must be taken based on a Member State's 'own constitutional requirements'. In the case of the UK, the question arose as to whether the British Government could issue the official notification that launched the withdrawal process mentioned in Article 50(2) on its own – as an exercise of so-called 'prerogative powers' in the area of foreign policy – or whether parliamentary consent would be required. This question was ultimately settled by the UK Supreme Court in the *Miller* case, in which it ruled that, due to the special nature of EU law, parliamentary consent was indeed necessary.

R (on the Application of Miller and Another) (Respondents) v Secretary of State for Exiting the European Union (Appellant) **[2017] UKSC 5**

86 … the EU Treaties not only concern the international relations of the United Kingdom, they are a source of domestic law, and they are a source of domestic

legal rights many of which are inextricably linked with domestic law from other sources. Accordingly, the Royal prerogative to make and unmake treaties, which operates wholly on the international plane, cannot be exercised in relation to the EU Treaties, at least in the absence of domestic sanction in appropriate statutory form …

90 The EU Treaties as implemented pursuant to the 1972 [European Communities] Act were and are unique in their legislative and constitutional implications. In 1972, for the first time in the history of the United Kingdom, a dynamic, international source of law was grafted onto, and above, the well-established existing sources of domestic law: Parliament and the courts. …

101 Accordingly, we consider that, in light of the terms and effect of the 1972 Act, and subject to considering the effect of subsequent legislation and events, the prerogative could not be invoked by ministers to justify giving Notice: ministers require the authority of primary legislation before they can take that course.

This judgment, of course, only applies to the constitutional system of the UK. Nevertheless, it creates a presumption that, given the wide-ranging effects that withdrawal from the EU on domestic legislation and individual rights would have in any Member State, parliamentary consent would likely be required elsewhere, too. Moreover and in contrast to the UK's 'unwritten' constitution, some Member States' constitutions explicitly presume or demand EU membership. Hence, the decision to leave the EU might even require constitutional amendment in these countries.

French Constitution, Article 88-1

The Republic shall participate in the European Communities and in the European Union constituted by States that have freely chosen, by virtue of the treaties that established them, to exercise some of their powers in common.

German Basic Law, Article 23(1)

With a view to establishing a united Europe, the Federal Republic of Germany shall participate in the development of the European Union that is committed to democratic, social and federal principles, to the rule of law and to the principle of subsidiarity and that guarantees a level of protection of basic rights essentially comparable to that afforded by this Basic Law. To this end the Federation may transfer sovereign powers by a law with the consent of the Bundesrat. …

Once a Member State officially issues the notification to withdraw, negotiations between the withdrawing state and the EU commence. Negotiations on the EU's side, as with most international agreements with third countries, are conducted by the European Commission with a mandate from the Council.

An important feature of the Article 50 TEU procedure is that it starts a two-year countdown during which a Withdrawal Agreement must be concluded. This time limit can only be extended by a unanimous decision of the European Council and the withdrawing Member State as per Article 50(3) TEU. The time limit is a way to put pressure on the withdrawing Member State to come to an agreement with the EU and not keep the entire Union in a state of uncertainty for too long.

In this context, the question arose whether a notification of the intention to leave the EU can be revoked and, if so, under which circumstances. There were concerns that opening up that possibility would undermine the effect of the time limit, giving the withdrawing Member State the opportunity to gain time for obtaining more favourable terms from the EU. This issue was settled by the CJEU in the *Wightman* case.

Case C-621/18, *Wightman v Secretary of State for Exiting the European Union*, ECLI:EU:C:2018:999

73 It follows, in the first place, that, for as long as a withdrawal agreement concluded between the European Union and that Member State has not entered into force or, if no such agreement has been concluded, for as long as the two-year period laid down in Article 50(3) TEU, possibly extended in accordance with that provision, has not expired, that Member State – which enjoys, subject to Article 50(4) TEU, all of the rights and remains bound by all of the obligations laid down in the Treaties – retains the ability to revoke unilaterally the notification of its intention to withdraw from the European Union, in accordance with its constitutional requirements.

74 In the second place, the revocation of the notification of the intention to withdraw must, first, be submitted in writing to the European Council and, secondly, be unequivocal and unconditional, that is to say that the purpose of that revocation is to confirm the EU membership of the Member State concerned under terms that are unchanged as regards its status as a Member State, and that revocation brings the withdrawal procedure to an end.

Thus, while a unilateral revocation is possible, the Court stressed that it needs to be 'unequivocal and unconditional' (ie, it must not be used as a tactic in ongoing withdrawing negotiations). At the same time, a Member State that decides to remain after all keeps all its rights, including any opt-outs that may apply to it.

The withdrawal agreement negotiated under Article 50 TEU must be distinguished from future agreements between the EU and its former Member State. According to

Article 50(2) TEU, the withdrawal agreement only has to take into account 'the framework' for the withdrawing state's 'future relationship with the Union'. Having become a third country from the point of view of the EU, future agreements would be concluded following the general procedure of Article 218 TFEU (Chapter 4). Nevertheless, any withdrawal agreement is likely to include a transitional period to ease the disentangling of the relationship between the EU and its former Member State and provide time for negotiating agreements establishing the future relationship with as little disruption and legal uncertainty as possible.

C. The External Dimension of Leaving the EU

Leaving the Union has also important external repercussions. In the first place, a Member State which had control over the levers of EU external action from within the Union subsequently becomes an object of EU external action. As a third state, it will have to negotiate agreements with the EU in the various areas of EU competence as described in the previous chapters. Moreover, that state can become the target of unliteral EU actions such as sanctions or international dispute settlement at the WTO.

In addition, leaving the EU to a large extent also redefines that state's relations with the rest of the world. As was pointed out in Chapter 4, the EU is an active international-treaty maker. In areas of exclusive competence, the EU concludes international agreements with third parties on its own, without the need for the Member States to be parties as well. Therefore, once a country leaves the EU, these international agreements no longer apply to it. In the context of Brexit, it was estimated that more than 700 treaties with third countries would cease to apply to the UK.[31]

It is then up to the former Member State and the respective third countries to negotiate either 'continuity agreements' to replace the erstwhile EU agreements or to negotiate new agreements between them. However, negotiating such agreements already during the Article 50 TEU process (ie, while a country is still a Member State) might violate the duty of sincere cooperation set out in Article 4(3) TEU,[32] as explained in Chapter 2).

More importantly, the withdrawing Member State will not know what it may be able to offer during such negotiations until it has settled its future relationship with the EU. For example, if a former Member State opts for staying in a customs union with the EU or align its regulations with EU rules in an EEA-style setting (see Chapter 13), that limits its freedom to reduce tariffs or adopt laxer regulatory standards in its relations with other third countries.

A particularly intricate issue is the disentanglement of a Member State from the EU's mixed agreements (see Chapter 4), since the withdrawing Member State is a party to these agreements – at least at first glance – in its own right.

[31] Paul McClean et al, 'The Brexit Treaty Renegotiation Checklist', *Financial Times*, 20 August 2017.

[32] J Larik, 'Sincere Cooperation in the Common Commercial Policy: Lisbon, a "Joined-Up" Union, and "Brexit"' (2017) 8 *European Yearbook of International Economic Law* 83, 103–04.

RA Wessel, 'Consequences of Brexit for International Agreements Concluded by the EU and its Member States' (2018) 55 *Common Market Law Review* 101, 119–20

At first sight, the situation could be easier in the case of so-called 'mixed agreements' (concluded by both the EU and its Member States with one or more third States or international organizations) as the UK, as one of the signatories, seems to be a "party" in its own right and bound directly under public international law. Yet, in the case of bilateral mixed agreements in particular the Member States and the EU are presented as a 'team'. This is often underlined by the preamble, where it provides that the agreement is concluded between the third country, of the one part, and the European Union and its Member States, of the other part, jointly referred to as 'the Parties'. Significantly, several mixed agreements include a clause defining the term 'Parties' as 'the Union or its Member States, or the Union and its Member States, in accordance with their respective competences, on the one hand, and (the third country), on the other'. Furthermore, just as in the case of EU-only agreements …, mixed agreements (again primarily bilateral ones) often have territorial application clauses defined in terms of the territory of EU Member States. …

While most mixed EU FTAs contain specific provisions for the termination of their operation, they do not provide for a special termination clause in case of withdrawal of a State from the EU. For some, this leads to the conclusion that 'the UK's withdrawal from the EU will not as such affect its capacity as a formal 'party' to mixed EU FTAs'. Perhaps the better question is to what extent they will continue to *apply* to the UK …

In that respect, it is essential to recall that these are not just international agreements that the UK entered into individually, despite the remark made by Advocate General Sharpston [in Opinion 2/15] that Member States are parties to the agreement as sovereign States, 'not as a mere appendage of the European Union'. As an 'integral part of EU law' – in the words of the EU Court – these agreements are closely connected to other EU legislation and policies. Moreover, many mixed agreements are concluded without a strict indication of what falls under EU competences and what is still in the hands of the Member States …

Thus, for bilateral mixed agreements (ie between the EU and its Member States and one third party) renegotiation or some other form of joint understanding on the continued applicability to the former Member State might be the best way to ensure legal certainty. For multilateral mixed agreements, including those setting up international institutions in which the EU participates (Chapter 6), the situation of the former Member State is more secure. For instance, leaving the EU will not change that state's status as a member of the WTO, NATO or the UN, for instance. Nevertheless, in certain instances, its term of membership may be affected. In the context of the WTO, for instance, tariff rate quotas that were negotiated for the entire EU would have to be split up.

Finally, it is important to note that – as we have seen in Chapters 4 and 5 – changes in EU membership may also have consequences under international law. In relation to EU agreements concluded with third states, at least a notification to those states (or members of other international organisations) may be required; occasionally, third parties may have to agree with changes resulting from the withdrawal of an EU Member State, for instance through an additional protocol.

V. The Broader Picture of EU External Relations Law

This chapter addressed both the accession to and withdrawal from the EU. As was shown, both processes are time-consuming, complex and require protracted negotiations. Even though both involve myriad technical issues, at their heart they raise both fundamental, if not existential, questions (What is 'European'? What is 'sovereignty'?) as well as highly sensitive political topics (How many new states can the Union 'absorb'? What should the future relationship with a state that decided to leave look like?). Having started with the six founding members, the Union's membership has more than quadrupled. It now includes states from the Atlantic to the Russian border, from the Mediterranean to the Arctic Circle, as well as former communist countries and countries that had not (re)gained their independence 30 years ago or have not known the many decades of peace enjoyed by other Member States.

At the same time, the referendum in the UK and its aftermath has shown that membership of the EU can come to an end. Thanks to Article 50 TEU, there is now a procedure to organise a withdrawal in a manner that minimises the potential for unravelling the European integration project more broadly and sets the stage for a friendly future relationship with states that choose to leave the Union.

As this chapter has shown, both joining and leaving the EU have strong external repercussions. Before a state can join the EU, it needs to go through the accession procedure to align itself with the EU's *acquis* and values. In that sense, its enlargement policy has been one of the EU's most effective forms of external action causing wide-ranging reforms in outside countries. For the EU, more Member States and more people have meant more capacity and greater global reach, including one of the largest markets in the world and a legal system that has become a standard setter in areas ranging from food safety to data protection. However, an expanded membership has also meant interests that are more diverse, which makes it more difficult to compromise.

At the same time, once a Member State decides to leave the EU it is, to some extent, treated as a third country right away, as it will have to negotiate the terms of its withdrawal with the rest of the EU. Once out of the EU, it will have become a third country and thus an object of the EU's external action. As the EU positions itself in an increasingly multipolar world, its membership will determine what kind of a community and what kind of an actor it will be on the international stage.

VI. Sources and Further Reading

Blockmans, S, *Tough Love: The European Union's Relations with the Western Balkans* (The Hague, TMC Asser Press, 2007).

Cremona, M, 'UK Trade Policy' in M Dougan (ed) *The UK After Brexit: Legal and Policy Challenges* (Cambridge, Intersentia, 2017) 247–65.

Fabbrini, F (ed) *The Law & Politics of Brexit* (Oxford, Oxford University Press, 2017).

Groenendijk, K, 'The Court of Justice and the Development of EEC–Turkey Association Law' in D Thym and M Zoeteweij-Turhan (eds) *Rights of Third-Country Nationals under EU Association Agreements. Degrees of Free Movement and Citizenship* (Leiden, Brill/Nijhoff, 2010) 39–61.

Hillion, C, 'The Copenhagen Criteria and their Progeny' in C Hillion (ed) *EU Enlargement: A Legal Approach* (Oxford, Hart Publishing, 2004).

Inglis, K, 'The Europe Agreements Compared in the Light of Their Pre-Accession Reorientation' (2000) 37 *Common Market Law Review* 1173.

Inglis, K, 'The Union's Fifth Accession Treaty: New Means to Make Enlargement Possible' (2004) 41 *Common Market Law Review* 937.

Larik, J, 'Sincere Cooperation in the Common Commercial Policy: Lisbon, a "Joined-Up" Union, and "Brexit"' (2017) 8 *European Yearbook of International Economic Law* 83.

Larik, J, 'The EU's Global Strategy, Brexit and "America First"' (2018) 23 *European Foreign Affairs Review* 343.

Larik, J, 'The New Transatlantic Trigonometry: "Brexit" and Europe's Treaty Relations with the United States' (2018) 40 *University of Pennsylvania Journal of International Law* 1.

Lauhlé Shaelou, S, *The EU and Cyprus: Principles and Strategies of Full Integration* (Leiden, Martinus Nijhoff, 2010).

Łazowski, A, 'And Then They Were Twenty-seven … A Legal Appraisal of the Sixth Accession Treaty' (2007) 44 *Common Market Law Review* 401.

Łazowski, A, 'European Union Do Not Worry, Croatia is Behind You: A Commentary on the Seventh Accession Treaty' (2012) 8 *Croatian Yearbook of European Law and Policy* 1.

Łazowski, A, 'Withdrawal from the European Union and Alternatives to Membership' (2012) 37 *European Law Review* 523.

Łazowski, A and Wessel, RA, 'The External Dimension of Withdrawal from the European Union' (2016) No 4 *Revue des Affaires Européennes* 623.

Maresceau, M, 'Pre-accession' in M Cremona (ed) *The Enlargement of the European Union* (Oxford, Oxford University Press, 2003) 9–42.

Maresceau, M, 'Turkey: A Candidate State Destined to Join the Union' in N Niamh Shuibhne and L Gormley (eds) *From Single Market to Economic Union. Essays in Honour of John A Usher* (Oxford, Oxford University Press, 2012) 315–40.

Odermatt, J, 'Brexit and International Law: Disentangling Legal Orders' (2017) *Emory International Law Review* 1051.

Phinnemore, D, 'Stabilisation and Association Agreements: Europe Agreements for the Western Balkans?' (2003) 8 *European Foreign Affairs Review* 81.

Smith, K, 'The Evolution and Application of EU Membership Conditionality' in M Cremona (ed) *The Enlargement of the European Union* (Oxford, Oxford University Press, 2003) 105–39.

Van Elsuwege, P, 'Good Neighbourliness as a Condition for Accession to the European Union: Searching the Balance between Law and Politics' in D Kochenov and E Basheska (eds) *Good Neighbourly Relations in the European Legal Context* (Leiden, Brill/Nijhoff, 2015) 217–34.

Van Elsuwege, P, 'Legal Creativity in EU External Relations: The Stabilisation and Association Agreement between the EU and Kosovo' (2017) 22 *European Foreign Affairs Review* 393.

Wessel, RA, 'Consequences of Brexit for International Agreements Concluded by the EU and its Member States' (2018) 55 *Common Market Law Review* 101.

Index